W9-CKD-272

BUCHANAN LIBRARY
George Mason University

Revolution and
Rebellion in the
Early Modern World

REVOLUTION AND REBELLION IN THE EARLY MODERN WORLD

Jack A. Goldstone

UNIVERSITY OF CALIFORNIA PRESS
Berkeley · *Los Angeles* · *Oxford*

University of California Press
Berkeley and Los Angeles, California

University of California Press, Ltd.
Oxford, England

Copyright © 1991 by
The Regents of the University of California

Library of Congress Cataloging-in-Publication Data

Goldstone, Jack A.
    Revolution and rebellion in the early modern world / Jack A.
Goldstone.
        p.   cm.
    Includes bibliographical references.
    ISBN 0-520-06758-4 (alk. paper)
    1. Revolutions—History.   2. History, Modern.   3. State, The—
History.   I. Title.
D210.G58   1990
904'.7—dc20   89-49052
                                                            CIP

Printed in the United States of America
1 2 3 4 5 6 7 8 9

The paper used in this publication meets the minimum requirements of American National
Standard for Information Sciences—Permanence of Paper for Printed Library Materials,
ANSI Z39.48-1984 ⊗

To my teachers—

S. N. Eisenstadt, George Homans, Nathan Keyfitz, and Theda Skocpol—

and to the Cambridge Group for the Study of Population and
Social Structure and the worldwide network of demographic scholars
they have stimulated and inspired:

omnes eruditi, conlegae, et amici

Contents

List of Illustrations

List of Tables

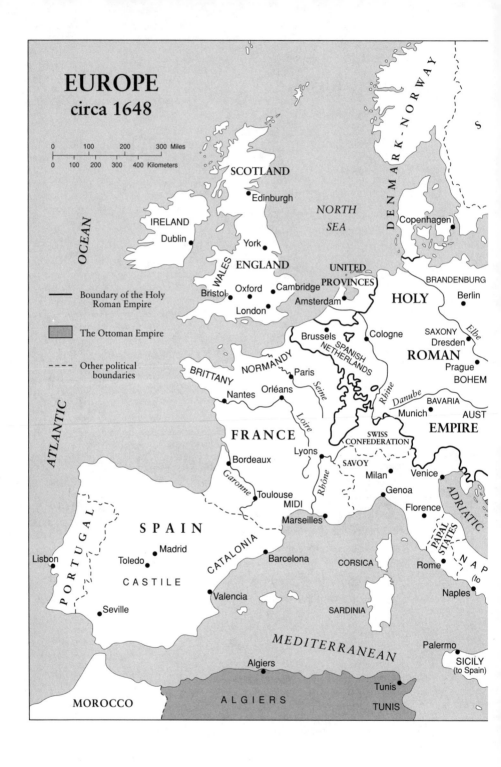

EUROPE
circa 1648

0   100   200   300 Miles
0   100   200   300   400 Kilometers

——   Boundary of the Holy
Roman Empire

▦   The Ottoman Empire

- - - -   Other political
boundaries

SCOTLAND

Edinburgh

NORTH
SEA

DENMARK - NORWAY

Copenhagen

S

OCEAN

IRELAND

Dublin

York

WALES   ENGLAND

Bristol   Oxford   Cambridge

London

UNITED
PROVINCES

Amsterdam

BRANDENBURG

Berlin

HOLY

Brussels   Cologne

SPANISH
NETHERLANDS

SAXONY

Dresden

ROMAN

Elbe

Prague

BOHEM

ATLANTIC

BRITTANY

NORMANDY

Paris

Nantes   Orléans

Seine

Rhine

Danube

BAVARIA

Munich

AUST

EMPIRE

FRANCE

Loire

Lyons

SWISS
CONFEDERATION

SAVOY

Bordeaux

Garonne

Rhône

Milan

Venice

Toulouse

MIDI

Marseilles

Genoa

Florence

ADRIATIC

PORTUGAL

SPAIN

Madrid

CATALONIA

Barcelona

CORSICA

PAPAL
STATES

Rome

N A P

Lisbon

Toledo

CASTILE

Valencia

SARDINIA

(to

Seville

Naples

MEDITERRANEAN

Palermo

SICILY
(to Spain)

Algiers

MOROCCO

ALGIERS

Tunis

TUNIS

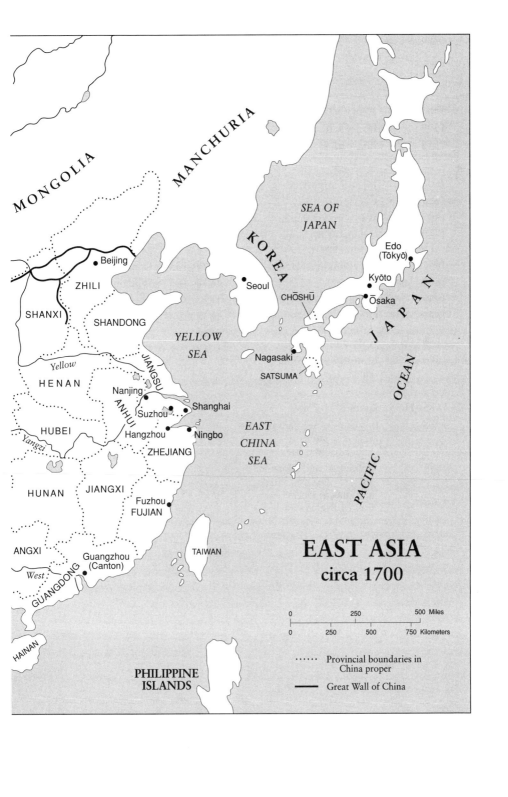

MONGOLIA

MANCHURIA

SEA OF
JAPAN

KOREA

• Beijing

ZHILI

• Seoul

Edo
(Tōkyō) •

Kyōto •

CHŌSHŪ

SHANXI

Ōsaka •

SHANDONG

SHANXI

YELLOW
SEA

JAPAN

Yellow

Nagasaki •

HENAN

Nanjing •

JIANGSU

SATSUMA

PACIFIC
OCEAN

Suzhou •

• Shanghai

ANHUI

HUBEI

Yangzi

Hangzhou •

• Ningbo

EAST
CHINA
SEA

ZHEJIANG

HUNAN

JIANGXI

Fuzhou •
FUJIAN

ANGXI

TAIWAN

West

Guangzhou •
(Canton)

GUANGDONG

EAST ASIA
circa 1700

HAINAN

| 0 | 250 | 500 Miles |
| 0 | 250 | 500 | 750 Kilometers |

PHILIPPINE
ISLANDS

····· Provincial boundaries in
       China proper

—— Great Wall of China

England

1500			1700		
	1485–1509	Henry VII (Tudor)		1702–1714	Queen Anne
	1509–1547	Henry VIII		1714–1727	George I (Hanover)
	1558–1603	Elizabeth I		1727–1760	George II
1600				1760–1820	George III
	1603–1625	James I (Stuart)		1776–1789	American War of Independence
	1625–1649	Charles I			
	1637–1639	War with Scotland	1800		
	1640	Calling of the Long Parliament		1815	Napoleon defeated
				1819	Peterloo riots
	1641	Rebellion in Ireland		1829–1831	Captain Swing riots
	1642–1649	Civil wars		1830–1837	William IV
	1649	Execution of Charles I		1832	First Reform Bill
	1649–1660	Oliver Cromwell, Lord Protector of the Commonwealth		1838–1848	Chartist agitation
				1846	Corn Laws abolished
	1660	Restoration of Stuart rule		1867	Second Reform Bill
	1660–1685	Charles II			
	1685–1688	James II			
	1688	Invasion by William of Orange; James II abdicates and flees			
	1689	William III and Mary (Stuart) declared king and queen; Declaration of Rights enacted			

France

1500			1800		
	1560–1589	Wars of Religion		1800–1815	Napoleon I (Bonaparte)
	1589–1610	Henry IV (Bourbon)		1815	Bourbon Restoration
	1598	Edict of Nantes—Protestant Toleration		1815–1830	Louis XVIII (Restoration Monarchy)
1600				1830	Revolution of 1830
	1610–1643	Louis XIII		1830–1848	Louis Philippe (Orléans) (July Monarchy)
	1643–1715	Louis XIV			
	1648–1653	The Fronde		1848	Revolution of 1848
	1675	Revocation of the Edict of Nantes		1848–1851	Second Republic
				1851	Coup of Louis Napoleon
1700					
	1714–1775	Louis XV		1851–1870	Napoleon III (Bonaparte)
	1770–1775	Reforms of Maupeou and Terray		1870	Franco-Prussian War; Napoleon defeated; start of Third Republic
	1775–1792	Louis XVI			
	1787	Calonne declares need for fiscal reform			
	1789	Meeting of the Estates General; fall of the Bastille; rural riots			
	1792	Louis XVI executed			
	1792–1799	First Republic			
	1795	Robespierre executed			
	1795–1799	Rule by the Directory			

Ottoman Empire

1500			1700	
	1520–1566	Süleyman I The Magnificent; conquest of Hungary, N. Africa	1711	Ottoman victory over Peter the Great at Pruth, gains in Russia
	1596	Ottoman victory over Hapsburgs; thousands of *tımar* holders dismissed	1789–1807	Selim III, modernizing reforms
			1800	
			1804	Serbian revolt
1600			1807–1808	Selim III and Mustafa IV deposed by army
	1603	Military revolts; celali revolts in Anatolia begin	1821–1830	Greek revolt
	1623–1640	Murat IV	1831–1839	Revolt by Muhammad Ali, governor of Egypt; he gains autonomy
	1620–1629	Loss of Iraq, revolts in Egypt		
	1629–1632	Rebel forces take control of Anatolia and Istanbul		
	1632–1640	Murat IV regains control of Istanbul, attempts reforms.		
	1648	Sultan Ibrahim strangled in his palace		
	1648–1656	Janissaries rule Istanbul, celali rebels rule Anatolia		
	1656–1683	First Köprülü grand viziers restore order		
	1659	Defeat of last celali rebel, Abaza Hasan Paşa		
	1669	Conquest of Crete		
	1683	Ottomans lay siege to Vienna		
	1683–89	Failure of seige, major losses		
	1689–1691, 1699–1702	Köprülü viziers again appointed, lead reconquest of Belgrade		
	1699	Treaty of Karlowitz recognizes loss of Hungary, Transylvania, Morea		

Imperial China

	1368	Founding of Ming Dynasty	1700
1500			
	1522–1582	"Single Whip" tax reforms	
	1573–1582	Grand Secretary Zhang Juzheng	1800
1600			
	1604–1627	Donglin academy formed, persecuted	
	1631–1644	Rebellion of Li Zi-cheng	
	1630–1647	Rebellion of Zhang Xianzhong	
	1644	Li takes Beijing; last Ming emperor hangs himself	
	1644	Manchus take Beijing, establish Qing dynasty	
	1644–1681	Manchus conquer China	
	1661–1722	Kangxi emperor	

1700

1736–1795 Expansion into central Asia

1796–1804 White Lotus Rebellion

1800

1839–1842, Opium Wars
1856–1860

1850–1863 Taiping Rebellion

1853–1873 Nian and Moslem rebellions

Preface

The Duke de Liancourt, loyal servant to King Louis XVI of France, softly entered his master's bedroom the night of July 14, 1789. Louis had been informed that angry crowds in Paris had taken the Bastille, but seemed unruffled and went to bed early. Concerned that the King did not realize the extent of the danger, Liancourt sought to rouse him to action. "What then," asked the King, "is it a revolt?" "No sire," answered Liancourt, "it is a revolution."

This story may be apocryphal, but it makes an important distinction. Louis's question was whether the attack on the Bastille might be a "mere" revolt—the kind of angry crowd outburst that frequently flares up, only to be violently put down. From early modern times to our own, riots, demonstrations, and vandalism frequently disturb the peace, but remain scattered episodes; they do not generally overturn governments. Louis hoped that the events of July 14, 1789, would be simply another such episode. Liancourt, however, thought otherwise. He judged the day's events as evidence that the pillars of the French state had grown rotten and that the government was tottering. The monarchy itself was in grave danger; thus the fall of the Bastille heralded "a revolution."

What we might call "Louis XVI's problem" has been a problem for statesmen and social scientists ever since: how do we tell, amid the swirl of current events, whether an outburst of violence is a passing storm or the beginning of a cataclysm? In other words, how can we tell when a state is truly threatened by revolution?

In the late twentieth century, revolutions have become familiar to us, for revolutions and rebellions have created our world. A revolt against English colonial rule gave birth to the United States. The Soviet Union emerged from a revolution in Russia. The great states of Asia—China, India, and Japan—took their modern shape from rebellions and revolutions, against Imperial, British, and Shogunal rule, respectively. In Western Europe the revolutions and rebellions of the early modern era (c. 1500–1850) left an indelible mark; and in Latin America and Africa, most nations began their modern political life through revolutions. More recently, revolutions have transformed politics in Eastern Europe.

Yet we do not understand revolutions well. America's failure to anticipate and then respond effectively to revolutions in Vietnam, Iran, and Central America has been a study in frustration. At the same time, the U.S.S.R. came to grief in Afghanistan's revolution, while its efforts at internal reform, to its great consternation, spawned rebellions in the Soviet Union and revolutions in its Warsaw Pact allies. Revolutions and rebellions still burst onto the world stage unexpectedly, creating shocks and crises, from the still-unfolding revolutions in Iran and Central America to the struggling democracies of East Asia and Latin America, from the instability of communist rule in Eastern Europe to the prospects for change in South Africa.

This volume examines the causes of revolutions and major rebellions in the early modern world. It analyzes periods of history very much like our own—periods of *worldwide* state crises. I focus mainly on the English Revolution of 1640 and the French Revolution of 1789. Yet the English Revolution was part of a wave of revolts from 1600 to 1660 that stretched across Portugal, Italy, Spain, France, central Europe, and Russia, even to Ottoman Turkey and Ming China. Although the century and a quarter that separated the English Revolution from the French Revolution was largely free of crises, in the years from 1789 to 1848 governments again shook and fell, not only in France, but all across Europe and in the Middle East and China. The central question I address is why these waves of crises occurred on such a broad scale, reaching from England to China, in these particular decades.

The details of the causal model that I develop apply only to the early modern period. But its basic principles may be useful in understanding even today's (and tomorrow's) crises. In the last part of this volume, I return to the present to consider some of the issues surrounding modern revolutions, and the reasons for America's international decline.

My approach has two main features. First is an analysis of how worldwide population trends affected early modern societies. Most political scientists and historians have underestimated the role of demography in political crises by thinking only about aggregate population changes. They have thereby overlooked the disproportionate impact that even moderate overall population change has on particular groups—urban workers, landless peasants, the young, and noninheriting offspring of elites—as well as the massive indirect effects of population change on prices, government revenues, and income distribution.

Second, this volume develops a *conjunctural* model of state breakdown. Much social theory is one-sided—political history is isolated from, or submerged under, economic history. Cultural forces are often neglected. Moreover, the various social actors—states, elites, and regionally distinct rural and urban popular groups—rarely all receive due attention. This volume stresses that social order is maintained on a *multiplicity* of levels. A theory of state breakdown must thus address how changes in economic, political, social, and cultural relations affect states *and* elites *and* different popular groups.

Uniting these two elements—demographic analysis and a conjunctural causal framework—creates some surprising results. Grasping how population changes and their impact on prices simultaneously unbalanced a wide range of state, elite, and popular social institutions allows us to predict the timing of early modern state breakdowns all across Eurasia, and with greater precision and understanding of their particular features than any existing theories of revolution or early modern crises. In addition, this approach provides powerful insights into a number of puzzles in early modern history—the "boom" and "bust" of university enrollments, the rise and fall of aristocratic and monarchic power and prestige, and, most importantly, the alternation of periods of state crisis and stability. It also highlights some of the profound similarities and differences between European and Asian development.

The result is a simple theory of revolutions. In this theory, revolution is likely to occur only when a society *simultaneously* experiences three kinds of difficulties: (1) a state financial crisis, brought on by a growing imbalance between the revenues a government can securely raise and the obligations and tasks it faces; (2) severe elite divisions, including both alienation from the state and intra-elite conflicts, brought on by increasing insecurity and competition for elite positions; and (3) a high potential for mobilizing popular groups, brought on by rising grievances (e.g., regarding high rents or low wages) *and* social patterns that assist or predispose popular groups to action (e.g., large numbers of youth in the population, increasingly autonomous rural villages, growing concentrations of workers in weakly administered cities). The conjunction of these three conditions generally produces a fourth difficulty: an increase in the salience of heterodox cultural and religious ideas; heterodox groups then provide both leadership and an organizational focus for opposition to the state.

This theory leads us to ask, regarding the timing of revolutions and rebellions, what historical conditions would lead to these different kinds of difficulties arising simultaneously, and why would such conditions occur all across Eurasia in some periods but be absent in others? Revealing answers lie in the broad-based impact that sustained population growth (or decline) had on the economic, social, and political institutions of agrarian-bureaucratic states.

This simple theory also has implications for the nature and outcome of revolutions. By arguing that revolutions are the result of multiple problems, arising from long-term shifts in the balance of population and resources, it suggests that no quick resolution can be obtained simply by a change of government. Therefore the fall of the old regime and its replacement by a new government should not be expected to end a period of social difficulties. Instead, the immensity of continuing problems is likely to create further conflicts. The breakdown of the old order may provide a zesty period of competition for popular support, marked by promises of freedom, democracy, and popular rights. But in practice, a society convulsed by severe problems is more likely to find solutions in stern authority and, in some cases, by the last resort of politics—civil and international war. Revolutions therefore create great debates about freedom but often shrink from establishing it. Uncovering the deep and multiple causes of revolutionary crises may help suggest why revolutions liberate ideas but tend to enslave men and women.

This theory of revolutions has further implications for the belief that revolutions have been carriers of historical progress. Revolutions have often been depicted as struggles between the "bad" defenders of a dying social order and the "good" builders of a new one; successful revolutions should therefore put an end to outmoded ideas and institutions and usher in a new era. In the theory of revolutions presented here, however, revolutions are not provoked by a battle between the past and the future, or between good and evil; they are instead provoked by imbalances between human institutions and the environment, governed by those factors that affect population and its sustenance, such as disease, weather, and the productivity of the soil. In this ecological battle, gains come slowly, and the political crises that indicate underlying difficulties will not necessarily lead to a "new" world.

Thus if population decline after a revolution restores a traditional balance of people and resources, traditional institutions may be revived. This makes it possible to suggest some reasons why after the English Revolution of 1640, which was followed by fifty years of declining or stagnant population, England in many respects experienced a revival of traditional monarchic, aristocratic, and high Church prestige, even though all of these institutions had been overturned during the revolution itself. On the other hand, renewed or sustained population/resource imbalances may lead to further revolutionary outbursts; this makes it possible to suggest some reasons why after the French Revolution of 1789, which was followed by continued (if slower) population growth, France experienced further revolutionary crises again in 1830 and 1848, despite the changes in political and agrarian organization brought by the Revolution of 1789.

These observations should not be taken to imply that there was no escape from ecological pressures. Economic innovation, both in the organization of labor (what is often called the "rise of capitalism") and in the tools of production, was to liberate most of Europe from such pressures by 1850, England somewhat earlier, Eastern Europe somewhat later. But in the years prior to 1850, economic progress and revolution were not at all synonymous; their relationship was more problematic. As I shall argue below, revolutions and rebellions could accelerate or retard and reverse economic progress. And although certain narrow elements of economic growth (e.g., the rise of newly affluent groups competing with traditional elites for privileged positions) could contribute to revolutionary conjunctures, it was often where broad-based economic progress was greatest that revolutions and rebellions were *least* likely to occur.

This approach has a major advantage and two major disadvantages. The advantage is that in focusing on population movements and their consequences, particularly as measured through price movements, we are forced to deal with measurable quantities. The causal explanations I offer in this book assert a particular relationship between sets of numerical data and are therefore falsifiable. Much comparative history has something of an ad hoc quality that makes it difficult to test. In my explanations, if the data or the analysis is found to be faulty—in particular, if our estimates of past population and price trends should significantly change—then much of the argument of this book would be demonstrably wrong. As a college freshman, I had a professor (the late physicist Richard Feynman) who drummed into me the precept that if one had an explanation that no facts could prove wrong, then one did not have a triumph, but a tautology. For a theory to be right, it must be able to withstand being confronted with facts that could decide whether the theory is right or wrong. I hold to a certain satisfaction that the explanation offered in this book can be tested, and therefore could possibly be right.

The first disadvantage is that the mathematical models, and the methods of testing them, may be unfamiliar ground for many readers. However, the main arguments should be clear from the text. Furthermore, because the data for the Asian cases are weaker than for the European cases, I have dispensed with the mathematical models entirely in addressing those cases. Thus readers who are inclined to skip over the mathematical elements in the analyses of the European cases can easily confirm their understanding by reading the Asian case studies, where essentially the same causal argument is deployed.

The second disadvantage is that because I ground my argument in changing demographic trends and rely on demographic data, there is a danger that readers will attach too much weight to those trends and suppose that I am espousing demographic determinism. I should make clear that the argument of this book is not merely demographic, but is a demographic/*structural* analysis, in which what matters is the impact of demographic trends on economic, political, and social *institutions*. Demographic trends alone determine nothing. Where I find similar consequences of demographic trends, it is only because I also find broad similarities in *institutions* in different historical settings.

Writers of comparative historical studies typically face a dilemma: on the one hand, if they treat each of several cases equally, they will necessarily treat them briefly, to keep within manageable bounds. This approach can produce case studies that lack depth and fail to deal fairly with the specialist literature. On the other hand, treating each case in detailed fashion would produce an impossibly lengthy, and impossibly dreary, tome. I have thus chosen a somewhat unbalanced compromise in organizing this work. I have treated the case of the English Revolution at length, building a full mathematical model, testing it, and engaging current debates among specialists in English history. I have then treated the French Revolution somewhat differently, still engaging the current heated historical and sociological debates, but using only very slightly the mathematical analysis developed for England. In discussing the cases of the Ottoman crisis and the Ming-Qing transition, I then proceed much more rapidly, providing briefer analyses of the origins of these political crises and examining how they resembled or differed from those of Europe. I hope the result, though it will fully satisfy neither specialists nor comparativists, will yet prove engaging to both.

A comparative historical work such as this one of course relies on the research of specialists. And specialists will find little that is novel, and much to cavil at, in my accounts of particular events. However, specialists often approach comparative works in a way that is of little benefit to them. For example, a historian of England might read this book's introduction, and its chapter on England, to see how well my treatment informs him or her regarding that one case. Such an approach will yield little, for I am not attempting in each chapter to compose a case history that surpasses the work of specialists. What I am attempting in each chapter is to emphasize those elements that are common across cases—that is, those elements that seem to be consistently related to early modern state breakdowns. Thus an English historian might find, in my treatment of the Revolution, that economic and demographic forces are overemphasized and details of political or Puritan doctrine are given insufficient attention. That would certainly be correct, were I attempting a complete description of each case. But my goal is to help historians and social scientists understand what forces, broadly speaking, created general waves of state breakdown in certain periods, and stability in others. Thus the most useful way for an English (or French, or Chinese, or Ottoman) specialist to approach this work is to take for granted that there will be differences in the treatment of England (or France, etc.) from what he or she might prefer, and to focus instead on the *other cases*. The specialist should then ask, are there interesting similarities between the other cases and my own? Do these similarities force me to reconsider, and better identify, the elements that I thought were unique to my case? If so, then this volume will have been worthwhile.

I also apologize if I have slighted or overlooked research that any reader feels to be of special interest. For the past decade I have tried to keep abreast of all the major research on English, French, early Ottoman, and late Ming demographic, economic, social, and political history, as well as being aware of research in these fields on Western Europe in general and on the Middle East, China, and Japan from 1500 to 1800. This is, of course, simply an impossible task. My files still bulge with citations to hundreds of additional works I would yet like to consult. I have stopped only because I believe my interpretation of this material is now firm enough to stand against future research. I thus offer my interpretation, despite knowing that my coverage of any particular case is doomed to remain incomplete.

During the writing of this book I have had so much help and encouragement from colleagues and students, and from institutions that provided opportunities to present these ideas, that I feel like no more than a front man for a vast collaborative enterprise. No doubt many who have had a hand in debating and influencing my ideas would differ with this final expression of them. And no doubt I have failed to remove all the errors and missteps from which they tried to save me. Still, I wish to thank those individuals without whom this book would not have been written: Rod Aya, Daniel Chirot, Randall Collins, S. N. Eisenstadt, Arnold Feldman, Gary Hamilton, Michael Hechter, George Homans, Christopher Jencks, Nathan Keyfitz, George Masnick, Joel Mokyr, Charles Ragin, Roger Schofield, Theda Skocpol, Paul Starr, Arthur Stinchcombe, Charles Tilly, Frederick Wakeman, Jr., Harrison White, Christopher Winship, and E. A. Wrigley. I am also grateful to the organizations that supported my work with released time, funding, and hospitality: the College of Arts and Sciences, the Center for Urban Affairs and Policy Research, and the University Faculty Research Grants Committee, all of Northwestern University; the Group for the History of Population and Social Structure at the University of Cambridge, England; the Program on Population Studies at the University of California, Berkeley; the Center for Chinese Studies at the University of California, Los Angeles; the Division of Humanities and Social Sciences at the California Institute of Technology; the American Council of Learned Societies; and the Research School of Social Sciences of the Australian National University.

Thanks are also due the University of Chicago Press, Cambridge University Press, the American Sociological Association, and Sage Publications for permission to use passages that previously appeared in the *American Journal of Sociology, Comparative Studies in Society and History, Sociological Theory,* and in *Sociology in America,* edited by Herbert Gans (Beverly Hills, CA: Sage, 1990).

My research assistant, Jon Shefner, was an effective and good-humored tracker of details, uncovering errors and providing useful suggestions. The supporting staff at Northwestern University and the

University of California, Davis—June Weatherly, Nancy Klein, Barbara Williamson, and Wava Haggard—played a vital role in moving manuscripts through various incompatible word processors. Thanks are due them for persistence, accuracy, and cheerfulness through it all. A special note of appreciation is due my editor at the University of California Press, Naomi Schneider. Her patience, perseverance, and encouragement were indispensable to the whole enterprise.

For Chinese words, I have used the Pinyin romanization (with the help of Don Price, whose assistance I gratefully acknowledge). For Ottoman terms, I have used modern Turkish romanizations (with the help of Stanford Shaw, whose assistance is also deeply appreciated). For quotations from works in French, I have rendered my own English translations.

J.A.G.
Davis, California
March 5, 1990

ONE

The Central Problem:
How To Explain the
Periodic Waves of State Breakdown
in the Early Modern World

I think God Almighty hath a quarrel lately with all Man-
kind . . . for within these twelve years there have the strangest
Revolutions and horridist Things happen'd not only in
Europe, but all the world over.

—James Howell

A. STATES IN CRISIS

For nearly 350 years scholars have wrestled with the "general crisis of
the seventeenth century." Certain facts are not in dispute. The first half
of the seventeenth century saw a widespread slowing and eventual halt
to the steady increases in population and prices that began around 1500.
In addition, rebellions and revolutions shook regimes across the Eurasian continent, most notably the English Revolution; the Fronde in
France; the anti-Hapsburg revolts in Catalonia, Naples, Sicily, and Bohemia; the Khmelnitsky revolt in the Ukraine; the celali revolts in the
Ottoman Empire; and the collapse of Ming rule in China (Parker and
Smith 1978; Aston 1967). But there is *no* agreement on how to explain
these facts. Historians contest fiercely over the causes, the connections,
and the significance of these events.

Some have argued that the seventeenth-century crisis marks a turning
point in the history of capitalism. Others have suggested that what occurred was mainly political, a crisis of absolutism. Certain scholars have
found a worldwide depression in the seventeenth century and have
sought to explain it. Yet others have noted that trade grew rapidly in
some markets, and thus claim that a general depression is illusory. These
debates have proved inconclusive, despite marshaling some of the keen-
est minds ever applied to historical studies (most of the key contribu-

tions are presented in the collections edited by Aston 1967; Forster and Greene 1970; and Parker and Smith 1978; other important works are Anderson 1974; de Vries 1976; and Wallerstein 1974, 1980).

A fundamental defect in these debates is that all arguments tend to be strongly Eurocentric. Reflecting the biases of both Marx and Weber, on the one hand they assume that events in the West marked important structural changes, demonstrating the dynamism of Europe; on the other hand, the equally major political rebellions and regime changes in the East are given only minor attention and are often dismissed as mere peasant uprisings or dynastic changes. In fact, the political rebellions in the Ottoman Empire and China involved the same broad spectrum of elite, urban, cultivator, and heterodox ideological struggles against a fiscally weakened state that characterized Western political crises (for China, especially, see Wakeman 1986). Moreover, the Eastern crises resulted in arguably *greater* changes in state power, class structure, and local government than most Western crises of the period. Thus, at the very least, the history of the general crisis in the East should be more closely examined by Western scholars. At most, and I shall argue the point strongly, Eurocentric notions of the seventeenth-century crisis, which posit a crisis of capitalism that led to dynamic structural changes in Europe and extended to, but caused far less change in, peripheral areas in Asia, should be discarded altogether. To grasp the nature of social change in the seventeenth century, we need to recognize a worldwide crisis of agrarian absolutist states that affected both Eastern empires and Western monarchies.

The same is true of the turbulent period from 1770 to 1850, which had its most memorable moments in the French Revolution but also included Pugachev's revolt in Russia; the European rebellions and revolutions of 1820–1821, 1830, and 1848; the Greek, Balkan, and Egyptian revolts within the Ottoman Empire; and the start of the bloodiest revolt in history, the Taiping rebellion in China. Hobsbawm (1962) has quite reasonably christened this period the "Age of Revolution." Viewing all of these events, one might reasonably conclude that the entire early modern period was simply one of successive crises.

Yet in the years from 1660 to 1760, full-scale political breakdown was curiously rare (Rabb 1975). There were isolated peasant revolts, elite rebellions, and dynastic changes, but revolutionary civil wars were absent from Europe and the Ottoman and Chinese empires. This stability occurred even though the two main alleged engines of revolution— war and the growth of capitalism—roared even more strongly than in the preceding century. This period was one of massive wars, from the "Second Thirty Years' War" (1688–1714), spurred by the ambitions of Louis XIV, to the Seven Years' War (1756–1763), employing the largest and most sophisticated armies that Europe had yet seen. This period was also one of enormous development in capitalist enterprise: in England, the vast majority of enclosures—perhaps two-thirds or more of all enclosures between 1500 and 1850—took place in this century (Wordie 1983); in England, France, and the Netherlands, the rural putting-out industry, which rendered the worker dependent on the suppliers of capital, grew rapidly, displacing the independent artisan in many crafts (de Vries 1976); and throughout the world, the volume of overseas trade grew exponentially, as intra-European trade was joined to vast colonial and imperial trading networks in the Americas, the Levant, and the Far East. I shall further detail, and attempt to measure, these trends later on. Yet it should be evident that the presence of war and the growth of capitalism persisted from 1660 to 1760. State breakdown did not persist. We thus face a problem of historical explanation: why was state breakdown, not merely in Europe but on a worldwide scale, clustered in two marked "waves," the first culminating in the mid-seventeenth century, the second in the mid-nineteenth, and separated by roughly a century, from 1660 to 1760, of stability?

Attempts at comparative study of Asian and European state breakdown in the early modern period have been rare (Mousnier 1970b, 1984). But as we shall see, there are remarkable similarities in the originating patterns of state breakdown in Eastern and Western absolutisms: state fiscal crises linked to inflation; intra-elite divisions over social mobility; and popular uprisings, partly autonomous and partly elite orchestrated, that pressed basic economic demands so fiercely as to lead to changes in political, social, and economic organization. In seventeenth-century China, just as in seventeenth-century England, there was even a faction called the "Levellers," who proclaimed a new age of equality of all men and influenced the popular revolts that accompanied the fall of the Ming. Nonetheless, after the state breakdowns of the mid-sixteenth century, Europe's economic advance accelerated through discoveries and innovations, while Asian economies grew only quantitatively, becoming oddly fixed in their economic and administrative techniques. Thus two more historical questions arise: Why did the near simultaneous state breakdowns in major Asian empires resemble, in their origins, the state breakdowns in Europe? And to the extent that they had similar origins, why were the long-term outcomes so different, leading to that divergence in development commonly known as the "rise of the West?"

STATES AND STATE BREAKDOWN

No doubt, some readers are already impatient with my juxtaposition of vastly different societies and the ill-defined term "state breakdown." Yet the states of early modern Eurasia—including the European monarchies, Russia, China, the Ottoman Empire, and Japan, in roughly the sixteenth through the nineteenth centuries—were not greatly different from each other.[1] The Eurasian states comprised more or less bureaucratic assemblages of officials, under the direction of a single hereditary ruler, and claimed sovereignty over well-defined and usually contiguous territories. Their economies were overwhelmingly agrarian, and the income of states and elites mainly depended, either directly or indirectly, on taxes and rents on land.

By "the state" I mean the institutions of centralized national-level rule-making and rule-enforcing power, including the individuals who controlled those institutions when acting in their official capacities. For early modern states, this included the hereditary ruler and the ministers, legislative assemblies with national powers, royal or imperial tax collectors and judges, and those military forces directly subject to central control. Thus by "the state" I denote only a part, although usually the dominant part, of the total set of political actors and institutions. In early modern societies a variety of other groups and individuals also might have exercised judicial or administrative powers, such as the ability to collect taxes or fees, enact regulations, and administer punishments for violations. Such groups—including regional parliaments or estates; county, municipal, and village authorities; churches and their religious judges; and lay and religious seigneurs—though subordinate, were somewhat independent of the central executive authority and on occasion collided with it. Thus state breakdown generally involved the collapse of the central authority's ability to dominate in a confrontation

---

1. Throughout this book, I use "Eurasia" to denote only the temperate regions north of a line drawn roughly from the easternmost end of the Mediterranean Sea through the Caspian Sea, the Himalayas, and the southern border of China. I thus exclude most of Syria, Mesopotamia, Persia, the Indian subcontinent, and Southeast Asia. These latter regions were often differently administered than the regions north of this line; moreover, their economic and demographic histories are less complete. For these reasons, and to keep this study within manageable bounds, I make no claims about whether the argument developed in this book applies to these southern lands.

with other politically powerful actors, rather than the breakdown of all political institutions.[2]

These societies also exhibited sufficiently separate political and religious authorities that the relationship between the two was problematic. Although specific individuals, above all, rulers, might exercise both political and religious authority, and though the state might seek to determine religious practice and appoint religious leaders, there existed a semiautonomous elite outside of official state office who acted as custodians of a well-articulated moral tradition (Eisenstadt 1980b). In Europe this condition arose because of the presence of the Catholic priesthood; in the Ottoman Empire it arose because of the presence of the Greek Orthodox Church and of the many Islamic religious schools, pious foundations, and their scholars and mullahs; in China it arose because the Chinese literati, although providing the empire's officials, never placed more than a fraction of their members in office and retained an informal role in local education, administration, and ceremonial functions that gave them a partly autonomous role in Chinese society; in Japan it arose because of the separation of the roles of the shogunal administration (which governed) and the imperial court (which remained the sacral center of society).

"Elites" were families of exceptional wealth or status, usually literate, but not necessarily state officials. They were somewhat differentiated by their pursuit of various paths to wealth and status, such as through land, arms, trade, administration, or religion. Such differentiation never constituted a clear-cut division of labor, however, and most elite families showed diversified portfolios of pursuits.

Because of the diversity of elite interests, the relationship between the state and elites was always problematic. Elites expected states to perform certain tasks of government that provided diffuse benefits: orchestration of successful military campaigns; maintenance of internal order; regulation or provision of certain collective goods, such as coinage and transportation networks; and provision of status- and wealth-enhancing opportunities to elites through regulated access to military and

2. M. Weber (1978) and Mann (1988) ascribe to states a monopoly of legitimate force; but this is a false characterization of early modern states, which existed in tension with semiautonomous sources of legitimate authority at the regional level or among groups subject to religious law. My definition follows Weber and Mann in ascribing to states the centralized national rule-making and rule-enforcing authority, but it differs in recognizing that the state shares political space with other actors and authorities. My definition therefore allows for a routine degree of tension and potential conflict that fuels political dynamics.

civil offices (sometimes including regulated access to elite education and training). To perform these tasks, the state required resources gained by taxation, land-ownership, or other sources of revenue. Yet the concentration of resources in the hands of the state posed certain problems. If the level of resource provision was too low, the state could not perform its tasks; if the level of resource provision was too high, the excess might be used to increase the wealth and power of rulers at the expense of broader elites. Elites therefore generally supported state actions that appeared consistent with the performance of expected state tasks, but opposed state actions that threatened an excessive concentration of power in rulers at the expense of broader elite interests. For its part, the state generally sought to perform its expected tasks in a manner sufficient to avoid widespread elite attacks, while seeking to increase its resources to enhance its wealth and power relative to domestic elites and international competitors (Levi 1988). This continuous tension over state resource control was usually managed by negotiation between the state and elites. State crises occurred when these latent conflicts escalated into overt struggles.

Of course, there was also routine tension between the population at large and the state. Rural and urban groups in early modern society looked to the state to ensure maintenance of roads, bridges, and irrigation works; bread at affordable prices and adequate employment; protection from banditry, foreign conquest, and elite exploitation; and administration of local justice. A certain amount of taxation was generally accepted as the price of these collective goods. In fact, these services were usually provided by local or religious authorities rather than by state officials, often for fees collected in addition to state taxation. Nonetheless, common people generally regarded their king or emperor or sultan as the ultimate guarantor of local order. The state was generally blamed when these services deteriorated, or when taxation reached levels that threatened traditional peasant living standards. Under these conditions, popular groups might revolt to demonstrate their grievances against the state; or they might revolt in the name of the king against local elites, decrying the latters' "failure" to comply with the presumed wishes of the king to protect the common folk.

Popular groups also contested with elites for resources, while being dependent on elites for guidance and protection in matters of politics, justice, religion, and material welfare. As with the state, popular groups ordinarily accepted status distinctions and resource extraction by elites as consonant with elite protection and guidance. Yet as with the state, this relationship should be considered one of "routine tension," for elites generally sought to maximize resource extraction and popular groups to minimize it, and elite definitions of adequate and effective guidance and protection often differed from popular views.

The societies studied in this book differed from most earlier agrarian empires in having widespread internal markets, so that the prices and distribution of goods were widely affected by supply and demand. Prices were meaningful in that they affected the access to goods and services for a wide variety of actors. Thus rulers had to acquire food for armies and many other services at prices set by the market; elites' earnings from rents or productive enterprises depended on the market price of their products; urban workers' incomes depended on a market-influenced wage; and peasants' access to land depended on market-determined rents. Of course, many actors used political power to influence the market and attempted to hedge or evade market restrictions. And peasants who had secure landholdings adequate to provide for their families might have participated in the market only marginally, to acquire occasional tools or luxuries or to earn small amounts of cash to pay taxes. However, in each of these societies the market was so widespread that it substantially influenced the incomes and opportunities of many actors, including all of the politically important ones.

In sum, in all of these societies there was (1) an agrarian economic base; (2) a hereditary ruler and officials who administered a territorial state, but who remained in some tension with semiautonomous local, regional, and religious and cultural authorities; (3) a literate elite extending beyond the circle of officialdom who followed a variety of pursuits, and who remained in some tension with the state over the adequacy of state performance and the level of state resource extraction; (4) urban and rural popular groups who were subject to cross-cutting allegiances and resource extraction from both elites and the state; and (5) reasonably well functioning internal markets wherein prices affected the access to goods for a wide variety of social actors.

This is not to overlook such matters as wide differences in the resources of states, in the autonomy of elites, and in the content of religion, all matters to be addressed in due course. It is only to say that for all of these societies one can reasonably speak of "states," of "elites," of conflict between "secular rulers" and "religious groups," and of "prices" and refer to things not impossibly dissimilar across societies.

I shall refer to the revolutions and rebellions examined in this book as cases of *state breakdown*. By state breakdown I mean a particular *combination* of events, but not quite a revolution. The term "revolution" is frequently used with little care; as a result, it has become vague and slippery. Moreover, since the French Revolution, this term has picked up overtones of radical political change that are out of place in referring to many political crises that occurred before 1789. Let me therefore carefully define the subject of this book.

Some authors (e.g., Huntington 1968) define revolution in the extreme sense of a violent and permanent overthrow of government and elites, based on mass participation, that establishes new political and economic institutions, a new status structure with new personnel, and a new set of legitimating symbols and beliefs. This model fits the twentieth-century Russian and Chinese Communist revolutions reasonably well, the French Revolution of 1789 somewhat, and most early modern state crises hardly at all. It is thus not very useful for discussions of the early modern period. The use of the term "revolution" has been further muddled by such phrases as "unsuccessful revolution," "social revolution," "abortive revolution," and "elite revolution," all of which are meant to imply something distinct both from each other and from such events as coups, civil wars, and popular rebellions. Because there have been few events that fit the extreme sense of "revolution," yet many cases of governments being overthrown or temporarily disabled, there have developed almost as many varied definitions of "revolution" as there are analysts and cases of state crises.

Of course, the term "crisis" is equally ambiguous. Scholars often use the term to denote any threat to law and order and thus have found "crises" in a bewildering variety of times and places. As the term is loosely used, a "political crisis" may denote a crisis of confidence in the government, a state bankruptcy, a coup d'état, an elite revolt, a peasant rebellion, an urban riot, or a civil war. I shall use *state crisis* specifically to describe a shift in elite or popular attitudes toward the state. That is, a state crisis is a situation in which politically significant numbers of elites, or popular groups, or both, consider the central state to be operating in a manner that is ineffective, unjust, or obsolete. Such a state crisis may stem from actual failures of governmental performance, such as bankruptcy, defeat in war, or inability to suppress local disorders. Or it may stem from changing economic conditions or reckless governmental actions that cause elites or popular groups to lose confidence in, or withdraw their allegiance from, the state. Either way, elite or popular groups consider the state incapable of performing necessary tasks of governance; the result is that the state loses the allegiance necessary to govern. But a state crisis is not bankruptcy or military defeat *per se*; states often survive such problems without losing the allegiance or confidence of elites and ordinary subjects. For example, Spain in the late sixteenth century, and France at the end of Louis XIV's reign, suffered military setbacks and state bankruptcies. But elites rallied around the state, and widespread popular disorders did not arise. A state crisis occurs when there has been a standing suspicion that the state is ineffective or unjust; such concrete events as a fiscal crisis or military reversal are then taken as the definitive proof of this suspicion. It is thus the shift in elite or popular attitudes toward the state, not a particular event, that marks the crisis of state authority.

Much of the political science literature describes such a shift in attitudes as a crisis of "legitimacy" (Zimmerman 1979, 1983). I prefer to avoid this term; it does not capture my meaning—in part because legitimacy has legalistic connotations that suggest a "legitimate" government is duly constituted whereas an "illegitimate" government is illegally constituted. These considerations are often irrelevant. Moreover, "legitimacy" is inadequate because this term generally focuses attention only on matters of justice and ignores state effectiveness. Political allegiance depends on the extent to which elite and popular groups view the state as just and *effective* in performing the duties of governance. Even legally constituted governments can become perceived as ineffective or unjust, while even illegally formed governments (such as those produced by revolutions or coups) can be perceived as effective and just in their actions. Moreover, even an unjust state may be perceived as so effective that it maintains the allegiance of key groups; and even a just state may be perceived as so ineffective that it loses that allegiance. In sum, a state crisis exists when politically significant numbers of elites, or popular groups, or both, no longer maintain allegiance to the existing state (as it operates as a set of institutions, not just its incumbents), regardless of how the state was formed and regardless of whether this shift in allegiance is due to the state acting unjustly or merely ineffectively, or to changes in the economy or international environment of which the state is victim.

A state crisis usually indicates a situation of imbalance—in the eyes of influential elites and of large numbers of ordinary people, the state is either failing to perform the expected tasks of governance, demanding too many resources for that task, or both. Thus the routine tension over state performance and state revenue escalates to unusually high levels. What will result from this crisis, whether it will pass lightly or lead to overt conflict, depends on the flexibility of state authorities, on the unity and organization of elites, on the mobilization potential of popular groups, and on the precise relationships among these actors, including their financial, organizational, military, and ideological resources. A state crisis may lead to revolution; but it may also lead to an unsuccessful attempt at revolution (as in Prussia in 1848) or to a successful reform (as in the English reform crisis of 1830–1832).

This book seeks to explain a particularly severe kind of state crisis, which, as noted above, I call *state breakdown*. State breakdown occurs when a state crisis leads to widespread overt conflict, including a combination of elite revolts, intra-elite struggles, and popular uprisings. A state crisis may be resolved peacefully if elites shore up state power, or if reformers succeed in rectifying state injustices. Or a state crisis may be resolved with a coup d'état if important elites are united and able to achieve desired changes without popular mobilization. But if elites are highly alienated from the state, command substantial resources, and are divided among themselves, a state crisis may lead to elite revolts and sharp intra-elite conflicts. And if popular unrest is waiting in the wings, conflict between the state and elites may open the doors to popular uprisings or to mobilization of the population to support competing factions. Struggles for power among different groups may then lead to civil war.

State breakdown thus refers to a condition of grave disorder, with a collapse of state authority. Such a situation is sometimes called a revolution. However, I shall reserve the term "revolution" for those cases where state breakdown is followed by substantial changes in political and social institutions and in the ideology used to justify those institutions.

To sharpen these definitions, and to clarify the differences between the wide variety of political crises that have occurred in history, it is useful to adopt some simple notation borrowed from vector algebra.[3] Let us divide the notions of state breakdown and revolution mentioned above into several constituent elements. We then have a range of factors that might be present or absent in a political crisis: (1) widespread elite or popular belief that the state is ineffective, unjust, or obsolete, producing widespread loss of confidence in, or allegiance to, the state; (2) an elite revolt against the state; (3) popular revolts—either urban, rural,

---

3. The application of this technique to holistic comparisons in the social sciences is developed at greater length in Ragin (1987).

or both—against state or elite authority; (4) widespread violence or civil war; (5) a change in political institutions; (6) a change in the status and power of traditional elites, chiefly landlords in agrarian societies; (7) a change in basic forms of economic organization and property ownership; and (8) a change in the symbols and beliefs that justify the distribution of power, status, and wealth.

We can then describe a given historical event by a string of ones and zeros, which designate whether a given element among the eight factors above was or was not present. Thus the Russian and Chinese Communist revolutions (counting the revolt of the Dumas in Russia as an elite revolt) would merit a complete row of ones: $(1,1,1,1,1,1,1,1)$. The French Revolution differs slightly, for even if one counts the loss of seigneurial power of French landlords as a significant change in landlord power, there was no significant change in property ownership or in the forms of economic organization. Thus we would designate the French Revolution $(1,1,1,1,1,1,0,1)$. Stability would be noted by a complete row of zeros: $(0,0,0,0,0,0,0,0)$. A peaceful reform of government could be designated $(1,0,0,0,1,0,0,0)$. This definitional system is extremely versatile. Thus one can describe an ordinary coup $(0,1,0,0,0,0,0,0)$ or an elite revolution $(1,1,0,0,1,1,1,1)$ without confusion. A dynastic civil war that posed no challenge to the state per se, and was only a contest among elite leaders for succession, as frequently occurred in the Ottoman and Mughal empires, could be specified as $(0,1,0,1,0,0,0,0)$, while a secessionary civil war, such as the American Civil War, could be designated $(1,1,0,1,1,0,0,1)$. More importantly, one can express the differences between such diverse historical events as the English Revolution of 1640 $(1,1,1,1,1,0,0,1)$, the Ming-Qing transition $(1,1,1,1,1,1,0,0)$, and the French Revolution $(1,1,1,1,1,1,0,1)$ more precisely than by arguing whether or not the first two were "truly" revolutions. In fact neither was exactly like the French Revolution, nor like the other, although all shared many of the same features.

This definitional system is capable of specifying 128 different kinds of events, ranging from stability to extreme revolution. Of course, many of these definitionally possible events have no attested empirical contents. For instance, I know of no popular rebellion that succeeded by itself without associated elite revolts or elite leadership in creating institutional change $(1,0,1,1,1,1,1,1)$. But this notation allows us to speak more precisely of the varieties of political change without being bound by the accumulation of meanings that have surrounded the word "revolution." In particular, we can specify that by *state breakdown* is meant any event that involves a crisis of central state authority, elite revolts, popular uprisings, and widespread violence or civil war: (1,1,1,1,x,x, x,x). The x's in the last four slots mean that these may be zeros or ones. Thus the object of explanation in this book is a severe crisis involving the first four elements in combination, whether or not this crisis produces the kind of changes we might wish to call a revolution. In particular, my goal is to explain why this severe kind of state crisis periodically erupted all across northern Eurasia in certain decades but was generally absent in others.

In this book I examine, in varying degrees of detail, a number of instances of state breakdown in the early modern world. I consider mainly four cases: the English Revolution in 1639–1642; the French Revolution in 1789–1792; the Anatolian rebellions in the Ottoman Empire (starting roughly in the 1590s, with disorder peaking at the assassination of the sultan in 1648 and ending with the suppression of Abaza Hasan Paşa's revolt in 1658); and the fall of the Ming dynasty in China (c. 1644). In addition, I more briefly examine the Fronde and the revolts in the Spanish Hapsburg Empire in the mid-seventeenth century; the revolutions of 1830 in France and of 1848 in France and Germany; the Taiping rebellion in Qing China, and the Meiji Restoration in Japan. Perhaps only one or two of these events, depending on one's point of view, deserve to be called "revolutions." However, all were instances of state breakdown. I also explore the relative tranquility of the late seventeenth and early eighteenth centuries in Europe and Asia. My primary goal is to show how a common causal pattern lay behind all these events. But in chapter 5 I shall return to important differences.

Before laying out the causal framework, it is worth noting some of the problems in current historiography, and some lacunae in the theory of revolutions, that this framework seeks to redress.

PROBLEMS IN HISTORIOGRAPHY

At present, the historiography of early modern political crises is in turmoil. For both the English and French revolutions, "revisionists" have blasted once widely accepted explanations based on long-term social change. For both cases, an influential and learned school of thought now insists that these revolutions in fact had no long-term social causes; instead they were brought on by purely political conflicts and exacerbated by chance conjunctions of unfortunate circumstances.

Until recently, most scholars viewed the English Revolution of 1640 as the culmination of extensive changes in English society. In an influential synthesis, L. Stone (1972) argued that the Stuart state was financially and administratively weak; that social mobility in the preceding century had augmented the importance of the gentry and lessened that of the peerage, creating struggles to broaden access to political power while weakening one of the supports of the throne; and that unresolved religious conflicts left England with a Church that had limited appeal to an increasingly independent gentry, creating a deepening problem of Puritan disaffection. Given the weakness of the state and the growing range of political, social, and religious conflicts, some form of major crisis was inevitable. Although Stone rejected arguments that traced the revolution to the growth of capitalism and the triumph of an English bourgeoisie, able proponents, including Hill (1961), B. Moore (1966), Anderson (1974), and Wallerstein (1980), put forth versions of this Marxist view. Though differing in emphasis, these authors shared Stone's view that the revolutionary crisis could be understood only by tracing its long-term social causes.

In recent years, however, key elements of both these approaches have come under attack. Examinations of parliamentary debates have shown that the political conflicts of the revolution were hardly a long-term running battle over royal versus parliamentary prerogatives; instead Parliament showed little tendency to criticize the Crown or to limit its authority before 1629 (Russell 1979). Similarly, studies of Puritanism show that the Puritan clergy, following their disciplining and co-optation by Elizabeth and James I, were quite cooperative with the Crown until the Arminian assault of the 1630s (Richardson 1973). Work on rural capitalism has uncovered evidence that by the early seventeenth century the Crown was a leader in raising rents, enclosure, and the search for profits (Thirsk 1967a); the image of an anticommercial Crown facing an aggressively entrepreneurial "bourgeois" gentry thus appears false. Moreover, the House of Lords appears to have played a major, even dominating, role in many of the parliamentary maneuvers of 1640–1642, casting doubt on the "rise of the gentry" (C. Roberts 1977a). In short, the old synthesis appears eroded. Still, all that has been accomplished is criticism; no alternative long-term explanation has appeared in its place. Revisionist scholars thus conclude that there were no long-term causes, and that the crisis of the 1640s, far from being inevitable, was a simple product of policy errors of the 1630s in the context of England's unique political institutions, namely, a dependence on the cooperation of Crown and gentry in local and national administration. This system could not survive a monarch that systematically antagonized the gentry and bungled its political appointments and policies. It was thus simply Charles I's mistakes that produced the revolution (K. Sharpe 1978b).

A strikingly similar trend in scholarship has affected studies of the French Revolution. The dominant synthesis for the last century has been the Marxist view that this was a "bourgeois" revolution in which an emerging capitalist class asserted its rights against a conservative Crown and nobility. This synthesis was and still is vigorously defended by an influential group of French scholars—Mathiez (1928), Lefebvre (1947), Soboul (1975), Mazauric (1970), Godechot (1970, 1971), and Vovelle (1984). Yet a new generation of American and French scholars has largely abandoned this view, for its elements have been undermined by critical scrutiny. Most damaging is the evidence that the capitalist bourgeoisie played a relatively limited, largely provincial, role in the revolution; the revolution's leaders in Paris were drawn from professionals and, to a rather large degree, the nobility (Eisenstein 1968; Egret 1968). G. Taylor (1972b) has shown that both nobles and prosperous nonnobles shared similar economic profiles. Doyle (1972) has presented evidence to question the old notion that eighteenth-century France was marked by a "feudal reaction." C. Lucas (1973) has suggested that conflicts within the nobility were as important, if not more important, than conflicts between nobles and bourgeoisie. Furet and Richet (1970) have argued that the conflicts that fatally weakened the French state were not between distinct classes but rather among the varied elements of the absolutist administration, drawn from different status groups and increasingly divided in their access to power and social prominence.

French absolutism relied on a congeries of separate but overlapping institutions—parlements and provincial estates, aristocratic provincial governors and recently ennobled intendants, court officers and private financiers, an army dominated by gentlemen officers, and a civil administration dominated by judges and lawyers. Keeping this administration in operation required a skillful hand in both economic and political policies. Furet (1981) has argued that a combination of severe weather that weakened the agricultural economy and the inability of Louis XVI to handle the multiple conflicts within the ramshackle but extensive and expensive French state led somewhat fortuitously to state breakdown. Not a crisis of capitalism but rather a crisis of absolutist administration brought down the old order. Thus the French Revolution, like the English, has been reduced from the culmination of long-term underlying social changes and stresses to the bad luck and misdirection of an un-happy monarch, unable to meet the managerial demands of France's uniquely complex administrative system.

While the sharp criticisms of the revisionists have satisfied the urge to unearth new facts and to uncover false impressions, the total effect has been deeply dissatisfying to many historians, who now see the most momentous events in English and French history construed as mere ac-cidents. Unwilling to abandon the satisfying old syntheses, yet shaken by the revisionist attacks, many scholars find themselves in a quandary. In regard to the English Revolution, Sayer (1985, 3) notes Marxists' troubled response to critiques of the Marxist interpretation: "The 'bour-geois revolution' is extraordinarily difficult to pin down in England. The 'classic ground' obstinately, infuriatingly, refuses to fit the classic models. The usual strategy for dealing with this is to retain the models . . . whilst variously 'ad hoc-ing' away England's 'peculiari-ties.' " Non-Marxists complain that "at present there seems to be no generally accepted interpretation of the English Civil War, and little has been done in the search for a new synthesis other than to demolish the old" (Carlton 1980, 168). What remains is a "chaotic and centrifugal state of social history today, which is flying off in all directions with no large structure to hold it together . . . . Nothing is left but a ragbag of miscellaneous topics, all fascinating in themselves, but without anything to bind them together" (L. Stone 1984, 47). Regarding the French Revo-lution, Behrens (1974, 637) similarly has noted that "it has often been pointed out, and is now publicly admitted, that the orthodox explana-tion of the Revolution in terms of a class struggle will not stand the test of facts. [But] now that the orthodoxy is discredited we do not know what to believe . . . . In the days of Mathiez and Lefebvre's ascendancy we thought we knew. Now there is no coherent explanation."

Old certainties of Asian history have also fallen under a barrage of new research. Traditional Asian history, from Chinese dynastic histo-rians to the Arab historian Ibn Khaldûn, explained recurrent state break-downs through the dynastic cycle: imperial families eventually produced weak heirs and corrupt followers, and then succumbed to more vigorous challengers. Modern historians, under the influence of Marxist com-parative history, have long reiterated this theme, adding that the cyclic history of the dynastic period was due to the "feudal" character of tra-ditional Asian societies and the absence of Western "rationalization" and progress.

However, recent scholarship on the Ming and Qing economy has undermined many historians' most cherished myths regarding Asia's lack of change and of economic rationalization. Evidence of advanced commercial enterprise in the sixteenth and seventeenth centuries in China is so great that Chinese historians now speak of this period as containing visible "sprouts of capitalism." Under the Qing, Chinese trade was evidently regulated by local merchant associations whose enforcement of contracts, regulation of weights and measures, and freedom from state interference in commerce equaled or exceeded anything found in the absolutist West (Myers 1982). As early as the sixteenth century, China exhibited regionally specialized agriculture, particularly in rice and cotton, serving vast markets. Moreover, the fall of the Ming dynasty was marked by changes in administration, in land law, and in rural class relations. Specifically, increased centralization, uniformity of taxation, collapse of the power of local landlords and transfer of their authority to the bureaucracy, and abolition of serfdom and its replacement by formally free tenant cultivators (Wakeman 1985) exceeded the changes produced by the English Revolution and paralleled those in France centuries later. Progress in commerce and rationalization may have differed from that of the West, yet the difference can no longer be framed in terms of a complete absence of economic change and rationalization in China. Similar changes have been noted in Ottoman history. These events are described in more detail later. However, it should be evident that the old shibboleths of the "unchanging East" are done for.

In sum, once widely accepted explanations of early modern history are now in tatters. The English and French revolutions, it is argued, were little more than large-scale historical accidents. The evidence for early sophistication and growth in Asian economies leaves it a mystery why the Asian empires experienced simple "dynastic" crises, and why they later fell behind Europe in economic and political development. The basic contrast that once made sense of world history—between an early modern West that progressed by inevitable revolutions and an early modern East mired in traditional stagnation—no longer receives support from historical research.

One might expect that historians searching for better explanations of the seventeenth-century crises would undertake careful comparisons of Eastern and Western political history. Yet at present, such comparisons are almost entirely lacking. A number of modern scholars have endeavored comparative studies of Asia and the West: Braudel, Chirot, Collins, Elvin, Hajnal, G. Hamilton, E. L. Jones, Laslett, McNeill, Mousnier, North, Skocpol, Wallerstein, and Wong. However, all of these studies have limitations and many deal only tangentially with politics. Braudel (1967), Elvin (1973, 1984), Hajnal (1965, 1982), E. L. Jones (1981b), Laslett (1971), and North (1981) deal chiefly with economic and demographic history; Mousnier (1970b) deals with peasant revolts, and Wong (1983) with administrative capabilities. Chirot (1985), Collins (1980), and McNeill (1982) deal with overall political and economic development but, despite their significant insights, still rest within an essentially Weberian framework of Western rationalization. Skocpol (1979) compares the French Revolution with the modern Chinese Revolution of 1911–1949; she thus pulls these events out of temporal context and fails to shed light on the coincidence of major political upheavals and divergent political and economic developments in the early modern period. G. Hamilton (1984) maps the divergent paths of cultural development in China and Europe and traces their implications for long-range economic change. However, the political upheavals of the Ming and Qing do not figure in his accounts. Wallerstein (1980, 1989) and his colleagues have examined the process of the Ottoman Empire's incorporation into the European trade patterns from the seventeenth to the nineteenth centuries; however, they have not directly addressed the problem of Ottoman state breakdown. In short, historians have yet to examine the major political breakdowns in imperial China and Turkey, and their connections to long-term economic and political development, through comparison with state breakdowns of early modern Europe.

Another curiosity is also apparent. Historians have long recognized that early modern European history shows a concentration of political crises in the period 1550–1650, followed by a century of stability, then another concentration of crises in the period 1750–1850. And they have drawn freely on theoretical accounts of revolution by sociologists and political scientists in their attempts to explain these events (Forster and Greene 1970; Zagorin 1982). Yet the reverse has not occurred; no theorist of revolutions has begun with the empirical clustering of early modern revolutions and attempted to build a theory of political crises consistent with this fact.

THE LIMITS OF THEORY

Historians of early modern revolutions who turned to social science for explanations (L. Stone 1972; Zagorin 1982) found theories designed chiefly to explain the widespread violence that occurred in the developing world after World War II, violence that was considered symptomatic of the strains of "modernization." From the 1950s to the early 1970s, most social scientists viewed revolutions as merely the largest events on a scale of political violence that ranged from individual illegal acts, through riots and rebellions, and ultimately to revolutions. They thus focused on generalized models of social "strain" (Smelser 1963). They differed over whether these strains stemmed from individual frustration and discontent (C. Davies 1964; Gurr 1970) or from systemic "dis-equilibrium" (C. Johnson 1966) or "imbalance" (Huntington 1968) in the development of different social and political institutions. However, analysis of individual-level angst and systemwide disequilibria left little room for an examination of how specific political institutions had worked, or failed to work, in particular historical contexts. Thus social theorists simply plucked elements of complex historical narratives and used them illustratively, often out of context, in building and testing their theories. In turn, historians simply plucked elements of these theories and used the terms to couch their descriptions of particular crises. With a few outstanding exceptions (B. Moore 1966; Wolf 1969), careful comparisons of how political crises had developed in various historical settings, and how they were similar or different, were not undertaken.

This situation changed markedly in the 1970s. The historically grounded work of C. Tilly and his collaborators (Tilly et al. 1975; C. Tilly 1978) challenged the validity of general theories of violence, ar-guing that more attention needed to be paid to how conflicts developed and how resources for opposition were mobilized in specific historical contexts. Paige (1975), Eisenstadt (1978), Skocpol (1979), and a host of other scholars developed a new "social-structural" perspective on revolutions (see Goldstone 1980, 1982, for a detailed survey). These works generally focused on a few cases and presented extended narra-tives and analyses. Their goal was not to provide a universally applicable theory of revolutions or of political violence; instead they explicitly sought to understand how different episodes of political violence varied and how historical context mattered to the causes and outcomes of state breakdown. Despite the richness of this work, however, it is not quite applicable to the problem of explaining the "waves" of political crises in the early modern period.

Charles Tilly's (1967, 1978, 1986) work on rebellion and revolution in Europe examines the organizational basis for popular protest and how changes in state-civil society relations affected the form and intensity of collective behavior. Yet Tilly treats these explanatory changes as long-term *continuous* processes—the growth of state power and the spread of capitalist organization of production. Though his work brims with insights on which I shall draw, it thus does not address the *periodic* "waves" of state breakdown.

Skocpol's (1979) work is among the most influential of recent theories of revolution. Comparing the French, Russian, and Chinese revolutions, she noted that each revolution occurred when the state faced pressures from wars with more advanced capitalist states. She also observed that in each of these countries there was some combination of structural weaknesses that created the potential for revolutionary crisis: backward agriculture that could not support a competitive military (Russia); autonomous elites who could block the state's attempts to raise taxes and centralize power (France and China); and strong peasant villages that could readily mobilize for attacks on landlords in the event of a weakening of the central government, under either traditional village leaders (France and Russia) or communist party organizers (China). The conjunction of pressure from abroad, structural constraints on state actions, and peasant organization that abetted effective rural uprisings produced revolutions. Skocpol's theory has not escaped criticism. Gugler (1982) and Dix (1983) have suggested that Skocpol understates the role of urban workers in bringing about revolutions. Eisenstadt (1978) and Sewell (1985b) have argued that cultural differences, which Skocpol neglects, played a large role in shaping revolutionary possibilities. However, Skocpol must be given credit for bringing three observations to the forefront of current studies of revolution: (1) revolutions arise from a conjunction of events—state crises, popular uprisings, and elite actions—each of which may have different causes and therefore must be separately investigated and explained; (2) states are not merely objects of revolutionary struggles but also actors in the social drama whose actions and options are crucial in precipitating revolutionary crises; and (3) revolutions are often the product of international forces that impinge on particular states and interact with their particular institutions.

Unfortunately, this work so far has had little impact on comparative studies of early modern history. The major comparative studies by Anderson and Wallerstein are still wrought in a solidly Marxist framework that subordinates state actions to class struggles. Skocpol's work, which does focus attention on the state and on international military competition, is a valuable corrective. Yet it turns out to be poorly suited to explain the pattern of state breakdowns in the early modern world.

The incidence of war itself provides little guidance to the long-term recurrence of revolution. Much has been made of the impact of particular wars, such as the Thirty Years' War, which preceded the seventeenth-century state breakdowns in England, France, and Spain, and World War I, which led to the Russian Revolution of 1917. Yet little attention has been paid to the even larger wars that did *not* produce state breakdown. From 1688 to 1714, Louis XIV brought Europe into almost continual armed conflict, leading some historians to label this period the "Second Thirty Years' War." France suffered extensive defeats in these wars, which were fought with larger armies and cost far more than the first Thirty Years' War. Yet despite defeat and bankruptcy, neither France nor any other of the combatants experienced revolutions. Similarly, the immediate outcome of the enormous conflicts of the Napoleonic Wars (1799–1815) was not revolutions in the major European powers but rather increases in the authority of conservative states in England, Prussia, Austria-Hungary, and Russia. Furthermore, insufficient attention has been paid to those revolutions that erupted in times relatively *free* of war, such as the revolutions that erupted in Belgium, France, Italy, Poland, Switzerland, Germany, and Austria-Hungary in 1830 and 1848. As these cases make clear, the incidence of war is neither a necessary nor a sufficient answer to the question of the causes of state breakdown.

From 1550 to 1815, there were few decades in which Europe was free from major wars. Moreover, the scale and cost of warfare was constantly growing. Yet in these centuries state breakdown was sharply cyclic, including a peak during the relatively peaceful (in terms of interstate conflict) mid-nineteenth century. How then should we view the connections between war and revolution?

Military pressure, of course, depends on the nature of war, as well as its incidence. The "military revolution" of the sixteenth century has been blamed for increasing the costs of war to a ruinous degree. Yet martial technology was almost unchanged from 1550 to 1850; once earthwork fortifications had countered the invention of the siege cannon, and the musket had replaced the bow, the chief element of war remained the infantryman, equipped with musket or pike. Artillery gradually supplanted cavalry, but the pace of change was slow (van Creveld 1989, 97). What changed most dramatically was the scale and cost of war. These trends, in turn, were related to broader trends in the economy: changes in the size of populations meant changes in the number of men eligible for service, and changes in prices enormously affected the costs of putting those men under arms. And in the periods 1550 to 1650 and 1750 to 1850, European nations experienced unusual bouts of population growth and price inflation. Thus, for example, the increases in military costs in the sixteenth and seventeenth centuries occurred largely because of a doubling in major states' populations and a fivefold increase in price levels; these trends combined created a tenfold increase in the costs of larger armies and their provisions (G. Parker 1976, 206).

We can therefore follow Skocpol in noting that the pressure of fighting, or preparing for, international conflicts can undermine state finances. Yet we must insist that it is not the mere incidence of such conflict that is crucial; such incidence does not correspond to the cyclic pattern observed for early modern state breakdown. What does matter is how the cost of meeting military pressures impinges on states. And in the early modern era, as I detail in the following chapters, those costs depended chiefly on cyclic trends in population and prices.

Moreover, in the early modern period the comparatively advanced capitalist states—the Netherlands in 1566–1648 and England in 1640–1688—were as likely to suffer revolutions as their adversaries. Thus a theory that sees state breakdown as primarily owing to military pressure from more advanced capitalist states fares poorly for this period. In addition, as noted above, Skocpol largely neglects urban tumults, which were crucial to state breakdown in these centuries. She also neglects the impact of cultural differences, without which one can hardly comprehend the varying effects of state breakdown in early modern Europe and Asia. Crucial deficiencies, therefore, have limited the impact of Skocpol's work on the comparative history of early modern Europe and Asia.

Problems in the theory of revolutions have also been explored in more narrowly focused studies. Trimberger (1978) extended the structural theory of revolutions to cover cases of "revolution from above." She noted that Japan in 1868 and Turkey in 1921 both experienced state breakdown and new institution-building, yet in each case the struggle for power was relatively brief and confined to elites. She maintained that this kind of elite revolution also was due to states coming under pressures from more advanced states abroad, but each occurred where there existed, instead of the structural weaknesses cited by Skocpol, a highly professional bureaucratic elite, devoted to government service rather than to ownership of land, which had the flexibility to reshape institutions to meet external pressures. Goldfrank (1979) has used a structural approach—emphasizing the place of Mexico in the international system, conflicts among the elites, and regional variations in the organization of peasants—to examine the origins of the Mexican Revolution. Abrahamian (1980) has used a similar approach, albeit emphasizing urban organization rather than the organization of peasants, to analyze the recent revolution in Iran.

Wolf (1969), Paige (1975), Migdal (1974), J. Scott (1976), and Popkin (1979) have waged a debate over the factors that govern peasant participation in revolutions, with Scott stressing cultural factors, Paige stressing the economic relations of cultivators to landlords, Midgal and Wolf stressing the penetration of villages by capitalist organization and the impact of population growth, and Popkin emphasizing peasants' calculations of advantage within the traditional village. All of these factors no doubt play a role, but their primacy in specific situations has not been resolved. One thing does appear clear, however: peasant participation in revolutions is rarely a simple protest against traditional exploitation. Instead, peasants act when they have the opportunity, which involves village mobilization and weaknesses in landlord or state control, and when the terms of traditional exactions are changing, which may be caused by population shifts, changes in marketing or agricultural practices, or changes in the state's and elites' opportunities and needs.

Regarding urban actors, Rudé (1964) has studied police records of revolutionary crowds and found that, far from being irrational mobs, these crowds were made up chiefly of established workers and artisans seeking to defend their economic interests. Further studies of workers' movements by Calhoun (1983b) and Aminzade (1981) demonstrate the manner in which revolutionary movements have drawn power from workers' defense of traditional rights. Rejai and Phillips (1983) have examined revolutionary leaders and found that leaders rarely precipitated revolutionary crises; instead revolutionary situations—state breakdown and conflicts over authority—gave scope for individuals who would likely have followed traditional professions to emerge in revolutionary roles.

Increased attention has also been devoted to the outcomes of revolutions. Skocpol (1979), Eckstein (1982), Walton (1984), and Tardanico (1985), examining mostly twentieth-century revolutions, have identified a number of factors that influence revolutionary outcomes. They suggest that socialist governments are most likely to emerge when economic resources are concentrated in a few capital-intensive centers, when mass mobilization is extensive, and when external pressures from capitalist countries are modest; capitalist governments are favored outcomes when the reverse situation holds.

This volume of work has been impressive in its insights. Current theories of revolution stress variety. Ranging over a large number of cases and problems, scholars have adopted multicausal, conjunctural explanations. They trace variation in revolutionary conflicts and outcomes to differences in military pressures, differences in the autonomy of elites and of peasants, variations in the resources of states, and changes in the opportunities and pressures imposed on nations by shifts in the international economy. Recent work in the theory of revolutions is also impressive for its willingness to depart from traditional views. For example, Skocpol downplays class conflict, denies that the French Revolution was chiefly a "bourgeois" revolution, and stresses the autonomy of the state. (Indeed, Marxist theories of the modern capitalist state have increasingly conceded an autonomous and critical role to state managers.)

Yet most of this effort is concerned with explaining twentieth-century revolutions, in which the collisions of international colonial and economic forces with traditional regimes played a major role. Where theorists of revolution have looked back as far as 1789, they have, like Skocpol, sought comparisons to more modern events. The theory of revolutions has yet to address early modern political crises in their own right. As a result, recent developments in the theory of revolutions have been of limited relevance to studies of early modern history.

Most historians of early modern revolutions and rebellions have retreated from the Marxist synthesis since it too often has been at odds with the findings of research. Yet recent theories of revolution have considerable flaws of their own, and only limited applicability to early modern Europe. As a result, studies of early modern revolutions and rebellions lack a common framework. To some scholars, this lack of synthesis is unsettling. J. Fletcher (1985, 37–38), whose studies of Mongol history span Eurasia, has recently asked, "Is there an early modern history? Or are there only histories? . . . Without a macrohistory . . . the full significance of the historical peculiarities of a given society cannot be seen." McDougall (1986, 20), contemplating the impressively wide-ranging findings of historians, has asked, "Can the [historical] profession long survive without some overarching structure to house and organize our sprawling warehouse of special knowledge? Or will it collapse under its own weight?" To date, theories of revolution have not provided an adequate framework for examining the state crises of the early modern world. It is no surprise, therefore, that many historians of early modern revolutions and rebellions, feeling far richer in facts than in overall frameworks, criticize social scientists for their misleading or inadequate offerings.

TOWARD A COMMON FRAMEWORK

Large states of the early modern period, whether monarchies or empires, faced certain common constraints. They needed to raise sufficient revenues to support their armies and reward their retainers. They needed sufficient allegiance from the elites to secure loyal officials for government service and, perhaps more importantly, to secure loyal local authorities in an era when centrally appointed officialdom rarely penetrated below the county level. And they needed to provide sufficient stability and sustenance for the working and cultivating population so that the latter could pay their taxes and other obligations and yet not be inclined to support rebellions. Thus any train of events that simultaneously led to fiscal deterioration, elite factionalism and disloyalty, and a major decline in popular living standards or undermining of popular traditional rights, threatened the ability of states to maintain their authority. In the sixteenth century such a train of events did begin, on a worldwide scale.

A DEMOGRAPHIC/STRUCTURAL MODEL OF STATE BREAKDOWN

Put simply, large agrarian states of this period were not equipped to deal with the impact of the steady growth of population that then began throughout northern Eurasia, eventually amounting to population increases in excess of the productivity gains of the land. The implications of this ecological shift went far beyond mere issues of poverty and population dislocation. Pressure on resources led to persistent price inflation. Because the tax systems of most early modern states were based on fixed rates of taxation on people or land, tax revenues lagged behind prices. States thus had no choice but to seek to expand taxation. This was all the more true as population increases led to the expansion of armies and hence to rising real costs. Yet attempts to increase state revenues met resistance from the elites and the populace and thus rarely succeeded in offsetting spiraling expenses. As a result, most major states in the seventeenth century were rapidly raising taxes but were still headed for fiscal crisis. Moreover, elites were seeking to secure their own relative position. Population growth increased the number of aspirants for elite positions, and their demands were difficult to satisfy given the fiscal strains on the state. Elites thus were riven by increasing rivalry and factionalism, as pursuit of positions and resistance to state demands led to the formation of rival patronage networks in competition for state rewards. Finally, population growth led not only to rural misery but also to urban migration and falling real wages, owing to the especially rapid expansion of youth cohorts that accompanied the population growth. Thus both urban workers and rural artisans staged food riots and wage protests.

Ideological battles flared as well, for state weakness, elite competition, and popular discontent combined to fuel religious conflicts. In these periods, the states' fiscal difficulties undermined their financial support for established churches, and the attempts to use the churches to buttress their increased demands for taxes and other resources led to entwined religious and political opposition. Dissident elites and dissatisfied artisans were thus widely recruited into heterodox religious movements. As all of these trends intensified, the results in each case were state bankruptcy and consequent loss of control of the military, elite movements of regional and national rebellion, and a combination of elite-mobilized and popular uprisings that manifested the breakdown of central authority.

Naturally, these trends showed numerous national and regional variations. Yet, as I demonstrate in the following chapters, the evidence for these trends is strong even in diverse settings. Thus this framework offers a way to understand the political crises of the early and mid-seventeenth century across northern Eurasia, and to explain their common features.

The growth in population that occurred throughout the temperate regions of Eurasia from about 1500 is well known but still not adequately explained. Climate records show a distinct warming in the later Middle Ages that lasted until around 1600, at which time population growth rates also slowed (Galloway 1986). In addition, from 1500 onward the recurrent visitations of plague, which reappeared in Europe roughly every thirty years since the fourteenth century, ceased. In discussing specific cases below, I present the specific population data, as well as the controversies over causation, for each nation. But it is generally well established that a combination of favorable climate and receding disease led to a doubling of the population in most regions between 1500 and the early 1600s.

These conditions did not last. The climate turned distinctly cooler and more variable after 1600; plague returned, accompanied by smallpox, typhoid, and other infectious diseases. By 1650, outside of a few exceptional pockets of growth, population increase had halted worldwide. There followed a century of high mortality, in which population in most regions stagnated or declined. Yet for those who lived, conditions, paradoxically, improved. With population nearly constant, agricultural improvement immediately raised per capita food supplies; food prices thus widely stabilized or fell. With the labor force not growing but trade and output increasing, real wages began to climb upward. Elite composition stabilized, and elite incomes and royal revenues were no longer eroded by inflation. On the contrary, landed elites and states took advantage of favorable conditions to retrench. The age of Louis XIV was one of short lives and high mortality; but it was also an age of stable prices and relative domestic peace for those who survived, not only in France but across the continent.

Some time in the late seventeenth century, the peak of poor climate and epidemics was passed; by the early eighteenth century, the population had recovered its early-seventeenth-century levels and then began to surpass them. By the second half of the eighteenth century, pressure on the land, and accompanying inflation, were evident throughout Europe and China. Renewed expansion of the cities and of the pool of aspirants to elite positions, combined with falling real wages, led to concentrations of the ambitious and the impoverished in European capitals. In nations with weak financial structures and high expenses, such as France and China, administrative structures were crumbling by the end of the eighteenth century. In nations that had used the favorable interlude of 1660–1760 to streamline expenses and expand their incomes, such as England and Prussia, administrative structures held, although they faced recurrent elite and popular protests throughout the first half of the nineteenth century, culminating on the continent in the revolutions of 1848.

After 1850, railroads and steamships combined with cheap American and Russian grain to end the specter of population outstripping food supplies in Europe. However, in Russia and China population growth continued to exceed agricultural expansion, and land hunger contributed to state breakdowns in both countries in the second decade of the twentieth century. But these events take us far beyond the early modern era.

This model of state breakdown emphasizes demographic changes. Yet it does not rest on those changes alone. The key process is how demographic changes affected critical aspects of the social structure. Thus for each case examined in this book, we shall look at evidence pertaining to the following questions: (1) How did population change? (2) How did shifts in the balance between population and economic output affect prices? (3) How did price changes affect state income? (4) How did population and price changes affect elite incomes and the recruitment of families and individuals to elite positions? (5) How did population and price changes affect the income and employment conditions of the general population, both cultivators and landless laborers? And (6) how did changes in the relative income of states, elites, and popular groups— and their attempts to cope with those changes—affect ideological alignments, including allegiance to established churches or heterodoxies? Because this explanatory framework combines attention to both demographic change and the ability of various social structures to respond to such change, it is not a demographic model but rather a demographic/*structural* model of state breakdown.

Moreover, while this framework emphasizes material changes as the *cause* of state breakdown, these material changes dictated no particular outcomes. I argue in chapter 5 that state reconstruction offered a variety of choices to elites, and that whether such reconstruction involved radical change or the strengthening of traditional institutions *depended chiefly on particular cultural frameworks and the development of elite ideologies*. Clearly, material and ideological factors influenced both the causes of state breakdown *and* the outcomes. However, this framework suggests a particular balance of material and cultural forces; it gives a predominant role to material factors in bringing about state breakdown, but a predominant role to culture and ideologies in shaping state reconstruction.

WAS DEMOGRAPHIC CHANGE AN INDEPENDENT FORCE IN HISTORY?

There is increasing awareness that early modern populations controlled their fertility. Restrictions on marriage, and the practice of infanticide, meant that populations were not simply controlled by their "animal instincts." One may thus ask whether it is proper to consider population change as an exogenous factor in early modern history, or whether population change should itself be considered as dependent on changing economic or cultural conditions.

Recent detailed studies of historical populations allow us to firmly answer this question—long-term changes in population size before 1850 were dominated by *independent movements of mortality*. Populations did control their fertility, but this was only a secondary process, undertaken in response to mortality changes. Thus a population experiencing low mortality, and hence rapid growth, would try to slow down that growth by restricting marriage and childbirth. Conversely, a population experiencing high mortality, and hence population decline or stagnation, would encourage marriage and try to avert population decline. But until about 1770 in England, and until about 1850 elsewhere, fertility control worked only to moderate the impact of mortality changes. In every case in this book for which there is detailed information—England and France prior to 1800, and Germany in the nineteenth century—independent mortality movements governed whether or not total population grew. As Wrigley and Schofield (1981, 244) note for England, prior to 1750 "mortality was clearly the more important influence on growth rates." The rule for early modern populations was simple: when mortality was low, the population grew; when mortality was high, the population declined or stagnated. Fertility control merely affected the rate of growth or decline.

I present evidence that supports this claim in some detail in the case studies that follow. Yet we may well ask what caused the worldwide mortality shifts that led populations to alternately grow and stagnate in unison all across Eurasia.

The very breadth of population movements—which moved in the same direction, although at different rates, from England to China—suggests that the answer cannot be found in local economic conditions or culture patterns. Indeed, long-run mortality was clearly independent of such economic conditions as prices and food supplies. Wherever the data for population, food prices, and wages exist, we consistently find that periods of population growth were precisely periods of relatively high food prices and low wages; whereas in periods of low food prices and high real wages populations stagnated. The reason for this pattern is simple: if population size moved for its own reasons and food supplies were relatively stable, then a growing population and rising demand would lead to higher prices, and a stable or declining population to lower prices. Similarly, a larger population and more laborers, if they faced relatively stable employment opportunities, would drive down real wages. Thus the patterns in the data clearly suggest, as Wrigley and Schofield (1981) and R. Lee (1980) note for England, as Dupaquier (1979) and Armengaud (1976) note for France, and as W. Lee (1977) notes for Germany, that population moved independently, for reasons exogenous to the agrarian economy. In R. Lee's (1980, 547) words, "in preindustrial Europe, as far back as records will take us, population swings were largely autonomous, not a response to economic variations."

Mortality did not respect income. The long-term mortality trends of English peers and French dukes were quite similar to those of the English and French populations as a whole. We are thus forced to seek a cause of mortality change that roamed freely across national borders, different cultures, and income groups. Scholars have hence come to believe that the critical determinants of long-run mortality change were long-run movements in the incidence of disease.

A focus on disease helps make sense of the coincidence of European and Asian population trends, for, as McNeill (1977) remarks, by the thirteenth century Europe and Asia had become linked through a confluence of disease pools. From the time of the Black Death in the fourteenth century, disease swept out of central Asia westward to the Middle East and Europe, and eastward to China. At the same time that the Black Death was ravaging Europe and the Middle East, massive epidemics accompanied the fall of the Yuan dynasty in China (1368). And in the late sixteenth and early seventeenth centuries, when plague returned to Europe, this time accompanied by smallpox and typhus, devastating disease epidemics were again reported in the Ottoman and Ming empires (Dols 1979; Dunstan 1975).

Once a new disease entered a vulnerable population, it did not merely kill off a portion of the population and then disappear. Instead it remained endemic, raising mortality levels for generations, until the virulence of the disease diminished as the population gained resistance. Thus the original impact of the Black Death in 1347 was exacerbated by repeat outbreaks every decade or two until the late 1400s. And the incursion of plague and smallpox from the mid-seventeenth century was followed by repeated outbreaks until the early eighteenth century. These waves of disease helped keep population growth low throughout the fifteenth century, and stagnant from the mid-seventeenth century to the early eighteenth.

We know almost nothing, however, about what signals the outbreak of a new virulent disease. We may ask, in our own day, what accounts for the new plague brought by the AIDS virus, and what its effect would have been had modern medicine not identified the virus and its mode of transmission? The origins of such killers as bubonic plague, smallpox, and syphilis remain something of a mystery. And why such diseases erupt in worldwide pandemics in some centuries and recede in others is unknown.

It is possible that the answer lies in part in worldwide shifts in weather. The periods of high mortality in early modern history occurred during periods of cooler and more variable weather than characterized periods of low mortality, as indicated by tree-ring growth (Galloway 1986, 7). It may be that cooler weather forced people to spend more time indoors, increasing risks of disease transmission (Post 1985), or that cooler weather led to changes in the migratory behavior of disease-carrying insects and rodents. It also may be that more variable weather—violent alternations of hot and cold, irregular seasons, and severe storms—weakened people's resistance to infection.

At present, these weather-related hypotheses are merely speculation. What we do know is that in the early modern period population growth was controlled chiefly by mortality movements, and that long-term mortality was determined chiefly by outbreaks of virulent disease. High long-term mortality levels were not due to high food prices or low real wages and thus appear to have been independent of economic factors. Mortality levels rose and stayed elevated for generations, as disease outbreaks repeated with slowly diminishing severity. Mortality levels then fell and remained low until the next major disease incursion. The rate of population growth or decline in particular regions was of course somewhat affected by local economic and cultural conditions. During good times, population growth was most rapid in areas with plentiful land to settle, such as Eastern Europe and Russia. But good times and bad times came in unison to all with the movement of contagious disease.

Such ebbs and flows in disease outbreaks are also found many centuries earlier. An unknown plague swept the Roman Empire in the late second century and recurred for several generations. No other epidemic is then recorded until a plague, probably bubonic, wreaked havoc in the Mediterranean and Western Europe under Justinian three centuries later (E. Jones 1974, 134; Le Roy Ladurie 1981).

These episodes of disease incursion may be somehow linked to global weather patterns, or caused by some little-guessed mechanism governing the activity of bacterial and viral agents. In either case, we may take the long-term movement of mortality, and hence of population, in the early modern period as a major independent force in history.

Taking the long-term movement of population as a starting point, we may then ask what were its economic, social, and political consequences.

By relating demographic change to prices, and thence to state incomes, elite recruitment, and popular living conditions, we can develop a potent causal framework for analyzing the timing and nature of state crises.

POST-MALTHUSIAN AND NONLINEAR ASPECTS
OF POPULATION CHANGE

The notion that population change was at the root of large-scale historical change has often been considered, and just as often been quickly dismissed. This dismissal stems from two conventional modes of thought: a crude Malthusian view of population change, and linear thinking about causation in history. Lest the preceding model be lightly dismissed, both these modes of thought should quickly be debunked.

Malthus's view of population change is often crudely presented as a belief that population increase results simply from the uncontrollable passion between the sexes. Population would therefore increase until food supplies were exhausted, leading to starvation and disease and a terrible reversal of the previous increase. Malthus in fact recognized that individuals could choose to limit births, and that prudence could keep population in check (Wrigley 1969, 35). But in its crude popular version, Malthusian theory predicted recurrent bouts of starvation as shortages of food provided a sharp limit to population increase.

We now recognize that this crude picture does not apply to early modern history. Populations were not constantly reproducing to the point of starvation. Periods of relatively low population pressure alternated with periods of higher pressure, but in general, popular control of fertility through restrictions on marriage or infanticide kept populations well below the Malthusian limit. Those who consider the crude Malthusian view the *only* way to envisage the role of population in history may therefore believe that since this theory has been overturned, they are free to dismiss *any* role for population growth in explaining historical change.

Yet historical demographers and economists have developed rather more sophisticated views of the causes and effects of population growth in history. First, it is recognized that population is not driven merely by births; bouts of epidemic disease may raise or lower long-term mortality, leading to periods of population stagnation or growth. Second, it is recognized that food supplies did not pose strict limits to growth; food supplies sometimes grew faster than population increased, sometimes slower, but in the long run the growth of food supplies has generally exceeded population increase (Boserup 1981). Third, it is recognized that long before food runs out, *distributional* effects take over. That is, even though food supplies may be adequate for the population as a whole, an increase in the labor supply that lowers wages, or a slight reduction in food supplies that raises prices, may leave some sectors of the population considerably worse off. That is, even though the population as a whole is well within any "Malthusian" limit, changes in the *relative* supply of food and labor may make it difficult for many to afford to buy enough food or other items of consumption (Sen 1981).

We are all familiar with the last effect—when demand for homes increases, the price of houses goes up long before we "run out" of housing. Similarly, early modern societies experienced periods when population was growing faster than food output; the result was not crude Malthusian starvation, but rather a shift in prices that led to a redistribution of income and opportunities.

This last point sums up what we might call the post-Malthusian view of population dynamics in early modern history, the view that informs this study. That is, I shall not be looking for periods of starvation driven by runaway births. Instead, I begin by noting that exogenous mortality shifts, probably due to incursions and moderations of epidemic disease, led to some periods when population stagnated or fell and to some periods when population grew strongly. What I shall be looking for are the *distributional* effects as societies adjusted, badly or well, to changes in the *relative* balance of food and people. These changes—in prices, and in the welfare of different sectors of society—are the politically important effects of population change.

Nonetheless, those tied to linear thinking about historical causation may still dismiss the role of population increase. Such increases, after all, were gradual and not enormously large. Events such as revolutions and rebellions are both large and sudden; their very nature seems to call for a different kind of explanation. Let us consider these problems under two headings: first, the size of historical causes and effects; second, their suddenness.

The matter of size is simple: to someone bound by linear thinking, a ten percent change in a causal factor should lead to a ten percent change in its effect, a doubling of the cause to a doubling of the effect, and so on—simple proportionality. Yet history is notoriously *nonlinear*: most causal factors affect different groups very differently (Abbott 1988). Moreover, simple causes may combine and interact, greatly multiplying their effects.

Population increases have a particularly nonlinear effect on *marginal* groups—that is, groups who face some sort of boundary conditions, such as peasants who are seeking to gain new lands, or younger sons of elite families who are seeking new elite positions. In any overall growth of population, those groups pressed outside some boundary grow far more rapidly. To visualize this effect, consider a circle with a boundary region. We might say those inside the boundary are peasants with land, or sons who will inherit elite positions; those outside the boundary are landless peasants, or younger sons with no position to inherit. What happens if the circle expands? If there is no growth in the bounded area, even a slight expansion of total population will lead to a manyfold increase in the numbers outside the boundary. Even if the bounded area grows (new lands are brought into production or new elite positions created), any growth that is less than the total population increase will still lead to a disproportional increase in the marginal groups. Thus, in the example sketched below, we start with only ten percent of the population in the marginal region. Yet if we double the size of the circle, we end up with fifty-five percent of the population in the marginal region. That is, even though the total population has only doubled, the *marginal* population increased eleven times! Even if we allow the bounded area (the supply of land or elite positions) to expand by half, we still find that doubling the total population results in increasing the excluded group six and one-half times, from ten to sixty-five. In sum, increases in total population generally produce a much, much larger increase in marginal populations—that is, in those groups competing for some relatively scarce resource—than in the population as a whole. The increase in competition is therefore much greater than the increase in overall population, by itself, would suggest.

Total Pop.	100	Total Pop.	200	Total Pop.	200
In boundary	90	In boundary	90	In boundary	135
Marginal	10	Marginal	110	Marginal	65

To this effect, we must add the interaction of multiple causes. As noted earlier, shifts in demand and supply lead to shifts in prices. In particular, growing demand for a scarce item, such as land or food, leads to price inflation. In early modern history a doubling of population usually led to a substantial increase in prices—anywhere from a doubling to a quadrupling was common. Consider then the financial impact of the growth of marginal populations on a government. What is the impact of a doubling of population on the costs of providing poor relief for workers without land, or of creating additional elite positions for younger sons who lack positions to inherit? Even in the last case in our simple example, where the marginal population increased only six and a half times, when one multiplies this by a doubling or quadrupling of prices, the financial burden imposed by growth of the marginal group increases by a factor of thirteen to twenty-six! This result is worth repeating: when one considers the impact of population growth on the size of marginal groups, *combined with* the increase in prices that population growth usually brings, the financial costs of supporting such marginal groups may increase thirteen to twenty-six times, even if the total population only doubles. That is nonlinear response with a vengeance!

Failure to consider such responses can lead to foolish dismissals of the impact of inflation or population growth on states and elites. For example, English historians might note that the English monarchy's revenues tripled from 1540 to 1640, a rate about the same as was seen in price increases. Thus, they conclude, the monarchy "kept up" with prices, and inflation was not a problem. But they fail to note that this inflation was accompanied by an increase in population that led to larger armies. If the size of the army doubled in line with population growth, while prices tripled, the cost of keeping the army would rise by a factor of *six*, leaving the Crown far short of "keeping up." Similarly, some historians might argue that as the population doubled from 1540 to 1640, and the number of peer families slightly more than doubled, there should have been no increase in "unsatisfied demand" for peerages—after all, they increased more than proportionally to population. But as we now realize, simple proportions do not capture historical change. In this example, if the population was growing slowly before 1540, then there might have been only one surviving younger son unable to inherit a title per ten peer families; if the population was growing more rapidly in the next hundred years, then by 1640 there might have been *three* surviving younger sons with no chance to inherit a title per ten peer families. The doubling of peer families would then create a sixfold increase in the number of younger sons unable to inherit a title, who would be seeking new positions. When these population dynamics are understood, it can be seen that the doubling of peer families would greatly increase, not merely satisfy, the demands for new positions. In short, linear or proportional thinking overlooks much of the effect of population change.

The problem of the suddenness of revolutions or rebellions likewise derives from proportional thought. That is, one might think that a sudden event must have a sudden cause. To dispell this notion, let us consider the causes of earthquakes, also sudden events. Prior to an earthquake, heat and kinetic energy from the earth's core create pressures on the earth's crust. Fault lines develop, and pressure builds along these faults. At some point, a small block that had been keeping the crust on either side of the fault in place, despite the pressure, breaks off. The earth is then free to move, and a sudden release of pressure occurs—an earthquake. What has caused the quake? The immediate cause was the breaking off of a block along the fault that held the pressure in check. But the breaking off of that block, of course, was itself caused by the cumulating pressure along the fault. Thus the pressure caused both the "trigger," or sudden releasing event, and the movement of the earth that followed. The sudden earthquake, in other words, was the result of long-term cumulating forces acting on a structure (the crust and its faults) that resisted pressure for a time, then suddenly gave way, releasing the pent-up forces.

The causes of revolutions and major rebellions operate in ways that seem remarkably similar to the forces that build up to cause earthquakes. That is, in the years before such a revolution or major rebellion, social pressures for change build. Yet the existing social and political structures for some time resist change (even though pressures and deformations may be visible). Suddenly, however, some response to the mounting pressure—a state bankruptcy, a regional rebellion—occurs which weakens that resistance (like a block breaking off along the fault). At that point, there is a sudden release of the pent-up forces and a crumbling of the old social structures—a revolution or major rebellion. More concretely, the Scots and Irish rebellions in Great Britain in 1637–1641, and the state bankruptcy and calling of the Estates General in France in 1789, were themselves responses to the mounting social and fiscal pressures in those societies. Yet these particular events also served to unleash far greater social pressures, which overwhelmed these states and led to revolutions.

The causes of revolutions and major rebellions therefore need not be sought solely among sudden events. Such events can be considered as "triggers," or "releasers," of pent-up social forces, but they are not the fundamental causes. Indeed, such "releasing" events are themselves generally the result of cumulating social pressures. A long-term cumulative factor, such as population increase, can therefore readily lead to a sudden event. What matters is whether the existing social and political institutions are flexible enough to move easily in response to such pressures. Where institutions are flexible, as in modern democratic states, pressures can usually be absorbed through electoral realignments and policy changes. Where institutions are relatively inflexible, as in hereditary monarchies or empires with traditional systems of taxation, elite recruitment, and economic organization, the result is more likely to be revolution or rebellion. The key to this study, therefore, will be to trace how cumulating pressures on relatively inflexible regimes led to crises, and conversely, how the cessation of such pressures led to periods of relative stability.

A last impediment to grasping the role of population in history is the view that causes come from a particular direction. That is, the causes of revolution might be sought from the top down (problems in the nature or capacity of states) or from the bottom up (in the discontent or actions of the populace). Yet again, both of these "linear" approaches distort historical reality.

As students of revolutions and major rebellions know well, the reason these are such "big" events is that they are instances where social institutions break down *at a variety of levels.* That is, there is a crisis of national government, but there are also crises of local government. There are conflicts with the state, but also regional conflicts and even conflicts within families. There are elite rebellions, but also a variety of rural and urban popular movements. To trace all of these events from one direction, whether top down or bottom up, is virtually impossible. What is needed is a search for causes that operate *on a variety of social scales—* national, regional, local, even familial. Scientists have invented a term for phenomena that show similarity on different levels or scales of operation: structures with this property are called "fractal." Societies do not operate simply from the top down or the bottom up; instead they exhibit similarity of organization on a variety of scales—national governments are complemented by similar state and local governments; national elites are complemented by similar state and local elites; large cities and businesses are complemented by similarly organized smaller cities and businesses. To explain revolutions and major rebellions therefore requires a causal approach that recognizes this fractal character of societies.

A major virtue of focusing on population pressures is that these pressures operate at all levels of society—nationally and locally, even within families. Although the causal pathways are somewhat varied, as I discuss below, by starting with population dynamics we may avoid a top-down or bottom-up approach to causal explanation and instead focus on factors that operate simultaneously across many levels.

In sum, the model of this book takes a post-Malthusian and nonlinear approach to population dynamics. That is, I shall focus on the *distributional* effects of relative shifts in population and resources, rather than on massive shortages for whole societies. And I shall emphasize that the impact of population growth is not simply proportional to changes in overall population, but often many times greater, particularly for marginal groups or when combined with price changes. Moreover, it is not necessary to look for sudden or unidirectional causes for revolutions and rebellions. Instead, it may be more useful to examine the impact of cumulating forces on inflexible institutions, and to pay attention to such forces at a variety of levels of society.

A NEW SYNTHESIS

This causal framework offers a new synthesis in several respects. First, it provides a synthesis of economic and political history quite different from the existing Marxist model. The latter, which has come to be called "*the* social explanation" of early modern revolutions, argues that the motivation for change came from shifts in the relations of production identified as the growth of capitalism, which produced conflicts between social classes that undermined states. I argue instead that the motivation for change came from ecological shifts in the relation of the population size to agricultural output, which produced diverse conflicts between elites and states, among elite factions, and between popular groups and authorities. These conflicts revolved around a variety of axes, including national and local political authority, status, and economic and religious issues. This causal framework is thus a "social" explanation of state breakdown that does not attach primary importance to the growth of capitalism or class conflict.

Second, this work synthesizes the "new" social history of demographic and social history with the "old" history of revolutions and state crises by mapping the diverse links between them. I draw on changes in population, urbanization, prices, income levels and distribution, social mobility, and education and relate these changes causally to major political crises.

Third, this framework is used to account for similar episodes of state breakdown in Europe and in Asia. It thus offers a synthesis of Eastern and Western history in the early modern period.

Fourth, this framework calls attention to *cyclic* forces in early modern history. Most long-term histories focus on a secular process, for example, the growth of capitalism, of democracy, or of the state. Yet the early modern period shows marked cycles in numerous aspects of social, economic, and political life. I argue that explanation of early modern history therefore requires a synthesis of secular trends *and* cyclic processes.

Fifth, this framework synthesizes both structural and cultural approaches. It does so not by simply merging them or by pointing to both sorts of explanatory factors. Rather, I argue that material and structural factors played the key role in producing state crises; however, once begun, cultural factors played the key role in producing certain processes and *outcomes*. Thus structural and cultural factors both played important, but quite distinct, roles.

Sixth, the methodology used is a synthesis of quantitative statistical methods and the case-centered approach typical of qualitative comparative historical research.

I begin by examining the disputes surrounding the origins of the English Revolution. Chapter 2 uses the English case to show in some detail how demographic change affected early modern polities. For comparison, I then briefly examine two contemporary political events: the state breakdown known as the Fronde in France, and the state breakdown at the peripheries of the Spanish Hapsburg Empire, in Catalonia, Portugal, Naples, and Sicily. Chapter 3 presents the controversy over the French Revolution and attempts to resolve several problems by extending the approach used to explain the English Revolution. Chapter 4 then turns to the state breakdowns in seventeenth-century Ottoman Turkey and Ming China, demonstrating the numerous similarities in their causes to the state breakdowns of the West. I also briefly examine two nineteenth-century cases of state breakdown in Asia: the Taiping rebellion in China, and the rather different and unique case of Japan's Meiji Restoration. Chapter 5 considers why the outcome of early modern state breakdowns differed so greatly between Europe and Asia. This chapter, which focuses on the role of ideologies and cultural frameworks in the unfolding of revolutionary crises, attempts to integrate political breakdowns, cultural frameworks, and economic history to suggest a reason for the rise of the West, and the relative decline of the East, between 1600 and 1800. Finally, chapter 6 draws conclusions for an understanding of state crises in the modern world, including problems of Third World development and the declining international power of the United States.

The claim that it is possible to offer a common causal explanation for the periodic breakdown of states in widely diverse settings may evoke considerable skepticism. It is valid skepticism, given the simple positivistic models of social change that have been offered in the past and the current confusion about the methods and goals of explanatory social science.

It is true that many sociological attempts to discuss historical change have been inadequate. I believe this is because of self-made barriers that are partly the product of twentieth-century social science and partly inherited from the grand masters of sociology, particularly Marx, Durkheim, and Weber. These barriers take two main forms: (1) a focus on *secular*, to the exclusion of *cyclic*, processes in history, and (2) a tendency to simplify social variety into exclusive bipolar categories.

Those uninterested in methodological and theoretical controversies may wish to skip directly to chapter 2, where the substantive argument begins. But in light of the confusion generated by past discussions of history and social science, a brief examination of the issues involved in the comparative-historical method may be of interest to some readers.

B. SOCIAL THEORY, SOCIAL SCIENCE, AND COMPARATIVE HISTORY

> One does not apply theory to history; rather one uses history to develop theory.
>
> —*Arthur Stinchcombe*

Social theory has often hindered attempts by sociology to contribute to our understanding of history. It has done so by taking what should be *empirical* problems and raising them to the level of *theoretical* disputes. Unfortunately, as these problems are unresolvable at this level, theoretical discussions have tended to be endless and inconclusive and to divert attention from real historical issues. All too often, social theory has misleadingly classified historical change solely in terms of the "progress" of simple secular processes. And far too often, social theory has

misleadingly addressed historical causation in terms of simple dichoto-
mies. It is therefore necessary to show how these theoretical blinders can
and should be cast aside.

In addition, both historians and social scientists are often hampered
in their pursuit of theory by a misunderstanding of the nature of "science," owing to their unfamiliarity with the practices of the natural
sciences. Far too many historians and social scientists ignore the diversity
and richness of modern science, believing that the model for "proper
science" is eighteenth-century physics. This unduly narrow view of science, inspiring hopes or fears when scholars talk of making history more
"scientific," has driven an unnecessary wedge between history and social science. I shall argue that history and sociology can create a distinct
sphere of inquiry—comparative history. This endeavor has its own problems and techniques, and must be understood and defended for what it
attempts in its own right and not as a variant of other fields.

THE BARRIERS IMPOSED BY SOCIAL THEORY

SECULAR AND CYCLIC PROCESSES IN HISTORY

Classical social theory saw social change as linear. Struck by the ongoing
"great transition" to modern technical and political organization, nine-
teenth- and early-twentieth-century social theorists—most notably
Marx, Durkheim, and Weber—saw all past change as a prelude to the
"great" change. The five hundred years that intervened between the
passing of manorial and political feudalism in the fourteenth century
and the arrival of industrial capitalism and parliamentary democracy in
the nineteenth century were thus classified as a long (and consequently
troubled) period of "transition." This view is still with us. Charles Tilly
(1984a, 1985) recently undertook the courageous task of drawing an
agenda for early modern European social history. He suggests (1984a,
49) that we focus on the "growth of national states and the development
of capitalism." Yet to speak of "growth" and "development" implies
continuous secular processes and reflects the classical obsession with the
movement from feudalism to capitalism. Crucial this change certainly
was; yet exclusive reliance on this metaphor of continuous movement
distorts our view of the key centuries in which this change took place.

The era from the Hundred Years' War to the revolutions of 1848 was
not merely a time of transition. It was a period of distinct economic and
political formations: an agrarian, urbanizing, commercial economy and

a semicentralized, partly bureaucratic, dynastic state, in which hereditary monarchs ruled with the aid of appointed officials. In this book
I refer to such formations, following Skocpol (1979), as *agrarian-
bureaucratic states*. The degree of commercialization and urbanization
varied, as did the degree to which officialdom—generally recruited from
a distinctively educated and landed stratum—was subject to the monarch's control. But the economic and political system was quite distinct
from the largely local, subsistence, nonurban economies and feudal polities that preceded it, and from the industrial economies and democratic
polities that followed. The major European states in these centuries had
much in common, in political and economic organization, with the
agrarian-bureaucratic states of the Ottoman and Chinese empires that
were their contemporaries.

In these centuries, social and political changes had their own distinct
patterns. While some changes were under way in which industry and
democracy later took root, these were not the only changes in society.
In fact, social change in the early modern period can only be understood
as a product of linear, or secular, processes *and cyclic processes*.

It is enormously difficult to fit the history of the early modern period
into a simple secular framework, for the centuries between 1250 and
1850 show relentlessly *cyclic* patterns. In regard to state-making on the
European continent, the late medieval crisis and early struggles with the
popes gave way to the stronger Renaissance states of the fifteenth and
sixteenth centuries. Yet by the seventeenth century these states experienced widespread political crises, facing rebellions and revolutions on a
vast scale. In the late seventeenth and early eighteenth centuries states
grew stronger still, with absolutism strengthening its grip in France and
Germany; but the late eighteenth and early nineteenth centuries were
again a period of state crises, with absolutism everywhere defeated or
forced to make concessions (even in Prussia, if only slight) to some form
of constitutional order. In regard to the growth of capitalism, we find
an expansion of the market economy and urbanization in the High Middle Ages, followed by a decline with the onset of the Black Death. The
sixteenth and early seventeenth centuries were a period of great commercial expansion; the late seventeenth century, on many indices, a time
of stagnation. In the eighteenth century, expansion resumed. Even if we
examine an index of "capitalism" as precise as the proportion of English
farm laborers who were nonhousehold hired wage-earners (as opposed
to traditional in-household farm servants), we find that this ratio rose
markedly in the sixteenth century, then *fell* in the late seventeenth and

early eighteenth centuries, before expanding definitively in the late eighteenth and early nineteenth centuries (Kussmaul 1981, 97–98). And if we look at such vital factors as population and price levels, a similar cyclic pattern forcibly presents itself. How, given the fundamentally cyclic character of so much of early modern history, can we be content to focus primarily on *secular* changes?

Two answers have been offered to this question. Both are unsatisfactory. The first is to assert that all the cyclic movements observed were merely internal dynamics of a secular process. Thus in the growth of capitalism one must be aware of the "crisis of feudalism" in the fourteenth century, the "crisis of capitalism" (sometimes specified as mercantile capitalism) in the seventeenth century, and the "crisis of capitalism" (specified as the birth of industrial capitalism) in the nineteenth century. The periodic crises, visible in the political as well as the economic spheres, were generated by internal contradictions in the development of capitalism itself. This is the answer offered by Hobsbawm (1965), Wallerstein (1974), and Anderson (1974). I deal further with this notion later on, when discussing particular cases. But it is now widely recognized that the mechanisms by which the "crises of capitalism" are supposed to account for political and demographic crises— making politics dependent on class struggles and demographic growth dependent on income levels—are inconsistent with the historical record of European revolutions and of population change. The question of *why* capitalism should undergo periodic internal crises has thus proved one of the thorniest, least soluble problems in the Marxist analysis of world history.[4] Moreover, from 1500 to 1850 China and Ottoman Turkey had

4. The contortions that arise from viewing the seventeenth-century crisis as a "crisis of capitalism" are evident in authors as different as Ruggerio Romano and Theodore Rabb. Romano (1978, 205) states that "the 'capitalist' experiment of the sixteenth century ended in the return of the feudal type of economy." Rabb (1975, 99) comments that "capitalism had made no striking gains at the expense of feudalism." Both comments are ridiculous. By the end of the seventeenth century, agrarian labor in Western Europe was essentially free, although the land was still under seigneurial (but not *feudal*) justice and dues; political control was exercised by state-appointed officials and centrally commanded and paid armies; cities had expanded to a degree undreamed of in feudal Europe; and internal and overseas trade had reached new heights with the exploitation of sea routes to Southeast Asia and the New World. Yet after 1700—and this is what Romano and Rabb point out— the power of monarchies and the social and economic dominance of the landed nobility increased all over Europe. In short, Europe after 1650 was no longer feudal, nor yet capitalist; it comprised agrarian-bureaucratic states with commercial economies. Since there is no room for such a category with its own dynamics in the Marxist view, debates become meaningless. One can claim that since Europe was no longer feudal after 1400, it was "essentially" capitalist, as argued by Wallerstein and Braudel; one can equally claim that since Europe was not yet capitalist before 1850, it was "essentially" feudal, as argued by Romano, Rabb, and most historians of Old Regime France, following Soboul

the same cyclic trends of state building and state breakdown, and of population and prices, as Europe, in almost exact synchrony. Yet their economies were only very weakly integrated into European trade before 1800. (In subsequent chapters I examine how small their links with Europe were, compared to their domestic economies.) In the early modern era Ottoman Turkey and China were powerful, substantially independent, and noncapitalist economies. How then can one explain political and demographic cycles that are found on a worldwide scale by pointing to the dynamics of a process—the growth of capitalism—that occurred only in Europe?

A second answer is to ignore that these cyclic movements occurred on a worldwide, synchronized scale in the early modern period and instead treat each fluctuation or crisis as a local phenomenon. Thus English population movements are explained in terms of English agriculture, French political crises in terms of the development of the absolutist state, and Chinese peasant rebellions as part of the dynastic cycle, even though the timing of population movements, political crises, and peasant rebellions generally coincided almost exactly across all of these states.

While historians might indeed insist on the uniqueness of each crisis, this view gives rise to occasional paradoxes. As J. Clark (1986, 24–25) has rightly pointed out, historians analyzing seventeenth-century England often describe the period from 1540 to 1640 (or to 1688–1689) as marking the final decline of royal and aristocratic prestige and the crucial turning point in the liberation of Parliament from king and aristocracy. At the same time, historians analyzing nineteenth-century England describe the period from 1740 to the Reform Bill of 1832 in precisely the same way. They cannot *both* be right. Unless, that is, the late seventeenth and early eighteenth centuries marked a revival of the power and prestige of the monarchy and aristocracy, so that the battle fought in the seventeenth century needed to be fought again in the nineteenth. Allowance of cyclic elements in political and social trends resolves the paradox.

(1977b). By arguing whether to assimilate early modern European society to one or the other of two social formations that did not exist—except in the most partial, local, and fragmentary manner—after 1400 and before 1850, scholars can only be diverted from understanding the dominant social relations of the period.

Nor is this a problem only for Western historians. For most of its imperial history, China too was an agrarian-bureaucratic state and thus difficult to fit into Marxist categories (unless one accepts "Asiatic despotism" as adequate). As Rowe (1985, 284) relates, the Chinese scholar Tao Xisheng, facing the same predicament as his Western Marxist counterparts, "found himself forced to declare virtually all of China's recorded history [over 2,000 years!] a 'transitional age' suspended between two Marxist social formations."

As another example, historians of sixteenth-century England trumpet the "discovery" of the poor that led to the Elizabethan poor laws (Beier 1989). But historians of the nineteenth century, discussing the New Poor Law of 1834, similarly note the sudden "discovery" of the poor and attribute it to a rise of social conscience associated with industrialization. These claims would be of some interest to historians of poverty in eighteenth-century France (Forrest 1981; Fairchilds 1976; Hufton 1974; C. Jones 1982), who note that in this period the French "discovered" the problem of poverty, and that indeed it was "perhaps the most serious social question which faced Enlightenment France" (C. Jones 1982, 29). What is going on? The answer to this paradox is again resolved by a focus on cyclic forces. In the sixteenth century, population growth flooded labor markets, leading to previously unknown, widespread unemployment among the able-bodied. This new social problem then attracted attention. It faded after 1640, when population stagnated throughout Europe and labor markets tightened. It returned in eighteenth-century France, and in nineteenth-century England, when population growth renewed and again flooded labor markets, producing again a wave, not seen for several generations, of massive unemployment and underemployment among the able-bodied. In short, the problem of unemployment, not merely poverty, was not "discovered" by this or that society. It was a *real* problem that periodically recurred as a consequence of cyclic forces—in this case, population growth.

Classical social theory emphasized secular social change and the differences between Western Europe's and Asia's cyclic development. Yet early modern history *everywhere* shows evidence of cyclic changes. We could strain to keep the theory intact by tracing all the cyclic patterns to some contortions or internal contradictions of secular processes and thus fit history to the theory. But as discussed below, it would be a poor fit indeed. Alternatively, as Arthur Stinchcombe suggests in the epigraph above, we could investigate the history to learn the nature of the cyclic processes and, where needed, use the history to develop better theory, blending secular and cyclic change. That is the course I follow in this book.

Other pitfalls posed by social theory also lie in wait.

THE PERNICIOUS "PROBLEM OF ORDER"

One reason for the slow development of social theory is that social theorists often start by seeking to solve "the problem of order": how can individuals create and maintain patterns of group behavior that transcend the lives and intentions of the individuals involved? (See T. Parsons 1937 for the classic formulation of this problem.) Yet it is absurd to reduce all the complexities of social behavior to a single "problem of order." Do natural scientists attempt to solve "the problem of nature"? No. Though a grand unified theory may be the holy grail of some physicists, most scientists—biologists, chemists, geologists, astronomers, zoologists—get on with the business of solving the *myriad* of distinct problems presented by nature, using a *diversity* of models and theories to solve their particular problems. Perhaps, someday, models developed for different problems will be shown to have common elements, and a reduction in complexity can be achieved. But the first order of business is to solve specific problems in research; reduction is an elegant final course, not the initial step.

Yet sociology seems to have gotten it backwards. The interminable arguments over whether "*the* social order" is based on conflict or consensus, on whether "social change" is founded primarily on material or ideal factors, and on whether "micro" or "macro" behavior is the fundamental object of sociological concern, reflect this notion that there is *a* problem of social order that, once solved, will allow all social behavior to be explained and understood. It should be evident by now that no such single solution is possible. History and current experience present *many, many* kinds of social order—that is, sustained patterns of multiindividual behavior. Some are based on conflict, others on consensus; some instances of social change may be primarily rooted in material changes, other instances may be primarily rooted in ideological factors; most show a mixture of both. *The only way to find out where a particular social order or social change of interest is on the scale of these factors is by close empirical examination.* In other words, the problem of order is not a single problem, and hence not amenable to solution by theoretical clarification and reduction. It is an empirical problem—or rather problems, for there are many actual social orders, and hence many *different valid* solutions to their description. The useful task, on which cumulative progress can be made, is to identify particular behaviors, or social orders, of interest, and seek to establish how *they* are developed and maintained, being aware that different answers are likely to hold at different times and places. To seek first a univeral answer is to endorse a fruitless and primitive monism.

To compound its difficulties, sociology often adds the error of Manicheanism to its monist view of the social order. That is, if there is *one* problem of order, and a single solution, then everything other than that solution is considered an evil deception. Modern social theory tends to divide its adjectives into opposed pairs, declaring one element of the pair to be essential or fundamental, the other to be secondary at best, mere superstructure or even illusion at worst. Too often, sociologists treat "micro" and "macro," "ideal" and "material," and "conflict" and "consensus," as mutually exclusive categories, rather than as ideal types that denote extreme ends of an empirical scale. Since reality is dominated by various mixtures in the middle, arguing about the polar extremes merely diverts attention from real social processes.

To give an example, consider the terms "micro" and "macro". As Alexander and Giesen (1987) have pointed out, this is a purely conceptual distinction; in the real world, there are not separate "micro" and "macro" behaviors. All *social* behavior involves both individual actions *and* socially generated resources—language, symbols, or institutional arrangements.

Yet debates about this distinction have steered sociology on the wrong course. Scholars use exchange theory to explain the microfoundations of macrostructures (Homans 1961), or "structuration" (Giddens 1976, 1979) or "linkage" (Alexander and Giesen 1987) theories to emphasize that microactions are constantly generating and maintaining macrostructures, and vice versa. But they have *not* escaped from the dichotomous concept itself. And there lies the nub of the problem. For social behavior is not merely an interplay between "micro" and "macro" levels. *Society exhibits order on a multiplicity of scales.* Indeed, many aspects of social structure are neither micro nor macro; they are *fractal*.

Geometry has recently embraced the term "fractal" to denote structures that show similar features, regardless of the scale on which they are observed. For example, a shoreline is indented with bays and inlets; but each bay has its own little bays and inlets, and so on. It is the same with society. At the national level one finds national political authority, national business firms, national political parties, national status hierarchies, national unions, national voluntary organizations, and the like. But within the nation are provinces that look and act like little nations; within the provinces are counties and municipalities that are similarly structured; within the municipalities are local voluntary groups, local clubs, local business firms, and the like, which are in some ways similarly structured. Even families—as settings for authority, conflict, coalition formation, and intergenerational conservation of property—have certain characteristics in common with larger societies. Social order is thus reproduced and maintained, in a largely self-similar fashion, across a variety of scales. *A focus on the micro versus macro distinction excludes an awareness of this whole phenomenon.*

Of course, society is not fractal in the same way as a natural formation, which may be identically self-similar across different scales. Precisely because social structure is the product of human intent and historical accident, rather than of self-replicating natural forces, a key problem is to establish *to what degree* social order is similar across different scales and different dimensions (e.g., political, economic, kinship) of a given society. To emphasize this distinction from the natural sciences, and keep *social* intention in mind, we could describe social structure as "near-fractal": a structure that is ordered—by a combination of conscious intent and historical accident—on a variety of levels, and whose ordering principles on those levels are largely, although problematically, self-similar.

Once this near-fractal character of society is recognized, a host of empirical problems present themselves. To what extent are the structures of society on various scales and dimensions congruent? For example, a nation-state with elected officials usually has state and local governments with elected officials, and voluntary associations and labor unions with elected officials. Conversely, nation-states dominated by a party apparatus and party-appointed officials usually have party-appointed officials in charge of provincial and local governments, unions, and the like. Yet there are exceptions. How is it that precisely at the time political structures of greater democracy were becoming established in nineteenth-century England, economic structures of greater authoritarianism—the factories—were simultaneously developing? Even today, although publicly held firms elect their officers, voting is weighted by share ownership, as opposed to the equal vote of all participants that is preferred in the political system. How do these variations manage to subsist? Are they holdovers on the way to a more congruent future? Or are they stable? To what extent does socialization in family units, which are undemocratic, impede later appreciation of individual rights and responsibilities? Is the movement for "children's rights" an inevitable extension of national norms into the lower levels of the fractal hierarchy?

These issues are of crucial importance, for example, in judging the prospects for successful restructuring in the Soviet Union and China: to what extent can each avoid fractal congruence and maintain party-dominated political organizations in the same society with "free" business firms and elective unions? This crucial problem of modern politics immediately springs forth when one considers the fractal structure of societies. Yet it is completely obscured (and hence ignored) by the traditional micro versus macro categories.

Indeed, the key dynamics of social reproduction and social change generally operate at the level of coherent groups—families, peasant villages, urban working classes, regional elites, business firms, and local governments—that mediate between individuals and the society as a whole. Are these dynamics micro or macro? Of course they are neither, and explanation is lost, rather than gained, by trying to fit them into one category or the other. Jettison the theoretical blinders that confine us to one or the other end of the scale, and the rich reality in the middle is revealed for empirical examination.

Casting aside these blinders is of the greatest importance for the task of this book, for the analysis of state crises is greatly handicapped by focusing on only the macro or micro levels. Macroanalysis focuses on the nature of state structures, particularly the relations of various classes to the state and of the state to other states in the international arena. Microanalysis focuses on the mobilization of individuals, particularly the rewards and penalties accruing to ordinary individuals who participate in revolutionary movements. All these factors are important. But they miss the very nature of major state crisis, which is *a breakdown of order on a variety of social scales.*

Thus state breakdown typically involves not only breakdown of the central government but failure of provincial and municipal governments as well. For example, at the same time that the English and French monarchies were having financial difficulties and struggling with fractious parliaments (or parlements), in 1640 and 1789 respectively, many English and French municipal governments were nearing crises because of their heavy debts and were struggling with fractious freemen and city corporations. Explanations that focus only on the national government level miss the scope and depth of revolutionary crises.

Moreover, state breakdown typically involves not only conflict between the state and elites (the focus of Skocpol's [1979] work), but also conflict *within and among different elites.* And not only conflict among elites at the national level, but also conflict among local elites at the county, town, and parish levels. Indeed, conflict among elites often reaches down to the level of the family, with fathers and sons, or siblings, divided by the crisis.

Similarly, working upward from the "ordinary individual's" attitude toward the government overlooks the fact that popular conflicts can take forms other than uprisings against the state; revolutions also generally show a host of conflicts rooted in lower-level social structures that more directly touch popular groups than conflicts involving the national government. For example, peasant conflicts often involve revolutionary and counterrevolutionary peasant villages pitted against each other, while urban conflicts involve various groups of workers and urban elites on opposing sides. A microfocus on the rewards and penalties facing the "ordinary" individual often misses the dynamics of peasant and urban worker activity, which is mediated by different kinds of local organization.

This book approaches the problem of state breakdown as a problem of explaining the breakdown of institutions *on a multiplicity of scales.* My goal is to explain the crisis of the state as a crisis of both national and local authority; to explain elite conflicts as a set of nested conflicts that occur on local, regional, and national levels; and to explain popular activity as involving conflicts that differ according to their regional and rural or urban settings. Such a widespread breakdown of order is typical of major state crises. *Thus the critical problem is to explain why institutions should break down simultaneously on a variety of scales and dimensions at a particular time.* Approaches that are either macro or micro at best address only part of this conjunctural problem. The causal framework of this book, which begins with the impact of demographic and price changes on social structures at various levels, is useful precisely because it illuminates how conflicts and instability can develop simultaneously throughout the varied and multi-tiered structures of a society.

Similarly, the question of whether social order and social change are based on material or ideal factors—or some wishy-washy blend of both—is often posed as a theoretical query that can be answered and then used to guide empirical inquiry. The same is true of the question of whether social order is based on conflict or on consensus. With the question posed in this fashion, *any* answers can only lead to rejection of empirical variation out of hand. It may be that in some cases, or for certain aspects of a complex social process, material factors (or conflicts) *do* dominate; in other cases, ideological factors (or consensus) may do so. To assume that it is *always* material factors (or conflicts), or *always* ideological factors (or consensus), or *always* both that provide the key to social dynamics is to theorize historical variation out of existence.

In short, theory can never solve "the problem of order," and indeed sociology committed perhaps its biggest error in approaching its task in this fashion. We have erred wherever we have used theoretical categories as rigid frames to shape our empirical inquiries, rather than as flexible molds to be shaped by the data.

Some sociologists do tend to begin with theoretical categories and then rigidly apply them to history; this understandably confounds and distresses historians. The latter's tendency to treat sociologists as people describing the world by viewing it through the wrong end of a telescope therefore has some foundation. Yet sociology need not operate that way. Social theory that is responsive to historical variation, and can help to explain that variation, gets to the heart of historical issues.

Comparative history is *not* the application of social theory to history. What then is it?

COMPARATIVE HISTORY: A MANIFESTO

Mais ce n'est pas l'histoire!
> —*Pieter Geyl, commenting on Arnold*
> *Toynbee's* A Study of History

VARIATION IN HISTORY

Eighty-seven years ago, Mantoux (1903, 122) wrote that "the particular, whatever occurs only once, is the domain of history." This view, often expressed earlier and echoed since, has remained dear to historians' view of what they do. Yet we must be clear what this means. The "particularity," the "uniqueness," is the property of a sequence or collection of events. The task of all historical inquiry is to explain those particular sequences of events that have occurred. However, this task would be quite impossible if all of the components, if every aspect, of such sequences were totally unique.

Consider the history of a nation, such as England. If every moment in English history were *utterly unique, in all aspects*, what value is there in talking of England? Presumably, *some* aspects were common to the society that existed in the southern two-thirds of the island of Britannia over several centuries. Language, form of government, and ethnic heritage all changed somewhat, but not so much that they were totally different at any given moment from what they were at the next.

Even though historical sequences are unique *in toto*, it is therefore possible to recognize *some aspects* of those sequences that are similar to those of other times and places. The historians' claim of the uniqueness of particular sequences then generates a useful problem. For we face not an a priori theoretical assertion of absolute incomparability but rather an empirical task: investigation of the *degree* of difference between non-identical, but possibly similar, collections or sequences of events. History, in short, shows both continuity *and* change. It is thus possible to ask questions such as the following: In *what* respects did England's eighteenth-century monarchy differ from that of the seventeenth century? *What* changes occurred in England's economy from 1750 to 1850, and were these changes greater than those in the preceding century? If such questions are unanswerable in principle (and no practicing historian would claim this, except in the heat of debate with recalcitrant social scientists), then the "history of England" can have no meaning.

If there is both change and continuity in history over time, the same variation is found over *space*. An eighteenth-century traveler from England to France would recognize certain features of the landscape—monarchy, nobility, and agricultural techniques—as differing in detail from the English analogues, but they would not be completely unrecognizable. One can therefore ask about the differences between English and French forms of government (or agriculture, or income, or religion) in the eighteenth century. Again, the historical claim of uniqueness is a matter of degree, to be established by empirical inquiry.

Here too, our conceptualization of events has been a slave to a simple, mutually exclusive categorization generated by a priori theorizing. Historians and social scientists tend to argue over methods as if there were only two ways to look at history—either every historical sequence is unique or else there are general principles or "laws." Neither position is quite true. The reality (and again, this is something every good historian knows and practices) is that of historical *variation*. Elements with greater or lesser continuity over time vary and combine in distinctive ways across time and space. Doing history—that is, reconstructing, describing, and explaining particular sequences of events—is almost always a matter of identifying *which particular aspects* of a complex situation are changing and which are remaining more or less the same, and then attempting to answer the question of why.

CASES AND CRITICAL DIFFERENCES

What distinguishes comparative history is its use of the *case-based* method to study historical variation. A historian might present a long-term history of Europe, or of disease, or of income distribution that spans several countries or several centuries. Such general histories, long-term histories, or world histories are *not* comparative history. They have in common with it an interest in large-scale historical variation, and a necessary recourse to secondary sources. But they differ in approach. The long-term or general history attempts to recount what happened within a given, possibly very large, time frame.

Comparative history is more focused, and much more thematic, than such general long-term or large-scale histories. Comparative history begins with questions such as the following: Why did Japan respond more successfully than China to Western incursions in the nineteenth century? Why did serfdom vanish after 1500 in Western Europe, while something very much like it expanded in Eastern Europe? Did ideology play different roles in communist and noncommunist revolutions? Such questions arise from noticing a critical difference in the record of historical variation—two sequences of events that seem to share some characteristics but are strikingly different in others. It may be that the apparent similarities are, on close inspection, illusory. Or it may be that only a small, but crucial, factor separated quite similar situations and led to striking differences. What makes comparative history interesting is that the answer in each case is not known in advance. It is an empirical inquiry to discover what happened and why.

The central goal of comparative history is thus not merely to find analogies or generalities in historical experience. It is to find *causal explanations of historical events*. Given that historical *variation* reveals both continuity and change, comparative history proceeds by asking *which* elements of the historical record were crucial. Thus to study merely the history of two cities, or of two countries, is to practice parallel, but not comparative, history. The latter depends on identifying some key difference between the cases and asking which of the many distinct elements in these cases were responsible for the *particular* difference in question.

It is common to take different countries as cases. But this is certainly not necessary. Traugott (1985) recently analyzed the forces on each side of the barricades in Paris in 1848—his cases are the insurgents, on the one hand, and the members of the Mobile Guard, on the other. His comparison of these two groups is the basis for his argument that the Mobile Guard remained loyal to the government not because of its class makeup but chiefly because of its socialization under military-style training and discipline between February and June of that year. Similarly, Calhoun's (1982) study of the English working class takes as its cases the artisanal workers of the early nineteenth century and the factory workers of the late nineteenth century; by identifying the differences between these groups, he is able to challenge E. P. Thompson's (1963) earlier claims of continuity in a single English working class. And Brustein (1985, 1986) has used regions as cases to shed light on patterns of French political protest in the seventeenth and eighteenth centuries.

Both historians and sociologists often ask "sociological" questions of the historical record, such as what was the pattern of social mobility in nineteenth-century Marseilles (Sewell 1985a)? Or they may turn to history to question features of the present-day sociological terrain, such as how did physicians become such a powerful profession in America (Starr 1982)? Answers to such questions draw on *both* the historians' skills of analyzing primary sources and the sociologists' knowledge of social processes. Such inquiries therefore do produce a blend of the sort Abrams (1982) envisaged, which goes under the name of social history or historical sociology. Though enormously valuable, this specialty is distinct from comparative history, which rests on the case-based approach. In this sense, comparative history is only a part, although perhaps the most controversial part, of a broader historical sociology. (More wide-ranging analyses of historical sociology are provided by Skocpol 1984 and by Hamilton and Walton 1988.)

ROBUST PROCESSES IN HISTORY

Comparative history often starts with apparently similar situations, among which there are nonetheless striking differences that call for explanation. Yet the reverse pattern of historical variation also sometimes arises—that is, in historical situations that seem markedly different, *similar* sequences of events unfold. There are striking similarities between the French Revolution of 1789 and the Russian Revolution of 1917, despite their vast separation in time and enormously different historical settings. Thus the comparative historian may also approach historical variation from the angle of *significant similarities*: why, in contexts that seem to differ widely, are similar patterns of events observed?

Examination of similar sequences of events in different historical settings has provoked enormous controversy and even scorn. Comparative history has been given a bad name by attempts to overextend limited generalities to lawlike findings. Such pretensions marred the otherwise valuable work of Marx and the Hegelians, including, in his own way, Arnold Toynbee. Suspicions have also arisen that, in seeking generalities, comparative history is disdainful of facts. But good comparative history does the opposite on both counts: it seeks limited generalizations and draws its strength from careful use of historical details.

First, it should be recognized that comparative history cannot simply "use" historical narratives as data. This is because historians do not tell us what happened in a particular time and place; rather, they *argue* about what happened. At any given time, certain patterns of events may be generally agreed on, others hotly disputed. Given the nature of historical evidence and the problems of reconstruction, it could hardly be otherwise. That is why it is essential for comparative historians to engage fully the secondary literature of the cases they study in order to be aware of the historical arguments, uncertainties, and issues at stake. A comparative historian does not approach historical scholarship as a miner approaches a mine. Instead, he or she approaches the literature as a historian would, to engage in a conversation about what happened.

Second, identifying similar sequences of events in different historical contexts is not the same as seeking general laws independent of historical context. Rather, identifying such sequences is more like a geologist's activity in mapping different regions and discovering similar fossils in similar rock strata at widely divergent places. The geologist will then hypothesize that a common process occurred in both places and will attempt to carefully reconstruct what that process was. But this process is not a "law" in the same sense as the law of gravity.

A law is a relationship that holds regardless of varying initial conditions. It is true that to make predictions, one must know the initial conditions of a system. Thus to predict the motions of two gravitationally bound bodies, one must know their masses and the distance between them. But gravity per se, and the inverse square law of its operation, do not depend on those masses or positions. The initial conditions are merely parameters that can vary without affecting the operation of the law. The law is *independent* of the initial conditions. The geologist's claim that a similar process occurred in different sites, however, is precisely a statement about initial conditions. It is a claim that at some particular times in history, physical laws, such as gravity leading to the sedimentary deposition of rocks and chemical reactions leading to fossilization of animal remains, must have acted on sufficiently similar initial conditions in distinct sites to create a similar rock or fossil bed.

What the geologist has found is evidence of a "robust process." Such a process is not a law but a combination of *characteristic initial condi-*

tions with particular laws that produces a characteristic outcome. It cannot be used to make precise predictions, for it has no parameters to be plugged into a "law" that then predicts precise outcomes. Thus the geologist would not hope to predict the precise number and location of fossils in a particular sort of rock. Geological processes act in historical context, with initial conditions that are never exactly alike. Yet the geologist would predict the *types* of fossils, and their rough proportions, if he or she knew that the rock was formed at a time when certain species lived. That is, if the initial conditions were similar (even though not identical), then regular laws would produce similar (though not identical or exactly predictable) results.

Similar robust processes also occur in history. This is because most men and women do act in a discernibly consistent or rational fashion. Indeed, we rely on this consistency every day. We count on generals not to betray their countries, and on bankers and bureaucrats not to defraud or destroy their organizations. Of course, there are traitors and saints; yet we label these individuals with special words to indicate their exceptional nature. If most generals were traitors and most bankers were saints, these words would lose their meaning; and, needless to say, history would be very different.

Thus the key to historical explanation is knowing that, in a given situation, most people will react in some consistent fashion. This does not mean that all people have the same goals. In some groups of individuals, honor may be so important that an honorable defeat is valued more than a base victory. In other groups, spiritual status is more valuable than material rewards. The point is that we do not consider all human action to be random or inexplicable, because we believe we can discover what a given person or group of persons values. We then expect, in most cases, a certain consistency in their behavior.

This does *not* imply that everything that happens occurs because someone intended it. On numerous occasions—such as when so many people simultaneously seek the same quiet stretch of country trail that it ceases to be a quiet country trail—people make choices that, because of the simultaneous or reactive choices of other people, or because of the lack or misunderstanding of information, lead to results other than what the actors originally intended. Rational-choice theory makes this discrepancy explicit and examines the consequences (Schelling 1960; Olson 1965). This kind of analysis can be extremely useful, for it is quite valuable to be aware of the kinds of circumstances in which the intended acts of individuals, in their interaction, produce collective outcomes that no one intended or foresaw. Yet what makes daily life, and social science, possible, is our belief that if we can identify certain sets of salient initial conditions that confront a particular actor or group, we can expect that they will react in a particular (though not identical) fashion that produces a characteristic (though not completely predictable) outcome.

A splendid example is the work of Skocpol (1979) on revolutions. Skocpol identifies a historical process that led to social revolutions in France, Russia, and China. The process involves the collapse of state power owing to failure to cope with external pressures from competing states, and to peasant rebellions mobilized at the village level. Though monarchs and peasants sought changes in their respective conditions in each case, the combination of their actions produced social revolution of a kind that neither monarchs nor peasant villagers intended.

Yet to merely describe this process is only a beginning. The key parts of Skocpol's work consist of tracing how the processes unfolded in her several cases. She notes that the processes differed in specific details. For example, states failed to cope with external pressures either because of inadequate economic development (as in Russia in 1917) or because powerful elites blocked changes necessary to improve state efficiency (as in Imperial China and Old Regime France). What makes accounts of this kind convincing is that they show how state leaders, faced with the situations of limited resources and external pressures, were trapped into taking actions that angered elites and led to state paralysis. This created openings for peasant rebellions from below. Again, Skocpol demonstrates how villages in Russia and France with local autonomy and organization reacted spontaneously to the opportunity of state paralysis, whereas villages in China, which lacked autonomy from local elites, could not react similarly until the Japanese invasion and mobilization by the Chinese Communist Party had created a village-level organization in China that was autonomous of local landlords. There is no single cause, or single combination of causes, that created social revolutions. Skocpol presents no "law" of revolutions that would apply in all contexts, regardless of initial conditions. Instead, she delineates a *specific historical set of conditions* that occurred in similar fashion in several places. Under those conditions—a situation of state paralysis and peasant organization, which could be produced by slightly differing combinations of causes—the reasonable actions of state leaders, elites, and peasants would likely result in social revolution. The identification of the critical elements of their respective situations that led actors to take similar actions, even though the situations were not in all respects identical (nor were the consequences), is the essence of good comparative history.[5]

A robust process in history is a sequence of events that has unfolded in similar (but neither identical nor fully predictable) fashion in a variety of different historical contexts. Yet, it is not a mere "limited historical generalization" or an analogy between different events. The statement "European monarchs in the seventeenth century were crowned" is a limited historical generalization. But we have no idea what produced the recurrent events—is mere coincidence an adequate explanation? Or did the choice of coronation as a symbol of monarchy have roots in a process of symbol manipulation and inheritance of a common symbolic heritage? If so, then there is a robust process *behind* and responsible for the limited generalization. Similarly, one may note an analogy in the contestations of power between the French Assembly and French monarchy in 1789, and between the Petrograd Soviet and the Provisional Government in 1917, and label this situation "dual sovereignty." But is the resemblance coincidental, or is it significant? What makes such an analogy historically meaningful? It is meaningful if we can identify a process of initial conditions leading to similar choices by actors in the two situations—that is, a causal process connecting the similar elements in each situation. As Stinchcombe (1978, 117) has pointed out, "the causal forces that make systematic social change go are people figuring out what to do." Thus a robust process is less than a law but more than a limited historical generalization or analogy. It is a causal statement, asserting that a particular kind of historical sequence unfolds because individuals responded to particular, specified, salient characteristics in their respective historical situations. If the salience of those characteristics is great, then one can reasonably expect that in a wide variety of historical contexts, actors will respond somewhat similarly to them, and their likely actions can thereby be predicted or explained.

---

5. Skocpol, in her own explicit methodological statements, has claimed to be applying J. S. Mill's "method of differences." Yet as critics (Nichols 1986) have shown, she does not comply with Mill's method, which calls for all cases to be identical except on the one factor being examined. Skocpol's argument points to clusters of conditions, rather than individual factors, as responsible for social revolutions, and her cases are far from identical with respect to their other features. The search for "robust processes," I believe, is a better characterization of Skocpol's method. Skocpol is thus among those many innovative scholars whose actual methods are far superior to their avowed methodologies.

Enormous confusion has arisen because of the belief of many historians and social scientists that pointing to robust similarities in history
is akin to alleging the existence of predictive, determinate laws. Historians argue that since historical sequences are unique and subject to
accident, the search for causally meaningful regularities is a hopeless,
misguided quest. Social scientists, in contrast, argue that the search for
causal regularities should be conducted across large numbers of cases,
testing for valid predictions and for exceptions that might invalidate
these predictions. But *both* these views err, for they fail to grasp the
difference between robust processes and laws.

To give an example from natural science, Darwin's theory of evolution by natural selection presents a process: when certain initial conditions exist—species with variation among individuals who are in
reproductive competition—the law that progeny inherit the traits of parents creates a process whereby traits of the reproductively successful
individuals are diffused throughout the population, giving rise to new
species. But one can adduce exceptions: laboratory mice (or other do-
mesticated species) do not experience natural selection. Their reproductive success is controlled by their owners, and individual variation is
purposefully minimized (among laboratory mice) or moved in specific
directions (such as particularly attractive or valuable features of animals
or crops). These exceptions, though, do not invalidate the theory of
evolution. Precise, determinate prediction is also not at issue. The theory
of natural selection makes no prediction of any particular new species,
or of the precise time of its emergence.

Evolutionary biologists are quite aware that predicting the future is
impossible, since, as S. Gould (1988, 32) observes, "the contingencies
of history permit such a plethora of sensible outcomes." Nevertheless,
Gould continues, given a set of initial conditions, "we can explain after
the fact with as much potential confidence as any science can muster."
As I. B. Cohen (1984, 96) notes, "Darwin showed that the way of progress in all of the sciences was not necessarily mathematical in style
.... [His was the] first major scientific theory of modern times that
was causal, but not predictive."

The power of Darwin's theory is that, by pointing to a simple process
that has unfolded, in similar fashion, in a number of different circumstances, a large number of details of the historical record can be related
to each other in a manner that had previously been unrecognized or
misunderstood. The validity of the theory of natural selection depends
on whether it can be shown that, for a number of species, the variety of

present species *did* develop through the diffusion of new traits from prior species. This means a close examination of the fossil record to see if the evidence conforms to the alleged process. One tests an alleged process by examining if, in the actual historical sequence that it is intended to explain, the details of what occurred are consistent with that process.

Similarly, the geological theory of plate tectonics—which details how the earth's crust is divided into plates that move along the earth's surface, pushed out by new rock forming in the oceans from midsea ridges and absorbed by deep-sea trenches—does not allow one to predict when or where an earthquake will occur. What it does explain (and predict) is that earthquakes are (and will be) more frequent in certain regions, those sites along the boundaries of moving crustal plates. Again, the theory is not a mathematical relationship; it is the identification of a process— the motions of crustal plates—not previously recognized. Once identified, knowledge of that process can then be used to explain certain phenomena, including the distribution of earthquakes across regions, the existence of seafloor ridges and trenches, and the age of the rocks on the ocean floors. It is not prediction of a particular earthquake that offers "confirmation" of the theory but rather evidence of certain patterns in the geologic record: seafloor rocks are younger than crustal rocks and are older as one examines specimens further from the midsea ridges; and crustal rocks show great deformation and evidence of stress along long fault-line regions that trace an outline of crustal plates. Again, the value of the theory is not that it predicts any one specific event (it does not), or that it explains every detail of the past pattern (it does not). Rather, the value lies in the identification and explanation of the connections among a great many details of the geological record that were not previously recognized or understood.

The essence of historical explanation, even in the natural sciences, is thus relating events to each other through a *process*. That process may rely on very simple regularities of behavior, or "laws." Yet mere identification of the laws does not provide the theory. The observation that parents pass traits to their offspring is not the same as the theory of natural selection. To identify the process, one must perform the difficult cognitive feat of figuring out *which aspects* of the initial conditions observed, in conjunction with *which simple principles* of the many that may be at work, could have *combined* to generate the observed sequence of events.

What has confused the debate is Hempel's (1942) assertion that if one knows the laws and the sequence of events, one simply applies the law to obtain explanation. But this is *emphatically* not so. In history, the observed sequence of events features uncontrolled initial conditions, that is, an endless number of events of unknown relevance. How then can one know which initial conditions are the relevant ones to use in explanation? One can possess all the relevant laws, and all the relevant data, and still be helpless without knowledge of the process by which they are related. Before Darwin, people knew of the fossil record and knew the principle of inheritance. But they did not know how to combine them until Darwin elucidated the process of natural selection.

How then, if not through prediction, do we test an alleged robust process? As with studies of geology or evolution, the allegation that a particular process in human history occurred in specific historical settings requires a detailed examination of the historical record of those cases. A process can be considered robust if its workings can be traced in different contexts—that is, if in different historical circumstances actors nonetheless met with situations that, in certain respects, were similar, and hence acted, in certain respects, in similar ways. The "certain respects" are presented in terms of a model that abstracts and simplifies certain details of the complex and varied reality. But the validity of the demonstration depends on whether those actual historical details are consistent with the alleged process. George (1979) has described this mode of proof as *process tracing*—showing that observed outcomes could reasonably be expected to result from the sequence of actions likely to be taken in the specified situation.

This emphasis on tracing of causal processes sharply differentiates comparative history from correlational studies that use many cases, such as the cross-national research often conducted in political science or sociology. Any limited generalizations found in this latter fashion, though useful, are only hypotheses whose basis in causal processes remains to be demonstrated. In this sense, comparative histories and large-data-set correlational analyses are complementary, but not competitive or substitutes for one another.

Good comparative history must therefore "sink a huge anchor in details" (S. Gould 1986, 47). By confronting the historical details and demonstrating previously unrecognized connections between them, comparative history makes its mark. Of course, as with geology or evolution, it is not possible to explain *all* the details of a historical sequence. Elucidation of a process that connects *many* details of what happened is sufficient to produce a work of great value.

A SUMMATION

Comparative history does not mine history to develop laws. Let us instead list what comparative history *does* do. (1) Comparative history uses case-based comparisons to investigate historical variation. (2) It seeks to engage in historical debates by offering *causal* explanations of particular observed sequences of events. (3) It may develop such causal explanations either by identifying critical differences between similar situations or by identifying robust processes that occurred in different settings. Outstanding comparative histories often do both. (4) It uses simplifying models, but this does not mean it is precisely predictive. (5) It validates its findings by process tracing, rather than simply by correlation. (6) It sinks an anchor in historical details, for its validity rests on how well the relationships it describes correspond to, and make sense of, those details. While its findings may have some predictive value, and may be generalizable, that is not the critical test. Instead, (7) the test of the worth of a work of comparative history is whether it identifies and illuminates relationships heretofore unrecognized or misunderstood in particular sequences of historical events that have occurred.

As Geyl said of Toynbee's efforts, in words that apply to all comparative history, "but it is not history." True enough; it is not the reconstruction of what happened in a particular place at a particular time from the remaining evidence. Nor is it a broad chronological narrative, of the sort recognized as general national or world history. It is a different endeavor, with different goals and methods. Yet it shares history's concern for getting the sequence right, and for human action. It seeks to engage in the same conversation with historians as they argue about those sequences. No less than history, comparative history seeks to explain why certain things happened and how the world we live in today got to be as it is.

This book claims that there were robust processes behind the waves of state breakdown that swept across Eurasia in 1560–1660 and 1760–1860. This book also claims that an awareness of those processes helps to resolve many of the problems in current analyses of the English and French revolutions, and of the Ottoman Empire and China. But pointing out these similar aspects is only part of the story. For although similar processes across Eurasia led to state breakdown, there were critical differences that affected the outcome in each case. In Europe, these differences were mostly structural differences that determined whether the outcome of crisis would be successful, or unsuccessful, attempts at revolution. But between Europe and Asia (or, more accurately, between northwestern Europe and Asia), there were cultural differences that affected the response to crisis—whether state reconstruction would be innovative or traditional. Understanding the robust processes and the critical differences therefore explains, first, why crises took place all across Eurasia in the same chronological periods and, second, why the detailed unfoldings and outcomes of those crises sharply differed.

This claim can only be judged by weighing the substantive argument and the evidence. Let us therefore plunge into the historians' conversation regarding the English Revolution.

TWO

State Breakdown in Early Modern Europe: The English Revolution

I have seen in this revolution a circular motion of the sovereign power. [It] moved from King Charles I to the Long Parliament; from there to the Rump; from the Rump to Oliver Cromwell; and back again . . . to the Long Parliament, and thence to King Charles II.

—*Thomas Hobbes*

In 1639 Scottish troops repulsed an English army seeking to impose the king's authority; the next year the Scots crossed into England. From 1639 to 1642, England experienced the characteristic elements of state breakdown: a state crisis, as Englishmen refused to pay the Ship Money levies in 1639 following the army's failure to defeat the Scots, leaving the government bankrupt; an elite rebellion, as many county leaders refused to obey the king's writs to join the Royal Army, instead cooperating with Parliament to raise an alternative force; and popular disorders, as merchants, shopkeepers, and craftsmen forcibly wrested control of London from the aldermen, as crowds in the city prevented the bishops from attending Parliament and forced the king and his family to leave London for fear of violence, as rural riots in the fens and Crown forests frightened conservative elites while anti-Catholic riots intimidated the king's supporters, and as large-scale uprisings threatened royal authority and English landlords in Ireland. By 1642, English, Scots, and Irish were choosing sides (or seeking to avoid involvement) in what would become a civil war between royalist and parliamentary forces. These events mark the opening stages of what is called the Great Rebellion or the English Revolution.

From 1642 to 1649, civil wars swept Great Britain, culminating in the defeat and execution of Charles I, the dissolution of the House of Lords, and the abolition of the episcopacy and authority of the Church of England. England was then ruled by Oliver Cromwell, the leader of the parliamentary army, who took the title of Lord Protector of the English Commonwealth. Yet these extreme measures, as well as the more centralized rule and greater taxation imposed by the victorious parliamentary forces, were highly unpopular. Conflict continued between radicals and moderates, between the central government and local authorities, and between the army and civilian leaders. In 1660, just over a year after Cromwell's death, the Protectorate was acknowledged as a failure, and Charles II was called to take his father's place on the English throne.

A. THEORETICAL CONTROVERSIES, DEMOGRAPHIC AND ECONOMIC TRENDS

Few events have received closer scrutiny from historians, or created more heated debate, than the English Revolution. The key issue is whether or not this conflict marked a permanent break with the past, setting England on a course to become the first industrialized nation. Both Whig and Marxist historians have answered in the affirmative, but recent revisionists have argued that the civil war was simply a temporary political breakdown, interrupting the continuity of, but not substantially changing, the "English Old Regime" (a phrase borrowed from J. Clark 1986).

As is often the case in debates about state crises, even the revisionists have been unable to free themselves from the assumptions of their opponents. All of these writers have maintained a false dichotomy in framing English history. On the one hand, for both Whigs and Marxists, the period from 1500 to 1850 was one of continuous progress. Whig historians emphasize how growing gentry assertiveness and parliamentary independence steadily weakened royal authority, while Marxists emphasize how capitalist development surged steadily forward. For both groups, long-term social changes produced major crises in 1640 and 1688, and led to breakthroughs of constitutional or capitalist progress. On the other hand, for revisionists, the period was one of little fundamental change and much continuity, with the major crises being chiefly political struggles that, until 1832 at least, were not products of any underlying social change. In short, for these various groups of historians, the entire period from 1500 to 1832 is characterized either by steady secular progress or by an absence of change.

The alternative that I present here, which seems to have eluded previous authors, is a framework of *cyclic* social pressures. In this view, long-term social changes—propelled by population increase—eroded royal authority and social stability during the period 1500–1640, resulting in state breakdown. However, from 1660 to 1750, as the population stabilized, these long-term social and economic trends reversed. Thus, even though the period from 1660 to 1750 was dominated by political struggles, largely over the intertwined issues of imperial policy, dynastic succession, and state religion, the pressures leading to state breakdown had receded. Hence these struggles never threatened the maintenance of royal authority or the existing social structure; indeed, in this period royal authority and elite dominance were retrenched. Then, from 1750 to 1832, long-term demographic and economic trends repeated the earlier pattern of the sixteenth and early seventeenth centuries; again, social stability and royal authority were eroded. In the nineteenth century, the new resources created by the industrial revolution allowed England to avoid state breakdown, but these pressures still led to a major reformation of political institutions and to a shift in the composition of the elite. In sum, by avoiding an all-or-nothing view of these vital centuries and by applying a cyclic concept of long-term social and economic trends, we would expect that political events would show different patterns in different periods—an approach that captures more accurately than existing orthodox or revisionist views the changing dynamics of English history.

The Marxist view, which identifies the events of 1640–1642 as the first major procapitalist revolution, has been the most widely accepted among comparative historians (Anderson 1974; B. Moore 1966; Wallerstein 1984). It has several virtues, as it links English history to that of the Continent and accounts for some of the similarities between the English and the French revolutions. However, its major assertions have now been so fully contradicted by detailed local studies, and by analyses of elite alignments and Crown policies, that the view is no longer tenable.

The Whig view, shaped mainly by Macaulay (1913–1915), S. R. Gardiner (1970), and Trevelyan (1953), is favored by most contemporary historians (e.g., R. Ashton 1978; Aylmer 1965; Hexter 1978; Hirst 1978; Rabb 1981; L. Stone 1972; Woolrych 1980; Zagorin 1969). These scholars emphasize constitutional and religious conflicts and therefore see the crisis of 1640–1642 as the culmination of specifically English long-term trends: the growing independence of Parliament (particularly the House of Commons), the increasing conflicts between Puritanism and the Church of England, and the broadening stream of

English constitutional and common law (from the Magna Carta to the legal scholarship of Sir Edward Coke), all colliding with the Stuarts' aggressive use of royal authority.

Though focusing on religious and political conflicts, the Whig view has also been given social and economic underpinnings by Lawrence Stone. In 1500 England was ruled chiefly by the king and the several dozen great aristocratic families who held the titles granted to peers of the realm: barons, viscounts, earls, marquises, and dukes. This small aristocracy provided the king's courtiers and ministers; sat in Parliament as the House of Lords; represented the king throughout the countryside as lord-lieutenants; and dominated the counties through their vast land-holdings and generous patronage, centered on their great country estates. This aristocracy was supported by the roughly 5,000 families who, though not titled, were considered "gentlemen." This gentry class included knights and squires with their own country estates, lesser landlords, and distinguished members of the learned professions, especially lawyers. The gentry served the Crown and aristocracy as retainers, as members of Parliament in the House of Commons, and as royal judges and officials, and administered the counties as justices of the peace, sheriffs, and commissioners of the subsidy (the main form of parliamentary taxation). Below the gentry were the vast majority of Englishmen: farmers who leased land from the aristocracy and gentry, ranging from prosperous "yeomen" who might also own land to petty husbandmen; merchants; shopkeepers; artisans; and, on the lowest rung of the social ladder, landless laborers.

Lawrence Stone (1965, 1972) argued that the century prior to 1640 was a time of fiscal and military decline for the Crown and much of the aristocracy, whereas the gentry was becoming wealthier and more numerous. Rising prices, sales of Church and Crown lands, and expansion of the professions enriched existing gentry. These same trends allowed many enterprising yeomen and merchants an opportunity to acquire wealth, whereupon they or their heirs entered the gentry. The decline of the Crown and aristocracy relative to the gentry made it possible for the latter—from their positions in the House of Commons and as justices of the peace—to challenge the king and to forcefully resist efforts to increase royal revenues and authority.

Yet this view too has its faults. The long-term trends cited are generally valid; but if accepted at face value, they explain far too little. That is, the Whig view of history explains why the English state broke down in 1640. But it does not explain why the English state was restored, in most of its traditional respects, in 1660. Moreover, it is difficult, if not impossible, to understand why from 1689 to 1800 the Crown and aristocracy again took command of England. In short, if one grants not only the direction of the cited trends to 1640 but also their apparent strength and permanence as argued by the Whig historians, then it seems impossible to accept the significant and well-documented reversal of many of those trends after 1640. Most fundamental for our purposes, to the extent that the Whig view of the breakdown of 1640 rests on uniquely English characteristics, for example, the weakness of the English monarchy relative to the growing strength of Parliament, Puritanism, and English constitutional tradition, the temporal overlap of the English Revolution and state breakdowns throughout Europe and Asia becomes a mere and inexplicable coincidence. English history is thus cut off from the history of political crises in seventeenth-century Eurasia of which it seems a logical part.

Revisionist historians (e.g., Christiansen 1976; J. Clark 1986; Elton 1974b; Fletcher 1981; Kishlansky 1977; Miller 1979; Morrill 1976; Russell 1979; K. Sharpe 1978a) have properly criticized Whig historians for finding a questionable continuity in constitutional struggles, for overestimating the diminution of the Crown and the aristocracy in the seventeenth century, and for attributing long-term goals to actions that, on close inspection, appear more the product of short-term struggles or sheer royal incompetence and errors. Revisionists claim that "the failure of Charles's government was not rendered 'inevitable' by deep divisions in society or inherited stresses . . . but was conditioned by the inability of the King and his ministers to operate any political system" (Elton 1974b, 2:160). Yet the revisionist view—which identifies the events of 1640 as the outcome of flawed royal policies, and the civil war as a struggle that changed little and was sharply repudiated by elites afterward—also fails to satisfy the appetite for historical explanation. If the English Revolution had been an isolated episode in world history, we could perhaps be satisfied in attributing it to one monarch's misjudgment. But it was one of many contemporaneous episodes of state breakdown. Surely something at the time must have forced monarchs to take inappropriate measures; otherwise we have to conclude that in the period 1640–1660 bad judgment reached epidemic proportions throughout Eurasia.

Moreover, the events in England encompassed much more than a struggle against the king: county elites fought each other; popular revolts occurred in London, in royal forests, and in the fens; new religious sects emerged; and people spoke of a crusade to take freedom all across Europe. The revisionists leave us grasping to understand why the conflict initiated in 1640 was so much more violent and longer in duration than that experienced in 1688–1689. After all, in 1688–1689, England faced a monarch who was hated for pro-Catholic and tyrannical policies; it also faced a foreign invasion and dynastic struggle, elements absent in 1640. Yet the events of 1688–1689 by comparison constituted a peaceful revolution; if the events of 1640 were also mostly a reaction against misguided royal policies, why did they precipitate a much broader conflict?

In short, the origins of the English Revolution and its relation to contemporary state crises remain a problem. Unfortunately, the current "solutions" are sufficiently suspect to disturb anyone interested in either revolutions or comparative history; a growing and talented revisionist school of English historians (Elton 1974b; K. Sharpe 1978b; Russell 1979; Morrill 1976) revels in denying that any long-term social causes of the revolution existed, while their Whig opponents insist on a view of the revolution that stresses uniquely English historical trends, thus cutting English events off from the numerous parallel crises occurring throughout the world. Marxists offer a broad theory that integrates the revolution with European social, economic, and political history. But as I show below, this view fails when tested against historical detail.

In the following sections, I first examine in some detail the failings of the Marxist view, particularly as manifest in its more recent Neo-Marxist variants. This examination is warranted inasmuch as the Neo-Marxist view has dominated recent comparative histories of this period (B. Moore 1966; Anderson 1974; Wallerstein 1980). I then proceed to build a model of the causes of state breakdown in England in the 1640s that incorporates elements of both the Whig and the revisionist views. My model departs from these other viewpoints by, first, placing their insights in the context of a cyclic view of long-term social and economic changes and, second, relating these changes to trends that can be discerned not merely in England but also throughout Europe and Asia.

PROBLEMS IN NEO-MARXIST THEORY

The orthodox Marxist view, set forth most cogently by Dobb (1946) and the early work of Hill (1940), relates the emergence of capitalism to the rise of a distinctive bourgeois class—including agrarian capitalists among the landed gentry and commercial capitalists among the growing overseas trading companies—who chafed at the restrictions on their activity imposed by a still largely feudal monarchy and aristocracy. By this account, conflict between the rising capitalist class and the conservative feudal class lay behind the revolution.

However, this view was severely undercut by the work of such historians as Trevor-Roper (1953), Hexter (1961), Pearl (1961), L. Stone (1965), and Zagorin (1969). These scholars demonstrated that it is impossible to identify a distinct bourgeois class in seventeenth-century England; that great capitalist entrepreneurs in shipping, mining, and commercial agriculture were found throughout the older nobility as well as the newer gentry; and that the greatest overseas merchants of London were closely tied to the Crown by a variety of offices, special privileges, and patronage networks and, indeed, generally supported the king in his struggles with Parliament. Instead of conflicts between classes, conflicts between the Crown and county elites dominated early-seventeenth-century politics. Specifically, as myriad local studies (Gleason 1969; A. H. Smith 1974; H. Lloyd 1968; Everitt 1968, 1973; Morrill 1974, 1976; Fletcher 1975, 1981; P. Clark 1977; W. Hunt 1983; Barnes 1961) have revealed, local conflicts were so intense and varied that the ruling classes cannot be simply split into royalists and parliamentarians. Rather, it is necessary to speak of the elites as fractured into numerous conflicting groups, whose diverse local rivalries overlapped with and flowed into the overarching conflicts between Parliament and the Crown. Wherever one looks in mid-seventeenth-century England, one almost never finds conflict between classes; instead one finds conflict within classes and shifting coalitions—among the Crown, lords, gentry, merchants, and popular groups—that cross and obscure class lines.

Neo-Marxist sociologists, in gradual progression from Barrington Moore, Jr., through Perry Anderson and Immanuel Wallerstein, have thus sought to revise the orthodox Marxist view by putting aside the notion of a distinct bourgeois "class" as the necessary spearhead of revolution.[1] In its place, they argue that the diffusion of capitalist economic relations throughout society—particularly the agricultural improvements associated with the spread of enclosures and a vast increase in overseas trade—gradually undermined traditional English life, provoking sharp conflicts over commercial practices and the control of political institutions. In particular, they claim that landlords' enclosure of arable fields, by expropriating cultivators and converting the land to

1. This is also the direction taken in Hill's (1975, 1980) recent work.

pasture, produced both rural riots pitting small farmers against enclosing landlords and political struggles pitting enclosing landlords against
the conservative, traditional, monarchy. In this view, though both sides
drew support from merchants, lords, gentry, and small farmers, the conflict was nonetheless between proponents of new market-oriented practices and defenders of traditional feudal-style economic habits, with the
latter supported by the Crown.

This story is told, in varying forms, by B. Moore, Wallerstein, and
Anderson. Thus Moore (1966, 9, 11–12, 14) observes that

> during the sixteenth century the most significant [enclosures] were "en-
> croachments made by lords of manors or their farmers upon the land over
> which the manorial population had common rights" . . . . The peasants were
> driven off the land; ploughed strips and common alike were turned into
> pastures . . . . Those who promoted the wave of agrarian capitalism . . . were
> among the main forces opposing the King and royal attempts to preserve the
> older order, and therefore an important cause . . . that produced the Civil
> War.

Wallerstein (1980, 142) points to a split within the ruling gentry class
"between the new capitalists and the old aristocrats" as commercial
practices spread. Anderson (1974, 142) is even more forceful: "The English monarchy was felled at the center by a commercialized gentry [and]
a capitalist city," which faced in Charles I's rule the attempted "political
refortification of a feudal state." But can we really trace the conflicts
that felled the Crown to the spread of enclosures and overseas trade?

LANDLESSNESS AND POPULAR DISCONTENT

Recent studies by geographers (Fox and Butlin 1979; Butlin 1982; Yelling 1977; Broad 1980; Charlesworth 1983; Rowley 1981; Darby
1973b; Bridbury 1974; Beresford 1954, 1961; Kerridge 1967) have
greatly expanded our knowledge of enclosure beyond the once exclusive
reliance on the documents of the royal enclosure commissioners. These
geographically based revisions were much needed, for as Butlin (1982,
48) summarizes, "we have known for some time . . . of the highly du-
bious nature of the returns to the commissions of enquiry and the trivi-
ality of many of the cases of enclosure . . . brought before the Exchequer
in the sixteenth century."

Contrary to B. Moore's (1966) claim, the type of enclosure held to
have important social and political consequences—the enclosure by a
landlord of common fields in order to turn out tenants and create sheep

pasture—constituted only a small portion of enclosures, and these occurred primarily from 1450 to 1520. Sir Thomas More's wry comment
that "sheep ate men" had some truth as a retrospective summation in
1516, when More's *Utopia* was written. But it fails badly as a description
of the following 120 years. As discussed below, England's wool trade
entered a century of virtual stagnation after 1550, while population
growth led to a booming market and rising prices for grain. Thus from
1550 "there was a retreat from large-scale sheep farming" (Charlesworth 1983, 14) and a shift in land use from pastures to arable grain
fields.

It is the English Midlands that are usually alleged to have seen disruptive enclosure of arable fields and conversion to pastures in the sixteenth and seventeenth centuries. But the vast majority of the Midlands
remained in open fields until the late eighteenth century (McCloskey
1975, 125; M. Turner 1980, 1984). From 1550 to 1650, enclosures for
grazing took place only in a few exceptional areas, chiefly the heavy clay
vales of the east Midlands where land was best suited to fattening livestock (Charlesworth 1983; Thirsk 1967a). In other parts of the Midlands, as Broad (1980) relates, the reverse trend was more common, and
there was much conversion of pastureland to arable land. Indeed "in the
Midlands there was a general trend toward expanding arable land at
the expense of grassland; . . . for instance at Bittesby in Leicestershire,
. . . in 1640 the arable area was fourteen times as large as in 1572. . . .
Up to the middle of the seventeenth century there was little or no transformation of arable land to pasture on enclosed land" (Maddalena 1974,
321). Skipp (1978) found that in northern Warwickshire the proportion
of cultivated land devoted to grain rather than to pasture grew from
one-third to nearly two-thirds during the seventeenth century. In 1621
a speaker in the House of Commons declared that "there is not want of
corn land at this time, but want of pastures and cattle for much woodlands and barren ground are become fruitful cornland instead of pasture" (Thirsk and Cooper 1972, 122). Contemporary authors on
agriculture, such as Tusser (1573) and Norden (1607), defended enclosures for their productivity in growing grain.

We must recognize also that by 1550 enclosures were rarely the work
of the manorial lord who possessed all or virtually all of the enclosed
lands. Instead, tenants usually initiated and agreed to enclosure in order
to increase the intensity of cultivation. Studies of the Chancery rolls of
the sixteenth and seventeenth centuries reveal that scores of enclosures
by agreement were initiated by yeomen and copyholders and benefited

TABLE ONE   DISTRIBUTION OF LANDHOLDINGS OF
ENGLISH LABORERS, C. 1540–1640

(a) Data from 447 holdings on 28 manors

Percentage of Holdings of Each Size (in acres)

Period	Cottage w/garden	Under 1 acre	1–1¾	2–2¾	3–3¾	4–5
Before 1560	11	31	28	7	11	11
1600–1610	35	36	13	6	5	5
After 1620	40	23	14	8	7	7

(b) Simulation: 100 families in 1535, net reproduction rate 1.2, wtih partible inheritance

Percentage of Holdings of Each Size (in acres)

Period	Cottage w/garden	Under 1 acre	1–1¾	2–2¾	3–3¾	4–5
c. 1540	11.0	31.0	28.0	7.0	11.0	11.0
c. 1600	31.6	28.5	21.9	8.1	4.9	4.9
c. 1630	41.1	26.3	18.9	7.0	3.3	3.3

SOURCE: Data in (a) from Everitt, 1967b, 402.

all concerned (Spufford 1974; Leonard 1962; Hey 1974; Thirsk 1967a; Yelling 1977).

It is true that in many areas of England large commercial farms displaced the family subsistence holding. And some Marxist scholars, despite the lack of evidence for direct expropriation, have insisted that this displacement is the only mechanism that could have produced the observed change in landholdings. For example, Lachman (1987) cites Everitt's (1967b) data, which are presented in the upper half of table 1. As the table shows, the proportion of laborers holding only a cottage increased from 11 percent before 1560 to 40 percent after 1620. This marks an almost 300 percent increase in the relative size of the landless, while the population as a whole increased by only 75 percent. Thus, Lachman argues, landlessness increased far more rapidly than population grew, and therefore only expropriation could have been responsible for the observed pattern.

Yet this shift in landholding was *not* a result of expropriation by manorial lords. As Spufford (1974, 85) argues, based on her detailed analysis of shifts in landholding in sixteenth- and seventeenth-century

Cambridgeshire, "vulnerability to seigneurial and legal factors did not underlie the change." Rather it was the gradual outcome of population increase and subdivision of tenements, factors that together made for smaller, uneconomical holdings. Holders of such diminished properties often sold out to other copyholders during times of economic difficulty. Thirsk (1961) and Everitt (1967a) have similarly found in Suffolk, Lincolnshire, and Bedfordshire that husbandmen commonly divided property among surviving heirs, leading to shrunken holdings. Thirsk (1961, 70) cites Edward Lande, an octogenarian of Dent, who in 1634 declared that "if a customary tenant died . . . without having [a] will, then it descended to all his sons equally to be divided amongst them . . . . By reason of such division of tenements, the tenants are much increased in number more than they were, and the tenements become so small in quantity that many of them are not above three or four acres apiece." Everitt (1967b, 399) adds that "small holdings were either divided up amongst children, and subdivided again till they shrank to mere curtilages, or else bequeathed to the elder son alone, so that the younger children were left propertyless."

These two factors of population growth and land division are sufficient to account quite precisely for Everitt's data on changes in landholding. The view that demographic increase could not have accounted for the changes fails to understand that landlessness was a property of the marginal population; and it is a simple arithmetic rule that in any instance of population growth on a limited resource, the *marginal* population will grow many times faster than the whole. Thus, to fabricate a simple example, if five farmers have seven sons, and all keep their farms intact, two sons will be landless. If the next generation grows at the same rate, the seven sons will have ten sons of their own. If the five farms are still kept intact, there will now be five sons who are landless. From the second to the third generations, total population has grown from seven to ten (a 42 percent increase), but the landless population has grown from two to five (a 150 percent increase). In short, if landlessness was due to population increase on limited land, we would *expect* that the landless group would increase much more rapidly than the total population.

We can be far more precise in our calculations. From 1540 to 1630, England's population increased by 75 percent (Wrigley and Schofield 1981, 208–209). Assuming roughly thirty years per generation, it is easy to see what effect this growth would have on landholdings.[2] To increase

2. The rough estimate of thirty years between generations was calculated as follows: Wrigley and Schofield (1981) give the mean age of males at first marriage as twenty-

by 75 percent in three generations, the population must have had a net reproduction rate of 1.2. This means that for each generation, 80 percent of the fathers had only one surviving son, and 20 percent had two surviving sons. Let us make the simplest possible assumption: for those 80 percent of fathers with one surviving son, the property was handed down intact, and for those fathers with two surviving sons, the property was divided equally between them. The lower half of table 1 presents the pattern of landholdings that would result, starting from the 1560 distribution that Everitt (1976b) found and calculated on the basis of this growth rate and inheritance pattern.

As can be seen, this simplest possible demographic model provides a nearly exact fit. Indeed, the data show that large landholdings (more than three acres) were *better* conserved than a simple inheritance model would suggest. This indicates that some large parcels were likely kept intact and younger sons were simply sent from the household to settle in new areas, a result consistent with the data on migration during this period (P. Clark 1979a). The diminution in holdings before the revolution is thus consistent with the observed rate of demographic growth. Again, there is no need to postulate that expropriation occurred. Population increase and inheritance division were quite sufficient in and of themselves to produce shrunken holdings.

When landholdings no longer fully supported their families, tenants went into debt to purchase food and supplies. Following a bad harvest, many tenants then had to sell their holdings to more fortunate neighbors, whose larger holdings or smaller families had allowed them to avoid debts and accumulate surpluses (Spufford 1974, 1976; Everitt 1967b; Thirsk 1961). Although rising rents and entry fines are often blamed for dispossession, only the smallest tenants, under pressure from growing families and their farming of unviably subdivided plots, thus lost out. From 1550 to 1600 rentals and entry fines in fact generally lagged behind inflation, causing losses to landowners while allowing copyholders and yeomen whose holdings produced surpluses to earn profits and enlarge their holdings (Charlesworth 1983; Russell 1979; M. Campbell 1942). As W. Hunt (1983, 34, 38) notes in his study of Essex, one of the counties most involved in commercial farming,

---

eight during the seventeenth century, based on family reconstitutions. Flinn (1981, 112) notes that the mean interval to the first birth was just over a year, with the second birth coming a little more than two years after that. Assuming that half the infants were male, the first male sons were born, on average, to fathers who were thirty years of age.

it [is] impossible to blame the encloser for the dispossession of the small farmer. . . . The evidence . . . would suggest that Marxists, and progressive historians in general, have considerably exaggerated the role played by violence and fraud in the decline of the English peasantry. Instead, the mechanisms of accumulation of holdings [were] gradual, dependent on how and when the land of the middling peasant came on the market. Usually the middling peasant gave up his holding or sold off part of it through . . . economic misfortune or indebtedness.

In particular, the farmer on a small acreage was more liable to run into financial difficulties as a result of a bad harvest (Charlesworth 1983, 15).

Although rural disorders were increasingly common in late Tudor and early Stuart England, cultivators and tenants were not the chief source of unrest. The last major protest by cultivators in southern and eastern England was Kett's Rebellion in 1549 (Cornwall 1977; Charlesworth 1983). After Kett's Rebellion, the courts developed "principles concerning the admission of copyhold [and] what constituted an unreasonable fine" (Croot and Parker 1978, 40). The initiative in farm improvement then passed to the tenantry, scores of whom moved up into the ranks of landowning gentry. It was not until 1600 that landowners generally began raising rents as fast as, or faster than, prices rose (Kerridge 1962; L. Stone 1965); but at that point rising rents were generally paid by a prosperous tenantry that had already enlarged its holdings and was profiting from commercial farming (Charlesworth 1983).[3]

Sharp's (1980) recent study of the enclosures of the western forests, a model of the new local history, is exemplary. The old view is that these enclosures constituted an arbitrary elimination of the common rights of small cultivators, who rose to defend their immemorial rights by rioting. Yet a close examination of the legal proceedings shows that

the disafforestations, rather than being arbitrary enclosures, were excellent examples of enclosure by agreement; substantial freeholders and copyholders were asked to grant their consent to the enclosure and the consequent extinction of their rights to common in return for compensating allotments of land. Contrary to accepted opinions . . . the property rights of . . . freeholders and copyholders were scrupulously protected in quite elaborate legal proceedings. (Sharp 1980, 127)

If not cultivators, who then was responsible for the rural tumults of the late sixteenth and early seventeenth centuries? Sharp found that it was

3. Yeomen tenants found their loyalty to gentry tried by rising rents, but the issue was one of sharing profits, not expropriation. The prosperity of small farmers after 1600 is described by Hoskins (1953).

not the dispossessed copyholders and yeomen cultivators who protested but rather the already landless squatters in the forests, primarily artisans who relied on grazing, game poaching, and wood gathering to supplement their incomes.

Numerous local studies (Appleby 1975b; Walter 1980; Walter and Wrightson 1976; P. Clark 1976) reach the same conclusion: from the mid-sixteenth to the mid-seventeenth centuries, the main source of rural unrest was not the inhabitants of open-field farming areas where land was enclosed. Rather, population growth (England's population rose from just over two million in 1540 to five million in 1640) had created another England: pockets of squatters and landless artisans who occupied forests, fens, and common lands and whose numbers were fueled by the migration of excess population from the tilled-field areas. These squatter communities, on the fringes of the older settled areas, were the main sites of riot and disorder. For their livelihood, these people relied on dairying, poaching, and gathering of firewood and charcoal in the waste and forest areas, as well as on metal, wood, and textile work. They thus had to buy their grain at the market. As the settled communities sought to expand their cultivated lands in order to feed the growing market brought by population increases, they enclosed the waste and forest where the communities of artisans and squatters had settled, provoking riots (Appleby 1975a, 1975b; Beckett 1982; Lindley 1982). Moreover, rising food prices spurred grain riots by rural artisans, events that occurred with increasing frequency in the late sixteenth and early seventeenth centuries (Charlesworth 1983; Walter 1980).

The contrast between the marginal and settled communities is nicely drawn by Underdown (1981, 75) in his study of Somerset and Wiltshire from 1590 to 1640.

> The dairying and textile area was characterised by weak manorial structures, rapid population growth, high rates of migration and vulnerability to food shortages in bad harvest years . . . . Recurrent food shortages provoked riots, [and the] region was the scene of constant instability and disorder. By contrast, like the dairying country, the downlands had been affected by the growth of a market economy, and by the consequent trend to partial enclosure. But through it all, the bonds of neighborhood, institutionalized in Church and manor court . . . survived. The fielden villages . . . were more stable.

Thus, the traditional community did not automatically disintegrate at the adoption of capitalist agriculture. Nor were cultivators inspired to protest the loss of land. Most popular disturbances in the late sixteenth and early seventeenth centuries were caused by rural artisans and squatters protesting the loss of waste and forest to arable fields, food scarcity, and high prices.

Most importantly, studies of the management of Crown lands have shown that the Crown, far from opposing enclosures, was by 1630 perhaps the largest encloser in England (Thirsk 1967a, 1976). True, the Crown did collect some fines from enclosers in the 1630s, but these were more a public expression of piety than an expression of Crown policy. Pressed by growing financial needs, the Stuarts spearheaded enclosure projects to convert waste to arable land, often in partnership with local gentry. The Crown and gentry then split the profits from the enclosure and rental of reclaimed fens and royal forests (Thirsk and Cooper 1972, 109; Lindley 1982; Charlesworth 1983). For example, in Lincolnshire in the 1630s a group of gentry joined the Crown in a fen drainage project; the same gentry emerged as the core of the royalist faction in the country during the civil war (A. Fletcher 1981, 312). In the north, the Crown led the way after 1600 in raising rents and entry fines, positioning itself in the forefront of the region's movement toward market rents (Appleby 1975a, 591). If enclosure for improvement, leasing, and profit is taken to be a mark of commercial progressiveness, then in light of the Crown's activity it makes little sense to portray the seventeenth-century crisis as a conflict between a progressive commercial gentry and a conservative anticommercial Crown.

We must also consider Wallerstein's (1980) claim that changes in overseas trade, not merely in domestic agriculture, created the critical conflicts leading to revolution.

PATTERNS OF OVERSEAS TRADE

Wallerstein (1980, 142) suggests that conflicts arose in England between "the new capitalists and the old aristocrats." He notes that these groups were both part of the ruling landlord class, but he blames the frictions within that class on the challenge raised by the newly risen elements of the gentry—"risen" in the sense that they gained in wealth relative to the old aristocrats by exploiting the opportunities provided by expansion of the world economy in the sixteenth century. Wallerstein further contends that the political crisis of the 1640s was a crisis in the whole capitalist world economy, which entered a period of contraction and stagnation in the period 1590–1640 after a century of growth. For Wallerstein (1980, 121), as long as the world economy was expanding, the tensions between the newly rising gentry and the older elements of the elite could be contained; but "once the economic limits of the expansion were in view, the struggle of defining who had a right to control the state-machinery became acute." Hence the revolution. However, the economic downturn created a long-term problem as well: "the continuing economic difficulties [after 1660] forced a de facto compromise between the two factions lest the political strife get out of hand, and the lower strata . . . begin to assert themselves." Hence the stability of the later seventeenth and early eighteenth centuries. Wallerstein's theoretical framework is elegant and he has many insightful things to say about economic development in this period; yet, these insights do not readily translate into an explanation of the origins of state breakdown.

One problem is the connection between the world economy and the rise of new elements in the gentry. Prior to 1650, England was not a net exporter of grain; in 1640 woolen cloth still accounted for 80 percent of the value of all exports (R. Davis 1967). England's connection to the world economy in this period was thus largely through the textile trade. But the majority of those who entered the gentry through farm enterprise did so through arable agriculture, whether by producing grain or by renting cropland to farm tenants. Their profits came from the increased domestic demand for food and land produced by England's growing population. Moreover, up to the year 1640 there was no stagnation in grain prices and rents; indeed, rents rose more rapidly after 1590 than before (Kerridge 1962). Neither the increased wealth of the gentry nor conflicts within the gentry can thus be traced to expansion and contraction in the world economy in the period 1500–1640.

If we turn our attention to England's overseas trade and suggest that it was nonetheless a "lead" factor in the economy as a whole, we find it hard to explain the timing of the revolution. The expansion of England's overseas trade ended in the 1550s; in the 1570s, the Antwerp market for cloth, the hub of England's export trade, collapsed in the Netherlands Revolt against Spain (R. Davis 1967; Minchinton 1969). English merchants had to seek new markets, which they did with only limited success. From 1560 to 1590, the volume of cloth exports was only two-thirds the level of the 1550s (Coleman 1977); "a boom in textile exports in the first half of the century . . . had been followed by a protracted decline in overseas sales during the third quarter of the century" (Supple 1959, 23). Trade then struggled to retrench and stagnated for over seventy-five years, until a new resurgence followed after 1650 (R. Davis 1973). If Wallerstein's theory were correct in asserting that contraction of overseas trade produced fatal conflicts, whereas continued stagnation led to compromise, the revolutionary crisis should have occurred in the late sixteenth century and should have been followed by a period of stability during the subsequent trade stagnation from 1600 to 1650. For that matter, the presumed "continued economic difficulties" in the later seventeenth century that Wallerstein claims were necessary to force a compromise simply did not exist. After 1650, England experienced an unprecedented trade boom. By 1686, the gross tonnage of shipping entering London had skyrocketed to *more than five times* the volume of 1600 (B. Dietz 1986, 128). The wool export trade, which showed no growth from 1550 to 1650, suddenly doubled in value in the latter half of the seventeenth century (Coleman 1977, 63–67, 160). If a long stagnation was necessary to force a compromise between England's elite groups, the massive expansion in England's overseas trade *after* 1650 should have loosened the constraints that held back open conflict. But this was not the case: the crisis of 1688–1689 revealed no conflicts within the elite comparable to those of the 1640s.

Finally, in the revolution many "new capitalists" were not enemies of the Crown but rather its close allies. Overseas trade was in the hands of royally chartered monopolies: the Levant Company, the Eastland Company, the East India Company, and the Merchant Adventurers. The men who profited from these monopolies generally supported the king. Studies of merchant allegiance during the revolution (A. Fletcher 1981; R. Ashton 1979; Pearl 1961; Manning 1976; Farnell 1977; Robert Brenner 1973) show that it was the merchants in *domestic* trade, not the major overseas merchants, who supported Parliament in the 1640s. The king's supporters also included many "new" families who gained from office, invested in land (often purchased from the Crown) for commercial profit, and partnered with the Crown in local projects for fen drainage and forest improvement (Zagorin 1969). Profit, rather than enterprise per se, seemed to guide the political attitudes of industrial centers. While clothing districts struggled and leaned toward radicalism, the coal trade centered in Newcastle was burgeoning, and "Newcastle . . . provides a clear case in point of a commercial and industrial center that sided with the King rather than Parliament" (Howell 1979, 112).

Although the Crown came into conflict with the leadership of London in 1640, one would have to ignore Crown history in the whole of the sixteenth and seventeenth centuries in order to depict this situation as the culmination of conflicts between "commercial capitalist" forces in

the capital and an anticapitalist or feudal Crown. From the mid-sixteenth century to the 1620s, the royal state and the commercial capital
supported each other and benefited from each other's growth. Under
the early Stuarts a close partnership bound the Crown and the commercial oligarchy: the Crown relied on the London mayor and aldermen
to raise loans and disburse royal funds; in return the oligarchs received
concessions in customs farming, royal monopolies, and trade agreements
(F. Fisher 1968; R. Ashton 1961). It was the intractable financial difficulties of the Crown in the 1620s and 1630s that shook this whole
mutually supportive arrangement. Charles I's need for money led him
to seize many landholdings of the city, the titles of which were simply
declared defective. Many chartered rights were revoked or declared expired and reestablished only in return for loans or cash payments (R.
Ashton 1979). When the Crown demanded massive new loans in 1640,
the aldermen simply replied that the royal credit and finances did not
merit further advances, forcing Charles to call Parliament. But the conflicts between the Crown and the city of London were not conflicts
between long-standing opponents. The city's enmity was that of a long-
standing business partner who is suddenly defrauded by an impecunious
associate.

   In short, B. Moore, Anderson, and Wallerstein seek to explain the
English Revolution as pitting those groups with increasing capitalist interests against a "conservative Crown" and "old aristocrats," with this
conflict set against a social background of widespread cultivator dispossession and unrest. Yet by 1640 virtually every member of the elite,
regardless of the age of their titles, was involved in commercial practices,
for a century and a half of inflation had eliminated the holdings of those
landlords who had not converted their leasings to market rents. And the
purported conservative Crown and widespread cultivator dispossession
and unrest need not be explained, for in the late sixteenth and early
seventeenth centuries they simply did not exist. They are historical chi-
meras that have preoccupied us for too long.

   To explain the outbreak of the English Revolution, we need to explain
what actually did happen. Three factors stand out as crucial: First, there
is the fiscal distress of the state. A shortage of money led the Crown
into policies and projects that created opposition. Many of these projects
were highly commercial and progressive—rent increases to market levels
on Crown lands, partnerships to enclose and exploit fens and forests,
and sale of trading privileges for international and domestic commerce.
Other projects were conservative and feudal—tighter rules of wardship

to bring revenue to the Crown, requirement of gentry to take up knighthood, and sale of titles and offices. But all of these policies had in common the search for increased revenues. Without fiscal distress the Crown would not have needed to so greatly antagonize the elites; without fiscal distress the Crown would not have needed to submit its fortune to Parliament in 1640. Thus, we need to know, and the Neo-Marxist theories do not tell us, why the Crown's tax and financial system became increasingly inadequate toward the mid-seventeenth century.

Second, there are the multiple, often highly localized, intraclass conflicts. One of the striking phenomena of the English Revolution is how the unity of the upper classes against the Crown rapidly dissolved with the advent of popular uprisings in London, in Ireland, and in the fen and forest regions in the period 1641–1642 (A. Fletcher 1981; Manning 1976; Kishlansky 1977). Yet the pattern of conflict is not one of sharp and clear divisions; instead myriad local struggles differently shaped the conflict in different locales. From 1640 to 1660 shifting coalitions and conflicts produced such grave disorder that only Cromwell's military rule, and later royal restoration, brought stability. By the mid-seventeenth century, interests in commerce and the leasing of land at commercial rates were almost universal among the elite; why, then, were the upper classes so fractured into multiple competing interests that they were unable to agree on a means to rule England?

Third, there is the growth of popular disorders among the lower classes. Hill (1980, 129) is certainly at least partly correct in stating that "what mattered in the English Revolution was that the ruling class was deeply divided at a time when there was much combustible material among the lower classes." The English Revolution became a revolution, not merely an effort by Parliament to restrict the Crown, when popular disorders in London and in the countryside presented an extraordinary dilemma to the elite: should authority be returned to the king in order to put down the disorders, or should Parliament itself take authority and encourage and attempt to profit from popular opposition to the king? The latter course would have been impossible had there not been numerous members of the middling classes—artisans and small merchants—in London who were willing to follow Puritan preachers and parliamentary leaders in opposing the traditional order. If popular protests were chiefly the work of artisans, small traders, and urban merchants, not of cultivators, what then was the cause of popular disorder and opposition to the Crown?

Other Marxist-inspired social theorists, specifically Skocpol (1979),

Wolf (1969), and Paige (1975), have provided superb studies of revolutions that occurred at later dates than the English Revolution and chiefly in the developing world. Unfortunately, these studies offer only limited help in explaining the English Revolution, for they deal chiefly with peasant revolutions. None of these writers gives great attention to the reasons for uprisings by artisans and urban groups, the kind that played a key role in England. Skocpol does argue that fiscal crises that precipitated state conflicts with elites lay at the heart of major revolutions, and this insight is certainly applicable to the English case. But if we ask why a fiscal crisis arose in mid-seventeenth-century England, Skocpol's answer does not apply. In studying the French, Russian, and Chinese revolutions, Skocpol (1979, 50) found that state fiscal crises arose when relatively backward states faced "intensifying military competition with nation-states abroad that possessed relatively much greater and more flexible power based upon economic breakthroughs to capitalist industrialization or agriculture and commerce." Yet in comparison with its major adversaries—Spain and France—Stuart England was not markedly backward economically or lacking in capitalist development. The crisis of 1640 was provoked by a small war with backward Scotland, a country ruled by the English monarch. If not pressures from more advanced states, what was the source of fiscal decay? Moreover, Skocpol's discussion of state crises focuses on conflicts between state administrations and autonomous elites; but we need to explain not only the conflict between the king and Parliament but also the severe intra-elite conflicts among the gentry. On this issue Skocpol provides little guidance.

The contributions of sociology and comparative history to an understanding of the English Revolution are thus sadly deficient. The best recent theorists of revolution, who have focused on more recent events, offer arguments that largely fail to apply to seventeenth-century England, while historical sociologists who do address the seventeenth century continue to rely on a Neo-Marxist view that is too often at variance with the facts.

Moreover, *all* participants in the debate are bound by a linear view of history, so that the revolution must be classified as either a crucial break with the past or a relatively insignificant interruption in the continuity of the English Old Regime. They lack a cyclic framework that could explain how long-term social trends created *both* a substantial weakening of the English Crown, Church, and aristocracy in the century before 1640 *and* a reversal of this pattern, that is, renewed strength in the Crown, Church, and aristocracy, in the following century.

Given the rich lode of social, economic, political, and demographic findings that have been unearthed in the last decade, we can do better. Let us first consider long-term patterns of life and death as we work toward an explanation of why state fiscal collapse, severe intra-elite divisions, and popular urban and artisanal disorders converged in mid-seventeenth-century England, at the same time that other state break-downs occurred throughout Europe.

DEMOGRAPHIC CHANGE AND ITS ECONOMIC CONSEQUENCES IN ENGLAND, 1500–1750

LIFE AND DEATH

From 1300 to 1500 life and death in England were almost evenly matched. Even after the Black Death in 1348–1349, the plague made chronic returns, and population recovered only slowly. By 1500 England's population may still have been below its fourteenth-century peak (Hatcher 1977; Gottfried 1978). But in the following century and a half, life gained the upper hand: from 1500 to 1650 England's population more than doubled, growing from just over two million to over five million (Wrigley and Schofield 1981; Cornwall 1970).

Contemporaries were well aware of the dramatic change. By 1575 Humphrey Gilbert already claimed that "England was pestered with people," and the political commentator Hakluyt remarked that "throughe oure longe peace and seldome sickness we are growen more populous than ever heretofore" (cited in Chambers 1972, 135). By 1624 Richard Eburne, vicar of Henstridge, recommended colonizing New-foundland to reduce "the excessive multitude of people" (Underdown 1973, 17).

Local studies (Gottfried 1982; Appleby 1975c) and examinations of national parish register data (R. Lee 1980; Wrigley and Schofield 1981; Goldstone 1986a) have led scholars to conclude that "if any particular factor must be singled out as the most important in this renewed demographic growth it was probably the decline in mortality rates from 1480 to 1520" (Gottfried 1982, 71). Indeed, as R. Lee (1978, 168) notes in his study of mortality and population change from 1250 to 1700, "exogenous changes in mortality . . . appear to account for virtually all the variation in population."

The low mortality in the sixteenth century was especially marked for youth aged one to nine years (Wrigley 1969; Wrightson and Levine 1979). Finlay's (1981b, 69) detailed study of eight parishes in central

England found that from 1550 to 1599 mortality for children aged one to nine years was only 75 percent as high as it was in the seventeenth century. As a result the population grew not only larger but also younger, and each new generation was crowded with more teens and young adults than existed in the preceding generation (Coale 1956).

However, after 1650 mortality rose to its earlier levels. Despite increases in agricultural output and higher real wages, incursions of smallpox and typhus and the return of the plague thinned the ranks of the young (Wrigley and Schofield 1981; Skipp 1978; P. Clark 1977; Appleby 1975c; Landers and Monzos 1988). Population growth ceased; indeed, the population fell to under 5 million and stayed at that level until 1700, before slowly recovering. From 1650 to 1750 England's population grew only from 5.2 million to 5.7 million, a gain of less than 10 percent. As youth cohorts shrank in size, the population grew older, and families smaller. By 1670 the contemporary observer William Coventry was driven to remark that "corn and cattle were being produced to excess and the population was not increasing rapidly enough to consume it" (cited in Thirsk 1976, 89). Only after 1750, when the shift toward younger ages for marriage boosted the birth rate, did a new surge of population occur (Wrigley 1983; Goldstone 1986a).

Population growth was closely linked to urbanization. In the sixteenth and early seventeenth centuries, propelled by the overall demographic increase, excess population from the countryside streamed to the towns. London grew from 50,000 inhabitants in 1500 to 400,000 in 1650. Other towns doubled and tripled in size over the same period. But in the following century, when England's overall population growth nearly ceased, London's growth rate fell by two-thirds, while most smaller towns stagnated or declined (Finlay 1981a; Finlay and Shearer 1986; Clark and Slack 1976; P. Clark 1981; A. Dyer 1979).

Was the growth of London in the sixteenth and seventeenth centuries chiefly due to the overall population increase? Or was it more dependent on growth in overseas trade during an expansionary phase of the European world economy, as Wallerstein (1974, 1980) contends? This claim is easily checked. Coleman (1977, 37, 50, 63–67, 160) provides data on England's exports from 1450 to 1750. Table 2 shows the results of a time-series regression of London's growth from 1500 to 1750 on both England's overall population growth and the growth of exports.[4]

4. Regressing the logs of the variables allows one to directly observe effects on percentage rates of change (Wonnacott and Wonnacott 1979). Population data are decade

TABLE TWO   REGRESSION RESULTS FOR THE GROWTH
OF LONDON, 1500–1750

Variable	Regression Coefficients[a]
ln (population)	2.66
ln (exports)	.303
Constant	N.S.
Rho	.754
R^2	.999

[a] GLS corrected for first-order serial correlation. For all coefficients shown, $P < .01$.

These two factors together explain nearly all of the variation in London's growth during this period. The data also allow us to ascertain their relative contributions to that growth. Computation of the separate impact on London of each factor from the coefficients in table 2 shows that over 80 percent of London's growth in the century and a half preceding the revolution was due to the increase in England's overall population.

Indeed, prior to the Industrial Revolution changes in the economy had little impact on population trends. From 1500 to 1750 mortality took the lead in determining population increase or decrease, and repeated inquiries in early modern English demographic history have shown that mortality shifts were independent of changes in harvest quality or real income (Appleby 1975c; Skipp 1978; R. Lee 1980). Mortality shifts among the peerage were virtually identical to those among the general populace (Hollingsworth 1965). As Wrigley and Schofield (1981, 354) conclude, "the dominant influences on mortality trends appear to have been exogenous to the economic system." Therefore, as Chambers (1972, 6–7) has remarked, "we are driven to conceding an independent role to population change as an autonomous variable, a cause rather than an effect."

The extraordinary population growth during the period 1500–1600 has often been noted by historians and social theorists. Yet its signifi-

averages from Wrigley and Schofield (1981); London population at decade intervals is estimated from de Vries (1984). Exports are an index estimated at decade intervals from Coleman (1977), based on the total volume of cloth exports from 1500 to 1630 and on the total volume (in pounds sterling) of all exports from 1640 to 1750. This index actually overstates the prosperity of the cloth trade from 1500 to 1640, since the volume measure takes no account of the decline in the value of cloth relative to agricultural products during this period. Still, the index shows exports sharply depressed from 1560 to 1630.

cance for political events in the seventeenth century has usually been misunderstood. While writers on revolution since Aristotle have expressed the view that excessive population growth can be politically destabilizing, their reasoning often has been crudely Malthusian.[5] They argue that population growth leads to a decline in living standards, popular discontent, breakdown of traditional society, openness to radical ideas, disorientation, and violence (Aristotle 1967, 77; Keyfitz 1965; Taeuber 1948; C. Johnson 1966; Migdal 1974). These arguments are not entirely false—real wages did fall in England as population grew, so that by the early seventeenth century they reached their lowest level in the entire period 1500–1750 (Phelps Brown and Hopkins 1962b). And Puritanism did find most of its adherents among the populace in the towns and "marginal" regions, the sites of rapid population growth, artisans struggling with falling wages, and frequent disorders (Clark and Slack 1976; Thirsk 1976; Underdown 1981). But popular suffering by itself never explains the occurrence of state breakdown and revolution. As C. Tilly (1976, 1978) and Skocpol (1979) have eloquently argued, diffuse popular discontent can express itself in a variety of ways; it is unlikely to have any political impact against a strong state supported by a unified elite. The crucial factors that lead to state breakdowns are state fiscal crisis, elite opposition, and intra-elite conflicts.

We thus should immediately disavow any "social breakdown" notion that population growth led to revolution merely by creating diffuse discontent. Paupers do not make revolutions. If a new synthesis of basic demographic data with a theory of political crises is to be valid, it must show a connection between demographic change and state fiscal distress and between demographic trends and elite conflicts, both with the Crown and among the elite themselves. I agree with Harris and Samaraweera (1984, 127) that "each of the steps intervening between population pressure and conflict needs to be examined in some detail . . . . To understand the link between population change and [political change] we must examine the mediating institutions."

Scholars who assess the impact of population change have often erred by focusing exclusively on change in the overall size of a population. However, demographic change also has powerful *indirect* effects. Changes in the balance of population and resources can shift relative and general prices, leading indirectly to income redistribution and pressure on state finances. Thus, we need to look carefully not only at

---

5. Weiner (1971), McNeill (1977), and Choucri (1984) are sophisticated exceptions.

population movements but also at changes in prices and their impact on existing institutions.

POPULATION GROWTH, SCARCITY, AND PRICE INFLATION

Population growth is often a benefit for a society. Where there is virgin land to bring under the plow, where education is widely available and there is a shortage of skilled administrators and officials, and where growing industry is able to provide opportunities for skilled labor, a growing youth and young adult population provides a needed impetus to the economy. But none of these conditions obtained in England during the late sixteenth and early seventeenth centuries. Most importantly, new arable land could only be gained by converting existing forests, fens, and commons that already provided the livelihood of artisan and dairying or pastoral communities. Food production thus was hard pressed to keep pace with growing population.

The clearest evidence of scarcity is shown in the movement of food prices, which rose 600 percent between the early sixteenth and midseventeenth centuries (Coleman 1977). The rise in food prices was part of a general rise in prices known for its magnitude as the "price revolution" (Ramsey 1971; Outhwaite 1969).

Some scholars, including Neo-Marxists (Wallerstein 1974, 77–84), have followed Marx and later E. Hamilton (1934) in attributing the price inflation to the influx of silver bullion from the Americas. But this explanation is now recognized as inadequate. Chemical assays of European coinage show that American silver formed only a small percentage of Europe's money during the "price revolution" and was hardly evident at all in any coinage except that of Spain and Italy, where inflation was in fact much *less* than in England or France (Gordus and Gordus 1981). Recent studies of the total volume of imports show that the amount of bullion imported from America in the sixteenth century was too small to account for the economic growth and the rise in prices in Europe; and in the late seventeenth and early eighteenth centuries, although much larger quantities of bullion were imported, prices remained flat (Morineau 1985; Cross 1983). Recent estimates of the change in England's stock of coinage suggest that England's money supply grew by less than 50 percent in the sixteenth century, while prices rose fourfold (Challis 1975). Although the increase in bullion no doubt made a contribution, the major source of inflation lay elsewhere.

Figure 1 shows long-term population and price trends in England.

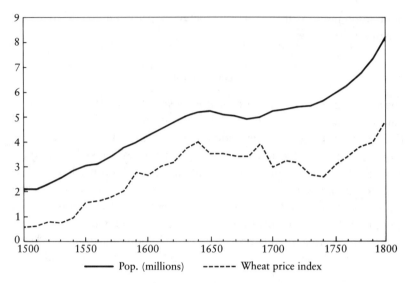

Figure 1. English population and prices, 1500–1800

Note: Wheat prices are shown as an index of decade-average prices, adjusted so that prices in 1641–1650=4.0.

Throughout the early modern period, prices, particularly grain prices, rose and fell in close harmony with population change. It is easy to see why population increase would raise the price of food. With limited supplies of land and fixed technology, grain output could respond only slowly to rising population. Thus when population was growing, demand would tend to exceed supply and prices would rise.

But population growth would also increase the supply of labor. Thus we might expect that the cost of labor (i.e., wages), and of manufactured goods heavily dependent on labor, such as cloth, would go down. What actually happened in the sixteenth and early seventeenth centuries, however, is that the price of *both* food and manufactured goods rose, although food prices rose much faster.

The source of this general rise in prices is much debated. Yet a new consensus is emerging that change in the *velocity of money*, rather than in bullion imports, allowed the general price level to rise (Miskimin 1975; Riley and McCusker 1983; Riley 1984; Lindert 1985; Glassman and Redish 1985; Goldstone 1984, forthcoming). Very briefly, population growth in the early modern period brought with it greater urbanization and economic specialization; these trends in turn brought changes in the density of exchange and an expanded use of credit, which greatly increased the velocity of monetary circulation. Hence population growth led to an expansion of purchasing power and market demand. When the supply of goods and services failed to grow accordingly, prices in general rose.

Grain prices showed the largest shifts, for the shortfall in grain did create a large *relative* increase in the price of foodstuffs. Thus from the first decade of the 1500s to the 1640s, grain prices rose by over 600 percent, while the price of manufactured goods rose by only 200 percent (A. G. R. Smith 1984, 436). Wages too rose by about 200 percent, or only one-third as fast as the price of grain. Thus the relative value of cloth, and of workers' wages, fell by about half in relation to food.

Grain prices, however, were the key to the economy. In an agrarian society where most people spent over half their income on food (such as bread and beer, both derived from grain), grain prices were at the heart of daily life (R. Stone 1987, 32). From the workers who had to feed their families, to the farmers whose lease payments were supposed to reflect the prices of their products, to the king who needed to purchase food to provision the armies, grain prices concerned the entire kingdom.

From 1400 to 1500, when high mortality kept the population stable, prices had remained virtually constant: prices in the first decade of the 1500s differed merely 5 percent from their level in the last decade of the 1300s. Then from 1500 to 1640, when mortality fell and population more than doubled, grain prices soared (Coleman 1977; Phelps Brown and Hopkins 1957). In the following century, from 1640 to 1740, mortality again increased and England's population remained stable. Prices remained stable as well, even though after 1650 bullion imports resumed and actually surpassed their sixteenth-century level (Morineau 1968, 1985; Doyle 1978). In sum, price change from 1500 to 1750 followed the pattern of population change, not of bullion imports. Thus the price increase of the sixteenth and early seventeenth centuries has been "firmly placed on the doorstep of the demographic boom" (Chambers 1972, 27).

A SIMPLE MODEL OF PRICE MOVEMENTS

Population growth increased the demand for grain, putting upward pressure on food prices, but agriculture was not static. Enclosures of fens and forests and the spread of new agricultural practices—for example, convertible husbandry, which rotated land from grain production to pasture—were increasing England's agricultural output in the sixteenth

TABLE THREE   REGRESSION RESULTS FOR ENGLISH
PRICES AND WAGES, 1500–1750

	Regression Coefficients[a]	
Variable	ln (prices)	ln (wages)[b]
ln (population)	2.24	−1.78
Harvest	.0187	−.00892
t		.0624
t^3	-4.54×10^{-5}	
Constant	2.97	5.78
Rho 1		.716
Rho 2		−.406
R^2	.990	.927

[a] For all coefficients shown, $P < .01$.
[b] GLS corrected for second-order serial correlation.

and seventeenth centuries (Kerridge 1967). Food became more expensive, but, unlike their counterparts on the Continent in the sixteenth and seventeenth centuries, ordinary Englishmen rarely starved (Appleby 1978).

We can construct a simple model to examine how population change and agricultural change explain shifts in prices. Other things being equal, population growth should cause an increase in prices. However, as improvements in agriculture, transportation, and marketing increase the supply of grain and reduce the cost of bringing it to consumers, technical change should create a tendency for prices to fall over time. In addition, one other element is needed to model price movements. Prices were highly unstable from decade to decade because short-term changes in weather could drive harvest quality, and prices, into sharp short-term swings. Hoskins (1964, 1968) studied such harvest fluctuations in England in this period and produced a rough index of short-term variations in harvest quality, based on the fluctuations of prices around the long-term moving average. Including Hoskins's measure of harvest quality in the model effectively filters out the short-term impact of weather on prices, leaving the underlying long-term shifts in prices to be explained by population and agricultural and marketing changes.

Table 3 shows the "best fit" estimation results for a regression of decade-average wheat prices on population, harvest fluctuations, and long-term technical change, the latter represented by the passage of time (t).

The model suggests that if population were constant, grain prices would tend to fall at an accelerating rate: roughly 2 percent per decade around 1600, 3 percent per decade by 1650, and 8 percent per decade by 1750.[6] However, each 1 percent increase in population brings an increase in prices of slightly more than 2.2 percent. Thus, population increase of more than 1–1.5 percent per decade before 1650 would lead to rising prices. From 1500 to 1650 England's population was often rising by more than 5 percent per decade; in the years of most rapid price increase, the later sixteenth century, it was generally rising by roughly 10 percent per decade (Wrigley and Schofield 1981). Thus, despite improvement in agricultural output, population growth dominated price movements during the "price revolution" of 1500–1640.

A similar calculation shows that the price of labor, as well as of grain, responded sharply to population changes. The response of real wages to population movements, also shown in table 3, indicates that if population were constant, real wages would tend to rise by over 6 percent per decade, reflecting secular trends toward greater productivity. Yet a 1 percent population increase would lower real wages by nearly 1.8 percent. Thus population growth of over 3.3 percent per decade would lead to falling real wages. During the period 1500–1650, then, population changes dominated wage movements and real wages fell; conversely, when the population was stable from 1650 to 1750, real wages rose.[7]

In short, despite farming improvements, the population boom in the period 1500–1640 brought a steady rise in prices. The demographic and price changes were gradual: total population increased by about 1

6. A variety of specifications were tested, using varied indices. The use of price indices for mixed grains, bread, and a mixed market basket of consumables gave virtually the same results as the use of wheat prices. A linear model for prices gave results that were not too different from the "accelerating change" model—the coefficient for population was 2.76 (instead of 2.24), and the secular price decline was a steady 4.5 percent per decade—but the "accelerating change" model better fit the data. This acceleration reflects the increased agricultural improvement of the period 1650–1750 (Kerridge 1967); there is reason to think that over the course of the eighteenth century agricultural improvement slowed (Deane and Cole 1969; Allen and O'Grada 1988; Jackson 1985).

7. Wage data are decade average real wages for building workers in southern England, from Phelps Brown and Hopkins (1962b) as emended by Goldstone (1985). These estimates are quite consistent with R. Lee's (1980) results using slightly different data for the period 1540–1800. Lee found that a 1 percent population increase lowered wages 2.2 percent (versus our 1.8 percent), and that the "absorption rate" for population growth without wage deterioration was 4 percent per decade (versus our 3.3 percent).

percent per year, and grain prices by 2 percent. Yet, the cumulative effect from 1500 to 1640—a rise in population from roughly two to over five million and a rise in grain prices of 600 percent, in just over four generations—was massive, shifting resources and creating challenges throughout English society.

To understand the impact of these changes, we must realize that they posed different problems for different actors. Let us therefore consider the distinct responses of the state, elites, and popular groups.

B. THE DEVELOPING CRISIS OF THE TUDOR/STUART MONARCHY, 1500–1640

POLITICAL CONSEQUENCES OF POPULATION CHANGE: THE STATE

A curious lacuna exists in sociological studies of early modern state crises. All writers agree that the financial crisis of 1640 was a crucial element in the breakdown of the English state; financial crises were also of critical importance in the Fronde and the French Revolution of 1789. But what causes state finances to crumble at some times, and to be sufficiently robust to support even massive wars at others? In England, why did state finances, strong under Henry VII, deteriorate and yield to crisis in the early seventeenth century?

Anderson (1974) and B. Moore (1966) subordinated matters of state finances to class conflicts in explaining state crises; in reply, Skocpol's (1979) study of the French, Russian, and Chinese revolutions stressed the autonomy of the state from class divisions and drew attention to the impact of international political competition on state finances. Wallerstein (1980) blamed a downturn in overseas trade in the early seventeenth century for the English monarchy's fiscal debacle. Yet the English fiscal crisis of the seventeenth century cannot be blamed simply on class conflicts, trade shifts, or international pressures.

The political tenor of the English fiscal crisis can only be understood by noting initially that the English Crown had been struggling since the mid-sixteenth century. It was normal for the Crown to borrow in order to finance wars and to repay those loans in peacetime, chiefly by means of parliamentary land taxes. The customs duties and income from Crown lands, along with other ordinary revenues, would then pay the Crown's basic core of peacetime expenses. But from the mid-sixteenth century, ordinary revenues lagged behind expenses, forcing recurrent peacetime deficits. Thus the Crown was forced to sell assets, levy forced loans, and seek parliamentary grants even in peacetime. By the early seventeenth century new expedients, such as monopolies, forest fines, and sales of offices, which offended large segments of English society, were required to balance the books. And by the 1630s, despite these expedients and more effective land taxation (under the rubric of Ship Money levies), the Crown still had to borrow heavily merely to cover its peacetime expenses. Thus the state's fiscal structure had gravely deteriorated well before 1640.

This is not to say that Crown finances deteriorated in a straight-line fashion from 1500 to 1640. There were occasional victories in the battle against inflation, as respites due to peace or good harvests, reforms in administration, or, infrequently, adjustments of customs revenues produced short-lived surpluses in royal accounts. But despite these intervals of increased solvency, the inexorable pressure of rising expenses overtaking relatively inflexible revenues could never be kept at bay for long. Not a single monarch from 1540 to 1640 was able to avoid leaving ever greater debts, and fewer assets, to his or her successor as the Crown turned to land sales and ever greater borrowing to meet its financial needs.

Under James I, the efficiency of Sir Lionel Cranfield (later Earl of Middlesex) helped to reduce royal expenses and raised the yield of several taxes; combined with the peace of James's early years, the treasury's annual accounts looked healthier than they had been in years: by 1618 the ordinary revenues showed a surplus of £40,000. Yet this prosperity was illusory, for it was built on a long-term structure of debt: "despite [Cranfield's] impressive reforms, the royal debt had risen from about £700,000 to £800,000" in that year "and was to rise further by a similar sum over the following year." Moreover, "the ordinary revenue of future years had already been anticipated to the extent of £117,000 in 1619" (R. Ashton 1984, 233). As Ashton adds, "the savings achieved had been impressive but insufficient." To understand why, despite efforts at reform, the Crown could not escape this spiral of debt and fiscal crisis in the century prior to 1640, we need to look more closely at Tudor and Stuart finances.

Class conflicts do not explain the fiscal crisis, for in England *all* classes both cooperated with the Crown and sought to limit royal taxation. What needs to be explained is why the balance struck between the Crown and the elites, who collected land taxes, provided loans, and paid customs duties on trade, provided increasingly inadequate revenues throughout the Tudor and early Stuart periods. One cannot point only to decreasing trade, which stagnated from the 1550s, for the failure to raise more revenues from the land was equally crucial in the Crown's plight. Indeed, it was tax evasion and resistance by the landed classes that wrecked the Crown's ability to pay for war. And it was not exceptional military pressures that caused the crisis. The Crown spent heavily for war in the sixteenth and seventeenth centuries, in the fight against Spain and France and the subjugation of Ireland. But these were routine, rather than exceptional, state expenditures. Pressures were much heavier in the later seventeenth century, when England was involved in lengthy wars with France, than in the early Stuart period. Charles I's finances collapsed when he tried to prosecute a war to discipline small, backward Scotland. It was thus not increasing military pressures but rather a *decreasing ability to finance even relatively modest military costs*, due to both the large and recurring peacetime deficit that had exhausted credit and the resistance of the elites to further taxation, that marked the crisis.

Some revisionists have claimed that there was in fact no fiscal crisis but merely a political crisis, for Parliament should have passed land taxes to help Charles pay for the Scottish wars. Parliament's refusal to cooperate, not the Crown's fiscal mismanagement, was thus to blame for the royal penury. Yet this short-term view overlooks the fact that a major reason for Parliament's intransigence was the gentry's offense at the various fiscal expedients the Crown had used to deal with its financial difficulties in the preceding decades. Hence the question we need to answer is not merely why the Crown was short of cash in 1640, but why the Crown's finances steadily deteriorated throughout the entire century before 1640.

We can begin to answer this question by noting that while the state may not have been a class actor, it was nonetheless an economic actor; thus its fiscal health was intimately linked to the long-term movements in population and prices that affected the economy. An examination of the working of the English tax system and of its response to these long-term trends unlocks the origins of the fiscal crisis.

CROWN EXPENSES AND REVENUES, 1500–1640

The Crown was perhaps the worst placed of all players in the English economy to deal with sustained inflation. The two main expenses of the Crown—fighting wars abroad and supplying patronage for its supporters at home—grew steadily more burdensome as population growth pushed up both the size of armies and the number of claimants for favors, while price inflation gradually multiplied these costs severalfold. Moreover, many of the Crown's revenues—particularly income from Crown lands and customs, and even parliamentary taxation—were adjusted only at long intervals and thus failed to keep pace with rising prices. The Crown's attempts to raise its revenues were often unwelcome, for many elites were too concerned about maintaining their own positions in the face of inflation and heightened elite competition to come to the rescue of the monarchy. As W. Hunt (1983, 170–171) points out, many gentry "refused to recognize the fiscal crisis that a century of inflation had produced."

The main expense of the Crown in the sixteenth and seventeenth centuries was military campaigns: to keep Ireland in subjugation, to patrol the Scottish border (until 1603), and to fight continental wars against the Catholic powers. The Crown thus needed to purchase enormous amounts of food to provision armies. Under the Tudors the counties were responsible for mustering the militias for self-defense and supplying their equipment, but for fighting abroad the Crown had to hire soldiers and supply them with pay and food during campaigns. "The main burden of victualling then fell on the government" (Corvisier 1979, 33–36; C. Davies 1964). In 1544, Henry VIII led 48,000 men into the field in France, accompanied by 20,000 horses—a force two-thirds the size of the city of London. Armies of 20,000 men, more than equal to the size of Bristol or Norwich, were frequently sent to northern France or to the Scottish border. Elizabeth I often faced the need to send troops to Ireland to maintain English authority, and James I sent expeditionary forces to the Continent in the Thirty Years' War.

For the most part these armies did not live off the land but were expected to buy their food out of their wages. Tudor food policy increasingly reflected the need to provision armies, which, with rising food prices, was a growing concern (Pearce 1942; C. Davies 1964). Throughout Western Europe, "price inflation meant that the cost of putting each . . . soldier in the field rose by a factor of five between 1530 and 1630" (Parker and Smith 1978, 5; G. Parker 1976). To wage war, or even to prepare for it, the Crown required a massive increase in revenues. But the financial system left to the Tudors by Henry VII was poorly suited to attain such increases.

Henry VII had looked back on 120 years of stable prices from 1380 to 1500, during which time the Crown had accumulated land and revenues, when he announced to Parliament that he expected to be able to pay his ordinary expenses—upkeep of the royal household and salaries of royal officials, pensions, and the administration of justice—"on his own," that is, out of the rentals of Crown lands, customs duties, and court fees and fines. In addition, the land taxes levied by Parliament to meet "extraordinary needs"—that is, military expenses—were more than sufficient. Henry VII in fact made a slight profit on his wars, collecting more from Parliament than was spent (Schofield 1964). This comfortable situation slowly unraveled in the following century and a half of inflation.

Some scholars have discounted the role of inflation in the erosion of state finances by noting that, on average, the income of the Crown over the Tudor and early Stuart years kept pace with inflation. Yet to merely "keep pace" with inflation is tolerable only if real expenses do not increase. And population growth greatly increased the two major expenses of the Crown: war and patronage. I consider the increase in patronage expenses in the following section on the expansion of the elites. For now, it is sufficient to note that as population grew throughout Europe in the sixteenth and early seventeenth centuries, so too did the manpower available to be put under arms. And as armies grew, so too did the *real* expenses of the Crown. Because the fleets and armies (the latter used most often in Ireland) of Elizabeth and the early Stuarts were far larger than those of Henry VII, their income had to more than keep pace with inflation if they were to meet expenses. If *real* military expenditure doubled and market prices rose by a factor of five, then royal income would have had to rise by a factor of *ten* to meet expenses without incurring a deficit. Thus, even if income had kept pace with inflation, there would still have been a massive deficit (50 percent) relative to expenses.

The cruelty of population increase, then, was that it raised real costs *and* prices simultaneously, imposing a double burden on Crown finances. And those finances were very slow to respond to increased Crown needs.

Most of the items of ordinary royal revenues were adjusted only at long intervals. The Crown had leased its lands for long periods (often three lifetimes, or ninety-nine years) for fixed cash rents. In a time of stable prices, long leases brought the Crown loyal and dependable tenants; but in a time of inflation such leases were disastrous. In order to meet rising expenses the Tudors thus used Crown lands for their value as assets, rather than as sources of revenue: land was either sold to meet war expenses or given away (sold at a nominal value) to favorites and officials as rewards. While these policies provided ready cash to meet short-term needs, in the long run they diminished the Crown's revenues and resources (Schofield 1964, 236; Wyndham 1979). Customs duties also remained set at fixed nominal prices for decades. Moreover, dues on wine and cloth were imposed on the quantity rather than on the value of the goods traded. So as prices rose, "customs realized a smaller and smaller proportion of the true value of the wares" (A. G. R. Smith 1984, 118). An extraordinary tightening of the customs under Elizabeth retook some ground, but reliance on customs duties (chiefly on woolens) never made up for the loss of landed income during a century when the woolen trade was stagnant (1550–1650) and when the real value of textiles and other manufactures was falling by 50 percent compared to the cost of foodstuffs. While ordinary revenues shrank, the growth of the royal bureaucracy and the increases in rewards and pensions to offset the effect of inflation meant that by the mid-sixteenth century "the majority of government departments were annually overspending their assigned income in substantial quantities" (Alsop 1982, 2).

Faced with a recurring deficit in ordinary accounts and a diminishing stock of land, the Crown turned to Parliament for tax revenues. But here the Crown faced even greater difficulties in increasing revenues to keep pace with growing expenses.

Parliamentary taxes consisted of the "subsidies" and "fifteenths and tenths," both designed to provide "extraordinary assistance" to the Crown in times of unusual need, such as war. They were voted by the landed gentry meeting in Parliament and assessed and collected by local county gentry acting as unpaid justices of the peace. The fifteenths and tenths, taxes at fixed amounts assessed on villages, had no capacity to respond to inflation. The subsidies were in theory a very different matter. A tax on landed incomes and movable goods, with a small levy on the wages of those without property, subsidies were meant to fall chiefly on the rich and to rise with their incomes. In fact, the assessment of the subsidy was made precisely by those on whom the tax was meant to fall most heavily, the wealthy landed families of the counties.

As food prices rose, the value of land increased accordingly. Rent records show a rise of 600 to 1000 percent in rent levels from the 1540s to the 1640s (Kerridge 1962; R. Allen 1988). Yet this increase in gentry income remained beyond the reach of royal taxation. From the 1540s, county gentry consistently underassessed their lands; thus the value of the subsidies fell more and more out of line with gentry wealth. Indeed, by the end of the sixteenth century underassessment was so widespread that, in general, "the richer the taxpayer, the less his true wealth was captured by the subsidy assessments" (Schofield 1988, 253).

In the 1540s, subsidy assessments may have been at 80 percent of the market value on landed estates; by the 1590s they had often fallen to 3 percent or less (Schofield 1964, 188). Sir Walter Raleigh observed that the incomes entered in the subsidy books represented "not the hundredth part of our wealth" (P. Williams 1979, 74). By 1603, the real value of a subsidy to the Crown was less than one-third of its value in 1568. The decline in valuation continued through the first half of the seventeenth century, until in 1628 a subsidy's real value was one-sixth what it had been in the mid-sixteenth century (Schofield 1964, 185–194; Hill 1961, 52; W. Hunt 1983, 274). By the 1620s, what had been the means to sustain extraordinary military expenditure in the early sixteenth century was insufficient even to meet the Crown's peacetime expenses (K. Sharpe 1978a; Russell 1979).

Mann (1988, 82) estimates that the *real* income of the Crown fell by almost 15 percent from the 1560s to the 1580s, at a time when military engagements in Ireland and war with Spain demanded far greater real expenditures. Even Elizabeth's fiscal prudence and the drive to increase revenues in the last decade of her reign, which increased real revenues to 10 percent above the level that had prevailed when she took the throne, fell far short of the Crown's needs. Thus Elizabeth bequeathed a sharply reduced stock of Crown land, and a large stock of debt, to her successors.

The Crown's responses to fiscal strain included debasement of the coinage, sale of Crown lands, and borrowing from the city of London and the international money market. By 1600, repeated use of these expedients had nearly exhausted them. Debasement of the currency had reached such an extreme in the 1540s and 1550s that the Crown had been forced to recall and recoin much of the currency, which was no longer being traded at face value (Challis 1978). In 1570 Elizabeth undertook a recoinage that stabilized the silver content of the currency, and debasement was discarded as a tool of state finance. Crown lands were sold in every decade from the 1530s, until Crown holdings shrank from a high of 20–30 percent of England's land in the 1530s to roughly 5 percent in the early seventeenth century (Mingay 1976). With its capital shrinking and operating deficits growing, the Crown was forced into more extensive and regular borrowing. James I relied heavily on the international money market, but during the period 1615–1617 lenders began to refuse further credit, and the government was kept afloat solely on loans from the city of London (Kenyon 1978). By the 1620s, city officials refused to lend on the security of the customs duties, as had been past practice, and insisted that remaining Crown lands be offered as collateral. By the 1630s, despite the extraordinary expedients adopted by the Crown to raise money, only the customs farmers could still be counted on to provide loans (D. Thomas 1983, 121–122).

Because parliamentary levies had become an increasingly inadequate means of taxing the incomes of the landed gentry, in the early seventeenth century the Crown turned to other means to tap their wealth. These included the sale of honors and ranks, with the rank of baronet created explicitly to sell to wealthy gentry (L. Stone 1965, 91). Knighthoods were granted in unprecedented numbers, most for substantial fees. In addition, Charles I fined eligible gentry who did not take up knighthood (L. Stone 1972, 122). Royal claims to old forests were revived; for example, in 1634 the Crown made the extraordinary claim that two-thirds of the county of Essex had once been royal forest, and that therefore the titles of the current landowners were in question. The Crown demanded 20 percent of the current value of the land from its owners in compensation (W. Hunt 1983, 267–268). Rockingham Forest's limits were extended from six to sixty miles, resulting in massive fines to the earls of Westmoreland and Salisbury (Hirst 1986, 173). Money was extorted from merchant associations and the city of London by declaring their royal charters invalid or expired, and by demanding fees in return for renewal of their chartered privileges (L. Stone 1965, 1972; R. Ashton 1961). Merchants in a wide variety of goods were allowed to trade only by obtaining (for a hefty fee) the right to operate with royal monopolies. As noted earlier, the Crown also pursued the enclosure and commercialization of fen and forest lands on a profit-sharing basis. And in the 1630s the Stuarts greatly expanded the imposition of Ship Money levies. In Tudor times there had been a small tax levied on port towns during war for naval support; Charles I developed this into an annual tax on land, levied throughout the nation.

Elizabeth I had managed to finance a war with Spain by levying parliamentary taxes even in peacetime under the valid excuse of war preparations. She also drastically curtailed royal household expenses and tightened customs collections. These measures allowed her to build a war chest in the 1570s sufficient to finance the war with Spain. Had population growth and inflation ceased in 1600, perhaps the tax system could have been restored, debts reduced, and financial crisis avoided. But from 1600 to 1640, England grew by 25 percent in population, from four to five million inhabitants; London doubled in size from two hundred thousand to four hundred thousand; and grain prices rose until, in the 1630s, they reached double the level of the 1580s (Wrigley and Schofield 1981; Finlay 1981a; Hoskins 1964, 1968). The expenses of the Stuarts rose accordingly, while the real yield of taxation continued to dwindle. Thus, although Charles I's nominal revenues in the 1630s (including Ship Money) were almost 150 percent higher than those of Elizabeth I in the 1560s, his *real* income showed an improvement of only 10 percent (Mann 1988, 82)—this to rule over a nation whose population had risen by two-thirds and whose gentry, always hungry for patronage, had tripled in number. Increases in the Crown's real expenses thus far outran increases in its real income.

By the 1630s, despite the expedients of Ship Money, forest fines, and sales of offices and titles, Crown finances were a fragile and tottering structure. Crown lands were nearly gone, and the subsidy was hardly worth the trouble incurred in getting Parliament's cooperation to levy and collect it. Heavy indebtedness kept the monarchy afloat as long as there was peace, but the cost was high. By the 1630s, the unpaid Crown debt reached over £1 million; interest could be paid only by constant extension and rescheduling of debt and by assignment of future revenues to cover current borrowing. In the late 1630s, half the Crown's ordinary revenue was hypothecated to cover current debt obligations, and sources of credit were getting harder to come by. The balanced budgets of the 1630s were thus "positively misleading"; the balance was achieved only by exhausting the Crown's credit to cover its current peacetime expenses (R. Ashton 1960, 43). Any extraordinary expenses meant instant financial disaster.

The Crown's financial difficulties were not limited to England, but extended to Scotland and Ireland. Just as the Stuarts' attempts to increase their revenues in England provoked growing concerns about Englishmen's liberties and property, so in Scotland and Ireland the king's subjects were on the defensive. As Scotland was primarily Presbyterian, and Ireland primarily Catholic, fears took root that the Anglican monarchy in London planned to despoil the smaller, nonconforming kingdoms (Russell 1987).

In Scotland, Charles took over feudal duties owed to the nobles and modified the terms of their tenures to give greater profits to the Crown. He issued royal monopolies and abolished elections for the Edinburgh town council. Most offensive, he revoked the nobility's titles to their lands (which he promised to reinstate for a percentage payment to the

Crown). At the same time, he sought religious conformity with English practice by imposing a new prayer book on the Scottish clergy. Religion had always been a source of tension, both within Scotland and between the English and the Scots. Charles's combination of religious impositions *and* economic predation from London, however, overcame the tensions between the Scottish nobility and the Scottish clergy, and created a unified opposition to the king. As Stevenson (1973, 52–53) points out,

> the whole experience of the seventeenth century in Scotland shows that ecclesiastical issues alone, and ministers and their followers alone, could never bring about a revolution . . . . The act of revocation [of land titles] . . . proved decisive in convincing the Scottish aristocracy of the virtues of presbyterianism, to which they had hitherto been singularly blind . . . . Revolt based on religious and other grievances gained power to shake the throne only through the support of the nobility. If the Scots nobles had remained loyal to the Crown, hatred of Charles' religious innovations among the ministers and their lay supporters might have led to disturbance and disorder, but not to the revolution which in fact took place.

Charles's general campaign to increase economic and religious controls provoked a formal covenant among the Scots to oppose the king's policies.

Similar measures inflamed Ireland. Ireland had been a net burden on the royal exchequer under James I, but in the 1630s this situation could no longer be tolerated. The Crown sought to raise funds through investment in Protestant colonization and plantations in Ireland, while the lord deputy, Strafford, increased the Crown's centralized administrative control. However, Strafford's efforts to bolster the Crown's resources and authority alienated every interest in sight, from radical nationalists to conservative landowners (Russell 1988).

Charles first attempted to discipline the Scots, but his armies—poorly paid and ill disciplined, with little enthusiasm for the fight—failed to restore his authority, and when the Scots entered England and demanded indemnities, Charles was unable either to repulse or to satisfy them (Stevenson 1973). His credit exhausted, and unable to raise funds, Charles called a meeting of England's Parliament, only to be reproached for his conduct rather than succored. Even after working out a tentative, and humiliating, settlement with Parliament and the Scots, Charles could not obtain peace. The Protestant religious settlement that the Scots sought alarmed the Irish; they then rose in 1641 to claim their own religious liberty and end the founding of Protestant plantations (Russell 1988). The Irish rising polarized England's Parliament, leading to renewed confrontation with the Crown and, eventually, to civil war. Thus, Charles's attempts to deal with his fiscal difficulties by acting throughout Britain in the same manner as he did in England lay the basis for a general British uprising.

The Scottish rebellion was the occasion of the monarchy's collapse, but the fiscal crisis was the fundamental cause. The lack of resources to pay an army and satisfy demands for patronage and the exhaustion of the Crown's assets and credit both prompted royal policies that provoked opposition and made the Crown's situation precarious. For "no seventeenth century state could avoid war indefinitely, and even if [Charles] had avoided the self-inflicted wound of the Scottish rebellion the first breath of war from any other quarter would have blown down the whole house of cards" (Woolrych 1980, 240).

The fiscal crisis of 1640 was thus not a mere short-term problem brought on by a few decades of depressed trade or bad harvests. Nor was it created by the opposition of the gentry to the policies of a backward feudal Crown. Short-term expenses, in a healthy monarchy, could always be bridged by loans or the sale of Crown assets. And the Crown had worked for decades by 1640 to update its taxation and tax collecting, to commercialize its remaining landholdings, and to participate through licensing and royal monopolies in whatever profits were still to be made in overseas and domestic trade. The crisis of 1640 was of revolutionary import precisely because its roots lay in the failure of the entire structure of Crown revenues to keep pace with a century and a half of inflation, during which time Crown assets and credit had already been pressed to exhaustion. Even parliamentary taxation, had Charles sought it throughout the 1630s, would not have solved the problem unless the whole nature of parliamentary taxation were changed. Taxes on landed assets at old valuations would not have provided sufficient funds; a massive rise in tax rates based on current gentry income was needed. But this was not likely to be voluntarily or easily achieved. By the seventeenth century, inflation had eroded the old structure. The lines were now drawn whereby the Stuarts could achieve financial solvency only at the cost of a political crisis.

A MODEL OF FISCAL STRAIN IN AN EARLY MODERN STATE

The relative impact of short-term and long-term economic factors can be assessed in a simple time-series model of how we would expect state finances to respond to inflation in a state where taxes are relatively inflexible. Short-term problems, such as a run of bad harvests, occurred frequently in English history, creating a sharp rise in prices and much popular protest. Similarly, a short-term fall in trade might hurt the ability of the Crown to increase its income. But my contention is that such effects were less important than the cumulative rise in prices at a rate greater than increased revenues could match.

For any early modern state the chief cost was the expenditure for war, an activity that could only rarely be avoided. Thus, if prices rose at a time when revenues were difficult to increase, mounting fiscal distress was inevitable. We can capture this relationship by formulating a variable for long-term, cumulative inflation effects as follows:

Long-term price pressure in nth decade after the base period

$$= \prod_{i=0}^{n} e^{k(X_i - B)},$$

where X_i is the rate of inflation in the ith decade after some base period, k is a positive constant, and B is the maximum rate at which ordinary revenues can be increased without attacking elite privileges or levying new taxes.

In this variable, if X_i (the rate of inflation) is generally larger than B (the maximum "manageable" rate of inflation), then $(X_i - B)$ will generally be positive and the impact of inflation will grow exponentially over time. That is, fiscal pressures will grow slowly at first but then become more and more severe. However, if the rate of inflation is less than the "manageable" limit B, then $(X_i - B)$ will generally be negative; the fiscal situation will then very quickly improve.

Two additional factors must be taken into account. First, in those rare decades when England was not at war, fiscal pressures were greatly relieved. This peace dividend can be represented by a dummy variable, with value 1 for those decades when England was at peace and 0 otherwise.[8] Second, long-term and short-term price effects can interact; that is, a large short-term price rise may have little effect if long-term price pressure has been low, but it may have a critical effect if long-term price pressure has been high. Thus, we should also add an interaction term to our model to allow for these combined effects.

This model of English Crown finances in the period 1500–1750 is shown in figure 2. In order to estimate this model and test whether it

8. Decades with eight or more consecutive years of peace were the 1500s, 1570s, 1610s, 1680s, 1720s, and 1730s.

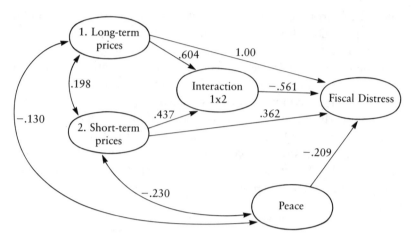

Figure 2. Prices and state financial distress, 1500–1750
Note: R²=.716

indeed captures the pattern of state financial response to inflation, we need somehow to measure state financial distress. Unfortunately, fiscal distress in premodern states is extremely hard to measure via the kind of internal documentation common to modern states. The key to state survival was adequate credit, and records of credit worthiness are misleading. Interest rates, for example, were manipulated so that a distressed Crown might not pay high interest but simply force customs farmers or other sources to loan the state money at a specific rate. A government might also escape obligations by forcing creditors to accept as payment for old high-interest debts newly issued bonds bearing a lower rate of interest. Such measures suggest a level of financial difficulty not evident simply from interest rates or income figures. Indeed, a state's financial difficulties were reflected less in the rate of interest it paid than in the degree of political risks it was forced to accept in order to acquire funds or escape its obligations.

These problems suggest a solution, however, for we can roughly fix a government's state of financial distress by examining whether or not it needed recourse to such forced measures. In fact, there was a regular pattern in the escalation of Tudor and Stuart revenue-raising measures, a pattern of steps that together constitute a Guttman scale of financial distress.

We can fashion a five-step "desperation scale" as follows:

1.   Adequate income and credit; no extraordinary measures required to meet expenses.

2.   Rescheduling of debts or stop-payment orders required because of inadequate funds for short-term obligations.

3.   Current income and credit chronically inadequate for current expenses; government fills gap with partial bankruptcies or repudiation of debts, sales of Crown assets, and forced loans.

4.   Major shortfalls of income relative to expenditures; measures under step 3 are supplemented by attacks on the privileges of elites for financial gain or by major new taxes (e.g., Ship Money, excise).

5.   Total bankruptcy, indicated by complete failure of credit; the state must acknowledge its needs to the elite and submit to their conditions in order to gain funds needed for continued existence; otherwise such crucial obligations as military pay cannot be met.

This ascending scale of fiscal distress captures the kinds of difficulty, and the levels of political conflict, brought by financial problems. It is admittedly a crude measure. Yet it offers the virtue of simplicity of application to early modern European states: one need only ask, for a given decade, did the state default on short-term obligations? Did it need to resort to forced loans, sales of Crown property, partial bankruptcies, or other partly self-destructive means to meet its financial needs? Was it driven to attack the privileges of its own supporters, the national elite, or to adopt major new taxes? And, finally, did the state reach a point where credit was simply exhausted and it could not raise funds to pay even its most critical bills? These questions deal with highly visible events that receive wide coverage in political and economic histories; noting the presence or absence of such events allows us to roughly plot the fiscal strain on early modern states over time.[9]

Most importantly, this scale measures fiscal strains according to their *political* impact. The actual amount of debt or deficit is not important, if adequate taxes cover the interest payments, if currently accepted taxes (e.g., subsidies) can be easily raised, or if royal wealth or land is sufficient to back up such debt. What matters politically is whether royal

9. My assessment of changes in English fiscal distress is based on the financial histories of F. Dietz (1964), Dickson (1967), and W. Kennedy (1913).

wealth is diminishing, so that the Crown becomes more dependent on its creditors; and whether currently accepted taxes are failing to keep pace with expenses, so that the Crown has to take steps that antagonize elites in order to pay its bills, initiate substantially novel (and harder to justify) kinds or levels of taxation, or do both.

Returning now to our formula for assessing long-term fiscal pressures, the task remains of estimating B, the maximum "manageable" rate of inflation, and k, the magnitude of the inflation effect. For the Tudors and Stuarts, we can estimate B from the increases in Crown income. It is interesting to note that the rate of increase of the Crown's nominal peacetime revenues was roughly the same both before the revolution and after the Restoration. In the eighty years from 1551 to 1630, nominal ordinary Crown revenues rose from £170,000 to £600,000, a gain of roughly 250 percent. The revolution, and new taxes imposed by Parliament, then abruptly doubled state income, putting revenues back into balance with prices and expenses. Thereafter, in the seventy years from 1660 to 1730, government peacetime revenues rose from £1.5 million to £5.8 million, a gain of 280 percent (Palliser 1983; Ashton 1960; Coleman 1977). (I return to the English financial system after 1650 in Chapter 3.)

Thus, both before the revolution and after the Restoration, government peacetime revenues rose at roughly .5–2 percent per year. To the extent that this increase was available for needed increases in real expenses, such as administering Ireland, expanding naval and military capacity, and financing increased credit, the monarchy could prosper; to the extent that this increase was consumed by inflation, the monarchy would be unable to increase its expenditures and credit to meet real needs except by recourse to politically dangerous expedients or wholesale revamping of the tax system.

Given the increase in ordinary revenues over the period 1550–1750, an annual inflation rate of .1–.2 percent clearly would not have cut too deeply into revenues; an inflation rate of around 1 percent would likely cause trouble, as increased revenues would nearly be consumed by inflation. The slow but steady deterioration in Tudor and Stuart finances suggests that we look for a B of around .5–1.0 percent as the threshold of accumulating difficulties. We can in fact estimate B by running a number of regressions; we thus leave both B and k to be estimated from the model.

The results of estimating the relationship between inflation and state fiscal distress in England are shown in figure 2 and table 4. The strength of the model is high and robust for a range of values of k and B. With a value of B of .5–.7 percent per year, and a value of k between .25 and .75, this model of the causes of the fiscal crises accounts for roughly 70 percent of the variance in state fiscal distress from 1500 to 1750. This robustness of the model tells us that we have basically caught the right shape of the relationship between price inflation and state financial condition. Further evidence that the model has substance is that if the parameters B and k are moved outside of this range, the fit of the model to the data, as shown in the values of F and R^2, quickly falls off.

It is interesting to note that the long-term price pressure effect dominates the other factors; even the peace dividend has a modest impact in comparison. Moreover, the interaction of long-term and short-term effects has a negative coefficient; this implies that a simple linear combination of long-term and short-term price effects overestimates financial distress. Since it is the short-term pressures that have the widest fluctuations, this result can be interpreted as moderation of the effects of short-term pressures. That is, if short-term prices suddenly move rapidly, whether up or down, their total effect on fiscal distress will be less than a simple linear response. Again, the impact of long-term cumulative pressures appears to be the crucial factor.

In short, it is apparent that the Stuart financial crisis arose from an inability to cope with cumulative inflationary pressures due to inflexibility in the early modern English tax system. This view not only describes the nature of the crisis of 1640 but also yields a simple and robust model that accounts for 70 percent of the decade-to-decade variation in state fiscal conditions over the entire period 1500–1750. I suggest that this model is widely applicable to European states in the period 1500–1850.

The Crown's disaster in Scotland confirmed the belief of many Englishmen that the Crown was no longer just or effective. Thus, the calls to contribute Ship Money in 1639 met with almost universal rebuff. Charles was then forced to call Parliament to seek succor.

However, the measures that Charles pursued to delay his fiscal reckoning—the monopolies, sales of honors, and nonparliamentary taxation (e.g., Ship Money)—had alienated the elite. Rectification of royal behavior was thus demanded as the price for parliamentary support. Yet even this demand was only the beginning of the conflict, for Charles's stubbornness and duplicity stoked the divisions that had been developing

TABLE FOUR   REGRESSION RESULTS FOR MODEL OF STATE FINANCIAL DISTRESS, 1500–1759

	Values of k, B[a]							
	.5, .5	.5, .7	.25, .7	.75, .7	.5, .1	.5, 1	.5, 1.2	1.5, .7
Long-term prices[b]	.952	1.00	.873	1.08	.779	.976	.836	1.02
Short-term prices[c]	.416	.362	.470	.307	.553	.281*	.234*	.228
1 × 2	−.471	−.561	−.503	−.633	−.516	−.672	−.639	−.604
Peace	−.177*	−.209	−.201*	−.230	−.189*	−.280	−.323	−.272
F(4/21)	12.55	13.27	11.93	11.85	5.60	7.93	4.38	6.91
R^2	.705	.716	.694	.693	.516	.602	.456	.568
D-W	1.87	1.92	1.85	1.77	1.34	1.52	1.23	1.37

[a] Standardized regression coefficients; all are significant at the $p < .05$ level *except* those marked with an asterisk (*).
[b] Long-term prices $= e^{k \, [(\text{short-term prices}) \, - \, B]}$.
[c] Short-term prices $=$ average annual percentage change in wheat prices, each decade.

among the parliamentary elites. Financial decay was not the sole source of political crisis; it was foreshadowed and exacerbated by conflicts and disaffection among the elite.

POLITICAL CONSEQUENCES OF POPULATION CHANGE: THE ELITE

One of the striking aspects of the English Revolution is the way that the gentry, though fairly unified against the king's excesses in 1640, suddenly fractured into a host of national and local factions in the years 1641–1642. Why were intra-elite conflicts so much sharper and more intense than they had been in the days of Elizabeth, or than they were in the late seventeenth and early eighteenth centuries? Certainly part of the reason is the greater extent of political crisis posed by Charles's bankruptcy, the Scots' invasion, and uprisings in Ireland, in London, and in the countryside. But at least part of the answer is also to be found in the extraordinarily strong personal competitiveness and insecurity that afflicted the gentry in the early seventeenth century.

Much has been written about social mobility preceding the English Revolution, both of individuals and of groups (L. Stone 1976). However, simply observing the volume of social mobility tells little about its political consequences. More precise terms are needed.

The prerogatives of high status usually include property, power, and precedence. If vacancies in the elite hierarchy of ranks and positions are expanding in pace with the number of qualified aspirants to such positions—whether due to mortality among the elite creating sufficient openings, or due to state expansion creating additional positions—then newcomers can enjoy elite prerogatives without displacing existing members, and conflicts need not arise. Indeed, co-optation of newcomers may strengthen the entire group. Let us call this simple *absorption*. In contrast, conflicts and competition may arise if downward mobility threatens existing elite families. Let us call this loss of position by traditional elite families *turnover*. Another source of conflict may arise if upward mobility elevates so many newcomers to elite wealth or status that substantial numbers of the elite—old and new—are excluded from prerogatives they consider their due, such as official positions, honors, or royal favors. Let us label this phenomenon of "crowding out" *displacement*. Social mobility per se, therefore, need not lead to conflict. What matters is whether social mobility leads to *turnover* and *displacement*.

In the early Stuart years, social mobility played an important role in social conflicts. But it was not the simple expansion of the gentry and of honors that created difficulties; it was the combination of several generations of population increase, inflation, and state fiscal difficulties that produced considerable turnover and displacement.

GROWTH IN NUMBERS

Population growth produced turnover in the elite hierarchy by two paths: directly through changes in family size and indirectly through changes in prices. When family size had been stable, families could provide for their sons by direct succession; little population increase meant few or no younger sons surviving to adulthood, few daughters surviving to marriage and requiring dowries, and few additional elite-based families for whom succession did not provide a ready place in society. However, population growth meant increasing numbers of surviving younger sons and daughters. Among parents, the problem of providing for larger families depleted resources, while among young adults there grew an increasingly competitive scramble for possessions or official positions that would conserve status.

In the century before the revolution, the reproduction rate of the peerage rose even more rapidly than that of the population in general, and large surviving families became more common (Hollingsworth 1965). Sir Thomas Payton described his household at Knowlton Court, after his sister's death, in the following sad terms: "She has left me seven children, all young, who have no surviving friend but myself. I have another sister who expects every day to be a widow with nine children. My wife and myself have eight children to employ our . . . care about. I have a brother . . . who together with his wife and six small children are supported almost entirely by myself, and whose callings and livelihood I must inevitably provide for" (Everitt 1968, 54). Although extreme, Sir Thomas's predicament was by no means wholly exceptional. Thus "one necessary result [of increased fertility] was a downward social mobility among non-heirs which caused intense competitiveness and divisiveness among the British upper class" (de Vries 1976, 11).

It should be emphasized, as noted earlier in regard to the problem of landlessness, that the impact of population growth on marginal groups —in this case, younger sons—is much greater than that on the population as a whole. When a population is just barely reproducing itself,

TABLE FIVE   SURVIVAL OF SURPLUS SONS UNDER
VARYING GROWTH RATES OF THE GENTRY

Generation	No. of Gentry Families (index 1st gen. = 100)	No. of Surviving Surplus Sons (index 1st gen. = 10)
1	100	10
2	105	10.5
3	110.25	11.0
4	115.75	34.7
5	133.1	39.9
6	153.1	45.9
7	176.1	17.6
8	184.9	18.5
9	194.1	19.4

NOTE: Net reproduction rates: 1.1 (10% per generation) for generations 1–3 and 7–9; 1.3 (30% per generation) for generations 4–6.

the problem of surplus younger sons is nil. Yet at even moderate growth rates, the problem of younger sons rapidly escalates.

We can see this effect in a simple numerical example. Consider a gentry population in England that went from a net growth rate of 10 percent per generation for three generations, to a growth rate of 30 percent per generation for the succeeding three generations, and then returned to the earlier rate. Let us further assume that about one-half of the surviving younger sons, through success in trade or the professions, achieve gentry status themselves; the rest drop out of our example. We then have the pattern shown in table 5.

Note that though the number of gentry families doubled, the number of younger sons more than quadrupled and then fell off by over 50 percent! In other words, the swing in the number of younger sons, because it occurs on the margin, is much greater than the swing in the rate of growth of the gentry as a whole. The impact of population growth on families trying to maintain their patrimony intact, and on the volume of young gentry without estates seeking court patronage or church positions, thus was far greater than a simple consideration of overall population growth would imply.

Added to the direct impact of population growth, however, was the impact of sustained inflation. Steadily rising prices affected families differently according to their respective market positions, good fortunes, and entrepreneurial skills. While it might be thought that high prices oppress the poor more than the rich, "in an age where the largest land-owners were members of a class whose social activity involved various forms of conspicuous consumption" this conclusion is not necessarily valid (J. Gould 1962, 316). Landlords who, like the Crown, had let their land at long leases for fixed rents and who had to support large families might see their estates dwindle as they sold their lands to meet expenses; others who were able to shift leases to short-term rents, or were able to buy lands from the Crown and other landlords and fill them with new tenants at higher rents, stood to prosper. Even yeoman tenants, if they farmed for the market and paid long-term fixed rents, stood to gain, perhaps enough to buy their own land and establish footholds in the landlord community. Over two or three generations, the small or middle-sized landholding could be expanded into a respectable estate, or it could dwindle to nothing (Palliser 1983; H. Lloyd 1968; Hoskins 1963; Bow-den 1967a). Thus the period 1500–1640 was one of extraordinary so-cial mobility, both upward and downward. L. Stone (1972, 110) has described this as a century in which more individuals and families were "rising and falling than at almost any other time in English history." The volume of land sales steadily rose, reaching two and a half times the level of the 1560s in the period 1610–1630, a degree of land turnover "without parallel in either the later Middle Ages or the late seventeenth and eighteenth centuries (L. Stone 1965, 37–38).

The result was that the gentry was changing in composition with unprecedented rapidity. In Shropshire the gentry grew from 48 families in 1423 to 470 families in 1623; in Staffordshire the gentry grew from 200 families in 1583 to 1,100 families by 1660. In Yorkshire, from 1603 to 1642, there occurred a disappearance and replacement of more than one gentry family in four in a space of forty years; in Northamptonshire, by 1640, barely a quarter of the 335 local gentry had been resident in the county before 1500, and more than a third had settled there since 1600 (Everitt 1968; L. Stone 1965; Mingay 1976). In Essex in 1600, only 15 percent of the county's politically prominent families had ac-quired their estates before 1485; in Hertfordshire the figure was 10 percent, and in Norfolk and Suffolk, 42 percent and 31 percent, respec-tively (W. Hunt 1983). In Sussex by 1640, only half the county's leading families had been settled there for more than three generations (A. Fletcher 1975).

One contemporary observer in Northamptonshire in 1641 remarked,

"The number of nobility and gentry is greatly overgrown. Now there is increased a very great number, more especially since the beginning of King James . . . . Whereas in Queen Elizabeth's time there was but two or three knights in the shire, now there is sixty, besides many pretended esquires and gentlemen" (cited in Everitt 1968, 58). This increase posed substantial problems for an elite whose stable relationships were based on public recognition of a status hierarchy and deference. As an inscription from Grafton Manor in Worcestershire, dated from 1567, expressed, "Whyle everi man is pleased in his degree, there is both peace and uniti; Salaman saith there is none acorde, when everi man would be a lorde" (cited in Palliser 1983, 60).

The overall bias of this mobility was upward; far more new families entered the elite than left. We lack precise figures, but rough estimates of the number of gentry families are as follows: in 1540 there were 6,300 gentry families; in 1600, 16,500; in 1640, 18,500; in 1688, after the civil war, 16,400; and in 1760, 18,000 (L. Stone 1965, 767; Aylmer 1961, 331; Speck 1977, 297). In sum, the number of gentry families in England virtually tripled in the century preceding the revolution, and then stabilized for the following century.

Of course, there were exceptions in both time and space to the pattern of rapid mobility found during the period 1540–1640. In counties such as Cheshire, Kent, and Cumberland, the new opportunities brought by rising prices were seized by existing local gentry rather than by newcomers (Morrill 1974; Everitt 1968). Thus in Kent, one of the most commercialized of English counties, the proportion of gentry in 1600 whose families had been established in the county in 1500 was still 75 percent (W. Hunt 1983).

In addition, the rate and nature of mobility varied at different levels of the social hierarchy and across different reigns. Mobility into the aristocracy occurred mainly in the years before and after Elizabeth's reign. In the 1530s and 1540s, sales of the Church lands that the Crown had acquired in the English Reformation formed the basis for new landed fortunes. This was largely a simple expansion of the peerage, fueled by new resources shifted from the Church to secular lords and gentry. Then during Elizabeth's reign the queen's circumspection in granting titles meant few new admissions to the higher ranks (Palliser 1983).

But while few were admitted to the peerage, the years from 1540 to 1600 saw a vast expansion of the gentry. During this period, rising prices and rents fixed for long leases allowed many yeomen and small gentry to increase their fortunes, while growing family size meant many junior branches of older families sought to acquire new estates to maintain their gentry status. At the same time, for many old established gentry, inflation and larger families reduced resources, leading to land sales and loss of social positions. It was during these decades in particular that a great deal of turnover accompanied social mobility.

After 1600, this pattern reversed; mobility into the gentry slowed, while mobility into the peerage increased. By 1600, many landowners were able to find tenants willing to pay for new shorter-term leases at higher rates and were poised to profit from the continued boom in land (L. Stone 1965). The opportunities for thrifty yeomen and low-ranking gentry to rise diminished, and wealth flowed to those who had already gained estates. However, from 1603 to 1629 the Stuarts' readiness to grant honors and titles in exchange for cash led to a huge expansion of the upper social ranks: knights, baronets, and peers (L. Stone 1965, 759). Yet the latter trend halted in 1629, when Charles I stopped the sale of ranks and sought to restore a more traditional, stable, social hierarchy (L. Stone 1972, 125–126)

We again need more precise terms to describe these patterns. We need to distinguish between *entry* into the elite and *ascent* into its higher ranks by those who had recently entered. Conflicts could arise as a consequence of either kind of mobility, or of an imbalance between the two. In the 1530s and 1540s there was considerable absorption of newcomers into the elite, but with a balance of both entry and ascent, and little displacement or turnover. Then from 1550 to 1600 inflation had its main effects, as rapid entry by newcomers claiming gentry status, and turnover by declining families, disrupted traditional county hierarchies. However, little ascent occurred to disturb the peerage. After 1600, however, there was far less entry, as the profits created by inflation flowed to established gentry rather than to their tenants. But this flow of profits and the generosity of James I and of Charles I's early years lifted the lid on ascent for nearly three decades, reshaping the upper gentry and the peerage, and inflaming the desire for further upward mobility. Then from 1629 to 1640, ascent too was virtually halted.

These shifts in mobility help explain why social conflicts grew stronger under the Stuarts. The slowdown of entry after 1600 meant that there was little expansion to satisfy those who wanted "in" to the elites; those left "out" thus grew restive. Moreover, though James I's reign saw considerable ascent, the fiscal restraint practiced by Elizabeth, and by Charles I after 1629, meant that the increase in upper-rank positions remained smaller than the increase in the number of the gentry: from 1540 to 1640 the number of peerages merely doubled, and seats in Parliament increased by only one-half, whereas the number of gentry families had tripled (A. G. R. Smith 1984, 387; L. Stone 1965, 758). Thus there was considerable displacement at the upper levels of the hierarchy, and the elite waged fiercer struggles for parliamentary seats and for the patronage offered by the Stuarts.

In short, social mobility was indisputably high from 1540 to 1640. But this fact alone tells us little about social conflict. There were considerable differences in the patterns of social mobility across the century before the revolution. In the 1530s and 1540s, much of the mobility reflected simple *absorption* as the Crown put former Church lands on the market and created new opportunities. Then, from 1540 to 1600, inflation and larger families created difficulties for some elites, while economic expansion created opportunities for newcomers. As will be discussed later, rapid turnover among the justices of the peace was one result. However, at court, Elizabeth's reluctance to grant titles limited "official" recognition of this mobility, thus deferring problems. James was only too glad, though, to recognize mobility when confronted with the evidence in cash, and he thus freely dispensed new ranks and titles. Yet even James's generosity left many suitors dissatisfied. The vast expansion of the gentry in the late sixteenth century, and the shifts in fortunes among all elites, had left many claims for changes in status unsettled. By the early seventeenth century, many yeomen were upset at the rise in rents, which excluded them from advancement; many elites, of all ranks, were upset that they had yet not received desired rewards and recognition; and many elites of all ranks were upset at those upstart new gentry and peers who had successfully claimed new titles, as well as court and county positions.

After the revolution social mobility sharply diminished. Where there had been "a rapid natural increase in the number of the aristocracy between 1580 and 1630, . . . by 1660 all such increase had ceased" (Hollingsworth 1965, 32). After 1660 the number of peer and gentry families remained frozen, with new entrants barely balancing the extinction of existing families (McCahill 1981; Speck 1977; Cannon 1984). Local studies confirm the impression of overall stability: In Warwickshire, Styles's (1978, 143–144) study of the heralds' visitations of 1619 and 1682–1683 found that "it is in the earlier, much more than in the later visitation, that we find records of new and minor families." "It thus looks very much as if . . . rapid mobility [was a] temporary phenomenon peculiar to the late 16th and early 17th centuries" (L. Stone 1965, 161; J. Jones 1978).

This stability does not mean that the land market became frozen or that individual mobility ceased after the revolution. In Lincolnshire and Lancashire the land market after the civil war was highly active (Blackwood 1978; Holderness 1974). The expansion of trade after 1660 lifted many merchants, who acquired landholdings and moved into the lower gentry. And much land, especially near London, was purchased in small pieces by metropolitan lawyers, officials, and merchants for country homes. But on the whole, it appears that there was a trend of consolidation of large estates (Habakkuk 1979; Speck 1977; McCahill 1981; Beckett 1977; Roebuck 1980). The years from 1660 to 1760 thus "saw some further shifts in the distribution of landed property, although nothing on so great a scale as in the hundred years before 1640 . . . certainly the changes created no new class of landed proprietors, nor any great rift among the ranks of the existing landowners" (Mingay 1976, 69).

It is therefore difficult to maintain that the extraordinary social mobility of the period 1540–1640 was associated specifically with the growth of "capitalism." After all, the years 1550–1640 were a period of stagnation in the cloth trade and a time when England still depended on food imports. It was in the century after 1660 that England became the leading economic power in the world economy, and a major exporter of grain as well as of manufactures. But during this latter century of capitalist expansion social mobility was modest. The great pressures and opportunities that account for the exceptional social mobility from 1540 to 1640 stemmed from increased family size, rising prices, and the Crown's financial difficulties. After 1660, when population stabilized and prices stagnated, these pressures and opportunities diminished; and while capitalism flourished, social mobility was sharply reduced. Indeed, recent studies of the demographic and inheritance patterns of the gentry have shown that, much more than legal devices such as strict settlement, it was the shrinkage of gentry family size due to high mortality that led to the conservation of large estates (Bonfield 1981; Clay 1981a; Roebuck 1980). Instead of provision of marriage portions and support payments for younger sons burdening estates, high mortality led to much collateral inheritance. Stone and Stone (1984, 75–76) found that in Northamptonshire, Hertfordshire, and Northumberland, "during the demographic slump of 1650–1740 about half of all landowners failed to produce a male heir to succeed them." Thus, the "demographic trends of the period were tending to concentrate property ownership into fewer hands" (Clay 1981a, 38).

Wallerstein (1980, 122) has suggested that the decline in social mobility after 1660 was intentional: "Is not the compromise of 1660 an agreement to . . . stabilize the unsettling mobilities of the sixteenth century?" But it is difficult to imagine the dominant strata agreeing to increase their mortality and to depress the price of grain—the crucial factors in maintaining the stability of landed estates, as Bonfield (1981), Clay (1981a), Thirsk (1967a), and Mingay (1976) have shown—in order to achieve social stability. In this case Wallerstein rather overstates the ability of the dominant strata to manipulate long-term social trends. The evidence instead suggests that autonomous mortality shifts and associated price changes governed the stability of the elite.

COMPETITION AND CONFLICT

The immediate consequence of the enormous upward and downward mobility of the elite in the sixteenth and early seventeenth centuries was heightened competition and factionalism. Although "as a class, landowners were firmly based and flourishing, as individuals they were highly insecure" (Kiernan 1980, 119). The result was "intense competition for jobs and patronage as an increased number of claimants for elite positions faced an economy and a royal administration unable to accommodate them all" (L. Stone 1976, 51).

The new members of the gentry elite did not form a new economic or social class. In their sources of income (chiefly rentals from lease of landed estates) and in their social and political aspirations they sought to assimilate into the landed elite. New gentlemen, or gentlemen newly risen to knighthood or the peerage, sought, above all, recognition of their place in the traditional order. Thus there was an enormous demand for new appointments to county offices. As A. H. Smith (1974, 47) notes for Norfolk, "The foremost gentry began to vie with each other for pre-eminence while those in the second rank jostled to improve their status . . . . Gentlemen clamoured for the principal offices . . . to assert their prestige: elections [to Parliament] were contested; keen competition developed for the deputy lieutenancies; demand for a place on the Bench caused a rapid expansion [and turnover] of the commission of the peace." Kishlansky (1986) has shown that, prior to the late sixteenth century, members of Parliament were chosen largely by acclamation, as counties easily selected their most eminent gentry to serve in Westminster. But by the late sixteenth and early seventeenth centuries, social mobility and competition had blurred the hierarchy of local status, and selection became more difficult. In a number of counties, parliamentary contests disrupted traditional patterns of patronage and primacy; such contests were bitter precisely because they were not merely about possession of an office but about a candidate's honor and standing in the community.

Had the royal bureaucracy or the Church been able to secure positions for the existing elite and for newcomers to the gentry and peerage, the expansion of the elite may well have strengthened ties between the Crown and the elite ranks. But such was not the case. "In terms of institutional development, the whole period from the early years of Elizabeth I to the eve of the Civil War is a relatively static one" (Aylmer 1961, 3). Newcomers increasingly jostled older elites out of accustomed positions. In Norfolk, where once it was so customary "for son to succeed father on the commission of the peace that the absence of the next generation indicates failure of the line . . . or failure of fortune," by the late sixteenth century "nearly half the magisterial families . . . provided a justice for only one generation" (A. H. Smith 1974, 59). Similar displacement by newcomers is visible in the Crown bureaucracy, where Aylmer's (1961) sample of 194 officers serving in the period 1625–1642 revealed that one-third came from the families of merchants, yeoman, or other nongentry. L. Stone (1965, 743) has gone so far as to assert that "the hostility of the majority of the Peers to Charles I in 1640 can be ascribed in large measure to the failure of the King to multiply jobs to keep pace with the increase of titles."

As mentioned earlier, population growth inflicted a double blow on state finances, both by raising prices and by increasing real expenses through larger armies and larger volumes of young men seeking patronage, thus producing a manifold increase in needed revenues. Population growth inflicted a similar double blow on elites. Inflation created mobility opportunities, so that the number of elite families increased more rapidly than the population. But this effect was multiplied by the direct effect of lower mortality: the much larger number of surviving younger sons, for whom patronage was especially crucial. My earlier numerical example demonstrated that when reproduction rates rose, the number of surviving younger sons increased *twice* as fast as the number of gentry families. Since the number of peer families doubled and the number of gentry families roughly tripled in the century before 1640, when we combine these two trends we find that the number of younger sons of peers and gentry who were completely dependent on royal patronage or professional jobs must have increased by a factor of four to six by the early seventeenth century. When we add the more than fourfold increase in prices, we can see that to maintain patronage for the same proportion of younger sons in 1640 as in 1540, and at the same *real* level, the Crown would have had to spend sixteen to twenty-four *times* as much, in current pounds, as it had a century earlier! Demographic change, through its joint price and marginal population impact, thus had an enormously greater impact on demands for patronage than would be guessed by considering overall population increase alone.

Limits on available land, civil and ecclesiastical offices, and royal patronage led to increasingly polarized factional battles between patron-client groups for available spoils (Morrill 1974; Hirst 1975; A. Fletcher 1975; A. H. Smith 1974). When one gentry family appealed to the king for promotion, a competing gentry family might appeal to a county peer or a friend at the court to defend their interests. Local conflicts between Catholics and Anglicans, between newly arrived and older gentry, and between partners of the Crown in fen-draining and forest projects and those excluded from such projects were waged through pursuit of office and influence, with rival factions backing different candidates (K. Sharpe 1978b; C. Roberts 1977a; W. Hunt 1983). "In this way the tensions and divisions between the leading councillors exacerbated relationships in the county while local rivalries and quarrels heightened tensions at Court" (A. H. Smith 1974, 48). The famous division of England into "court" and "country" is more aptly described as a division into factions—some closely dependent on the king, others less favored by royal appointments and projects—that arose throughout the ranks of the elite and appeared at every level of governance (Russell 1979).

Even though James I greatly increased spending on patronage, paying out perhaps ten times as much as Elizabeth, this represented only a *doubling* of patronage spending in real terms (L. Stone 1965, 775). This increase was far from sufficient to cope with a tripling in the number of gentry families, and the even greater increase in the number of younger sons in need of court assistance. Under Charles I, the state's fiscal troubles meant a cutback in patronage spending to merely twice that of Elizabeth in current pounds, or *less* in real terms, despite a vastly increased number of applicants for royal favor. This was displacement on a massive scale indeed. Thus "the numerical increase in all ranks . . . and the glaring injustices of the distribution of titles tended to set the whole governing class at loggerheads" (L. Stone 1965, 124).

The problem of younger sons seems to have added both manpower and desperation to both sides in the revolution. Hirst (1986, 18) notes that the "disproportionate number of younger sons staffing the Parliamentary bureaucracy in the 1640s and 1650s . . . suggests that at least some expectations [from the Crown] had been frustrated." Yet young men desperate for positions also characterized the royalist side. Everitt (1969, 49) points out that "the situation [in 1642] seems to have been aggravated by the remarkable surplus of landless younger sons in the King's armies, with no estate to root them in the countryside, no career but the army open to them, and little to support their pretensions to gentility." In short, the large number of younger sons among the gentry as a whole, for whom the Crown was unable to provide patronage or positions, created a large body of men willing to take sides to establish a claim on their futures, and hence brought an exceptional volatility to these years.

After 1660, as noted above, social mobility declined sharply. It should not be surprising that from that date, competition among local elites also visibly declined. In marked contrast to the situation in the late sixteenth and early seventeenth centuries, after 1660 the number of appointments of justices of the peace was *more* than sufficient to meet demand; indeed, many places on the local bench went vacant for lack of interested candidates (Rosenheim 1989). And in the early eighteenth century, the proceedings of local commissions show much bipartisanship: "despite party differences, there existed an under-appreciated but substantial level of unanimity, solidarity, and capacity for compromise among all the levels of the county elite of Augustan England" (Rosenheim 1989, 125).

Another indicator of changes in intra-elite conflict is the level of civil litigation. One might expect that as commerce rapidly expanded after 1660, the level of litigation would likewise increase. Yet this was not the case; instead, the level of civil litigation closely followed the trends of social mobility and competition: "In 1640, there was probably more litigation per head of population going through the central courts at Westminster than at any time before or since. But one hundred years later in 1750, the common law hit what appears to have been a spectacular all-time low" (Brooks 1989, 360). The drop in litigation was especially marked among the gentry: between 1640 and 1750, the number of gentry who appeared in the Court of Common Pleas as plaintiffs or defendants dropped by over 65 percent. When social mobility rose again from 1750 to 1830, as I discuss later, the level of civil litigation rose as well (Brooks 1989, 362, 384). It thus appears that legal contests among the gentry depended more on the prevailing level of social mobility and competition than on the extent of England's commercial activity.

While most mobility studies have focused on the landed elite, it is worth noting that the same pattern is found among urban elites. Thus Clark and Slack (1976, 118) note that "until the later seventeenth century, the indications are that there was a rapid turnover in the economic elite of the greater urban centers" and considerable conflict among urban leaders. But then there follow "the beginnings of a permanent financial interest" and a period of stable urban oligarchies.

Wallerstein (1980, 121) attributes the conflicts among England's seventeenth-century elites to "the economic expansion of the sixteenth century permitt[ing] the clear emergence of the bourgeoisie as a social class whose relationship to the dominant status-groups was unclear." Though we must reject the notion of a distinct, emerging "bourgeoisie social class," we can agree that rising prices and expanded opportunities for profit created a situation in which the dominance of traditional leading county families became "unclear." The increase in upward and downward social mobility meant that prerogatives of office and county control were no longer secure; instead, claims to precedence were contested by an increasing number of individuals aspiring to elite status. Claims for recognition and advancement were put forth by court officers, country gentry recruited from the enterprising yeomanry, and domestic and international merchants, who were all divided and in conflict. Moreover, we can agree with Hochberg (1984) that opposition to the Crown was strongest in the most commercial counties, chiefly the southeast and those regions connected via coast or river to major trade routes. After all, it was precisely these areas that offered the greatest opportunities for yeomen and gentry to profit from rising prices and to achieve mobility; such areas also had the largest number of gentry who owed their position to their own efforts and thus were more interested in safeguarding their property from Crown interference than in supporting traditional authority.

Still, the key question is why there was a price rise and economic expansion that provided opportunities for extraordinary social mobility in the sixteenth and early seventeenth centuries. England's role in the world economy expanded much more in the period from 1650 to 1750, when exports tripled and England took a leading position in trade, than in the period from 1550 to 1650, when exports stagnated and the country slowly emerged from the shadow of Spain and Holland. Yet in the later period social mobility was modest. The extraordinary mobility from 1550 to 1650 depended on the opportunities provided by rising prices. Price movements, in turn, depended not on international trade (bullion imports, particularly the traffic of the East India Company, brought a far larger volume of precious metals through England after 1650 than before [Chaudhuri 1968]) but rather on the expansion of England's population. And population movements depended on exogenous shifts in mortality, most likely due to changes in the incidence of infectious disease. Thus, if it is agreed that intra-elite conflicts in the English Revolution were caused by increased social mobility that produced competition over status and standing within the elite, then evidently autonomous population movements provided the critical lever that pried loose the traditional pattern of landholding and elite standing.

To be sure, mobility patterns do not allow us to predict the precise allegiance of particular individuals. Although some studies (Antler 1972; R. Ashton 1978, 80) have shown a slight tendency for Parliament's supporters to be more "recently arrived" than their royalist counterparts, most attempts to determine the loyalties of specific individuals from their class backgrounds have failed. Yet much as the physicist, while incapable of describing the exact trajectory of individual particles in a gas, can nonetheless deduce the overall motions of an aggregate of particles if their temperature is known, the historian or social scientist may be on firmer ground in describing the behavior of large aggregates. And in this regard, it appears that the recomposition of the elites that followed the massive changes in population and prices had the effect on the elites *as a whole* of increasing insecurity and sharpening local and national divisions. In short, as rising temperature agitates a gas, so rising social turnover and displacement fractured the elites into numerous factions incapable of formulating a unified response to a severe political crisis.

When the Crown admitted bankruptcy and appealed to Parliament for help in 1640, attitudes toward the Crown reflected experiences of the previous decades. Although there was widespread opposition to the king's foreign policies, to his manipulation of forest fines, sale of titles, and imposition of Ship Money levies, there was no firm foundation of elite unity. Instead of harmony, an atmosphere of competition and adversarial interests prevailed (Kishlansky 1977; A. Fletcher 1981).

The Scots' invasion, royal bankruptcy, and popular unrest constituted a political crisis, but one arguably less severe than the crisis posed by Henry VIII's conflict with the pope, or by James II's flight and William III's invasion in 1688. Yet only in the 1640s did the state crisis lead to civil war. The 1640s were exceptional in that consensus among the elite on how, and by whom, the crisis should be managed could not be achieved. Yet the English state, lacking a written constitution and an established bureaucracy, depended on precisely such a consensus for its very existence. Confronted with the pressing problems of occupation by a Scottish army, popular uprisings in London, and rebellion in Ireland, the myriad divisions among the elite gave rise to adversarial politics that paralyzed the government (Kishlansky 1977). A reluctant recourse to open conflict thus became necessary to cut the Gordian knot of elite rivalries.

In the 1640s, local conflicts thus fueled the national divisions among elites. "The split between Royalists and Parliamentarians . . . provided the opportunity for pursuing an old battle under new banners" (Howell 1982, 76). In the counties, gentry "saw this as the ideal moment for a trial of strength between those who claimed pre-eminence for themselves in the community" (Morrill 1974, 34; Everitt 1973; H. Lloyd 1968; A. Fletcher 1983). This situation is in striking contrast to 1688, when, after a generation of relative price, family, and social stability, the elites were able to face a comparable political crisis with far greater unity of purpose than could be found in the 1640s.

It is desirable, however, to obtain a measure of the degree of rivalry and competition among elites that does not depend as heavily on gross economic factors as the two indicators usually employed: social mobility and land sales. Such a measure might help us to determine whether intra-elite conflicts and rivalries changed in scale from the early to the late seventeenth century. Let us therefore look at one major setting for elite recruitment: the universities and Inns of Court.

UNIVERSITY EXPANSION AS AN INDICATOR OF ELITE SOCIAL
MOBILITY AND COMPETITION

Tudor and Stuart England saw an expansion of education at all levels, as printing and the growth of urban audiences created a market for popular culture (Levy 1982). But although the growth in overall literacy was part of a long secular trend, higher education showed a peculiar pattern of boom and bust. From 1540 to 1630, Oxford, Cambridge, and the Inns of Court (the centers for advanced study of the common law) expanded their annual enrollments by 400 percent (L. Stone 1974; Prest 1972). After the revolution, however, enrollments dwindled; by 1750 enrollments at Oxford and Cambridge had dropped to 50 percent of their respective levels in the 1630s (L. Stone 1974; Prest 1972; Knafla 1972; Lemmings 1985).

This pattern is clearly not a simple result of overall population changes; up to the year 1630 enrollments rose much faster than total population, whereas after 1630 enrollments fell drastically while the total population was constant. Collins (1981) has argued that the boom represented a credentialing "crisis," in which the growing numbers seeking a degree outpaced the employment opportunities for trained specialists. Indeed, there is wide consensus that the universities "prepared too many men for too few places (Curtis 1962, 27)." Yet the boom and the following bust are readily understood as a consequence of the high degree of social mobility and status competition experienced by the late Tudor and early Stuart elite. Although for a portion of enrollees a degree was an important goal leading to a career in law or in the Church, many more enrollees were seeking a "cultural" credential—social integration into the elite and polish to confirm one's standing as a gentleman (Kearney 1970).

The increase in university enrollments had two sources. The largest percentage increase came in the form of younger sons of peers, baronets, and knights, a category that increased fourfold from 1580 to 1639 and reflected higher survival rates among elite families (L. Stone 1974). For these youths, university education offered the hope of lucrative court or Church positions and preservation of status. However, the largest increase numerically was in sons of yeoman, merchants, and lesser gentry who were seeking to raise or affirm the status of their families. In 1577 William Harrison observed that many yeomen "do buie the lands of unthriftie gentlemen, and often setting the sonnes to . . . the universities, and to the Inns of the Court, . . . do make their sayde sonnes by that means to become gentlemen" (Palliser 1983, 90).

University education thus became a talisman, confirming status in a time of rapid social mobility and competition where claims to precedence were frequently contested. By the 1630s, university education among the gentry was nearly universal: whereas in 1562, less than half of the justices of the peace in six counties surveyed by Gleason (1969) had attended the universities or Inns of Court, by 1636, 84 percent had done so.

After the revolution, however, when social mobility virtually ceased, the need for cultural certification diminished. When sons were generally the sole inheritors of family estates, and family positions were generally uncontested by newcomers, the demand for university education dropped; private tutors and a European tour sufficed for education (Stone and Stone 1984, 264–266). When county hierarchies were stable and status assured, formal credentials had less value. Thus, Landau (1984, 378–379) finds that in Kent in 1679–1761, in contrast to the pattern prior to 1640, only one-quarter to one-third of the justices of the peace had attended universities or the Inns of Court.

The demand for credentials evident in the universities in the late sixteenth and early seventeenth centuries, and the boom and bust pattern of enrollments, thus forms a useful indicator of the degree of social competition among the elite.

PAUPERS, PURITANS, AND THE "MIDDLING SORTS"

Two ingredients of the revolution were a royal financial crisis and a sharp sense of competition and dissatisfaction among elites. Yet a third and crucial ingredient was the existence of a vast body of traders, artisans, apprentices, and workers—the "middling sorts"—who formed a mobilizable body that parliamentary leaders could marshal against the king and his allies in London. The first stirrings of the crowd were spontaneous demonstrations in London and the countryside. Part of the elite viewed these demonstrations as threats to social order that required the iron hand of the Crown, foremost defender of the traditional order. As Lord Saville saw the delicate situation, in a strong request for compromise, "I would not have the . . . parliament lessen [the king] so much as to make a way for the people to rule us all" (cited in Morrill 1976, 36). Thus popular tumults helped the king attract a royalist party in 1642, where none had existed in 1640. Yet another part of the elite saw popular disorders as an opportunity to frighten the king into compliance with their demands for concessions on taxation, choice of ministers, and religious and foreign policy (Hexter 1978; W. Hunt 1983). Thus, whether as threat or as resource, the high mobilization potential of the populace, especially in London, was a key factor in the origins of the revolution (Manning 1976; Pearl 1961; Lindley 1982; A. Fletcher 1981).

A fourth ingredient, of course, was politically radical Puritanism. Puritanism had originally arisen as a peaceful reform movement within the Anglican Church. In Elizabeth's time, many important bishops were Puritans, and as late as King James's reign, Puritan preachers advocated obedience to the king as a cardinal virtue (Woolrych 1968; Richardson 1973; A. Fletcher 1975; W. Hunt 1983; Kenyon 1978; P. Clark 1977; McGiffert 1980). But in the 1620s and 1630s, Puritanism became allied with political radicalism. Why did this change occur, and why did it attract members of the middling sorts and the elite?

PAUPERS AND DEMONSTRATION EFFECTS

Paupers played no role in the English Revolution except as spectators. However, that does not mean they are unimportant to understanding the revolution. From the Poor Laws to the sermons of Puritan preachers, elites showed a growing concern with poverty in the late sixteenth and early seventeenth centuries. To understand this concern, we need to note the major changes in the nature of poverty that followed England's massive population expansion.

In the early sixteenth century, poverty was hardly unknown. But the poor fell into readily comprehensible groups: the aged, the mentally or physically handicapped, the widow and her family. Young men of working age and families with the male head of household present were not among the poor. Over the course of the sixteenth century, however, this situation changed. As land and employment failed to keep pace with the growth of population, substantial numbers of men and their families were unable to keep above the line of dependence on charity (Pound 1971). Their growing numbers are recorded in studies of migration in the late sixteenth and early seventeenth centuries (Slack 1974; Beier 1974; Kent 1981), which show an astounding increase in the number of entire families migrating, as well as a vast increase in the number of young men roaming from place to place in search of work. Much literature from the sixteenth and seventeenth centuries comments on the growing armies of "hardy beggars" and "masterless men" (Hill 1972, 1975). As Coleman (1977, 18–19) notes, "The great increase in rogues, vagabonds and thieves complained of in 1573 . . . in the House of Commons testified to an economy failing to provide employment in the face of population growth."

The problems posed by these men went well beyond problems of theft and beggary, which of course also greatly increased (J. Sharpe 1982; W. Hunt 1983). Grain riots, which occurred with increasing frequency in the late sixteenth and early seventeenth centuries, were perceived by elites as threats to the social order (Walter 1980; Walter and Wrightson 1976; Hill 1972). The adoption of the Poor Laws in the late sixteenth century, intended to contain the problem by taxing the counties to provide support for the poor, meant that local communities were increasingly taxed as poverty increased. Especially after the stagnation of the cloth trade from the 1570s, and then much more so after the continued population growth and price inflation of the early seventeenth century, support of the able-bodied poor reached proportions that "the individual parish was not really designed to encounter, let alone solve" (Walter 1980, 73). For example, in many Essex parishes the poor rates (the levy on taxpayers to support payments to the destitute) doubled and tripled from the 1610s to the 1630s (W. Hunt 1983, 236).

The problems posed by the poor, therefore, were those of increasing social disorder and high economic costs of support. To both the middling sorts and the elite, the vast increase of poverty was a burdensome nuisance and a demonstration that something was seriously amiss in their society. Problems on this scale required a prescription for social reform to protect property and the social order. Puritanism, which offered such a prescription, therefore appealed to the middling groups—small manufacturers and clothiers, farmers and yeomen—as well as to landlords in those areas most threatened by disorder. The growth of poverty thus played a crucial role in setting the stage for the revolution, not because the poor themselves were Puritan or revolutionary, but because the "demonstration effects" of poverty—increased vagrancy, disorders and grain riots, and rising costs of poor relief—drove a variety of groups from different classes to embrace a prescription for greater order and social reform. This common ground formed the basis, when Crown authority faltered, for a broad-based alternative alliance loosely organized around Puritanism and opposition to the Church and Crown.

Again, as with Crown fiscal difficulties, I do not suggest that popular difficulties simply increased in a straight line from 1540 to 1640. There were decades in which real wages rose slightly, such as the 1560s; and there were particularly severe decades, such as the 1590s, when lean harvests created enormous distress. But it is not the level of real wages or poverty *alone* that mattered for political crisis. Popular mobilization potential only mattered when it combined with state fiscal distress and elite opposition to the Crown; it was then that there arose the opportunity, and leadership, for significant popular action.

Real wages did show a steady decline from 1500 to the 1630s, but the difficulties of workers did not become politically dangerous until they combined with three critical trends that accelerated sharply after 1600. First, whereas prior to 1600 rents had generally risen more slowly than prices, allowing yeomen and husbandmen to profit from inflation, thereafter landlords succeeded in jacking up rents more rapidly. Thus discontent among small farmers increased and was added to the discontent of those involved in manufacture. Indeed, in many areas these malcontents were one and the same, people who participated in both agrarian and manufacturing pursuits according to the season or size of their families. Second, after 1600 elite competition for favor and conflicts over foreign policy and taxation became intertwined with conflict over the authority and ritual of the Church. Elite disaffection with the Church provided a common ground between elites aggrieved at the court, rural squatters and artisans aggrieved at court-supported landlords who were seeking to enclose forests and fens, and urban craftsmen and merchants aggrieved at rising excise taxes and royal monopolies. Third, the growth of towns, particularly the increase in the number of freemen, together with greater elite competition, unsettled oligarchic dominance of municipal governments. Elite appeals to popular support became a larger part of urban politics in such centers as Norwich (J. Evans 1979) and set the stage for popular revolt in London (Pearl 1961).

To understand how these three diverse trends combined to create a significant cross-class opposition to established authority by the 1630s, let us look more closely at Puritan beliefs.

PURITAN IDEOLOGY AND ITS APPEAL

Puritanism is a misleading label. The term was disowned by most prominent leaders whom we would today call "Puritans." As early as the 1620s, John Pym objected to the abusive connotations of the term "Puritan" as applied to zealous Protestants (A. Fletcher 1981). The Crown used the term to label its enemies as traitorous extremists (Russell 1979); thus, as Lucy Hutchinson wrote in her memoirs, "if any were grieved at the dishonor of the Kingdome . . . or the unjust oppressions of the sub-

ject . . . he was a Puritane; . . . and if Puritane, then enemy to the King
and his government . . . such false logick did the children of darkness
use" (cited in Lamont and Oldfield 1975). The ideology that we now
term "Puritan" was in its day better understood as "lay Anglicanism"
or "zealous Protestantism" (M. Schwarz 1982).

Zealous Protestantism originated as a reform movement within the
Church, with no opposition to the Crown. Elizabeth appointed many
reform bishops, and lay preachers stressed "the preservation of the traditional social and political hierarchies and . . . the preservation of traditional values" (L. Stone 1972, 102). Here is William Perkins in 1612,
one of the most noted of the reforming clergy: "God therefore hath given
to Kings, and to their lawful deputies, power and authority not only to
command and execute His own law, . . . but also to ordain and enact
other good and profitable laws of their own, for . . . their people" (cited
in Woolrych 1968, 91). Puritan preachers such as Thomas Adams, Robert Bolton, and John Downame were equally eloquent and sincere in
their defense of royal authority. As Collinson (1982) points out, Elizabethan Puritanism was a conservative movement, championed by men
who were themselves the authority in their respective locales. Until the
1630s, when royal policies were attacked, it was the abuse of authority,
never the authority itself, that was challenged. As K. Sharpe (1978a, 23)
remarks, "revolutionary puritanism was . . . a child of a decade beyond
the 1620s."

Desires for reform of the Church came partly from the Church's own
failure to meet the challenges of population growth and inflation. In
many parishes, the Church's "patrons . . . were content to leave stipends
[for clergy] fixed at the exiguous levels of a century before" (Hirst 1986,
63). Thus many clergy had no more than a day laborer's standard of
living. In addition, sprawling parishes, such as those of Sussex and Kent,
and burgeoning towns meant that parish churches and organizations
established to meet the needs of sixteenth-century communities were
simply overwhelmed by subsequent growth. They thus catered inade-
quately to their congregations, and indeed, "too many people were outside the reach of the Church in their most impressionable years" (Hirst
1986, 62). The influence of the established Church grew thin on the
ground, while a host of social disorders increased. People thus turned
to ideologies that offered hope of a cure for social ills.

The ideology that appealed to the middling sorts and numerous members of the elites was a "culture of discipline." Faced with increasing

problems of poverty and vagrancy and of theft and popular disorders, Puritan preachers prescribed sobriety, self-discipline, and zeal in pursuit of morality. Their "Puritan ethic" had little to do with capitalism.

> If the capitalist spirit consists of a relentless drive to accumulate wealth and a willingness to take risks in the pursuit of higher profit, then preachers did everything within their power to stifle it . . . . The puritan utopia would not look much like capitalism . . . . Insofar as capitalism required . . . a large class of families dependent on wage labor, [Puritan preachers] stood squarely against it. Their social ideal is far closer to that of Thomas Jefferson . . . . A godly commonwealth would be a society of independent producers—like that of Massachusetts. Diligent labor would assure a moderate prosperity. . . . There would be no exploitation, since . . . usury and oppression, like witch-craft and idolatry, have no place among god's people.
>
> (W. Hunt 1983, 127–128, 138–139)

To the Puritans, there were two classes of men: the poor, who lacked means of support, and the independent householder, who enjoyed a modest prosperity. The danger was of men slipping from the second category into the first by lack of effort or discipline, or by excess of vice. Unfortunately, sermons decrying drunkenness as the devil's work and preaching discipline did not solve the social problems of the day— namely, too many hands for too little land and too little work. As un-employment rose in the 1620s and 1630s, and as wages continued to fall and disorders to increase, zealous Protestants concluded that they were fighting a strong adversary; thus scapegoats were sought for the continuing decay of the economy and the social order.

A target was easy to find. "It was difficult for a Protestant gentle-man of the day to conceive of a threat to his liberties that did not in some way emanate from the Romish Beast [the pope]. There was con-sensus that the Englishman's rights were adequately protected under the Constitution . . . . Hence the perceived threat must have originated from an external source. And where else but from the throne of the Anti-christ?" (W. Hunt 1983, 202). If the poor were multiplying and becom-ing unruly, if the social hierarchy was unstable, if the Crown was going bankrupt, then evil must be at work. And since the welfare of the king-dom ultimately depended on the king and his policies, the problems of the day must be due to the errors of Crown policy, specifically, flirtation with popery. The king's Catholic wife, the corruption of the court as reflected in the king's sale of honors and offices and manipulation of monopolies and taxes, and, last but not least, the court-led Arminian movement to restore greater ceremony and episcopal authority to the

Anglican Church—these were innovations that smacked of popery and alliance with England's enemies. If the Crown had been solvent, if the economy had been sound, and if the social order had been stable, then perhaps William Laud's church reforms would have been praised as a means to augment the authority and prestige of the Church. Instead, the resemblance between his reforms and the Catholic Church led to his being pilloried as part of a papist conspiracy, the cause of England's fiscal and social problems.

To understand why Puritanism developed a revolutionary appeal, it is important to recognize that Puritanism was a crusade—against corruption, Catholicism, and popery—offered as a panacea to cure the nation's evident ills. Thus, "there was an obsessive anti-Catholicism amongst most Parliamentarians" (Morrill 1976, 15). Pym saw himself as fighting the pope as much as the king of England (Russell 1979; A. Fletcher 1981; Clifton 1973). In the nation at large, Puritan preachers "channel[ed] hostility that might have been directed against the rich in general toward that section of the upper class that clung to the old religion or displayed obtrusive loyalty to the Crown . . . . Catholics, and by extension Royalists in general, were scapegoated for hardships that men and women could not otherwise comprehend. [Thus, for example,] weavers blamed Catholics for the crisis of the cloth trade" (W. Hunt 1983, 309), a crisis that in fact was due to excessive demand for food that reduced the relative value of their product and their wages, and to excessive competition for work that pushed down the level of employment. Fears of a "popish plot" were a crucial element in mobilizing gentry and the middling sorts in support of Parliament (Hibbard 1983). Revolutionary Puritanism is thus more accurately described as an amalgamation of English Protestant nationalism, a defense of traditional English ways and economic prudence, and an attack on all innovations in royal policy that smacked of popery, rather than as a purely religious phenomenon. It drew its crusading urgency from the fiscal and social problems of the day.

Of course, the Crown was not insensible of such problems. And many policies adopted by Charles I in the 1630s had some success in dealing with disorder, particularly the detailed Orders and Directions issued by the Privy Council in 1631, which galvanized local justices of the peace into taking greater care to control food supplies, vagrancy, and poor relief. But the royal administration was never able to fully implement such policies, for "the governing elites began to split apart . . . the new advocates of efficiency, austerity and discipline [within the court] fought

the older, easy-going, routinely venal bureaucrats . . . . In the Privy
Council, Protestants fought Catholics and crypto-Catholics . . . . The
episcopal bench was split, [and] many of the lay courtiers and officials
were jealous of the increasing interference by the bishops in secular administration and policy" (L. Stone 1972, 127). Most importantly, the
Crown was dealing with a deep-rooted structural problem: the imbalance between a growing population and an economy that was not increasing its output of grain and its supply of jobs at an equal pace. Thus
no amount of court cajoling could prevent the decline in real wages and
recurrent harvest shortfalls. Instead, the social problems became the basis for policy disputes that divided both the court and local elites.

The dependence of revolutionary Puritanism on widely perceived social problems is evident in the fate of Puritanism after the Restoration,
when population stability led to stable prices, rising real wages, and
sharply diminished social mobility. As Walzer (1974, 300, 312, 316)
has noted,

> Puritan ideology was a response to real experience . . . a practical effort to
> cope with personal and social problems. The disappearance of the militant
> saints from English politics in the years after the Restoration suggests . . . that
> these problems were limited in time to the period of breakdown . . . as the
> conditions of crisis and upheaval in which [radical] Calvinism was conceived
> and developed did not persist so Calvinism as an integral and creative force
> did not endure . . . . After the Restoration, its energy was drawn inward, its
> political aspirations forgotten; the saint gave way to the non-conformist.

But in the early seventeenth century, the appeal of Puritanism reached
across class lines.

THE POPULAR ELEMENT IN THE REVOLUTION: SOCIAL CHANGE AND THE PURITAN COALITION

By the early seventeenth century much of the English countryside was
leased to large tenants, who closely supervised their hired labor. In these
areas, which included most of midland England, the potential for cultivator revolts was low. Thus, as noted earlier, in the late sixteenth and
early seventeenth centuries the chief source of popular tumults was not
settled cultivators but rural artisans, squatters in marginal fen and forest
communities, and city dwellers, particularly in London.

Underdown (1985) and A. Hughes (1987) have recently offered evidence of an association between the ecological conditions of particular
regions of England and the regional pattern of parliamentary support.

In Warwickshire, Somerset, and Derbyshire, they found that even though the gentry was mostly neutral or royalist, the clothiers, yeomanry, and towns supported Parliament, allowing the minority of parliamentary gentry to control those counties (A. Hughes 1987, 151). In all these counties, though the open-field arable regions showed strong loyalty to the royalist cause, the wage-dependent and squatter populations of the forests, fens, and wood and pastoral regions strongly supported the parliamentary gentry.

It was precisely the forest, fen, and wood and pastoral districts, as well as the clothing districts and towns, that suffered most from the shift in prices that raised the cost of bread relative to wages and the price of manufactures. It was also precisely these areas, recipients of the migration of excess population from the settled areas, that were more unstable, often the site of food riots in bad harvest years. And, in 1642, it was "the fens and forests again [that] erupted, . . . and by 1642 parts of the eastern counties were in a state of virtual rebellion" (Underdown 1985, 136).

Underdown further argues that it was precisely in areas where the influence of the Church and gentry was weak, where living standards were under attack, and where crime was most rapidly increasing that the middling sorts were most likely to be drawn to Puritan culture. It should be clear that this situation reflects a differential impact of population increase and price inflation on certain communities. In the towns, clothing districts, and forest and fen regions, we have precisely those groups most vulnerable and adversely affected by the demographic and price trends. It was the middling sorts in these areas that were most willing to follow the parliamentary leadership against the Crown and established Church.

If we are to understand how a minority of parliamentary gentry was able to hold out against, and defeat, a king who still had the loyalty of much of the established county leadership, we should not underestimate the power of the *coalition* that developed between distinct popular groups—drawn from the middling classes—and the parliamentary party. This coalition did not reflect common interests so much as it represented a convergence of distinct interests on a common overall goal.

For the parliamentary gentry, the chief interest was a restored balance of royal and parliamentary rule that would respect private property, limit the use of the royal prerogative, and defend English Protestantism against corruption and popery. For the middling sorts of the towns, clothing districts, and forest and fen margins, the chief interests were cheaper bread, steady employment, a ministry that would address their problems and help maintain order in communities under strain, a reduction in the burden of taxation, and, in the forest and fen regions, a halt to the expropriation and commercialization of squatter lands by the Crown and its allies. But for both groups, the way to attain these goals was the same: chastise the king and defend Parliament.

In sum, we again face the impossibility of understanding the elements of the English Revolution in isolation. The essential characteristic of the revolution is that social order broke down on a *multiplicity* of levels, producing conflicts and new social alignments. Conflict between king and elites over fiscal matters was intertwined with factionalism among the elites; and this factionalism was intertwined with popular grievances. The result was that popular allegiances reinforced the split in the elites and made possible a parliamentary party capable of prosecuting a war against the king.

MEASURING MASS MOBILIZATION POTENTIAL: REAL WAGES, AGE STRUCTURE, AND URBANIZATION

As we have noted, the competition among the elite was reflected in the vogue for university experience and the expansion of enrollments. But if elite social mobility and status competition can be roughly gauged by the growth of university enrollments, how can we estimate the political mobilization potential of the populace at large?

The key factor behind popular disorders was the rise in grain prices, reflected in falling real wages. As discussed earlier, throughout the period 1500–1750 both grain prices and real wages closely paralleled changes in England's population. By the 1640s, real wages reached their lowest level anytime in English history after 1300, falling to 50 percent of their early sixteenth-century level. However, falling wages did not mean a bonanza for capitalists. The relative value of manufactured goods fell as well, and the stagnation of the cloth market in the late sixteenth and early seventeenth centuries meant fewer opportunities for profit. Moreover, the fall in wages was not limited to the wages of day laborers; the fall was equally marked for craftsmen (Phelps Brown and Hopkins 1962b), who generally earned three times as much as day laborers. In short, craftsmen, artisans, shopkeepers, and tradesmen all faced the same problem: the cost of food was escalating far more rapidly than the value of their labor and their wares.

The political consequences of these grievances were exacerbated by the increase in size of the capital. From 1500 to 1640, London grew eightfold, from fifty thousand to four hundred thousand inhabitants. Had grain and employment opportunities been plentiful, such growth need not have posed difficulties. But the growth of London pulled scarce grain supplies from throughout southeast England, leading to a proliferation of riots to stop the movement of grain. "Grain riots in Norfolk, Essex, Kent, Sussex, Hertfordshire, Hampshire, and the Thames Valley were commonly provoked by the fear of siphoning off local food supplies to meet metropolitan demand. Elsewhere, urban demand played a similar role in provoking disorder . . . . The needs of Bristol help explain the cluster of riots in Gloucestershire, Wiltshire, and Somerset" (Walter and Wrightson 1976, 27).

Recent theorists of revolution have so often stressed the role of peasants in great social revolutions that the urban component of popular action has been unduly neglected (Skocpol 1979; Wolf 1969). Some scholars have therefore pointed to the crucial role of urban groups in modern revolutions—in Russia, Iran, Nicaragua, and Cuba—as a corrective to peasant-focused views of the past (Bonnell 1983; Gugler 1982; Dix 1983). It is not the past, however, but our theories that show too little of early urban revolts. The crowds of London in 1640–1642, of Paris in 1789–1794, and of Berlin and Vienna in 1848 were as much a driving force behind state breakdowns as were rural uprisings. In early modern *and* modern revolutions, the concentrated mass mobilization potential of urban centers deserves close scrutiny. Cities are particularly explosive during eras when population growth collides with limited economic and state resources, for it is when real wages fall and urban police administrations have difficulty keeping pace with urban expansion that the mobilization potential of urban crowds is most likely to be realized.

In mid-seventeenth-century London, economic difficulties and sheer ungovernability owing to the city having grown much faster than its legal and police administration created an enormous potential for disorder. Modest merchants, shopkeepers, and craftsmen were infuriated at the rise of the poor rates, the imposition of taxes, Crown infringements on guild property and monopoly restrictions, and the fall in the relative value of their wares. These groups found widespread support for social and political reform from the apprentices and artisans concentrated in the city. A petition in support of abolishing episcopacy was said to have been signed by over thirty thousand apprentices; crowds of apprentices also surged around Parliament, threatening the king and harrying the bishops (Manning 1976; Pearl 1961; S. Smith 1973). The

early Puritan sects "drew much of their support from economically depressed minor tradesmen and shopworkers living mainly in the [London]
suburbs" (Clark and Slack 1976, 72).

Aside from the level of grievances, there was the problem of the inability of the mayor and aldermen to maintain control of the city; as
Manning (1976, 71) notes, by the 1630s "London had grown too fast
for its machinery of government, with the forces of repression at its
disposal, to be able very easily to control its population and maintain
order." In December 1641, when Parliament confronted the king, and
crowds in London manifested their support, the mayor hurried to the
palace to inform the king that "apprentices and other inferior persons"
were raising a tumult and threatening to take the Tower of London, and
that matters were beyond his control (Manning 1976, 76–79). The king
and his family were forced to flee London, and the bishops were kept
from Parliament, out of fear of harassment and possible attack from the
city crowds.

Lindley (1986, 118–119) points out that in London in 1641–1642
there took place "popular mobilisation on an unprecedented scale."
Pearl (1961, 236) notes that "through their circulating petitions, their
demonstrations, their Puritan preaching and their secular Tavern clubs,
[the populace of London] created a movement which made a considerable contribution, underestimated by historians, to Pym's victory over
the Crown." Not that contemporaries so underestimated London's role.
The popular leader Richard Baxter observed that "the war began in our
streets before the King and Parliament had any armies" (cited in Hirst
1986, 212).

Both the shift in relative prices, which depressed real wages and raised
grain costs, and the enormous growth of London were direct consequences of England's population growth. In addition, another dimension
of population change—the growing size of the youth cohorts, a product
of the manner in which population increased—contributed to the mobilization potential of the populace.

There is an extensive literature on the role of youth in radical political
movements (Moller 1968; Gillis 1974; Eisenstadt 1963; Cohn and Markides 1977; Esler 1972; K. Davis 1971). The basic finding of this research is that "a crucial problem in understanding anti-regime
movements lies in the disproportionate participation of the young in
these movements . . . . A central feature of rebellions in many countries
during the past century has been the prominent role played within them
by the young" (Cohn and Markides 1977, 462). Given the leading role

of the young, small changes in the age distribution of a population can have a marked effect on popular mobilization.

Let us note that even in times of widespread discontent, the participation of people in demonstrations or opposition movements depends to some extent on how great they perceive the support of that opposition movement to be. The more timorous among the discontented may only join an opposition that appears widespread and successful, whereas the bolder dissidents may join a movement while it is still relatively small. Thus the bold lead, and the more timorous follow; the outcome depends on whether the bold are numerous enough to win over the timid. As Trotsky (1932, 177–178) reflected in his analysis of the Russian Revolution, "the difference in level and mood of the different layers of the people is overcome in action. The advance layers bring after them the wavering and isolate the opposing. The majority is not counted up, but won over." If younger cohorts are bolder than their elders, then when youth cohorts grow larger relative to older groups, the behavior of the population as a whole may show a change in mobilization behavior.

For a simple demonstration of this effect, let us construct a population in which people over 25 years of age are unlikely to join an opposition movement supported by less than one-quarter of the entire population over 15 years old. Let us also say that people over 35 years old are unlikely to join an opposition movement unless it contains at least half of the over-15 population. Now suppose the age distribution of the over-15 population is as follows:

age		
	16–25	25%
	26–35	20%
	>35	55%

We then have a stable distribution: even if most of the under-25 cohort joins an opposition movement, the opposition is still unlikely to grow spontaneously to encompass the population as a whole.

But suppose the age structure shifts slightly so that the new distribution is as follows:

age		
	16–25	30%
	26–35	25%
	>35	45%

A movement that has the whole-hearted support of the under-25 group will now attract the 26–35 group as well; and this addition will attract the over-35s, since it is now large enough to surpass the point at which the older cohort will join. In this latter case there is an unstable distribution: if the opposition grows large enough among the under-25 group, it will attract the bulk of the whole populace. While this sketch is highly simplified, it illustrates how, given the greater propensity of the young to join opposition movements, a shift in the age structure can affect the volatility of the whole population.[10]

The extraordinary youthfulness of England's population in the 1630s thus very likely contributed to the mobilization potential of the population. It is striking to note that in the late sixteenth and early seventeenth centuries, the portion of the population aged 10–29 was generally equal to or greater than the entire over-30 population, whereas by the 1690s it had sharply declined, becoming 20 percent smaller than the older group. Moreover, the cohort that reached ages 26–35 during the 1630s was the largest youth cohort of the entire period 1500–1750.[11]

In Parliament itself, where a large number of peers' sons sat and the recess of the 1630s meant that the older members best recalled the struggles of the 1620s, the opposition was generally older than the king's supporters. But it was quite different in the country at large, especially in London. There, "the radicals . . . came from the younger generation." Contemporaries such as Thomas Edwards, William Dell, and Richard Baxter all tell of the young as most open to conviction and new views; Edwards emphasizes that "it was 'many young youths and wenches [who] all of them preach universal redemption' " (cited in Hill 1972, 152). Baxter commented that "the headiness and rashness of the younger inexperienced sort of religious people made many Parliament men and ministers overgo themselves to keep pace with these hot spurs" (cited in W. Hunt 1983, 289). Hill (1972, 296) adds that the "leaders of the democratic sects . . . all were under thirty when the civil war ended. . . . Part of the ebullience [of the period] springs from the youth of the actors. . . . It was a young man's world while it lasted." The role of youth in the English Revolution is also emphasized by S. Smith (1973, 1979) and Farnell (1977).

Clearly, I am not suggesting that the growth of London and the youthfulness of the population alone led to radicalism. Many large cities and

10. Cf. Granovetter (1978) for more sophisticated models of threshold behavior.
11. This finding and the age-ratio data used in this chapter were computed from unpublished data on the age distribution in England since 1541 compiled by E. A. Wrigley and R. S. Schofield of the SSRC Cambridge Group for the History of Population and Social Structure, in Cambridge, England. I am indebted to them for making their data available.

youthful populations lead politically stable lives. Indeed, if real wages are above average, then urban growth and a youthful population can be stabilizing factors, as urban growth attracts families to better circumstances and a youthful population enters the labor force under favorable conditions. However, if there is a precipitous drop in real wages, then the size of the capital and the youthfulness of the population can increase the mobilization potential of the populace. This complex relationship can be captured mathematically by suggesting that mass mobilization potential depends chiefly on real wage levels, with exacerbating or ameliorating interactions from urban growth and the age structure. We can thus estimate mass mobilization potential (MMP) as follows:

$$MMP = (\text{Average Real Wage/Real Wages }) \\ + ([\text{Average Real Wage/Real Wages}] - 1) \\ \times (\text{Urban Growth}) \times (\text{Age Structure})$$

The first term here is the ratio of the real wage in a given decade to the average for the period under study (in this case, the period 1500–1750). With this model, when real wages are at or near the average wage for the period, this term is near unity. When real wages are substantially below the average for the period, this term rises rapidly, leading to growing MMP; conversely, when real wages are above the average for the period, this term falls rapidly.

The second term is a corrective for interaction effects. If real wages are above average, the correction is negative, and urbanization and increases in youth reduce MMP. However, if wages are below average, the correction is positive and urban growth and youthfulness exacerbate the stresses of falling real wages. The measure of age structure is the ratio of the population ten to twenty-nine years of age to the population aged thirty years and over. The measure for urban growth is a weighted measure of the long-term growth of London. However, the impact of urban growth on political mobilization potential has been much debated; thus the latter measure deserves a brief explanation.

Studies of early modern France (Lodhi and Tilly 1973; Rule and Tilly 1972) have shown that short-term rates of urban growth are not good predictors of political volatility. It is not merely the flow of recent migrants that makes cities volatile; what matters more is that individuals are concentrated in a structural setting that facilitates collective action (Kelley and Galle 1984). I suggest further that it is not merely the urban setting that facilitates collective action; instead, what matters is the relative capacity of the state administrative institutions (police, but also food distribution, censorship, and informal political integration through provision of services) to cope with the potential for collective action of urban assemblages.

Unfortunately, for the early modern state it is difficult to measure the rate of administrative control; what we do know is that by 1640 (as the lord mayor complained to the Crown) London had outrun its administrative machinery. For our purposes of examining early modern states, we can take as an approximation that the more rapid is a city's long-term growth, the more difficulty an administration will have in keeping pace, so that mobilization potential is likely to increase. Thus the contribution of urban growth to mobilization should be measured not in terms of short-term increase but rather in terms of a cumulative retrospective of long-term increase. I have chosen to use as an indicator, for a given decade, a weighted average of London's growth over that decade and the preceding two and three decades. Thus, in the above formula for MMP, "urban growth" in the ith decade equals

$$.5(\text{London}_{i,i-1}) + .33(\text{London}_{i,i-2}) + .17(\text{London}_{i,i-3})$$

where $\text{London}_{i,j}$ is the ratio of London's population at the end of the ith and jth decades.[12]

This model of MMP corresponds to a situation in which the average wage is a customary "living wage"; any time wages are above that level, mobilization potential is low and fairly stable. However, whenever wages fall below that level, grievances and mobilization potential rise rapidly. The model also assumes that changes in real wages reflect grain prices and work availability, which are both important factors in food riots and urban artisanal protests, and that state administrations are slow in adjusting to changes in urban size. This model seems to be a good starting point for a preindustrial economy and polity, as existed in early modern England.

It must be recalled that this measure is an indicator not of violence but rather of mass mobilization *potential*. Such potential is unlikely to erupt into widespread conflict unless other conditions of state breakdown are present—visible state weakness and elite opposition—that conduce to popular mobilization and collective action. Thus, it is nec-

12. London's growth was fairly smooth; thus, extending the growth measure further back has no effect on the results calculated here. If growth were highly irregular, it would be worthwhile to use a measure with greater smoothing.

essary to consider the *joint* impact of trends regarding the state, elites, and mass mobilization potential in seeking to explain state breakdown.

DID THE ENGLISH REVOLUTION HAVE SOCIAL CAUSES?

Neo-Marxists have argued that the social causes of the English Revolution lay in the changes wrought by the growth of agrarian and overseas capitalism. However, these arguments are difficult to sustain. By the mid-seventeenth century, virtually every group among the elite—including the Crown—was involved in commercial exploitation of their land or in collection of profits from trade. Rural conflicts chiefly involved artisans protesting grain shortages, high prices, and the extension of arable land, not cultivators protesting unlawful enclosures. Further, in the early seventeenth century enclosures were more often instances of collaboration than of conflict between Crown and gentry. Finally, as overseas trade stagnated from the 1570s, the largest overseas traders maintained their support of the Crown in return for royal monopolies. England's economy grew more commercial and capitalist after 1500, but the hypothesized causal links between this growth and state breakdown are absent. Whig historians have argued that constitutional and religious struggles underlay the revolution. But they have not been successful in demonstrating that such struggles were rooted in long-term social causes that presaged an eruption into open conflict in the mid-seventeenth century, or in explaining why a state fiscal crisis and popular uprisings were particularly likely to develop in those decades. Recent revisionist historians have therefore argued that the English Revolution had no long-term social causes at all but rather was the result of errors of judgment and administration by Charles I.

Yet all parties have failed to examine closely the links between the inability of English economic, fiscal, and social institutions to adjust to the sustained population growth of the years 1500–1640 and the causes of state breakdown. State finances, the stability of the elite hierarchy, and popular employment were all adversely affected by population growth and consequent inflation. These relationships are schematically shown in figure 3.

I have suggested ways to measure changes in all three of these areas by using a rough scale of state fiscal distress, employing university enrollments as an indicator of elite mobility and status competition, and constructing a compound estimator of mass mobilization potential. Each

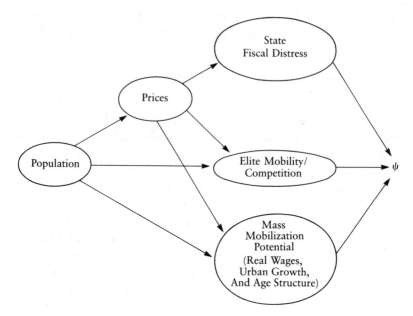

Figure 3. Political demography of early modern England: Basic Relationships

of these three indicators is graphed (as normalized Z-scores) in figure 4. Clearly, each set of scores is somewhat higher in the early seventeenth century than in earlier or later periods; however, the changes are not of remarkable proportions.

In any case, the crucial factor making for state breakdown is not that any one of these factors was high. After all, states survive bouts with bankruptcy, elite divisions, and popular disorders when they occur separately. My claim is that the mid-seventeenth century was exceptional in that *all* of these factors, being driven by the underlying force of population growth in the preceding century and a half, created a synergistic stress that caused the breakdown of state power. In terms of a causal model, such a synergistic combination can be represented by an interaction effect. Thus, if our model of the origins of the revolution is correct, we should find that the interaction product

$$\Psi = \text{Fiscal Distress} \times \text{Mobility/Competition}$$
$$\times \text{Mass Mobilization Potential}$$

rises to a distinctive peak in the mid-seventeenth century, unmatched by a similar rise in either the sixteenth or eighteenth centuries. I have named

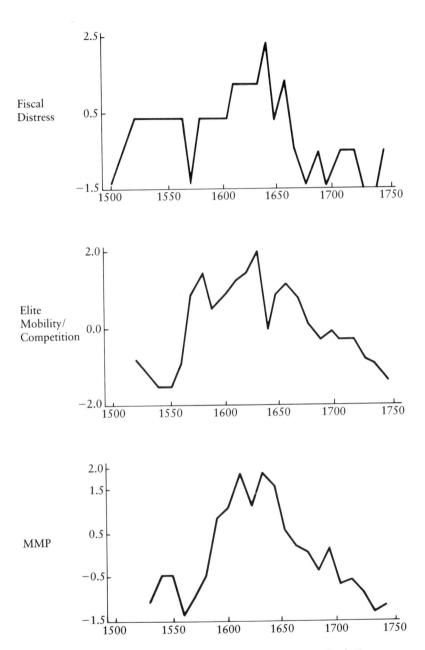

Figure 4. Fiscal distress, mobility/competition, and MMP in England: Z-scores, 1500–1750

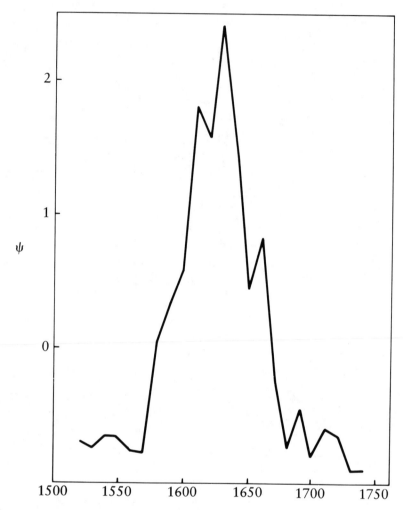

Figure 5. Pressures for crisis (*psi*) in England, 1520–1749

this function by the Greek letter Ψ, serviceable as an acronym for "*po-litical stress indicator*," hereafter *psi*.

The course of the function *psi* from 1520 to 1750 is depicted in figure 5. This function sharply distinguishes the period of mounting crisis and revolution in the early seventeenth century from other periods in early modern English history.[13]

13. The graph should be mentally adjusted for one slight problem in the data: in the 1640s Charles used the town of Oxford for his headquarters, causing university enroll-

This data analysis makes clear that the early seventeenth century was a period of unique social character, and that its uniqueness lay precisely in an unusual combination of factors. However foolish Charles may have been, the differences between the early seventeenth century and the centuries that immediately preceded and followed it were not merely in the realm of royal policies. The constitutional struggles and religious conflicts of the time were underpinned by an extraordinary combination of decaying finances, rising elite mobility and competition, and falling real wages, all propelled by rising population. This combination of ills reached a peak in the middle third of the century unmatched at any time throughout early modern English history. The English Revolution was in part a religious, in part a constitutional, and in part an economic conflict. What is undeniable from the preceding analysis is that these conflicts combined to reach fatal acuteness precisely when English society was undergoing a unique level of social and economic stress, a stress that can be precisely defined and measured through the function *psi*. The *psi* function clearly differentiates the mid-1600s from the preceding and succeeding centuries as a period of exceptional predisposition to state breakdown. The burden of proof thus shifts heavily to those who continue to claim that the breakdown of the English state in 1640 occurred in an "ordinary" situation unaffected by long-term social and economic changes.

Of course, conflicts continued to arise in England; in 1688 many of the same issues reappeared as an aroused gentry faced a king suspected of harboring Catholicizing and tyrannical intentions. But instead of elite unity shattering in the face of popular uprisings, order was maintained through a relatively peaceful change of rulers (Prall 1972; J. Jones 1978). This containment of crisis was at least partly due to the greater social peace that then prevailed: by 1688 England had behind it a generation of sharply reduced social mobility and urban growth, stable prices, and rising real wages. Party conflicts over national policy continued to divide England in the early eighteenth century (Colley 1982), but in the counties and the towns stable oligarchic rule increasingly replaced the contention of the seventeenth century, while rising real wages replaced the difficulties of earlier times (Plumb 1967; Clark and Slack 1976).

---

ments there to suddenly dwindle. If one uses only Cambridge enrollments to follow university enrollment for the 1640s, the peak of the *psi* curve would occur in the 1640s, instead of the 1630s.

DID THE ENGLISH REVOLUTION HAVE
CAPITALIST ORIGINS?

A committed critic, on first reading the preceding argument, insisted that "none of the results you present contradict any of these [Neo-Marxist] theories. In fact Wallerstein or Moore or Anderson could easily account for the results presented by substituting 'commercialization in agriculture' for population in the path diagram of figure 3 (assuming as I think reasonable that the two are correlated). All the consequences of the model also flow from commercialization of agriculture so that their predicted effect on *psi* would be the same in the demographic structural and Neo-Marxist models." This is a serious charge, and one that deserves consideration. Let me therefore go over the model and arguments presented to clarify whether we have merely presented a plausible alternative to the Neo-Marxist models of the English Revolution, or whether they have been in some sense refuted.

All the Neo-Marxist models claim that the English Revolution was a triumph for capitalism, which in the English context translates, in particular, to the commercialization of agriculture. The revolution is in fact attributed to conflicts between those who opposed the further development of commercialization in agriculture and those who supported it, with the latter as victors. Thus, it is essential for all Neo-Marxist theories that the commercialization of agriculture, following the revolution, proceeded at a rate greater than or at least equal to that before the revolution. Hence for any index of the commercialization of agriculture, Neo-Marxist theories depend on a track of steady growth or acceleration after 1660.

We can observe, however, that the variables that are crucially tied to the revolution—prices, social mobility and competition, and mass mobilization potential—all show a sharp *reversal* in trend after the revolution. Before the revolution, prices rise, social mobility and the turnover of land are extensive, urban growth is extremely rapid, and real wages fall. After 1660, prices fall, entry into the peerage and gentry sharply declines in volume, urban growth rates fall, and real wages rise. If the commercialization of agriculture is responsible for the trends before the revolution, how can the continued or more rapid commercialization of agriculture after 1660 also be responsible for a complete reversal in the trends of these key variables?

The reason that population changes effectively explain the movement of prices, social mobility, urban growth, and real wages in the period

1500–1750 is that population growth is rapid until 1650 and then drops to nearly zero. Population growth thus follows a different path over time than the commercialization of agriculture, and one cannot substitute the latter for the former in any model and achieve the same results. Population growth follows a *cyclic* path, as do the key variables that led to state breakdown. Commercialization of agriculture and expansion of overseas trade were certainly important factors in the economy. But they followed a different path than population, accelerating after 1650 while demographic and price trends reversed course.

This difference in direction emphasizes our earlier claim that population trends were largely autonomous. After the revolution England's overseas trade, particularly with Asia and America, expanded dramatically, the rate of enclosure increased, and the commercialization of agriculture grew. Indeed, these trends are commonly pointed to as evidence that the revolution marked a breakthrough for capitalism. Yet despite this heightened economic activity, population growth slowed to a crawl, prices stabilized, urbanization rates declined, and social mobility virtually ceased. Capitalism, in its various guises, sprang forward. But it was the movement of population, not of capitalism, that was correlated with the politically crucial social and economic trends of early modern England. We must therefore carve out a central niche for the consequences of demographic change, rather than of capitalism, when we investigate the long-term causes of state breakdown in the English Revolution.

WAS THE ENGLISH REVOLUTION INEVITABLE?

It is fair to ask precisely what the mathematical model presented above means. Does the rise in *psi* in the 1630s mean that the revolution was inevitable? Was there nothing Charles I could have done to save his throne? And since the broad conditions I have identified—fiscal difficulty, high social mobility, and popular grievances—seem recurrent in English history, indeed can be found to some degree in every reign from 1550 to 1650, one may well ask why the revolution occurred in the 1630s and not earlier. Was Charles I merely making the worst of a long-term ecological shift that created problems but need not have produced an acute crisis? In short, how much (or how little) does the demographic/structural model actually explain?

EXPLANATION IN HISTORY

There is a vast literature on the problem of explanation in history. Without entering those debates here, I can clarify what I am offering in the way of explanation.

As an illustration, consider the following circumstances: A person, call him John, stumbles and falls in his apartment; he strikes his arm on a table, injuring himself. Observing this sequence of events, how can we explain it?

If we try to explain the *ultimate* outcome—why John injured his arm—we have to take into account a host of details: why John could not avoid the table, why the table was located where it was, why the table was hard enough to cause injury rather than padded, and so on. But we can step back and ask a simpler question: why did John fall?

We could guess that John was merely clumsy. But let us say we notice that other people in John's building also stumbled at the same time. We might then guess that an explosion in the basement, or a nearby train wreck, shook the building. But suppose we examine the basement and the neighborhood and find no evidence of such events. So we still have to ask why John *and other people in the building* all stumbled at the same time.

Let us say we notice that people in other buildings also fell. We might say, Aha! an earthquake. We could then check some additional hypotheses: Did more people stumble on the upper floors of buildings than on lower floors? And are there cracks around the foundations of some buildings? Or are there items that fell from shelves? If we find these confirming data, we would feel confident in saying that John stumbled because there was an earthquake.

But let us take a close look at this explanation. Was it inevitable that John stumbled just because there was an earthquake? No. If John was exceptionally agile, he might have avoided falling. And if the furniture in his room was differently arranged, or if he was nimble, he might have stumbled but not injured his arm. So what does this "explanation" offer?

When we explain John's fall by saying, "There was an earthquake," what we mean is that under such conditions most people could reasonably be expected to lose their balance and stumble. Certainly not *all* people *have* to fall in such conditions for this explanation to have value. What is important is whether *most* people would. Indeed, if someone did *not* fall during an earthquake, we might look for evidence of exceptional balance or good luck.

Knowing there was an earthquake thus does not allow us to make a deterministic prediction. But it allows us to decide between two descriptions of what happened: (1) John was operating under ordinary conditions, so his fall was most likely due to clumsiness or accident; (2) John was operating under exceptionally difficult conditions, so his fall was most likely caused by those conditions throwing him off-balance. For most of us, it is precisely the ability to decide between these two descriptions that constitutes being able to explain why John stumbled.

Of course, if we want to explain why, given the earthquake, John hurt his arm rather than some other part of his body, or how he might have escaped without injury, we have to enter a debate about John's athletic ability and the arrangement of the furniture. Such a debate is relevant, but knowing that an earthquake occurred allows us to better understand why John stumbled, and why he stumbled (along with his neighbors) at a particular time.

The demographic/structural explanation of the English Revolution is much like identifying the "earthquake" behind Charles I's fall. Certainly, Charles's fall was not inevitable. But he was operating in background conditions that were exceptionally difficult. Stressful conditions are what the *psi* model reveals. Thus one cannot fairly say that Charles's actions alone were responsible for the crisis. It is of course relevant to debate Charles's policies and the particular conditions he faced during the period 1639–1642. But it should be clear that one need not show why the revolution *had* to happen in order to offer a useful explanation of why it *did* happen. It is enough to show that conditions were such that it would have taken extraordinary skill to avoid a crisis. And if those conditions were generally found across Eurasia, then they are useful in explaining not only why Charles I stumbled but also why he stumbled, along with other monarchs, at a particular time.

Thus, the *psi* curve is like a seismographic reading; it measures the shaking of a society at its foundations. And although such shaking increases the likelihood that there will be some falling at the top, it neither makes a fall necessary nor makes the precise details of what will happen predictable.

Still, we need to ask why the *psi* curve, since it is derived from broad ecological forces that operated across many decades, points to the 1630s and 1640s as being unusually unstable.

ENGLISH SOCIETY AND INSTITUTIONAL RESISTANCE

We often speak of population pressure, but pressure on what? Society is not a basket that fills up with people and then bursts. Society com-

prises a complex set of institutions designed to coordinate the reproduction, rewarding, and repression of individuals and families.
Ecological change has an impact when it disrupts the ability of those
institutions to function.

Among the critical institutions of early modern England were taxation to sustain the Crown, status systems to regulate local authority and
relations between households, and land and labor markets to provide
employment and income. If all of these institutions were to fail at once,
society would indeed shake. How well could they stand up to ecological
change?

We have already noted that as population grew faster than the
economy, land and labor markets failed to sustain a stable equilibrium.
The result was rising prices, in evidence from the early sixteenth century.
There followed state fiscal difficulties, elite mobility and competition,
and popular discontent. Why, then, did it take so long for pressures to
build to crisis levels?

The reason is that England's institutions had some ability to respond
to stress. What *psi* measures is not the raw ecological pressure—the
movement of population or prices—but rather the strain on institutions,
as shown by political, social, and economic behavior.

Thus, the Crown could survive rising prices for some time by selling
its assets. Only when sales of Crown land had nearly exhausted this
resource, and the Crown lacked the security for continued borrowing,
did financial strains become acute. It was at this point, which occurred
in the early seventeenth century, that new means of revenue creation
were needed, hence the sale of offices, monopolies, and Ship Money
levies. One cannot measure the Crown's financial health simply by its
ability to pay its current bills. The issue is what *reserves* the Crown had
to meet the inevitable contingencies that confront states, and what *credit*
backing it had to support its borrowing.

Revisionists have pointed out that no financial crisis was necessary
in the 1630s because Ship Money was at first satisfactorily collected
and the Crown paid its bills. In the event of a war, like the Scottish War,
Parliament should have provided needed funds. But this characterization
overlooks three facts. First, the bills were paid in large part by borrowing
against future revenues. The Crown had few reserves or credit to finance
any large expenditures precisely because many decades of bridging the
gap between rising expenses and lagging revenues had exhausted those
reserves. If the Crown had not raised millions of pounds from land sales,
the fiscal crisis would likely have come sooner. Second, Ship Money was

paid because it was appropriated for a particular purpose—the badly needed refurbishing of the navy. As soon as taxpayers judged that Ship Money would go to another, unpopular cause, such as bailing the king out of the Scottish War, their tax payments stopped. This was hardly fiscal stability. Third, the willingness of Parliament to provide taxes for war depended on the unity of the parliamentary elite and their loyalty to the Crown. The Crown had had difficulties gaining new revenues from Parliament for several decades and had alienated its supporters through its arbitrary revenue exactions and failure to satisfy demands for patronage. To assume that Parliament would adequately provide for the Crown's needs because, traditionally, it *should* have done so is to ignore important changes in the situation of the elite, changes owing to the same pressures that created the Crown's difficulties.

The fiscal component of *psi* measures the distress factor of these institutional constraints on the Crown. The component rises slightly when the Crown is forced to borrow. It rises more when the Crown is forced to rely on sales of land, manipulations of the coingage, or forced loans because regular taxation and borrowing are insufficient to pay its bills. This was the recurrent situation of the Crown from the late sixteenth century. The fiscal component rises still further when the Crown takes actions that directly confront the traditional privileges or prerogatives of elites, such as attacking the rights of corporations, depreciating the status of individuals, or relying on irregular and novel forms of revenue raising. And the fiscal component peaks when the Crown finds itself bankrupt and with no other recourse than to appeal for succor to the elite.

Price inflation and increases in military and patronage expenses—all fueled by increased population—acting on relatively inflexible traditional revenue sources lay behind the erosion of state finances. But the rate at which financial erosion occurred was determined by the economic and political resources of the Crown. The *psi* measurement of fiscal difficulty is thus less a financial measure than a *political* measure: to what degree did existing Crown assets and revenue sources and the cooperation of the elites allow the Crown to meet its expenses? In this sense, the Stuarts were in far worse shape than the Tudors, and Charles I was in worse shape than James I.

Of course, elite cooperation interacts with fiscal conditions—that is why *psi* is an *interactive* measure. If elites are united behind the Crown even bankruptcy need not precipitate state breakdown, since elites can adopt reforms to improve the Crown's situation, as the Restoration Parliament did for Charles II. It is pointless to debate Charles I's fiscal situation in isolation. Given that the old subsidies and the fifteenths and tenths had been reduced to a fraction of their former value, Charles I's finances were determined by the degree to which the elite cooperated in voting unprecedently large numbers of subsidies, or in accepting new sources of revenue. Thus, it is crucial to ask why elites were more restive in the 1630s than in the 1580s.

Many historians have pointed out that the volume of social mobility in England rose sharply when Henry VIII sold off church lands to eager buyers in the 1540s. But as I have insisted, the mere volume of mobility is not what mattered. The expansion of the elite in the mid-sixteenth century was largely a process of absorption; the newcomers who gained from purchase of Church lands did not yet pose a threat to the established elite. That challenge came only from the long decades of inflation from 1540 to 1640. Over these three generations, those who suffered from inflation lost land and influence; those who gained—new peers and rising gentry—sought a larger share of both, creating turnover and displacement.

The problem was not merely a large number of newcomers, for there were many new peers in both the 1540s and the 1640s. The problem was that by 1600 there had developed, at many levels of the elite, an imbalance between those who sought elite positions and the number of positions available. This was evidenced in the dramatic increase in turnovers on the county bench, in the contests for precedence on the bench and for parliamentary seats, and in the pursuit of legal and university credentials to fuel competitive office seeking. It is sometimes argued that the sale of offices under James I should have solved social problems by more widely dispensing the grace of offices and titles. This would only have been the case, however, if the sale of offices had simply absorbed newcomers, without either threatening prerogatives of established elites or leaving dissappointed suitors behind. As we have seen, both types of stress-inducing events occurred. The Crown's sale of offices and distribution of patronage created a court faction that was in constant conflict with the established local "country" gentry who felt threatened by their loss of influence. And the sale of offices did nothing for the hundreds who emerged from the universities with minimal prospects and turned to radical politics.

Again, what *psi* measures is not the volume of mobility but rather the competitive pressures for elite positions. It does this by focusing on university enrollments, rather than on numbers of the elite or on the recency of their elevations. Throughout Europe, early modern history shows periods of credentialing crises in which elites, competing for scarce positions, sought the competitive advantage of a degree. Such an acute situation was particularly marked in England in the early seventeenth century.

Psi's last component is labeled "mass mobilization *potential*" because popular grievances are no more than potential sources of disorder. The population becomes an effective political actor only when the weakness of the central authorities, or the encouragement of the elite, allows popular mobilization to spread. Some historians of the English Revolution discount the impact of popular actions, noting that the London crowds were orchestrated by Parliament, and that the food rioters posed no major threat to elites. The implicit contrast is with France, where the crowds of Paris or the peasants of the countryside are viewed as more autonomous and forceful actors.

But this is a false contrast. As discussed in the following sections, French peasants' and Parisians' actions depended on the encouragement of dissident elites and the weakness of the Crown no less than was the case in England. No doubt the village organization of the French countryside, and the dependence of French landlords on royal protection, meant that confrontations between peasants and landlords were far sharper in France during times of state crisis. But as Underdown's (1981) work on the Clubmen shows, one should not underestimate the ability of the English yeomanry to act autonomously. In many shires, the allegiance of the middling sorts—yeomen, small clothiers, and artisans—to Parliament was what enabled dissident gentry to hold their county for the parliamentary cause. Nor were the crowds who attacked Catholic elites in Essex, or the London mobs who harried the bishops and created fears for the safety of the king, inconsequential.

Their motivation came largely from the shortage of jobs and the collapse of real wages as the traditional economy failed to provide for the expanding population. Poverty was only an *indirect* threat to Parliament's supporters, but its impact should not therefore be discounted. Increasing poverty and disorder and rising poor rates led honest artisans, small merchants, and independent yeomen to seek personal security through either faith in a godly reformation of society or a simple chastening of the king who had ruled alone the last dozen years. Either way, sympathies among the middling sorts ran strongly for Parliament rather than for the Crown. But the root cause was the inability of the economy to absorb the growing population. Thus again, *psi* measures not merely the ecological change but the ability of the economy to cope with such change, as indicated by the ability of the economy to sustain real wage levels. And it measures factors such as the youthfulness of the population and the concentration of the population in cities, each with increased political impact in times of duress. Still, such mass mobilization potential comes to little unless elite and state circumstances are conducive to action. Hence, this component of *psi* must also be considered as part of an interactive measure of the likelihood of state crisis.

What made the 1630s an extraordinarily difficult period was that by this time *many* English institutions were failing, exhausted by the ecological pressures confronted since the 1520s. Wages reached new lows, which frightened even the God-fearing working class and lower middle class with the specter of poverty; competition for professional positions produced not only a generation of educated men with few prospects in the royal and Church establishments but also sharp competition for precedence among newcomers in the counties; and the Crown sought new revenues that would make it more independent of a fractious Parliament.

While one can point out measures that might have mitigated the ill effects of any one of these factors, it is extremely difficult to think of how Charles I might have coped with *all* of them. How could he have increased revenues when prices were rising, Crown lands were almost exhausted, and elites were uncooperative? How could he have won elite cooperation when the elites were so numerous and divided that to offer patronage to one family was to offend two others? And how could he have kept a lid on popular unrest in times of severe distress if the elite were not united in their desire to support the Crown's authority?

What was so devastating about population growth, in the context of England's economy and institutions, was that it simultaneously created so many interlocking and mutually reinforcing difficulties. If the Crown had possessed less land, or if James I had not been able to expand Parliament and the county benches to accommodate some of the mobility of the sixteenth century, the crisis might have come sooner. If Charles could have avoided war for another decade, the crisis might have come later. What the *psi* curve tells us is that the ability of English institutions to cope with the ecological change deteriorated rapidly in the early seventeenth century. The political ground was shaking. The details of Charles's fall—the loss of the civil war and his eventual execution—reflect in large measure the resources of the players and the "arrangement of the furniture" of England in the 1640s, once the crisis had begun. But the broad forces that created a situation in which all of Charles's choices were difficult and any policy was fraught with danger revolved around the failure of England's institutions to provide for the population expansion of the preceding century.

Historians have sometimes dismissed long-term factors behind revolutionary crises by asking what factors would have led people to seek revolution. Upon finding that no one consciously sought revolution, they comfortably declare that therefore no long-term factors existed (J. Clark 1986, 70–71). But changes that transformed people into revolutionaries are not what we should seek, for the seventeenth-century crises all across Eurasia were generally unsought by the actors. People accepted the need for change only reluctantly and often sought to delay change or to avoid it altogether. Crises arose not because people wished for a crisis but because long-term factors had made existing institutions unworkable. Conflicts then arose over who was responsible for that deterioration, and how to pick up the pieces. Thus, the key question about the seventeenth-century crisis in England is not what factors made people want change but rather what factors forced change onto people who were fundamentally conservative by making their current positions untenable.

What is often neglected is that while no one wanted revolution, no one wanted the conditions of the early seventeenth century either: a Crown that had to resort to a multiplicity of nonparliamentary means to raise funds even to maintain itself in peacetime; growing tension between factions in the court and the counties as increased numbers of elites struggled to establish a place in unstable status hierarchies and patronage networks; and enormous problems of poverty, underemployment, vagrancy, and crime. Solving these problems would have required the close cooperation of Crown and elites in changing the institutions of government finance, elite recruitment, and economic organization.

Yet the resources did not exist for a solution that would have benefited all parties. Given the increase in real costs associated with a doubling of population and a tripling of the gentry, multiplied by the fivefold increase in prices, maintenance of the Crown's real fiscal resources relative to its growing burdens would have required nearly a dozenfold rise in Crown revenues. This is something the fundamentally conservative gentry could hardly conceive and were not disposed to grant. At the same time, the failure of the economy to cope with population growth meant that the problems of regulating poverty and vagrancy became an obsession for justices of the peace and a point of contention between local and central authorities over who was responsible for the growing burden, and evident disordering, of traditional society.

Was the English Revolution inevitable? No—and certainly not as it occurred in all its details. But some sort of crisis was extremely likely, and more likely in the second quarter of the seventeenth century than at any time in the century before or after, because in those years population expansion was shaking England's economic, social, and political life on so many levels. Perhaps Charles might have kept his head, and even his throne, if he had acted differently. But Charles was ruling in an explosive situation, and any number of false moves or accidents could have led to state breakdown.

Still, as we noted in our example, diagnosing an earthquake is much easier if we also examine what happened to the neighbors. Let us, therefore, examine two of England's neighbors in the seventeenth century, France and Spain, and see if similar seismic forces appeared.

C. COMPARISONS: FRANCE AND SPAIN IN THE SEVENTEENTH CENTURY

The long-term social changes already discussed are familiar, in broad outline, to historians of the English Revolution. Of course, these general trends cannot explain many of the details of the English Revolution as it later unfolded. That explanation requires a close analysis of the contending parties and their resources, and of events after 1642, from the shifting factions among the gentry to the policies of Charles I and Oliver Cromwell and the hazards of war. Historians of England therefore often pass over these general trends and clothe their analyses in factors unique to England: the shift of power from nobles to gentry, the growth of parliamentary power buttressed by constitution and common law, the weakness of the Tudor/Stuart state, and the growth of Puritanism (Hexter 1978; L. Stone 1972; Aylmer 1965; R. Ashton 1978). But the English Revolution was only one of a number of political crises that occurred in the mid-seventeenth century. If we are to identify what was truly unique about the English experience, and what was merely a national variation on a more general historical process, we need to examine to what degree the general processes we have discussed—demographic shifts and their economic, social, and political consequences—were felt throughout Europe.

CONTRASTING CASES

France and Spain provide an interesting set of comparisons and contrasts. In France in the 1640s and 1650s, noble revolts, peasant uprisings, and rebellion in Paris—collectively known as the Fronde—drove the king from his capital and deprived the Crown of authority in the countryside. Royal authority was only restored in the 1660s. Spain, too, underwent state breakdown of a sort in these decades, but with significant differences. In the seventeenth century the Spanish monarchy was based in the heartland of the Iberian Peninsula, in the kingdom of Castile. But the monarchy also ruled Portugal, Catalonia, and, in southern Italy, the kingdom of Naples and Sicily. In the 1640s Spain experienced royal bankruptcy and provincial rebellions in Catalonia, Naples, and Sicily, and a secessionary coup d'état in Portugal. However, Spain was exceptional in that its core territory of Castile was peaceful. In the "crisis of the seventeenth century" Castilian elites did not join in revolt against the Crown, nor did urban disorders drive the court from the capital at Madrid. In Spain, the breakdown of state power occurred primarily at the periphery. Can our model of state breakdown help explain these phenomena?

THE FRONDE

The Fronde is sometimes seen as a lesser version of England's revolution, the downgrade being attributed to France's more modest development toward capitalism and weaker bourgeoisie (Porchnev 1963; Wallerstein 1974, 297). But France, which some see as maintaining a predominantly precapitalist and relatively backward agriculture throughout the Old Regime, was experiencing the same kinds of property and population shifts as occurred in England: commercialization of large farms (especially in northern and eastern France), shrinkage of peasant holdings, and an increase in landless wage laborers. And the same reasons can be cited: population increase and inflation leading smallholders into debt and to sale of their land to larger farmers (Jacquart 1974a; Le Roy Ladurie 1974a; Briggs 1977; J. Cooper 1978).[14] Again the question of

14. Wallerstein (1980, 90) agrees that trends in landholding were similar in England and northern France in this period. Robert Brenner (1976), however, stresses the differences, noting that in France, but not in England, the peasantry survived. Both are correct, provided one pays attention to the difference between individual and communal landholdings, and to regional differences. Northern France had roughly the same level of engrossment and large farms as England; in both areas, nonpeasant landholders held nearly 70 percent of the land (J. Cooper 1978, 23). Yet whereas French peasants in the

why cultivators rose against landlords is not illuminating; for, as in England, in the seventeenth century French commercial landlords still retained considerable power and jurisdiction over their tenants, the potential for autonomous peasant uprisings remained low, and, in the regions of capitalist agriculture where the interests of the landlords and tenantry were most opposed, the countryside was relatively undisturbed by rural uprisings. It was in the less commercial, largely subsistence and sharecropping regions of western and southern France, where landlords and their tenants had joint interests in opposing the exactions of the Crown, that the major peasant revolts occurred (Brustein 1986). Thus, the central question about the Fronde is why peasants and landlords, and state officials and urban dwellers, all simultaneously entered into fierce conflicts with the Crown in the mid-seventeenth century. Attention to demographic change and its impact on French institutions helps us follow the wide variety of conflicts.

From 1500 to 1650 France's population grew rapidly, though not quite as rapidly as England's. Population increased from perhaps twelve or thirteen million in 1500 to around twenty million by the mid-seventeenth century (Coleman 1977, 27; Goubert 1967, 1973a, 32–33). And many of the same trends as were seen in England during the sixteenth and seventeenth centuries were equally visible in France: a sevenfold rise in grain prices; a convergence of surplus rural population on

---

northeastern plains lost their individual plots, village common lands survived into the eighteenth century. The impoverished peasant thus could combine use of common land with labor on the lord's demesne to maintain a foothold in agriculture. In England where common fields were important, in the midland plain, they also survived into the eighteenth century; it was not until parliamentary enclosure in the period 1770–1815 that the peasantry in these regions disappeared (M. Turner 1980; Everitt 1967b; W. Hunt 1983). But in much of England, especially in the southeast, land was held "in severalty" (i.e., in individual plots marked off by hedges or enclosures) as early as 1500, and rights to pasture were individual, not common (Yelling 1977; Kerridge 1967). In these regions, when smallholders lost their individual holdings they had no recourse except to migrate or become artisans or laborers. In both England and northern France, population growth led peasants to lose individual landholdings, creating opportunities for commercial entrepreneurs (in France these were usually bourgeois and venal officeholders who invested in land); and in both countries, areas with village communal rights defended their commons largely intact to the late eighteenth century. The difference was that in England areas with communal village rights were always geographically fairly limited, whereas in northern France they were much more general. Thus, in northern France impoverished peasants continued to intertwine with commercial farms, while in England they largely migrated or became wage laborers. This is not to deny that this small difference had enormous implications for long-term agricultural improvement, for the claims of villagers who had common rights limited innovation with crops and crop rotations on commercial farms (P. Hoffman 1988). But these differences arose because village communal land rights had never been present in much of England, not because of the greater survival of peasant household property or of the absence of commercial farms and medium-sized properties in northern France.

Paris, which grew over 15 percent per decade from 1550 to 1650; and a sharp fall in real wages (Braudel and Labrousse 1970–1980; Baulant 1972; de Vries 1976).

The social and political consequences of population growth and price inflation were also similar to the English experience. The Crown's tax system, a congeries of different provincial levies and direct and indirect taxes that had been cobbled together during the fifteenth-century price stability, rapidly gave way to the rising costs of war (Bonney 1978a, 1981; D. Parker 1983). The yield of the major land tax, the *taille*, collected in periodically fixed cash amounts, had declined in real terms as prices rose. In many areas, "taxes did not keep pace with prices but fell conspicuously behind" (Le Roy Ladurie 1974a, 121; Mousnier 1970a). The monarchy's problems are evident from the budget accounts compiled by Lublinskaya (1968): from 1607 to 1622 expenses rose from 30 to 50 million livres, while direct taxation yielded a constant 11.3 million livres (or slightly less, since by 1622 taxes were 1.6 million livres in arrears). The monarchy thus had to resort to the same measures that had alienated the English elite and exhausted Charles I's credit: "the Crown was . . . impoverished by the sales and mortgaging of its lands" (Pennington 1970, 264). Forced loans were exacted, and venality of offices—the sale of offices for cash—reached new heights. In addition, elite privileges and investments such as the *paulette* (a fee paid to the Crown by officeholders to allow them to keep their offices in their families) and the *rentes* (a form of government bonds) were arbitrarily manipulated to profit the Crown (Pennington 1970, 264; Mousnier 1970a; Kimmel 1988). But these measures were still not enough: in the 1630s taxes were increased at unprecedented rates, which, by further burdening rural areas whose resources were already stretched by population demands, provoked provincial antitax rebellions (Mousnier 1970a; Briggs 1977; Le Roy Ladurie 1974a). Moreover, the sharp increases in taxes did more to swell discontent than to fill the treasury, for the requested sums rarely materialized from the overburdened countryside (Bonney 1978a, 173; D. Parker 1983, 64–65). The monarchy thus found itself bankrupt and dependent for its continued existence on loans from financiers.

Inflation posed problems for the nobility as well, for many nobles had "very inadequate machinery for adjusting to inflation" (Goubert 1973a, 129). "For those who had exchanged feudal or seigneurial dues originally levied in kind against fixed money there was no remedy," and many nobles were "forced to sacrifice part of their patrimony to survive," many sales being made to merchants and financiers (Briggs 1977, 8; M. Bloch 1966, 122–124). Moreover, increased family size often led to "the division and subdivision of family estates among children generation after generation" (Bitton 1969, 64).

Inflationary pressures for some posed profit opportunities for others, and merchants, tenant farmers, rich peasants, and many financiers took advantage of noble and Crown penury to acquire land, titles, and rank. The sixteenth century was thus, as in England, a period of exceptional social mobility among the elite. Bitton (1969, 2–3, 100) notes that "it was during . . . the late sixteenth and early seventeenth centuries that problems [of social competition] became most acute [due to] the high rate of infiltration across class boundaries." As in England, the position of the landlords as a class was secure, but within that class, divisions and competition festered. Official positions "became the object of fierce competition; [a] scramble to get jobs" ensued (Briggs 1977, 67). As in England, nobles and lesser landlords switched their allegiances to the Crown or to the opposition depending on which factor predominated: their financial interests in squeezing a settlement from the king or their fears of popular disorders (Mousnier 1979; Coveney 1977).

Displacement and turnover among the elite is visible in the replacement of the traditional nobility in the royal service by recruits from the Third Estate. The Crown, partly to raise revenue and partly to counterbalance the traditional nobility, created a virtual new class—the *noblesse de robe*—by selling roughly fifty thousand official posts during the late sixteenth century. This robe nobility did not merely grow alongside the older nobility; it rose to displace them on the highest councils of the land: in 1624, twenty-four of the thirty members of the French Council of State were robe nobles. And with the *paulette*, which, as noted earlier, made many offices the hereditary property of the officeholders, it became increasingly true that "through venality the bourgeoisie rose to govern France" (Kamen 1971, 179). Older nobles wrote to complain of the injuries "suffered by the nobility from the sale of offices . . . so that [they are] deprived of posts they formerly possessed, [which] fell into the hands of people of no birth, merit, or capacity" (Kamen 1971, 162). By the early seventeenth century, the sale of offices had virtually put the bureaucracy and judiciary beyond royal control. Thus, new officials—the intendants—were appointed to supervise the officials, and the *paulette* came under attack. The Crown thus found itself opposed by the robe nobility for attacking their privileges and by the traditional nobility for the special favor shown to the robe.

Noble opposition, from both the traditional grandees and the newer nobility of officeholders, was made more fearsome by the threat of popular revolts; indeed, "it was only because the political conflict so easily touched off risings in Paris and in the country that the state was brought close to anarchy" (Pennington 1970, 224). Rural revolts reflected the increased revenue demands of state taxation falling on a growing population that found it ever more difficult to feed itself: "the mid-seventeenth century . . . witnessed a rash of peasant uprisings provoked [by a shortage of] foodstuffs" (de Vries 1976, 162–163). Real wages fell as the labor force grew faster than employment; "the day's wage of the building craftsmen at the end of the sixteenth century would buy less than half of what it had commanded in the second half of the fifteenth" (Phelps Brown and Hopkins 1957, 292). The migration of landless peasants swelled the urban charity rolls, and there was "an enormous increase in vagrancy and begging" (Briggs 1977, 7). As in England, popular suffering did not merely create the potential for defensive rioting by the masses. The widespread perception of growing poverty and financial distress also gave to the elites a widespread feeling that the state was in need of drastic change; "early seventeenth century France was being swept by . . . powerful currents for . . . internal reformation" (Elliott 1984, 65).

Thus, state breakdown in France can be traced to factors quite similar to those in contemporary England: state fiscal crisis, exceptional elite mobility and competition, and heightened mobilization potential among the populace, especially in Paris, stemming from the strains of population growth on a preindustrial agrarian society. Contemporary state crises thus reflected similar demographic trends in states with broadly similar limitations.

However, the different contours and outcomes of the conflicts reflect significant differences in the resources of the combatants. The Tudors had reduced the power of the great lords, although they lacked a standing army and a large bureaucracy. Having relied on the support of the country gentry, Parliament, and London since the time of Henry VIII, the English Crown had few supporters to fall back on when its fiscal and administrative expedients undermined the confidence of Londoners and brought attacks from Parliament. Radical Protestantism, moreover, could cloak itself in nationalist appeals against a suspect papist administration. Hence, aside from marshaling reluctant traditionalists, who felt that defense of an objectionable king was preferable to the radical parliamentarians' courting of popular revolution, Charles I had few options. But in France the great older nobles—the dukes and princes—were still independent powers, and the Crown could exploit their resentment of the urban officeholding elite. Protestantism, though a serious threat to stability, could not pose as a nationalist ideology to lead the nation. Thus, unlike in England, there was no clear basis for a nationalist cross-class coalition against the Crown. Adroit manipulation of alliances and divisions among the princes, the *officiers*, and the populace allowed the French Crown to survive through feint, retreat, and eventual triumph (Coveney 1977; Mousnier 1970a; D. Parker 1983; Zagorin 1982).

In both countries, the seventeenth-century crises mark a period of breakdown of government due, in each case, to the failure of institutions to cope with extraordinary social and economic strains, succeeded by a struggle that essentially reinforced preceding political trends: in England, a monarchy that controlled its ministers, but not its purse strings, and hence required the cooperation of Parliament and country gentry to govern; in France, a monarchy whose standing army and royal taxation allowed it to govern by decree, but whose policies were limited by the interests, influences, and privileges of the nobilities of the robe and sword that staffed its complex web of military, civil, and juridical offices.

This view helps make sense of the simultaneous crises and divergent outcomes in England and France. Both countries experienced a cyclic crisis in the mid-seventeenth century, brought on by commonly felt demographic pressures and their consequences in agrarian states, and both therefore experienced state breakdown. But the preceding political alignments and the specific nature of the conflicts led to different resolutions of the problem of state reconstruction after each crisis. In England, although social conflicts and fiscal crises did not return on the scale of the 1640s after the reversal of the underlying demographic and social trends, the revolution did not resolve two key problems of English politics: the status of the established Church and the relation of the dynasty to that Church. Thus the 1680s were consumed by struggles over religious tolerance and the possibility of Catholic succession to the Crown. In 1688–1689, England worked out a solution to these problems. Private worship outside of the Anglican Church would be tolerated, but the monarchy and the Church would be indissolubly linked, even if slight alterations in the succession were necessary to achieve this latter requirement. Struggles over the succession did not immediately die out, as the Jacobite rebellions demonstrated (J. Clark 1985, 1986); however, the pattern of private tolerance and public orthodoxy was established. And Parliament's crucial role in achieving this outcome, in conjunction with William and Mary, helped to ensure its continued importance in English politics.

In contrast, in France the end of the Fronde quickly marked the reimposition of strict private and public orthodoxy. Louis XIV quickly moved to establish a web of patronage and royal office networks throughout France, united by loyalty to the monarch (Kettering 1986). Protestants were attacked as rebels, and the Edict of Nantes, which had established their toleration, already "in many respects a dead letter" in the 1670s (D. Parker 1983, 56), was formally revoked in 1685.

I return later to these events. At this point, I simply note that one can hardly make sense of these near-simultaneous crises, and their sharply divergent outcomes, by viewing both crises as struggles for capitalism that differed chiefly in their degrees of conflict. Nor can one account for their many similarities—state bankruptcy despite large tax increases vitiated by inflation, rapid social mobility and expansion of the elite that resulted in displacement and fierce divisions, and popular, particularly urban, unrest—or for their temporal coincidence, if both events are simply attributed to policy errors of particular rulers. However, if one views them both as responses to cyclic pressures, reflected through different national constellations of political and cultural divisions, much about them can be understood. In particular, the lack of any conflict between monarchical succession and the national Church since Henry IV's embrace of Catholicism meant that in France state reconstruction could be undertaken on the basis of an uncompromising allegiance to Louis XIV. The revocation of the Edict of Nantes and the demise of the Estates General, as well as of most provincial estates, followed naturally from the focus on the ruler as the source of national unity. But in England the continuation of such a conflict required a compromise, which was finally institutionalized in 1688–1689. The need to defend that compromise helped institutionalize Parliament, as well as religious toleration—a combination that would have momentous consequences.

PERIPHERAL REGIONAL REVOLTS IN THE SPANISH HAPSBURG LANDS

Seventeenth-century Spain shows a pattern different from that of either England or France. Like these countries, Spain experienced strong growth in the early sixteenth century, recovering from a late medieval population decline. But in the later sixteenth century, population growth slowed and then was abruptly reversed, as plague made a dramatic return. From the 1580s, there is clear evidence of declining births and population stagnation. A major epidemic hit in 1596; after 1610, the expulsion of the Moriscos (former Muslims who lived chiefly in Granada) further reduced the population. Thus, while England and France continued to grow well into the seventeenth century, Spain's population declined. In the core kingdom of Castile, population peaked at 6.7 million circa 1590, then fell to 5 million by 1665 (Lynch 1981, 2:135–36; Nadal 1984, 17; Kamen 1983, 98, 222–24; Ringrose 1983). Only the region of Catalonia, relatively untouched by the plague, continued to grow.

The consequences of this demographic trend were different movements in prices and wages from those occurring in France and England. Population increase and sluggish agriculture led to rising commodity prices up to the 1590s, but when population growth ceased, prices (in silver) stabilized and remained stagnant to 1650 (Elliott 1963a, 186; Lynch 1981, 1:372; Kamen 1983, 276). Price inflation thus ceased much earlier in Castile than in northwest Europe. In addition, thanks to the modest increase in the labor force, real wages never dropped as sharply as they did in France and England: "In Spain prices and wages stayed close together between 1500 and 1650. The Spanish worker kept his earnings more or less abreast of inflation throughout the period" (Mauro and Parker 1977, 56; Lynch 1981); and levels of real wages in Spain were several times those in England or France (Defourneaux 1970, 23).

Similarly, urban growth never reached the levels of England and France; indeed, net urbanization during the period was minimal. Although the total population of many towns doubled from 1500 to 1590, the trend then reversed, and many towns were smaller by 1650 than they had been a century earlier. Madrid grew, but at the expense of Toledo; Seville's population fell by a third from 1600 to 1650 (de Vries 1984; Ringrose 1983).

The situation of the nobility also differed from that in England and France. Population growth and inflation, along with the New World empire, created opportunities for profit, and a modest middle class of medium property holders arose, sent their progeny to the universities, and sought to acquire—by purchase or by educational investment—offices and noble status. There was thus an expansion of the nobility in Spain during the sixteenth and seventeeth centuries, especially in the lower ranks (Lynch 1981, 2:143). But, unlike the situations in England

and France, this was expansion with little downward mobility, and with a multiplication of offices and privileges for the older as well as the newer Castilian elite. Thus, expansion took the form of absorption, and did not involve turnover and enmity toward the Crown. In the seventeenth century "the Castilian aristocracy [was] still dominated by fourteenth century families" (Jago 1979, 61).

The lack of turnover was in part the result of royal policies that protected the nobility; but it also reflected high mortality, which meant smaller families and fewer downwardly mobile younger sons, and the decline of middle-class opportunities and expansion that followed the end of price increases in the 1590s.

In contrast to England, there was no great growth of a rural squirearchy challenging for control of the countryside at the local level; and Spanish agriculture was organized to protect the profits of the Mesta, the noble-controlled wool monopoly, and to preserve large estates (Dominguez Ortiz 1971). Also, whereas in England Henry VIII's sales of Church and Crown lands greatly increased gentry landholding, the Spanish Crown's modest land sales in the sixteenth century "left the pattern of Castilian landholding substantially unmodified" (Mantelli 1984, 204). Accessions to the nobility thus came chiefly from urban merchants and the legal profession. These groups were admitted to urban councils, where they formed an addition to the nobility but did not displace it; major offices were still monopolized by old noble families (Pike 1972; Phillips 1978). And in contrast to France, while offices were sold, the practice was on a very small scale: "At a national level venality made no serious impact at all. There was . . . no fear of subversion of the social and political order by the accession of the lower classes to posts of distinction" (Kamen 1980, 35; I. Thompson 1979). In addition, as offices and privileges were protected and expanded, the increase in honors "had little unsettling effect on Spanish society . . . . Existing grandees seem to have accepted the creation of new grandees so long as their own privileges remained untouched" (Kamen 1980, 250–251). Imperial expansion also created an outlet for new nobles, solving problems of competition: "In Italy the new Grandees could display their status without offending the time-honored rules of precedence accepted in Spain" (Kamen 1980, 251).

While the mobility that did occur was thus more easily accommodated, it is also important to note that the opportunities for mobility were fewer in Castile than in England or France, and they lasted a shorter time. The Castilian nobility was protected against inflation by two hedges. First, most land was held through short-term leases that could be readily adjusted for inflation (Jago 1979, 69; Lynch 1981, 1:134; Kiernan 1980). Second, noble estates were legally bound against sale by entails (*mayorazgo*); money could then be raised by mortgages (*censos*) without loss of capital (Kamen 1980). Thus England's "very rapid turnover of landed property [was] the reverse of the situation in Spain" (Kiernan 1980, 118).

Castilian nobles suffered problems of indebtedness and cash flow and by the early seventeenth century increasingly depended on Crown offices and patronage for income augmentation. But the Crown readily provided support to the nobility, and at the same time, competition from below faded. For while the nobility's rental incomes were reduced by the population reversal and decline during the period 1590–1650, the owners of middle-sized properties were hit far worse by the fall in rents and markets, and in many areas the rising middle class sharply diminished in size (Dominguez Ortiz 1971). After 1600, then, the nobility was able to secure its position largely without the threat of an expanding middle class; from the 1600s, all important court offices went to the traditional nobility (Kiernan 1980). Even the education system served this end. Although universities expanded greatly in the sixteenth century, by 1580 enrollment had peaked, reflecting the end of expansion among those seeking cultural credentials (Kagan 1974). By 1640 enrollments had fallen by a third, and places in the major colleges were reserved for the nobility. "Higher education in Spain had become a powerful instrument for perpetuating the social and political dominance of the aristocracy" (Lynch 1981, 2:141).

In short, compared to their counterparts in England and France, the Castilian nobility suffered far less from competition in the early seventeenth century. Protected by a favorable land situation (entails and short-term leases), Castilian nobles controlled the universities and Church and court offices and, from 1600 onward, enjoyed conditions in which stable prices and economic stagnation closed the opportunities for newcomers to rise and in which higher mortality meant diminished problems of internal competition for property and position (Jago 1979; Nader 1977; Kamen 1971, 1980). As noted earlier, these same demographic and economic trends appeared in England after 1650, with similar consequences for the elite, and contributed to aristocratic retrenchment. The entrenchment of the Spanish aristocracy in the seventeenth century can be better understood when it is realized that these trends in Spain began a half-century earlier.

Thus, of the factors contributing to political stress in the *psi* function—state fiscal distress, elite turnover and competition, and mass mobilization potential (falling real wages, urbanization, age composition)—all except the first moved in stabilizing directions in Castile from 1590 to 1640.

Of course, state fiscal distress was on the rise, for the Spanish Crown had taxed its own agriculture into lassitude and thus was forced to buy grain (and army mercenaries) on the world market, where prices continued to rise to 1640. The costs of war thus spiraled upward. However, the Crown did not attack the privileges or properties of the Castilian elite to raise funds. It did seek greater gifts and contributions from them but offered compensating rewards in power and offices. Although the Crown increased revenues from Castilian commoners through modest sales of offices and higher land taxes, unlike the situation in France these taxes increased no faster than the cost of living (Kamen 1980, 200). But in the 1640s, when these expedients failed to meet financial needs, the Crown turned outward, to its possessions in Catalonia, Italy, and Sicily, to increase its revenues. There its demands fell on societies demographically and socially different from Castile.

Catalonia, Naples, and Sicily had all experienced greater population growth than Castile through the sixteenth and early seventeenth centuries: Catalonia's population grew from under 300,000 in 1550 to around 500,000 in 1640, while its capital city, Barcelona, doubled in size (Vicens-Vivens 1969; de Vries 1984). The kingdom of Naples and Sicily grew from 1.87 million in 1500 to over 3 million in 1600, with the cities of Naples and Palermo nearly tripling in size, the former increasing from 125,000 inhabitants in 1500 to 350,000 in 1647, the latter from 48,000 in 1500 to 135,000 in 1625 (Cowie 1977, 28; Chandler and Fox 1974, 89; Felloni 1977, 2–3). In these areas, real wages fell, and food shortages and grain riots multiplied (Felloni 1977; Elliott 1963b, 1970).

In addition, the experience of the elite of these regions was different from that of Castile. The volume of social mobility, shown by purchases of nobility, was even greater in Catalonia than in Castile (Amelang 1982). But preferment of Castilian nobles for appointments in the Spanish Empire meant that local elites had their ambitions blocked. In Catalonia, "there were not enough offices to go around [hence] there was passionate rivalry between families for the few vacancies that did exist" (Lynch 1981, 1:213). Thus, as in England, demands for increased revenues in Catalonia fell upon an elite that was resentful that offices had not kept pace with the expansion in their ranks. Also as in England, some were willing to take advantage of popular discontent, especially in swollen cities, to pressure the Crown into concessions (Elliott 1963b, 1970). Similarly, while the Castilian elite were coddled, "in Naples it was the excessive tax demands of Spain . . . that alienated the propertied classes and drove them to rebellion" (Kamen 1971, 327; Stradling 1981).

In short, when we examine the Spanish monarchy, we find that a combination of differences in both demographic conditions and royal policy toward elites resulted in different regions having very different levels of the factors we have identified as crucial to state breakdown. In Castile these factors, except for state fiscal distress, were at comparatively low levels. And even the usual consequence of state fiscal distress—attacks on elite property and privileges—did not occur, the Crown instead turning outside Castile to seek funds. But in Catalonia in particular, and in Naples and Sicily to a lesser degree, all the conditions for state breakdown—a fiscally strapped Crown raising its exactions, an overgrown nobility partially displaced from its traditional prerogatives, and swollen cities experiencing a steady decline in real wages—were present. Thus, it should be no surprise that in 1640 "the heart of the monarchy, Castile, held firm . . . . Where France had its revolt at the center, Spain had its revolts at the periphery" (Elliott 1970, 109).

There were urban riots in parts of Castile in the 1650s, but these were responses to currency manipulations rather than to long-term wage declines. In addition, individual nobles who had had enough of war by the 1640s conspired against the Crown (Stradling 1981). But neither activity gained widespread support. At no time in the seventeenth century did Castile face the combination of elite revolt and popular unrest that threatened the English and French monarchies—largely because it never faced a combination of elite displacement and turnover with rapid net urbanization and widespread wage decline. These differences in demographic and economic trends had significantly different consequences for the political health of the states involved.

As in England and France, the contours of the crisis in Spain also affected the pattern of subsequent state reconstruction. After suppressing the rebellions in Catalonia, Naples, and Sicily, Spain's chief priority was to ensure allegiance to the Castilian Crown, and central control was strengthened. As in France, after 1660 state and Church united in a campaign to enforce public and private conformity, but the enforcement of conformity by the Inquisition was more intense in the Hapsburg lands. In addition, the early and extensive downturn in Spanish population, which had halted urban growth, shrunk local markets, diminished social mobility, and allowed the aristocrats to entrench their position, meant that Spain entered the late seventeenth century with a weaker economy, and even greater aristocratic dominance, than its northern neighbors. Spain's economy did recover after 1660, and Spain held on to its New World and Mediterranean possessions. But Spanish politics became an aristocratic tournament, the games of which were more challenging and rewarding than pursuit of commercial ventures. Since the aristocracy controlled the overwhelming majority of Spain's capital, and since that capital was employed chiefly in seeking political advantage, opportunities for more intensive growth were dissipated. Spain's population recovered after 1660, but the ensuing economic growth was merely recovery, not development. Spain remained a major European power, but heavy state centralization, oppressive religious control, and aristocratic dominance led to heated politics and a torpid economy, a combination that eroded Spain's former hegemony.

Let us now move ahead a century to consider the issues surrounding the origins of the French Revolution. Afterward, we return to the events examined in this chapter in the course of reviewing the overall patterns of population growth and political crises in early modern Europe.

THREE

State Breakdown in Early Modern Europe: The French Revolution

Les spécialistes persistent à ignorer le rôle aggravant que la pression démographique a pu jouer dans la crise de l'ancien régime.

[The specialists persist in ignoring the aggravating role that demographic pressure may have played in the crisis of the ancien régime.]

—*Jacques Dupâquier*

A. THEORETICAL CONTROVERSIES, DEMOGRAPHIC AND ECONOMIC TRENDS

EXPLAINING THE FRENCH REVOLUTION

Since 1789 the French Revolution—whether viewed as a model to emulate or as a menace to avoid—has been at the center of debates on political change. It is unfortunate, then, that students of politics who look for an explanation of why the French state fell in 1789 now receive no clear answers from historians.

For many years the dominant explanation was that the revolution stemmed from a social crisis (Mathiez 1928; Mazauric 1970; Soboul 1975; Godechot 1970; Kaplow 1965). Long-term changes in France's economy that increased the importance of capitalist practices and enterprises, and spawned distinctive bourgeois entrepreneurs, clashed with political and status systems that remained traditional. But the evidence for a "bourgeois revolution" has been progressively crumbling under severe criticism for several decades (Chaussinaud-Nogaret 1975; Cobban 1964, 1967; Doyle 1972; Eisenstein 1968; Forster 1963, 1971, 1976; Furet 1971, 1981; Furet and Richet 1970; Root 1982, 1987; G. Taylor 1964, 1972a, 1972b). Behrens (1985, 9) has recently remarked that "there is in fact no major item in the catalogue of long-term causes generally held responsible for the Revolution that is now left standing."

Baker (1987b, xi) concurs, noting that for the so-called bourgeois revolution, "longstanding historiographical interpretations have collapsed." Several scholars (G. Taylor 1972b; Doyle 1980) have thus opined that "the forces pushing France toward revolution were almost entirely political. There was no underlying social crisis" (Doyle 1980, 158). And the most respected modern syntheses (Doyle 1989; Schama 1989; Furet 1981) claim that the revolution was to some degree a chance event, due to the "convergence of several heterogenous series, surely a fortuitous situation" (Furet 1981, 25).

There is thus a remarkable parallel between recent trends in the historiography of the French and English Revolutions. In both cases explanations that have focused on long-term social changes, particularly the rise of capitalism and capitalist groups, have been undermined by decades of critical scholarship. As a result, a new generation of revisionist scholars has rejected any long-term economic causes for either revolution, adopting instead an explanation based on short-term political conflicts and the purportedly unique structure of French or English institutions. Historians of both revolutions have deserted what was once a common, unifying framework, in favor of more particularistic and contingent explanations. Rejection of the Marxist framework has meant greater fidelity to the evidence, but at a price—the resulting analyses have left national histories isolated and reduced to the vagaries of chance. A coherent early modern European history has largely disappeared.

The sociologist Theda Skocpol (1979) has offered a broad explanation of revolutions, based on international as well as domestic politics. Skocpol argues that the French Revolution was the result of France's inability to compete with England in sustaining the expenses of war, owing to a lagging precapitalist economy. When the Crown, in an effort to raise revenues, deadlocked with entrenched political elites who resisted state taxation, the resulting crisis allowed the pent-up grievances of France's volatile village communities to surface; rural uprisings then pushed the political crisis into social revolution. Her explanation rests not on the "rise of the bourgeoisie" but rather on the decline of France relative to its chief international adversary. This international pressure, combined with the ability of the French elite to block reform through their strategic positions in parlements and venal offices and with the ability of peasants to take advantage of the political crisis through their communal, partly autonomous, village organizations, was responsible for the revolution.

Skocpol's work is a powerful attempt to restore sociological explanation. It focuses on aspects of French institutions—for example, the weakness of the state in the face of international pressures and the crucial role of peasant villages—that were also found in other instances of social revolution, namely, Russia in 1917 and China in the period 1911–1949. Yet Skocpol's explanation also fails to place the French Revolution in the historical context of European state breakdowns. Skocpol's goal is not merely to explain why France had a political crisis but also why it had a *social* revolution. Since France was the only nation in early modern Europe to have a social revolution, as opposed to a mere state break-down, Skocpol's explanatory goal leads her to stress precisely how France's state and agrarian structures *differed* from those of other states. Her parallels are drawn not between the French Revolution and other early modern state breakdowns but rather between the French Revolution and social revolutions in twentieth-century states struggling with the beginnings of heavy industrialization.

Skocpol demonstrates that France in 1789 had two elements whose combination was unique in early modern Europe: (1) a landlord class that was strong enough as a whole to block the central government's efforts to raise taxes, but weak enough locally to be dependent on the central government for enforcement of its property rights, and (2) a peasantry whose partly autonomous, communal organization enabled it to act collectively against landlords. Thus, when the state, which kept these adversarial elements in balance, broke down, the result was social turmoil and social revolution. The fundamental contribution of Skocpol's work is the demonstration of what made France unique in early modern Europe, and why its revolution had elements in common with the later socialist revolutions in Russia and China.

But if we ask why the French state broke down in 1789, Skocpol's analysis is far less satisfactory. Certain aspects of her analysis need to be modified; others show lacunae that remain to be filled. As discussed later, in terms of the size of its manufacturing and commercial sector, France was not "lagging" behind Britain. France's output in trade and industry in 1789 was larger than England's. And it was not the rising cost of war, and French inability to pay, that led to the fiscal crisis. The American War of Independence, in real terms, was France's least costly war of the eighteenth century. We thus need to look elsewhere to understand why the French state survived twenty-five years of unsuccessful war in the period 1689–1714, another seven years of unsuccessful war from 1756 to 1763, and then, although much richer than before, was toppled by six years of successful war in the period 1778–1783, a war that was the only interruption in twenty-six years (1763–1789) of peace. Moreover, Skocpol's explanation tells us little about why conflicts *within* the elite were so intense, the very conflicts that caused the failure of the Estates General and ushered in the revolution. Finally, Skocpol's emphasis on rural uprisings leads her to understate the importance of unrest in Paris, which provided the crucial reinforcement to the National Assembly.

State breakdown in France in 1789 comprised a combination of elements: a state fiscal crisis, elite rebellion and sharp intra-elite conflicts, and urban and rural unrest. As we have seen, precisely the same combination occurred a century and a half earlier in the English Revolution and in the French Fronde (although only in 1789, owing to landlords' local weakness in confrontations with peasants, did rural uprisings successfully challenge elite prerogatives). Neither Skocpol's analysis nor the particularistic explanations of the revisionists shed any light on why this specific combination of elements occurred *in all three instances*. In addition, we have noted that the French Revolution was part of a wave of state breakdowns from 1770 to 1850 that stretched all across Europe, into Russia and China. Neither Skocpol nor the revisionists observe, much less explain, that state breakdown was widespread in certain periods of early modern history. They thus offer no guidance to understanding the periodic, systematic failures of early modern states and the place of the French Revolution in this pattern.

I argue in this chapter that the breakdown of the French state in 1789 was rooted in the same causes that gave rise to the crises of the seventeenth century. That is, following a period of demographic decline from 1660 to 1700 which brought an interval of stability, when population rose in the eighteenth century, France was again thrown into crisis by the inability of its economy, its system of taxation, and its mechanisms of elite recruitment to cope with sustained population growth.

Of course, French historians have long been aware of the eighteenth-century population increase. Indeed, many, such as Soboul (1977a, 35) and Labrousse (1958), have cited population growth as a factor adding to the strains on the ancien régime. However, these scholars have concentrated on the effects of population growth on the standard of living of the working class and the peasantry. They have not observed the effects that demographic change had on the state and on elites. As we saw in the discussion of the English Revolution, the impact of population growth on these latter two groups is even more important than that on the lower classes as a cause of state breakdown.

My goal in this chapter is to explain why political conflicts became particularly acute, and the French state particularly weak, toward the end of the eighteenth century. By focusing on the *multiple* causal paths by which demographic change acted on French society, I construct an account of the political crisis that connects politics and economics but does not depend on the type of secular social change cited in "Marxist" or "capitalist" theories of the French Revolution. Instead, by demonstrating the connection between the revolution and the *cyclic* forces of population and price changes, I hope to restore the proper links between the revolution and long-term economic patterns and firmly place the revolution in context with regard to both the seventeenth, and the late-eighteenth- and early-nineteenth-century, waves of state breakdown.

Two caveats are critical here. First, this argument seeks to explain only the breakdown or "crisis" of the Old Regime. If one thinks of the "French Revolution" as being chiefly the events from 1791 to 1815, that is, the struggles for dominance, the emergence of Jacobin leadership, the Reign of Terror, and the rise of Napoleon, then the revolution is not explained here. Instead, I examine those events briefly in chapter 5. And I state there, but want to make clear here as well, that one must keep analytically separate the story of the breakdown of the Old Regime— commonly thought of as the problem of the "origins" of the revolution—and the story of the unfolding of the revolution after the Old Regime lost the initiative, that is, after 1789. The factors that explain the breakdown of the Old Regime are not, in general, sufficient to explain what happened in the ensuing struggles over power and state reconstruction.

Second, to say that the French Revolution was rooted in long-term social changes that affected all of Eurasia in the period 1770–1860 is not to say that such social changes alone caused the revolution, or that those changes had the same effects everywhere. The impact of long-term social changes, as I indicated in discussing the contrasts between the English Revolution and the Fronde, always depends on the particular social and political structures exposed to those changes. In the period from 1660 to 1730, England and Prussia underwent major transformations in their political institutions and their economies; hence they each responded to the population pressures of the eighteenth and nineteenth centuries in their own specific fashions. France, as shown below, modified but did not replace its earlier economic and political structures under Louis XIV; thus his successors encountered fiscal pressures, intra-elite conflicts, and popular unrest similar to the events of the seventeenth century.

Imagine, if you will, a series of buildings on a level plain. Some are tall, others are low and heavy; some are fragile, others are sturdy. Seismic pressures accumulate and slowly shift the plain on which the buildings stand; we do not see the gradual accumulation of pressure, only the earthquake that follows. All buildings will be affected by the shock, but the consequences for each will differ with their constructions—some will topple, others will crack but remain standing. If we now ask why some buildings fell, it is vain to argue over whether it was the seismic shift or weak construction that led to their collapse; the proper answer is that it was the combination, the impact of the seismic forces on the buildings with their structural weaknesses. If we wish to know why the collapse occurred at a particular time, we should focus on the ebb and flow of seismic pressures; if we wish to know why certain buildings fell, given such pressures, then we should focus on the vulnerability of their construction to seismic stress.

In my argument, state institutions are like buildings on a plain, and population pressure is like the seismic pressure that shifts the plain on which the buildings are constructed. From 1500 to 1660, and from 1730 to 1860, population growth all across Eurasia created "seismic pressures" that undermined the foundations of states. This explains the synchrony of the state breakdowns. But if we are to understand why certain states collapsed, while others merely shook, we need to examine the particular structural vulnerabilities of those states.

To carry the metaphor a step further, after the shock of the mid-seventeenth century the English state was rebuilt along new, more flexible lines, partly because of rather unique and contingent events that had to do with a change of dynasty to protect the Protestant succession. The tax system was transformed by the Long Parliament, and again by William III. The resolution of elite conflicts was also transformed, as Kishlansky (1986) has shown. After 1688 parliamentary "selection," which simply recognized the leading families of the counties and thus led to battles over social precedence and personal standing that brooked no compromise, was replaced by parliamentary "election," in which elites competed on the basis of policies rather than personal standing. Party politics, which recognized the need to tolerate an opposition, replaced the ideal of a unified hierarchy from which all dissent had to be eliminated. Although the monarchy, the Anglican Church, and the prestige and wealth of the aristocracy remained, in important details the English state of the late eighteenth and early nineteenth centuries was quite different from that of the early Stuarts.

In contrast, following the Fronde, Louis XIV rebuilt the French state largely by adding new layers of administration, but without any change in the basic system of taxation or elite recruitment. Thus, whereas the architects of eighteenth-century English politics built a classic-appearing structure on a new foundation, Louis XIV and his ministers created a magnificent baroque façade but left the old weak foundations unchanged. It is no wonder, therefore, that when a new wave of population pressures appeared in the eighteenth century, the English state was able to stand the stress, whereas the French state crumbled.

This chapter explores the economic, political, and social structures of France from 1660 to 1789, with an eye to how those structures were vulnerable to population shifts. But let us first examine the ebb and flow of population pressures in this period, and their effects on prices and incomes.

POPULATION AND PRICES IN FRANCE, 1650–1789

THE PATTERN OF DEMOGRAPHIC CHANGE

Thirty years ago our knowledge of French population history in the seventeenth and eighteenth centuries began to emerge from its dark ages. We then knew little more about population or output than did contemporaries, on whose estimates most of our knowledge was based. We did have the pathbreaking regional monograph on Le Nord of Lefebvre (1972 [1924]), and the still-standard work on price history of Labrousse (1984 [1933]), but these rich data were subject to various interpretations. Only in the last few years have more solid population estimates emerged from the painstaking work on parish registers conducted by Henry and Blayo (1975), Dupâquier (1970), and their colleagues at the Institute nationale d'études démographiques (INED). And Lefebvre's work has been complemented by a large number of regional studies, including those of Goubert (1960), Le Roy Ladurie (1974a), Baehrel (1961), Jacquart (1974a), and P. Bois (1960).

We have already noted that the population of France grew markedly from 1500 to around 1650. There is general agreement that growth then stopped, and even reversed, for fifty or sixty years. Le Roy Ladurie placed the seventeenth-century maximum in 1636, suggesting the French population was "at least 10 to 12 percent higher then than its level in 1711" (1987, 267–268). Biraben and Bonneuil (1986, 950), examining eleven parishes in Caux, found that population peaked in 1639 at 17 percent above the level of 1700, fell slightly to 1660, and then dropped sharply thereafter. Dupâquier (1979, 9) reported that in the *élections* (tax districts) of Reims, Rethel, and Romorantin, population fell 30 percent or more between 1636 and 1665 (the 1660s being years of high mortality) and recovered only slowly, so that the population in 1700 was still 15–20 percent below its seventeenth-century peak. There is, however, some evidence that growth in several parts of France continued until the 1660s. Lemaître (1978, 38) found that baptisms in Ussel, in the Limousin, remained high from 1630 to 1670 before falling sharply; Le Roy Ladurie (1974a, 214) noted that in Languedoc population growth did not start to reverse until 1680. In Provence, Baehrel (1961, 235–236) found that population probably peaked in 1690 before declining until 1735. In the Vivarais, similarly, Molinier (1985, 233) found that the number of households peaked in 1693 and then fell to the 1730s. Biraben and Blanchet (1982, 1116) found that baptisms in Saint-Denis and Aubervilliers rose until 1648 before turning downward; Dupâquier (1979, 9) reported that in some districts near Caen and in Neufchâtel population was higher in 1665 than in 1636. Goubert (1967, 173; 1970b, 32) observed that the population in the Beauvais continued to rise from 1636 to 1647, and that in Brittany baptisms and marriages remained high until 1670. For France as a whole, growth thus slowed at different times. We can be confident, however, that a high level was achieved in the 1630s. This level was maintained or slightly exceeded in some areas until the 1640s, or, more rarely, until the 1670s or even 1690s, before the wave of growth was exhausted. Total population most likely peaked around midcentury, at a level 10–20 percent higher than that of 1700.

Although it was once thought that the demographic malaise lingered through the entire reign of Louis XIV, there is now strong evidence that population reached its nadir in the early 1690s and then began to recover. Rebaudo (1979) has presented data showing a national rise in baptisms and a contraction in deaths after 1695; he estimates that population fell from 1670 to 1695 and then expanded steadily. Scheaper (1980) has presented additional evidence, from studies of prices and industrial output, that indicates solid economic growth from 1690 to 1715. Dupâquier's (1979, 34–35) estimates for the population of France (in the territory of its modern-day borders) confirm this trend, showing an expansion from 21.5 million people in 1700 to 22.5 million in 1710.

Le Roy Ladurie's (1987) estimate that the mid-seventeenth century peak was 10–12 percent above the figure for 1711, and Dupâquier's estimate that the peak was 15 percent above the figure for 1700, yield a consistent estimate of 24.7 million for the population of France (in its modern borders) circa 1640–1660. Population then probably declined, with a sharp fall after the early 1660s, to a low point of 20–21 million circa 1695, before turning upward. For the eighteenth century, Dupâquier (1979, 34–35, 37, 81) provides decadal population estimates, based on data from the INED parish studies, that show population returning to a level of 24.6 million in 1740 and then surpassing that level and rising to 28.1 million in 1790. Thus, as in England, from circa 1640 to circa 1740 net population growth in France was likely nil. And in France, from 1660 to 1695 population actually fell to a depressed level of 20–21 million, 20 percent below the levels of circa 1640 and circa 1740. The curve of French population according to these estimates is shown in figure 6.[1]

The population growth of the eighteenth century was rapid but not evenly spread across time or regions. Growth was strong from 1700 to 1730, slowed markedly for two decades, then resumed and accelerated from 1750 to 1790. The total increase from 1700 to 1780—slightly over 30 percent—was not remarkable by European standards; England, Germany, and even Russia grew faster. But France was already the most densely populated large country in Europe (Dupâquier 1970, 156), and the approach to its peak population in the early seventeenth century was marked by enormous price inflation and by famine crises in every decade from the 1630s through the 1660s. Thus, for France to grow to, and then beyond, its seventeenth-century peak was to arrive at population levels that had previously proved hazardous.

Moreover, population growth was concentrated in those areas that were already France's most densely populated. Population increased only slightly in Brittany and some western provinces, perhaps only 1 to 8 percent from 1750 to 1790, while France as a whole was growing by 15 percent. Thus, there was an enormous focusing of growth in the northeast and along the Mediterranean littoral (Dupâquier 1978, 236; Le Goff 1981, 11–12). Lemoigne (1965) suggests a 100 percent increase

1. I must emphasize that the figures before 1700 are my own estimates based on Le Roy Ladurie (1987), Goubert (1970b, 1970c), and various local studies, as identified in the text. More conservative estimates by Dupâquier et al. (1988, 67–68) argue for a similar trend, but with an earlier and lower peak, circa 1630.

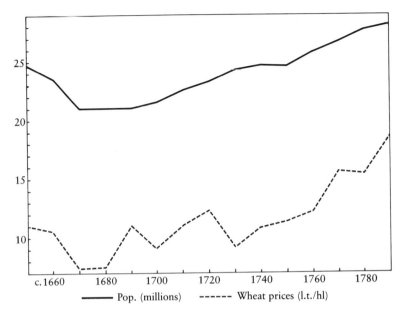

Figure 6. French population and prices, 1650–1790

in Alsace during the eighteenth century, and Palmer (1977) notes a similar increase in Le Nord in the years after 1750. There was also considerable growth in Langedoc; Frêche (1974, 311) reports an eighteenth-
century increase of 50–60 percent in the vicinity of Toulouse. This was
not because people were actually reproducing far more rapidly in the
north and south, and not at all in the west. Instead, this pattern most
likely reflects migration from poorer areas to the wealthier regions of
the northeast and the Midi as people searched for work. Dewald (1987,
46), studying patterns of village endogamy in upper Normandy, reports
that the fraction of marriages in his sample in which both partners were
from the same village fell from 73 percent during the period 1685–1694
to 49.5 percent in the period 1780–1789.

Demographic change involved aspects other than mere population
growth. The population grew markedly younger, as each new generation
was slightly larger than its forebears. In 1700 the ratio of those aged ten
to twenty-nine years to those aged thirty and over was probably not
more than 6:10, so that the dominance of the older adults over the
younger was clear. By 1750, the ratio had risen to 8.6:10 and stayed
near 8:10 for the remainder of the century. Thus the late eighteenth
century was a period in which the fraction of younger adults, relative to

their elders, had increased by nearly a half compared to the late seventeenth century.[2]

In addition to becoming younger, the population also became more urban. Dupâquier (1978, 245) estimates that from the period 1740–1749 to the period 1780–1789, small towns increased in size by 24 percent, middling towns by 20 percent, and larger cities by 38 percent, against a rural growth of only 8.3 percent. From 1700 to 1790, Paris grew from 530,000 to 700,000 in population, or over 30 percent, while Lyon rose from 97,000 to 150,000, or over 50 percent (Dupâquier 1979, 40, 91–92). Toulouse grew by roughly 50 percent from 1715 to 1790 (Frêche 1973, 268). Strasbourg swelled by 100 percent from 1697 to 1789 (Lemoigne 1965). From 1730 to 1780, Troyes and Reims increased by 50 percent (L. Hunt 1978, 10). As Soboul (1977a, 33) notes, "the eighteenth century was an age of urban expansion."

Why did France's population increase? A population can grow as a result of immigration, higher fertility, or lower mortality. In England the population grew slightly from 1700 to 1750 because of declining mortality. Growth then accelerated dramatically because of a rise in fertility, which in turn was caused by markedly earlier marriages by women (Wrigley 1983). The fall in marriage age probably reflected increased opportunities for employment by wage workers, who tended to marry young (Goldstone 1986a). But France followed a different path. Dupâquier (1978, 1979) reports that the age of women at marriage rose throughout the eighteenth century, while the rates of both marriage and fertility within marriage were stable or slightly falling. Thus, there is no evidence that France's growth was the result of higher fertility. And since there was little migration to France from surrounding countries, virtually all the demographic increase was produced by lower mortality.

Dupâquier (1978, 240) notes that infant and juvenile mortality data from the Parisian basin show a mortality decline after 1720 of the right magnitude to account for France's eighteenth-century growth. He adds that "adult mortality did not decrease in the second half of the 18th century" (Dupâquier 1970, 162). But this should not surprise us. The typical pattern in early modern populations, as we saw for sixteenth-century England, is that variations in mortality affect mainly the young.

2. Age structures after 1740 can be calculated from data presented by Henry and Blayo (1975). For the period 1670–1690, I have relied on R. Lee's (1974) estimates of the general shape of a "stationary" population in early modern Europe, along with the knowledge that France's population was nearly stationary from 1670 to 1690. Figures for the remaining decades were then interpolated.

It is for this reason that early modern populations became markedly younger as they grew: increased survival among the young was driving the growth.

PROSPERITY OR DECLINE?

The question of whether France was "rich" or "poor" in the eighteenth century relative to the late seventeenth century continues to be hotly debated. The fall in population in the late seventeenth century has led some historians to label the reign of Louis XIV as a time of misery, marked, in particular, by great mortality crises in the periods 1661–1662 and 1693–1694 (Mandrou 1978; Meuvret 1971). Mathiez (1928), following Tocqueville (1955 [1856]), also concluded that since France's population grew in the eighteenth century, this must have been a time of relative prosperity.[3] Recently, Doyle (1980, 158) observed that "the very fact that the population had increased from . . . the beginning of the century to . . . 1789 shows that there was spare capacity to meet growing needs." But all of these impressions rest on the assumption that mortality levels reflect general standards of living. We now know that for early modern Europe this assumption is false.

Studies of the short-term consequences of famine on early modern European populations by Lebrun (1980), Poussou (1980), and Watkins and Mencken (1985) have shown that recovery can be quite rapid; those who die are the infirm or elderly who would likely have died in the next few years anyway. Children who die are quickly replaced because mothers who lose one child bear others. Thus, famines are generally followed by a compensating fall in mortality and an increase in fertility. One may say that early modern European harvest failures concentrated deaths, creating mortality peaks, but they did not raise the long-term mortality levels. As Weir (1989b, 202) has observed, "recent accumulations of demographic evidence have provided convincing proof" that "subsistence crises cannot have been the prime mover" of long-term population change.

Instead, long-term mortality levels seem much more affected by epidemic diseases (Livi-Bacci 1989; Dupâquier 1989). We have noted, in

3. Tocqueville [1856] wrote that "the fact remains that the country did grow richer and living conditions improved throughout the land." Mathiez (1928) added that "an infallible sign that the wealth of the country was increasing was that the population was growing rapidly and the prices of commodities, land, and houses were steadily rising." Both citations are from Greenlaw (1958, xv).

discussing England, that there appears to be little or no connection between economic welfare, as measured in levels of real wages, and levels of mortality. Lebrun and Poussou similarly note for France that the great mortality episodes are much less correlated with harvest failures and high grain prices than was once thought. After 1660, the plague returned to much of Europe, accompanied by smallpox and typhoid. These diseases raised mortality, particularly among the young, in France and throughout Europe. Only after 1700 did mortality generally begin to fall.

The combination of severe harvest crises in the 1660s and the 1690s and high mortality in the period 1660–1690 had led some historians to conclude that the high mortality reflected generally poor economic conditions. But in fact the thirty years between these crises were remarkable for the low and stable prices of agricultural goods. In the mid-seventeenth century, there were harvest crises in the periods 1630–1631, 1648–1653, and 1661–1662 (Briggs 1977, 38). In the following entire century from 1662 to 1760, there were only two periods of crisis, 1694–1699 and 1709–1710, when bad weather created difficulties all over Europe (Briggs 1977, 38; Meuvret 1971, 88). But toward the end of the Old Regime, there were harvest crises in the periods 1770–1775, 1778–1779, 1781–1782, 1785–1786, and 1788–1789 (Sutherland 1986, 55). Thus, harvest crises were more common when the population level was relatively high and rising. When population was stagnant, grain prices were generally low and crises were rare.

Real wage trends tell a similar story. If we deflate Durand's (1966) wage series for Parisian building workers by wheat prices, we find that the food-purchasing power of wages rose nearly 50 percent from the 1650s to the 1680s. Yet mortality levels remained high. The same calculation shows that real wages in the period 1670–1689, when mortality was high and population was stagnant, were 37 percent higher than in 1770–1789, when mortality was low and population was rapidly rising. As in England, mortality levels appear to be independent of the standard of living.

We thus cannot accept the view that the high mortality of the late seventeenth century and the low mortality of the eighteenth century indicate greater prosperity in the later period. The chronic, long-term mortality levels that affected population growth were apparently the result of shifts in the virulence of disease. Disease took its toll on the rich as well as on the poor, and on the urban dweller perhaps even more than on the rural. In an age ignorant of sanitation, disease did not respect income. But if we reject the argument from mortality levels, how can we answer the question of whether France was richer or poorer toward the end of the Old Regime than under Louis XIV? Our information on French economic output in the eighteenth century remains sketchy, but it has been greatly improved recently by studies of yields by Morineau (1970a) and by studies of tithe records, summarized by Le Roy Ladurie and Goy (1982). In addition, the price data painstakingly developed by Labrousse reveal much.

The first point to make clear, however, is that any effort to assess simply the prosperity of "France" is misguided. For it is obvious that in the eighteenth century different sectors of the French economy were growing at dramatically different rates. Thus, some parts of the economy prospered while others did poorly. In addition, income was unevenly distributed and underwent further redistribution over the course of the century, so some groups prospered while others did not. In the following discussion, I present estimates of French economic growth. But it should be remembered that some gained enormously, while many others were left out or even lost ground during such growth. Thus, proper assessment of the social and political consequences of economic change will require, along with a look at overall growth, attention to the sectoral and income divisions of the economy.

Optimistic estimates of France's eighteenth-century agricultural growth, offered by some scholars (e.g., Toutain 1961), can no longer be accepted. There were pockets of progress: yields in Le Nord were comparable to the best in England, and in Cambresis tithe records show an increase in output of 50 percent over the century (Neveux 1980). Upper Normandy also shows considerable advance in agricultural techniques and output (Le Roy Ladurie and Goy 1982, 176). But these areas were exceptional. In most of France output rose only slightly through the eighteenth century. Lemoigne (1965) shows that grain production around Strasbourg failed to keep pace with the city's growth after 1750; Frêche (1974, 311) similarly shows that near Toulouse grain output rose only 5–15 percent, much less than population increased. In both Provence and the Vivarais, despite considerable population growth, cereal production was actually less in the late eighteenth century than in the late seventeenth century (Baehrel 1961, 91; Molinier 1985, 190). Nor was there a large increase in production from the improvement of previously uncultivated land. Labrousse (1970b, 429–430) estimates that additions to cultivated land from 1730 to 1789 amounted to less than 4 percent of the existing arable. Tithe figures drawn from across France have led Le Roy Ladurie and Goy (1982, 175–176) to conclude that cereal production rose only 20 percent in the eighteenth century.

Prices for farms, and for farming out of tithes, show an increase of 120–150 percent from the period 1730–1739 to the period 1780–1789 (Labrousse 1970b, 455–459), which might suggest major strides in output. But much of this increase was inflation, for the price of agricultural goods rose nearly 70 percent in the interval (Labrousse 1984). Moreover, we know that rents rose by only 100 percent in this period, so the price of farms was evidently going up faster than the returns they provided (Labrousse 1984, 2:379). The rise in farm prices tells us only that land was becoming relatively scarce, not that output was rising.

Le Roy Ladurie and Goy (1982, 176) do suggest, assuming France was able to feed its population at a constant level, that since the population rose 30 percent from 1700 to 1789, real output must have risen the same amount. Since cereal output rose only 20 percent, they conclude that the remaining increase came from maize, potatoes, rice, chestnuts, wine, olive oil, beans, and forage crops. Yet this seems unlikely—the numbers simply do not add up. If cereals were only 60 percent of total agricultural output, and rose by 20 percent, then for total agricultural output to nonetheless increase by 30 percent the output of all other agricultural goods must have risen by 45 percent, or more than twice as much as cereals. But the price of beans and hay rose as rapidly as, or more rapidly than, the price of cereals; this hardly indicates that they had become far more plentiful than grain. The price of wine did fall relative to that of grain, indicating markedly higher increases in output. But this may also reflect changes in demand, for as grain and legumes grew more scarce and expensive, per capita wine consumption might well have fallen. Olive oil was important in the Midi, as were chestnuts in the Massif Central and maize in the southeast. But none of these was a staple in the central and northeast regions, where most of the population growth was concentrated, and so could not compensate for the deficiency in cereals. Perhaps most conclusively, as we have noted, real wages were 37 percent lower in the period 1770–1789 than in the period 1670–1689. Thus a substantial portion of the population was consuming far *less* per capita at the end of the eighteenth century than at its outset. With this in mind, we have no reason to assume simply that total food consumption, and hence output, were keeping pace with population growth.

The conclusion that food production must have kept pace with population may also stem from the assumption that the peasantry was already miserable and impoverished under Louis XIV; thus, any further fall in food output per capita would have resulted in widespread starvation, which is not evident in the eighteenth century. In fact, this view rests on false premises, for the late seventeenth century was a time of relative prosperity for the peasants, and of relatively high real wages for workers. There was thus "room" for a decline in living standards without immediate starvation ensuing. And as Hufton (1974) has pointed out in her superb survey of poverty in eighteenth-century France, improvements in roads and state administration of relief meant that the burdens of food shortage were now more evenly distributed. So whereas before, a local shortage meant that a fair number of people actually starved, in the eighteenth century a large number of people survived but were chronically undernourished. Relative emancipation from plague and from famine thus did not bring better living standards. Quite the reverse occurred; as Hufton (1974, 15) notes, the lower mortality of the eighteenth century simply created "a greater number of poor than ever before."

Table 6 presents Labrousse's (1984) data on price increases, drawn from a national data pool, for a variety of goods. The first column gives the ratio between prices in the period 1780–1789 and those in the period 1730–1739.[4] For example, wheat prices increased 67 percent, beans rose 61 percent, and hay rose 78 percent.[5] The remaining three columns give the purchasing power, relative to the period 1730–1739, of a constant unit of wheat and of incomes derived from labor and land. Thus in the period 1780–1789, one unit of wheat could buy 3.7 percent more beans, but 6.2 percent less hay, than in the earlier period. Judging from the relative price of goods to wheat in the second column, it appears that most agricultural goods, with the exception of wine, were not much more plentiful relative to wheat in the 1780s than in the 1730s. Raw wool was cheaper relative to wheat, but flax was more expensive. Meat and tallow were slightly cheaper, but wood slightly more costly. There is no evidence that, on average, noncereal agricultural output increased more than twice as rapidly as cereal output.

In sum, France's cereal output rose by roughly 20 percent over the

4. I have used the baseline of 1730–1739 because until 1726 the French currency was highly unstable owing to monetary manipulation by the Crown. The price of wheat in *livres tournois* was virtually the same in the periods 1700–1709 and 1730–1739, but fluctuations in the silver content of the livre make it difficult to compare nominal prices for commodities in the first quarter of the eighteenth century with prices in later decades.

5. Price increases for other cereals—barley, oats, and rye—were nearly identical (Labrousse 1984, 1:175, 189, 229).

TABLE SIX   FRENCH PRICES, 1730–1789

	Percentage Increase in Prices, 1730–1739 to 1780–1789	Relative Purchasing Power in 1780–1789 Compared with 1730–1739 (in percent)		
		Wheat	Labor	Rent
Wheat	.67	100	75.4	118.6
Beans	.61	103.7	78.3	123.0
Hay	.78	93.8	70.8	111.2
Meat	.59	105.0	79.2	124.5
Wine	.12	149.1	112.5	176.8
Tallow	.55	107.7	81.3	127.7
Iron	.32	126.5	95.5	150.0
Wool	.47	113.6	85.7	134.7
Flax	.94	86.1	64.9	102.1
Wood	.73	96.5	72.8	114.5
Linen cloth	.33	125.6	94.7	148.9
Wool cloth	.24	134.7	101.6	159.7
Land (rent)	.98	84.3	63.6	100.0
Labor (salary)	.26	132.5	100.0	157.1

course of the eighteenth century. Other food and forage crops—beans and hay—did not become much more plentiful. Thus, a base estimate of agricultural increase is 20 percent. A more optimistic view, assuming that noncereal output grew faster than that of cereals (as seems likely for wine), raises this figure to perhaps 25 percent. But the evidence seems clear that the most important part of the agricultural economy— cereals, legumes, and forage crops—increased only two-thirds as much as the population.

Figure 6 shows how the trend of wheat prices followed that of population from 1650 to 1789. As we saw in the previous chapter for England, the trends match closely, indicating the close relationship between population change—including both overall growth, which boosts demand, and urbanization, which boosts the velocity of money—and food prices in a relatively inflexible agrarian economy.

These price changes cannot simply be attributed to changes in the money supply. Riley and McCusker (1983) and Riley (1984) have shown that there was little correspondence between French price movements and money stocks from 1650 to 1788. They report that in this period "the money stock grew most rapidly when prices were stable, and least rapidly when prices were rising" (Riley and McCusker 1983, 275). It appears that, as in England, changes in demand due to population shifts best account for the movement of prices.

It is instructive to repeat the exercise, undertaken with data on England in chapter 2, of deriving a more precise estimate of the relationship between price and population movements. Following Hoskins's (1964) procedure for England, I have computed a "harvest quality" index for France, derived from the difference between the average wheat price in a given decade and the average across the thirty-year period centered on that decade. If the decade-average price was within 5 percent of the thirty-year average, a harvest score of 0 was given. If the decade-average price was beyond this range, a point was then added (or subtracted) for each 5 percent increment above (or below) the thirty-year average price. For example, in the 1690s the average price of wheat was 20 percent higher than in the period 1680–1709; thus, this decade received a harvest quality score of 4. In the 1730s, the average price of wheat was 14 percent less than the average for the period 1720–1749; thus, this decade received a score of -2. As the movement of population and the harvest quality index for the period 1650–1789 are almost completely uncorrelated ($r = .045$), the index provides a way of separating the short-term price variation caused by harvest fluctuations from the long-term variation caused by population shifts.

Table 7 shows that by simply taking movements in population and in harvest quality, one can explain 93 percent of the variation in decade-average wheat prices in France from 1650 to 1789. (Harvest variation alone, incidentally, explains less than 20 percent of the variation.) In England, it was also necessary to incorporate a time trend (t) to account for progress in agriculture, which lowered prices. In fact, the best fit for England utilized a time-cubed trend, indicating rapidly accelerating agricultural progress toward 1750. But for French prices, the addition of a time-trend term to the equation, whether linear or polynomial, added nothing to the explanatory power of the model. Moreover, the time-trend terms were statistically nonsignificant. Thus, no time-trend coefficient appears in table 7, since for France there *was no* tendency for agricultural prices to fall before the end of the Old Regime. This is an interesting confirmation of Le Roy Ladurie's (1974a) suggestion that

TABLE SEVEN   REGRESSION RESULTS FOR FRENCH
PRICES AND WAGES, 1650–1789

Variable	Regression Coefficients[a]	
	ln (prices)	ln (wages)
ln (population)	1.94	−.86
Harvest	.0585	−.035
Constant	−3.72	7.26
Rho	.605	.466
R^2	.928	.770

[a] All coefficients significant at $p < .05$; GLS corrected for first-order serial correlation.

French agriculture during the Old Regime had an "histoire immobile," or a fixed ceiling.

However, aside from the impact of agricultural progress, grain prices reacted to population change in France in much the same way as in England. In both countries, if one controls for harvest fluctuations and long-term progress, the effect of a 1 percent rise in population was about a 2 percent rise in prices (2.24 percent in England and 1.94 percent in France, a difference that, given the crudeness of the data, is not significant).

Though French agriculture lagged behind population growth, the same was not true of trade and industry, which were booming. As can be seen in table 6, the prices for industrial products—linen cloth, wool cloth, and iron—became much cheaper in relation to wheat and hardly rose at all compared to wages. This was true even though some raw materials for these industries, for example flax and wood (for charcoal), were becoming more expensive. It thus appears that the output of industrial goods was handily keeping pace with demand. And demand for manufactures must have risen far more rapidly than population, since the more rapid growth of the cities meant increased demand for iron to make nails needed for construction and demand for more and better clothing than was worn by country dwellers. Markovitch (1976, 458–459) estimates that the volume of coarse (unfinished) wool cloth produced in France increased by 40 percent from the period 1716–1718 to the period 1785–1787, and this seems reasonable in terms of meeting a greatly expanded demand at a nearly constant cost (in terms of real wage equivalents). The increase in the volume of finished wool cloth was even higher: 76 percent from 1716–1718 to 1785–1787. Thus, total output was not only increasing but also shifting in the direction of higher value-added production. Labrousse (1970d, 548) adds that the production of linen at Rouen rose 66 percent from the 1730s to the 1750s. However, he finds that net growth from 1740 to 1780 was nil, owing to recession in the 1780s; this is a problem we address later.

Among the manufactured goods for which Labrousse provides price series, wool cloth shows the smallest price rise. This suggests that other manufactures were not growing as rapidly, relative to demand. Tallow for candles, in particular, shows more inflation. Léon (1970, 517) suggests that the metal trades increased their output by 200 percent in the eighteenth century, and Marczewski (1961, 371) offers the optimistic suggestion that total French manufactures grew at a similar pace. But these are only rough estimates and are probably inflated, as was our estimate of French agriculture before the study of tithe returns. It is prudent, in view of Markovitch's (1976) careful analysis of the wool industry, and in view of evidence that wool prices fell more rapidly than those of most manufactures, to take the increase in finished wool cloth output as an outer bound for the growth of all manufactures. Thus, a reasonable estimate for the eighteenth-century growth of manufactured products is 80 percent. This is more than three times the growth of agriculture and more than double the rate of population growth.

There is some further evidence for this growth rate in the wage regression shown in table 7. In England from 1500 to 1749, every 1 percent increase in population led to a 1.78 percent decline in real wages. In France from 1650 to 1789, though population growth still burdened the labor market, the resulting wage decline was only half as severe: a 1 percent increase in population produced only a .86 percent decline in real wages. This difference reflects that the English wage decline in this estimation occurred chiefly in the decades before the English Revolution, when industrial expansion was modest and unable to absorb the excess population generated in agriculture. In France, however, the wage decline is being measured for a later period, 1650–1789; and toward the end of this period, when population was rising, industrial expansion was considerable. Thus more (though clearly still not enough) of the "excess" population in France could be absorbed by manufacturing.

In addition to agriculture and manufacturing, France in the eighteenth century was making large gains from trade. The volume of trade, for which there are good data from customs records, rose from 215 million livres to 1,062 million livres in current prices, or 400 percent, including both foreign and domestic commerce (Leon 1970, 502; Crouzet 1970). Even allowing for inflation, which was about 69 percent in wheat prices from the period 1700–1709 to the period 1780–1789, this is remarkable growth. In real terms, it is still an increase of 196 percent.

How much did each sector contribute to France's total output? Estimates for agriculture's share in physical output in 1789 range from 57 percent (Marczewski 1965) to 73 percent (Perroux 1955). Dupeaux (1976, 105) maintains that agriculture's share in total output was 75 percent by value as late as 1830! Marczewski's estimate seems too low. The portion of the French population engaged in agriculture circa 1789 is estimated to have been 75–80 percent (O'Brien and Keyder 1978, 94; Mayer 1953, 91). The productivity of the remaining 20 percent would need to have been three times that of their neighbors in agriculture to account for a 43 percent share of production. In contrast, under Perroux's share estimate, the ratio of productivity in manufacturing to productivity in agriculture would be a much more reasonable 1.5:1. This is in fact the ratio preferred by O'Brien and Keyder (1978). Thus, I shall use Perroux's share estimate as a guide.

The contribution of trade is estimated by Riley (1986, 21) to have raised national output by an additional 6 percent. All of these estimates, of course, exclude the service sector of the economy, which is difficult to measure. Maza (1983, 81) shows that salaries for maids in Paris rose more rapidly than the normal run of wages, which suggests a rapid expansion of services. But in general, services do not generate the kind of output that can be taxed by an early modern government. Thus, for examining the political impact of economic growth, we can continue to concentrate on trade and the production of physical resources.

If we accept the growth rates for the agricultural, industrial, and trade sectors presented above, 25 percent, 80 percent, and 196 percent respectively, and project backward from Perroux's estimates of shares in 1789, we arrive at the estimate of 36.3 percent for total growth in France's economy from 1700 to 1789 in real terms. (I have deflated wheat prices by 69 percent and manufactured goods prices by 47.2 percent, as the latter rose in price more slowly. All nominal prices were then converted to bushels of wheat equivalent. These GNP estimates are shown in table 8 and explained more fully in the Appendix.) Thus it seems fair to conclude that France in toto was substantially richer in 1789 than in 1700. Even when we allow for population growth, there was a modest growth of 4.3 percent in real per capita output.

Yet most individual Frenchmen were not better off in 1789. This is because of the enormous discrepancy in shares. Roughly four-fifths of the population earned its living in agriculture, where output per capita had *fallen* by 4.3 percent over the course of the century. In contrast, the remaining fifth of the population, who earned their living from manufacturing and trade, worked in a sector where real output rose almost 30 percent per capita. Those who worked in the colonial trade of the coastal ports worked in a sector where growth was far greater still. For the urban, commercial, and manufacturing centers, the eighteenth century, especially before the late-century recession, was a time of rising prosperity and growing wealth. Of course, this commercial prosperity was further concentrated in the hands of merchants, shopkeepers, landowners, and professionals, all of whom had an advantageous position as beneficiaries of expanding markets. The urban wage earners initially shared in this expansion as employment opportunities increased, but they eventually found the value of their wages eroded by the rise in food prices.

Landes (1950) has analyzed this problem of unbalanced growth in an early modern economy. At first, the growth in population and in manufactures signals prosperity for all. Those in the manufacturing sector bid up the price of foodstuffs, which gives agriculturalists the income to buy more manufactures. Manufacturers can then hire more workers, absorbing the additions to the labor force. This is a period of rising prices and economic growth. However, if the agricultural sector continues to lag, prices for food will continue to rise to the point where workers will cut back on consumption of manufactures in order to feed their families. There then ensues an industrial recession brought on by underconsumption.

Hufton (1980, 323) has identifed the 1760s as the "crucial turning point in French economic growth. . . . [F]rom that juncture there seems to have been, in many regions, an evident imbalance between population and supply." Kaplan (1976, 2:489) notes that in the 1770s, the run of harvest shortfalls and sharply rising grain prices "led to a severe contraction in purchasing power, widespread unemployment in the countryside and in the cities, lagging wages, serious indebtedness, an extraordinary wave of business failures affecting petty artisans as well as great financiers, and an industrial recession."

In the remainder of this chapter I trace how these trends affected various elements in French society: the state, elites, urban artisans, and the peasantry. However, the main points of the discussion should already be clear. France in the eighteenth century was becoming wealthier, but it was an unbalanced growth that could not be sustained. The failure of agricultural growth to keep pace with population increase meant that expansion rested on a weak base. As scarcity of foodstuffs led to rising prices, the remaining purchasing power of the population was eroded, leading to a commercial recession. Moreover, the French state remained shackled to land taxes. Despite increased excise and trade taxes, the state was unable to tap fully the expanding incomes in manufacture and commerce. Continuing to rest chiefly on taxes on agricultural land, the monarchy found itself supported by an ever weaker, more tightly stretched economic base. Thus vulnerable, the Crown depended more and more on loans and on a small circle of wealthy financiers to meet its fiscal needs. When recession toppled the financiers, the monarchy itself was thrown into crisis. Unbalanced growth thus had both severe and unforeseen consequences.

In the next section, I briefly sketch the fiscal, elite, and popular responses to population and price trends under Louis XIV. I then examine these responses in more detail for the period from 1700 to 1789, showing how they shaped the crisis of the Old Regime.

FRANCE UNDER LOUIS XIV

Historians are sharply divided in their opinions of Louis XIV's reign (1643–1715). As noted earlier, many have construed the fall in population, the decline in wheat prices, and the famine crises of the 1690s and of 1709–1710 as evidence that Louis XIV exhausted and impoverished his country. But this view is directly contradicted by some acute observers. Vauban, and later Voltaire, looked back to the period 1660–1689 as a time when France was more prosperous than in the late eighteenth century (Jacquart 1974b, 180; Le Roy Ladurie 1974a, 235).

As we have seen, one's view depended on where one stood in the economy. For most French men and women, the key fact was that in the late seventeenth century, France produced roughly 4 percent *more* total agricultural output per capita than in the late eighteenth century. Perhaps more importantly, if we focus on cereals, French output in 1700 was 9 percent higher per capita than in 1789. As a result, wheat prices in the period 1660–1700 were lower than in either of the periods of higher population, that is, the early seventeenth and late eighteenth centuries. Whether measured in *livres tournois* or in grams of silver, the price of wheat in the period 1670–1689 was only about two-thirds as high as in the 1650s and 1660s. The poor harvests of the 1690s and again in 1709–1710 raised prices, but in the decade 1700–1709 prices were still 20 percent lower than in the 1660s (Baulant 1972, 40–41; silver conversion from Goubert 1973a, 75). Goubert (1970c, 337) describes the decades after 1662 as having "a habitually very low level of food prices."

These low prices particularly benefited two elements at opposite ends of French society: the Crown, and small peasants and workers. The incomes of large landowners fell, however, making them more dependent on the Crown for wealth and position. Thus, the three pillars of Louis XIV's absolutism—royal spending, noble dependency on the Crown, and a peaceful peasantry—were in large part achieved thanks to a favorable price trend produced by the demographic shift of the late seventeenth century.

The Crown, relative to the 1660s, found that in the 1670s and 1680s a given amount of money collected in taxes now purchased 50 percent more grain! This windfall allowed Louis XIV and his ministers to build a vast patronage network and the largest armies in Europe, without major increases in the nominal level of direct taxes. Beik (1985, 144–145) notes that in Languedoc "the inescapable conclusion is that taxes [in money] did not rise that much between 1633 and 1690, although they fluctuated greatly. The rise between 1600 and 1710 was massive, but once the threshold of 1632 was crossed, neither Richelieu, nor Mazarin, nor Louis XIV made significant gains except during brief emergencies." Bonney (1978a, 173), looking at royal revenues from all of France, finds that the yield from the *taille* in livres peaked in 1644. From 1660 to 1690 he estimates that the *taille* fell to roughly 30 million livres from its level of 40 million livres in 1665.

Still, by the 1690s these taxes no longer sufficed to meet Louis XIV's needs. Waging war on a vast scale almost continously from 1689 to 1714 required higher revenues. A capitation tax was levied in the period 1695–1698 and renewed in 1701. A *dixième* was imposed in 1710. In addition, the Crown borrowed vast sums from financiers, sold offices, and raised indirect taxes—the salt tax (*gabelle*), customs duties, and excises. By 1715, the Crown's debts had reached 2 billion livres, against an annual ordinary revenue of 120 million livres. Bankruptcy was thus inevitable (Mousnier 1951, 3–4; Briggs 1977, 218–220). What is remarkable, however, is not that Louis XIV's bankruptcy occurred, for this was a commonplace event in the finances of early modern monarchies, but rather that he was able to avoid bankruptcy for twenty-five years of war, while massively expanding the French bureaucracy and military efforts. In contrast, Louis XVI was driven to bankruptcy by a modest and victorious overseas war, which had followed almost two decades of peace. Clearly, the ability of France to sustain the expenses of war was greater under Louis XIV. And much of this ability can be traced to the windfall effects of cheaper grain and a wealthier per capita peasantry.

The smaller peasants and craftsmen also did well in the late seventeenth century; as Le Roy Ladurie (1978, 261) observes, this was "une epoque qui n'est pas trop mauvaise pour les petit gens." For the peasantry, the main concern was access to land. And with the population level down by perhaps 20 percent from the midcentury peak, land was available. Landlords repeatedly lowered their rents: in Montpellier, for example, rents measured in silver fell 15 percent from the period 1650–1669 to the period 1670–1689, then another 50 percent to the early eighteenth century (Morineau 1977, 182; Jacquart 1975; Goubert 1970c, 338–342). A smaller population also meant smaller families, so that the subdivision of properties that had impoverished the peasantry "was finally checked by the . . . Colbert period" (Le Roy Ladurie 1974a, 257). And for those who also had to support their families by engaging in wage labor, the fall in population created a tighter labor market, so that real wages were almost 40 percent higher from 1670 to 1700 (except during the bad harvest years of the early 1690s) than in the 1650s.

The lower prices for wheat did not hurt most small peasants, who fed their families with homegrown grain while supplementing their cash incomes with wage labor. In addition, higher cash incomes were available from viniculture. The late seventeenth century was a boom period in wine, for higher real wages greatly increased the market for ordinary wines made for daily consumption. The price of wine rose 50 percent from the middle to the late seventeenth century, and vines were planted everywhere they could grow (Goubert 1973a, 73–74; de Vries 1976, 67).

Sum up the situation of the peasantry in the late seventeenth century—land available at lower rents, a lucrative cash crop in wine whose value was steadily rising, the *taille* stable, and rising real wages for those who needed work—and it is not surprising that "after 1675 . . . there were indeed . . . a great many disturbances and petty local revolts, but on the whole nothing very serious. . . . [T]he revolts of 1675 were the last that can be considered great social and political movements" (Mousnier 1970b, 115). Le Roy Ladurie (1974b, 7) also comments on the "remarkable" disappearance, after 1675, of the peasant uprisings, which had been "almost epidemic" from 1548 to 1675. Given the favorable population and price trends, however, this new calm is not remarkable but a clear reflection of the forces of the market, which now favored peasants at the expense of landlords.

Landlords, faced with higher labor costs and a lower price for their cereal crops, were hurt badly. Some holders of small to medium-size estates went bankrupt and were bought out by wealthy aristocrats who, well positioned to endure lower prices, purchased the land at bargain rates. There was thus some concentration of land in the hands of the very wealthy during this period (M. Bloch 1966, 139–142; Le Roy Ladurie 1974a). But for the most part it was a period in which landlords looked to the state, rather than to their lands, to raise their fortunes. Louis XIV thus found local notables, who had been so truculent under Richelieu and Mazarin, more than willing to accept places in the official hierarchy in return for pensions and royal favor. As Cobban (1957, 1:14) remarks, "Louis had not so much suppressed the declining aristocratic elements in the state as bought them off at a high price, by the perpetuation of their exemptions from financial burdens and the grant of sinecures and pensions at the expense of the royal revenue."

There was a silver lining for landlords, however, in the form of reduced intra-elite competition. In the decades before 1650, rising prices had allowed modest proprietors to accumulate profits, which they used to buy their way into the elite. There was thus a vast turnover in the lower offices of the municipalities and courts, and a "penetration *en masse*" of the nobility by newcomers (M. Bloch 1966, 125). But after 1650 the opportunities to rise by commercial profits receded. Thus, the rates of social mobility sharply diminished. "After the great expansion of the elite which had characterized the earlier period, changes were now largely confined to shifts within the existing privileged groups" (Briggs 1977, 153). Salmon (1981, 255) notes that from 1653 to 1673, 66 percent of new councillors entering the Parlement of Paris were sons of councillors. Beik (1985, 91) notes that in Languedoc the "age of turbulence" in the turnover of royal officers "was largely over by 1660." The number of new councillors entering the Parlement of Toulouse was exceptionally low in the period 1661–1681; and Beik (1985, 93) considers "the fact that the same men ruled so consistently for so long may have contributed to the stability and regularity of Louis XIV's rule." This "stabilization of society" was largely a product of the new demographic and economic situation.

Louis XIV's success in building absolutism thus depended on a favorable economic conjuncture. He did not so much rebuild the French state as simply expand it. The basis of revenues remained direct taxes on the land, supplemented by indirect taxes and borrowing. The basis of elite recruitment remained family connections and royal favor. Louis purchased the loyalty of the elite with tax exemptions, pensions, and privileges. He could afford to pay because his land taxes fell on a peasantry that was, then, per capita, richer than at any other time in either the seventeenth or eighteenth century. The price of elite loyalty was also relatively cheap, for the fall in income from land meant that elites looked to the state for advancement. As a further benefit, higher mortality meant that elite families were not increasing in size, and falling prices meant that there were few newly enriched families seeking elite positions; thus, the size of the elite group whose loyalty needed to be purchased was stable.

But what would happen to Louis XIV's system if population growth began to outstrip production, so that the peasant tax base grew poorer per capita; if scarcity of grain drove up prices, so that existing taxes provided a lower real state revenue; and if rising prices and land scarcity allowed landlords to raise rents and get richer independent of the state, so that they no longer depended as much on royal favor for advancement? And what if the expansion of markets and falling real wages led manufacturers and urban professionals to gain wealth rapidly, so that the pool of aspirants to elite status dramatically expanded; and if the aspirations of this expanding pool of newly wealthy collided with the promise of privilege that had purchased noble loyalty under Louis XIV? And what if at the same time population growth and land scarcity raised rents, created a larger and poorer urban population, drove down popular living standards, and heightened the conflict between peasants and landlords?

Louis XIV's successors soon found out.

B. THE DEVELOPING CRISIS OF FRENCH ABSOLUTISM, 1700–1789

FRENCH FINANCES

Until recently, the loss of official fiscal documents in fires had made any study of eighteenth-century French finances difficult. However, ministers privately kept a close eye on state finances, as did foreign observers. By studying these private and diplomatic documents, Riley (1986, 1987) and Morineau (1980) have reconstructed state accounts for much of the century.

French royal income consisted of ordinary revenues from taxation and "extraordinary" income from sale of offices and royal assets and from loans. In the eighteenth century the direct taxes on land were chiefly the *taille*, but also the capitation and the *dixième* and *vingtième*.[6] The latter two were intended to be proportional taxes on all income but, as discussed later, in practice became simply additions to the *taille*. The annual "gift" of the clergy was also primarily a land tax, as agricultural tithes were the main source of church income. These direct taxes, and other landed revenue from such sources as royal domains and forests, made up just over half the ordinary royal income throughout the eighteenth century (Morineau 1980, 314).[7] The remaining ordinary revenues came from customs duties on trade and excise taxes on consumer products, including the salt tax (*gabelle*). The customs and excise taxes were generally farmed out, an arrangement in which the tax farmer provided the king with an agreed-upon sum, which was the estimated yield of the tax less the costs of collection and a profit for the tax farmer. Although this arrangement reduced the net yield to the treasury, it provided the Crown with regular and predictable revenues, while shifting the burdens of information gathering and collection delays to private financiers. (It also shifted the focus of resentment against indirect taxes from the Crown to the financiers, who were reviled for profiting from the public purse.) In the first decade of the eighteenth century, total ordinary income was about 120 million livres per year (Briggs 1977, 218; Forbonnias 1758, 4:167, 397).

However, this income did not suffice in times of war; thus, the Crown resorted to extraordinary or irregular sources of income: sales of offices,

6. The *dixième* and *vingtième*, because they were issued for fixed periods rather than for perpetuity, as were the *taille* and *gabelle* and other ordinary taxes, are often considered "extraordinary" taxes (Riley 1986, 55). However, since they were imposed with some regularity in the eighteenth century and were simply decreed collections (like the ordinary taxes) at fixed amounts, I have grouped them with the ordinary revenues in order to distinguish them from what were called *affaires extraordinaires*. These latter—including the sale of offices and loans—involved voluntary subscription, rather than imposition, and required later servicing; hence they raised current income at a deferred cost. Thus in this discussion, "ordinary revenues" means all revenues that provided an anticipatable regular income, even if some of these were for limited, and others for unlimited, durations.

7. I have included as indirect taxes those labeled by Morineau as "impôts indirects" and "autre." I have included as direct taxes both those that Morineau labels "impôts directs" and those cited as contributions of the domain, clergy, and the *don gratuits* of *pays d'états*, which were all primarily levies on the land.

anticipations of ordinary revenues from future years, and, above all, long-term borrowing. In war years, this extraordinary income could easily exceed the ordinary revenues. The security of royal finances thus depended on the ability to borrow in times of need. This in turn meant that the ordinary revenue had to be sufficient not only to pay the ordinary expenses of the Crown—salaries and household expenses, military and diplomatic expenses, pensions, and the costs of tax collection and local justice and administration—but also to provide an ordinary, or peacetime, surplus to cover interest on war debts. Thus in war, the king would borrow and spend more than his ordinary income; in peace, the king would service the loans by using the difference between ordinary revenues and ordinary expenses to fund the interest.

This process could be interrupted in two ways. If war was constant, so that the debt increased year after year, then eventually the margin of ordinary income over ordinary expenditures would become insufficient to service the debt, and bankruptcy would result. This is what happened to Louis XIV after the nearly continuous wars from 1689 to 1714. A second path to failure was if the ordinary revenues failed to keep pace with ordinary expenditures, eliminating the margin available for debt service in peacetime. There would then be insufficient funds to service the debt, and bankruptcy would also follow. This is what happened to Calonne and Louis XVI in the period 1787–1789.

THE SURPRISING FISCAL CRISIS OF 1787–1789

Contemporaries were shocked by the fiscal crisis of 1787–1789. Even today, historians are often confused about how this crisis developed, and have difficulty grasping why it touched off a political firestorm. Some economic historians, for example Weir (1989a) and E. White (1989), have pointed out that the debts of Louis XVI in 1789 were smaller, relative to both royal income and French economic output, than the debts of Louis XIV, who left France bankrupt in 1714. Yet the earlier bankruptcy did not lead to demands for reform of the monarchy. Weir and White therefore argue that the debt itself could not have been the real problem; rather, some other, more political factors in the relationship of the Crown to its creditors must have been responsible for the outcry touched off by the Crown's admission of bankruptcy in 1787.

Merely comparing the magnitude of the debt in 1789 with that in 1714 does not begin to explain the Crown's difficulties in the later period, however. Bankruptcy, after all, does not depend on the size of one's debts, but on one's ability to pay. What mattered in 1787–1789 was that the Crown had insufficient revenues to service its debts, even though its tax revenues were greater than ever. Contemporaries agreed that French taxation was unfair; they did *not* believe it was too low. Thus the Crown's shocking and (to contemporaries) inexplicable inability to service its debts created consternation among the French elite. Many members of the Assembly of Notables, to whom Calonne first revealed the monarchy's plight, simply did not believe the monarchy's accounts, nor did they accept the need for the fundamental reforms that Calonne proposed (Doyle 1989, 71–74). Instead, they decided this extraordinary claim of bankruptcy, and the accompanying request for broad new taxes, required consulting the nation's representatives in the Estates General. The fiscal crisis provoked a political firestorm not because the debt problem was unusually large, but because, to most Frenchmen, the Crown's inability to service its debts was *mysterious.*

The mystery stemmed from the failure of contemporaries, like many modern historians, to understand clearly the two paths to bankruptcy described above. The French elite realized that if their nation fought lengthy and expensive wars, as France did under Louis XIV from 1689 to 1714, financial exhaustion and bankruptcy were likely to follow. Thus contemporaries knew that the bankruptcy of 1714 was caused by Louis XIV's wars, and the losses to financiers and taxpayers in the ensuing financial shocks—the *lit de justice* of 1716, the currency devaluation during the years 1716–1725, and the collapse of John Law's system—could be understood as the normal losses that accrue to war and fiscal speculation. The Crown's policies might have been ruinous, but the reasons for the fiscal crisis were generally understood.

In contrast, the financial crisis of 1787–1789 seemed incomprehensible. France had been at peace not only since 1783, but for all except six years from 1763. Most elites saw that French manufacturing and trade had greatly expanded, and that peasants were heavily taxed. They therefore expected that, since France was richer than ever, the heavy taxes should have yielded enough revenue to easily service the Crown's debts. What elites did not realize was that that tax revenues had not grown apace with the growth of trade and manufacture, but had remained shackled to stagnant agriculture; that inflation had eroded the real value of taxation; and that population growth and heightened social mobility had greatly increased the Crown's ordinary expenditures on poor relief, administration and law enforcement, and patronage and pensions, so that the surplus in ordinary revenues and, therefore, the Crown's ability to service its past debts, were being eaten away. I shall discuss these matters in greater detail below. The key fact is that in 1787 the Crown had arrived at bankruptcy by a path—subtle erosion of the ordinary surplus—that most French elites did not comprehend, instead of by the more easily understood path of lengthy and ruinous wars.

We should also note that in the eighteenth century, the French Crown did not make its fiscal records public. People therefore judged the French Crown's fiscal strength and creditworthiness on circumstantial evidence: whether the kingdom was at war or peace, whether or not the economy was growing, and whether or not the monarchy was spending freely. French financial ministers, despite fiscal problems, therefore tried to keep up appearances. After 1763, the Crown continued to spend generously on pomp and pensions, paid generous rates of interest on its borrowing, and assured the French public that the American War of Independence had been adequately financed through public debt without any difficulties. Given the glowing circumstantial evidence of the late eighteenth century—a long period of peace since 1763, broken only by the successful and easily financed participation in the American War of Independence in the years 1778–1783; a larger economy, with greatly increased trade and manufacturing sectors; and a monarchy that seemed generous to its friends and creditors—by all customary expectations the monarchy should have been in excellent financial health.

Calonne's announcement that bankruptcy was imminent and a major revision in the tax system was necessary was therefore greeted in many quarters with shock and disbelief. As recently as 1781, Necker, then Louis XVI's director of the treasury, had published an account that showed finances to be sound. The announcement of bankruptcy in 1787 was unexpected and inexplicable in customary terms; many assumed that gross corruption, malfeasance, and irresponsibility of the Crown, or of Calonne himself, must have been at fault. Popular fascination with Necker's first public account of French finances (the *Compte rendu*), the controversy over Calonne's versus Necker's accounts, and the demands of the Assembly of Notables to see the fiscal records can be understood only when we realize that, by customary standards, French finances in 1789 should have been sound. The announcement that the ordinary accounts were in deficit by over 100 million livres a year therefore created a sensation (R. Harris 1979, 1986; Gruder 1984a).

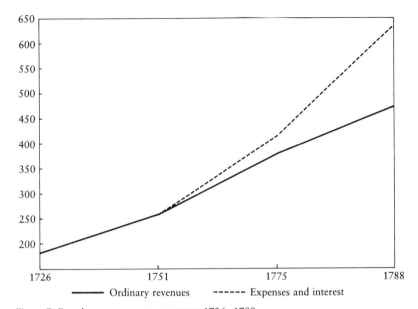

Figure 7. French revenues versus expenses, 1726–1788
Note: Both revenues and expenses expressed in millions of livres tournois.

In fact, to understand the genesis of the French fiscal crisis we need to look at the connections between population increase, inflation, and the French tax system in a manner rather different from that of the contemporaries of 1789.

The turning point in French finances appears to have occurred in the 1760s. Prior to the Seven Years' War, the French government had sufficient revenues to run a surplus in peacetime to service its debts. After the 1760s, "because the necessary expenses of government—defense, civil administration, the court—could not be forgone, and because the burden of debt service was so large, the treasury [had] to go to the capital markets each year to borrow large sums. The era of large peacetime deficits was at hand. . . . No longer were the ordinary revenues . . . sufficient to meet expenses" (Riley 1986, 232). The dilemma is clearly depicted in figure 7. But to understand it we need to ask, how rich was France, and how heavily was it taxed? How large were the debt burdens imposed by the Seven Years' War and the American War of Independence in relation to France's resources? Why were taxes not sufficient to meet the burden of debt service?

FRENCH INCOME AND TAXATION

France was certainly rich enough to meet its debts. Nor was the American War of Independence particularly ruinous: that war in fact cost less than either the Seven Years' War or the War of the Austrian Succession, relative to royal revenues (Morineau 1980, 325). The difficulty lay not in insufficient wealth but rather in the French tax system, which depended on revenues from the weakest sector of the economy.

Tables 8 and 9 present a summary of data on the growth of national income and taxation in France, compared with that of England (including Wales). All items were calculated in current livres or pounds and then converted to bushels of wheat at national average prices to simplify comparison.[8] I have divided total output into that from agriculture and that from industry and trade. In addition, I have divided taxes into direct taxes, which I have assigned here to the agricultural sector, and indirect taxes, mostly customs and excise, which I have assigned to industry and trade. In fact, some indirect taxes were paid by cultivators, particularly the French salt tax. Thus, table 8 probably underestimates the burden of taxation on agriculture in France.

In terms of total output, France was an extremely wealthy country; its total output (excluding services) in 1789 was equivalent to 975 million bushels of wheat, compared to under 300 million for England. In per capita terms, though, England was slightly richer, with real income about 13.5 percent higher per person in 1789. This reflects the faster growth in England, where real per capita output rose 18.5 percent from 1700 to 1789, compared to 4.3 percent in France.

Oddly, England's edge did not come from superior performance in agriculture. England's agricultural output did grow much faster than France's, at a rate of 46 percent versus 25 percent. But England's population grew much faster as well, so that in per capita terms both England and France suffered a fall in agricultural output of about 4 percent in this period.

In trade and industry, France's output was almost twice as large as England's (the equivalent of 306 million versus 164 million bushels of wheat), and France generated a larger total gain in output from 1700 to 1789 (the equivalent of 126 million bushels of wheat versus 88 million for England). Moreover, per capita growth in French industry, at nearly

8. These tables are similar to those prepared by Matthias and O'Brien (1976). However, the latter relied on estimates of French and English economic growth and population figures that are now out of date. The data sources and method of construction for tables 8 and 9 are explained in the Appendix.

30 percent, was quite respectable, although English industry had a markedly higher growth rate at 43 percent.

Why, then, did France seem so much poorer than England, since per capita agricultural performances were about equal and France was still making healthy gains in industry? The driving force was the difference in the weight of the two sectors. In 1700, trade and industry already accounted for 45 percent of England's total output; in France the proportion was only 25 percent. Even though in both countries the per capita growth of industry was rapid, while that of agriculture lagged, England had a much larger part of its economy in the "high" growth sector from the beginning of the century. Thus its total per capita growth was much faster. France was shackled not by poorly performing agriculture, or by poorly performing industry, but simply by a relatively large agricultural sector. The weight of this slow-growing (per capita) sector dragged down the growth rate of the entire economy.

There is a rich literature on the relative wealth and rate of growth of England and France in the eighteenth century (Ruttan 1978; O'Brien and Keyder 1978; Matthias and O'Brien 1976). O'Brien and Keyder in particular have argued that because French per capita growth rates in agriculture and industry were comparable to those of Britain, France actually did not lag in growth. But this claim ignores the enormous impact of the different *proportions* that agriculture and industry represented in the respective economies. France did lag in overall growth precisely because so much of its economy was still tied to agriculture.

Did this slower growth mean that France could afford less taxation than England? In fact, over the eighteenth century the per capita tax burden increased at about the same rate in both countries: in England, per capita taxes in real terms rose 85 percent, and in France they rose just over 79 percent. The English did pay much higher taxes in 1789 than the French, both as a percentage of total output (18.6 versus 8.71 percent) and on a per capita basis (7.34 versus 3.02 bushels of wheat per person). But the reason for this higher level was not that English tax rates had risen much faster during the century; it was that they had already been higher in 1700. Why, then, is France seen as so heavily taxed that it could stand no more? Why could France not simply raise its taxes to English levels (approximately 20 percent of GNP) and thus solve its financial difficulties?

Finding answers again depends on a sectoral analysis. England's agricultural output per capita had fallen by 4.0 percent from 1700 to 1789, because its population had surged. But direct taxes on land, relative to

TABLE EIGHT   FRENCH ECONOMIC GROWTH, C. 1700–1789

	Total		Agriculture		Industry and Trade	
	Livres tournois	Bushels wheat	Livres tournois	Bushels wheat	Livres tournois	Bushels wheat
GNP						
c. 1700	2.4 billion	716 million	1.8 billion	535 million	0.6 billion	180 million
c. 1726	2.8	807	2.0	582	0.8	225
c. 1751	3.8	895	2.6	626	1.1	269
c. 1775	5.4	962	3.7	660	1.7	302
c. 1789	5.4	975	3.7	670	1.7	306
% incr.	130.3	36.3	111.4	25.0	186.7	69.6
GNP/capita						
c. 1700	109.44	33.29	81.86	24.90	27.58	8.39
c. 1726	117.02	34.05	84.34	24.54	32.68	9.51
c. 1751	152.92	36.38	107.00	25.45	45.92	10.92
c. 1775	200.74	35.62	137.78	24.44	62.96	11.17
c. 1789	192.88	34.71	132.38	23.83	60.50	10.89
% incr.	76.20	4.30	61.70	-4.30	119.30	29.80

Royal taxes

	119 million	36.2 million	55 million	16.7 million	64 million	19.5 million
c. 1700	119	36.2	55	16.7	64	19.5
c. 1726	181	52.7	89	25.8	92	26.9
c. 1751	259	61.5	137	32.6	121	28.9
c. 1775	377	66.9	189	33.5	189	33.5
c. 1789	472	84.9	236	42.5	236	42.5
% incr.	296.64	134.66	331.13	155.07	267.26	117.28

Taxes/GNP (%)

	119 million	36.2 million	55 million	16.7 million	64 million	19.5 million
c. 1700	5.06	5.06	3.11	3.11	10.84	10.84
c. 1726	6.53	6.53	4.44	4.44	11.92	11.92
c. 1751	6.87	6.87	5.20	5.20	10.76	10.76
c. 1775	6.96	6.96	5.07	5.07	11.09	11.09
c. 1789	8.71	8.71	6.34	6.34	13.88	13.88
% incr.	72.19	72.19	103.97	103.97	28.11	28.11

Taxes/capita

	119 million	36.2 million	55 million	16.7 million	64 million	19.5 million
c. 1700	5.53	1.68	2.55	0.77	2.99	0.91
c. 1726	7.64	2.22	3.74	1.09	3.89	1.13
c. 1751	10.51	2.50	5.57	1.32	4.94	1.17
c. 1775	13.97	2.48	6.99	1.24	6.99	1.24
c. 1789	16.80	3.02	8.40	1.51	8.40	1.51
% incr.	203.48	79.54	229.87	95.16	181.00	66.24

Note: Rows may not add exactly because of rounding.

TABLE NINE ENGLISH ECONOMIC GROWTH, C. 1700–1789

	Total		Agriculture		Industry and Trade	
	Pounds sterling	Bushels wheat	Pounds sterling	Bushels wheat	Pounds sterling	Bushels wheat
GNP						
c. 1700	36.5 million	167 million	20.0 million	91.7 million	16.5 million	75.7 million
c. 1789	90.4	298	40.6	134.0	49.8	164.0
% incr.	150.4	80.2	103.0	46.1	201.8	117.1
GNP/capita						
c. 1700	7.26	33.29	3.98	18.24	3.28	15.05
c. 1789	11.95	39.43	5.31	17.52	6.51	21.48
% incr.	64.60	18.50	33.50	-4.00	98.50	42.80
Royal taxes						
c. 1700	4.34 million	19.9 million	1.48 million	6.79 million	2.86 million	13.1 million
c. 1789	17.0	56.2	2.99	9.87	14.0	46.3
% incr.	291.67	181.79	102.03	45.35	390.35	252.79
Taxes/GNP (%)						
c. 1700	11.90	11.90	7.40	7.40	17.33	17.33
c. 1789	18.61	18.61	7.36	7.36	28.16	28.16
% incr.	56.41	56.41	-0.48	-0.48	62.47	62.47
Taxes/capita						
c. 1700	0.86	3.96	0.29	1.35	0.57	2.61
c. 1789	2.22	7.34	0.39	1.29	1.83	6.05
% incr.	157.53	85.28	32.84	-4.43	222.41	131.97

Note: Rows may not add exactly because of rounding.

England's total population, had also fallen, by 4.4 percent. Thus, over 90 percent of the total gain in English tax revenues from 1700 to 1789 came from increases in indirect taxes, which by 1789 took over 28 percent of the output of industry and trade. In France, the distribution of tax increases was quite different. Of the total increase in royal revenues from 1700 to 1789, less than 50 percent came from indirect taxes, which by 1789 took under 14 percent of the output of trade and industry; slightly over 50 percent came from direct taxes, which fell mainly on agriculture. To state the contrast in another way, for every Englishman and Englishwoman in 1789, England produced 4 percent less agricultural output than in 1700, but also took 4.4 percent *less* in real taxes from its agricultural sector. For every Frenchman and Frenchwoman in 1789, France produced 4.3 percent less agricultural output than in 1700, but took 95 percent *more* in real taxes from its agricultural sector! Thus, although the English paid more per capita in overall taxes than the French, the perception that in 1789 French agriculture (and hence the peasantry) was overtaxed, compared to England, is most likely correct.

Could France have simply collected more taxes through indirect levies, as done in England, thereby relieving the burden on agriculture? The increase in France's royal taxes from 1700 to 1789 was equivalent to 49 million bushels of wheat. The increase in the output of trade and industry in this period was equivalent to 126 million. Thus, indirect taxes that captured merely two-fifths of the increase in France's industrial production would have yielded nearly the same amount without any increase in taxes on agriculture. England in fact did take such measures. There, the gain in trade and industrial output was equivalent to 88 million bushels of wheat; of this gain, 33 million bushels were taxed away. Another way of looking at this situation is to note that a deficit of 112 million livres per year led Calonne to call the Assembly of Notables to consider major tax changes. At that time, the indirect taxes yielded 13.9 percent of the output of industry and trade, or 236 million livres. If the taxes on this sector could have been raised to English levels, at 28.2 percent of output, they would have yielded an additional 243 million livres, or enough to solve the budget problem and yield a surplus.

Ironically, the vogue of physiocratic thought in France in the eighteenth century, which emphasized agriculture as the source of all wealth, actually undermined the French tax system. For the monarchy could have solved its financial problems if it had been able to raise taxes on commerce and manufacturing. This sector *was* growing fast enough to support the needed taxes. Thus, it is incorrect to say, as Skocpol (1979) does, that France could not afford war with England because England was a more advanced capitalist country. Though a small part of the total economy, France's industrial sector in 1789 was still almost twice as large as England's. Taxes on French industry at English rates would have allowed the Crown to avoid the fiscal crisis of 1787–1789. But the French tax system was based on land taxes. Even Calonne's reform proposals, along with most of the tax reforms discussed from 1763 to 1789, were at heart a uniform tax on land. Yet raising taxes on the land was not the answer. The agricultural sector was already being taxed at nearly the same rate as in England (6.3 percent versus 7.3 percent), and in the preceding decades taxes on agriculture per capita had risen 95 percent, while the products of the land per capita had fallen. A uniform land tax would have eliminated much injustice, but it would not have solved the basic problem of French finances. That problem was one of overdependence on land taxes when population growth was reducing the per capita output of land.

Since comparisons with England are standard, it is noteworthy that Behrens (1985) compared France to another continental monarchy, Prussia. Prussia was not richer than France, or a more advanced capitalist state, but it avoided bankruptcy despite its eighteenth-century wars. The reason is that Prussia had at least one advantage over France: vast empty spaces, left after the devastation of the Thirty Years' War. Much of this land was acquired by the Crown. These Crown lands, which Frederick the Great offered to peasants for settlement, yielded revenues that provided nearly 35 percent of the Prussian Crown's annual income (Behrens 1985, 79, 123–125). For Prussia, vacant lands provided the same kind of safety valve that the large industrial sector provided England—a way to productively employ a growing population in a manner that raised state revenues.

Thus, exclusive focus on comparisons with England slightly misrepresents France's central problem. It was not a case of "lagging capitalist development." Instead, it was a mismatch between France's tax system and its ecological conjuncture. England had an agricultural sector with diminishing per capita output, but raised its taxes from its growing industries. Prussia had a growing agricultural sector with large reserves of land relative to its population, which Frederick encouraged peasants to reclaim and cultivate, thereby raising revenues. France had an agricultural sector with diminishing per capita output, but its tax system still relied heavily on increasing state revenue *from that sector*. As already emphasized, the problem was not mere population growth per se but rather the collision of population growth with particular structural conditions: limits on land and technology that yielded diminishing per capita agrarian output *and* a revenue system that was overdependent on land taxes. In eighteenth-century France this collision led eventually to recession and state bankruptcy.

GROWING DEBTS, STAGNATING REVENUES

Louis XIV left, at his death, larger debts relative to royal income than France faced at the end of either the Seven Years' War or the American War of Independence (Riley 1986, 180; Bosher 1970, 23–24). These debts could not be paid out of existing revenues, so they were reduced by three measures. First, and least effective, was a *lit de justice* (chamber of justice) held in 1716. This tribunal claimed to punish financiers for extortion and make them remit a fair sum to the Crown. In practice, however, the chamber raised only 220 million livres, or about 10 percent of the outstanding debt (Bosher 1970, 10; Briggs 1977, 66). The second measure transformed the debt into a speculative commodity—securities issued under the John Law plan. The collapse of the market in these securities cut the real value of the debt by about half and lowered their yields to a level the Crown could afford to pay. The third measure was devaluation of the currency through reduction of the gold and silver content of the coinage. In addition, tax levels were raised by 50 percent from 1700 to 1726, with higher direct taxes making up most of the increase. Together, these measures rebalanced revenues and expenditures (Riley 1986, 100). However, they did nothing to strengthen the tax system itself. As Cobban (1964, 56) notes, "the great king [Louis XIV] had endowed France with a modern system of government while retaining a semi-medieval system of financing it."

From the 1730s to the 1780s, wheat prices in France rose almost 70 percent (Labrousse 1970e, 9). Compared to the period 1730–1739, prices were 18 percent higher in the 1740s, 23 percent higher in the 1750s, 32 percent higher in the 1760s, and 70 percent higher in the 1770s. After the long period of low prices under Louis XIV it was expected that, although prices would rise in times of war or harvest shortage, they would then return to "normal levels." In the eighteenth century, they did not. Scarcity in the agricultural sector propelled the prices of land and of grain steadily higher. Relative to these prices, the wages of labor and the price of manufactured goods steadily declined. As Riley (1986, 31) notes, in the eighteenth century the French people "consistently expected less inflation than they got."

The inflation posed problems for the Crown, problems that did not occur in England. There, slower population growth and faster increases in agricultural output kept prices stable; in fact, grain prices steadily fell from the 1700s to the 1740s, and in the 1750s prices were only 5 percent higher than in the opening decade of the century (Hoskins 1968). From the 1760s, English fertility sharply rose, the population started its dramatic increase, and the rate of agricultural progress slowed, as we noted earlier. England then joined France in experiencing rapid inflation in the last third of the century. But by that time England had already taken advantage of the long price stability in the early 1700s to convert much of its public debt to bonds known as "consols" at the low rate of 3 percent annual interest (Dickson 1967).

France, given its inflation, had to pay higher interest rates. In addition, the French borrowed badly. Much of the debt incurred in the eighteenth century was in the form of life annuities and *tontines* (G. Taylor 1962). These were a form of "gambling on lives" (Alter and Riley 1986). The subscriber paid the government a sum of money; in return, the government agreed to make an annual payment to the subscriber (or some other designated individual) for life. If the subscriber (or designated party) lived long enough, he or she would make a profit on the loan, possibly a large one. If the subscriber died young, the government reaped a profit. The government made estimates of life expectancy and adjusted the sums paid out, with the expectation, like the house in a gambling casino, that in the long run they would come out ahead.

Unfortunately, the French authorities were inept demographers. As mortality fell in the eighteenth century, the subscribers won more and more, which raised the real costs of these loans. The English and the Dutch reduced their dependence on these kinds of loans as unprofitable (Riley 1986, 173). But the French continued and so paid a higher rate of real interest than their neighbors. France was thus doubly penalized: because its inflation was higher, it had to pay a higher nominal interest rate; because it stayed with life annuities and was victimized by falling mortality rates, it paid higher interest rates than intended or necessary. In fact, in the latter half of the eighteenth century French *tontines* paid roughly twice as much to investors as comparable British annuities (Weir 1989a, 113).

Since France was paying a higher-than-market rate on its loans, money poured in from abroad. French authorities misinterpreted this influx as a mark of confidence in French securities, failing to recognize that they were paying premium rates for borrowed funds. Unfortunately, the ease with which these loans were filled in the first part of the eighteenth century encouraged the government to continue its reliance on borrowed funds, rather than taxation, to meet its expenses.

We have already seen why the cost of debt service in France was high. The other expenses of the Crown also rose steadily. Expenditures for the court were an exception; thanks to reforms by the Crown's ministers, this expense rose only 35 percent from 1726 to 1788, far less than inflation. But the other ordinary expenditures could not be so easily contained, for they represented vital political and military obligations. From 1726 to 1788 pensions increased by 327 percent; diplomatic and foreign service expenses by 235 percent; and public works and charity expenses, as the royal administration took over more local tasks and poverty increased, by 1,560 percent. The need to enforce order after the widespread grain riots of the 1770s, as scarcity became more common, and the need to protect vital trade routes produced higher peacetime military spending: from 1726 to 1788 the costs of the standing army and navy rose by 144 percent. Charges for short-term borrowing, fees, and emoluments to financiers also increased dramatically. Altogether, the ordinary expenditures, excluding debt service, had increased by 207 percent. This reflected a 21 percent rise in the real costs of government, amplified by 70 percent inflation (Morineau 1980, 312–314).

The figure of 207 percent was the increase in the regular peacetime costs of the monarchy. But to pay these rising costs, plus the costs of war, which were financed by growing debt service, ordinary revenues had to increase *still faster*. For if the ordinary revenues grew no more rapidly than the ordinary peacetime expenses, then the remaining margin available for debt service would be stagnant. This would mean that the Crown could not afford to service any additional debts. However, from 1726 to 1788 the ordinary revenues had in fact risen much more *slowly* than the ordinary peacetime expenses, by only 161 percent (Morineau 1980, 314–315).

Thus, the amount of debt the Crown could service out of current revenues actually diminished. The difference between the debt service that the Crown could afford and that which it undertook to pay for its wars was covered by more loans. In its last decade, the Crown was forced to borrow additional sums simply to service its already outstanding loans; this meant a pyramid of debt that could not be long sustained.

From 1775 to 1788, the combined costs of ordinary administration and debt service rapidly outpaced the increase in ordinary revenues. It was this gap, illustrated in figure 7, that impelled the Crown's ministers to seek drastic reform.

Why could the Crown not expand taxes sufficiently to meet added costs? As we have seen, England raised its taxes by increasing indirect taxes on its industries; if France had done the same, it would have raised enough money from its much larger industrial sector to cover its budget deficit. The problem of French finances was thus largely created by the Crown's continuing dependence for tax revenues on its agricultural sector, which was struggling with slow growth, and not on its industrial sector, which was rapidly expanding and could easily have borne a heavier tax load.

THE PROBLEM OF COMMERCIAL PRIVILEGE

The reason for this ill-advised dependence, as has often been pointed out by historians, was privilege. But it was not the kind of privilege that one usually associates with the ancien régime, namely, the privileges of the noble order. Insofar as most nobles gained their incomes from land and agriculture was already heavily taxed, raising the taxes on noble incomes would simply have made the tax system more equitable, without greatly raising its potential yield. Achievement of the latter objective required a massive shift of taxes from agriculture to the municipalities, where most of the profits from trade and manufacture were concentrated.

But as Behrens (1962) has pointed out, privilege in the ancien régime was not a monopoly of the nobility. Many of the major towns, including Paris, were privileged in being exempt outright from the *taille*. In addition, many other towns had purchased exemption in return for a fixed annual payment (Temple 1975, 75–76). Any raise in the potential yield of the tax system required a remodeling of the municipalities; this was what the attempted reforms of Terray and Maupeou were all about. Insofar as the landlords paid the taxes on the agricultural sector—either directly through the *taille réelle* or indirectly as lowered rents from their tenants, who had to pay the land taxes—the French Crown taxed its landlords as heavily as the English taxed theirs. The elements of French society that paid far less taxes than their English counterparts were the shopkeepers and professionals, merchants and manufacturers, and artisans and urban consumers in general. In short, it was indeed collective privilege that undermined French finances, but privilege of the commercial variety.

From 1726 to 1750, direct taxes, falling mostly on agriculture, rose over 70 percent in real per capita terms. The Crown did not attempt to raise them signficantly more for the remainder of the ancien régime. This was a logical decision because per capita output in agriculture probably peaked in 1750, and the increase in real direct taxes per capita from 1700 to 1750 already took 100 percent of the increase in real per capita agricultural output. Any further increase in real taxes would simply have lowered agricultural incomes in real terms. Authorities evidently recognized that the agrarian sector was already taxed near reasonable limits, since they were clearly reluctant to raise direct taxes any more than needed to cover inflation for the rest of the century.

Ideally, then, the Crown could grant some agrarian tax relief by lowering direct taxes and raising taxes on the municipal economy. Yet this could not be done by fiat. The municipalities (and all other privileged groups) had invested enormous sums in offices, charters, and statuses whose mark of privilege was exemption from direct taxes. Sharp reduction of the impact of direct taxes would enormously devalue those privileges. Since privileges were regarded as a form of private property (Bossenga 1986; Bien 1987), any unilateral act that reduced their value was tantamount to a seizure of property—in a word, despotism. Yet when we examine the tax system of the Old Regime, we can see why the Crown nonetheless sought to remodel the municipalities.

As already noted in our discussion of early Stuart finances, land taxes respond poorly to population growth in the context of limited land and productivity. As population grows, land is subdivided among peasants, making it more difficult to support a family. Subsistence farmers fail, and more peasants thus become landless or have to lease land. But those landowners who own more land than is needed to support a family can profit from rising prices for grain. Eventually, rents rise as well. Thus, wealth is polarized, with the small independent family farmers giving way to larger landowners, on the one hand, and increased numbers of landless laborers, on the other. The latter seek employment in the urban and rural manufacturing economy, which grows faster than the population as a whole. This is bad for land taxes: the rich are usually able to avoid full assessment by acquiring exemptions or using their influence with assessors, while the landless do not pay taxes on land. Thus, the bulk of the taxes falls on peasants struggling to maintain family farms in the face of larger families and higher rents, as both the increased profits of the landowners and the growing economies of the cities and of rural manufacture escape the tax bite. Hence a given level of taxation becomes both more inequitable and more out of touch with the actual sources of wealth in the economy.

We noted that, for the Stuarts, the main land tax, the subsidy, fell so much in real terms that it was necessary to return to Parliament to seek multiple subsidies, and that even these failed to meet expenses. Given that constant appeals to Parliament for subsidies provoked remonstrances and debates over policy, Charles I turned to remodeling town charters, issuing monopolies, and collecting and expanding levies without parliament's consent (tonnage and poundage and Ship Money). All of these measures earned Charles a reputation as a foe of liberty, without providing him sufficient revenues to avoid mounting debt and eventual fiscal crisis. The solution to the fiscal dilemma required a complete overhaul of the fiscal system, in which land taxes not only would be adjusted to reflect real incomes but also would play a much smaller role in revenues. War could then be financed by borrowing, with the debt service provided by the ordinary income drawn from greatly enlarged indirect taxes.

A very similar story can be told of taxes and politics in eighteenth-century France. The *taille,* which was the mainstay of the Crown in the seventeenth century, was eroded by inflation in the eighteenth century. Recognizing the political volatility of the *taille* and the problems of assessment, the Crown allowed it "to remain stagnant while incomes and wealth grew" (Riley 1986, 50). By 1775 the *taille,* the yield of which in nominal terms had not changed since the 1720s, provided only 15 percent of total revenues (Morineau 1980, 321).

The Bourbons added new taxes to make up the difference, chiefly the *vingtième.* This was intended to be a proportional tax on all income, as was the subsidy in England. But like the subsidy, the *vingtième* relied on the taxpayer to report the income on which the tax would be paid. The most influential were thus able to get away with the biggest underassessments. Sutherland (1986, 21) reports that "the princes of the blood ought to have paid 2.4 million livres in *vingtième,* but actually paid only 188,000 livres." A true *vingtième,* or one-twentieth, tax on French output would have yielded 190 million livres in 1750; the actual *vingtième* yielded 27 million livres. Clearly, the *vingtième* failed as a true proportional tax. But it is unlikely authorities ever expected to collect on the full value of incomes; their goal was the much more modest one of making up for the inflation erosion of the *taille,* and this they accomplished. Despite inflation, real direct taxes in 1750 were about 20 percent larger than in 1726.

Unfortunately, however, revenues then appeared to reach a limit. Indeed, Guéry (1978, 229) argues that real royal revenues peaked in the 1740s and then fell until the 1770s before regaining their earlier level in the 1780s. Riley (1987, 227) similarly sees no long-term increase in real royal revenues from the late 1730s to the 1760s. Morineau's (1980) data, which include only the ordinary revenues, suggest a very slight rise (10 percent) in real royal income from 1751 to 1775, although a larger increase of 27 percent from 1775 to 1789.

There were two reasons for this revenue stagnation. First, inflation meant that the Crown had to run just to stay in place. The *vingtième*, no less than the *taille*, failed to increase in yield with population and inflation, as people claimed that once the assessment had been made, the government had no right to change it (B. Stone 1986, 154). The *vingtième* therefore yielded the same amount in livres in the 1780s as in the 1750s, or about 36 percent less in real value (Riley 1986, 51). Thus the government, simply in order to maintain its real income, was forced to request a second and even a third *vingtième* be paid in addition to the first. In nominal terms, royal taxes rose almost 50 percent from 1751 to 1775, provoking no end of complaints. But this was sufficient to raise real royal income by only 10 percent, a clearly inadequate amount to cope with the rising costs of the Crown's eighteenth-century wars and administration.

Second, the distribution of taxes did not follow the distribution of income. Although the urban commercial and industrial sector was growing, "the *vingtième* . . . failed effectively to tap urban, industrial wealth, because the government refused from the start to incur the hostility likely to be provoked by any serious investigation into income and profits" (Temple 1975, 76). Thus the *vingtième* was far easier to escape by underreporting of income in trade and manufacture than in the countryside, where the income from land was established, in a way, from the records of the *taille* (Behrens 1985, 167). And, as with the *taille*, "the nobility soon found ways to buy exemptions, . . . so that the onus of paying the new taxes fell on the peasantry. . . . The new taxes became, in effect, additions to the *taille*" (Root 1987, 25).

All the major towns of France, and many of the smaller ones (the *villes franches*), had the privilege of exemption from the *taille* (Behrens 1985, 74; Temple 1975). The Crown raised revenue from the towns chiefly by sale of municipal offices, not just those of the mayor and councillors but also those conferring the right to sell wine, pork, and fish, or to supervise such sales. Although selling offices brought in much revenue, this was an ineffective way to improve royal finances. Sale of an office brought in a capital payment, but the Crown then was committed to pay an annual salary, or to alienate fees and payments that the officeholder was entitled to gain through the office. Thus, sale of an office was more like a loan than a tax because it committed the Crown to future payments or alienation of administrative revenue in return for immediate cash. It thus put the long-term ordinary accounts in worse shape, not better, unlike a true tax on urban and commercial wealth. In addition, sales of municipal and judicial offices put ownership of privileges squarely in the hands of those whose later cooperation would be needed to reduce privileges. Support for the Crown under the status quo was gained, but support for the Crown if reforms were needed was diminished.

It should be noted that the towns themselves had growing fiscal problems in the late eighteenth century. By the 1790s, many towns had sizeable debts, which required municipal tax reforms (Bossenga 1987). Again, the problem was not inadequate resources but rather an outdated system of revenue assessment. In the eighteenth century, towns had been forced to deal with growing expenses of two types: first, urban growth required an expansion of administration and service costs; second, towns borrowed to finance their own contributions and loans to the Crown, whose demands sharply grew (Bien 1987). The main source of urban revenues was excise taxes, known as *octrois*. But the *octrois* provided neither a fair nor a flexible system of taxation. They were essentially consumption taxes, and thus heavily regressive. Moreover, as with royal taxes, wealthy townsmen could gain privileges and exemptions. Holders of certain offices, or residents with sufficient influence, could arrange to bring certain items (such as wine from their own vineyards) into town for sales largely exempt from the *octrois*. Thus, as in France as a whole, most revenues were paid not by the wealthiest but by the middle classes and the working poor—the consumers of meat, wine, tallow, and other items that bore excise taxes. There were thus no great pools of urban tax wealth for the royal government to tap; instead, for the government to raise revenues from the municipalities it had to enter into the existing struggles among urban officials and their populations over town debt and taxation.

It is difficult to estimate total urban wealth, since France's towns were hosts to growing numbers of both the rich and the poor in the eighteenth century. But we do know that urban taxation per capita does not seem to have reflected the wealth of France's towns. We estimated above (see table 8) that for France as a whole, the annual royal tax burden in 1789 was 16.8 livres per person. Bossenga's (1987, 124) analysis of royal taxation in French municipalities notes that many towns paid no more than this average, and sometimes even less. Small towns such as Rocroi and Flêche paid as little as 3–5 livres per person in taxes. The rapidly growing trading center Marseilles paid about the same as the national average, at 17.2 livres per head. Larger towns, such as Orléans, Lille, and Lyon, paid about 50 percent more than the national average tax rate, at 24–29 livres per person. But should we believe that these towns were only 50 percent wealthier, on average, than the population of the French countryside? Only Paris, at just over 50 livres per head in 1789, appears to have paid a substantially higher than average tax. But again, even this figure is less than three times the average tax burden. Unless we believe that Paris—despite the concentration of wealth among its nobility and bourgeoisie, as well as its skilled tradesmen and retailers—was no more than three times wealthier, per capita, than the French average, then Paris too was substantially undertaxed.

Following the Seven Years' War, which had been financed almost entirely through loans, the Crown attempted to remodel the municipalities in order to increase the possibilities of raising royal revenues from this source. The existing municipal offices were declared void and their holders were offered compensation. In their place, a whole new system of municipal authority and justice was proposed, one that relied on elected notables, gave a larger role to manufacturers and professionals than to nobles and clergy, and, ideally, would be more amenable to royal fiscal guidance (Mousnier 1979, 1:598–604). But it was difficult to find qualified men to assume the new offices, and the Crown's need for money led to a revival of the old venality. Thus, these reforms were rescinded in 1771.

More fundamental efforts to increase taxes, particularly to increase or extend the *vingtième*, also met staunch resistance. This resistance was centered in the parlements. Thus in 1770 the minister Maupeou took on the parlements directly. The Crown sharply reduced the authority of the parlements and purged their memberships (Echeverria 1985, 16–18). New courts were created to take over the parlements' work. At the same time, the finance minister, Terray, wrote down a large portion of the outstanding war debt, suspending payments on short-term debts, substituting annuities at lower rates, and extracting money from the financiers (Doyle 1980, 47; Bosher 1970, 27). These measures did not restore fiscal balance, but they succeeded in increasing revenues and halving the annual deficit. By 1774, "this was still not a state of sound financial health, but the government had been given a new lease on life" (Echeverria 1985, 20).

This new fiscal policy was dramatically unpopular, of course. The members of the old parlements agitated against the suppression of their positions and authority. The populace, which blamed the Crown for high bread prices, and the elite, which feared royal usurpation of their offices and privileges on a broad scale, protested the dissolution of the parlements, decrying royal "despotism." At Louis XV's death in 1774, he was one of the most unpopular monarchs in memory, and his ministers Maupeou and Terray were left isolated. Louis XVI immediately dismissed the reform ministry and repudiated their policies. If the reform policy had succeeded, it seems possible that higher taxes on the municipalities would have followed, and a stronger fiscal system would have developed. But the measures aroused a storm of protest against "despotism" that resulted in their retraction. The tax system remained bound to the land and heavily unbalanced.

France thus entered the American War of Independence with basically the same tax system as existed in 1700. But the output per capita of her agrarian sector was lower. Not surprisingly, rather than try to raise taxes—economically impossible in agriculture, and politically impossible in the manufacturing sector—the Crown financed the war by borrowing.

The reason for the Crown's fiscal policy should be clear. Any increase in the direct taxes tended to fall on the land, and on the modest cultivators in particular, rather than on the larger landowners. Since the real product of the land per capita was decreasing in France after 1750, it was increasingly difficult for the peasants to pay the tax burden. Reluctant to raise taxes in real terms, the Crown turned to borrowing. Unfortunately, the rates it had to pay were high, and the real expenses of the Crown were rising, so borrowing expanded.

REVENUE SHORTFALLS, RECESSION, AND FISCAL COLLAPSE

The American War of Independence was not exceptionally costly. Morineau (1980, 325) estimates that French expenses in the war were 1.3 billion livres, compared to 1.8 billion for the Seven Years' War and 1.2

billion for the War of the Austrian Succession. In real terms (i.e., bushels of wheat equivalent), the American War was France's least expensive war of the century, costing only half as much as the Seven Years' War. Since France overall was richer during the period 1776–1789 than during the earlier wars, payment of the costs should not have been impossible. But the costs were to be paid not by "France" but rather by the monarchy, which relied heavily on taxes on agriculture, which was, per capita, the poorest sector of the economy.

After experiencing the bad harvests of the 1770s and the war years of the late 1770s and early 1780s, the Crown might have expected prices to return to lower levels, ordinary expenses to then fall, and a margin for debt service to appear. But with the long-term pressure of population on resources, prices continued to rise and were 15 percent higher in the period 1786–1788 than in 1779–1780 (Labrousse 1970e, 9). Thus, there was no "peace dividend." Instead, from 1775 to 1788 the ordinary expenses of the Crown, excluding debt service, rose from 257 million to 372 million livres (Morineau 1980, 315). Half of the increase was due to inflation and to increased costs for charity and poverty relief (the latter ballooned from 5.4 million to 33.3 million livres). These factors were directly attributable to the growth of population exceeding the growth of the economy. The other half of the increase came from the costs of a larger standing army and navy (the former needed in part to deal with increasing vagrancy and local disorders [R. Schwartz 1988]) and from the need to pay higher fees and miscellaneous charges to financiers and others who provided assistance to the Crown. Only 10 percent of the rise in ordinary expenses came from increases in pensions, and none at all from higher court expenses. Thus from 1775 to 1788, ordinary Crown expenses increased by 115 million livres. At the same time, amortization of the debts assumed for the American War added 107 million livres per year to the Crown's interest charges. But the major direct taxes rose by only 13 million livres!

The Crown was able to raise miscellaneous revenues and income from the domains between 1775 and 1788 by 90 million livres per year (Morineau 1980, 315). Had ordinary expenses simply held constant, this would have allowed the Crown to manage the American War debt. But in fact this increase in revenues was swallowed by the increase in ordinary expenses, leaving no margin to service outstanding debts. By 1788 the combination of ordinary expenses and debt service charges exceeded ordinary revenues by the unheard of, for peacetime, sum of over 100 million livres (Morineau 1980, 314–316). Calonne, therefore, had no choice but to continue to register new loans, just to meet interest charges and to cover current expenditures.

The Parlement of Paris objected vigorously to this peacetime extension of borrowing, writing seventeen sets of remonstrances in this period (Doyle 1970, 445). In 1784 the Parlement, puzzled that even though the war had ended the Crown continued to seek new loans, condemned "the obscurity and confusion in the expenditures" (R. Harris 1986, 60–63).

As we noted, popular perceptions were that Crown finances should have been *improving* in the 1780s. The American War was over by 1783, and government loans had been well subscribed. French government accounts were of course secret, but the Crown ministers, particularly Necker, had kept up an image of financial strength to encourage lenders to trust the Crown. Thus, when Calonne announced that the deficit had grown so large that new taxes were needed, the response was surprise, even shock. Elites certainly knew that the current tax system was inequitable; they did not realize, and hardly believed, that the system as a whole was inadequate for legitimate royal expenses. Hence when Calonne sought to have new taxes approved by an Assembly of Notables, they objected to his accounts and demanded to see the records before approving new taxes (Gruder 1984a).

The final blow to Crown finances was the economic recession of the 1770s and 1780s. Riley (1987, 237) believes that the French economy ceased to grow in real output after 1770. Indeed, from this date food scarcity increased and wheat prices sharply rose. If Riley is correct about the stagnation of output, then continued population growth would have created a 6 percent fall in real per capita income from 1770 to 1790. This is certainly consistent with the fall in real wages, which were on average 15 percent lower in the period 1770–1789 than in 1750–1769. This fall in real income led to lower demand for less essential goods. Wine prices fell to a disastrous level, and business activity of all kinds was depressed (Labrousse 1958, 70; 1970d).

The recession led to the bankruptcy of several prominent Crown financiers (Bosher 1970, 190). Under the conditions of the late 1780s, when the Crown continually needed to borrow to meet current expenses, as well as simply to pay the outstanding interest on its debts, the failure of the financiers was a fiscal death knell. They had been the lenders of last resort to bridge daily expenses (Bosher 1970, 96–97). With Calonne's inability to persuade the notables to approve new taxes, and with his continued requests to the Parlement of Paris for new loans casting doubts on the monarchy's credit, it was proving increasingly difficult to find new long-term loans. Short-term loans and anticipations from the financiers were thus necessary to give the Crown any room to maneuver. With their unavailability, the monarchy literally could not cover its daily bills. The Crown had no choice but to capitulate to demands for reform, and it recalled Necker to preside over the arrangements to convene the Estates General.

In sum, one cannot blame the fiscal crisis of 1787–1789 on the magnitude of the American War expenses. Nor can one say that France was economically too poor, or too backward, to support those expenses. France's trade and industrial sector had grown strongly; only its agricultural sector had seen a decline in output per capita. The monarchy's fiscal problems came chiefly from its overreliance on that declining sector. Bad harvests and high food prices led to recession in the 1770s and 1780s, but France had had recessions before. This one caused a fiscal crisis only because the government had already become so dependent on borrowing, and had stretched its credit so thin, that the bankruptcy of a few financiers was sufficient to strip it of its final props.

France had not become heavily dependent on borrowing, or unable to service that debt, because of overall poverty. France's overall economic output rose 36 percent in the eighteenth century, a modest but real increase of 4.3 percent in per capita terms. The problem was that while the trade and manufacturing sector was growing almost three times as fast as agriculture, the Crown only managed to raise the rate of taxation on trade and industry by less than 30 percent. In contrast, during the same period, England faced a similarly declining per capita output in agriculture but was able to raise the rate of taxation on its commerce and manufacturing sector by over 60 percent, and thus to service its loans.

France remained overly dependent on direct taxes, levied mostly on land. And such taxes responded poorly to the changes in the economy that followed from the demographic changes of the eighteenth century: higher prices, a larger urban and manufacturing sector, a poorer per capita agrarian sector. Shackled by this dependency, the French government was forced to borrow. To do so, it offered lucrative loan terms, but, faced with lagging revenues, it was before long unable to raise revenues fast enough to service its debts. The fiscal crisis was created when population growth that raised prices and overburdened agriculture collided with a tax system that, hedged by "commercial privilege," directed taxation away from manufacturing and commerce and onto the land.

The Crown and leading political thinkers had attempted to improve the financial situation. Indeed, from the 1760s onward there was a continuous stream of proposals for reform and an attempt to reorganize the administration and finances. But these were defeated by the resistance of the elites, particularly the Parisian and provincial parlements.

Part of the problem was that contemporaries did not understand the cause of their plight. The leading elites, concentrated in Paris, saw all around themselves a thriving urban economy, which they believed indicated a richer France. They saw that the peasantry was poor and were puzzled by how, in a country so rich and fertile, the cultivators could be forced to go without food. They were not ready to recognize that population growth had crowded many peasants into plots too small to feed their families, or that increased landlessness and falling real wages lowered the incomes of about one-third of the population. Population growth was considered a positive good, and not a source of such problems as landlessness, unemployment, or inflation (Fox-Genovese 1976).

Everyone was aware of inflation, of course; but they did not attribute it to rising population. Instead they attributed the rise in grain prices to the evils of speculation. Popular belief had it that the government connived with the grain speculators, and there was an element of unintended truth in this view. In the 1760s, influenced by the physiocrats, Louis XV freed the grain trade from royal control. The goal was to reduce prices and want by encouraging the free market to allocate local surpluses to regions of scarcity. Had France been running a general grain surplus, a free market would likely have accomplished precisely that goal. But Louis XV had the misfortune of embracing a free market view just when demographic growth and lagging agriculture were pushing France into conditions of greater scarcity. Harvest shortfalls became more common, more widespread, and more severe as the load on agriculture increased. In the years 1770–1789, only three harvests were truly abundant (Doyle 1989, 14). As a result, the market's free rein meant unfettered price increases in times of shortage. In the period 1767–1770, France had the largest harvest shortfall since 1709–1710. Prices skyrocketed, more severely than even in 1789, and food riots spread throughout France. In 1769, Terray restored controls. In 1774, Turgot again freed the grain trade from royal control, but again high prices and popular discontent followed. After Turgot's fall from favor, Necker restored grain controls in 1776. But they were then withdrawn in 1787 by Calonne, just before another harvest failure led to a huge surge in prices. The experiment in free market enterprise failed, but it lasted long enough to saddle the Crown with the responsibility for high prices (Kaplan 1976).

Since rising prices were blamed on speculators and royal mismanagement, there was no support for the notion that taxes should rise with every rise in prices. Indeed, this principle was forcibly opposed by the parlements, who had a "static conception of state finances" (B. Stone 1986, 154). In 1787, the Parlement of Rouen stated in an *arrêt* that it was "an error" to believe that taxes must "increase gradually with the taxpayers' revenues." To think otherwise "would be to profess that false and imprudent maxim, that the state's debts, instead of being amortized through order and savings, must grow in proportion with the taxpayers' properties" (B. Stone 1986, 154). Similar views were expressed by all the parlements.

Many of the proposals for reform, including those presented by Calonne to the Assembly of Notables, stressed a reduction of privileges and a substitution of a uniform land tax for the *taille*, the irregularity of which among regions and among different classes of taxpayers was widely recognized. The difficulty here lay in the refusal of the parlements to accept the king's judgment on what would be a fair reorganization of direct taxes. The Parlement of Paris insisted that "the constitutional principle of the French Monarchy is that [new] taxes be consented to by those who must pay them" (B. Stone 1986, 89). The king could have raised the level of the *taille* by decree, but, as already noted, that would simply have increased the burden on the poorest of the *taille* payers, who were already in straitened circumstances. Thus, what was needed was a new tax, or system of taxes. And here the Parlement of Paris was correct: the Crown had no precedent for introducing new taxes without first obtaining the free consent of the parlements and provincial estates.

The Crown's efforts to solve its fiscal problems led to a series of confrontations with the parlements. In the 1760s, the parlements' responsibilities for the grain trade were reduced by the free market policy. When prices rose, the parlements championed the right of the people to have bread at reasonable prices. As noted earlier, after the Seven Years' War the parlements opposed the continuation of the *vingtième*. And in the name of preserving the local customs and liberties of each province, they fought the centralizing and nationally uniform plan proposed by

Maupeou. Doyle (1974, 250) notes a particularly revealing instance of conflict between the Crown and the Parlement of Bordeaux. In an effort to increase revenues from the royal domain, the Crown in 1791 proclaimed that all of the alluvial lands of the Gironde and Dordogne rivers and the Medoc coast "appeared to have been usurped" from the royal domain. Proprietors were ordered to produce their titles or else cede the lands to the Crown, which would then exploit the properties by leasing them to developers. This ploy is reminiscent of Charles I's efforts to raise revenues by declaring one-third of Essex to have been "usurped" from royal forest. It was similarly unsuccessful. The Parlement of Bordeaux remonstrated vociferously and was summoned to Versailles, where the king managed a graceful concession, acceding to the rights of private proprietors over all lands not actually covered by navigable waterways. This was but one of the many small incidents in which the Crown appeared to be arbitrarily threatening the property of its subjects, and in which the parlements came to the rescue as upholders of law and tradition and of liberty and property. The many remonstrations of the parlements against the taxes, fees, reforms, and loans sought by the Crown, all of which raised the cry of resistance to royal "despotism," were thus not aimed "against a status quo going back to Louis XIV, but rather in defense of a status quo threatened by the ever-increasing encroachments of a revenue-hungry government" (Doyle 1972, 104).

By the late 1780s, the parlements were increasingly hesitant to register royal loans, whose mounting scale in peacetime merely endorsed their criticism of the Crown's fiscal irresponsibility. In 1787–1788, when Calonne announced that the deficit had reached over 100 million livres and new taxes were needed, the parlements continued their defense of liberty and the traditional constitution by refusing to register any taxes not approved by the Estates General (Doyle 1974, 268; B. Stone 1986, 89). Calonne sought to override this rebuff by convening the Assembly of Notables to approve new taxes; but they too were "shocked by the disclosure of financial need," and similarly refused to act in place of the estates (Gruder 1984a, 326). With the failure of the financiers, any further delay was impossible, and plans went ahead for the convocation of the Estates General.

Yet, as in Stuart England, the fiscal crisis was only one element of political breakdown. The Crown's efforts to alleviate its fiscal distress, though insufficient to avoid bankruptcy, had succeeded in antagonizing the French elites, making the convocation of the Estates General a risky proposition. Moreover, those elites were deeply divided internally over how French politics should be restructured in the wake of the crisis.

ELITE COMPETITION AND CONFLICT

That the French elites were seriously divided at the time of the monarchy's failure in 1789 is not doubted. Indeed, the essential point of transformation of that financial crisis into a crisis of the entire political order was the breakdown of the Estates General. The Estates had been called to vote on reforms needed to restore the effectiveness of the monarchy. Instead, a large portion of the Third Estate, with some breakaway members of the nobility and the clergy, responded to royal pressures by calling themselves the "National Assembly" and claiming executive power.

This sequence of events was in many respects similar to that experienced in England after 1640. There too, the English Parliament was called to provide fiscal support for the monarchy. Instead, antagonized by royal pressures, a large portion of the House of Commons, with some members of the House of Lords, claimed executive power, in particular the right to control the militia.

In both cases, these divisions were not primarily the products of disagreement on fiscal issues. In England, the deliberations of the Long Parliament initially exhibited a great deal of unity on the issue of curbing royal abuses. But once the king resisted Parliament and sought to arrest some of its leading members, unity began to break down. At this point, the simmering social and religious conflicts of the preceding decades surfaced, fueled by the unfulfilled aspirations of downwardly mobile younger sons of peers, the ambitions of underemployed Puritan ministers, the protests of the small shopkeepers and apprentices of London, the fears of spreading disorder in Ireland, and, above all, the divisions among county families into "court" and "country" factions through contests over local power and social precedence. These conflicts became more important than the pressing fiscal business at hand. The latter soon gave way completely to the broader question of how far supporters of reform dared go in challenging royal authority. Similarly, in France the *cahiers* of the electors of the Estates General showed considerable unity on curbing the abuses of privilege and on reforming finances. But once the Estates General met and began to organize itself, the fiscal issues were quickly eclipsed by issues grounded in the social conflicts of the preceding decades. In France, this meant particularly the extent to which the nobility should be given separate status and disproportionate authority relative to the rest of society.

In both England and France, the initial crises were therefore amplified by claims and conflicts outside of strictly fiscal issues. These claims and conflicts raised fundamental questions about the future of the traditional Church and state. In both cases, the national assemblies, ostensibly convened to deal with fiscal crises and under pressure from the Crowns not to challenge royal authority, fractured internally over the degree to which the traditional order should be reinforced or, alternatively and independently of royal influence, reshaped. In both crises there were considerable differences within the elite in their acceptance of, and attachment to, traditional authority and social hierarchy. An explanation of these differences is thus essential to understanding the political breakdown that occurred in each case.

For the French Revolution, as for the English Revolution, much has been written about the role of social mobility in the decades preceding the political crisis. Two basic hypotheses have been seriously considered by historians; the present consensus is that both are incorrect. The first, with a focus on the ease and volume of social mobility *by individuals* across status lines, suggested that England's stability in the eighteenth century was due to ease of social mobility, whereas the conflicts in France in 1789 were owing to the pressures built up within a rigid and inflexible social hierarchy. By this account, high levels of social mobility contributed to stability, low levels of social mobility to conflict and crisis. The second hypothesis, the "social" or "Marxist" interpretation, assumed that individuals did not move freely across class lines and viewed social mobility as the result of an increase in the relative wealth and status of one *social class* relative to other social classes. For the English Revolution, this phenomenon was labeled the "rise of the gentry"; for the French Revolution, it was designated the "rise of the bourgeoisie."

We now know that in fact the volume of social mobility in England was much greater in the decades before 1640 than in the late seventeenth and early eighteenth centuries. As noted in chapter 2, the latter period encompassed a great revival of aristocratic fortunes and a nearly complete "freezing" of the number of peers and gentry. The professionals and businessmen of England gained wealth after 1650, but as Stone and Stone (1984) have shown, there is little evidence that this wealth translated into political power or social precedence in the counties. Moreover, as discussed later, it is now accepted that in eighteenth-century France there was easy and large-scale movement from the Third Estate into the nobility through the purchase of ennobling offices. The first view is thus completely refuted by the evidence: there was more individual mobility in the times that led up to crisis than in the stable times that followed, and in particular, there was more individual mobility during the eighteenth century in France than in England.

The Marxist or social interpretation has also faltered because, in both England and France, it is virtually impossible to identify a distinct "rising gentry" or "bourgeois" class that, collectively, had both different relations to the economy and different fortunes from the rest of the elite. In England, the lords remained as dominant over the gentry in the seventeenth and eighteenth centuries as in the sixteenth, and members of both groups were similarly involved in industry and commercial agriculture. In France, the economic resources of wealthy nobles and wealthy commoners were nearly indistinguishable, with both investing heavily in land, large-scale trade and industry, and government offices and bonds (G. Taylor 1964, 1972b). It is true that the growth of trade and manufacturing, and increased opportunities in commercial agriculture, provided the resources for many *individuals* to rise relative to their fellows. But these people then usually acquired places in the local gentry or, perhaps, titles (in England) or ennobling offices (in France), and so "rose" out of their respective classes of origin. Thus, the expansion of the commercial sector created more individual mobility. But this was a resource used to self-advantage by individuals of all social groups, not the province of a particular class, and hence commercial expansion was not responsible for a "rise" of one class relative to others.

The failure of these two hypotheses had led some to conclude that no "social interpretation" of elite conflicts in these cases of state breakdown is viable. But this assessment is not warranted. As we have seen in discussing England, much progress can be made by going beyond the simple notion of "social mobility" into the more specific notions of "turnover and displacement." That is, the mere expansion of the elite need not be a problem. Conflicts of the kind that might divide elites in their allegiance to the traditional order and create factions among them are more likely to arise when the number of qualified aspirants for elite positions increases more rapidly than the number of places bearing traditional elite prerogatives. Under these conditions, social mobility generally means that some families obtain elite positions at the expense of other families who traditionally held them. This combination of upward *and downward* mobility is "turnover." In addition, still other families who feel entitled to a share in elite prerogatives are denied; they are "displaced" by the sheer volume of vying aspirants.

Under conditions of sustained population growth and fiscal stringency, the situation of "turnover and displacement" mobility—where the number of elite aspirants rises faster than the number of appropriate positions—is likely to arise. Under conditions of demographic stagnation—where elite families usually have only one surviving son each, or even fail to reproduce, and so create "vacancies" in the social hierarchy—such mobility conditions are less likely to occur.

In the preceding chapter, we saw that this kind of social explanation of conflicts within the English gentry helps make sense of why county-level rivalries were particularly acute in the early seventeenth century. In England, social power and precedence were realized in the form of appointments to the county bench, selection to Parliament, and royal appointments to Church and state offices. As the number of well-to-do country families increased, the Crown was besieged by requests for appointments to the bench and for positions in court. Parliament expanded, but contests for selection grew heated as established social hierarchies were disturbed by the rise of new local families. Competition for such honors led to competing patronage networks, linking factions in court to factions in the counties. These divisions later fueled the divisions between monarchists and parliamentarians after 1640.

In Old Regime France, social power and precedence were realized somewhat differently. The legal status of "nobility" had far more importance than in England, while local-level power was less important. Thus, in France elite divisions were more likely to crystallize around the issue of nobility, whereas in England they crystallized around county leadership. Nonetheless, the underlying process of conflict formation was the same: an excess of qualified applicants pursuing a less rapidly expanding number of elite positions.

In the following sections I suggest how a focus on the "turnover and displacement" aspects of social mobility provides a more successful explanation of elite social conflicts in Old Regime France than either the simple "low mobility produces conflict" view or the Marxist interpretation based on differences in fortunes among distinct social classes.

ELITE GROWTH

Le Roy Ladurie (1987, 333) tells us that "a freeze in social mobility" was perceptible in France after 1650. This stagnation was largely due to the decline in grain prices. He notes that a study of small farmers south of Paris "failed to find a single case of upward social mobility during the first half of Louis XIV's personal rule [1661–1688], whereas so many examples are to be found during the Renaissance when, in around 1500, a peasant often had needed no more than a bit of luck and a good perpetual tenancy to become rich." He further adds that "under Fouquet and Colbert, even the big farmers did not perform terribly well where social climbing was concerned. Around the capital, they no longer pulled off those modest thrusts toward the towns, toward commerce and office, that their predecessors of the sixteenth and seventeenth centuries had managed. . . . After 1650, . . . the families of the rich ploughmen of the Ile-de-France remained stuck . . . they neither rose nor fell."

This situation changed dramatically with the return of rising prices, as well as the expansion of towns, manufactures, and trade in the eighteenth century. "In an era of rising demand and prices, almost anyone with a modicum of business sense was acceding, at least between 1730 and 1770, to modest wealth" (C. Lucas 1973, 108). Merchants could take advantage of the fact that trade and manufacturing expanded at a faster rate than the rest of the economy; commercial tenant-farmers could take advantage of the fact that, until 1770, prices rose more rapidly than rents. Numerous individual cases of social mobility have been documented, including families of merchants and prosperous peasants who rose to nobility in three generations (Forster 1981; Chaussinand-Nogaret 1985, 32, 37–38). Chaussinand-Nogaret (1985, 28–30) estimates that a minimum of 6,500 families were ennobled in the eighteenth century via office or royal favor. By this estimate, these *anoblis* were one-quarter to one-third the total of roughly 25,000 noble families in France in 1789. Gruder (1968, 177) estimates that from 1715 to 1789 the number of nobles (including junior members of noble families, who were noble if the father had hereditary nobility) increased from 190,000 to 400,000. Thus, the number of nobles more than doubled, while the population as a whole rose by slightly less than one-quarter. As a result, the proportion of nobles in the total population rose by three-quarters, from .84 percent to 1.42 percent. This meant that for every 1,000 non-noble taxpayers in 1715, there were 8 nobles who were tax-exempt and seeking royal favors. But in 1789, for each 1,000 non-noble taxpayers there were 14 nobles who were tax-exempt and seeking royal favors.

The growth of the nobility came from absorption of the most successful members of the Third Estate. In this sense, Cubells (1982, 196)

notes, ennoblement "played the role of a decapitation of the bourgeoisie." Since there were no prohibitions (as there were in Prussia) against
commoners acquiring land, and even seigneuries, they did so with gusto
(Lefebvre 1947, 10; Labrousse 1978, 159). Social historians record that
"the bourgeoisie were infiltrating into the nobility on a hitherto unprecedented scale" (Blacker 1957, 49). To be sure, the volume of new
nobility was impressive, but not unprecedented; the sixteenth century
was also a time of massive social mobility, and as C. Lucas (1973, 97)
observes, "noble complaints about the debasement of their estate sound
very much the same whether written in the 1780s or the 1580s." Still,
as Shulim (1981, 367) notes, "it seems quite clear that the rise of members of the Third Estate into the Second Estate [i.e., the nobility] in the
eighteenth century was relatively easy, rapid, and continuous."

The main route of entry into the nobility was through purchase of
an ennobling office. Necker estimated that there were four thousand
ennobling offices by the end of the Old Regime, from those that offered
gradual nobility if the office stayed in the same family for two or three
generations to those that offered immediate personal and hereditary
nobility (Barber 1955, 109).

Yet while the number of offices was large, the number of prospective
purchasers grew still larger. "Demographic factors contributed to increase the pressure for social promotion from the lower end of the elite,"
and "it appears that . . . the established channels of social promotion
within the law courts and administration which led from one to the other
became progressively clogged" (C. Lucas 1973, 108). Mousnier (1979,
2:344) comments that "by the end of the eighteenth century, *avocats*
[lawyers] could no longer hope to become magistrates. There were too
many *avocats*, and many of them were needy." By the 1760s, the prices
of many offices had risen beyond the reach of the local *avocat* or notary
who sought promotion, and the cost of obtaining command of a regi-
ment had passed beyond the reach of most of the provincial nobility
who looked to advance through military careers. Doyle (1984, 858)
notes that at one point in the 1780s no less than four thousand hopefuls
pursued 113 notarial offices in Paris. Members of the provincial parlements sought to keep their offices in the family, rather than make them
available on the open market. Even "the merchant or financier, enriched
by banking, manufacturing, or colonial trade, could no longer count
after (say) the 1750s on crowning his career by the purchase for himself
or his children of an hereditary office of state or a commission in the
army" (Rudé 1980, 72).

Hence, when calling for a "career open to talent," frustrated would-be social climbers were "not calling for a new age, but a return to the conditions of the 1730s and 1740s" (C. Lucas 1973, 118). In France, the nobility was open, but, as Furet (1981, 108) concludes, "the opening in the ranks of the nobility [was] too wide to preserve the cohesion of the order, and yet too narrow to accommodate the century's prosperity."

One indicator of scarcity of offices is their rising price. "State service could not be expanded at will. As capital accumulated and culture became more democratic, the build-up of ambitions among wider groups of the population ran into the problem of numerical limits. Saturation point was reached without gratifying everybody's aspirations" (Chaussinand-Nogaret 1985, 129). Rising demand and limited supply meant that office prices, like the price of land, rose twofold and even threefold during the period 1700–1789, a rise "far steeper than that of basic commodities" (Doyle 1984, 855).

As noted, some of the provincial parlements virtually closed their ranks to outsiders in the eighteenth century; this closure of the market led to a fall in the price of those provincial positions when they did change hands. Some scholars (e.g., B. Stone 1986, 57) have therefore concluded that the level of aspirations to office declined. But Doyle (1984, 843), in systematically examining the prices of offices in the courts and municipalities, found that they generally rose 300 to 600 percent from 1710 to 1790; in some particularly prosperous towns, such as Bordeaux, the rise was even greater, a nearly tenfold increase. And prices continued to rise steadily up to the end of the Old Regime. Doyle (1974, 28) reports that the cost of a court counselor's position in Aix rose over 30 percent in the two decades before 1789; in Bordeaux, the cost of the office of *secrétaire du roi*, which conferred immediate hereditary nobility, rose more than 100 percent from 1740 to 1780; and that of a position in the *cours des aides* rose by over 70 percent in the same period.

This "clogging" of the arteries of promotion has led some historians (Hampson 1963, 10–11; Lefebvre 1947, 15) to accuse the Old Regime of staging a feudal reaction to halt mobility. In fact, the amount of closure varies considerably according to where one looks. The parlements were probably the most closed to outsiders by the late eighteenth century. By the 1760s, the parlements of Dauphine, Provence, and Rennes were virtually closed, hereditary fiefdoms, with that of Rennes still largely held by long-standing noble families (Barber 1955, 113;

Meyer 1978, 305). However, the parlements of Perpignan, Metz, Pau, Douai, Bordeaux, Dijon, Bensançon, and Rouen continued to admit considerable numbers of commoners (Egret 1968, 44–46; Shapiro and Dawson 1972, 172). The parlements of Nancy, Grenoble, Aix, Toulouse, and, most importantly, Paris were closed to commoners but could still be entered by those of relatively recent nobility. At Paris, "perhaps eight out of every ten could do no better than claim a noble status gained in the course of the seventeenth and eighteenth centuries" (B. Stone 1986, 30).

Elsewhere in the royal administration, opportunities for advancement remained open. Gruder (1968, 222) reports that among the royal *intendants*, though all were noble, there were more new nobles at midcentury than in 1714, and still more under Louis XVI. She adds that by the latter's reign, half of all *intendants* were from families whose nobility was acquired through purchase of the office of *secrétaire du roi*. Bien (1978, 155) notes that this particular office was almost always purchased by commoners. He notes that for all cases in which records of the purchases survive, provincial purchasers were invariably commoners, as were 261 of the 266 purchasers in Paris. These commoners included sons of merchants, municipal officers, professionals, and wealthy farmers. At the very highest levels, ministerial posts remained open to talent. "Far from closing, the doors to ministerial office seem to have been open to a wider and more diverse social range in the later eighteenth century than in the late seventeenth" (Doyle 1972, 108). Even in the army, the fraction of field marshals and lieutenant generals who were born commoners rose from 1.7 percent in 1750 to 7.9 percent during the period 1781–1789.

There was thus considerable social mobility, which fed the ambitions of those who had gained wealth and sought recognition and higher status. But positions were too few to keep pace with demand, hence there was considerable displacement of those with elite aspirations. As Chaussinand-Nogart (1985, 129) notes, infiltration of the nobility was sufficient to unsettle older noble families, but the middle classes "wanted a tidal wave." With this evidence of displacement, is there also evidence of downward mobility, permitting us to speak of "turnover"?

DIFFERENCES IN FORTUNE

Rising prices and a growing market created opportunities for profit, but they were not opportunities that all elements of the populace were equally able to exploit. Many nobles as well as commoners (many of whom, or their sons, became noble) shared the movement toward greater wealth. But others, in both classes, were left behind. The same can be said of the peasantry and the clergy. The army too, assaulted by rising prices, by the flood of demands from old and new nobles for career opportunities, and by the need to adapt to new standards of professionalization and technical and engineering expertise, was rent with internal divisions. Demographic increase and price inflation generally meant that while some became richer, many others became poorer. A heightening of stratification by wealth thus ran through every social and professional grouping of the Old Regime.

The Nobility. "If we were to take their claims seriously and grant them all the privileges they claim for themselves, it would become necessary to compose a special set of laws for them, nay, set aside for their use a separate country in this world and a separate paradise in the next—for the insolence of these little country *gentilshommes* is so extreme that it just isn't possible to live in peace with them. They are savage animals . . . the most violent and insolent in this world." But the author of these lines does "not see the *gentilshommes* as eternal oppressors against whose exactions there is no remedy except bloody revolt. No . . . the nobility is a paper monster, ridiculously poor, ignorant, and inept, living out the last phase of its historic existence, clinging to empty honors and ridiculous titles, and really quite weak, ready to be pushed out of the way." These sentiments were not voiced toward the end of the Old Regime but rather in 1613, by the jurist Loyseau (quoted in Huppert 1977, 10, 33). Writing at another, but similar, time of rapid social mobility, turnover, and displacement, he gives voice to the sentiments we have sometimes associated with the eighteenth century. In both periods, ambitious members of the Third Estate sought to discredit the traditional nobles who looked down on them and competed with them for royal offices. Yet the nobility was no more dead and dying under Louis XVI than under Louis XIII.

It was, however, sharply divided. The professional descendants of Loyseau, the members of the parlements and the royal courts, were almost uniformly ennobled by the late eighteenth century and prided themselves on their nobility. Moreover, they (and the court nobility of Versailles) prided themselves on their fine manners, their graceful conversation, their knowledge of the world, and their service to the king. They too looked down on the uncouth, poor, rural nobility, whose only pride was in their birth, and whose attachment to superficial marks of rank, such as carrying their swords while tilling their small rural holdings, was considered slightly ridiculous. The more sober representatives of the law courts even looked down on the cavalier morals of the military nobility, whose gambling, drunkenness, and duels were no longer considered the epitome of "living nobly" (Huppert 1977, 87). In return, the nobility of the army and the countryside sneered at the ennobled financiers, whose "nouveau riche" avariciousness, they believed, was ruining France (Cobban 1964, 55; Behrens 1985, 170).

The divisions of outlook and manners reflected economic divisions. The nobility that served in the royal household and manned the parlements was far wealthier than the average noble. Most of the members of the Parlement of Bordeaux had total annual incomes in 1790 of 8,000–16,000 livres, and a few had incomes of over 30,000 livres (Doyle 1974, 53). By comparison, Chaussinand-Nogaret (1985, 52–53) estimates, based on a sample of noble incomes from thirteen *généralités*, that about 40 percent of the nobility had incomes of from 1,000 to 4,000 livres, and another 20 percent had incomes of less than 1,000 livres. In the Beauvaisis, in the relatively wealthy core of agrarian France, north of Paris, "out of 109 nobles, 70 . . . possessed incomes of not more than 1,000–2,000 livres, and 23 had only 500 livres—27 sous a day, less than the income of a country priest" (Mousnier 1979, 1:148). The poverty of some nobles, and the riches of others, reflected in each case a combination of apt or ill investments, family size, and fortune.

Many of the nobility were dynamic exploiters of opportunities in mining, trade, and manufacturing. The giant Anzin mining works, which by 1789 employed four thousand workers, and the Le Creuset foundry were begun by grand seigneurs (Chaussinand-Nogaret 1975, 275–276; Mousnier 1979, 1:189). Nobles also invested in shipping and wholesale trading companies, formed banking syndicates, and speculated on the Paris stock exchange (G. Taylor 1962). The large trading companies— the Compagnie de Commerce du Nord, the Compagnie de la Guyane française, and the Compagnie des Indes—were all directed by nobles. Chaussinand-Nogaret (1975, 274) argues that the most modern aspects of commercial capitalism—specifically, finance and overseas trade and mining and metallurgy—were in the hands more of the nobility than of the non-noble bourgeoisie.

Some nobles also profited from the land in this time of rising grain prices (Forster 1970; Fiette 1982). But initially this was only true for those who directly exploited their domainal lands or gained dues in kind.

Those who earned their incomes mainly from rents fared poorly for most of this period, for leases were usually given out at fixed rents for periods of nine years, or even of several decades, and it took a long time for rents to catch up to rising prices (Goubert 1973a, 129). Compared to the preceding decade, in the 1740s rents were 4.7 percent higher, while grain prices had risen 18 percent; in the 1750s and 1760s rents rose faster than prices but still failed to recover their 1730s real value. Thus, in these decades the profits of the land went to tenants rather than to landlords (Labrousse 1984, 2:379). Only after 1770 did rents dramatically rise, and these gains in real rent levels often accrued to bourgeois or to newly ennobled landlords who acquired the lands of those who had suffered during the decades of lagging rents (Huppert 1977, 112–114).

Since rent levels were resistant to change, but grain prices were rising and real wages were dropping, the way to profit was to control land that could be directly exploited with paid labor. Thus, in the eighteenth century French seigneurs attempted to expand their domainal lands, often seeking to appropriate part of the village communal lands through partition (*triage*) (Mousnier 1979, 1:184). Seigneurs also sought to restrict peasant access to woodlands, which, with the rising price of firewood, were becoming one of the most profitable parts of many seigneurial holdings. Where direct exploitation of domain lands was significant, revenues from marketing of produce dominated, and seigneurial dues were only a small part of noble income (Forster 1971, 38). However, where domain lands had largely been rented out, landlords sought to compensate for lagging rent levels by taking seigneurial dues, which had either been commuted to cash fees or else lapsed, and enforcing their collection in kind, which was far more profitable than cash fees (Milward and Saul 1973, 49, 257; Gillis 1970, 38). In such cases, revenue from dues could amount to half or more of seigneurial incomes (Mousnier 1979, 1:186–188). These attempts to partition the commons and to tighten control of woodlands and collection of dues have sometimes been labeled a "feudal reaction" on the part of the nobility. But there was nothing "feudal" about this behavior; the aim was simply to adapt to new market opportunities and shifts in prices that reduced the relative value of existing leases. English landlords in the late eighteenth century took exactly the same measures—appropriated common lands and tightened enforcement of rules against wood gathering—when English prices for grain and wood began rising (Snell 1985, 174–180).

Though some nobles were able to increase their domains and hence their revenues, other families were squeezed by lagging rent, on the one hand, and growing families to support, on the other. Lower mortality meant more surviving children, and as this burden was not evenly distributed, the family with limited land and income but many children could quickly find its heirs reduced to poverty. As Hufton (1967, 50) notes, "when more children were surviving infancy, fathers of large families could look forward to much effort if they were to conserve for their names any sort of wealth. No matter how rich the family, children in large quantities were a very mixed blessing. [Younger sons] were dependent upon parental skill . . . in finding them a position in the church, the army, to a lesser extent the navy, and the law courts." Mousnier (1979, 1:167) adds that "almost everywhere the need to ensure a firm economic base for the family . . . entailed the attribution to the eldest son of the major share in inheritance. The younger sons had to be content with a small share, often resigning themselves to bachelorhood, a mediocre career, and an early retirement, usually to the country; and it was they, probably, who gave the gentilshommes their reputation for poverty." In some provinces, where inheritance laws dictated division among surviving sons, larger families meant rapid dispersal of family wealth. René de Chateaubriand, recounting his family's fall into poverty, wrote that they "grew poorer through the inevitable effects of the country's law." Following Breton practice, the eldest son took away two-thirds of the property; the younger ones divided among themselves a single third of the paternal inheritance. As the land was further divided among their children, their descendants "came to the sharing-out of a pigeon, a rabbit, a duck pond, and a hunting dog. For all this they were still *high knight and powerful lords* of a dove-cote, a frog-pond, and a rabbit-warren" (cited in Kaplow 1965, 47).

In times of demographic stagnation, when the number of surviving males was roughly the same from generation to generation, a family with an excess of children could likely find heiresses and widowers to balance its fortune. Poorer noble families could often place a son in the household of a wealthier family. But in times of demographic growth, when each generation produced roughly 10–15 percent more surviving sons than the preceding one, financial pressures mounted. And since these pressures squeezed much harder on some families than on others, some families suffered misfortunes while others managed to prosper. But the latter may have been fewer in number than the former. In the eighteenth century, the bankruptcy of poor noble families was common, and poor nobles were sufficiently numerous that contemporaries believed most *gentilshommes* were poor (Hufton 1967, 53; Mousnier 1979, 1:192). In addition, Mousnier (1982) notes that the opportunities for poor noble families to place their children in the households of wealthier nobles diminished, and that traditional ties of patronage and loyalty consequently began to break down.

Larger families also increased social conflicts. Poor noble families had traditionally been able to secure places for their children in the army and in the Church, where they received preference in royal appointments. But as non-noble and recently ennobled families joined the ranks of aspirants for such positions, nobles "came into competition with those men whose station in life in all respects other than the possession of [ancient] nobility was identical to theirs" (C. Lucas 1973, 119). The positions that old nobility had traditionally dominated thus became more difficult to obtain precisely when they were most needed. Hufton (1967, 50) notes that toward the end of the eighteenth century, "as their need to find an income for their sons independent of the family land grew with rising costs and larger families, the noblesse became increasingly defensive of their monopoly of these positions."

The downward mobility of many noble families—owing both to rents eroded by inflation and to larger families, which divided inheritances and created impoverished younger sons—led to sharp clashes with upwardly mobile families, recently ennobled, who sought marriages and offices appropriate to their new stations. "Nobility" as a personal virtue was once associated with honor and service; but in the late eighteenth century (as also in the sixteenth), old noble families stressed that nobility was a quality of breeding and noble birth, or of "military virtue," which those of common origins could not attain with the mere purchase of a title (Schalk 1976; C. Lucas 1973). Social distinctions were preserved by hypergamy, a situation in which women (who carried a dowry) could marry into families of higher status but men were denied the same opportunity (Mousnier 1979, 1:73). Thus "in Paris a wealthy *roturière* [common-born female] married a duke and was presented at court; in the provinces a *roturier* [common-born male], however rich he might be, had difficulty marrying the daughter of a ruined marquis (Barber 1955, 99–105).

Most important was the persistent claim that certain positions, in the army and the Church, should be closed to all except those of long-standing nobility. This claim led to the Ségur Ordinance of 1781, which restricted army commissions to those with three generations of noble lineage, and reserved places for noble offspring in the military schools.

Divisions between the downwardly mobile country nobility and the upwardly mobile *anoblis* also surfaced, as we see next, in the selection of
delegates to provincial estates and the Estates General.

The Bourgeoisie. "By and large, the bourgeoisie accepted the status hierarchy with which it was confronted, and sought to improve its position
by means of the approved channels of mobility" (Barber 1955, 12).
Unfortunately, by the late eighteenth century these channels had become
clogged, and many bourgeois aspirants to higher careers were stalled
and frustrated.

The term "bourgeois" has no precise meaning, as its legal significance
varied with the granting of different privileges to different towns
(bourgs) in the course of the monarchy. By the eighteenth century, however, the term referred to any citizen who paid taxes in a major town,
and who therefore enjoyed the privileges of that city. The term thus
excluded the poor who paid no taxes, but included professionals, businessmen, officials, and landowners who lived in the town. These groups
enjoyed roughly the same sources of income as nobles—land, bonds,
and offices—and were often wealthier than the country nobility (G.
Taylor 1964). In addition, the privileges of bourgeois status were considerable: exemptions from the *taille*, the franc-fief, troop quartering,
and the corvée. One can thus well agree with Forster (1980, 183) that
"there was no 'noble class,' only 'noble privileges,' " many of which
were shared by the bourgeoisie.

But much as the nobility was internally divided by differing economic
fortunes, so too was the bourgeoisie. The great wholesale merchants of
the seaports and the great manufacturers of Paris and Lyon had fortunes
from hundreds of thousands to millions of livres; they had little in common with the doctors, lawyers, small retailers, and minor officials of
the provincial towns (Barber 1955, 28–29). The differences in fortunes
made for differences in mobility, as the wealthy bourgeoisie bid up the
prices of ennobling offices beyond the reach of the average career officer. Thus, the *avocats* and notaries who hoped to gain entry to the
higher courts of the parlement and the upper ranks of royal administration found themselves bypassed by the sons of colonial merchants and
financiers (Doyle 1980, 135). Cobban (1964, 59) remarks that "as the
commercial and financial classes were rising, so, it seems, the class of
venal officers was declining. The inevitable result was a conflict between
the rising and declining groups, which particularly took the form of a
struggle for control of the towns."

The town administrations, after several rounds of attempted reforms of the municipal offices and the courts, were in disarray in the last decades of the Old Regime. "On the eve of the revolution, there was complete confusion in this sphere." In some towns, new officers carried out functions; in others, new offices were purchased and merged with the old order, and prereform administrations were reestablished. "But even more numerous were the towns where the [new offices] had been neither taken up nor merged [with the old]." There the king's intendant appointed municipal officers (Mousnier 1979, 1:604).

The constant reform efforts had devalued many former offices, while the clogged channels of promotion left few avenues for career advancement. Outbid for advancement by the wealthy bourgeoisie of trade and finance, and with town administrations increasingly in the hands of royal appointees, the *avocats*, notaries, and minor officials of the towns were enraged at the closure of opportunities and the depreciation of their educations and career investments. But this anger was more the result of conflicts within the bourgeoisie than either conflicts with nobles or the lack of opportunities for the bourgeoisie as a whole. In examining the *cahiers de doléances*, or lists of grievances, drawn up by members of the Third Estate on the eve of the 1789 elections to the Estates General, Shapiro and Dawson (1972, 170) found that the members who were most radical in their demands for equality were from precisely those towns where there were the most opportunities for social mobility through purchase of ennobling offices. Failure of the lower bourgeoisie to keep pace with the wealthier bourgeoisie, rather than closure of opportunities to the order as a whole, evidently created pockets of radicalism. As Doyle (1980, 135) observes, "on the eve of the Revolution, the bourgeoisie was just as divided between rich and (relatively) poor as was the nobility."

The Clergy. The Church stood to profit from the rise in prices, for much of its income came from tithes on agrarian production. Tithes were ill regarded in the eighteenth century, however, for while they rose in value, the peasants saw that local curés remained impoverished (Gagnol 1974, 176). The reason was that tithes were collected by the chapters and dioceses of the Church, while the curés depended on benefices and cash salaries.

The bishops and abbots of the richest abbeys and orders were almost invariably noble and enjoyed high incomes and wealthy life-styles. The ordinary clergy were almost invariably commoners, whose incomes depended on their specific appointments. In Angers, curés' incomes ranged from under 400 livres per year to over 3,000 livres (McManners 1960, 139); in Dauphine, similarly, incomes ranged from under 300 livres per year to 2,600 livres (Tackett 1977, 119). The differences came from variations in the benefices that were attached to certain parishes.

The ordinary clergy were abused by this system in many ways. First, promotion became, as McManners (1960, 139) notes, "a lottery within a lottery." Personal favor, rather than merit, determined promotion, and since parishes varied so widely in incomes, a new appointment could mean either a tenfold or a hardly noticeable increase in income. One *vicaire* of Angers wrote bluntly in 1789, "Don't you think that all curés ought to be equal, both in tithe and revenue?" (cited in McManners 1960, 139).

Second, many curés had no protection against rising prices. In the west, in Brittany, Lower Normandy, Nantais, and Upper Maine, the parish clergy usually had some land, and 20–40 percent of them had reasonable incomes of over 2,000 livres. But in the northeast the curés were far poorer, with 60–80 percent (excepting those in Paris) having incomes of under 1,200 livres (Tackett 1984, 666). And in southern France many, if not most, curés were without benefices and thus subsisted entirely on their fixed cash salaries. "With the rise in prices after 1740, all of the congruists [clergy dependent on salary] found their incomes being progressively eroded" (Tackett 1977, 126–127). Their incomes were raised twice by royal decree, in 1769 and again in 1786. These raises kept the level of the congruists' salaries in line with the overall movement of prices. But in the long intervals between raises, the curés' real incomes declined.

Third, the curés on fixed incomes watched as tithe holders, who were usually absentee landlords, not only profited but also escaped taxation. The clergy were exempt from the *taille*, but liable for the *capitation* and *vingtièmes*. But these burdens were not levied evenly. McManners (1960, 223) notes that in Angers "the higher clergy underassessed themselves for taxation [while] the parochial clergy had paid out half a million [livres] on their behalf." Tackett (1977, 237) observes that in Dauphine also, the Church overassessed the curés on their salaries and underassessed the landed incomes of the priors and tithe holders. In the northeast as well, the higher clergy favored themselves through underassessment of taxes at the expense of the curés (Tackett 1984, 666).

Not surprisingly, the curés chafed at their treatment. From the 1760s, they began to express a desire for rationalization of the Church, for abolition of the special privileges of the abbeys and orders, and for greater equality between the pastoral and elite clergy (McManners 1960, 220–222; Tackett 1977, 231). Since out of the 296 deputies of the clergy elected to the Estates General, 208 were curés, their grievances eventually had a major impact in 1789.

We have noted that, in general, in times of rising prices landed incomes are most difficult to assess, and generally escape fair taxation, whereas the earnings of those on fixed salaries are eroded. In eighteenth-century France, the clergy was divided into two groups: those with generous landed incomes from tithes and benefices versus those with minor or no benefices, who largely depended on fixed salaries. Thus, these general processes had the effect of polarizing the institutional structure of the French Church and creating sharp divisions between upper and lower clergy.

The Army. The army was a microcosm of French society, and indeed, in no other institution in Old Regime France were the rivalries of different elite groups more clearly revealed.

The army was the preferred career of the traditional nobility, and the refuge for those among the poorer country *gentilshommes* who could not make a living from their lands. Corvisier (1979, 102) estimates that perhaps 20–25 percent of the French nobility had military experience. All general officers in the army were noble, and any non-noble promoted to that rank also gained noble status.

After 1763 and its defeat in the Seven Years' War, the French army underwent a series of reforms designed to enhance its professionalism and effectiveness. Able officers who had been promoted from the ranks during the war were encouraged to remain in the army. And recruitment for the artillery corps was aimed at gaining skilled officers with backgrounds in engineering. Both of these processes increased the role of *roturiers* in the officer corps. By 1789, almost 20 percent of the army's officers were of *roturier* origin (Barber 1955, 120).

But this increased presence of common-born officers did not mean that the army had become a path of mobility. Quite the reverse was true. The Crown could no longer afford to take on high-ranking officers who could not afford their own pensions and outfitting costs; thus, the ranks of colonel and above were virtually closed to nonwealthy aspirants, whether noble or *roturier* by birth (Barber 1955, 118; Corvisier 1979, 163–164). In addition, as a cost-saving measure the number of companies was reduced, and in 1776 venality was abolished. These measures reduced the number of captaincies, which had been the favorite rank of the provincial nobility. The change to merit-contingent promotions and the abolition of venality outraged wealthy nobles and recently ennobled families who could no longer purchase positions for themselves or their offspring (S. Scott 1978, 27). The upper ranks of the army thus became a closed preserve, consisting of long-standing officers, some of whom had risen from the lower ranks, and newer officers from the wealthiest noble and recently ennobled families who had purchased positions in the decade following the Seven Years' War.

The entry points to a military career thus shifted downward, to the company level and below. And at these lower points, competition became fierce. "Banned from the highest ranks, the lesser nobility opposed—with a bitterness all the greater—all access by wealthy commoners to company-officer ranks" (Corvisier 1979, 169). The grievances of the nobility, and their evident poverty, moved the Crown to make special allowances for scions of long-standing noble families who sought military careers. As noted earlier, not only were places reserved for them in the military schools, but also, in 1781, the Crown decreed that all new officers had to have three generations of inherited nobility (Shulim 1981, 367). Even with these protective measures, the provincial nobility faced a limited future. All regimental commands (colonels) and higher offices were monopolized by the wealthy court nobility; poorer nobles "stacked up" in the grades of captain, major, and lieutenant colonel (S. Scott 1978, 22).

The prospects for *roturiers* became even worse. From 1763 to 1776, a wealthy financier or wholesale merchant who had acquired ennobling office could hope, through wealth and connections, to acquire a captaincy or even a colonel's position for himself or a son. Even a modestly successful businessman might hope to launch his son on a military career by equipping him for a lieutenancy. Such prospects were now gone, and even those who had entered the officer corps found it harder to advance. "Young middle-class men of talent had to be content with sub-ordinate officer and non-commissioned positions" (Corvisier 1979, 169).

The end result of all these adjustments in military recruitment was that "increasing competition and declining opportunities for advancement served only to intensify rivalries among officers; [hence] the line army, despite its unique organization and functions, reflected the divisions that existed in society as a whole" (S. Scott 1978, 22, 207). The senior officers were chiefly court nobility, including some recently ennobled "counting-house colonels" from financiers' families, who acquired their positions through influence at court. The junior officers were chiefly provincial nobility, who resented their superiors and chafed at the limits on their own advancement. Noncommissioned officers were drawn from bourgeois families and the enlisted ranks; these subordinate officers were embittered by the 1781 royal decree, which effectively cut off their career aspirations. These contentions did indeed "reflect the divisions that existed in society as a whole." They represented the clash between downwardly mobile provincial nobles, whose rent revenues lagged behind inflation and who had younger surviving sons for whom they could not provide, and court nobles, who dominated the general officer corps. They also embodied the clash between the wealthy bourgeois families, who had "made it" in the middle decades of the century and who were able to purchase ennobling office and respectability by placing family members in military careers, and the still-aspiring bourgeois or recently ennobled families, who now found the officer corps closed to their offspring. The clash was made worse by the penury of the monarchy, which resulted in cost-saving measures that further reduced opportunities for advancement. The twin forces of population expansion and the consequent rise in prices, which produced both vast expansion of aspirants to elite positions and royal penury, thus created divisions even within the officer corps of the royal army.

FACTION AND DISSOLUTION

The elite of French society was thus divided horizontally and vertically toward the close of the Old Regime. The horizontal division was into groups with different degrees of privilege—the nobility, the clergy, and the bourgeoisie. More importantly, the vertical division was by wealth and opportunity. For the upper stratum in each privileged group—the court nobility, the bishops, and the wealthy financiers and wholesale merchants (many of whom became noble in the course of their careers)—society was open to their talents and generous in its rewards. But for the lower stratum in each group—the provincial nobility, the curés, and the lawyers, notaries, retailers, and lesser municipal officers—society appeared to neglect their talents, to discriminate unfairly against their services, and to foreclose any success in their futures. It was precisely these latter groups, however, that were most numerous and so dominated in the selection of representatives to the Estates General.

The conflicts within each privileged group burst forth in 1787–1789, in a series of controversies over the composition of the Estates General.

In the provinces, where preliminary elections were held for provincial estates, many provincial nobles asserted their claims to have a separate status and excluded even the recently ennobled from their ranks. In Brittany, moderate urban nobles from Rennes and Nantes tried to forge an alliance with prominent members of the Third Estate, but "the needy and narrow-minded country squires who flocked in droves to the capital of Brittany did not expect to cede any of their prerogatives; [instead they] expressed their intransigence and the hatred which they bore the opulent bourgeoisie" (Egret 1965a, 143). In Franche-Comté, the older noble families sought to exclude from the noble meeting of the provincial estates any families who had not been noble for at least a century, or four generations, thus excluding nearly 85 percent of the nobles of the province. In Artois, they limited the Second (noble) Estate to families with six generations of nobility and a seigneurie, thereby excluding 75 percent of the nobles (Doyle 1980, 120). In Provence, the Second Estate was limited to fief-holders, thereby excluding 50 percent of the members of the Parlement of Aix. Nobles who had been so excluded then allied with the municipal officers and leading members of the province's Third Estate in a movement to overturn the authority of the province's estates (Egret 1965b, 158).

Elections to the national Estates General were no less troubled. Everywhere, the summons to noble electors went only to those with fully transmissible hereditary nobility, thus excluding the many thousand recent purchasers of personal nobility: "members of rich and ambitious families who had paid good money to escape from the Third Estate and now found themselves pushed brusquely back into it" (Doyle 1980, 152). Faced with the provincial problems over degrees of nobility, Necker decided that all hereditary nobles, irrespective of the length of their ancestry, should have a vote for noble delegates. But in several districts this resulted in breakaway factions of older nobles, who elected their own delegates and required the Estates General to choose between their deputies and those of the other noble electors.

Overall, however, "the noble elections were a triumph for the natural but hitherto silent majority among the nobility—provincial, poor, relatively inarticulate, politically inexperienced, but determined to use this unlooked-for opportunity to disavow those who formerly usurped its [leading] role" (Doyle 1980, 153). In other words, the delegates to the Second Estate were, overwhelmingly, precisely those nobles whose downward mobility in the preceding decades predisposed them most strongly to seek reinforcement of leading status and privileges for their order. Chaussinand-Nogaret (1985, 172) opines that the delegates were far more conservative than the electors as a whole because the deputies "belonged almost entirely to the military caste and had been elected less for their opinions than the prestige of their uniform."

These sinking members of the noble classes faced their counterparts in the elections to the Third Estate, for these returned "a landslide victory for the non-commercial, professional, and proprietary bourgeoisie" (Doyle 1980, 155). Eighty percent of the Third Estate delegates were lawyers, notaries, or officeholders, and three-quarters of the delegates were from moderate-sized towns (Sutherland 1986, 40). These were precisely the members of the bourgeoisie most concerned about blockages to mobility, and about the pretensions and privileges of the nobles. These delegates complained that the costumes of the Third Estate representatives were demeaning compared to those of the Second, and that they should not have to kneel when the king appeared at the Estates General if the Second Estate was not also so compelled (Harris 1986, 454–456).

Finally, as observed earlier, the elections to the First Estate produced an overwhelming victory for the curés.

Under these circumstances, it should be evident that the Estates General were likely to split apart. For they threw together precisely those factions of each order with the greatest accumulated grievances. None of these groups was pleased with the current social and political hierarchy, but they had very different ideas about what needed to be rectified. The alliance of the Third Estate with the curés, against the nobility, was a clear alliance of sympathies between two groups who felt abused by the privileged. And while some of the leading court nobility were willing to ally with the Third Estate to seek a more rational, meritocratic social order, the refusal of the Second Estate as a whole to act jointly with the Third Estate, or to surrender any of its prerogatives, reflects the determination of the provincial nobility to avoid social submersion or outright relinquishment of their leading role, as they had been forced to do in the army and in the royal administration during the previous decades.

The result of all these machinations among groups—a breakaway combination of the Third Estate, most of the First, and a small number of leading elements from the Second in the National Assembly, leaving behind a "rump" composed chiefly of conservative provincial nobles— revealed the underlying social divisions in the national elite. But these were not chiefly divisions between "noble" and "non-noble." Rather, they were divisions between successful and unsuccessful nobles, and between successful and unsuccessful bourgeois. The Estates General gave the less successful elements in both groups a chance to take the national stage; each group thus sought to rectify their fortunes. The impossibility of simultaneously improving the lot of both the lesser bourgeoisie (which would have required a more meritocratic society) and the lesser nobility (which would have required greater "affirmative action" for nobles based on birth) made a united front between these groups an extremely unlikely prospect.

Unfortunately for the Crown, at the very time the Estates General were breaking apart, so too was the army, and for the same reasons. During 1789 many high officers were on leave or at the Estates General. Remaining in charge were officers of fortune and provincial majors and lieutenant colonels. Thus, "during a period when discipline was rapidly disintegrating, those officers most interested in maintaining it were away from the men under their command, and those left behind in charge were often the least likely to take the drastic measures to preserve a hierarchy which had long been prejudiced against them" (S. Scott 1978, 83).

In discussing the English Revolution, we noted that in the twenty years following the initial split of the elite in the Long Parliament there unfolded another skein of divisions and conflicts, reflecting the many divisions among the elite. The same sort of sequential splintering occurred in France, where the divisions in the Estates General were rapidly succeeded by divisions among the revolutionary parties. The federalists who opposed Jacobin rule after 1792 were predominantly drawn from the upper bourgeoisie (Edmonds 1983, 29). As L. Hunt (1984, 176) notes, "the moderates of Bordeaux and the royalists of Amiens were just as much or even more 'bourgeois' than the republicans of Toulouse." Divisions between, on the one hand, the petty professionals and officials who dominated the National Assembly and benefited most from the expansion of central authority and the openings provided by the revolution and, on the other hand, the large manufacturers and trading bourgeoisie, who needed above all else local order and resented the interference from Paris, the costs of the war, and the disruption of business, fueled federalist, Bonapartist, and even royalist sentiments. Thus in the south and west, where smaller merchants, artisans, and, especially, lawyers and municipal officers were most influential and faced few threats from either rootless poor or wealthy notables, local sentiment remained republican. But in the major cities and in the wealthier regions of the north and east and of Languedoc, where a large number of wealthy notables faced a growing threat from the poor and from middle-class radicals, strong desires for a "republic of order" and rightist sentiments emerged (L. Hunt 1984, 143–146). The continuing conflicts of the revolution were not simply "bourgeois" versus "aristocratic" or "revolutionary" versus "reactionary" struggles; they represented long-standing divisions within the elite, particularly within the bourgeoisie.

YOUTH AND THE RUSH FOR CREDENTIALS

Before ending our discussion of the French elite, it is worth noting two other aspects of elite competition and conflict. First, the change in age structure resulted in more youth taking and seeking positions of responsibility. Many historians have noted that this enlarged youth cohort contributed to the radical atmosphere and impatience with traditional institutions that existed toward the end of the Old Regime. Second, the competition for elite positions led, as in the seventeenth century, to a rush for credentials for such positions.

Lynn Hunt (1984, 217) has commented that the radicalism of the French Revolution was fueled by the youth and marginality of its leaders; during the period 1793–1794 in particular, unusually young men exercised power. Hampson (1978, 85) remarks that in the provincial estates of Arras there was a split between "wise men of age and experience and young hotheads," with the latter organizing and putting through a radical slate of delegates to the Estates General. Meyer (1978, 283) adds that in Rennes youth played a leading role in the resistance of the parlement to royal pressure, with young nobles and law students joining forces to oppose the royal officials. Egret (1968, 47–48) notes that the minimum age of twenty-five for members of parlements was widely disregarded in the late eighteenth century, when very young sons were admitted "from families whose fathers were always in a hurry to find them positions." In both Paris and Dijon, councillors under age thirty-five were in the majority, and "all the contemporary memoires outdo each other in insisting that this majority of young men exerted a decisive influence on the debates of the [Parlement of Paris] in 1787 and 1788. The First President of the Paris Cours des Aides deplored 'their headlong and rash actions' " (Egret 1968, 47). And in the Estates General, Sutherland (1986, 41) informs us, liberals were to be found chiefly among the younger generation.

We have already noted that relatively youthful leaders took over positions of responsibility and contributed to the radicalism of the English Revolution in the years after 1640. Such leaders were available, and youth, in general, took a large role, because the political crisis occurred just when the youth cohort in the population was exceptionally large, relative to the number of older adults. In this respect, the French Revolution closely resembles the events in mid-seventeenth-century England. For in France the years from 1740 onward were decades with an age structure in which the youth cohort (ten to thirty years old) was relatively large compared to older adults.

We have also noted that in England, and in Europe in general, the late sixteenth and early seventeenth centuries saw an expansion of higher education far in excess of the increase in population as a whole. We explained this as a credentialing "crisis," in which turnover and displacement mobility, by increasing competition for elite positions, sharply raised the demand for educational credentials.

In Old Regime France, the same phenomenon occurred. The chief credential for admission and promotion in the higher ranks of royal service was a law degree. The overwhelming majority of the royal intendants were trained in the law (Gruder 1968, 18). The same was true for the majority of Third Estate representatives to the Estates General (Sutherland 1986, 40). And just as in England enlarged youth cohorts and competition for places led the universities to turn out too many men for too few places, producing ambitious and marginal preachers and lawyers, so too the French universities turned out too many lawyers. "Throughout the century government administrators had expressed alarm at the spread of education" (Lefebvre 1977, 48). Such fears were well placed, for the universities did issue forth a flood of graduates, creating a situation in which "lawyers were too numerous for the work available" (Doyle 1980, 134).

The pattern of demand for higher education in France closely follows that of social mobility. In the sixteenth and early seventeenth centuries, when mobility was high, complaints about an excess of students were common. Chartier (1982) reports that Richelieu's testament complained of the ill effects of too many students, who destabilized the social order. Chartier (1982, 395) adds that during this period "texts abound which denounce the excessive number of universities and deplore the problem of too many students." But with the stalling of population growth and prices after 1660, and the consequent decline in social mobility, the demand for credentials fell. The matriculations in law at the leading French universities (Paris, Orléans, Dijon, Caen, Bourges, Avignon,

Point-à-Mousson, Poitiers, and Toulouse) fell by one-third from the 1680s to the 1710s. But from the 1730s, when social mobility again increased, they rose sharply. Matriculations increased by 77 percent from the 1730s to the 1780s, while the population climbed only 16 percent (Kagan 1975). It thus appears that the demand for higher education in the eighteenth century, as in the seventeenth century in England and France, closely followed and reflected the competition for places among aspirants to elite positions.

By 1789, three generations of demographic expansion and rising prices had created widespread turnover and displacement in every social and professional group of the Old Regime. These phenomena created divisions and conflicts that wrenched the Church and the army, embittered the municipal and professional bourgeoisie and the provincial nobility, and resulted in a split within the Estates General. These events were sufficient, when combined with the fiscal crisis, to create a major political crisis. But this crisis was further expanded by the actions of the lower classes.

POPULATION, POVERTY, AND THE PATTERN OF POPULAR UNREST

French historians have long noted that population growth led to increasing hardships for the peasants and the working classes. However, to focus on population growth alone is to examine only one element of the demographic changes of this period. For the population was not only growing larger; it was also becoming younger and more urban. It is these three trends together, combined with the inability of the rural economy to grow in pace with the population, that increased the likelihood of popular action in the event of political opportunity.

Moreover, as the French population was spread among varying social structures, with marked differences both between peasants and urban groups and among peasants of the north, the west, the center, and the Midi, the impact of demographic changes, and the conflicts that they generated, varied among different sectors of the populace.

THEDA SKOCPOL AND THE COMPONENTS OF THE REVOLUTIONARY CRISIS: SOCIAL STRUCTURES AND DYNAMIC FORCES

At this point, it is useful to draw some distinctions between the approach used here and the analysis of Theda Skocpol in *States and Social Revo-*

lutions (1979). Skocpol argues that the French Revolution was the product of two movements with distinct origins: a state crisis, rooted in international competition and domestic blockage of state expansion; and a rural crisis, rooted in the actions of peasant communities. It was thus *structures* within French society—an elite-blocked state and peasant communities organized to provide a basis for coordinated popular action—that created France's vulnerability to social revolution.

But identification of these structural features does not constitute a sufficient explanation of the Revolution. One must also ask what forces buffeted these structures and turned potential vulnerability into crisis. Although Skocpol points to international military competition as the key force, this is also not sufficient, for the real costs of France's involvement in the American War were, as noted earlier, far less than the cost of either the Seven Years' War or the War of the Austrian Succession. International war was a constant feature of the Old Regime. We need to examine *dynamic* forces, which arose over the course of the eighteenth century, to explain why the vulnerable structure of the French monarchy finally gave way in 1789.

Skocpol claims that the French state crisis was due to France's inability to compete with the more advanced capitalist state of England and, in particular, to the state's inability to expand taxation given resistance by elite-controlled parlements. I agree wholeheartedly with this view of structural blockage and would modify this aspect of Skocpol's approach in only two ways. First, the "inability" to compete did *not* rest mainly on France's economy being more backward or less capitalist than England's. The culprit is, instead, the *relation of the state* to the French economy. England's state relied more on indirect taxes that tapped urban and commercial wealth; France relied more on direct taxes on the land. Thus, even though both countries had growing urban and commercial sectors, England's state benefited from this growth far more than did the French monarchy. Second, it was not the costs of war with England alone that led to crisis, since the American War was less expensive than France's other eighteenth-century wars. The difficulty was that population growth—through inflation, larger military forces, and mounting costs of poverty relief—pushed up Crown expenses faster than revenues increased, so that by the end of the century the government had insufficient disposable revenue to service its loans. In short, where Skocpol sees as the source of trouble a backward economy undone by the costs of war, I see a backward tax system (too much a land-based tax system) undone by the mounting population and inflationary pressures of the eighteenth century. The conflict between the Crown and French elites arose not because the monarchy was attempting to squeeze out more revenues than the economy could bear, but rather because the elites had benefited from price trends and controlled increased resources that the Crown, struggling with rising prices, sought to tax. The *structural* blockage pointed out by Skocpol thus had its effect in the context of *dynamic* forces buffeting the fiscal system.

In addition, Skocpol's emphasis on state structure and rural community structure fails entirely to explain two key aspects of the crisis: first, why the elites fragmented internally and, second, why the urban populace of Paris was so ready to act to defend the Assembly and the revolution. We have shown how the effects of population growth and resulting price inflation led to turnover and displacement among the French eighteenth-century elite, creating markedly different conditions than prevailed under Louis XIV. Before considering in detail the problem of urban action, it is important to examine Skocpol's analysis of rural uprisings. For it is the area of peasant action that reveals the greatest differences between Skocpol's structural approach and the view of this book that social-structural features must be seen as operating in the context of *dynamic* forces.

For Skocpol, peasant grievances were always "structurally" present. She draws on M. Bloch's (1966) observation that peasant disorders are as common in agrarian societies as strikes are in industrial ones in order to make the point that peasants always have reason to rebel. Therefore, when the political crisis of 1789 paralyzed state authority, it was to be expected that peasants would rise up and express their grievances. All that they needed was the ability to organize and to act collectively, supporting their resolve through the communal structure of the peasant village. For Skocpol, then, to explain peasant actions in 1789 one must point only to the "broadly similar structural features characterizing agrarian social relations across all France" (Skocpol 1979, 122).

But this view cannot explain important variations in French peasant actions. First, peasant "revolts and contestations" do not spread evenly across French agrarian history; as Le Roy Ladurie (1974b) and Mousnier (1970b, 115) have observed, peasant unrest largely died out between 1675 and 1730, then resumed and increased throughout the eighteenth century. Thus, peasant unrest shows a cyclic pattern that closely corresponds to the cycle of population and price pressures. Second, peasant unrest showed different motives, and different patterns, in different parts of France. For example, peasant actions in 1789 were relatively weak in Brittany, moderately revolutionary in Languedoc, and fierce in Burgundy (D. Hunt 1983; Brustein 1986). In short, a view of peasant unrest in which a constant level of grievances is maintained across time, rooted in similar peasant "structures" across France, does not conform to the evidence of temporal and regional variations.

In place of Skocpol's view of a constant level of grievances and of similar rural structures, I suggest that we see rural France in the eighteenth century as affected by dynamic forces that receded from 1660 to 1730 and then mounted to the end of the century, acting on a mosaic of diverse rural structures. This view is, of course, hardly innovative; I am merely following the insights of French historians of the rural world. But it is important, given the significance of Skocpol's work, to insist that her outstanding insights into the vital role of social structural features not obscure the similarly vital role of dynamic forces and regional variations. Let us therefore take a closer look at rural conditions toward the end of the Old Regime.

THE BURDEN ON THE LAND

Although peasant actions in 1789 are often thought of as following the events in Paris, particularly the taking of the Bastille on July 14, rural unrest was evident from early in the year, with disorders breaking out in Brittany in January, and spreading to Paris by April. "The Estates-General, therefore, were elected, and met, against a background of riot, disorder, and popular anxiety which left few parts of the country untouched" (Doyle 1980, 167). While the political crisis gave the peasants an opportunity, and a motivation, to express their grievances, "the peasantry of 1789 was not some blind, impersonal force, but rather a movement of working people whose experience had given them the inclination and the tools to act" (D. Hunt 1983, 138).

For many peasants, the critical experiences were land hunger and growing poverty. Dupâquier (1978, 245) points to five trends that evidence growing rural distress: (1) the age of marriage rose, indicating difficulty in accumulating the resources needed to start a family; (2) real wages fell; (3) the "floating" population increased, along with the volume of long-distance migration; (4) towns grew faster than the overall population, indicating emigration from the countryside; and (5) unemployment increased. Kaplan (1976, 1:86) adds that while there were no large-scale famines in eighteenth-century France, the incidence of grain shortages increased, with problems in 1709–1710, 1725–1726, 1738–1742, 1766–1775, and 1788–1792. Thus, difficult years rose in frequency from just over one in eight (nine bad years out of sixty-five) in the first two-thirds of the century to more than one in two (fifteen bad years out of twenty-seven) from 1766 to 1792.

The failure of cereal production to keep pace with population growth meant a "broadening of the base of the social pyramid perhaps more than even before" (Hufton 1974, 15). For in most areas of France, and particularly the densely populated northeast plains, the citizens depended on bread (Lefebvre 1947, 27). Keeping an animal on the village commons provided insurance against disastrous expenses and, if the animal was a cow or goat, offered milk or cheese. It did nothing, however, to provide a family's daily bread. Thus, a family either owned enough land to grow sufficient grain or else had to purchase grain on the market from wage earnings. And in the eighteenth century, as population grew, fewer and fewer families had enough land, and increasingly more were forced to buy their grain.

Robert Brenner (1976) has argued that the French Crown protected the peasants from expropriation, and we are accustomed to thinking of France as a nation of rural smallholders. But this is not an accurate portrait of France in the late eighteenth century. The Crown did protect the communal lands of villages and their animals, but it could not protect the family holding of the individual peasant from the vicissitudes of rising rents, subdivision among family members, and indebtedness (Root 1987). In the eighteenth century the majority of the land was owned by absentee owners: the Crown, the Church, and noble and bourgeois landlords. And the fraction of the land that was owned by peasants was generally subdivided into plots too small to support families. Thus, the dominant forms of agricultural participation by the French peasantry were cash tenancy and wage labor, not independent family farming (Brustein 1986, 148–149). As Lemoigne (1965, 63–65) notes in discussing the flow of migrants from the countryside to Strasbourg in the late eighteenth century, "the search for work and for bread became the dominant preoccupation of a population that was becoming proletarian."

The majority of peasant families were hard hit by the sharp rise in rents after 1770 and by the escalation in food prices relative to wages. In fact, the areas of France most affected by the wave of peasant actions in 1789 known as the "Great Fear" were precisely those areas most affected by landlessness and inadequate-sized tenancies, while those areas with either more widespread peasant landownership or larger and more adequate leasehold properties (e.g., Brittany and Bas Languedoc) were less affected.

Poverty was not evenly spread throughout France. Migration streams converged on three areas: in the northeast to the vicinity of Paris, in the west to Anjou, and in the south to Haute Languedoc (Hufton 1974, 74–75). These areas thus "concentrated" the landless. As we noted in discussing seventeenth-century England, such long-distance migration is evidence that there was insufficient land in many regions to provide a livelihood. Fairchilds (1976, 104) informs us that in the period 1725–1733, only 17 percent of those arrested for beggary in Aix-en-Provence came from areas not contiguous to Provence; by 1771–1789, 33 percent of those in Aix who were receiving poor relief came from such areas. The volume of long-distance migration by those in need had sharply risen.

In the late eighteenth century, landlessness, or insufficient land to support a family, was an increasingly common problem: "50 to 90 percent of holdings, depending on the region, were insufficient to maintain a family of even two or three children" (Hufton 1974, 187). In some areas, such as northern Burgundy, "day laborers made up three quarters of the inhabitants of the villages" (Mousnier 1979, 1:269). As there was not enough work for all, the landless either took to the roads in search of work or turned to beggary or crime.

There had always been poverty in early modern societies, of course. But it was a poverty of the unfortunate—the old, sick, lame, widowed, orphaned, demented, or temporary victims of local harvest or employment problems. Such individuals were the objects of Christian charity. They were not a threat to the social order; indeed, they anchored that order by providing a relief function for the Church, an opportunity for almsgiving, and a moral category compared to which the poor but healthy worker could feel well off.

The difficulty of the late eighteenth century was that population growth in excess of land and work opportunities created a permanent group of able-bodied underemployed who depended on assistance to survive. This group did not meet the normal requirements of Christian charity; and it was a group into which any healthy worker could fall, thus descending to the level of the lame and sick in need of help. It was a group whose growth in the late eighteenth century overburdened the traditional mechanisms of charity in France (Fairchilds 1976, 17). These unfortunate therefore became a burden to the state. And because, unlike the infirm, they often turned to vagabondage, the problem of petty crime increased and posed a threat to the propertied classes.

In Languedoc, average annual arrests for beggary rose by 28 percent from 1768–1775 to 1776–1786 (C. Jones 1982, 145). In Aix-en-Provence, looking at a longer span, in the 1720s an average of 151 beggars were arrested per year; in 1773 alone the number arrested was 2,631. Beggars "flooded its churches and street corners" (Fairchilds 1976, 132). The royal government sought to deal with this problem by greatly expanding the *maréchaussée* and by issuing sterner orders for the imprisonment of beggars and vagabonds, with new *arrêts* issued in 1764, 1767, and 1777 (R. Schwartz 1989, 249; Engrand 1982; Fairchilds 1976, 149–150). But local authorities, especially the parlements, resisted these efforts, partly because they had no desire to imprison people simply for seeking work and partly because they lacked the resources to build and maintain penal facilities on the scale required. Moreover, they blamed the Crown for the problem in the first place. "The idea that the evils of the fiscal structure lay at the root of poverty and vagrancy gained a new vogue" after 1770 (Forrest 1981, 17).

Unfortunately, the Crown had no means to deal with the problem of the poor. Everyone talked about it; C. Jones (1982, 29) suggests that the changing nature and dimensions of poverty formed "perhaps the most serious social question which faced Enlightenment France." Jones also suggests that the failure of traditional Christian charities, and the evidently economic nature of the problem, contributed to the change in *mentalités*, prompting a search for rational and secular solutions to social problems. The idea arose, later to play a major role in the revolution, that all Frenchmen held a "right to subsistence" (*le droit a la subsistance*) that should be guaranteed by the state (Forrest 1981, 27).

But the imbalance of population and resources was persistent and grew worse toward the end of the Old Regime; thus, the problem of poverty resisted solution. "Beggars and vagabonds remained objects of fear and hatred in rural areas" (Forrest 1981, 13). Petty crime increased (C. Jones 1982, 37), and "gangs of criminal vagrants . . . under the guise of begging, terrorized the . . . farmsteads of the *pays de grand culture* in the Orléanais and the Beauce" (C. Jones 1982, 147).

REGIONAL DIFFERENCES IN SOCIAL STRUCTURE AND PEASANT ACTION

Some regions were more affected by population pressure than others. Brustein (1986), in a brilliantly suggestive paper, has pointed out the vast differences in the nature of tenancy, landlord-peasant relations, and village structure across different parts of France. Following his lead, we can roughly divide France into four sections: the northeast (essentially

the Seine basin), the west (Brittany, Lower Normandy, and the Amori-
can Massif of the Lower Loire), the center (the Massif Central), and the
Midi (the Mediterranean south). Of course, within each region, and even
within each department, there were variations both in land and village
organization and in income distribution and farming patterns that ran
counter to the regional norm, making local exceptions to any regional
pattern common. However, with the understanding that these regional
divisions are only a crude way of sorting out general differences, they
are still a useful guideline for considering differences in rural peasant
actions.

Brustein notes that peasant violence against seigneurs was greatest in
the northeast. There was some antiseigneurial action in the Midi and
the center, though less severe. And there was very little such action in
the west, which in fact was notably counterrevolutionary and procleri-
cal. These different regional responses reflect, as emphasized throughout
this argument, a *combination* of population pressures and structural
conditions.

As noted earlier, population grew less in Brittany than elsewhere in
France in the eighteenth century. Nières (1984, 509) suggests an increase
of 15 percent from 1700 to 1780. Although nobles owned most of the
land in Brittany, there was little increase in competition for tenancies.
Much of the land was open waste used chiefly for grazing; the remainder
was leased out (usually for a mix of in-kind and cash payments) in enclosed parcels of four to five hectares, each large enough to support a
family. Indeed, throughout the *bocage* of the west and southwest, the
tiny farm typical of the northeastern peasant was rare, and larger holdings predominated (Moreau 1958). Wage labor was not common, outside of a few textile-producing districts in the present-day departments
of the Sarthe and Vendée; instead, family farms employed resident farm
workers (*domestiques*) who received most of their compensation in kind
(Brustein 1986, 151). There is little evidence of progressive impoverishment, or of complaints of unfair land concentration in the local peasant
cahiers (Sutherland 1982, 57; Le Goff 1981, 151).

In the western regions, in general, common waste for grazing was
generous, and enclosed farms were typical. Thus, there were few conflicts with landlords over rights to the common. And since farmhouses
were scattered, with small hamlets separated by enclosed fields as the
norm, communal organization was based on the parish and centered on
the curé, rather than based on the nucleated village and centered on the
village assembly, the more typical orientation of the open-field areas of

the northeast. Unsurprisingly, Brittany and the west were for the most part quiet in 1789. And when the revolution turned to radical attack on the Church and nobility, these regions proved conservative and even counterrevolutionary. There were differences in income between owner-occupiers and tenants, and between wage earners and those who owned or leased land, and these differences led to different reactions to the policies adopted by the revolutionary government regarding the Church, agrarian reform, and military recruitment. The activities of the Vendéans and the Chouans against the revolutionary government reflected these divisions (C. Tilly 1967; G. Bois 1960; Sutherland 1982). But there were not the conflicts over access to land, and over the levels of cash rents and wages, that prevailed in more demographically burdened and commercially developed areas of France, and thus not the same degree of antagonism toward rural landlords.

Provence, Languedoc, and other parts of the Midi, along with the central region, had somewhat higher levels of peasant-landlord conflict. Whereas the typical form of peasant landholding in the west was share-cropping-tenancy, in the more commercialized Midi a combination of small-scale freeholding and wage labor prevailed. Peasants owned half to two-thirds of the land, and only 10 percent of the peasantry was completely landless (Baehrel 1961, 397–400). The warm climate, diverse soils, and access to the sea made it possible to cultivate a wide range of commercial products: olives, vines, and fruit, as well as wheat. Since peasants generally owned their own land, and since in the Midi taxes were paid by both peasants and noble seigneurs (who were liable for the *taille réelle* on their nonexempt properties), there was only moderate friction between peasants and seigneurs over issues of rents, landownership, and taxation. "Seigneurial relations in the region lacked the tinge of violent animosity which colored the atmosphere in many areas of northern France" (C. Jones 1982, 38).

In the more mountainous central regions, leaseholding was more common, and poor soils meant less commercial activity. Peasant landowning was again widespread; for example, in Ussel, in the Limousin, 60 percent of the land was owned by peasants and communes, and only 17 percent of families were landless (Lemaître 1978, 95). Still, the quality of the land was poor, so as population grew, these regions participated in the commercial economy of the Midi by sending forth streams of migrants and seasonal wage laborers.

Though direct conflict between tenant cultivators and their landlords was thus muted, there certainly were animosities in the region, for the combination of rapid population growth and active markets in this area meant that land scarcity and rising prices imposed severe hardships on those peasants with growing families who sought to expand their holdings by lease or purchase, and on those peasants who depended on wages. The populations of Provence and of the neighboring regions of the Massif Central grew rapidly in the eighteenth century. Subdivision of land through inheritance led to the impoverishment of many families. Arthur Young (1971 [1792], 121), a contemporary observer, noted that much peasant poverty arose from "the minute division of their little farms among all the children. . . . I have, more than once, seen division carried to such excess, that a single fruit tree, standing in about ten perch of ground, has constituted a farm, and the local situation of a family decided by the possession."

Population pressure also drove up the price of grain relative to other products, and in relation to labor. From 1725 to 1785, wheat prices in Provence rose 70 percent. But wages rose far more slowly, while wine prices failed to increase after the 1740s (Baehrel 1961, 534, 563; Labrousse 1970d, 537). The increasingly wealthy bourgeoisie of the towns, who profited from rising prices and growing markets, were expanding their landholdings at the expense of the smaller peasants. The net result was rising antagonism, not so much between tenants and seigneurs, which was not a common relationship, but between peasants and townsmen and between rich and poor. As C. Lucas (1978, 7) notes, 1789 in the Midi saw not so much antiseigneurial actions as extreme local conflicts of all sorts. Popular risings were "basically familiar food riots," but these were "immediately transformed into a general assault of the poor on the wealthy." Much as in the English Revolution, the conflicts between royalists and revolutionary forces were firmly rooted in local conflicts that erupted in time of national crisis. Lucas describes these conflicts as more similar to those in the Greek city-states—pitting the urban oligarchs and rural largeholders against a combination of rural smallholders and urban and rural laborers—than to the starker landlord-cultivator conflicts of the northeast.

In sum, the west had little population pressure and an agrarian structure that, though poor, could maintain its pattern of dispersed family farms. The Midi faced considerable population pressure, including that of migrant labor from the central regions. Its commercial smallholding and limited wage-labor agrarian structure thus came under stress, intensifying conflicts between the better-off and the worse-off inhabitants. But the form of that conflict reflected local agrarian structures and thus featured a myriad of conflicts based on local market position, rather than sweeping conflicts over access to land or seigneurial rights.

The northeast, however, was preeminently the region in which a greatly increased population faced a fixed supply of land, and in which the dominant forms of cultivation—cash tenancy and wage labor—made the rural population acutely vulnerable to increased prices and falling wages. Conflicts between seigneurs and peasants were thus severe.

In the great open plains of the north and east, grain cultivation for market was the primary form of agriculture. To provide fodder for the animals needed to pull the plows, however, there were also common grazing lands, usually grass but in some areas forested. Because grazing lands were scarce, common pastureland was valuable and closely regulated by the community. Animals also grazed on the fallow and on the stubble remaining after the harvest. Some woodlands were preserved for hunting, but also to provide wood for fuel and construction. Because of the value of the land and the dominant role of the nobility and clergy from medieval times, peasants owned a smaller portion of the land than in any other region of France.

The peasantry held only about three-tenths of the land, and many, probably a majority, had too little land to support their families (Sée 1958, 50; Lefebvre 1977, 34; J. Cooper 1978, 23). "The heads of families who were landless accounted for 75 percent in the coastal plain of Flanders, 70 percent in certain villages in the vicinity of Versailles" (Lefebvre 1977, 34). In Upper Normandy, "peasant property had virtually disappeared by about 1620" (Dewald 1987, 5). In northern Burgundy, the majority of the peasantry depended chiefly on wage labor (Saint-Jacob 1960). Most peasants thus supported themselves by a combination of farming very small plots of land, leased from ecclesiastical, noble, and bourgeois landlords, and wage labor on the farms of nobles and wealthy peasants. There were generally a few wealthy peasants in each northeastern community, owning and leasing a hundred or more acres of land, whose financial well-being was in sharp contrast to their neighbors' circumstances.

As in the south, population growth led to subdivision of family inheritances and to rising rents and grain prices. Giesey (1977, 274) notes that, for all except nobles, "the coutume [i.e., custom] de Paris, which influenced other coutumiers, classified four-fifths of the *propres* (family immovable wealth) as the réserve héréditaire, which should be divided equally." Vovelle (1980, 86), in a sample from the Beauce in 1810–1820, after the revolutionary land redistribution, found that half the farms were tiny plots that collectively held only 7 percent of the land. Dallas (1982, 206–207), for the same area and time period, found that the median peasant holding was only .99 hectare. Rising grain prices were beneficial for those who still held enough land to feed their families and market their surpluses, but by the late eighteenth century these individuals represented but a small minority of northeastern peasants. The majority depended to some degree on wage labor to secure their food, and thus they were badly hurt by the rising price of bread.

The northeast was thus distinct from the west, where tenancies were large, open grazing was widespread, and wage labor was rare. It was also distinct from the south, where landownership by peasants was more common, vines and olive cultivation made smallholding more profitable, and adjacent mountain grazing lands were available. The key features of the northeast were a shortage of grazing land, which meant that common lands were scarce and valuable, and a relative shortage of land for cultivators, which meant that tenancies were small and wage labor was widespread.

The impoverishment of the northeastern peasants, despite their laboring in the agriculturally richest portions of France, was common knowledge among contemporaries. As already noted, many blamed the problem on the government's excessive taxation. Yet as we have seen, the *taille* actually fell in real terms over the course of the eighteenth century. A greater problem was the *dixième* and *vingtième*, which the bourgeois and nobles were largely able to shift onto the backs of the peasantry. In total, direct taxes per capita on the agricultural sector doubled over the eighteenth century, while output per head stagnated (see table 8).

Still, direct taxes on land were not paid by the majority of peasants, since they were landless laborers. These people were far more affected by the rising price of bread and by the struggles over the commons.

We have already noted that, in the Paris region, grain prices rose some 70 percent from 1726 to 1789, while wage levels rose only by about 26 percent (Labrousse 1984, 2:491). The effect was particularly pronounced in years of bad harvests, which affected the plains around Paris in 1768–1771, 1775, 1784, and 1789 (Labrousse 1984, 1:112). In these years, grain shortages triggered riots, in which those seeking to buy bread attacked grain convoys, warehouses, and bakers, confiscating bread and forcing the owners to take a "fair"—that is, sharply below-market—price (L. Tilly 1971). As noted earlier, the political impact of such shortages was worsened by the government's indecision over the role of markets. Hoping that a free market in grain would encourage production and alleviate shortages, the Crown promulgated free trade in grain in 1768. However, recurrent grain crises and ministerial shuffles led to the freedom of grain markets being revoked in 1770, restored in 1774, revoked in 1776, and restored again in 1787. Since prices inevitably rose whenever grain markets were freed because of the imbalance between population increase and stagnant production, the main effect of these actions was to saddle the government with blame for collusion with grain speculators to raise prices.

Generations of observers have claimed that France's peasant problem was due to the backwardness of French agriculture, a system seen as burdened by traditional open-field organization and remnants of feudal dues. Yet recent research has shown that, at least for the French northeast, this view is merely a myth. In reanalyzing Arthur Young's data, Allen and O'Grada (1988) have demonstrated that wheat yields in northeastern France circa 1770 were not significantly different from those of contemporary England. Morineau's (1970a) earlier study of English and French yields reached the same conclusion. In both England and northeastern France, wheat yields were approximately twenty-two to twenty-three bushels per acre. Moreover, comparisons of open-field and enclosed lands in eighteenth century England have shown that the open-field system was not backward and had similar yields to those of enclosed farms; enclosure was more a means of changing land use and raising rents than of increasing yields (Allen and O'Grada 1988). Most of England's agricultural improvement from 1650 to 1750 came not from raising yields on extant arable lands but rather from bringing formerly pastoral lands in upland areas into grain production (Goldstone 1988). Since the French northeast was already dominated by grain, no gains by this means could be expected. And the French upland pastoral areas in the south, west, and center were too far from markets, and in areas of too little rainfall, to be converted to arable until the railroads and new fertilizers of the nineteenth century ushered in such changes (Price 1983a). Thus, French agriculture in the northeast was doing as well as contemporary agriculture anywhere. Irrational cultivation or traditional hindrances cannot take the blame for the ecological imbalance.[9]

9. The examination of French agriculture, its progress and impediments, is a complex enterprise, and a considerable specialized literature has developed on this topic. I have

The heart of the problem of peasant poverty was a rapid and considerable population increase in a country that, given contemporary technology, was reaching the limit of its agricultural output. As grain supplies grew more slowly than the labor force, it was inevitable that grain prices would rise and wages would fall.

In northeastern France, the last refuge of the small peasant was the common grazing provided by the village. By keeping a pig or, more rarely, a sheep or a cow, a peasant accumulated a small piece of self-reproducing capital, which could be sold when emergency needs for cash arose. As landholdings for many peasants shrank or disappeared, access to the common became the slender barrier between solvency and destitution (Root 1987, 111).

The rising importance and commercial value of the northeast's common lands provided a focus for peasant-landlord conflicts. In the eighteenth century, landlords sought to extend their holdings by claiming (or usurping) portions of common land and converting them to arable (Gauthier 1977, 167–170). Titles to common land were often difficult for villagers to prove, and violations by landlords were difficult to prosecute (Root 1987, 267). Landlords with seigneurial rights could also claim part of the commons if the whole were divided and dispersed to the individual villagers, a process known as *triage*. This was actually a procedure that landless villagers favored, as securing small scraps of land improved their situation. In the course of the revolution, many poor peasants pressed for such partition (provided that former landlords were excluded). But it was in the interests of the better off and more influential among the peasantry to preserve the commons, for those with large flocks gained disproportionate benefits from the free use of common grazing lands. They were assisted by the royal intendants, who saw village common land as essential to the finances of the village community—tax arrears and repairs to the church and communal buildings were often financed by leases on portions of the commons, or by loans secured with the common lands. Where commons were fully partitioned, rural villages could go bankrupt, an outcome that the royal administration strived to avoid. Thus, even though agrarian reformers in the court urged that the common land be dispersed to private hands to encourage more intensive use, the intendants encouraged the peasant community,

---

addressed the issues discussed here, including the comparison between England and France, in more detail in Goldstone (1988).

whose village assemblies were often dominated by the better-off peasants who provided employment to their neighbors, to fight landlord attempts to appropriate communal lands (Root 1987, 180–183). As an example of the continuity of such struggles across the years before and after 1789, C. Tilly (1986, 25) notes the case of Perroy de la Forestelle of Burgundy, who sought to enclose the local meadows and forests in order to exclude villagers. Not only did local peasants successfully resist his efforts, but when the revolution came, Perroy was tried and executed for hostility to the revolution.

Struggles over common lands were one focus of northeastern conflicts; a second was struggles over access to arable land and its products. The most obvious indicator of these struggles is the rise in rents. Until the 1770s rents lagged behind prices (Goubert 1970c, 338–342). But from 1770 onward, rents shot forward. Labrousse's (1984, 2:379) national rent index shows a rise of only 21.6 percent from the 1730s to the 1760s, followed by a further increase of 63 percent in the two decades before the revolution. Thus, landlords were taking advantage of the scarcity of land toward the end of the Old Regime to extract as much as possible from their tenants. In addition, remnants of feudal exactions, often collected in kind—the *lods et vents*, the *banalités*, and the *cens*— were pressed into service, to different degrees by different seigneurs, in order to extract more grain and livestock from the peasantry. These exactions were most resented in the northeast, where peasants already held the smallest and least secure tenancies, and where common lands were most valuable and most under threat.

The great wave of peasant unrest that erupted in 1789 was therefore foreshadowed by rising conflict and increasing misery in the last decades of the Old Regime. The Crown was widely blamed for local grain shortages and high prices; the calling of the Estates General promised delivery from these evils. The rising population, landlessness, and poverty of the northeast and the Midi had led to an increase in crime and brigandage in the late eighteenth century (LeRoy Ladurie 1974b; Agulhon 1976). When the harvest failed in 1788 and vagabonds took to the roads in increasing numbers, what more natural thought could have occurred among the peasantry than that the seigneurs, who had been raising rents, pressing old dues, and usurping the commons, would seek to use these brigands to derail any forthcoming relief from the Estates General?[10]

10. Markoff (1985, 1988) demonstrates that peasant uprisings were most marked precisely in those districts that lay along major roads *and* where the statements of peasant

Thus, a wave of panic and violence, aimed mainly at seigneurs and justified by fear of brigandage, swept through those areas that had suffered
most from the pressures of the preceding decades. The resulting destruction of seigneurial records and chateaux stiffened the resolve of the National Assembly in Paris in its dismantling of the seigneurial regime.

How are we to interpret the role of the peasantry in 1789? Were they,
as Soboul (1976, 437) suggests, unwitting promoters of capitalism and
antifeudal in their opposition to the seigneurial regime? Or, as Furet
(1981, 94) argues, if we view the seigneurs' attempts to raise rents, press
old dues, and usurp commons as responses to market opportunities, and
hence as capitalistic behavior, should we conclude that "the peasant
resistance against the *seigneurie* may well have been not anti-aristocratic,
or 'anti-feudal,' but anti-bourgeois and anti-capitalist"? If we wish to
take both views, then we can join Le Roy Ladurie (1974b, 11), who
remarks that in opposing the seigneurial regime, the Burgundian peasantry of the eighteenth century "were anti-feudal because they were anti-
capitalist."

All these views, however, are flawed by the failure to take sufficient
account of regional variation. It was precisely in the west, where the
nobility and feudal practice remained most entrenched, that antiseigneurialism was weakest. One might respond that it was the corrosive
influence of the growth of capitalism that led to antiseigneurialism. But
in the Midi, which was fully commercialized, popular unrest took a more
varied, less purely antiseigneurial form. And in the northeast, the question of whether revolts were antifeudal or anticapitalist oversimplifies
a complex set of relationships between seigneurs and tenants, both of
whom were seeking to adjust to scarce land and excess labor.

I have argued that the peasant unrest of the late eighteenth century
should be viewed as a consequence of an ecological crisis that affected
different agrarian structures to different degrees and in different ways.
The cause of the crisis was the rapid population growth that pushed on
a relatively fixed supply of land and slowly growing agrarian output.
The result was land scarcity, rising rents, and falling wages in those
areas most affected. But the actors who were embedded in those agrarian
structures, though all aware of the growing crisis, viewed it in different
ways. To the physiocrats and their reforming allies in Paris, the problem

---

grievances collected in the *cahiers* in 1789 show the greatest concern about communal
rights, taxation, public welfare, and other national issues that they hoped would be settled
by the Estates General.

was excessive taxation and poor practices in agriculture. To the rural landlords, the problem was excessive taxation and royal mismanagement, which raised prices and forced them to raise their incomes to maintain their standards of living. They were also aggrieved by the increased competition for social standing created by rapid mobility, which likewise forced them to seek higher incomes to purchase offices and status. To the peasants, the problem was not only excessive taxation and royal mismanagement (on which the Estates General promised relief) but also, in large part, the greediness of landlords and grain speculators, who collected excessive rents, dues, and tithes and charged excessive prices. *None* of the actors embedded in the agrarian structures was familiar with the concept of diminishing returns, and none had the political arithmetic needed to understand how the entire panoply of their woes derived from the inability of the agrarian, social, and tax structures to cope with the rapid rise in population.[11] Thus, each group of actors fixed their own explanation, and their own villains, for the crisis. Only when we understand how *all* groups were caught in a cyclic crisis can we grasp how so many different social relationships seemed to dissolve into conflicts all at once.

By stressing the cyclic crisis, I do not mean to overlook the secular changes that were at work. Certainly, capitalism expanded in the eighteenth century, as in the sixteenth and seventeenth centuries. By making landlords, tenants, and workers increasingly dependent on the market, especially in the northeast and in the Midi, though less so in the west, the growth of capitalism intensified the impact of ecological crisis in those areas. The crisis was, after all, manifested most clearly in a shift in relative prices—rising for land and grain, falling for wages; thus, its impact was greatest in those areas most sensitive to price movements. But one cannot therefore say that the growth of capitalism *caused* the crisis. Commercial farming had already squeezed out most of the peasant subsistence farming in northeastern France by the mid-seventeenth century (Dewald 1987; Jacquart 1974a). And from 1650 onward, the expansion of vine cultivation for market was essential to families throughout the Midi and Rhône Valley. What seems to distinguish the reign of Louis XIV from the period of 1730 to 1789 is not that the former was less commercial than the latter but that the earlier period

11. One outsider did perceive the source of the troubles. Arthur Young (1971 [1792], 134–135), following his travels in France, wrote that France suffered from "too great a populousness" for its agricultural progress, for which reason "the prices of provisions are as dear in France as in England, while [the wages] of labour are 76 per cent lower."

was one of stable and reasonably prosperous commercial exchange, whereas in the latter period the terms of exchange inexorably tilted against the peasantry. This shift in the terms of exchange was a result not of commercialization per se but rather of marked changes in the relative quantities of the main elements of the economy—land, grain, and labor. These changes were the product of rapid population growth and a more slowly growing agrarian economy. Capitalism was gradually changing the agrarian structure of France, or, more accurately, of the northeast and the Midi. But its main effect was simply to render these regions more vulnerable to the kind of ecological crisis that arose in the late eighteenth century.

In addition, we should acknowledge another secular change, also particularly marked in the northeast: the decline of local landlord political power. In the eighteenth century, the Crown sought to "substitute for seigneurial tutellage the tutellage of the Crown" (Root 1982, 290). Interposing royal justice, royal taxes, and royal bureaucracy between the seigneur and the peasant community, the Crown reduced the ability of the seigneur to act as the leader and master of the rural community (except in Brittany, and to a lesser degree throughout the west, where the local seigneurs better defended their local privileges). With the seigneurs' political power constrained, the peasantry took its cues from its own leading members in the village assemblies, and from the royal intendants. In attempts to improve centralized rule, the latter encouraged the villages to emancipate themselves and, interestingly, to resist local seigneurial exactions that were no longer justifiable and in accord with the laws of the province and the nation (Root 1987, 193). Thus, in 1789, when central authority faltered while awaiting the action of the Estates General, local landlords had no political resources to resist peasant assaults on the seigneurial regime.

Before concluding our examination of rural conditions, it is instructive to contrast French peasant revolts in 1789 with those of the mid-seventeenth century. It is sometimes argued that in the seventeenth century peasant actions were chiefly anti-tax revolts against the state, while in 1789 peasant actions were chiefly antiseigneurial revolts against landlords (Doyle 1980, 199–200). This contrast is valid, but it does *not* imply that the crises were of a fundamentally different nature. In both periods, France was suffering from a cyclic crisis of population pressure, inflation, and peasant impoverishment. But because state responses and rural structures were slightly different in these two periods, the peasant responses were slightly different as well. These differences should be viewed as variations on a single theme, rather than as distinct kinds of crises.

In the seventeenth century the state reacted to fiscal pressures by seeking massive increases in the *taille* (an attempted quadrupling from 1632 to 1648) and an extension of the *gabelles* (salt taxes). Moreover, local landlords were still powerful and dominated peasant actions. Hence in those regions where landlords and peasants had mutual interests—the west and southwest which were characterized by sharecropping, and the Midi, where the *taille* was assessed on land and thus affected both landlords and peasants—the state faced united resistance to its drastic efforts to raise taxes, and rural uprisings were widespread (Mousnier 1977). In contrast, where landlords and peasants had more sharply conflicting interests—the areas in the northeast characterized by cash tenancy and by the assessment of the *taille* on individuals, which exempted noble landlords but not their tenants—strong local landlords successfully prevented peasant revolts (Brustein 1985). Thus, reaction to the mid-seventeenth-century crisis took the form of anti-tax revolts in the west and south, while tensions in the northeast were suppressed by strong landlord control.

By 1789 the state had turned to massive borrowing, rather than further increases in direct taxes, to cope with fiscal pressures; hence there was no sharp provocation for a united tax revolt in rural areas. But local landlords were now no longer strong enough to prevent peasant uprisings. Dependent on a strong central state, they were left defenseless when the state crumbled in 1788–1789. Peasants in regions of growing population and dependence on wage labor, who faced rising grain prices, land shortage, and—in the northeast—conflicts over the commons, were spurred in 1788–1789 by the crisis of the state to revolt against landlord exactions. Thus the reaction to the late eighteenth-century crisis took the form of revolts in the regions of the greatest pressure on the land and the greatest conflicts between peasants and landlords, namely, the northeast and the Midi. In both periods, the underlying pressures for crises were similar. It was chiefly changes in the state's reactions and in the strength of local landlords that produced different patterns of regional unrest.

As stated earlier, recurring waves of ecological crisis largely explain the timing of France's waves of peasant revolts in the mid-seventeenth and late eighteenth centuries. However, an explanation of the exact shapes of those revolts requires close attention to variations in agrarian structures, both over time and across regions. Though rural conflicts in the late eighteenth century were fueled by France's population increase, this increase was not of the same magnitude or of uniform consequence throughout the country. The degree of conflict in each area reflected a combination of population pressure *and* structural vulnerability to such pressure. Where that combination consisted of rapid population growth, agrarian structures that put the burden of such growth chiefly on seigneurial tenants, and locally weak landlords—that is, in areas of northeastern France—we find the most severe agrarian uprisings of the revolution.[12]

THE BURDEN ON THE CITIES

Spectacular as the peasant uprisings were, L. Hunt (1978, 3) has argued that "the urban revolution was the mainstay of the national revolution: the peasantry could regulate the pace of change, accelerating it by revolt as it did in 1789, obstructing it by disinterest or hostility as it did in 1793–94. But without the Parisian Revolution the National Assembly would have been stillborn, and without the urban revolution in the provinces the national revolution would have died in infancy as it did in 1848 and 1870." The cities shared in the burdens of the last years of the Old Regime, and in the uprisings that ended it.

"The State," wrote Montesquieu in 1748, "owes all its citizens an assured food supply." For the next forty years the French monarchy tried to live up to that goal, especially for the population of Paris. But the expansion of population and stagnation of output made provision of sufficient food supplies an impossible responsibility.

12. Markoff (1985), using a completely different theoretical framework, undertook an empirical examination of the correlation between peasant unrest and regional attributes by *baillage* (judicial district) in France in 1789. He found that six factors are positively correlated with unrest: population of the largest town, length of major roads, central administration (i. e., being in a *pays d'élection*), the presence of open fields, the proportion of grassland, and being in the Mediterranean south (the Midi). These factors correspond quite closely to the broader results of the analysis presented here: Town population and road lengths reflect commercialization, which increased vulnerability of the peasants to price shifts. Being in a *pays d'élection* generally meant being in a region of *taille personnel*, where nobles and most bourgeois were exempt from the *taille* and the burden of other direct taxes was most easily shifted onto the peasantry. Open fields and a high proportion of cultivated grassland were characteristic of the northeastern plains, where open fields devoted to grain were balanced by carefully cultivated commons for grazing, which became a focus of peasant-landlord conflict. And the Midi, though of a different agrarian structure than the northeast, was still burdened by population growth and price pressures, which resulted in conflicts, although of a different character than those in the northeastern plains. In sum, Markoff's results nicely confirm the preceding analysis of France's varying regional vulnerability to the ecological crisis.

As wages and employment opportunities diminished, purchases of bread took more and more of workers' resources. Labrousse (1984, 2:491) found, in sampling a wide variety of wage series across France, that from the period 1726–1741 to 1771–1789 almost half the cases showed a salary rise of less than 11 percent; over three-quarters showed increases of less than 26 percent. In comparison, Labrousse's (1984, 2:598) cost-of-living index for this time frame, combining series for rye, beans, wine, meat, firewood, and wool, shows a rise of 54 percent. Since his series includes no figures for urban rents, his estimate of worker hardships may be understated. In 1777, Jean-Marie Roland, inspector of manufactures in Picardy, lamented, "Workmen today need twice as much money for their subsistence, yet they earn no more than fifty years ago when living was half as cheap" (cited in Doyle 1989, 14).

Difficulties affected not merely the poorest citizens, but also the settled workers of the guilds. The wages of masons rose no faster than those of ordinary day laborers (Labrousse 1970d, 2:561). All workers were thus affected by the fluctuating and rising prices of grain. Urban poverty grew in Bayeux, Strasbourg, and Amiens, among other cities, as local population growth outstripped available food supplies (Hufton 1967, 11; Lemoigne 1965, 54; Engrand 1982, 382). Only the seaport towns, where income from the colonial trade was still expanding and food needs could be met by seaborne imports, avoided the general suffering.

The problems of heightened social competition and blocked mobility, created by a growing number of aspirants for a limited number of places, as earlier discussed in relation to the elite, were also found further down the social scale. Kaplow (1972, 36) notes that

> the theoretically easy progression from journeyman to master was made still more difficult by the tendency of many guilds to favor sons of masters by requiring less of them than of an outsider in the way of apprenticeship and the production of a masterpiece. In addition, many guilds restricted the number of apprentices a master might have at a given time so as to keep the trade in the hands of a limited number of families. Numerous otherwise qualified persons were in this manner prevented from becoming masters and were forced to remain journeymen throughout their working lives. . . . [T]he poverty of these workers was likely to be extreme and their mobility nil.

These difficulties grew steadily through the last decades of the Old Regime. In 1775 food riots raged; in 1785–1786 there were worker protests in Paris and Lyon (Rudé 1975, 7–8; Kaplow 1972, 41). Though the authorities did all they could to keep Paris supplied with grain, this privileged position simply attracted more migrants from all over France, intensifying the problem (Gillis 1970, 176). In 1788–1789, the harvest failure led not only to grain shortages and higher prices but also to the complete collapse of the already weak demand for manufactures, as all available purchasing power was diverted to procure food. The populace of Paris demanded that the government act to provide bread. Distrustful of the Crown, whose on-and-off control of the grain market was blamed for rising prices, they looked to the parlements, and to the Estates General, for economic changes that would restore employment and affordable loaves. The contemporary author Louis-Sébastien Mercier wrote that "all Paris is parlementaire. . . . Since they had no other organs, the people thus see in the parlement the assembly of magistrates ready to speak for them and to defend them" (cited in Kaplan 1976, 2:442).

As in London in the 1640s, the Crown had no means to deal with popular disorders of the magnitude that ensued in 1789. Paris was as well policed as most modern cities. Although it had swelled to over 700,000 inhabitants in 1789 as a consequence of migration to the capital (Rudé 1973, 173–175; Kaplan 1976), its police force of 1,500 men, together with the 3,600 French Guards stationed there, constituted a ratio of roughly one law-enforcement officer for every 140 inhabitants (Sutherland 1986, 63; Cobb 1967, 437). In Paris in 1968, the ratio was one law-enforcement officer per 187 inhabitants; in most American cities in the 1960s, it was around one per 200 (A. Williams 1979, 63–64).

For the Parisian police in 1789, the problem lay in the scale of the difficulty confronted. While adequate in force for the task of fighting crime and quelling local fights, the police faced a city in which roughly half to two-thirds of the inhabitants "were on the borderline of want or below it" (Cobb 1967, 437). Hence "there was virtually no way they could contain individual desperation and public danger issuing from urban hunger" (A. Williams 1979, 295). The situation was even worse in the provinces, for there "underlying every aspect of the functioning of the eighteenth century [provincial gendarmerie] was its numerical weakness" (I. Cameron 1977, 51).

In addition, it is important to consider the nature of the civic unrest. More was at issue than the preservation of order and royal authority against political opponents or rebels. The police (and the army) were reluctant to act against Frenchmen voicing demands that they themselves considered valid, demands to remedy an economic situation so dire that its nature was evident to all. Many of the French Guards "were quar-

tered in Paris and worked at various trades during their off-duty hours"
(S. Scott 1978, 54–55). The regular troops were mostly recruited from
urban areas: only about a quarter of the enlisted men in 1789 were
former peasants; the rest were chiefly sons of tradesmen and shopkeepers
(S. Scott 1978, 19). These troops, during the course of military exercises
and leaves and through part-time work, had "numerous and frequent
contacts with civilians, usually from the same social background; [such
contacts were] a common part of military life for most soldiers" (S. Scott
1978, 40–44). Moreover, they too were subject to price pressures, for
"the soldiers' pay was insufficient" to cope with mounting living costs
(S. Scott 1978, 55). So many soldiers in Paris shared the view of their
fellow Parisians that royal mismanagement was responsible for the crisis
that "discipline . . . deteriorated rapidly" in June 1789 (S. Scott 1978,
55). Elsewhere, the story was similar: in Alençon, "the intendant wrote
on 2 April that the *maréchaussée* were much in agreement with the local
people and were anxious to see lower bread prices." In Picardy, the
military commander noted that "the soldiers show little willingness or
resolve" (Lefebvre 1973, 26). In Poitou, officials complained that "the
soldiers . . . have always exhibited repugnance for forcibly opposing
popular disturbances whose cause is the dearness of grain" (S. Scott
1978, 49).

The discipline of the troops was not actually put to the test in 1789,
largely because their officers had little faith in their performance. And
after the fall of the Bastille, widespread desertions, alliances with the
National Guard, and declarations in support of the revolution by soldiers confirmed their officers' fears. "The soldiers of the line army generally could not be depended upon to obey their officers and defend the
established regime against the Revolution. The men in the ranks were
too close to the people in the streets and too alienated from their superiors to be expected to repress a movement from which they could
gain so much" (S. Scott 1978, 60–61).

In sum, food shortages and high prices brought the Crown more than
simply massive popular disturbances supporting the Parlement of Paris
and Estates General against the monarchy. The very nature and perva-
siveness of the crisis undermined the ability of the police and army to
maintain order. Facing civic disorder on a huge scale, and with repressive
forces that largely shared the grievances that prompted those disorders,
the Crown had little choice but to capitulate to the calls for change.
Throughout the revolutionary *journées*, the urban crowds held the upper

hand, for the monarchy no longer had the moral authority, or the disciplined repressive capacity, to resist them.

IDEOLOGICAL DIMENSIONS OF THE ECOLOGICAL CRISIS

The mention of moral authority in the preceding paragraph shifts us to new ground. Even before the monarchy had fallen, it had lost the initiative in French politics and had been thrown on the defensive. In part, this initial weakening of royal authority was due to the financial crisis—a monarchy that could no longer pay its daily bills or raise loans needed to seek the help of its leading citizens. But there was also an ideological component, a belief among the general populace that the monarchy alone was no longer competent to lead. Charles Tilly (1978) has described a revolutionary situation as one in which two separate powers vie for the ultimate authority in society, a condition that he calls "multiple sovereignty." In France, even before the revolution, the authority of the king had diminished, and people looked to "the nation" or "public opinion" as the ultimate arbiter of political dispute (Baker 1987a). Multiple sovereignty in this sense thus arose before 1789, foreshadowing the conflict between the National Assembly and the monarchy. In discussing the origins of the revolution, therefore, one cannot ignore the question of how the sole sovereignty of the monarchy was eroded, and how the popular view of royal authority changed from "absolute" to "arbitrary."

The ideological origins of the French Revolution have been debated as heatedly as the material causes. If the growth of capitalism was responsible for the crisis, then it is logical to expect a clash between "bourgeois ideology" and a feudal and absolutist ideology to have played a major role in the revolution. But evidence of this ideological clash cannot be found. The language of the Enlightenment was used as much by the nobility to protest the arbitrary authority of the Crown as it was by the bourgeoisie (Hampson 1978; 1983, 62–63). Indeed, "by the end of the Old Regime, Enlightenment ideas and terminology pervaded the discourse of all factions and political opinions" (Sewell 1985b, 63). And the most active spokesmen for the revolution, from the Assembly to the Parisian press, were not the leading lights of the Enlightenment; indeed, the latter were the recipients of royal pensions, often of noble status, and proponents of enlightened despotism rather than bourgeois revolution (Darnton 1970). Yet it is certain that France, after 1750, underwent what Baker (1987b) has labeled a change in its "political culture," and that this change shaped the revolutionary struggles. I have more to say about the revolutionary struggles that followed 1789 in chapter 5. At this point, I simply wish to show how the ecological crisis, and its effects on French institutions, contributed to the ideological currents that swept French society from 1750 to 1789.

The key question is not simply, how did the Enlightenment arise and take wing in France? For the Enlightenment, like Puritanism in England a century and a half earlier, was *not* inherently revolutionary. Puritanism, as we noted in chapter 2, initially began as a reform movement that sought royal sponsorship and manifested great respect for authority. And the similar ideology of Pietism in Germany provided the basis not for revolution but for strengthening absolutist rule. Thus, to understand the impact of Puritanism, one must ask, quite specifically, why did Puritanism become revolutionary in England in the 1630s and 1640s? The answer, as shown in the preceding chapter, is that the institutions of the English monarchy were clearly seen to be disintegrating, a disintegration attributed to royal corruption, incompetence, and even disloyalty to the English national religion. The failure of the monarchy, which was largely due to its inability to cope with the pressures brought by the seventeenth-century ecological crisis, led to a refashioning of Puritanism, from a reform ideology seeking royal sponsorship to a reform ideology posing an alternative justification for national rule.

Quite analogously, the European Enlightenment began as a reformist movement. And indeed, in Prussia and Austria-Hungary in the eighteenth century it remained reformist, with enlightened monarchs Frederick the Great and Maria Theresa using Enlightenment ideology to justify the rationalization of the military, education, and administration in a manner that increased royal authority at the expense of traditional local privileges of nobles and estates (Koch 1978; Behrens 1985). The key question, therefore, is why did the Enlightenment *in France* turn revolutionary? And the answer, I suggest, is found in events in France similar to those that occurred in seventeenth-century England: the monarchical institutions and social order were stripped of public respect because of the inability of French authorities to handle the pressures of France's ecological crisis.

Fiscal weakness and repeated borrowing, failure to satisfy the aspirations of elites for mobility and rewards, and rising landlessness and urban poverty, despite evident wealth among the commercial and urban elite, persuaded Frenchmen that the Old Regime was deeply flawed. Under Louis XIV, France had appeared strong and prosperous; under

Louis XV, France appeared weaker, and its government mean and penny-pinching; under Louis XVI, much of France's population appeared penurious, and its government incompetent.

To a large degree, these diverse perceptions reflect the different circumstances of these monarchs: Louis XIV governed in a time of low and stable prices, slow urban growth, and rising real wages; his successors faced steadily rising prices, a peasant population that, in per capita terms, was becoming poorer, and a privileged elite that was becoming richer off trade and markets and thus had no sympathy for or identification with the growing fiscal difficulties of the Crown.

We have already noted that population pressure and rising prices shifted the terms of economic exchange away from peasants and workers and in favor of landowners, giving rise to more severe rural conflicts. The shift in prices, which provided profit opportunities for urban and rural elites and undermined the royal tax system, similarly shifted the terms of economic exchange away from the monarchy and in favor of the elite. For as the former grew financially weaker, the latter grew financially stronger and more independent. This shift had its consequences in the realm of political discourse as well, for elites began to trust more in their own opinion, which they interpreted as *l'opinion publique,* and less in the decisions of the Crown, which still pretended to absolute power and thus absorbed all the blame for the social and economic distress brought on by the demographic cycle.[13]

In short, late-eighteenth-century France was a society experiencing the operation, with a vengeance, of the law of diminishing returns. But it was innocent of the very concept and thus had no understanding of what was happening. All that was evident was that virtually every group, every class, and almost every locality—from the monarchy to the urban poor, and from the professional elite to the peasantry—faced problems that had been absent from the 1660s to the 1730s. Thus every group, including the royal ministers, found reason to blame the existing institutions.

13. Doyle (1980, 78–95) has noted how public opinion gained its power from the prestige and clientele attached to Parisian salons. The rise of public opinion thus mirrored the rise of elite independence from the orbit of Versailles. Maza (1987) has shown how public opinion was fed by the publication of accounts of trials—the *mémoires judiciares*—which, because of their official nature, escaped censorship. Lawyers often used their trials, and hence the *mémoires,* as occasions to compose briefs for liberty. This is but one example, although a very concrete and interesting one, of the ways in which professionals were seeking to manifest their independence from Versailles.

Yet the result was not a sudden turn to radicalism. We can understand more about the ideological shift by noting how much of this criticism was essentially conservative all the way up to 1788. The path from what Vovelle (1978) has called the *sensibilité pré-révolutionnaire* to the *sensibilité révolutionnaire* was slow and winding. Initially, it was not royal authority per se, but perceived abuses of that authority, that drew criticism.

The *philosophes* of eighteenth-century France had a linear view of history, which virtually excluded ideas of sudden rupture or revolution; rational progress, not revolution, was their essential notion. Thus, they favored authority and reform from above (Soboul 1982, 411). The most profound influence was that of Montesquieu, whose notion of a well-ordered state was a balance of rights and responsibilities among the various social strata. Thus, the chief criticism of the Crown was not that it was outmoded but that it had become despotic. And defense of "liberty" against "despotism," until 1788, was mostly a defense of particular traditional "liberties," whether of officeholders or of property owners, against the Crown's attempts to expand its authority and increase its revenues.

This resentment of unbridled authority was evident in the problems faced by the Crown in the area of religion. Anticlericalism had grown in France with the corruption of the Church, whose episcopate grew distant from parish and curés, and whose tithes were often leased out and collected by secular absentee landlords. As one example of this disenchantment with the Church, in the late eighteenth century Masonic lodges began to adopt the names of abstract virtues rather than traditional religious titles, the latter having lost respectability (Halèvi 1984). Moreover, the authority of the Catholic Church had begun to fail all over Europe as a result of the progress both of philology, which held the historical content of the Bible up to a new and critical light, and of natural science (Hazard 1963). It is hard to overestimate the impact made by the return, in 1758, of Halley's comet, an event predicted decades in advance by the English astronomer. Comets had always been interpreted as divine portents; their reduction to a predictable natural phenomenon was a major step in the demystification of the world. Yet the attacks on the authority of the Church had been underway since the late seventeenth century. Hazard (1963, xviii) notes that "virtually all those ideas which were called revolutionary round about 1760, or, for the matter of that, 1789, were already current as early as 1680." The religious problems faced by the Crown were not so much created by the Church's authority as by the Crown's attitude toward the Church's authority.

France was flanked on both west and east by European states—England and Prussia—distinguished for their religious tolerance. Both had state religions, but both observed freedom of conscience for their citizens. France did not. From the Edict of Nantes to the revolution, the French state was constantly in conflict with its citizens over adherence to Catholicism in general, and to the dictates of the papacy in particular. In seeking to enforce a particular orthodoxy in the conflicts over Jansenism and over the Jesuits, the Crown found itself attacked by the parlements for putting loyalty to Rome ahead of loyalty to the French nation (Van Kley 1975). Religious differences did not inherently threaten royal authority—Frederick the Great did not tremble for his throne because he, a Protestant, allowed some of his subjects to practice Catholicism. But by its own acts of religious intolerance, the French Crown tarnished its claims to be the defender of French freedom.

The notion that the Crown did not respect the liberties of its subjects, as evidenced by the religious conflicts, was reinforced in the struggles over taxation and the authority of the municipalities and parlements. The essential problem was that the Crown needed to change the tax system drastically if it was to gain its share of France's growing commercial and professional wealth and thus keep pace with inflation. But its attempts to implement change clearly infringed on the traditional liberties of its most influential subjects. Thus, the Crown was attacked in the name of tradition. Even in the *cahiers* drawn up in 1788, as G. Taylor (1972a, 481) notes, "far more important than concepts of natural rights, popular sovereignty, and the separation of powers as mandates for change was tradition—legal, constitutional, and institutional." The most far-reaching and apparently radical demand in the *cahiers*, the call for uniform taxation without regard to social rank, was in fact no more than a call for the enforcement of the principle of taxation contained in the *capitation* and *dixième* of Louis XIV. Even the Jacobin clubs, noted for their radicalism, were hardly radical in the beginning. Michael Kennedy (1982, 303) states that "until 1791, the clubbists were monarchist, almost to a man. . . . Not until 1792 can Jacobinism be associated unequivocally with Republicanism."

The sea change in attitudes toward traditional rights took place only in 1788. The defense of traditional liberties had taken concrete form in the call for a meeting of the Estates General. Since the monarchy was no longer able to keep Frenchmen, or even itself, economically sound, the collective wisdom of the "nation" would have to be tapped. Yet how were the Estates to be constituted? Following the pattern of the 1770s and 1780s, the Parlement of Paris sought liberty in tradition, calling in 1788 for the Estates General to be "regularly convoked and composed, according to the forms observed in 1614" (Baker 1987b, xxi). But at this point, when tradition was about to triumph, the realization set in that traditional forms would straitjacket most of the elite.

The liberal magistrate Malesherbes wrote in alarm, "What is the Estates-General which you propose? . . . It is an old debris of ancient barbarism; it is a field of battle where three factions of a single people come to fight together; it is the clash of all false interests against the general interest" (cited by Gruder 1968, 253). Malesherbes's view was quickly adopted by members of the bourgeoisie and liberal nobles, who realized that the traditional composition of the Estates General would likely hand power to the most reactionary group in French society—the poor but numerically predominant country nobility—especially if the latter allied with conservatives in the Church. And indeed, the provincial nobility seized the opportunity offered. As we have seen, in many regions in 1788 the older nobility excluded recent entrants into the order from the selection of noble delegates to the provincial and national estates.

Then, and only then, did criticism of the Old Regime turn away from tradition and adapt the language of the Enlightenment to the goal of radical reform. "It was only when the established order had collapsed completely, and when it became obvious that institutions must be recast afresh from their very foundations, that the attitudes propagated by the Enlightenment were to lead Frenchmen in really new, uncharted—in fact, revolutionary—directions" (Doyle 1980, 84). As G. Taylor (1972a, 489) reminds us, "The Declaration [of Rights] is not the Enlightenment. It is an adaptation of Enlightenment words, phrases, and concepts to a revolutionary situation that the philosophers had neither intended nor foreseen. It is the Enlightenment radicalized, reorganized, by the men of 1789."

Thus, the ideological origins of the revolution cannot be found in a fount of modernizing sentiment. Instead, the erosion of royal authority, which was rooted in the societywide problems induced by the ecological crisis, first gave rise to a "traditionalist" defense of civil society. Men did not reject the monarchy because of the growth of enlightened ideas. They rejected the monarchy because it was obviously failing to provide solutions to widespread and pressing social problems: "If Enlightenment ideas at times gave direction, provided a certain content, and supplied the language for their criticisms and claims, these did not operate as a direct literary influence but helped to confirm attitudes already in mind" (Gruder 1968, 637). Those attitudes were straightforward: the failures of the monarchy, whether attributed to corruption, incompetence, closed-mindedness, or abuse of traditional liberties, had to be rectified if the evident social problems were to be solved.

Only when the ultimate crisis finally arose in 1788, as royal bankruptcy forced an abdication of the political initiative to the Estates General, did it become clear that "traditional" forms and liberties no longer fit a society in which the elite had been transformed by three generations of rapid expansion and social mobility. At that point, improvisation was necessary. And also at that point, the shift in political culture that followed the erosion of institutions emerged as the dominant factor shaping ensuing events. A rejection of tradition began, which was further accelerated by the need to utilize Church assets to solve the state bankruptcy, the flight of the royal family, and the need to mobilize the entire nation for war with Europe. But the growing radicalization of the revolution is the story of what happened following 1789. That is the story we return to in chapter 5. My goal now is merely to clarify the forces that led to the crisis of the Old Regime.

MODELING STATE BREAKDOWN IN EIGHTEENTH-CENTURY FRANCE

In the previous chapter I presented a simple model of state breakdown in the English Revolution. I suggested that state breakdown in England was due to the interaction of three factors—state fiscal distress, elite mobility and competition, and heightened mass mobilization potential—all of which had been increased by the collision of demographic expansion with relatively inflexible agrarian technology and fiscal and social institutions. By graphing the product of the indicators of these factors—a product labeled the function psi (Ψ)—the pressures for state breakdown were charted.

In the present chapter, I have argued that precisely the same factors were responsible for the breakdown of the French state in 1789. Can we chart the pressures for state breakdown through the psi function for France as readily as we did for England?

INDICATORS OF SOCIAL CHANGE

For England, I used a simple 1-to-5 scale, denoting the measures used by the Crown to raise revenue, as an indicator of fiscal distress. The same scale can be used for France in the period from 1650 to 1789, although the French Crown was generally at a "higher" level of distress than its English counterpart.

I measured changes in the level of social mobility and competition in England through changes in the level of matriculations at Oxford and Cambridge. This measurement was predicated on the notion that social mobility and competition created a demand for credentials that would offer an advantage in the competition for offices. Thus, expanding enrollments indicated both larger numbers of aspirants, hence greater demands for elite positions, and increased competition among the aspirants for places. For France, Kagan (1975) has assembled a decadal series of matriculations at the major French universities in the faculties of law from 1680 to 1789. Since legal training was the chief credential sought for bureaucratic or judicial office, matriculations in law are an appropriate indicator of fluctuations in the numbers of place-seekers. I therefore use this measure for France in the same manner as matriculations at Oxford and Cambridge were used for England.

The third component of *psi*, mass mobilization potential (MMP), poses greater difficulties. In England, cultivators were generally too dispersed, too divided, and too closely supervised by local landlords to pose a threat in most areas. It was only in more marginal areas, where local landlord supervision was less and peasant communities more independent, such as the royal forests and the fenlands, that rural disorders were significant. Thus I focused on London, where urban concentration and youthfulness of the population compounded the problem of falling real wages, in examining the mobilization potential of the populace.

In France, failure to include the mobilization potential of rural cultivators in our analysis would be grossly misleading. The magnitude of the state breakdown in 1789 was a product of the actions both of the Parisian crowds *and* of the peasantry, particularly in the northeast and the Midi. We thus need some measure of the changing potential for peasants to act against seigneurs.

Aside from real wages, which fell for agricultural workers and rural artisans in close parallel to their fall in the towns (Labrousse 1984, 2:492), the chief point of contention among the peasants was land.

Shortage of land allowed landlords to raise rents, condemned many families to depend partly or wholly on wage labor, made the imposition of seigneurial dues far more painful, and triggered fierce battles over the commons. One simple way to measure land scarcity, given that the cultivated acreage barely increased in the eighteenth century, is to use population itself as a proxy. But this is not quite accurate. As long as the cities and rural trades could absorb population growth, pressure on land would be reduced. And as long as productivity could be increased by further application of labor, land shortage would not reach a critical stage. A more accurate indicator, not only of scarcity but also of landlord exploitation, is the real rent per acre charged by landlords. To the extent that rents rose more slowly than prices, tenants actually could gain from price increases, and their land was more valuable. However, as land became scarce, landlords were able to charge a higher rent. When rent levels rose faster than prices (i.e., the situation was one of rising real rents), terms of trade were shifting away from tenants and in favor of landlords. Thus, real rents seem to be a reasonable proxy for peasant mobilization potential against seigneurs. They also have the essential characteristic of being available in a decadal series, thanks to Goubert's (1970c, 338–442) and Labrousse's (1984, 2:379) efforts, whereas other relevant data, such as the level of *cens*, *banalités*, and other dues, are not.[14]

How, then, do we assemble these data? I assume that the effects of variation in the age structure—i.e., that a population with more young people is more likely to take the risks of protest—applies to both peasants and urban workers. I also assume that rural mobilization potential and urban mobilization potential are not additive in their effect but, instead, multiplicative. That is, having both a high urban potential for unrest *and* a high rural potential is not merely twice as bad as having one or the other, but many times worse. In addition, lower real wages, since they followed the same trend for peasants and urban workers, had a similar impact on both groups. This reasoning leads to a multiplicative form for mass mobilization potential, that is, the same form as used for England but with an additional term for real rent levels. This latter is normalized, like real wages, as a ratio to the average real rent for the

14. Of course, increases in real rents could also result from increases in productivity that raised the real value of land. However, increases in productivity were modest at best in this period. Since real rents fluctuated far more than productivity (real rents doubled from the period 1730–1739 to 1780–1789, while productivity grew no more than 20 percent), we can be confident that, in examining fluctuations in real rents, we are seeing changes in the market for land rather than in the value of output.

period, so that when real rents are at historically "high" levels, the mobilization effect is compounded by age effects. Conversely, when real rents are at historically "low" levels, the mobilization effect is reduced by age effects, for younger families benefit most by being able to take up new leases at lower rates.

This form of MMP also has the desirable property that if real wages rise while real rents rise, a situation indicating opportunities in the wage sector that counterbalance a shortage of land, the two trends offset each other's impact on MMP; whereas if real wages fall at the same time that real rents rise, indicating declining prospects in both wage earning *and* tenant farming, their respective effects on MMP are compounded. For example, an excellent harvest, which reduces grain prices, would in fact raise the real value of rents paid; however, it would also raise real wages. Thus, in this measure, since these effects offset each other, a good harvest does not trigger a rise in MMP. However, a long-term deterioration in the terms of trade away from labor would lower real wages and raise real rents; this trend would show up in this measure as increasing MMP.

The resulting formula for MMP in France is as follows:

$$MMP = (\text{Real Rents}/\text{Avg. Real Rents})$$
$$\times (\text{Avg. Real Wage}/\text{Real Wages})$$
$$+ (\text{Avg. Real Wages}/\text{Real Wages} - 1) \times \text{Urban Growth}$$
$$\times \text{Age}$$
$$+ (\text{Real Rents}/\text{Avg. Real Rents} - 1) \times \text{Age}$$

THE PSI MODEL OF STATE BREAKDOWN IN EIGHTEENTH-CENTURY FRANCE

Figure 8 plots *psi* for France from 1680 to 1789. It shows a low but rising level of pressures for crisis during the reign of Louis XIV. Pressures became considerable in the later years of the Sun King, then declined into the 1720s, but rose dramatically after 1750. Recall that this is simply a graph of bare data series: state borrowing/taxing behavior, law matriculations, real wages and rents, urban growth, and age structure. But it seems to accord quite precisely with the feeling expressed by many contemporaries and historians that the Old Regime sharply came under pressures after 1750, which mounted relentlessly until 1789. This suggests that the *psi* function does in some way capture the situation facing the French state over the course of the eighteenth century.

Moreover, the *psi* model demonstrates, as it did for England, that the

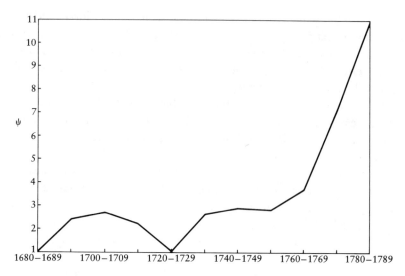

Figure 8. Pressures for crisis (*psi*) in France, 1680–1689 to 1780–1789

situation in the 1780s was not a "normal" period, socially and economically, in which state breakdown must therefore have resulted from accidents or the incompetence of the ministers or of the monarch. Instead, the social and economic situation of the late eighteenth century was demonstrably and quantitatively growing more difficult for governance.

Psi measurement is, of course, a crude technique for assessing pressures for state breakdown. It does not include regional measures that reflect different rural structures. It thus must be supplemented by regional analysis, as we have done above, to show why certain areas responded differently to *psi* pressures. However, it does help us answer the question of why peasant unrest was modest from 1675 to 1730, then mounted to the crescendo of 1789. *Psi* also lacks an ideological component. Ideological shifts—doubts about the merits of the Old Regime and a search for a rational alternative—had dramatic consequences, especially after 1789, which we shall examine in chapter 5. But I think it is fair to say that these ideological shifts were at first a consequence of the pressures shown in the *psi* model: expansion and heightened competition among elites and the erosion of fiscal and social stability fed an emergent public opinion highly critical of the Crown. In short, if we ask *how* the weaknesses of the state and the grievances of peasants and elites were translated into action, rural structures and ideologies opposed to the existing social order undoubtedly played a crucial role. But if we focus on *why* the state weakened and grievances became acute at the particular historical moment of the late eighteenth century, the answer lies in the inability of France's economic, social, and political institutions to cope with the diverse effects of demographic change. The failure of institutions at several levels—from the agrarian economy to elite recruitment to central state finances, as shown in the *psi* model— was the reason for the breakdown of the ancien régime.

Let us pause for a moment to take stock of what we have accomplished. For over a century, Marxist-inspired historians and social scientists have explained the French Revolution as a consequence of the growth of bourgeois capitalist forces. Although criticism of this model has by now undermined virtually every facet of the Marxist argument, its demise has unfortunately not advanced our understanding of events. For, once deprived of a material basis, the French Revolution has come to seem a somewhat fortuitous occurrence. Whether viewed as a purely political crisis or as a compound of political and economic misfortunes, the difficult question remains why the French monarchy failed in such spectacular fashion, in a set of struggles pitting diverse social groups against the monarchy and each other, at the end of the eighteenth century. Without a material base, the key problem of the *conjunction* of diverse crises—agricultural, political, and social—in 1789 seems insoluble. In the words of Vovelle (1984, 55), attributing the popular aspect of the revolution only to a subsistence crisis "would mean viewing the French Revolution as nothing but a combination (possibly fortuitous) of movements which were in any case uncoordinated and unconnected."

The ecological model I have suggested solves this problem, quite fully. A focus on how rising population and stagnant agriculture created rising prices for grain provides entry into the various corners of French society. For the monarchy, rising prices undermined a tax system hamstrung by dependence on direct taxes on land. This led to the monarchy's clashes with the towns and elites over loans and taxes. Among the elite, rising prices created distress for some and opportunities for others. The combination of growing population and growing profit opportunities created a vast expansion of qualified aspirants for elite positions. This expansion explains not only the rising social mobility of the eighteenth century but also the increasingly acute competition, perceptions of blockage, and struggles for status that characterized the period after 1750. Finally, among the workers and peasants population growth explains the problems of land scarcity, unemployment, and declining real wages, all of which intensified toward the 1780s. A vast panoply of research on diverse social trends—including changes in state finance, social mobility, education, migration, urbanization, poverty, landlord policy and rural conflicts, and shifts in mentalities—can thus all be connected to one simple trend, namely, the demographic expansion and its diverse effects.

Viewing the ecological crisis as a whole explains the increasing problems of harvest shortfalls and subsistence crises and of widespread migration and poverty in the latter part of the century. To the old problem of whether France before the revolution was growing richer or poorer, this view offers the more subtle answer that it was growing richer in total but its agricultural sector and wage earners were growing poorer *per capita*. There was growing wealth in France, but price shifts led to its concentration in the hands of the landowning, trading, and upper professional elite, at the expense of both the Crown and the general populace.

Moreover, this model explains the crisis without presuming it was aimed at, or brought about primarily by, any one social group. Instead, it pictures the crisis as one in which all social groups were caught up, where none fully understood the causes. Thus, each group drew freely on its own perspective for explanations of the crisis, producing a diverse array of opinions, from the traditional and reformist elites to the traditional urban worker and the peasantry (Rudé 1980). The model also suggests that the erosion of social institutions under the pressures of the ecological crisis, an erosion evident to all in the form of highly visible social problems, gave rise to extensive criticism of the state and Crown, which in turn shifted political discourse in new directions.

Most importantly, although this model is not "Marxist," it nonetheless provides a common framework for understanding the French Revolution, the English Revolution, and the Fronde. All three can be interpreted in the same context of periods when ecological pressures collided with relatively rigid institutional structures, giving rise to widespread conflicts. In each case, the precise institutional structures were somewhat different; thus, the shapes of the respective conflicts, and their outcomes, varied considerably. Yet, it is possible to explain certain common aspects of all three crises—the state's fiscal difficulties, the severe intra-elite cleavages, the urban and, in some areas, rural unrest—as characteristic of the strains imposed by rapid demographic expansion on early modern agrarian states. And it is possible to explain why these crises occurred when they did—the English Revolution and the Fronde in the mid-seventeenth century, the French Revolution at the end of the eighteenth century, with a period of relative political quiescence from 1660 to 1750—by reference to easily charted patterns of population movement. Finally, it is possible to formulate parsimoniously a function (*psi*) that explains the timing of *both* the English and French revolutions with reference to only a few critical variables.

While these explanations are worthwhile accomplishments of the ecological model, they leave several questions unanswered. I have argued that the English Revolution and the Fronde were part of a "wave" of demographically induced political crises that spread across seventeenth-century Europe. I have also suggested that the French Revolution was situated at the beginning of another such wave, which broke across Europe from 1770 to 1850. Thus, it is important to look briefly at the European revolutions of the nineteenth century to see if there is additional evidence of the already identified pattern of demographic trends and their economic and political consequences. That task is taken up in the remainder of this chapter.

C. COMPARISONS: THE NINETEENTH-CENTURY WAVE OF EUROPEAN REVOLUTIONS

The year 1789 opened an "age of revolution" in Europe (Hobsbawm 1962, 137). In the 1820s there were revolutionary movements in Greece (against Ottoman rule), Spain, and Naples. The latter two, as well as the revolutions in South America against Spanish rule, were a consequence of the power vacuum left when Napoleon's troops were driven from Spain and Italy. Then, despite the more than thirty years of international peace that followed Waterloo, during the period 1830–1834 there were revolutions or rebellions in France, Belgium, Poland, and Ireland, as well as a serious constitutional crisis in England. And from 1847 to 1852 there were revolutions or serious revolutionary crises in France, Italy, Germany, Austria, Hungary, Bohemia, Switzerland, and Romania.

These crises have been relatively neglected by modern scholars, compared with the voluminous analyses of the English and French revolutions. But there is reason to pay serious attention to these events, particularly those of the 1830s and of the period 1847–1852. These were, after all, the revolutions that Marx and Tocqueville knew firsthand, and the only ones that Marx explicitly analyzed (Calhoun 1989).

Moreover, although writers such as Grenville (1976, 19) and Namier (1959) have argued that these revolutions were not "real" struggles, but merely coups d'état in France and unsuccessful elite rebellions elsewhere (a view that Marx did not share), recent research has overturned these superficial views. It is now clear that, except perhaps in Prussia, these nineteenth-century crises were full-fledged cases of state breakdown. Elites and popular groups rebelled against the authority of states who could not marshal the resources to defend themselves. Only Russian and Prussian troops prevented the dismemberment of the Austrian Empire. In France, the events of 1830 and 1848 were not merely quick coups. "Social protest was absolutely central and vital to the movements of 1830" (Church 1983, 8); and indeed, such social protest continued throughout the period 1830–1834 (Bezucha 1983). Rule and Tilly (1975) and Margadant (1979) have shown that from 1848 to 1851 conflict in France was widespread as different groups struggled for control of Paris and Paris struggled for control of the provinces.

The nineteenth-century revolutions are interesting not only as further cases of state breakdown, but also because they pose particular theoretical puzzles. They occurred just as industrialization was beginning in Europe, and during a period of sustained peace. Analysts of these revolutions must, therefore, explain the relationship between the revolutions and the advance of industrial capitalism, and explain why such widespread revolutions occurred in the absence of the stress of war. Earlier writers have left these problems unsolved.

Marx (1935, 1964), of course, ascribed the struggles that toppled the French Restoration Monarchy (1815–1830) and the July Monarchy (1830–1848) to class conflicts brought on by the advance of capitalism. He argued that conflicts pitting ambitious bourgeois against conservative aristocrats felled the Restoration Monarchy in 1830. Then, a split developed between the bourgeoisie of finance, who supported the ensuing July Monarchy, and the bourgeoisie of commerce and industry; this led to the collapse of the July Monarchy in 1848. However, in a few months both branches of the bourgeoisie joined to consolidate their power through ruthless suppression of the working class, which sought a proletarian revolution of its own.

But these characterizations of class conflicts, as in the cases of the English and French revolutions of earlier centuries, have not withstood scholarly scrutiny. Nobles played a leading role on *both* sides in all of the nineteenth-century revolutions, and "no simple pattern of class conflict . . . can satisfactorily explain the outbreaks of 1830. Vertical divisions were . . . just as important as horizontal ones and, in any case, such divisions varied quite considerably from country to country" (Church 1983, 10). In France in 1848, factional rather than class divisions divided the elite into legitimists, Orléanists, and republicans (Jardin and Tudesq 1983), and Traugott (1985) has shown that there were no class differences between the workers who manned the barricades of Paris and the workers of the Mobile Guard who fought against them. Elsewhere in Europe, elite rebellion in 1848 rested almost entirely on the actions of students, professionals, and officials, rather than on the actions of the commercial and industrial bourgeoisie (Langer 1966, 100).

But if Marx is an unreliable guide to the origins of these crises, recent theoretical perspectives do not fare much better. Skocpol's (1979) work suggests that revolutions come when structurally "blocked" or divided states are subjected to unmanageable international pressures, in particular defeat or ruinous expenses in war. Yet the period from 1815 to 1850, under the "concert of Europe," was perhaps the high point of cooperation and peace on the Continent in the early modern era. So how could it then also be a high point of domestic crises? As Howard (1976, 95) has noted, "for the best part of forty years [Europe's armies] were kept far busier in repressing riot and revolution at home than in fighting, or preparing to fight, one another."

The revolutions of 1830 and 1848 are particularly interesting in light of the thesis advanced in this book. Marxist theories of revolution stress the corrosive effects of the growth of capitalism on early modern society. New classes drawing wealth from commerce and industry attacked the traditional landed elite. At the same time, the expulsion of cultivators from the land, combined with factories that undercut traditional labor, led to misery that was especially concentrated in the cities. The "dangerous classes" then provided the raw material for political unrest. In contrast, I have argued that early modern revolutions were not simply a response to the growth of capitalism. Instead, state crises occurred when *traditional* political, economic, and social institutions were unable to cope with cumulative population growth. This theory produces the following, perhaps surprising, prediction. If capitalist economic organization was more productive, providing more jobs, more elite positions, and more output for consumers, then areas where capitalism was most advanced should have been *least* vulnerable to simple population pressure. Conversely, areas that were more bound by traditional institutions should have been more vulnerable. Thus, the revolutions of 1830 and 1848 provide a sharp test of the demographic/structural theory versus Marxist theories of revolution. If the latter are correct, then those areas where industrial capitalism made the greatest incursion should be the areas of greatest unrest; if the former is correct, then those states or regions that were *least* affected by industrial change, and hence most vulnerable to population pressure on resources similar to that of earlier times, should have experienced the worst unrest and crises.

Of course, circumstances were not so simple. Some states that had little capitalist penetration, such as Russia, also had ample land for settlement and so had an outlet for population growth. In other cases, both capitalist development and population growth were present, and we must carefully examine their interaction. And of course, capitalism and population increase need to be examined in light of both changes in state organization and elite conflicts. Nonetheless, my argument is that throughout Europe, those areas where capitalism was most entrenched—the industrializing northern counties of England, the mining and factory towns of northeast France, and the Junker agribusiness estates east of the Elbe—showed the least disturbances. It was in the most *traditional* regions—the agrarian counties of southern England, the craft and artisan neighborhoods of Paris and Lyon, and the family farm areas of Brittany, the Midi, and southwest Germany—that popular unrest was most severe.

Of course, one cannot focus on popular conditions and disorders alone to explain these crises. As with the earlier revolutions, these events were conjunctural: state crises were produced by a combination of state weakness, elite conflict, and popular disorders. Indeed, as C. Tilly and his collaborators (Tilly, Tilly, and Tilly 1975; Rule and Tilly 1975) have shown, popular unrest was tightly focused on periods in which elites challenged and unsettled state authorities. We thus need to explain the actions of elites and the struggles over state power.

The following sections seek the causes of state crises in four cases: France in 1830 and in 1848, England in 1830–1832, and Germany in 1848. I argue that where the conjunction of population growth and institutional constraints resembled that of earlier centuries, one finds the same trends—elite competition and conflict, falling real wages, urban concentration, rural landlessness, and an increasingly youthful population—that created the earlier crises. However, history did not precisely repeat; there were three main changes.

First, state revenue systems had generally been improved in the eighteenth century (and in France, in the early nineteenth century under Napoleon); thus states were more resistant to fiscal crises (Stearns 1974, 67). States did face fiscal problems over pay, patronage, and corruption, but these problems did not lead to utter bankruptcy. Since states were more fiscally sound, the degree of breakdown of the central authorities was far less than in earlier crises.

Second, elite mobility and competition showed much displacement of aspiring elites, but very little turnover. Hence, there were great pressures to expand the access of marginal elites to politics and social positions, but little counterrevolutionary pressure from elites who had lost earlier status and sought to turn back the clock and create reactionary regimes. The lack of counterrevolutionary forces meant that the moderate leaders of these revolutions did not experience the kind of extended struggle between the Right and the Left that usually produces greater radicalization (a process discussed in more detail in chapter 5). In these revolutions, unlike the great English and French revolutions, reformers did not have to ally with popular radicals to overpower a strong counterrevolutionary elite. Instead, the revolutionary crises produced broader elite access to politics, and a reconciliation of the old government elite and the reformist opposition. This left only a struggle pitting the coalition of reformists and old elites against the now-isolated radical revolutionaries. The new regimes were able to suppress the latter and consolidate relatively conservative, although reforming, governments.

Third, the growth of industrial capitalism did provide increased resources, and hence a defense against population pressure. Thus, as I later demonstrate, it was precisely those occupations and regions *least* affected by factory production that suffered most in this period and exhibited the most unrest. Indeed, the expansion of resources permitted by capitalist growth *after* 1850, by raising real incomes and removing the persistent threat of food shortages, as well as by providing a growth of government and private positions for educated youths and elites, ended the early modern era of demographically driven political crises. It was because of England's earlier development that she escaped this era after 1830, almost a generation ahead of continental Europe.

In short, I argue that it was not the incursion of the "new"—capitalism and modern social life—but rather the persistence of the "old"—relatively inflexible systems of elite recruitment, labor markets, and land use, unable to cope with the pressure of growing population—that was responsible for the nineteenth-century crises. Let us, then, first investigate the movements of population, production, prices, and associated trends in France, England, and Germany, before turning to the particular cases.

POPULATION GROWTH AND ITS IMPACT ON NINETEENTH-CENTURY FRANCE, ENGLAND, AND GERMANY

If population growth alone created crises, England would have suffered the worst in the early nineteenth century, and France the least. From 1800 to 1850, the population of England and Wales increased by 92 percent (72 percent for all of the United Kingdom, including Ireland) (Wrigley and Schofield 1981, 534–535; Gash 1979, 369). In the half-century from 1816 to 1864, Germany's population rose 61 percent, led by Saxony (96 percent) and Prussia (72 percent). The states of southwest Germany, which experienced massive emigration in the 1850s, show slower net growth in the period 1816–1864 but still reveal massive increases before 1850. Despite the emigration, these states' *net* population growth from 1816 to 1864 ranged from 24 percent (Württemberg) to 33 percent (Bavaria) to 43–45 percent (Baden and Hesse) (W. Lee 1979, 144; Köllmann 1976b, 10). France grew more slowly but continued to add 1.5 million to 2 million souls each decade to an already crowded landscape, her population rising by 31 percent from 1800 to 1850 (Armengaud 1976, 235). Yet as I have insisted, it is not population growth alone but rather an imbalance between population and resources that produces crises. Here, France was seriously disadvantaged, Germany mildly so, and England clearly ahead.

France's economy, *on average*, kept pace with its population in this period. But harvests and output were subject to large fluctuations, and France's output, though running ahead of population demands in good years, fell behind in bad ones. France entered the nineteenth century with its population already pressing on the limits of its production. The further growth of the population, and the slow growth of the economy, meant that this difficult situation underwent no fundamental change. France thus continued to face grain crises of the kind that haunted the last decades of the ancien régime. Particularly severe crises occurred in the periods 1816–1817, 1828–1832, and 1846–1847 (Price 1981, 199).

Germany, at the end of the Napoleonic Wars, faced varying pressures

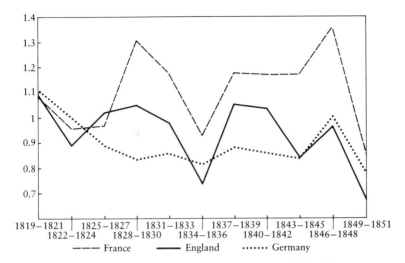

Figure 9. Grain price movements in France, England, and Germany, 1819–1851

Note: The grains are wheat for France and England and rye for Germany. The prices are shown as an index, adjusted so that for all countries, prices in 1819–1827 = 1.00.

across different regions. "While the thinly populated agrarian regions of the north and east were able to absorb the [demographic] increase without great difficulty, in the west and south a serious problem of overpopulation arose . . . creating land hunger among the peasantry, [and] intensifying the crisis in the artisan trades" (Hamerow 1958, 20). The latter effects were particularly evident after 1830, from which time population pressures on the land in the southwest were acute.

England, aided by its agricultural revolution, food imports from Ireland, and the growth of its manufacturing sector, coped better with population increase. But its success was more evident after 1830. In the 1820s some regions, particularly in the southeast, show strong evidence of overcrowded labor markets and grain shortages.

These varying trends show up fairly well in the movement of grain prices in each nation, depicted in figure 9. Throughout Europe, the vast amounts of credit created by governments to pay for the Napoleonic Wars inflated prices, but from 1820 to 1848 price trends again reflected the balance of consumer demand and supply. In France grain prices *rose* steadily, with crisis peaks in 1830 and 1847; except for the favored years 1834–1836, prices were consistently higher than in the 1820s. In Germany prices fell to the mid-1830s and then rose, gently at first, but ultimately increasing more than 25 percent by 1848. In England prices show various ups and downs, but the overall trend is *lower* prices after the 1820s.

The pressure of population on the land also gave rise to other patterns in the first half of the nineteenth century, familiar from our examination of earlier periods of population growth: rapid urban expansion fueled by migration from the countryside, falling real wages due to saturated labor markets, and sharply rising university enrollments as the number of aspirants for elite positions again expanded faster than the number of available positions, creating increased competition for credentials and offices.

Paris doubled in size, Lyon and Marseille nearly did so, and Toulon tripled between 1800 and 1850 (Jardin and Tudesq 1983, 270, 372). Altogether, the percentage of France's population living in towns with more than 10,000 inhabitants rose by more than half, from under 10 percent to nearly 15 percent of the total population (Price 1972, 11); the number of people living in the twelve major cities more than doubled, from just over 1 million to 2.5 million. London nearly tripled in size, from 864,000 to 2.4 million, while the number of people living in towns with more than 20,000 inhabitants grew an incredible 320 percent. Berlin, benefiting from rising status as Prussia grew, expanded from 200,000 inhabitants in 1819 to 380,000 in 1848. Vienna also grew rapidly, from 232,000 inhabitants in 1800 to 400,000 in 1846. In Prussia as a whole, the population living in truly large cities of over 100,000 inhabitants rose two and a half times—from under 200,000 to 500,000—in the three decades from 1816 to 1848 (A. Weber 1963, 43–46, 73, 82, 95).

Everywhere "urban institutions and social services failed to keep pace with the headlong and unplanned expansion" (Hobsbawm 1962, 245). In particular, "everywhere on the continent the civil police was inadequate for the task" of keeping order in the explosive cities (Langer 1969, 111). Except for England, which introduced a modern constabulary after 1830, Europe's monarchs in the first half of the nineteenth century relied on some combination of army troops and civil militias to deal with large disturbances, instruments that often proved unreliable in times of broad social crisis (Church 1983, 149). And such disturbances became almost inevitable, as "increased numbers of urbanites rapidly outstripped urban employment opportunities" (Gillis 1977, 176).

Figure 10 maps the early-nineteenth-century trends in real wages. Wage trends in this period are notoriously slippery, since income moved

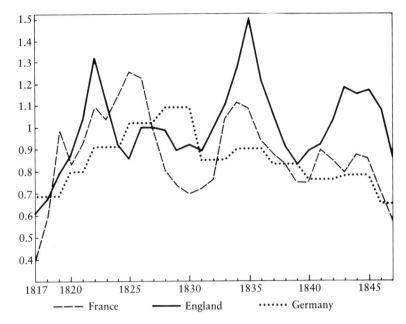

Figure 10. Real wage movements in France, England, and Germany, 1817–1847

Note: Real wages are shown as an index, adjusted so that for all countries, real wages in 1820–1829=1.00

differently for different kinds of workers and for different regions of the same country. I offer a more circumspect treatment of these issues later. But the trends in this graph are not misleading. They show wages of construction workers in England and in Germany, and of a mix of workers in France. In all countries, the years to 1827 were prosperous for workers; thereafter a severe crisis struck France, and milder drops in income occurred in 1830 in England and Germany. There was recovery in the mid-1830s, but in France and Germany wages then steadily drifted downward, falling precipitously in the crisis of 1847–1849. By contrast, though English wages show ups and downs after 1830, the trend in real wages is flat and sustained at a higher level than in the 1820s. The overall picture is one of improvement in England, admittedly with some ups and downs and some stagnation in the 1840s, but one of increasing difficulty in France and Germany, with particularly sharp periods of misery in 1828–1830 and 1847–1849 in France.

Urban misery, however, is not enough to provoke crises, unless elites unleash the high mass mobilization potential of aggrieved workers through their own attacks on the state. Such attacks are particularly likely when the number of aspirants to elite positions is growing faster than the number of places, leading many frustrated would-be leaders to challenge the state. In the early nineteenth century, "the peculiarities of . . . economic growth did not provide adequate employment opportunities for the educated" (Gillis 1974, 72). To be more precise, there were employment opportunities galore on the bottom rungs of educational ladders, where the vast expansion of popular journals and schools provided low-level points of entry to the professions. But there was no such expansion in the upper reaches of state office, university life, and law and medicine. Ever larger cohorts of youth left the schools and universities only to find themselves crowded into the outer reaches of the bureaucracy and the professions (Church 1983, 11; Stearns 1974, 43).

In France, attendance at lycées, the elite preparatory schools, nearly doubled from 1816 to 1830, and then rose by half again to 1848 (Prost 1968, 33; P. Jones 1981, 13). In Germany, the number of university students tripled from 1800 to 1830, before dropping in the 1840s as it became evident that graduates were failing to find jobs. "In both Germany and France, industrial development was still proceeding too slowly to absorb more than small numbers of educated youth" (Gillis 1974, 75). Nor did state administrations expand to take the new generations. The exception to this pattern was England. There, too, university enrollments increased: Oxford and Cambridge enrollments, which had grown less than 10 percent from the period 1740–1749 to 1790–1799, suddenly doubled by the 1820s and maintained that level through the 1840s, before again expanding after 1850 (L. Stone 1974, 90–91). Yet England greatly expanded its civil service after 1830, while expanding industry drew ambitious men away from formal school competition (which still stressed classical preparation for careers in the Church) with the promise of more worldly rewards.

To differing degrees, European monarchs in the early nineteenth century thus faced the same constellation of problems—grain crises, surging urban populations, falling real wages, and expanding cohorts of educated aspirants to elite positions—that undid some of their predecessors in the mid-seventeenth and late eighteenth centuries. How well did they cope? An answer requires a closer look at the material and political resources in each country. The reward, however, is an explanation that makes sense of national, temporal, and even regional variation in political crises in the early nineteenth century.

FRANCE: FROM REVOLUTION TO REVOLUTION TO REVOLUTION

In 1789 France was fundamentally transformed. Or was it? The long-standing belief that the French Revolution marked a caesura in French history has recently been questioned, as contemporary scholars (Furet 1981; Forster 1980; Bergeron 1981) have returned to Tocqueville's view that France in the late eighteenth and early nineteenth centuries saw more continuity than change.

STABILITY UNDER NAPOLEON

Although bankruptcy continued to haunt the National Assembly and the Directory, Napoleon made major changes in France's administration that solved, albeit briefly, some of the problems faced by the Old Regime.

We noted that the Bourbons had relied too heavily on land taxes, which were already at maximum practical levels, and too little on indirect taxes, that is, excise taxes and customs. Napoleon attacked this problem directly. No new land taxes were levied, and, although their administration was tightened up, taxes on real estate remained stable from 1791 to 1813. Sumptuary taxes, levied on carriages and conspicuous housing features (doors, windows, chimneys, and so on), provided a modest supplement to the *octroi* to defray local administration. But the major tax gains came from big increases in indirect taxes on tobacco, liquor, and salt. The yield from these taxes quadrupled from 1806 to 1812. During the Napoleonic Empire, only a third of tax revenues in France came from land taxes. The remainder came from excises, stamp and registry taxes, and customs duties. By 1806, the Old Regime's problems of constant debt were replaced by adequate revenues and fiscal solvency (Bergeron 1981, 38–39).

The vast expansion of the state under Napoleon also solved the problem of frustrated elite aspirations. The new departmental structure, requiring staff for 130 *départements*, "was well-calculated to rally families and form personal loyalties to the Emperor"; the new administration joined sons of the "comfortable bourgeoisie [and] the old aristocracy," providing an outlet for "sons, sons-in-law, and nephews of ministers, senators, state councillors, generals, prefects" (Bergeron 1981, 30). The opening of military careers to talent, and the enormous size of the imperial armies, completed the job of creating sufficient opportunities for everyone of talent or ambition.

The revolution did not destroy the old nobility; Napoleon preserved it while conferring equal status on talented newcomers to the administrative and military elites. The Napoleonic Empire thus ended the period of turnover and displacement and created an era of upward mobility that was primarily achieved through simple absorption, hence stabilizing in its effects.

Hampson (1963, 251) notes that of roughly 400,000 nobles in 1789, only "some 1,158 were executed, and 16,431 fled the country." Even those who fled were often able eventually to repurchase confiscated land under assumed names, and Napoleon tended to appoint former nobles, including repatriated émigrés, to office (Cobban 1957, 2:26). Forster (1980, 186) has recently concluded that "large landlords of the Old Regime, noble or not, were not destroyed—nor even permanently hurt—by the Revolution." In almost half of France's departments, pre-revolutionary nobles remained the *majority* of the wealthiest landowners; in only a handful of departments did they vanish from the ranks of the economic elite (Bergeron 1981, 126–129). Napoleon reinstituted a titled nobility, based on state service and drawn from the military and national and local administration, including a fair portion, about 22.5 percent, drawn from the old nobility (Bergeron 1981, 69). "It was all a bit of a social crossroads, but the combination of new solidarities also made for homogeneity"; in Paris, in the faubourg Saint-Germain, "the highest civil and political officials now lived as neighbors . . . along with numerous survivors of the good society of the noble faubourg, both those who had stayed in place and those who had returned from the emigration" (Bergeron 1981, 120, 122). Even in various localities outside of Paris, from which Forster (1980, 189) examined a sample of several thousand notables, "it appears that the social and occupational structure of French society remained remarkably stable . . . between 1789 and 1810."

In lieu of fiscal weakness and social turnover and displacement, the Napoleonic Empire enjoyed fiscal solvency and social absorption. Thus, two elements that had led to the crisis of the Old Regime were overturned. So too was the third, for the success of the imperial armies and the demand for labor in workshops turning out the supplies of war—from boots and uniforms to munitions—sharply reduced mass mobilization potential.

From 1789 to 1794, price increases outstripped wages, and recurrent food shortages kept angry crowds in the streets (Cobb and Rudé 1965, 257). But after 1794, France was enriched by war plunder, its coffers and granaries filled with levies from subjected states in the Netherlands and the Rhineland. Although the proliferation of war credit and military spending led to a surge of inflation in 1800–1820, wages rose faster than prices in this period, so that real salaries improved and conditions under the consulate and Napoleonic Empire were better than those during the last years of Louis XVI (Lefebvre 1965a, 133–134). Indeed, Vidalenc (1970, 353) remarks that "the memory of high salaries at the end of the Empire came to hold a role in the formation of the Napoleonic legend." Napoleon himself "always thought that his popularity rested not only on military victory but on the abundance and low price of bread" (Bergeron 1981, 101). Thus, as Jardin and Tudesq (1983, 41) point out, Napoleon scrapped free trade in grain when the need arose, and the government acted swiftly following the bad harvests of 1810–1811 to redistribute grain.

In the countryside, peasants in some areas acquired land from sales of Church and émigré lands and from division of communal property, and they benefited from the abolition of tithes and feudal dues. But for French peasants as a whole, these gains were small (Vidalenc 1970, 353). The major gains for peasants were the decline in real rents as inflation reduced their real payments, and the opportunity to send their sons to possibly lucrative military careers rather than being forced to provide for them on their tiny farms (Palmer 1977, 99–100).

In sum, the empire temporarily solved the problems of the Old Regime. Fiscal crisis and elite conflict were stemmed by a shift to indirect taxation and a vast expansion of state civil and military jobs. Mass mobilization potential was reduced by the gains brought by success in war. These gains included spoils from conquered territory, which kept taxes low and increased grain supplies, and provision of an outlet for millions of Frenchmen away from home, thus relieving pressure on the land and keeping real wages high in France. But the success of these measures could be sustained only as long as military success continued, and as long as the expansion of elite aspirants did not outgrow the new Napoleonic administrative system. The costly failure of the Russian campaign of 1812–1813 forced Napoleon again to greatly increase taxes, while the defeats of 1814–1815 left France with debts totaling nearly eight hundred million francs. Fiscal difficulties thus returned. More importantly, there were no fundamental changes in the underlying economic and social structures that would prevent the recurrence of old problems and conflicts if France were again confined to her old borders and her population continued to grow.

"The Revolution of 1789 had not produced a new world or even a new France. Institutions of government and administration and the persons in positions of power were different, but . . . the revolution . . . had left largely untouched the fundamental aspects of French life—economic activity, social structure, distribution of population. . . . France in the 1830s was, as it had been in the 1780s, agrarian, rural, far from centralized, divided by language and distance, populated largely by peasants, and dominated by an aristocracy of landowners" (Pinkney 1986, 3). Palmer (1977, 100) adds that "the agrarian crisis was unresolved, and was not to be 'solved' until industrial growth drew peasants into factories and cities." Price (1981, 199) concludes that "the decline in the tax burden brought about by the Revolution, [and its modification of] the distribution of resources . . . temporarily relaxed the pressure of population, postponing the major crisis for another half a century. The intervening period saw recurrent crises and a gradual process of pauperisation in many areas accompanying the growth of population and in the absence of a radical improvement in agricultural methods and yields."

These comments by diverse scholars accurately depict the dilemma of the Restoration and the July monarchies, which faced the continuous population growth of the nineteenth century in very nearly the same context of economic constraints and an inflexible land-and-office-based status system that had created insoluble crises for the ancien régime. France and other European states in the nineteenth century were indeed, as Marx and Engels argued, haunted by a specter. But it was not the specter of communism. It was the specter of continuous demographic increases in a setting of economic and social structures that could not yet adequately provide for such growth. In the nineteenth century, revolutions did not arise as birth pangs of a new order; instead, states relived the nightmares of the old.

ECONOMIC CONSTRAINTS

From 1791 to 1851, France's population grew by 32 percent, from twenty-seven million inhabitants to just under thirty-six million (Dupeaux 1976, 37). Although France led the rest of Europe in controlling fertility and its birthrate sharply declined after 1800, mortality fell sharply as well, so that the margin of births over deaths remained positive, and new youth continued to swell France's population. Moreover, the control of fertility was chiefly an initiative of a minority of well-off families in the north and east (Weir 1982, 190–200). Among the poor, and throughout the south and west, reduced mortality was not offset by birth control; indeed, population increases in Brittany and the Midi were exceptionally strong (Jardin and Tudesq 1983, 239). Agulhon (1983, 9) remarks that by the 1840s the rural departments of France, despite emigration to the cities, "were then more highly populated than ever before or since."

How well could France's still predominantly agrarian economy cope with this burden? Recall that from 1770 to 1795 France suffered from recurrent severe grain shortages (with major crises in the early 1770s, late 1780s, and early 1790s) and from a depression in manufacturing, brought on by declining demand for consumer goods as real wages fell and foodstuffs absorbed an ever-larger proportion of family budgets. Thus, even if French agricultural output had increased by one-third in the first half of the nineteenth century, keeping pace with population growth, this increase merely would have sustained the difficult conditions of the late eighteenth century, when a bad harvest could send the country into an economic and political paroxysm. An end to France's vulnerability to ecological crises would have required either larger increases in agricultural output, on the order of 40–50 percent from 1800 to 1850, or a substantial transformation of the economy to make it less dependent on agriculture.

Neither occurred. In the 1830s, 80 percent of Frenchmen still lived in rural villages of less than two thousand inhabitants, and of the 20 percent who lived in cities, many were still "enmeshed in the agrarian economy and rural society" (Pinkney 1986, 4). As late as 1845, two-thirds of the French labor force worked predominantly in agriculture, and even the large number of rural dwellers who supported themselves primarily by handicrafts engaged at least part-time in seasonal agricultural labor (O'Brien and Keyder 1978, 94; Mayer 1953, 91).

Agrarian output did improve in the early nineteenth century, but the degree of improvement has been the subject of fierce debate. Optimists (Newell 1973; O'Brien and Keyder 1978; Lévy-Leboyer 1968) have claimed a rise of 55 to 70 percent from the early nineteenth century to the 1840s. Pessimists (Vidalenc 1970; Morineau 1970a; Clout 1980; Grantham 1978; Crouzet 1980; Price 1981; R. Cameron 1970) insist that there was virtually no increase at all in yields, and little in output.

Such divergent claims, ranging from 0 to 70 percent increases, reflect the difficulty of making judgments on the basis of fragmentary evidence. The data are from regions that differed widely in output, and from years that differed widely in harvest quality. The selection of different years and areas for benchmarks produces widely different results. Nonetheless, a consistent picture—not as extreme as the pessimists' case, but leaning in their direction—emerges when one brings together data on yields, agricultural practices, prices, and the occurrence of grain crises.

Much data on nineteenth-century French yields can be found in official sources: the *Récoltes* (harvest data) requested by the government in the early nineteenth century, and the agricultural censuses from 1840. In addition, for the late eighteenth century, Allen and O'Grada (1988) have reconstructed yield figures for various regions from Arthur Young's (1971) data. However, the *Récoltes* have proved misleading, for their base year is 1816–1817, a devastatingly bad year in which harvests were disrupted by bad weather and the depredations of occupying armies following Napoleon's defeat at Waterloo (Grantham 1978, 313; Allen and O'Grada 1988; Morineau 1970b, 177). When we compare yields for this year with the yields of the census of 1840, which was a fairly good year, we gain the illusion of great progress that has fed the optimists' visions.

Optimists also gained hope from comparisons of wheat yields in northeast France with those in England, for the former were within 10 percent of the latter by the 1840s. Unfortunately, this fact is not evidence of progress, for as early as the eighteenth century, possibly even the seventeenth century, wheat yields in the northeast compared favorably with English yields, particularly in Le Nord and Pas de Calais and in parts of Normandy (Morineau 1970b; Allen and O'Grada 1988). What held back French output was the poor productivity of the French lands outside the northeast and the major river valleys. Yields in these areas, which were for the most part too acidic in soil or too arid in rainfall to support improved crop rotations, and which covered two-thirds of the country, were generally 50 percent, and rarely more than 67 percent, of the yields in the northeast (Galassi 1986, 93–94; Grantham 1978, 320–326).

If one uses the late eighteenth century rather than the "disasters of 1814–17" (Grantham 1978, 313) as a baseline, there is little evidence of any increase in yields before 1850. When Allen and O'Grada (1988) compared their estimates of French wheat yields in the northeast in an "average" year in the 1780s with the official *Récoltes* of 1850–1851, they found no increase in yields at all for the more fertile loam soils, and increases of only 8–15 percent for the mountain and heath soils. There were substantial yield improvements in the stony soils (50 percent) and chalk soils (70 percent), but these were only a tiny fraction of the land cultivated for wheat. There was thus virtually no improvement in yields for the bulk of the fertile land of the northeast. For the west, south, and center of France, Heffer, Mairesse, and Chanut (1986, 1278) report that the 1852 agricultural survey showed wheat yields in these regions were still lagging, with no more than 50–67 percent of the output per hectare achieved in the northeast.

Evidence of stagnation in yields is reinforced by evidence of stagnation in agricultural practices. Throughout the early nineteenth century, small farms, communal regulations, substantial fallows, and primitive implements remained prominent in French agriculture. Fragmentation of landholdings got *worse* over the early nineteenth century: in 1825, holdings assessed for land taxes at fifty francs or less (approximately ten hectares and under) accounted for 34 percent of the value of all landholdings; by 1858, their share had risen to 37 percent (Heywood 1981, 362). Traditional communal rights that hindered agricultural improvement, such as *parcours* and *vaine pâture*, remained widespread. Even in 1866 the French government thought it more politic to regulate rather than abolish the latter (Clout 1983, 25; Laurent 1976, 668). Fallow lands still took up 27 percent of the arable in 1840, compared to 6 percent under cultivated fodder (Price 1981, 53). And "the inquiry of 1848 revealed that the principle harvesting tool throughout France was still the low productivity sickle" (Price 1975a, 12). In the Pyrenees, an officer charged in 1836 with drawing up a report on the area found it sufficient simply to recopy the report of an intendant from 1698, appending the statement that agriculture "appears to have been since a very ancient time in the same state as it is today" (cited in Vidalenc 1970, 355).

England's breakthrough in agrarian productivity depended on planting fodder crops (chiefly turnips and clover) on fallows and on previously uncultivated rough grazing lands. These crops allowed larger animal herds and more manure, while the legumes further fertilized the soil. But in much of France, soil and climate were unsuitable for fodder crops; and even in the suitable soils of the northeast, the investment in seed and livestock required to raise yields could be recovered only if markets were available to sell the increased output of meat. Poor transportation and low urban incomes meant restricted markets, except in the vicinity of major cities, such as Lyon and Paris, where such investments did in fact occur (Grantham 1978). These bottlenecks would be broken decisively only after the railroads brought fertilizers that allowed fodder crops to be grown and higher yields to be achieved on more of the arable; resulting lower grain prices then raised demand for meat, which justified further investments in livestock and improved meadow cultivation (Shaffer 1982, 128; Clout 1983, 61). In the first half of the nineteenth century, however, this process had barely begun. Only haltingly after 1837, then more rapidly after 1850, was the landscape of French agriculture thus transformed.[15]

Still, we must recognize that some progress did occur before 1850. First, although wheat yields did not increase, the area planted in wheat rose by 20 percent from 1830 to 1848 (Jardin and Tudesq 1983, 169). Much of this was in west and south-central France, where wheat began to replace rye. Considerable progress was also made in reducing fallows. In the eighteenth century, roughly 33 percent of land in the northeast, and 50 percent in the south and west, lay fallow under simple two- and three-field systems. By 1840, fallows had been reduced to 20 percent of land in the northeast, and 27 percent nationally (Grantham 1978, 319; Price 1981, 53). If fallow lands were reduced from perhaps four of every ten acres of arable nationally in the late eighteenth century to under three of every ten acres in 1840, this would imply a 20 percent increase in the utilization of arable land. In addition, substantial gains were made in the Midi through expanded irrigation (Jardin and Tudesq 1983, 313; Clout 1983, 61).

Not all of this land use was for bread grains, of course; the decades from 1817 to 1846 saw a doubling in the acreage of potatos, along with increases in maize, tobacco, sugar beets, madder, oil seed, hemp, and mulberry trees (Price 1981, 64; Jardin and Tudesq 1983, 169–170, 313). These crops produced industrial raw materials, which could be converted to cloth and oil exports in exchange for grain from the Levant. Marseilles, in particular, became a food and manufacturing entrepôt, importing grain and processing flour and edible oils (Sewell 1985a).

Thus it would be incorrect to conclude that because yields stagnated, agriculture as a whole made no progress. Land reclamation, irrigation, crop diversification, and cultivation of the fallow added considerably to output. But there were limits on what could be achieved before the railway era. In 1852 national average wheat yields were hardly different from those of the Old Regime, at still under fourteen hectoliters per hectare. By 1882 this average had risen 30 percent, to eighteen hectoliters

15. For a more detailed comparison of English and French farming in the eighteenth and early nineteenth centuries, and more geographical detail on the obstacles to French progress, see Goldstone (1988), Morincau (1970a), and Allen and O'Grada (1988).

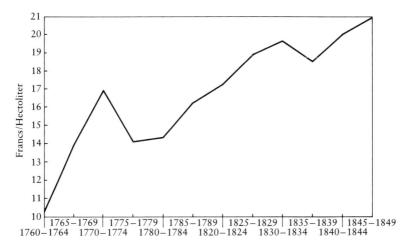

Figure 11. French wheat prices, 1760–1849

Note: Data are five-year averages, excluding the war decades of 1790–1819.

per hectare (Laurent 1976, 683). Clearly, although French agriculture made some progress before 1850, the "agricultural revolution" came afterward.

Was the progress before 1850 sufficient to keep pace with demographic growth? There are two indications that the answer is, not quite. The first indicator of food shortages is the long-run behavior of grain prices. Optimists note that after the extremely high prices of 1790–1820, grain prices in France fell and remained low to 1850. But this observation is misleading, for the high prices in 1790–1820 were largely a consequence of war, resulting first from wartime monetary and credit expansion, and then from the pressures of military occupation. If one examines five-year averages of the price of wheat from 1760 to 1850, excluding the war decades of 1790–1820, one finds a steady increase, as shown in figure 11. Indeed, the rise is so steady that no suggestion of a change in underlying conditions can be discerned.

The second indicator of continued shortages is the recurrence of food crises, which shook France in every decade of the Restoration and July monarchies: in 1816–1817, 1828–1832, 1837–1839, and 1846–1847. These were crises of the old type. They led to food riots and an evaporation of the spending power of the working class that cut demand and produced consequent depressions in manufacturing (Dupeaux 1976, 134). In short, the crises recreated the economic conditions of the early

1770s and late 1780s, thus demonstrating that France's agrarian economy was not yet capable of producing a steady surplus that could avoid frequent grave shortfalls.

From 1790 to 1850 France's population grew by a third. How much did food output rise? It is impossible to be precise, but clearly neither a total stagnation nor an agricultural revolution occurred. On *average*, the long-term trend of rising prices suggests that grain output lagged behind demand. However, the trend was not dramatic, meaning that in the early nineteenth century, as in the late eighteenth century, an average harvest fed France's population, though perhaps slightly less well as each decade passed. We might thus venture that total grain output rose by around 30 percent in these years. But more important for political analysis is that if *average* output only barely kept pace with population growth, a bad harvest would completely fail to meet demand; thus, harvest failures would continue to lead to enormous shortages and crises. That such crises actually occurred every decade, as in the late eighteenth century, shows how little fundamental progress had been made in the agrarian economy. France, in its balance of population and food supplies, remained on the critical edge.

The Restoration and July monarchies thus ruled over a society in which the ecological balance was not significantly different from that witnessed by Louis XV and Louis XVI: a population pressing on agrarian resources, able to feed itself in good years but not in bad; steadily rising grain prices; and great vulnerability to food riots and manufacturing depressions in the wake of poor harvests.

French industry in this period was more of a success story, at least in value of output. Again, estimates of output vary enormously, depending on which industries are included in indices of growth and on how they are weighted. Optimists (Markovitch 1970, 241; Levy-Leboyer 1968, 790–794; Marczewski 1961) offer indices showing that a doubling or tripling of the 1790s level of output was already achieved by 1850. Against these estimates are the more pessimistic conclusions of Crouzet (1970, 273), who finds hardly any overall growth in French industry from 1820 to 1830, and then only a 60 percent increase to 1850, most of which occurred after 1840. The reason for this slow growth was the continued dominance of traditional industries. Pinkney (1986, 12) states that even in the late 1840s, more than 80 percent of the value of cloth output came from domestic industries—especially woolens, linens, and hemps—which were caught in a "stagnation that lasted until 1840" (Crouzet 1970, 276). Although O'Brien and Keyder (1978) have, based on the optimists' output data, claimed remarkably high productivity levels for French industry in this period, Crafts (1984, 59) has effectively criticized these claims. The most sensible summary seems to be that of C. H. Johnson (1975b, 143), who notes that, despite considerable early growth, "1840 seems to have been a major turning point for French industry, and whatever 'revolution' it may have experienced was nurtured in the later years of the July monarchy and came to full bloom in the 1850s."

Let us grant that French industrial output still grew faster than both agriculture and France's population, as it had in the eighteenth century. But the ecological problem of interest is not whether industry grew faster than the population as a whole. The key question is whether industrial growth was rapid enough to absorb and employ that fraction of the population that could not find work in the slower-growing agrarian sector.

From 1800 to 1850 the number of French urban dwellers in cities of 10,000 or more inhabitants doubled, from 2.6 million to 5.2 million, increasing their proportion of France's total population from 9.5 percent to 14.4 percent (A. Weber 1963, 79). O'Brien and Keyder (1978, 94), who tend to be optimistic about the extent of industrial employment, estimate that from 1790 to 1846 the portion of the labor force outside of agriculture rose from 19 percent to 33 percent, which, given the total population increase, would mean more than a doubling of the nonagricultural population, from 5.2 million to 11.7 million. Mayer (1953, 91) gives a more conservative estimate, but still of the same order, with the nonagricultural labor force rising from 18 percent to 24 percent of the total work force. With the overall population increase of 32 percent, this implies a nearly 80 percent absolute increase in the number of nonagricultural workers.

The doubling of the nonagrarian labor force makes even the optimists' estimates of rising industrial output less impressive. Even if there was no productivity increase, we would expect that total manufacturing output would double with the doubling of the nonagricultural labor force, unless hours worked declined. Thus, the assertion that French industrial output doubled from 1800 to the 1840s implies no gains beyond those barely sufficient to balance the increase in the industrial labor supply. And if Crouzet (1970) is correct that output increased only 60 percent, this would imply massive un- and underemployment. I later consider the confirming evidence for this pessimistic assessment in terms of real wage decline. For now, it is only important to note that even if we accept the optimists' view to the extreme point of granting a doubling of industrial and commercial output in the early nineteenth century, France still does not escape from ecological pressures. The stagnation of agriculture meant that the nonindustrial labor force doubled as well. Thus, in an average year, employment would barely keep pace with labor growth. And in a year when harvest failure and rising food prices reduced the demand for manufactures, one would expect a massive shortfall of employment.

In sum, the growth in France's economy in the Restoration and July monarchies was at best barely sufficient to keep pace with demographic changes, in regard to both grain production relative to total population, and industrial growth relative to growth in the nonagricultural labor force. Thus, the basic ecological situation of the late eighteenth century was maintained. And the same pressures that made for political instability therefore remained.

STATE CONSTRAINTS, ELITE CONFLICT, AND MASS
MOBILIZATION POTENTIAL, 1815–1848

France's fiscal difficulties in making payments to the occupying powers after Napoleon's defeat required higher indirect taxes and sales of royal forests. The finance minister, Villèle, finally put French finances on a sound basis in the period 1821–1828. Villèle kept tariffs and excise taxes high, centralized and regularized accounting procedures, and reduced land taxes (Jardin and Tudesq 1983). Nonetheless, fiscal health and good credit were achieved more by cutting expenses to the bone than by increasing state revenues. Ardant (1975, 221) shows that state expenditures took a declining fraction of French GNP from the period 1803–1812 to 1845–1854. And Jardin and Tudesq (1983, 14) note that "tight fiscal policy led to an abrupt drop in the number of high positions in the army and in certain administrative agencies, thereby creating a new class of malcontents, such as officers on half-pay." Louis XVIII's first ministry cut fifteen thousand jobs from the government rolls (Spitzer 1987, 237). In addition, pay scales for the army were frozen at 1799 levels; by 1827 they were hopelessly out of date, with French officers receiving only one-half the pay of their British or Prussian counterparts (Porch 1974, 8).

Had France's status system changed and become less dependent on state office and landownership, the rise in population and the straitening of state finances need not have collided. If a new industrial bourgeoisie had risen to absorb aspiring elites, ambitious men need not have relied on climbing within the traditional professions and the civil service, or on the purchase of land, to make their way. But the bourgeoisie of the early nineteenth century "remained predominantly the bourgeoisie of the ancien régime. At the top level it was composed of professional men—lawyers, doctors, professors, scientists, publishers, higher civil servants, bankers, wholesale merchants, and only a few manufacturers" (Pinkney 1986, 19). Professional status was generally buttressed with real estate. The Napoleonic and Restoration nobility and local notables all relied on landownership to justify their self-presentations as responsible leaders of the nation. The qualifications to participate in French public politics—to vote for and to hold office in the Chamber of Deputies—were set in terms of direct taxes paid, which reflected traditional sources of wealth.

In the Restoration and July monarchies it was difficult for newcomers to penetrate the upper ranks of the national and local elite. As population increased in the early nineteenth century, France's youth cohorts grew larger still; indeed, "the ratio of youth to adults reached nearly the levels (75–80 percent) common in Asian and South American countries today. Not until 1870 did levels begin to drop toward the 35 percent now common in European societies" (Gillis 1977, 29–30). Elite education and the lower rungs of professional life were thrown open in the Restoration: the lycées expanded, the universities increased their output of medical and legal graduates, and a vast expansion of the publishing industry and the law courts provided "entry-level" positions to aspiring elites. But there were few additional opportunities for the new products of the imperial universities, who had been bred to be "good for nothing but careers in public administration and the liberal professions" (Spitzer 1987, 227). Any further rise of the new generation was blocked by entrenched members of the generation that rose under the Napoleonic Empire (Spitzer 1987; Sussman 1977; O'Boyle 1966). The same individuals who, as very young men, had responded to the Napoleonic call for talent now clung with great seniority to the top positions in the professions and the civil service, while old nobles and former émigrés dominated the Restoration court. The cutback in official positions, and the domination of very senior men with a marked royalist, clerical, and émigré tinge, resulted in a situation in which "the Restoration took on itself the onus of the partial, inconsistent, and irritating closure of the [career] avenues it had opened" (Spitzer 1987, 248–249).

As in the eighteenth century, rising prices led to a broad expansion and enrichment of the smaller commercial bourgeoisie. Daumard et al. (1973, 118), investigating the material goods left at death by inhabitants of Paris and several other major cities, found a steady increase in the value of householders' possessions—a 100 percent rise in Paris and a 50 percent rise in Toulouse—from 1820 to 1847. These families sought entry for themselves or their children into the elite of the professions and state offices. In response to this demand, the lycées expanded and a lower-level, intellectual middle class of lawyers, teachers, writers, doctors, and civil servants bloomed. But limited career prospects confined this group to the margins of professional and political life.

Sufficient social mobility to greatly increase the number of individuals who were within the lower orbit of the elite and aspired to more, combined with insufficient mobility into higher levels to satisfy the abundance of aspirations, led many low-level elite to opposition politics.[16] Throughout the 1820s, 1830s, and 1840s, the warning of Louis Philippe's prefect of the Seine (cited in Spitzer 1987, 224–225) was apt: beware of "the doctors without patients, the architects without buildings, the journalists without journals, the lawyers without clients, all the misunderstood, maladjusted, famished characters who, having found no seat at the banquet, try to overturn the table to get the plates. These are your makers of revolution, your high-priests of anarchy, your buccaneers of insurrection."

Of course, this warning was incomplete. Malcontented marginal elites may have been the core of the opposition leadership, but they could do nothing without popular support. Nor could their supporters hope to oppose a royal professional army if its loyalty and discipline had remained intact. These two additional essential conditions—military defection and popular mobilization—were produced by royal penury and the economic crises of 1827–1832 and 1846–1847.

The later Bourbons lost their support in the army through fiscal constraint and personnel conflicts. The freezing of salaries and the imposition of émigré officers led to "political opposition in the army [that] went hand-in-hand with frustrated ambition" (Porch 1974, 8). Veterans of the Napoleonic Empire, who recalled the openness of Napoleon's

---

16. Auguste Comte (cited by Spitzer 1987, 232–233) expressed the views of many when he wrote the following: "An intelligent, able, and well-educated young man cannot, now matter how hard he tried, find a way to make a living, while so many idle ignoramuses sleep on their piles of treasure. . . . [W]ould such a horrible abuse exist under a good government?"

armies to talent, chafed under officers drawn from the prerevolutionary nobility. When the economy crashed, this resentment gave way to blame and then to passivity or support for the opposition. Thus in 1830 many officers and men who had fought for the Empire were unwilling to fight for the Restoration regime (Jardin and Tudesq 1983, 99). Desertions were widespread in the July days; "when he abdicated on 2 August, the King had barely 1,350 men, many of them officers without regiments. . . . [V]irtually every garrison within fifty miles of Paris had declared for the provisional government" (Porch 1974, 35–36).

The popular groups that supported the opposition leaders, and before whom the royal army melted away, are sometimes seen as the victims of early capitalism—urban workers ground down by competition from factories and exploited by ruthless capitalist entrepreneurs. But this image is no more true of the early-nineteenth-century crowds of Paris than it was of those of the late eighteenth century. In Marseille, "in no case did new, large-scale mechanical technology invade a flourishing handicraft trade and bring hardship or precipitous decline" (Sewell 1985a, 31). In Paris, as Traugott (1985, 7) notes, "factory work was almost unknown." Nor did foreign enterprise undermine workers, for high tariffs protected France's internal markets from British competition (C. H. Johnson 1975b, 168). The revolutionary urban workers were predominantly the upwardly mobile migrants who, soon after entering the traditional artisan trades, found their futures threatened by overcrowded labor markets and their wages eroded by sharply rising grain prices. They were overwhelmingly from precisely those traditional trades—construction, cabinetmaking and joinery, locksmithing, and printing—that were least affected by factory competition, and that preserved the most autonomy for masters and journeymen from capitalist entrepreneurs. Those trades most influenced by early-nineteenth-century capitalist organization—textiles and mining—played little or no role in the revolutions of 1830 and 1848 (Tilly and Lees 1975, 188; Newman 1975).

In the early nineteenth century, French cities were swelled by a flood of immigrants from the overcrowded countryside. Dupeaux (1976, 142) notes that, in the rural areas, partition of inheritance continued to fragment landholdings: the number of smallholdings valued at less than twenty francs increased by 30 percent from 1828 to 1858. The only alternative for families seeking to preserve their patrimony, or for holders of inadequate parcels of land to support their families, was to seek industrial employment, whether in rural industry or through migration to the cities. And in such cities as Toulouse, Lyon, and Marseilles, migrants were overrepresented among those arrested for radical politics (Aminzade 1981; Stewart-McDougall 1984; Sewell 1985a).

Migrants are sometimes considered "dangerous" because they are thought to be isolated and anomic, rather than integrated into stable communities (Chevalier 1973). But France's radical migrants were corporatist and communal in their activities and were arrested for belonging to radical organizations, not for lone acts of deviance. The problem was that the old "church-based institutions in the center of the city were incapable of integrating the growing number of workers" (Aminzade 1981, 68). Thus, while inner-city natives remained under the control of Church and guild masters and largely legitimist in outlook, the new working-class suburbs were marked by independent working-class associations run by journeymen, who in times of economic distress opposed the authority of both guild masters and the state.

And times of distress grew more frequent and intense. The "superabundance of labor" (Bezucha 1983, 473) favored masters and entrepreneurs in hiring and setting wages; wherever possible, less-skilled workers were substituted for more-skilled (and more expensive) laborers, and nominal wages were held stable despite rising food prices. As already noted, real wages declined from 1820 to 1848. But this long-term trend was a modest problem compared to the extreme collapses in wages and employment that accompanied harvest crises. In Lyon, silk weavers' wages fell by 50 percent in the depression years of 1825–1830 (Droz 1967, 64); in the same period, "wage rates in the building trades of Paris fell off by 30 percent, in the metal industry by more than a third" (Pinkney 1972, 63). By 1829, in the major cities "nearly half the population was dependent on poor relief" (Church 1983, 18). In 1848, over half of Parisian workers were unemployed (Amman 1975, 23). It is thus no wonder that the early nineteenth century was a period in which, with every crisis, elites were stunned by the level of pauperization in their communities and held the Crown responsible for this social failure (Langer 1969, 181; Stearns 1974, 20).

Early-nineteenth-century France was much like late-eighteenth-century France. Population pressing on agrarian output led to rising prices. State fiscal constraint alienated elites, who looked to the state for employment and status. This problem grew worse as rising urban and commercial prosperity, built on rising prices and expanding markets, increased the number of aspirants for elite positions. Resentment in the army undermined the Crown's support, while an overcrowded countryside and overburdened urban labor markets provided potential recruits to the political opposition. When harvest crises drastically raised the price of grain and ensuing depressions in manufacturing threw hundreds of thousands of laborers out of work, the calls from the elite for change found a responsive audience. Thus, it is no surprise that when harvest crises occurred in 1829 and 1847, state crises followed. Indeed, given the similarity to late-eighteenth-century conditions, the real puzzle is why the revolutions of 1830 and 1848 were less drastic than the revolution of 1789.

THE REVOLUTIONS OF 1830 AND 1848

In figure 12, I have plotted the *psi* function for France and England from 1820 to 1847 on an annual basis. These curves are not directly comparable with the earlier curves for France and England, since in the nineteenth century there was no state bankruptcy in either country. Thus, these *psi* curves reflect only changes in the two other *psi* components: elite competition and conflict (measured by enrollments in French lycées and in England's universities of Oxford and Cambridge) and mass mobilization potential (based on data for urbanization, real wages, and age structure).[17] Nonetheless, they are interesting for what they indicate

17. Because these computations of *psi* are done on an annual rather than adecadal basis, some changes in the formula were used. In order to maintain comparability between England and France, elite school enrollments were measured as an index against the baseline of 1817–1819. The measurements that enter into mass mobilization potential—deviations from average real wages, urbanization rates, and youth ratios—are directly comparable across the cases.
    Elite competition was measured by the total enrollment in lycées and in Oxford and Cambridge in the ten previous years.
    The impact of wage movements and urbanization were measured on a more short-term basis. The contribution of real wages to mass mobilization potential depended not just on the current wage but also on the previous years' wages: a bad year coming after a good one was not tragic, but a bad year coming after several previous bad years could be catastrophic. Thus, the wage component of MMP is computed by averaging four years' wages, with the most recent two years getting two-thirds weight, and the two preceding years getting one-third weight.
    The urbanization component of MMP was based on the growth of London and Paris in the preceding decade, but it was weighted to emphasize more recent growth. The system of weighting used is as follows: growth rate in the preceding three years, one-half; growth rate in the preceding five years, one-third; growth rate in the preceding ten years, one-sixth. Since urban growth was steady in this period, the result is not very sensitive to weighting. I have used this scheme because I feel it is sensible to weight recent expansion more heavily than past, but the end result would not be much different if one simply used total urban growth in the preceding full decade or half-decade.
    The overall formula for *psi* is the same as used earlier, except for the lack of a fiscal strain component. This is equivalent to setting this component at the lowest level of the

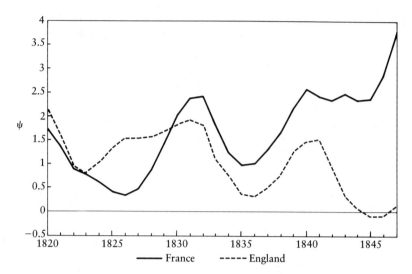

Figure 12. Pressures for crisis (*psi*) in France and England, 1820–1847

about fluctuations in instability over time, and about differences between England and France.

The *psi* curve for France shows a sharp drop following the period of Napoleon's defeat and France's occupation, indicating conditions with a high likelihood of stability in the early 1820s. There follows a peak of high *psi* in 1828–1832, and then a return of conditions favoring stability in the late 1830s. From 1839–1840 there is again a rise in *psi*, leading to a very high peak in 1847. In other words, the *psi* curve for France suggests episodes of instability, with the greatest instability circa 1847. The *psi* curve for England moves similarly, if less abruptly, until 1830 and then sharply diverges; there is a modest rise in the early 1840s, but on the whole the pattern for England indicates much greater stability after 1830 than does the pattern for France.

The main difference between France's nineteenth-century revolutions

---

fiscal distress scale—that is, unity. Thus in figure 12, *psi* = elite competition × mass mobilization potential.

The following data sources were used: for lycée enrollments, Prost (1968); for Parisian growth, A. Weber (1963); for French wages, the Kuczinski nominal wage series in Bruhat (1976), deflated by the wheat prices in Labrousse (1970e); for French age structure, Henry and Blayo (1975); for Oxford and Cambridge enrollments, L. Stone (1974); for London's growth, A. Weber (1963); for English wages, the Phelps Brown and Hopkins (1962a) nominal wage series, deflated by the wheat prices in B. Mitchell (1962); for English age structure, unpublished data made available to me by E. A. Wrigley and R. S. Schofield from their project on the population history of England (see chapter 2, note 11).

and that of 1789 is in the area of state finances. The fiscal reforms of Napoleon and Villèle had strengthened the state enough to avoid bankruptcy, though not enough to absorb a growing elite. Thus, elite resentment festered, but there was not the hostile judgment—widespread in the 1780s owing to the Crown's constant borrowing and then bankruptcy in a time of peace—that the entire monarchical structure was so corrupt and inefficient that it needed to be reformed. Instead, a change in the leadership and an expansion of political participation to include additional aspirants to elite roles were seen as sufficient to rectify the problems of the state.

In this sense of comparatively constrained response by elites, the pressures behind the revolutions of 1830 and 1848 were not as severe as in 1789. The conditions for some kind of crisis were present, but had the Crown and its ministers decided to compromise and follow the lead of the Chamber of Deputies, much as William IV in England compromised and followed the House of Commons on reform in the 1830s, we might be speaking today of the "reform crises" of 1830 or 1848 instead of the revolutions.

As it was, Charles X virtually committed political suicide in 1830 when, following the economic crisis of 1829–1830 and the election of a reform-minded majority in the Chamber of Deputies, he sought to avoid change by dissolving the Chamber, reducing the size of the electorate, and closing the free press (Jardin and Tudesq 1983). Faced with determined opposition by the king, the parliamentary opposition "called on the nation to resist, placing placards to this effect throughout Paris" (Rule and Tilly 1975, 65). In Lyon "without any knowledge of events in the capital . . . liberal leaders not only called for the immediate mobilization of the National Guard, but also encouraged the master silk weavers to close their shops and send their journeymen into the street" (Bezucha 1975, 121). When the army melted away in the face of the resulting popular protests, Charles X had no recourse but to flee.

Similarly, in 1848, when Louis Philippe's ministers resisted major reforms in the midst of widespread unemployment, the "leaders of the dynastic opposition who were planning the master Paris banquet actually called upon the populace to demonstrate, so as to make the function more impressive" (Langer 1969, 325–326). As in 1830, the combination of restricted mobility and economic collapse had discredited the regime with the middle classes. But in 1848, except for a few garrison troops, civil defense of the capital was in the hands of the National Guard, a middle-class militia, rather than the line army. Thus, when initial clashes between troops and demonstrators provoked angry crowds, "even the legions from the well-to-do sections . . . joined the opposition to the . . . regime and insisted on immediate reforms" (Langer 1966, 99). As one National Guardsman told Tocqueville (1970, 40), "We don't want to get shot for people who have managed affairs so badly." Facing a hostile capital, with his defense forces melting away, Louis Philippe, too, took flight.

In both cases, the attempt to persist on a conservative course and forcibly to repress opposition at a time when the elite had lost confidence in the regime, when the populace was suffering widespread unemployment, and when the military or militia was alienated and sympathetic to the opposition, produced a revolution. But the outcomes were somewhat different than in 1789. In the absence of a fiscal crisis requiring massive state reform, the moderate reform opposition in each instance sought merely to extend participation in, rather than reconstruct, the state.

Even more importantly, the respective struggles to consolidate authority had different opponents. In 1789 the main opposition to the new republic came from the allies, foreign and domestic, of the Old Regime. Provincial nobles who had suffered downward mobility during the years of inflation, whose defensive attitude was shown in such acts as the exclusion of recent nobles from provincial estates, the Segur Ordinance of 1781, and the refusal to merge with the Third Estate in the Estates General, saw the revolutionary crisis as an opportunity to regain their earlier influence. After 1790 they were joined by nobles from the court, the bishops, and financiers who sought to slow or reverse the revolution (Tackett 1989). Thus, counterrevolution from the Right was the main threat; and the chief response was continued mobilization of urban crowds against "the aristocracy." In the nineteenth century, however, as we have noted, mobility patterns, and hence elite conflicts, were different. There was much displacement, but little turnover. As Amman (1975, 26) states, "there seems to have been little downward social mobility among members of the propertied elite." This limited turnover was largely the result of effective birth control by the French elite in the nineteenth century (Weir 1982). In the crises of 1830 and 1848 there was not, as in 1789, a large cohort of disgruntled surplus sons of nobles and notables, calling for a return to *more* traditional status distinctions as a means to salvage their fortunes. The conservation of family fortunes by elite families, combined with the patronage of the imperial and monarchical regimes, preserved the status and influence of notables, even though it excluded newcomers. Cries for reform by the latter group were therefore widespread, but there were few fallen "losers" harboring countergrievances. Thus, in the nineteenth-century revolutions, "the situation did not seem to demand extreme action from the new republican government. There were no invading armies bent on restoring the old regime, and more significantly, no Frenchmen were prepared to defend" the old order (Price 1972, 1).

However, there were continued threats on the Left, from workers who demanded that the new republic do more to alleviate their wants. Thus, the revolutions of the nineteenth century "skipped over" the dramas of 1789–1794 and moved directly to the situation of the late Directory, in which a moderate regime, embracing both older notables and newcomers, sought to restore order and defend itself against the demands of restive urban and rural popular groups. Though in error about the causes of the revolutions, Marx was quite right in noting that the *process* unfolded in 1848–1851 much as in 1799–1801, with Louis Napoleon reprising the role of his uncle. In both revolutions, fears of continuing disorder led to the rise of a conservative, populist dictatorship.

After 1850, the growth of the industrial economy and rising real wages, national economic integration via the railroads, and greater use of fertilizers to boost agrarian output created the conditions for political stability that underlay Napoleon III's successful two decades of authoritarian rule. But in the first half of the century, the Restoration and July monarchies replayed the difficulties of the ancien régime. For the Old Regime economy still dominated, and population increase created the same imbalances, conflicts, and recurrent crises as were experienced in the past. The entire period of French history from 1750 to 1850 thus had a fundamental sameness of character. It was the last century of the early modern period, in which economic, political, and social institutions were highly vulnerable to the effects of population growth. The signs of industrial capitalism were certainly evident, but they would not create a new world until the late nineteenth century.

Marx believed that the revolutions of 1830 and 1848, particularly their urban worker component, represented the future. He argued that the grievances of the bourgeoisie against the monarchy stemmed from the barriers the regime erected to commercial enterprise, and that the grievances of the workers stemmed from their exploitation by capitalists. As we have noted, this view collapses under the weight of counterevidence. The grievances of the bourgeoisie against the monarchy were grievances of the *traditional* office-seeking and professional bourgeoisie, not of manufacturers; the most active groups in 1848 throughout Europe were lawyers, doctors, journalists, teachers, and civil servants (Stearns 1974, 41). These grievances stemmed from blocked mobility created by a large young generation facing elders who had risen under the Napoleonic Empire, and from lack of confidence in a regime that was unable to escape recurrent economic crises. But these crises, and the grievances of urban workers, were not a product of modern capitalism. Rather, their source was the traditional economy, swamped by population growth and unable to provide enough food and jobs to keep food prices stable and to prevent real wages and employment from falling. It was neither lumpenproletariats nor factory textile workers who manned the barricades on either side; instead, traditional artisans from the craft trades, seeking relief from massive unemployment, provided recruits for *both* the street insurrections and the *garde mobile* who defeated them (Traugott 1985).

In short, it was the shadows of the past, not the fires of the future, that hung over French politics in the early nineteenth century. Thus, the demographic/structural model makes better sense of the participants and their grievances during this period in France than is achieved by the Marxist view. The revolutions of 1830 and 1848 were not necessary breakthroughs but rather returns of cyclic crises.

This interpretation helps us better understand not only the events in France but also the contrast with England. For the advance of capitalism certainly had made greater strides across the Channel. And England did have a constitutional crisis in 1828–1832. But thereafter, the modest activism of Chartism was entirely different from the massive social conflict that arose in France in 1848–1851. And indeed, the *psi* model shown in figure 12 suggests that England was unlikely to suffer state breakdown in this later period. To understand why, let us take a closer look at the reform crisis and its results in England.

ENGLAND: REFORM AND STABILITY

There is a long history of debate on the relationship between reform and revolution. Tocqueville (1955) noted that Louis XV and Louis XVI had initiated many reforms in France and alleged that their reforms hastened, rather than delayed, the coming revolution. The Russian czars and the Chinese imperial court also implemented reforms in the last decades before their downfalls. These events suggest that reforms can be blamed for undoing regimes—they contribute to revolution rather than avoid it.

But this view overlooks two very successful reform movements in nineteenth-century Europe: the English reforms of 1828–1832 and the

Prussian reforms of 1807–1814. In both cases, the nations emerged *stronger* and *more* stable from their reforms. Equally significant, in France in 1830 and 1848, as we just noted, resistance to reform turned situations of political crisis into actual revolutions. We thus are confronted with an old puzzle: does reform hasten or deflect revolution? The answer to this question is straightforward but requires careful specification. In our examination of whether social mobility is destabilizing, we found that the critical question is not *how much* mobility occurred but rather *what kind.* Similarly, the critical question about reforms is not how many occurred but rather *what kind* of reforms and *in what circumstances.* In France under Louis XVI, in Russia under Nicholas II, and in China under the empress dowager, the reform regimes were already under tremendous strain. Louis XVI was facing enormous pressures from price inflation, population increase, and worker impoverishment; Russia was in danger of being overwhelmed by superior German military might; China was already partly dismembered by the Western Powers. But the reforms adopted by these regimes were all quite modest, entailing reorganization of central and local administration designed to give more power to the central government while offering advisory positions to dissident elites. There were no attempts to change the fundamental structures of power, status, or economic organization. In contrast, the reforms adopted by England and Prussia involved substantial changes in access to political power and status. In England, obstacles to full political participation by Catholics and Dissenters were removed, and the electorate expanded by more than was accomplished in France through the Revolution of 1830. A full, active (not merely advisory) sharing of power with new groups tied them to the old elite and separated them from lower-class protests. Similarly, in Prussia the opening of the civil service and army to talent, and the removal of restrictions on non-noble landholding, tied the talented members of the bourgeoisie to the regime. A genuine (if partial) broadening and sharing of power, rather than lip service acknowledgment of advice set against concentration of central power, marked the successful reforms.

In addition, England and Prussia made their reforms under pressures that, though real and insistent, were far more modest than those faced by France, Russia, and China. Prussia had been soundly defeated by Napoleon at Jena, but the state was still intact; England was facing difficult social and political pressures in 1830, but its fiscal structure was sound and its military firmly reliable. Thus, both cases of successful reforms were made in times of difficulty, but not of extreme duress. The reason that reforms hastened revolution in France, Russia, and China is so simple that it hardly bears repeating: the reforms were *too little and too late*. The successful reforms were more extensive in terms of power sharing and were undertaken while the regimes were still in positions of considerable strength.

Machiavelli (1952, 14), not Tocqueville, best described the realities of reform when he advised rulers that they should act while still strong, if reforms are needed, and not wait for overwhelming pressures to arise—for by then "you are too late for harsh measures; and mild ones will not help you, for they will be considered as forced from you, and no one will be under any obligations to you for them."

UNRESOLVED PROBLEMS: THE ENGLISH STATE AND
ECONOMY AFTER 1688

What pressures led to England's successful reforms? It is common to think of the revolutions of 1640 and 1688 as having "solved" England's problems by removing the constraints on economic growth and democracy (Trevelyan 1953). In fact, the Revolution of 1640 and Cromwell's Commonwealth accomplished little besides bloody conquests of Scotland and Ireland and massive tax increases. The Commonwealth was so disliked that the restoration of the Stuarts in 1660, in the person of Charles II, was greeted with widespread and unabashed joy. Moreover, in the ensuing decades the backlash against the revolution nearly enabled the later Stuarts to gain greater power (including a standing royal army) than had been exercised by Charles I (J. Jones 1978; Kenyon 1978).

Charles II's brother, James II, lost the throne in 1688, but more through an invasion than a revolution. Resentment of James among leading Englishmen, who feared that he would establish a Catholic dynasty on the English throne, created an opportunity for the Protestant William of Orange, who had collateral claims by marriage to the English Crown. When William, with a modest invasion force, set forth from Holland and landed in southern England, James panicked. Feeling deserted by his advisors and subjects, he fled, leaving the throne "vacant." Parliament embraced William and Mary as king and queen, and in 1689 passed the Declaration of Rights, articulating the conditions for their assumption of royal authority. Though not really a revolution—and, given James's panic and William's successful invasion, not really "glorious" for England—the so-called Glorious Revolution of 1688–1689 gained a reputation as the event that guaranteed English liberties. The key to this claim is the Declaration of Rights, which established certain rights of Parliament and limited religious persecution (Schwoerer 1981). The Declaration was critical in setting England on a course to religious toleration, even as other nations were in the process of extinguishing religious liberty—in Spain, by the Inquisition; in France, by revocation of the Edict of Nantes and a declaration of war on the French Huguenots; and in Austria and Italy, by the Hapsburg-led Counter-Reformation. However, despite the importance and novelty of certain elements of the Declaration, it was in essence a compromise adopted in a time of unexpected and extreme duress, and a product of negotiations between William and Parliament over disposition of the Crown. The Declaration did not transfer power to Parliament, but left executive power with the king; it did not guarantee equal rights to all religious groups, but merely set limits on persecution; and it did not guarantee freedom of the press, equal representation of Englishmen in Parliament, or many other "liberties" that we assume are essential to democracy. In short, the Declaration was a series of compromises that enabled William III to govern England in partnership with Parliament; it did not fundamentally resolve the problems of sharply limited democracy, inequitable taxation, and political restrictions on non-Anglicans.

The problems in the English polity were thus far from gone. But they were held in abeyance by conditions favorable to stability. As observed in chapter 2, stable population and prices after 1650 gave the Crown room to maneuver, diminished social mobility and competition, and reduced mass mobilization potential through higher real wages.

England experienced a longer period of price stability than occurred in France; it lasted from 1650 to 1750 and allowed the government to refinance its debt at more favorable rates. By 1750, the English Crown had consolidated most of its outstanding debt into government bonds (known as "consols") at an interest rate of 3 percent, less than half what the French Crown was paying. However, English public finance in the period 1650–1750 was not merely a matter of favorable terms of borrowing. Loans were important, but, as Brewer (1988, 338) notes, "an effective tax system was ... a necessary condition of the new credit mechanisms." From 1689 to 1714, England's wars "were on a scale England had never known before"; and they were fought with "larger armies *and heavier taxes* than England had ever experienced" (Miller 1983, 50; emphasis added).

This taxation involved a greater reliance on indirect taxes on the production and sale of goods, rather than on land taxes. After 1713, the land tax rarely provided more than 30 percent of Crown revenues (Brewer 1988, 341; O'Brien 1988). This shift in income sources greatly favored the Crown in a century in which the price of grain declined, while that of manufactured goods slightly rose.

English taxes had risen during the Commonwealth, again during the Restoration, and again following the Revolution of 1688. William III's average revenue was more than double that of James II, and four times that of Charles I (Miller 1983, 57). More importantly, however, since prices were stable, these increases were *real* revenue gains. And since the population was virtually constant and social mobility low, patronage and social control expenditures were stable; thus, the entire sum of increased revenue was available to support England's efforts in war.

Conditions also favored a revival of aristocratic dominance and stability. In the countryside, landlord patronage increased. Stagnant wheat prices meant that increases in farm income depended on capital to improve output. Thus, yeomen who lacked capital became more dependent on large landlords who could provide it. Indeed, the low wheat prices of these years meant that the independent farmer was often squeezed and bought out; estates were expanded and consolidated, increasing large landlords' domination of local towns and the countryside (Thirsk 1967a; Habakkuk 1979; Beckett 1982). Control of pocket boroughs by local lords also increased, consolidating the hold of the elite on Parliament and inhibiting electoral contests (Kishlansky 1986, 139).

Population and price stability also meant stagnant domestic markets, hence few opportunities for the rapid expansion of local commercial elites, such as occurred in early-eighteenth-century France. From 1688 to 1750, England's commercial growth was concentrated in a few large trading companies that profited from overseas trade. During this period, in most English towns it was not the manufacturers' but rather the *landlords'* influence that increased: rural landlords took over the leading positions in local government in the town corporations and boroughs (Cannadine 1980; Clark and Slack 1976). Moreover, the accumulation of elite fortunes was assisted by the marked population stagnation in these years among the peerage, whose mortality rose and whose birthrate fell considerably more than did those of the general populace. Thus, as noted in chapter 2, elite families often went without male heirs, providing numerous opportunities to merge elite fortunes or to co-opt rising members of the professions and international trade into landed families by marriage without disturbing existing lines of family influence. Although there was thus some absorption of professionals and wealthy merchants into the landed elite, the volume of mobility was low and did *not* result in turnover, that is, downward mobility of existing families (Stone and Stone 1984).

In addition, the long rise in rents, which had helped many modest gentry pull themselves up, now ended. From 1650 to the 1730s, rents generally fell (Roebuck 1980, 34; M. Davies 1977; R. Allen 1988). This shift favored the larger landholders with deeper reserves, while the gentry with small lease rolls suffered. This trend reinforced the power of the aristocracy in the countryside.

Finally, the literate and professional elite found new stability. University enrollments declined, as did admissions to the Inns of Court. Graduates thus more readily found livings in the Church, law courts, and the government. The vast expansion of the navy and the revenue bureaucracy from 1680 to 1725 provided additional official positions for every level of the social hierarchy (G. Holmes 1986, 269).

Popular conditions also improved. The stagnation of grain prices hurt small farmers, but it was to the advantage of workers, whose real wages rose by about one-third in the century 1650 to 1750 (Phelps Brown and Hopkins 1962b). And elite concerns about the masses changed dramatically, from worry about able-bodied laborers who could not find work or wages sufficient to earn a living, to anxiety about the morality of workers who seemed to earn too much money to preserve their discipline and who drank their excess wages away. At the same time, while London and the Atlantic ports continued to grow, London's growth rate was in these years only a third as high as in the preceding century, while most English towns grew little, if at all (Finlay and Shearer 1986; de Vries 1984). The total result of these trends was a marked reduction in popular disorders. Much as in France, where peasant revolts dramatically diminished from 1675 to 1730, so too in England, "for over a century between Venner's 1661 Rising and the late 1760s . . . popular forces . . . were astonishingly inert" (G. Holmes 1986, 258).

In short, from 1688 to 1750 England was marked by easier fiscal circumstances, low social mobility, and ready absorption of the few aspirants to elite positions, with this absorption occurring through civil service expansion and through marriages that filled the gaps left by a demographically moribund gentry. There was still concern about working-class behavior and provision for the ill and infirm, but between the flurry of legislation following the Elizabethan Poor Laws in the 1590s and the New Poor Law of 1834 lay a period—roughly from 1650 to

1750—when tight labor markets took care of the concern for the unemployment of the able-bodied poor. Stable population and prices thus combined to underpin a financially stronger state, to create a revival of aristocratic dominance, to contain elite conflicts, and to reduce popular grievances. However, these favorable circumstances ended in the mid-eighteenth century, and the unresolved problems left by the settlements of 1688–1689 once again became acute.

Despite the parliamentary "replacement" of James II by William III and Mary in 1689, William III—and his successors, Anne, George I, and George II—retained the key royal prerogatives to make war and command the militia, to appoint all ministers, peers, and bishops, and to summon and dissolve Parliament (Horwitz 1977, 14). Moreover, despite gains in the authority of the House of Commons during Walpole's ministry, George III's madness, and the war with Napoleon, by 1830 power still had not shifted entirely to the Commons. The reason was that the House of Lords still retained its influence and veto power. Even in the Commons, an increasing number of seats were from old towns that had shrunk to "pocket" boroughs, where there were so few voters that the patronage of an influential peer or local gentry family could determine the election. At the same time, vast new towns that had grown up since 1750, such as Manchester and Birmingham, were unrepresented. Thus, as far as the growth of democracy is concerned, even at the end of the eighteenth century the Commons was still checked by royal and peer authority, was itself not very democratic in composition, and was heavily dependent on landlord patronage. In the years when population and prices were stable, social mobility low, and fiscal problems modest, these factors were not major issues. But from 1760, as prices rose and wages fell, and as debts from the American War of Independence and the Napoleonic Wars mounted, there were increasing calls for reform of a state that, to many, seemed narrow, corrupt, and unrepresentative.

Patriotic fervor for the war against France, and the profits and higher wages that accompanied the war, reduced enthusiasm for change and sharply limited the appeal of radical and Jacobin agitation in the 1790s. But after the war, the calls for reform again grew, and they were intensified by concerns about religion.

Intertwined with constitutional issues and social and political conflicts among the elite, religion had been a major concern in the 1640s, and again in 1688. The problem was straightforward: what would be the religion of the state, and how would it be enforced on the people of the realm? Parliament's solution in 1689 was a compromise: Anglicanism was enshrined as the official religion of the nation and declared a requirement for state office, but tolerance of private worship was given to other faiths, "a formula combining toleration of worship with substantial exclusion from political participation" for non-Anglicans (J. Clark 1986, 145). This formula worked only so long as the elites were predominantly Anglican, and the Catholics and Dissenters neither too numerous nor too rich in resources. But by the late eighteenth century, these stipulations were failing. For the rise in population and prices had created commercial opportunities that Dissenters, in particular, had exploited. And as population grew, English dependence on Irish food supplies, together with the migration of Irish workers to England, made the persistently difficult Irish problem—hence, the role of Catholics in the United Kingdom—even more acute. Thus, the problem of what role non-Anglicans would play in English politics arose anew.

Finally, the way had not been fully cleared for the political triumph of capitalism in 1688. The development of English agriculture was rapid from 1688 to 1750, but it then markedly slowed. Domestic commerce and manufacturing henceforth were chiefly responsible for England's economic growth. But the centers of commercial capitalism were unrepresented in Parliament, where elections were controlled by landed gentry and pocket boroughs. The exclusion of Dissenters, combined with the absence of parliamentary representation for the new manufacturing towns, meant that the leaders of the industrial boom and the middle classes of the burgeoning manufacturing centers were without a political voice. Thus, legislation favoring landlords over manufacturing and labor interests remained dominant, creating frictions among the elite.

Among workers, the rising price of bread and falling real wages fueled anger against a government accused of indifference toward the laboring population. In fact, the adverse trends affecting laborers reflected the difficulties still faced by the traditional sectors of England's economy in the midst of rapid population growth. After a century of stability from 1650 to 1750, in which England and Wales grew by less than 10 percent, the population surged forward, nearly *tripling* from 5.7 million to 16.5 million inhabitants in the next century (Wrigley and Schofield 1981, 532–533). Agriculture could not keep pace. After 1760, agrarian output grew more slowly than the population (Crafts 1983, 187; Jackson 1985, 344–346). Despite the expansion of capitalist tenant farming, the small peasant holding was far from gone: in 1798, much as in France, fully one-third of all private rural landholdings in England and Wales remained less than four acres in size; over half were less than ten acres

(Soltow 1981, 64–65). And yields per acre stagnated (Allen and O'Grada 1988). England was able to increase its output substantially only by major changes in land use, converting former pasturelands to arable production and draining fen lands (Goldstone 1988; Grigg 1966). An adequate food supply depended increasingly on imports from Ireland (B. Thomas 1985a). Prices, particularly grain prices, rose sharply. By the 1780s wheat prices were 60 percent higher than in the 1740s; even after the inflation and postwar deflation of 1800–1820, wheat prices in 1825–1831 were still almost 40 percent higher than they had been in the 1780s (B. Mitchell 1962, 487–488). Although factory work brought higher wages in the north, both to manufacturing workers and to the agricultural workers who labored to feed them, in the south, towns and fields were burdened by excess hands, bringing rapidly falling real wages and rising unemployment. As Gash (1979, 2) reminds us, "when Chadwick looked for evidence of intolerable urban conditions . . . he found them in Bath, Brighton, Windsor, and Edinburgh," as well as in the new industrial towns. In 1829, the *Quarterly Review* warned its readers that if "the social plague of poverty and degradation among the peasantry is not stayed . . . it will inevitably draw after it a strong and dreadful explosion" (cited in E. Evans 1983, 146).

In short, in the early nineteenth century England again faced many of the same kinds of conflicts, albeit in less severe forms, that had occurred in the mid-seventeenth century: conflict over access to political authority among the elite, whose ranks had been not only expanded by the new opportunities resulting from population and price increases, but also divided by the limited opportunities resulting from state and religious discrimination; and unrest among urban and rural workers beset by falling wages and unemployment.

Let us ask, however, why problems were particularly acute in the years 1828–1832, and why conditions thereafter diverged from those in France.

THE REFORM CRISIS

The performance of the British economy from 1790 to 1850 was in striking contrast with the modest changes that occurred in France. As we noted earlier, by 1789 trade and industry already formed a larger part of England's economy than of France's. In the nineteenth century this trend intensified. By 1840, only 22 percent of England's labor force worked in agriculture, and agriculture accounted for only one-fifth of the United Kingdom's national product (E. Evans 1983, 412; Kuznets 1966, 88–90). In contrast, in both France and Prussia the labor force in agriculture, even in 1850, remained at *over* 60 percent; and in 1830, French agriculture produced one-half of national output (Hamerow 1983, 56–57; Kuznets 1966, 88–90).

British industrial leadership is evident in mechanization as well. In 1840, Great Britain had 72 percent of Europe's total steam horse-power—620,000 horsepower, as opposed to 90,000 in France. In per capita terms, the imbalance was even greater: 33.3 horsepower per thousand inhabitants in Britain versus 2.6 in France. In general, despite its much smaller population (England, Wales, and Scotland totaled less than half the population of France in 1830), nineteenth-century Britain was about thirty years ahead of France, and forty years ahead of Germany, in industrial output. Britain's textile mills first consumed 100,000 tons of raw cotton per year in 1830; France reached this level in 1860, and Germany in 1871. Britain first produced one million tons of pig iron in 1835; France reached this level in 1862, and Germany in 1867 (Hamerow 1983, 4–6).

As a result of this industrial growth in England, total output rose faster than population. Revisionist economic historians have now debunked the myth of a sudden dramatic "takeoff" in England's per capita output from 1780, presenting instead a picture of more gradual increase, interrupted by difficulties during the Napoléonic Wars (Crafts 1983; Williamson 1984). But economic growth still was rapid enough to prevent a fall in per capita output, despite rapidly rising population. Crafts (1983, 197) estimates that output per head was roughly constant from 1760 to 1800, and that it then rose 20 percent by 1830. Rising industrial production turned England into the "workshop of the world." And although, as already noted, England's agricultural output failed to keep pace with the tripling of population in the century to 1850, exports of manufactures allowed England to pay for imported food.

But British industrial dominance and economic prosperity were both concentrated in the industrializing districts of northern Britain. In the south, England remained agricultural; and there the growth in population in excess of the growth of the agrarian economy produced dire, if localized, effects.

Although the fraction of England's labor force in agriculture shrank, rapid population growth still meant a rise in the absolute numbers working in agriculture, from 1.7 million in 1801 to 2.1 million in 1850 (E. Evans 1983, 412). Industrialization did not therefore rely on driving people out of the countryside, contrary to what is sometimes thought. It was largely the sons and daughters of rural proletarians and farmers, not the field hands and farmers themselves, who flocked to the new industrial towns. Population growth, not a shift of population between sectors, accounted for the growth of the industrial labor force (C. Tilly 1984b; Levine 1984). Where the demand for labor was increasing rapidly, chiefly in the industrializing northern counties, real wages rose. But in those trades and southern counties where traditional agriculture and crafts were overburdened by population increase, suffering was apparent.

There has been an extensive debate over whether "average" wages in England rose during the Industrial Revolution (Hartwell 1972; Tunzelman 1985; Lindert and Williamson 1983; Crafts 1985; Mokyr 1988). Yet there is little disagreement that there were marked regional and occupational differences in workers' fortunes. Analyzing these regional differences is in many ways more useful than attempting to create an artificial "national average" wage.

In the north, Marx and Engels's bleak picture of factory workers as irregularly employed and suffering from frequently being tossed back into the "surplus labor force" now appears completely mistaken. Recent studies of the actual practices of eighteenth-century factories, both in England and in France, show that workers had regular, stable employment—or at least far more stable than putting-out or cottage craft work (Rosenbaud 1985; Haberman 1986; Boyson 1972). For Lancashire, Haberman (1986, 988) has shown that "the labor market did not operate like an auction," with employers bidding for interchangeable, anonymous labor; instead, the cotton spinners received seniority and enjoyed local long-term attachments. Factory wages were remarkably high: adult males in Lancashire mills made from fifteen to eighteen shillings per week in carding and thirty to forty shillings per week in fine spinning, compared to wages of under fourteen shillings per week in agriculture in the region, and wages of under nine shillings per week for agrarian workers in the poorer southern counties (Perkin 1969, 128–129).

However—and herein is the crux of the problem—even in England factory workers were but a small portion of the labor force. Factories could expand only as fast as capital to build them could be deployed, and the Napoleonic Wars gobbled up huge amounts of British capital (Williamson 1984). Thus until the 1830s the wars and their after effects, which involved huge subsidies to continental allies as well as the maintenance of naval and army expeditionary forces, constrained British growth and left the surplus English workers in dire straits. Moreover, the factories did not take over many traditional labor tasks, such as weaving, until late in the nineteenth century: "The handloom weavers were not exposed to the competition of the machine until the 1830s in Britain and the 1840s elsewhere. . . . In their case the population pressure made itself keenly felt. . . . Their problem derived from the fact that ever more unskilled and unwanted laborers resorted to the handloom in the hope of earning at least a pittance, with the result that they achieved that and nothing more" (Langer 1969, 184–185). Thus, from 1815 to 1830 the sheer numbers flooding the labor market, not factory competition, reduced the wages of handloom weavers from thirteen to six shillings per week (Langer 1969, 185).

This contrast between industrialized and traditional occupations—in which textile workers in factories earned high wages, while weavers, unaffected by industrial competition but burdened by population pressure, faced a drastic decline in income—appears in regional wage differences as well. The northern counties—those *most* affected by industrialization—had generally greater wage increases, even in agriculture, than occurred in the agrarian south. In 1833, for example, wages for field hands were eleven to twelve shillings per week in Lancashire, Yorkshire, and Lincolnshire, as well as in the home counties surrounding London and in Kent and Sussex; but they were under nine shillings per week in the southern counties of Somerset, Cornwall, Devon, and Wiltshire (Mingay 1972, 45), and under eight shillings per week in Dorset, home of Thomas Hardy's depressed agrarian laborers. These comparatively low wages in the south marked a startling reversal from the late eighteenth century. In the 1770s, weekly wages in the south had been 15 percent higher than in the north; but from 1770 to 1837 agrarian wages in the north had nearly doubled, while those in the south had stagnated (Perkin 1969, 128–144).

Recall that these are nominal figures; since the price of wheat, which still took half the income of even a well-paid northern worker in an average year, was rising, the real picture was even worse than the figures indicate (Horn 1980, 267–268; Botham and Hunt 1987, 387). In the late 1770s, wheat in England was approximately forty shillings per imperial quarter; in the difficult years of 1829–1831, wheat averaged over sixty-five shillings per quarter, before falling for most of the 1840s and 1850s (B. Mitchell 1962, 488). Thus, workers in the industrial north enjoyed earnings that rose considerably faster than food prices, but workers in southern agrarian counties where nominal wages stagnated, particularly Dorset and Wiltshire, experienced a 40 percent drop in real income (E. Hunt 1986; Snell 1985).

After 1830, the general rise in wages in England was so great that even the poorer regions gained (Lindert and Williamson 1983, 1985). The economy boomed: total national income, which had risen 17 percent over the 1820s, rose by 33 percent in the 1830s (E. Evans 1983, 392). But as Gash (1979, 3) notes about the years to 1830, "there is a strong case for thinking that it was the staggering growth of population more than any other single factor which kept wages low and fostered unemployment in the generation after Waterloo." Indeed, industrialization was responsible for improving conditions, in factories and fields, in the areas that did better during those years; given the enormous population increase, "without industrialization there might have been a social catastrophe" (Gash 1979, 3).

Conditions were particularly acute in the depression of 1829–1831, when harvests were poor and unemployment surged. Poor relief, which had been high from 1814 to 1823 and then dropped in the period 1824–1828, once again rose to the earlier distressing levels (E. Evans 1983, 401). The burst of attacks on machinery by workers, food riots, and the Peterloo riot that capped the years 1816–1819 had given rise to calls for reform, but these were muted in the prosperous years 1824–1828 (Gash 1979, 125). Thereafter calls for change were reechoed in the spread of violence known as the "Swing riots." These disorders, involving almost 1,500 incidents of machine breaking and food and wage riots, spread over more than a dozen counties, chiefly in the rural Midlands and southwest (Hobsbawm and Rudé 1969).

Though never a threat to the government, these rural disorders alarmed elites. So too did the cost of poor relief, which by 1831 had reached £7 million, or over one-third the cost of the entire national government's expenditures exclusive of debt service (Gash 1979, 195). "By February 1830 the Whig leader, Earl Grey, was talking of 'a state of general distress such as never before pressed on any country.' As radical leaders and opponents of reform alike knew, only high prices and unemployment could translate an intellectual case for constitutional change into a mass movement of incalculably threatening aspect" (E. Evans 1983, 204).

The populace widely assumed that a conspiracy of landlords was responsible for high prices. At the end of the Napoleonic Wars, when grain prices fell sharply, Parliament sought to protect farmers by passing the Corn Laws, which restricted imports of cheap grain. Although there were complaints from workers, these faded when prices nonetheless continued to decline in the early 1820s. However, when prices rose again after 1824, the Corn Laws were taken as clear evidence of landlord guilt. Since landlords controlled Parliament, through control of pocket boroughs and patronage, radical leaders such as Cobbett, Cartwright, and Hunt aroused a powerful response with their diagnosis that "the sufferings of the people were due to the inadequacies and extravagance of government, and the remedy lay in annual parliaments and universal suffrage" (Gash 1979, 93). For the working population as well as for radical leaders, high prices and unemployment were the misdeeds of corrupt government; reform thus meant work and bread at low prices. The failure of the agrarian economy of the Midlands and southwest to absorb the population increase, together with the limited expansion of industrial employment, meant that in 1830 bad harvests led to much "evidence" of the need for reform, and to a very high mobilization potential among the population at large.

The case for reform had been stated for some time by elites, who had grievances of their own against the political restrictions maintained by the government. Like France, England at the end of the 1820s had a surplus of educated youth confronting a shortage of government positions and a large middle class blocked by property qualifications—and, unlike France, also by religious discrimination—from political participation.

From the 1740s to the 1760s, freshman admissions at Oxford and Cambridge had fallen from 378 to 321 per year, recovering to 375 per year only in the 1770s. From 1780 to 1809, admissions increased slightly, averaging 416 per year. Admissions then exploded, averaging 850 per year in the 1820s, stabilizing for the next three decades at over 800 per year, and then growing mightily again after 1860 (L. Stone 1974, 90–91).

Yet, the doubling of graduates in the 1820s was not matched by openings in the Church and government. The British civil service increased by only one-third from 1780 to 1832, as the constraints of paying off accumulated war expenses limited expansion of government: 80 percent of British government expenditure in the 1820s was interest on war debt, and 8 percent was war pensions (Gash 1979, 103). The enormous expansion and professionalization of the British civil service occurred only after 1830. Thereafter, in the four decades from 1830 to 1870, the number of civil servants rose 250 percent, providing an outlet for numerous professional job seekers (E. Evans 1983, 285; Perkin 1969, 123).

Similar growth constraints undermined the established Church. The Anglican Church, resting on state authority, required an act of Parliament to establish new parishes and build new churches, and an act of the Crown to appoint new bishops. In times of economic constraints, Parliament moved slowly in expanding the physical establishment of the Church and redrawing parish lines. But Dissenting churches could and did spring up on their own to minister to new congregations as the needs arose. This difference in freedom of growth proved an enormous handicap to the established Church in the early nineteenth century. For in old towns like London, existing urban parishes were overwhelmed by increases in the numbers of inhabitants, for which they had neither sufficient room in the churches nor an adequate number of ministers. And the new factory towns, which now counted their populations in the hundreds of thousands, often individually remained a single, impossibly large parish. The Anglican Church, in the eighteenth century, had concentrated most of its resources in the then-richer and more populous south. The massive expansion of population, and the shift in demographic and economic weight to the north, caught the Church off-guard. There was thus a drastic "failure of the Church to adjust to the demographic changes that had taken place in English society" (Gash 1979, 61–62).

The new additions to the churchgoing population were therefore overwhelmingly drawn to Dissenting congregations, since the established Church simply did not change its traditional parish organization or expand its churches rapidly enough to accommodate the huge increase in numbers. This skewing in the distribution of churchgoers is crystal clear from the data on construction of chapels and churches: from 1688 to 1801, non-Anglican congregations built 7,116 places of worship, versus the 11,785 places of worship constructed by the established Church. But from 1801 to 1830, non-Anglicans built 26,186 places of worship, whereas Anglicans built a mere 428 (Perkin 1969, 1978). The stagnant parish organization of course lacked sufficient room to give new ministries to the increased number of Oxford and Cambridge graduates, much less to absorb the increasing numbers of individuals trained in Dissenting academies. The Dissenting churches thus came to dominate the churchgoing population of the expanding cities and northern counties, thus adding to their already strong presence among entrepreneurial elites (E. Evans 1983, 115).

J. C. D. Clark (1985, 89) has argued that "what destroyed the ancien régime in England . . . was . . . the advance of Dissent, Roman Catholicism, and religious indifference. Non-Anglicans grew from about 1/2 million out of 7 million in England and Wales in 1770 to slightly over half the churchgoing population at the 1851 religious census; and over half the population did not then attend church at all." The growth of non-Anglicans threatened the validity of the political system, which, despite the exceptions granted in the Indemnity Acts, was still based on political exclusion of Catholics and Dissenters.

The Dissenting and Catholic middle classes, and even many liberal Anglicans, were also increasingly distressed at the inefficiencies of government caused by the "Old Corruption" (Rubinstein 1983). The Tory government of the early nineteenth century had continued the former royal practice of assuring a loyal Parliament, administration, and judiciary by offering or tolerating extraordinarily generous privileges, patronage, and simple corruption. These rewards went to the electors in pocket boroughs, to party supporters in the Commons, and to placemen in the civil service, the legal profession, and the judiciary. Rubinstein (1983) notes that a small group of professional supporters of the government thus acquired enormous fortunes, in some cases hundreds of thousands of pounds. Of course, Dissenters and Catholics were excluded from such positions and the accompanying rewards. But they were joined in their resentment of this "Old Corruption" by many Anglicans who felt that the economic crisis could only be solved by an honest and economically efficient government. Thus, change was also demanded by those seeking economic reform of the government, and who believed that only a reformed Parliament could assure an efficient, less corrupt regime.

In short, by the late 1820s an educated elite, produced by an expanding population and a growing economy, had run into a wall of closed opportunities in a stagnant, corrupt civil service and the established Church. Moreover, the failure of the Church to shift its organization to keep pace with demographic change meant that self-made men and products of the Dissenting schools, influential by virtue of both their ties to Dissenting ministries and their key roles in commercial and industrial expansion, may have been formally excluded from politics but nonetheless had vast support throughout the growing network of non-Anglican congregations. Thus, the voices for reform—an agenda that included not merely the reform of Parliament and expansion of the electorate to give representation to Manchester and Birmingham, but also the opening of political opportunity to non-Anglicans and economic reform of the administration—formed a rising chorus.

When this chorus of dissent was combined with the shock given to the establishment elite by the unemployment, riots, and popular demonstrations of 1829–1831, the stage was set for confrontation. The members of the establishment in the Lords and Commons had two choices: they could resist the calls for change, out of fear that allowing Dissenters and Catholics into politics and redrawing the parliamentary map would undermine their authority, and perhaps all aspects of the traditional order; or they could open the door to the powerful forces knocking and hope that shared authority would be more lasting than an authority increasingly seen as corrupt.

In 1828 and 1829, the door of establishment order was opened: the Test and Corporation acts were repealed and the Catholic Emancipation law was passed, removing the political restrictions on non-Anglicans. But in 1830–1831, resistance prevailed when bills to reform Parliament were turned back. At this setback the population, which saw reform as a cure for unemployment and high prices, did not suffer passively. In October 1831, after the peers rejected the second Reform Bill, there was rioting in Bristol, and the Duke of Newcastle's castle was put to the torch. Middle-class political unions organized massive demonstrations (E. Evans 1983, 210). In contrast to events in France in 1830, the English army apparently remained loyal to the government. But fortunately, its loyalty was not put to the test. If William IV, like Charles X, had reacted to the crisis by dissolving Parliament and failing to call for new elections, and had he backed an unpopular conservative ministry and imposed censorship, it seems likely that the Whig leaders and middle-class reform opponents might have taken their protests to the streets. In this event, would the army have fired on mass demonstrations led by respectable citizens against an unpopular government? Would William have been forced to abdicate? Might there have been a revolution in 1832—not like that of 1789 in France, but like that of 1830—in England?

Though not an implausibility, we shall never know. Certainly, economic conditions were not as harsh all across England as they were in France, although in the agrarian south both the suffering and the relief efforts were similar to those across the Channel. Thus, figure 12, which assesses *psi* using an estimate of mass mobilization potential based on the wages of construction workers in London, rather than of weavers or field hands in the south, suggests that in the period 1830–1832 the potential for instability was much greater in France than in England. But elements of the political situations were similar: alienated elites and middle-class groups who were excluded from official politics galvanized economically distressed popular groups and faced a government discredited by severe unemployment and high bread prices. Fortunately for the monarchy, William IV called a new Parliament in 1832, which resulted in a strong reforming majority, and backed the reforming Grey ministry. The third Reform Bill passed later that year.

We thus speak of the Reform Crisis of 1832, rather than of the "Revolution." But the difference between what happened in England in 1832 and what happened in France in 1830 is a difference of degree, rather than of kind. Similar crises and confrontations arose, from similar causes. In both constitutional monarchies, rapid population growth and modest economic growth gave rise to greater elite expansion than existing political institutions could accommodate, and at the same time more new laborers were sent into traditional urban and rural labor markets than the respective economies could provide for. In both countries, elite demands for more open politics, combined with popular demands for work at higher wages and lower prices, produced irresistible pressures for change.

But after 1830 the differences between England and France grew more palpable. France remained for another two decades a country held back by its slow-growing agricultural sector, with a labor force of primarily agricultural workers and traditional artisans; it thus remained vulnerable to falling real wages as population grew, and to severe crises of bread price escalation and manufacturing unemployment in the event of bad harvests. The July Monarchy remained dominated by landed elites, and by an official and professional bourgeoisie. It was not until the Revolution of 1848 further opened political life that a tight alliance between the commercial bourgeoisie and official notables against the working class was cemented. Until 1848, France remained under the shadows of Old Regime institutions and demographically induced conflicts.

Britain emerged from similar shadows two decades earlier. The enormous expansion of the industrial economy in the 1830s and 1840s changed the conditions of the labor force; the vast expansion of the civil service and industrial economy opened positions for ambitious and talented men (if not yet women); and the opening of political participation and the vote to non-Anglicans and the middle classes cemented an alliance of propertied groups against popular agitation. Thus in the 1840s, while France again faced a major state crisis, England faced some difficulties and popular agitation from the Chartists, but nothing as severe as the crisis of 1830–1832. Chartism attracted workers during the depressions of 1837–1843 and 1846–1847. But these depressions, which in France came as the last blows in already worsening labor conditions, were in England merely interruptions to steady post-1830 labor improvements. And as G. Jones (1983a, 176) has pointed out, "Chartist agitation never had more than an outside chance of success, since enfranchisement of the middle class in 1832 placed a major obstacle in the way of chartist/middle class alliance." Thus, discontent was transient, and "the stabilization of the economy and the mid-century boom finally killed off all but a few beleaguered Chartist outposts" (G. Jones 1983a, 178).

To sum up, England's 1832 reform crisis was in many ways similar to France's crisis of 1830. Slightly different acts by the two monarchs could have resulted in even greater similarities: either reform in France or more severe crisis in England. In both cases traditional problems—the inability of political and economic structures to absorb population increases—lay behind the crises. Less severe fiscal strains than had occurred in England in 1640 or in France in 1789, owing to the improvement of state finances, meant that in neither case would there be a repeat of the total collapse of the state. But growing elite competition and conflict and rising mass mobilization potential, especially marked in France in 1830, meant some kind of crisis was likely to occur.

After 1830, however, English and French conditions sharply diverged. As shown in figure 12, despite England's greater population growth, the greater changes in England's economy meant that the forces making for instability declined in England, while they increased in France. Wrigley's (1972, 257) summation seems apt: "It was England's good fortune that the Industrial Revolution rescued her from what must otherwise have been a period of great stress due to the pace of population increase."

GERMANY: REGIONS OF CRISIS, REGIONS OF STABILITY

In the early nineteenth century, Germany was identifiable as a cultural zone, perhaps even a nation, but not yet as a state. Many sovereign entities, both secular and ecclesiastical, carved Germany into a political checkerboard. Thus one cannot speak of a "state crisis" in 1848; one must speak of many crises, varying in severity as demographic conditions and political institutions differed across regions.

In 1848, the areas most convulsed by revolt were in the south and west: Baden, Saxony, the Bavarian Palatinate, Württemberg, Hesse-

Darmstadt, and the Rhineland. Here peasants rioted on a scale similar to that of 1789 in France, while workers and urban professionals and students demonstrated to demand liberal regimes. Across the Elbe, in contrast, unrest was far less severe (Hamerow 1958, 107). "In all of northeast Germany, the flat lands were never turbulent at all" (Stadelmann 1975, 82–83). Only in Silesia were there serious popular disorders, and these involved mostly artisans rather than cultivators. There were uprisings in Berlin, led by students, professionals, and civil servants and supported by workers. But these were islands of protest in an otherwise relatively calm Prussia. Thus, Germany showed a marked regional pattern of protest in 1848: rural protests in the south and west backed by urban and worker protests that created severe crises, but only urban professional and worker protests in Prussia, which were quickly put down by armies drawn from the stable East Elbian countryside.

We thus have three questions to ask about Germany in 1848. First, why did state crises break out in 1848 but not earlier, in the 1830s, as in England and France? Second, why were the popular uprisings so much more severe in the southwestern states? And third, why did the "revolution" fail—or did it? Answers to all three questions can be found by examining the ecological balance and the institutions of elite recruitment and state finance.

THE ORIGINS OF THE CRISIS

Overall, Germany's population (excluding the German regions of the Austrian Empire) increased almost 40 percent from 1815 to 1845 (Hamerow 1958, 19). This increase was almost entirely due to a fall in mortality that particularly affected the young (W. Lee 1979, 145–149). Thus, as in other cases of early modern demographic increase, the population grew not only larger but also younger. Indeed, "the crucial expansion in this age group was primarily a phenomenon of the first half of the the nineteenth century" (W. Lee 1979, 156). Nonetheless, while population grew rapidly, total agricultural and industrial production increased far more, roughly doubling in this period (Franz 1976, 313; W. Lee 1979, 153). At first glance, then, it seems there should have been no ecological problem.

But regional patterns were very different. In northeast Germany, the growing population "could still be absorbed by an expanding agriculture" (Köllmann 1976a, 101). The process of settling the east, of felling forests, draining swamps, and establishing farms, was still ongoing: "at the end of the reign of Frederick II [1786] almost one-third of the cultivators were recent settlers" (Milward and Saul 1973, 57). Relatively thinly populated, with large manors interspersed with modest peasant properties, the East Elbian territories produced a considerable surplus in grain, mostly controlled by Junker landlords. But in the west and south a serious problem of overpopulation arose. In these areas, already densely populated and dominated by small peasant farms, demographic increase had led to the subdivision of holdings into uneconomical plots (W. Lee 1979, 160). As Hamerow (1958, 223) remarks, "in the west were the overworked holdings of a teeming peasantry more fertile than the soil." Peasants unable to find land to farm turned to handicrafts. But there were no large urban markets, such as those of Paris or London, nearby, nor did German crafts workers serve a seafaring merchant class bent on overseas exports. German artisans were thus penned into limited domestic markets, and were pinched further as population growth undermined the wealth of the townsmen and the smallholding peasantry who purchased craft products. Hence Germany was divided into a grain-surplus region in the east, which exported grain to London and the Low Countries as well as supported Berlin and Vienna, and a grain-shortage region in the southwest, where peasant farms were often too small to allow families to grow their own food, and where rural crafts often provided too little income to allow them to buy it.

The recovery from the Napoleonic Wars allowed some progress, and the spread of potato cultivation, which provided an adequate if bland diet from relatively little land, helped many families become self-supporting. Thus, in the 1820s and 1830s prices remained stable, and indeed, to the early 1830s there are signs of food overproduction (W. Lee 1979, 154). But by the late 1830s prices turned upward, increasing 30 percent from 1830 to the late 1840s (Borchardt 1976, 207). In addition, as peasants from the overcrowded southwest flooded labor markets throughout Germany, real wages, which had risen from 1800 to 1830, began to fall. In the 1840s, real wages for masons averaged 25 percent less than in the 1820s, and much less still during the crisis of 1847–1848 (Kaufhold 1976, 347; Kitchen 1978, 73). Unemployment increased as well, and by the 1840s the dismal reality of large numbers of the able-bodied poor, unable to find work and drifting to the rapidly expanding cities, was widely apparent (Stadelmann 1975).

Focusing on mass mobilization potential, it is easy to see why Germany was spared the widespread difficulties of France, or even the severe regional difficulties of England, in 1830. At that point, population pressure, though mounting, had not yet reached critical proportions. It was only after 1830 that prices began to rise and real wages to fall, trends that had begun decades earlier and had been severe in the late 1820s in England and France. In the 1830s and 1840s, however, growing landlessness and peasant impoverishment in the southwest, and over-crowded labor markets throughout Germany, jointly created popular grievances. Combined with the enormous expansion of the cities—Berlin, for example, lurched toward 400,000 inhabitants in 1850—and the increasing youthfulness of the population, mass mobilization potential moved sharply upward. The exception to this trend was in the rural northeast, where adequate land meant that peasants, though still compelled to offer labor to Junker estates, were not pressed to the same degree as in other locales (Hagen 1989).

Demography thus answers, at least in part, two of our initial questions about Germany: why unrest did not develop until the late 1840s, and why it was especially marked in the southwest. And it is important to note that demography serves us much better on these two issues than does attention to capitalist exploitation. In agriculture, it was precisely in the southwestern states where beneficent rulers had "pioneered in the elimination of personal servitudes and the extinction of manorial dues" (Hamerow 1958, 158). Small, relatively independent family farmers, whose feudal dues had long since been converted to cash payments, but whose access to land was rendered precarious by population increase, were the backbone of the peasant revolts of 1848 in Germany, much as they had been in northeastern France in 1789. In the east, where large capitalist estates geared to export production relied on still-enforced labor dues, peasants were quiescent.

This difference can be understood only by realizing that even the "feudally oppressed" peasants east of the Elbe, though legally more restricted, were in many ways economically better off than their western counterparts. Junker landlords needed peasants who could maintain plow teams to work their lands. And labor, rather than land, was the scarce commodity in the east. Thus, while the Junkers extracted considerable labor from the peasantry, the latter retained for their families' support considerable amounts of land. Recall that in France or England a family with twenty acres of land could support itself, and a family with forty acres generally operated a viable commercial family farm. And many peasants clung to landholdings of only a couple of acres, while most peasant laborers and cottagers had less than an acre. Compare this with Koch's (1978, 47) description of the Prussian peasantry in the 1650s, in the midst of the "second serfdom," in which he distinguishes between "peasants, possessing between 30 and 60 hectares of land [that is, 42 to 84 acres] and whose service obligation to the local lord consisted in supplying between two and four horses and one or two hired labourers" and "cottagers, [possessing] no more than 30 hectares of land," who were compelled to render manual service. There were also landless laborers, farm servants, and household servants who attended the lords directly. And land in Prussia was less fertile than in Western Europe, so more land was required to support a family. But the key point is that working estates by means of enforced labor dues *required* a peasantry that was capable of supporting itself and supplying farm animals. Otherwise, from whom would labor dues be extracted? Indeed, the available evidence from local studies shows that in the nineteenth century, tenant households in Junker-dominated Brandenburg were still secure in their landholdings and maintained a relatively high standard of living (Hagen 1986, 1989).

In contrast, the independent family farm placed no lower limit on the poverty of the peasant family. By the 1840s, the overcrowded peasantry of the southwest, though free, was in greater danger of being unable to support itself than the "unfree" but low-density peasantry of the east. Indeed, in the southwest it was often only an acre of potatoes that kept farm families from starvation.

And as in France and England, among workers it was the traditional artisans, not the factory workers, who suffered the most economically and participated in the urban revolts. Factory workers were an insignificant minority, constituting only a few percent of German laborers in the 1840s. But they enjoyed rising wages and steady employment in the early nineteenth century. In contrast, handloom weaving was still the most important craft occupation; there, wages fell to 1.5–2.5 marks per week, compared to 9–10 marks per week for industrial workers (Langer 1969, 185). Industrial workers became the aristocrats of labor, "while the once proud handicraftsman was sinking to the level of a propertyless, rootless, proletarian" (Hamerow 1958, 36). Hence "artisan masses . . . became the shock troops of revolutions, whereas the employees of iron foundries and locomotive works were as a rule only interested bystanders in the great events of 1848" (Hamerow 1958, 80).

Once again, traditional problems of demographic pressure on land and artisan labor markets, rather than the onset of capitalist factory production, best explains the popular component of the mid-nineteenth century crisis. Of course, that crisis was not merely a popular uprising but also a political movement in which professional elites played a crucial role. For, as in our other cases, population growth affected not only peasants and workers but also the elite.

From the mid-1830s to the late 1870s, "the landed nobility in the eastern provinces of Germany entered a period of unprecedented prosperity" (Sagarra 1980, 27). Rising prices translated directly into rising profits for the Junkers, who did not rely on cash rents but instead directly sold the produce of their estates on world markets. The ranks of landowners had been opened to commoners in the Prussian reform movement of 1807–1814, along with the civil service, and many former nobles lost their lands to wealthy non-noble buyers in the next decade (Hamerow 1958, 51). But by 1830 the social order in the east had stabilized, the newcomers having been absorbed into Junker society. "In the Restoration era the [landed] social order remained generally static and showed only limited signs of any tendency toward mobility" (Sagarra 1980, 27).

But such amiable stability was not found in the civil service or the urban professions. In the early 1800s Germany had, by Western standards, a tiny and economically weak commercial bourgeoisie. Those few who were successful had bought into Junker society in the late 1810s and 1820s. For the most part, the middle class was professional, and mobility was gained through the universities and the state bureaucracy. This path opened wide in the 1810s and 1820s as the reform movement sought talented non-nobles for leading offices. But offices grew in numbers more slowly than the pool of qualified aspirants. By 1830, the path to office was clogged, filled with frustrated aspirants competing for too few places.

We observed earlier in discussing England and France that as social competition increases among elites, the rush for credentials leads higher education to expand far more rapidly than the population grows. As in England and France in both the early seventeenth and early nineteenth centuries, so too in Germany the rush was on. The number of Prussian university students tripled from 1800 to 1830, creating "a glut of jurists and clerics by 1830" (R. Turner 1980, 112). The number of university students in Germany as a whole tripled as well (Jarausch 1982, 27–28). But while the universities boomed, "bureaucratic positions grew only slowly after the 1820s," leading to "a great disproportion between the demand for salaried state officials and the supply of graduates" (Jarausch 1982, 30; 1974, 555). As a result, "contemporary accounts abound with complaints about the great number of public servants and

aspirants to those positions; every year the figure of dissatisfied unemployed candidates grows, and despite all the warnings of the government continues unabated" (Jarausch 1974, 556). Although the Prussian
government restricted university enrollments in 1834 and a plateau was
reached, this expansion of the universities overloaded the professions
throughout Germany. By the 1830s, "a Prussian administrative trainee
of the *Assessor* rank waited an average of 6.6 years for his first salaried
post; by the 1850s the waiting period was over 10 years" (Gillis 1974,
75). Lawyers, doctors, academics, and theologians faced similar frustrations. As a result, many "turned to . . . journalism, where they gave vent
to their social frustrations" (Gillis 1974, 76). In the crisis of 1848, the
Frankfurt Assembly "was dominated by lawyers, professors, and civil
servants. . . . In a real sense, then, the political revolutions of 1848, rid-
ing on the back of lower-class agitation, were revolutions of professional
people" (Stearns 1974, 45).

Discontented intellectuals had much to point to in their complaints
against the government. "The dimensions of the social problems affecting Germany [gave] a wide section of society the feeling . . . that the
state . . . pays no heed to human beings" (Sagarra 1980, 55). Students
adopted the misery of the poor as a stick with which to beat the state
about its failures (Jarausch 1974, 551). Prophetically, the governor of
the Rhine Province reported to the Interior Ministry in 1844 that "the
disgruntlement and dissatisfaction which are becoming evident . . . emanate from . . . mostly the lawyers, doctors, and merchants. . . . I can well
believe that they would be prepared . . . to create an unrest which they
would then exploit in their own entirely private interest" (cited in Hamerow 1958, 60).

In 1848 the opportunity for political exploitation came. The previous
fall, potato blight and bad weather had ruined the harvest, leading to a
doubling of the price of grain. As in other traditional economies, the
harvest crisis, by reducing the income of the population, shut down the
markets for manufactures, leading to massive unemployment. In early
1848, rural uprisings and urban artisan riots were cheered by students
and professionals who took the lead in proclaiming the fault of the government and demanding an expansion of political rights and opportunities. As the growth of cities had enormously overreached the capacities
of the police (Langer 1966, 105), and the Prussian king was reluctant
to order the army into action against his own citizens, the revolution
seemed likely to triumph. In the smaller states of the southwest, monarchs fled or capitulated to radical demands.

But the revolution was halted, and then reversed, by the resolute ac-

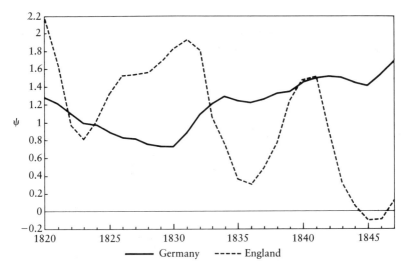

Figure 13. Pressures for crisis (*psi*) in England and Germany, 1820–1847

tion of the Prussian ministry and army. For, unlike the situations in France in 1830 and 1848, where the government lacked reliable troops, or in England in 1640 and France in 1789, where the government was bankrupt and needed to seek elite support for change, the Prussian government was financially secure and had the firm support of the officer corps. Just as in England, the Prussian state increasingly relied on excise, rather than land, taxes (Braun 1975, 269–272). It also controlled vast royal estates that provided a secure income. Thus, "Prussia was the only German state which found itself with a sound financial basis on the eve of the industrial revolution in mid-century" (Sagarra 1980, 9). In addition, the officer corps was drawn overwhelmingly from the landed Junker class of East Elbia, for whom the 1830s and 1840s were a period of stability and prosperity; thus, the Prussian armies remained firmly devoted to the king, not to the revolution.

In sum, Germany by the mid-nineteenth century encountered the common problems that traditional economies face with rapid population growth. Figure 13 compares the movement of *psi* in England and in Germany in the early nineteenth century, drawing on both mass mobilization potential and elite competition as measured by university enrollments.[18] In England, *psi* rises somewhat in the late 1820s, peaks

18. See the preceding note for computation of *psi* for England. For Germany, the following data sources were used: for German university enrollments, Jarausch (1982);

in 1830–1832, and then declines, albeit with a large "hump" in 1837–1842. In contrast, in Germany *psi* declines to 1830 but then steadily escalates. Thus, the *psi* model accurately captures the divergent trends of this period.

DID THE REVOLUTION OF 1848 FAIL?

Prussia, like early-nineteenth-century England but unlike France and the states of southwestern Germany, had two advantages when facing the crisis: first, a relatively stable financial situation, based on indirect taxation, and second, relatively limited regions of popular deprivation. In England, peasant suffering was concentrated in the agrarian south. In Germany, it was concentrated in the southwestern states, rather than in Prussia. Thus, military resources could be drawn from the stable regions and directed against the regions in revolt: Berlin and southwestern Germany.

What Prussia could not do, any more than England or France, was ignore the crisis and escape the need for change. The strength of the Prussian state allowed the Crown to meet its difficulties by adopting additional reforms, rather than succumbing to revolution. The peasantry was relieved of certain dues, and the professional middle classes were given a new constitution and Parliament, the lower house of which was elected on a franchise broader than that provided by the English Reform Act of 1832. These measures, which separated the middle classes from the lower classes, and the peasantry from the workers, brought social peace to Germany and greatly strengthened the leadership of the state. Though management of the new Parliament was occasionally difficult, German economic and military successes after 1850 resolved most problems. But it was not possible to turn the clock back. If the Revolution of 1848 "failed," it failed only in that it did not emulate the French revolutions in chasing a monarch from the throne. It did in fact lead to changes in the state and countryside comparable to those produced by the French Revolution of 1848, and thus it laid the foundation for a stronger, if sadly authoritarian (as in France, under Napoleon III), Germany. The lesson, again, is that demographic pressures in Old Regime

---

for German wages, the decadal average real wages given by Kaufhold (1976), amended to reflect the price data given by Borchardt (1976). Urban growth was based on the growth of German cities with over 100,000 population by 1850, and on the growth of Vienna, as given in A. Weber (1963). Age structure was roughly constant, as estimated from J. Hoffman (1839) and Prussia, Statistisches Bureau zu Berlin (1849).

states can generate the conditions for crisis, but the exact shape and outcome of the crises depend crucially on the precise resources and institutions of particular states.

STATE CRISES IN EARLY MODERN EUROPE: A SUMMATION

Figure 14 indicates, in a limited format, that the general correlation between demographic growth and state crisis, traced here for several specific cases, held quite generally for early modern Europe. The vertical bars indicate the *net* population increase, in percent, in various countries during three periods from 1500 to 1850. The first period runs, for each country, to the year in which it attained its early-seventeenth-century population peak. The second period runs to 1750; the third to 1850. An asterisk above the bar denotes that a major constitutional crisis, rebellion, or revolution occurred in that country during the period. Note that those states that deviated from the general pattern of crises in the seventeenth and nineteenth centuries—Sweden and Hungary—were also deviant in their respective patterns of population growth.

Figure 14 presents more questions than answers. Certainly, it is beyond the scope of this book to trace in detail the movements of population and prices, and of social mobility and real wages, in the countries I have not explicitly considered. Scholars familiar with Scandinavia, the Low Countries, Italy, and Central and Eastern Europe can no doubt analyze more skillfully and objectively the occurrences of state crises in these other locales. For now, I wish to consider some of my own doubts about the model of state crisis presented here and to offer some additional factors for examination.

VALIDITY

One advantage that the demographic/structural model holds over many social science theories is that it is easily falsified. That is, if the data on population growth, prices, social mobility, wages, and so forth that I have used prove erroneous, the validity of the model as an explanation of the English and French revolutions, and of the revolutions of the nineteenth century, is immediately undermined.

To be sure, the data utilized are far from secure. Controversy continues, and as I have noted, some very basic issues—such as the growth of French agriculture in the eighteenth and nineteenth centuries or the

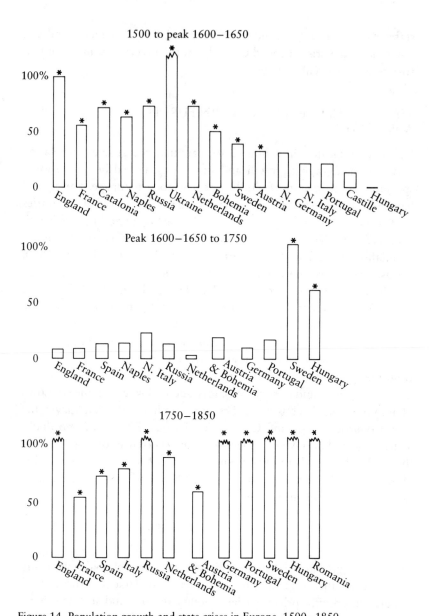

Figure 14. Population growth and state crises in Europe, 1500–1850

Note: An asterisk over the bar denotes a state crisis occurred during the indicated
time period. A broken bar indicates growth exceeding 100%.

movement of English wages after 1780—remain hotly debated. I hope that the importance of such information to explanations of the key political events of the early modern era will stimulate the collection of better data series. The confirmation or refutation of the model will then rest on sounder foundations.

PRECISION

It would be a grievous error to be overly precise in defining the periods of general crisis brought by demographic pressures. For example, I focus on the English Revolution of 1640. Yet the entire period from 1540 to 1640 was marked by recurrent political difficulties in England, from the Pilgrimage of Grace and Kett's Rebellion to the rebellion of the northern earls and the English Revolution. Similarly, in France the Wars of Religion in the late sixteenth century arguably constituted a more severe crisis than the Fronde in the mid-seventeenth century. I would thus prefer to consider the whole era of rising population and prices, and of turbulent social mobility and falling wages—an era that began in both countries in the early sixteenth century and culminated in the mid-seventeenth century—as prone to state crises, and then oppose that whole era to the period of stability that followed in the late seventeenth and early eighteenth centuries. The more precise one wishes to be about the exact timing of crises, the more the particular details of individual cases—the financial resources of the state, the degrees of social mobility and of wage deterioration, and the vicissitudes of the harvest—assume a governing role. The *psi* model appears to be at least a moderately accurate instrument for identifying and explaining periods vulnerable or prone to state crisis, but there is considerable room for its precision to be improved.

VARIABILITY AND UNIFORMITY

While I have argued that demographic growth in the context of early modern economic and political institutions gave rise to certain "robust processes"—inflation, social mobility, and popular difficulties—that were politically destabilizing, it is important to remember that these processes took place in diverse contexts. The processes did *not* override these contexts but rather were shaped by them. Thus, while I have dealt chiefly with the origins of state breakdown, I have taken pains to point out that the outcome of these destabilizing pressures varied with the structure of particular states. Hence the adjective "demographic/*structural*" is used to describe this model.

There is one particular variation in the operation of the model that, though implicit in what I have covered, deserves explicit mention. In the cases of England in 1640 and France in 1789, crises were brought by population growth that occurred generally, if not completely evenly, throughout the society. In contrast, in the cases of the Spanish Hapsburg domains in 1640–1648 and Germany in 1848, population growth occurred much more dramatically on the peripheries, and far less in the core regions, of these societies. This difference in the distributional characteristics of population growth produced distinctive patterns of crisis. In Spain, the center held firm despite rebellions at the periphery, where population growth created the greatest conflicts and difficulties. A similar pattern occurred in Germany in 1848, where stability in the northeastern heartland of Prussia enabled that state to hold firm against rebellions that were most severe in southwestern Germany, though they had a professional and worker component in Berlin. I mention this pattern because it is also an important consideration in the analysis of Russian crises. There too, in the cases of the Ukrainian revolts of the seventeenth century and the Pugachev revolt of the eighteenth century, population growth was far greater on the periphery than in the core area around Muscovy; and again, in each case the attempt of the central state to maintain or increase control over a rapidly growing peripheral region gave rise to a crisis, one in which the central state held firm.

This question of the extent to which effects of demographic growth on social, economic, and political institutions are localized, or spread broadly throughout a state or society illustrate an introductory point mentioned in chapter 1. I view societies as not simply the intersection of "micro" and "macro" forces but rather as *fractal* in organization—that is, as having nested structures that are similar on many levels. While I have noted here in some detail that differing local institutions influence the effects of demographic pressures, it is still an open question whether the processes I have recapped on the national or broad regional level can be traced on a smaller scale. Indeed, in order to understand state crises, we may well need to know to what extent a society with a low degree of fractal symmetry—that is, with greatly different institutions at different levels or in different localities—is more, or perhaps less, vulnerable to the kind of demographic strains I have analyzed. Merriman (1975a, 112) observed in a footnote that in the French department of Ariège, "three of the most insurrectionary cantons [in 1848] were becoming rapidly overpopulated between 1804 and 1841." Frankly, I would be quite surprised if the demographic/structural model produced uniform results at the cantonal level. But it seems worth investigating the various levels at which the political, elite, and popular components of the model continue to operate.

GENERALITY

The difference between the *generality* and the *validity* of a historical analysis is sometimes confused and thus is worth making clear. The *validity* of my model depends on whether the political consequences I have suggested are indeed traceable to the demographic, economic, and social processes described in the particular cases I have examined. In contrast, the *generality* of the model depends on whether such demographic/political linkages can be traced in *other* cases, or, even more broadly, whether the demographic/political linkages can be connected to still additional historical phenomena.

As an example of the latter possibility, consider the phenomenon of witchcraft. It has been widely reported that persecutions for witchcraft rose in the sixteenth century and waned after 1650 throughout Europe (W. Hunt 1983, 55). Many explanations have been offered for this rise and fall. But can it be linked to the population and price cycles I have highlighted? Could greater popular insecurity during the period of population expansion have contributed to paranoia? Could greater elite assurance and stability after 1650 have contributed to elite suppression of popular superstition? Again, I leave these matters to other scholars more versed than I in cultural history, but the linkages between the long cycles of population and economic history and cultural patterns do deserve close attention.

In regard to extension of the demographic/structural model to other cases of state breakdown or stability, it is clear that I have focused primarily on large, fairly autonomous states. The dynamics of smaller states, such as the Low Countries and Italy before unification, may be different. And the dynamics of states outside Europe also deserve consideration.

The question of generality raises an additional line of investigation that I next pursue in this book. I have argued that the great crises of early modern European history did not stem from the rise of capitalist economic and social organization. Instead, crises were produced by the cyclic forces of population expansion pressing on agrarian/bureaucratic states. If this view is correct, then the acid test of the model would be to examine states that did not develop Western-style capitalism and see whether they too had similar state crises. Thus, in the next chapter I examine early modern state crises in the Ottoman Empire and Ming China.

In addition, the present model of state breakdown, though not Marxist, is nonetheless materialist—I claim that it was changing population/resource balances that led to state breakdown. What of shifts in ideology, of the volition of individuals, of the role of culture and contingency in history? These matters are best examined by contrasting instances of state breakdown that occurred in quite different cultures. Thus, I defer consideration of these issues until chapter 5, after I have explored state crises in early modern Asian states.

FOUR

State Breakdown in Early Modern Asia: The Ottoman Crisis and the Ming-Qing Transition

[T]he population of the Ottoman Empire increased considerably in the sixteenth century. . . . [T]his increase in population exceeded the increase in the area of cultivated land. This
can be accepted as the underlying cause of social imbalance
and disorder.

—*Halil Inalcik*

The harm of overpopulation is that people are forced to
plant cereals on mountain tops and to reclaim sandbanks. . . . All the ancient forestry . . . has been cut down and
the virgin timber land of the aboriginal regions turned into
farmland. Yet there is not enough for everybody. This proves
that the resources of Heaven and Earth are exhausted.

—*Wang Shiduo*

We have now examined in some depth the classic state breakdowns of
early modern Europe. I have argued that these events were not due to
the growth of capitalism, or to fortuitous combinations of circumstances. Instead, they were caused by the incapacity of agrarian economies,
and of their attendant social and political institutions, to cope with the
pressures of sustained population increase. Clearly, if this argument is
sound, it should be just as valid for agrarian-bureaucratic states outside
of Europe.

This chapter examines two state breakdowns that occurred in Asia
contemporaneously with the "general crisis of the seventeenth century"
in Europe: the Ottoman crisis in Asia Minor, and the Ming-Qing transition. From 1590 to 1610, and again from 1622 to 1628, much of Asia
Minor was lost to the control of the Ottoman Empire. While the central
government suffered from financial crises, factional divisions, and cor-

ruption, provincial officials, disaffected soldiers, and impoverished peasants joined together in a series of revolts that threw off central rule. In
Istanbul, the army revolted in 1589, 1592, 1607, 1622, and 1631–1633,
as the government was unable to pay their wages. In 1648, in yet another
army revolt, the sultan was strangled, and in 1657–1658 Abaza Hasan
Paşa founded a rebel government that wrested much of Asia Minor from
the empire. The collapse of the Ottoman Empire was only prevented in
the last half of the seventeenth century by a new dynasty of grand viziers,
the Köprülü.

In virtually the same years, the Ming dynasty was afflicted with a
similar series of misfortunes. From 1590 through the first half of the
seventeenth century, the imperial treasury was continuously in crisis.
The government was unable to pay its troops, and unable to control the
factional struggles that incapacitated the bureaucracy. Rebel armies, led
by disaffected soldiers and swelled by peasants, seized whole provinces
in the south and northwest; urban riots and uprisings by bonded laborers
spread through the lower Yangzi basin. In 1644 the Ming emperor
hanged himself as the rebel army of Li Zicheng captured Beijing. On the
verge of setting up his own rule, Li was destroyed by the neighboring
Manchus, who had been invited to take power by Chinese officials unwilling to serve the rebels. The Chinese Empire was restored to order
only in the late seventeenth century under the new Manchu dynasty, the
Qing.

What is striking in both cases is that the crises were not merely peasant revolts or simple responses to harvest failures. Instead, the depth of
the crises reflected the conjuncture of difficulties at all levels of society:
financial crises and bankruptcy of the central government, paralyzing
conflicts and revolts among the elite, and popular uprisings, all culminating in extensive civil wars. Although their forms differed according
to the institutions, ideological frameworks, and actors involved in each
case, all the elements of state breakdown were present in both.

Moreover, as in Europe, the century following the seventeenth century crises was a period of relative tranquility. But also as in Europe,
after this interlude both the Ottoman Empire and China again underwent state breakdown. From the 1780s to the 1850s, the Ottomans
faced rebellions in the Balkans and Egypt that removed Greece from the
empire and gave substantial autonomy to Egypt. In the same period, the
White Lotus, Nian, and Taiping rebellions, though eventually defeated,
wreaked havoc over large parts of China.

In this chapter, I examine the causes of the seventeenth-century crises in Turkey and China. I then look quickly at the following period of stability and the return of state breakdown in the late eighteenth and nineteenth centuries. The statistical data for the Asian cases are somewhat weaker than for the European cases, and my discussion is thus necessarily more discursive. Still, I believe the evidence strongly supports the view that these political crises in Asia can be traced to the same causes as those in early modern Europe.

I also examine briefly the interesting and exceptional case of Tokugawa Japan, an agrarian/bureaucratic state that experienced virtually no population growth for over a century, roughly from 1720 to 1840, but then underwent state breakdown in the following generation, in a crisis known as the Meiji Restoration of 1868. However, Japanese institutions differed in crucial aspects from those of all the other states studied here; Japan thus provides "the exception that proves the rule" regarding the role of demographic factors in early modern state breakdown.

A. THEORETICAL CONTROVERSIES, DEMOGRAPHIC AND ECONOMIC TRENDS

AN UNCHANGING EAST?

The states of Asia have long been viewed, in both Western and Asian historiographies, as subject to different forces than operated in the West. The influential views of Karl Marx and Max Weber in Europe, and the traditions of classical scholarship in Asia, combined to depict the West as comprising inherently dynamic states, in contrast to a changeless series of dynasties in the East.

VIEWS OF CHINA

Despite their considerable admiration for Chinese art and literature, Westerners have long considered China an unchanging society, ruled for millennia by Confucian principles set down in the fifth century B.C. Noting certain continuities in official titles and outward appearances, while taking far too scant notice of centuries of profound struggles over ideology and social organization, Western scholars have often simply, and erroneously, concluded that nothing important changed in China for over two thousand years. For Marx, China was an example of "Asiatic despotism." As Moulder (1977, 15) notes, Marx considered that "property was underdeveloped in Asia. There was no nobility, no bourgeoisie. The state was the 'real landlord.' " Lacking the economic conditions for class struggle, history was "stationary." There were wars and rebellions, and dynasties rose and fell, but there was no *social* history. Max Weber (1951), too, saw Asian history as lacking the spark that produced dynamic social change in the West. And right up to the present, comparative analyses of China and the West (Wittfogel 1957; J. A. Hall 1985) have stressed the contrast between Western dynamism and Chinese rigidity.

The tendency of Western scholars to view China as essentially unchanging was strongly reinforced by classical Chinese historiography. We noted in chapter 1 that Western historians and sociologists have downplayed cyclic forces in European history, relentlessly pressing historical events into a pattern of secular change. Chinese historiography took exactly the opposite view, downplaying progress and forcing events into an oscillating, cyclic pattern (Feurwerker 1976, 14). Chinese historians built their view of China around the notion of the "dynastic cycle," a presumed tendency of any dynasty to decay over time, to suffer corruption and inefficiency, and then be overthrown and replaced. In this century Wang Yü-ch'üan (1936) and other scholars (see Meskill 1965) added problems of overpopulation and fiscal decline to the classical view of moral decay, but still emphasized a cyclic pattern—there was no long-term change, just the tendency to fall away from, and then return to, stable Confucian rule. These differences in historiographical traditions unfortunately became rigid frameworks for describing the history of each civilization. Western and Chinese historians, adopting each others' perspectives, came to consider that Western history was driven by forces of progress, while Chinese history was driven by completely different and separate forces that produced recurring cycles without secular change.

Recent scholarship has substantially altered the view that China was an unchanging society. China had periods of enormous technological flowering, economic growth, and military and naval expansion. Among many examples, one can point to the development of advanced iron metallurgy and canal transport in the Song dynasty (960–1279), the growth of a regionally diversified and specialized cotton-growing and textile-manufacturing industry in the Ming (1368–1644), and the doubling of cultivated land through extensive irrigation, land reclamation, and new crop adoption in the early Qing (Elvin 1973, 1984; Chao 1977;

G. Hamilton 1985; Metzger 1977; Myers 1974, 1982). Moreover, China's intellectual history was not simply a repetition of unchanging Confucian ideals; there were periods when Buddhism nearly eclipsed Confucianism, and the latter over much of China's history was rent by fiercely contending orthodox and reformist camps (B. Schwartz 1959). Examined closely, Chinese history represents not an unchanging scene but rather a kaleidoscope of change. Nonetheless, the grip of the "dynastic cycle" view of Chinese history remains strong, and despite the admission of considerable progress in China during certain periods, portrayals of the dynastic cycle still dominate leading texts in Chinese history (Fairbank, Reischauer, and Craig 1965, 1:117–118).

The notion that a separate dynastic cycle governs the course of Chinese history is quickly undermined, however, when Chinese and European history are brought into a comparative framework. The Yuan dynasty fell in 1368—precisely the same period as the late medieval crisis in Europe. The succeeding Ming dynasty fell to rebellions in 1644—again, precisely the same period as the European crisis of the seventeenth century. The next dynasty, the Qing, then experienced its worst rebellions—the White Lotus, Nian, and Taiping rebellions, which virtually brought its collapse—from the 1780s to the 1850s. This period of unrest coincided almost precisely with Europe's "age of revolution" from 1789 to 1848. The assertion that Chinese history was governed by completely different forces than European history seems less secure when it is recognized that the waves of political crisis and stability in both regions coincided closely over a period of five hundred years.

Recently, scholars of Chinese history (Atwell 1986; Elvin 1984; G. Hamilton 1985; Wakeman 1986; Wong 1983) have shifted from the earlier supposition that China experienced a distinctively stagnant, non-Western, pattern of history. They note that the parallel timing of state breakdown in Europe and China, plus the growing evidence of periods of great technical progress in China, raise two major comparative problems: Why did China experience crises in the mid-seventeenth and then in the late eighteenth and nineteenth centuries, at the same time as the European monarchies? And why, given the many respects in which Chinese technological innovation, commercial expansion, and economic growth put China ahead of the West in classical and medieval times, did China's development slow in the early modern period while that of Europe accelerated, so that China was eventually overtaken by the West? Similar questions arise when contemplating Ottoman history.

The Ottomans were closer to Europe than the Chinese, and were far more threatening. Ottoman achievements were thus vilified in the nineteenth and early twentieth centuries by nationalist European historians who were more concerned with the liberation of Greece and the Balkans from Ottoman rule than with an impartial assessment of Ottoman history (Karpat 1974a, 3–6). Their view of the Ottoman Empire as a despotic feudal state filtered into Western sociology, leaving the Ottomans represented in Marx as a case of Asiatic despotism and in Weber as a case of traditional patrimonial authority.

In recent years, however, Western and Turkish historians have taken a more sanguine view of the Ottoman Empire, restoring it to its rightful place as one of the great cosmopolitan empires of world history. Innovative in its political and social organization, it created a centralized state that successfully fought the European powers for centuries on three fronts—the Mediterranean, the Hungarian plain, and the Russian steppes—while also conquering the Arab world and contesting Persia for the Tigris and Euphrates basin. Far from merely repeating the traditions of the medieval Islamic world, Ottoman statecraft created new mechanisms of elite recruitment, military organization, and land use that unified and commercialized an enormously varied and complex society (Karpat 1974a; Itzkowitz 1972).

Still, Ottoman historiography is also haunted by a long scholarly tradition that emphasizes dynastic cycles. The great medieval Arab sociologist and historian Ibn Kaldûn (1332–1406) offered a theory of political change in the Arab world that rested on cycles of dynastic decay. He argued that Islamic states are strong only in their youth, when vigorous nomadic warriors conquer and discipline farming communities. However, invading nomads lose their martial virtues once they become rulers of settled agrarian societies. They then suffer corruption and decay of efficiency, and become vulnerable to conquest by more vigorous outsiders (Khaldûn 1967, 122–160). This theory still shows its influence in accounts of Ottoman history that picture the Ottomans as primarily Turkish nomad warriors who reached the limit of their conquests under Süleyman in 1566, then suffered a slow and inevitable decay (Hourani 1974, 72–73). The notion of a long decline serves in these accounts as an explanation of the vulnerability of the Ottomans to the more vigorous European states in the nineteenth century.

But to picture the Ottoman Empire as in continuous decline from

1566 to its demise in 1918—a span of over 350 years—distorts reality. The Ottomans developed a sophisticated and multiethnic administration for their agrarian society that made them a major power for several centuries in Europe and the Middle East. It is true that in the early seventeenth century the Ottoman state was severely disrupted by internal rebellions. But it underwent a considerable revival from 1650 to 1730, when it again acquired territories, terrified Europe, and consolidated its rule over the Middle East. Only thereafter, in the eighteenth and nineteenth centuries, did deterioration of Ottoman rule and widespread regional rebellions recur. Thus Ottoman history, too, shows the same wave pattern of disorder and stability—and again with the same timing—as occurred in Europe and China. And as with China, the Ottoman Empire was for most of its history a sophisticated society, economically and administratively equal to, or more advanced than, the monarchies of Europe. Only after the late seventeeth century did Ottoman development clearly begin to lag.

To explain these patterns in the history of early modern Turkey and China, we need to break down the historiographical barriers that have separated East from West. Instead of counterposing Eastern dynastic decay and Western dynamism, let us consider whether similar long-term forces operated across Eurasia, and investigate their effects.

DEMOGRAPHIC TRENDS AND
ECONOMIC CONSEQUENCES

Throughout the early modern period, the Ottoman Empire and China experienced the same demographic trends as Europe: population growth through the sixteenth and early seventeenth centuries, followed by roughly a century of decline and stagnation, and then renewed expansion from the early eighteenth century. And, as in Europe, food production failed to keep pace with population increase during the periods of growth. The Ottoman Empire and China thus experienced similar trends in prices, at roughly the same periods in history, as countries in the West.

THE ECOLOGICAL CHANGE

In both the Ottoman lands and China, the fourteenth century was a period of devastation. The spread of the Mongol empire from Eastern Europe to China in the thirteenth century had unified the northern Eurasian disease pool, particularly extending the range of the bubonic plague bacillus. This bacillus, originally endemic to ground rodent populations in the Himalayan foothills, spread across the Eurasian grasslands in the late thirteenth and early fourteenth centuries, eventually infecting rodent populations from England to Manchuria (McNeill 1977, 144–147). In the fourteenth century, for reasons that are still somewhat unclear, the bacillus erupted from its rodent hosts into human populations, creating the Black Death, which decimated populations across northern Eurasia. The depradations of disease were spread and exacerbated by war, for also in the fourteenth century the Ottomans drove the Mongols out of Asia Minor, and the Chinese, under leadership that would erect the Ming dynasty, drove the Mongols out of China.

In Asia as in Europe, the recovery from the plague and wars of the fourteenth century was slow; by the end of the fifteenth century the populations of China and the Ottoman Empire still had not entirely made up earlier losses. But in the sixteenth century, growth accelerated. In Asia Minor, from 1520 to 1580 overall population is estimated to have increased by 50 to 70 percent, while towns commonly showed increases of 100 percent or more. Istanbul, with a population slightly over 100,000 in 1520, swelled to a metropolis of 700,000 by 1600, including the suburbs beyond the city walls.[1] China's population appears to have risen from roughly 65 million in the late fourteenth century to 150 million by the late sixteenth century, reaching a peak of perhaps 175 million in the early seventeenth century. Market towns increased in number, while major urban centers such as Suzhou, Nanjing, and Beijing experienced substantial growth.[2] The cause of this spurt in growth is still debated, but evidence is accumulating that, as in Europe, the prime cause was a reduction in the mortality from infectious diseases, perhaps linked to favorable trends in climate.[3]

Chinese population data exist in profusion in official records. How-

1. There is some controversy over Ottoman population figures. The estimate on Asia Minor is from Barkan (1970). Problems arise because of incomplete data and uncertainty about the size of households (hane), a common unit in Ottoman records. However, local studies based on military counts of all adult males have repeatedly reinforced the finding of rapid sixteenth-century growth. In addition, urban studies confirm the pace of rapid increase. Anatolian population is discussed by Cook (1972), Erder (1975), Erder and Faroqhi (1979), and Faroqhi (1977). Urban growth is analyzed by Barkan (1970), Jennings (1976, 1983) and Faroqhi (1984). The population increase in market towns is described by Faroqhi (1979b) and Islâmoğlu and Keyder (1977).
2. These Chinese population estimates are taken from Ho (1959), Perkins (1969), and Geiss (1979). Urban growth in the sixteenth century is described by Marme (1981) and Shiba (1977).
3. The impact of disease in the Middle East and China is discussed by Dols (1979),

ever, except for those records compiled at the beginning of new dynasties or under exceptionally concerned emperors or ministers, the official figures are untrustworthy, since, as discussed later, local authorities often simply reported earlier figures over and over with little change. Thus, the data I report consist of estimates by modern scholars based on critical examination of official records, local gazetteers, and guidebooks for officials, as well as information in clan genealogies and literary sources. Virtually all of these sources report sustained growth during the sixteenth century, followed by a reduction in population circa 1650, setting in sooner in some regions, slightly later in others. Gernet (1982, 429) notes that "all the evidence leads us to think that the population of China increased constantly between the end of the fourteenth century and the middle of the seventeenth," although, as in Europe, the rate of growth was probably slowed in the late sixteenth and early seventeenth centuries by epidemics (Telford, n.d.b; Dunstan 1975). Estimates of China's population increase and price movements from 1500 to 1800 are shown in figure 15. The price data are somewhat more trustworthy than the population figures, since officials were quite concerned to get annual, and even monthly, price data on rice supplies from throughout the empire. Figure 15 clearly shows the now familiar pattern of increase in the sixteenth century, stagnation in the late seventeenth century, and resumed increase in the eighteenth century, with population and prices moving in parallel.

The official population figures for the Ottoman Empire are far superior in quality to the Chinese data, for the Ottomans collected two kinds of population data: tax registers of households and military registers of all men of military age. Indications are that these registers were scrupulously kept (Cvetkova 1977), but unfortunately, few registers from the sixteenth and seventeenth centuries have survived. Thus, we can only examine changes at long intervals, and interval estimates have to serve in lieu of graphs of long periods. However, all of the national estimates and local studies, based on the available data of official registers, point to strong growth in Ottoman population and prices in the sixteenth century, stagnation in the seventeenth, and resumption of growth in the eighteenth and nineteenth centuries. In short, the Ottoman Empire, too, fits the familiar pattern.

McNeill (1977), and Raymond (1972). Possible climatic causes are surveyed by G. Parker (1977) and Galloway (1986).

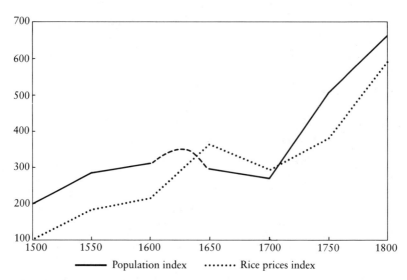

Figure 15. Chinese population and prices, c. 1500–1800

Note: Population is estimated to have increased slightly in the first quarter of the seventeenth century, then fallen, as shown by the broken line (see text).

There is, however, an important regional pattern for the Ottoman case. The Ottoman Empire had three main parts: the Balkan region of Europe, the Anatolian peninsula (modern Turkey), and the Arab lands of North Africa and the Middle East. Detailed discussion of the third is beyond the scope of our analysis, but the contrast between Anatolia and the Balkans is worth noting. In the sixteenth and seventeenth centuries, Anatolia was most pressed by population growth, while the Balkans, which were then recently conquered and devastated by war, had more available open land to settle. In the eighteenth and nineteenth centuries, this pattern reversed: Anatolia, parts of which had been devastated by the crisis of the seventeenth century, recovered quite slowly, while population growth in the Balkans rapidly increased. Thus, in the later period it was the Balkans that felt the greater impact of demographic increase. And as I discuss shortly, political rebellions followed the same pattern, centering in Anatolia during the seventeenth century and in the Balkans during the nineteenth.

For both the Ottoman Empire and China, the available evidence strongly indicates that the population growth of the sixteenth century was not accompanied by comparable growth in agriculture. In Ottoman Anatolia, cultivated acreage apparently increased by only 20 percent from 1500 to 1570 (Cook 1972, 13–14). Local studies find a marked decline in productivity per capita. In the Anatolian districts of Konya and Akşehir, for example, the number of rural taxpayers roughly doubled in the sixteenth century, while the wheat harvest rose a mere 15 percent. Increases in barley cultivation and gardening slightly alleviated, but hardly compensated for, the resulting deficit (Faroqhi 1984). By 1560, the Ottomans sought to halt the export of wheat, and surpluses to feed Istanbul could no longer be drawn from western Anatolia. Instead, the capital drew its supplies from Bulgaria, Thrace, and Macedonia (McGowan 1981, 12–13, 35).

In China, land under cultivation is estimated to have increased by less than 50 percent between the late fourteenth and mid-seventeenth centuries (Perkins 1969). Adoption of high-yield American crops, such as maize and sweet potatoes, and elimination of rice from the diet of the poor in favor of flour and potato products sustained population growth, but at a lower standard of living. Liu and Hwang (1977) estimate that land cultivated per capita fell by 33 percent from 1480 to 1600.[4]

These changes made the sixteenth and early seventeenth centuries exceptional, for after 1650 these trends reversed. In the late seventeenth century, population in both empires declined, most markedly in northwest China and eastern Anatolia.[5] Agricultural expansion then overtook stagnant populations. In China, average land cultivated per head rose perhaps 50 percent from 1600 to 1730 (Perkins 1969). But in the earlier period, pressure on scarce resources affected states, elites, and workers through its impact on prices.

THE PRICE REVOLUTION IN TURKEY AND CHINA

From 1489 to 1616, prices for rice, wheat, and barley—in constant units of silver—rose throughout Anatolia by some 400 percent (Barkan 1975, 11). In China, rice prices in silver tripled from the late fifteenth to the

4. Chao (1986, 85–89) estimates a slightly larger expansion of arable, a 52 percent increase from 1393 to 1581; however, he also estimates that population reached a peak of two hundred million, and so he argues for an even greater reduction in arable land per capita. Chao estimates that farmland per capita fell by more than 50 percent from the late fourteenth to the late sixteenth centuries.

5. In addition to the sources identified in notes 1–4, population stagnation in the Ottoman Empire after 1650 is noted by McGowan (1981), Owen (1977), and Sugar (1977); and in China by Shang (1981–1982). Istanbul stagnated as well, its population in 1700 being only 15–20 percent greater than in 1600 (Mantran 1962).

mid-seventeenth centuries, with far higher prices in peak shortage years (Cartier 1981, 464; Geiss 1979, 159–164, 198). The timing, and the degree, of the increases corresponded fairly closely with the movement of prices in Europe. And in both China and Turkey, grain prices gradually fell after 1660, drifting downward quite steadily through the early 1700s (Sahillioğlu 1983, 304; Cartier 1981, 457).

Few events of worldwide historical importance have been more fundamentally misunderstood than the great inflation of 1500–1650. Braudel (1966), E. Hamilton (1934), and Chaunu and Chaunu (1953), among others, noted the rise in silver imports from America to the Old World in the sixteenth century and attributed the bulk of the price rise to the inflow of silver.[6] But this attribution rests on both faulty data and faulty logic. We have already noted for both England and France that there was little or no relationship between bullion imports and prices for the period 1500–1800 as a whole. The same is true for Asia. However, many Western scholars have assumed that silver imports to China and the Ottoman Empire before 1800 simply reflected the New World silver trade, ignoring the far larger amounts of Asian silver that circulated from Japanese mines and Indian trade. In addition, these scholars have focused too much on the simple quantities of bullion being traded and have ignored the more fundamental changes that population growth produced in the structure of markets and in the balance of supply and demand.

In Asia, as in Europe, when population increased, many of those unable to secure land for farming turned to rural crafts or else migrated to the burgeoning cities and towns. In Anatolia and China, not only did the large cities grow, but the countryside also exhibited a vigorous growth of smaller market towns, as well as a subdivision of economic tasks that led to greater occupational specialization (Faroqhi 1984; Zurndorfer 1983). This growth was accompanied by an expansion in the use of credit. In China, merchant use of credit was common from the twelfth century on (Elvin 1973, 161–163), and there is evidence of widespread use of credit in the sixteenth-century Ottoman Empire (Jennings 1973; Cvetkova 1983b). In addition, both the Chinese and Ottoman governments sought to stretch their revenues through substantial currency debasements in the sixteenth and early seventeenth centuries. I have shown elsewhere how changes in urbanization and economic spe-

---

6. Wakeman (1986), Cartier (1981), Geiss (1979), and Atwell (1982) also emphasize the role of silver imports on Chinese prices. Inalcik (1978) and Wallerstein (1980) do the same for the Ottoman Empire and Europe.

cialization can create a dramatic rise in the velocity of circulation as the increased scope and density of trading networks encourage a more rapid turnover of money (Goldstone 1984, 1990). Also, as Miskimin (1975) notes, both expansion of credit and government currency debasement augment the velocity of money. Thus, from a variety of sources, velocity grew rapidly, financing the expanding demands of rising populations. Yet the output of agriculture, as a source of food and of raw materials for most manufactures, grew only modestly, leading to steady upward pressure on prices. From 1500 to 1650 grain prices rose in the Ottoman Empire and in China, as they had in England, by three to five times.[7]

Silver imports from the New World can have played only a small role in this rise. In the early 1580s, by which time Ottoman prices had already risen severalfold, Spanish coins made up but a few percent of the Ottoman money supply (Sahillioğlu 1983, 282). Nor did American bullion appear in the Ottoman currency; chemical assays of sixteenth-century Ottoman silver coins reveal that their silver is markedly different in composition from that characteristic of the New World silver deposits (Gordus and Gordus 1981). Thus, it appears that Ottoman coinage did not reflect a movement of New World silver into the Levant. In India, in the great trading center of Surat, the focus of the Indian Ocean trade in which Ottoman merchants took part, price movements were unrelated to silver imports (Brennig 1983). And as I discuss later, the scale of silver imports from the New World to China was insignificant compared to silver imports from Japan, and to the vastness of the Chinese economy.

That prices rose more rapidly than the volume of silver available is evident from the complaints in the late sixteenth and early seventeenth centuries by monarchs, urban merchants, and rural artisans that they *lacked* the hard coin they needed for purchases. After all, if a surfeit of silver was driving prices upward, monarchs could have contained inflation merely by reminting their coinage with a higher silver content. But states universally debased their coinage in this period, and both the mints and the merchants complained that a shortage of silver was hampering their operations.[8] In China there was an increasing reliance on copper

7. Admittedly, price data for Asia are not of the same quality as for England; however, all of the available evidence, which is now considerable, indicates that price increases were of the same order in all three areas during this period. Data on Ottoman prices are from Barkan (1975) and Faroqhi (1984); on Chinese prices, from Cartier (1969, 1981), A. Chan (1982, 234), Geiss (1979, 165–169) and Wilkinson (1980, 27).

8. Problems and complaints of currency shortages in the early seventeenth century are discussed for China by Wakeman (1986) and W. Peterson (1979, 69); and for the Ottoman Empire by Inalcik (1969a). For that matter, there were similar complaints in early seventeenth century England (Supple 1959).

coinage to meet the demand for a medium of exchange (A. Chan 1982, 282).

Moreover, the coincidence of trends between silver flows and price movements vanished after 1650. In the late seventeenth century, silver exports from America to Europe, and from Europe and Japan to Asia, surpassed those of the late sixteenth century, but prices were stable or declining in most nations (Morineau 1968; Chaudhuri 1963).

In short, between 1500 and 1700 price movements across Eurasia corresponded closely to the balance between population and food supply. In the sixteenth and early seventeenth centuries, population growth, accompanied by increasing urbanization and velocity of monetary circulation, pressed on limited food supplies and led to steadily rising prices. As the Ming minister of the Board of Works noted in 1638, "the vital problem lay in the production of grain, and it was the shortage of grain that had caused the rise of prices in all commodities" (cited in A. Chan 1982, 284).

The rises in population and in prices operated jointly to undermine government finances, reshape elite social mobility and competition, and precipitate popular uprisings.

B. THE DEVELOPING CRISES IN OTTOMAN ANATOLIA AND MING CHINA, c. 1500–1650

FISCAL DECAY

The Ottoman and Ming states both drew part of their incomes from varied trade and customs duties. But as essentially agrarian states, the bulk of their income was drawn from land taxes. In these states, land taxes were generally fixed, with assessments based on the estimated value of cultivated acreage. Such tax systems were extremely vulnerable to the effects of ecological change. First, as the population rose in each state, new land was brought into cultivation, old land was more intensively farmed, and a larger proportion of the population, lacking land, turned to commerce and handicrafts to make a living. None of these new sources of wealth was seriously brought under the land tax assessments. Local officials, whether Ottoman *timar* holders or Chinese gentry, when called on to update land registers, simply resubmitted past registers or else made only minor changes (Faroqhi 1979–1980, 35; R. Huang 1969, 87). Thus, as population grew, the tax system grew more and more out of touch with the composition of the economy; taxes shrank as a proportion of total output. Second, as families multiplied, individual peasant landholdings dwindled into uneconomical plots, while the poorest became landless laborers. As continued population pressure raised rents and drove down real wages, both the holders of minuscule plots and the landless had little choice but to sell and seek the aid and protection of large landlords. More and more land and labor thus passed under the control of local magnates, whose influence allowed them to evade or pay greatly reduced taxes on their land. Finally, as population pressure forced prices up, the costs of government—particularly the pay and provisions of armies, always the largest and most crucial items of government expenditure—steadily increased. The long-range effect of ecological change on government finance was to create an ever-widening gap between increasing costs and decreasing efficiency of taxation.

THE OTTOMAN STATE

The Ottoman state, in its heyday in the fifteenth and early sixteenth centuries, supported its army and civil administration by a highly centralized system of revenue assessment. All the land in the empire—including farmland, villages, towns, and cities—was considered to belong to the sultan, and was therefore state land (*miri*). The only exceptions were land belonging to pious foundations (*vakıf*s), which supported mosques and Islamic schools, and a very small amount of private land (*mülk*), generally former uncultivated or waste land (often swampland) that the sultan had granted to individuals to encourage them to invest in clearing or draining the land and putting it to productive use.

Revenues drawn from state lands were either sent to the sultan's treasury to pay for the central administration in Istanbul or assigned as stipends to military commanders, officials, and members of the provincial cavalry, who formed the backbone of the Ottoman armies. The sultan's officials surveyed the Ottoman territories, then set a tax assessment for each town and village. Though some dues were collected in grain, in other goods, or in services, the most important revenues were taxes paid in cash, fixed on the basis of the official assessment (Beldiceanu 1980b, 59–60). State lands were divided into estates (*tımar*s) of various sizes and graded according to the value of their revenues. The income from larger estates was devoted to the use of the sultan and the chief Ottoman officials; the income from smaller estates was granted to members of the provincial cavalry, who were responsible for providing their own equipment and attendants to accompany them on campaigns. Provincial governors and other officials who received large *tımar*s were also responsible for providing and equipping men for the army, in amounts proportional to the size of their *tımar*s.

*Tımar*s could include whole districts, groups of towns and villages, individual villages, or even portions of a single village. *Tımar*s also could include specified revenues drawn from particular taxes or dues. A grant of a *tımar* to an official or cavalryman thus amounted to a grant of particular revenues, drawn from the taxes and other dues assessed on localities. The largest estates were often noncontiguous, comprising revenues drawn from a variety of areas in the empire (Hutteroth 1980, 44).

Holders of *tımar*s, though they controlled the revenues in the area of their *tımar*s, did not in any sense own the land, which belonged to the sultan and could be reassigned at the sultan's pleasure. The provincial cavalrymen who held *tımar*s generally resided in the region of their estates when not on campaigns, but were more like local administrators than like feudal landlords. They were responsible for seeing that residents stayed on the estates and paid their taxes, and for maintaining law and order in the region of their estates. During campaigns, provincial governors would assign a certain number of *tımar* holders to remain in each district to collect revenues and maintain order (Shaw 1976, 26–27). But *tımar* holders did not have unlimited authority over the inhabitants of their estates; peasants and townsmen held hereditary usufruct rights to their farms and property, and were protected under the law by the sultan's courts.[9]

During the fifteenth and early sixteenth centuries, the granting of *tımar*s provided a sound foundation for Ottoman rule. The stipends, generally based on surveys and assessments made following the Ottoman expansion in the fifteenth century, were sufficient to maintain a powerful military and a loyal administration. In 1525, the Venetian emissary to Istanbul wrote: "I know of no State which is happier than this one. . . . It controls war and peace with all, it is rich in gold, in people,

9. The *tımar* system has sometimes been likened to feudal vassalage. However, as Weber first pointed out, it was a system of prebends, not of fiefs. The *tımar* holder had no land rights; he received only a temporary land grant from the sultan and was not owed reciprocal obligations from the latter. Subinfeudation was not allowed; all *tımar*s were held directly and solely from the sultan (M. Weber 1978, 1074–1075). The *tımar* system discussed here obtained only in Anatolia and the Balkans. In Egypt the Ottomans took over the Mameluke system of tax farming, while in the other Arab lands they appointed local notables as officials, recognizing their land claims in a modified form of the *tımar* system (Shaw 1975).

in ships and in obedience; no State can be compared with it" (cited in Steensgaard 1973, 74).

By the late sixteenth century, however, rising prices had destroyed this system. The real income from *tımar*s, the assessment of which remained fixed in cash at fifteenth-century levels, steadily dwindled by 2–3 percent each year. By the 1580s, "squeezed between the millstone of set stipends and rising prices," *tımar* holders could no longer afford to equip themselves for campaigning. Their *tımar*s were then revoked, and the income was reassigned to the sultan or to imperial favorites (Itzkowitz 1972, 90; Cvetkova 1983a, 181).

The ranks of the army, however, had to be maintained, and this was accomplished partly through the permanent expansion of the imperial troops—janissaries and palace cavalry *sipahi*s—and partly through the temporary recruitment and training of landless peasants as musketeers. These latter mercenary troops (*segban*s) were recruited for specific campaigns and then returned to the provinces, where they served in the retinues of provincial governors and landowners or, in some instances, formed independent bands of bandits. Expansion of the imperial troops, who received salaries from the imperial treasury, and their supplementation by mercenaries entailed an enormous increase in the burden of cash payments by the central government. While the number of *tımar* cavalry fell from 87,000 in the 1560s to 8,000 in 1630, the janissaries and palace *sipahi*s increased from 12,900 in 1527 to 67,500 in 1669, with the total of their annual salaries growing tenfold (Barkan 1975, 20).[10]

The cash needed to feed the imperial military machine was gained by assigning *tımar* lands, particularly the larger units, to tax farmers. But this practice did not remedy the decay of the *tımar* system. In order to protect their lands from taxation, local notables and commanders "donated" their lands to Islamic foundations. These *vakıf* lands then formed "trusts" that were administered by the families of the local notables and were kept off the tax rolls. In addition, tax farmers sought to have their leases converted into lifetime, or even heritable, rights to administer estates. Though technically still public lands, these long-term leaseholds (*malikâne*s) were in fact run for the benefit of the tax farmers rather than

10. As firearms grew in importance in the sixteenth century, some expansion of the musket-wielding janissaries and mercenary infantry was needed for defense of the empire, particularly against the Austrians (Inalcik 1980a, 286–288, Jennings 1980, 339–342). The expansion of the janissaries was thus a necessary evil. Still, the decay of the *tımar* system of revenue collection brought on relentless internal problems for Ottoman fiscal and provincial administration.

the government. "Malikâne virtually gave the [tax farmers] quasi-proprietary rights over extended territories"; and in some cases, where the tenants' hardship led them to abandon the land, tax farmers were able to get their territories recognized as *mülk*, or true private freeholds (Inalcik 1980a, 329; Stoianovich 1953, 398). Both *vakıfs* and *malikânes* thus became de facto private estates, which made a reduced contribution to the sultan's coffers (Inalcik 1972, 350–353; 1985, 100; Shaw 1976, 173).

In addition to the conversion of *tımar* lands to de facto private estates, newly cleared and cultivated lands (*mavat*) were given as freeholds to entrepreneurs who developed them for commercial cultivation. As all of these forms of private land control expanded in the sixteenth and seventeenth centuries, there developed the beginnings of "a new landlord class" (Inalcik 1980a, 329), which increasingly controlled larger shares of the empire's wealth, while the sultan controlled less and less.

The effects of inflation on the *tımar* system were thus pervasive and severe: the *tımar* cavalrymen became less effective as they could less afford the costs of campaigning; *tımars* that were assigned to court favorites or converted to *vakıfs*, as elites sought to protect themselves and their resources, were virtually lost for military purposes; and an increasing portion of public land was turned over to tax farmers, who remitted cash to the sultan to pay imperial troops but still grew harder to control, remitting smaller portions of the lands' output to the royal treasury and squeezing the peasantry for greater profits.

A particularly severe blow was dealt to the system in 1596, when the grand vizier, desperate for cash, dismissed thousands of *tımar* holders in order to convert their estates to *ilitzam* (tax farms) (Griswold 1985, 14). This move apparently reflected the failure of the *tımar* system to meet imperial needs, since by the end of the sixteenth century "the system had outlived its usefulness"; the sultan then increasingly relied on tax farming in former *tımar* lands (Karpat 1974b, 90; Abu-el-haj 1987).

The decay of the *tımar* system, however, was just one aspect of the generally "tardy and incomplete adjustments that the tax registers made for price inflation" (Faroqhi 1979–1980, 35). From 1520 to the 1580s direct taxes on most towns failed to keep pace with inflation, or even to expand with population; urban taxation per capita thus fell, in real terms, by well over half. Only the very modest market dues, which often increased by a factor of five in the sixteenth century, reflected the economy's expansion and price increases (Faroqhi 1979–1980, 43–45.)

As a result of these trends, central tax collections lagged further and further behind mounting expenses; by the late sixteenth century, the sultan's fiscal difficulties became extreme. From 1597 to 1648, the government's income in real terms (e.g. equivalent gold pieces) was only 50–60 percent what it had been in the early sixteenth century (Inalcik 1969b). From the 1580s there were recurrent revolts by janissaries, who demanded pay increases to help keep pace with inflation and protested payment in debased coin. Increasing military costs and falling revenues severely unbalanced the Ottoman budget. In 1527–1528 the central treasury had an annual surplus of seventy-one million *akçes*; this shrank to zero by 1581–1582 and eventually fell to a deficit of forty-four million *akçes* by 1669–1670 (Barkan 1975, 17).

It has sometimes been suggested that the Ottoman fiscal crisis was tied to a critical fall in trade with the West in the late sixteenth or early seventeenth century. Yet R. Davis's (1970) research on the English Levant trade argues otherwise. The Persian wars of the 1570s and 1580s hurt the Ottoman silk trade, but in the 1590s peace and trade were restored. The spice trade still flourished, bringing in customs revenues in 1582 that were four times what they had been a century earlier. The overall value of the Levant trade did not diminish in the early seventeenth century; indeed, England, the largest Western importer in the Levant, nearly doubled the value of her imports from the Ottoman Empire from the 1630s to the 1660s. In exchange, as Braude (1979, 441) shows, England exported an ever-rising volume of cloth to the Levant from the 1590s on. Mantran (1977, 217–218) observes that during the sixteenth century "the Cape route scarcely affected [Ottoman] trade"; the transformation of trade structures is not apparent until the late seventeenth century (Inalcik 1970a, 213; 1973a, 125–127; R. Davis 1970, 195, 202; Islâmoğlu and Keyder 1977, 43; DeGroot 1978, 10; Steensgaard 1973, 189–191). In short, the Ottoman fiscal crisis stemmed from more fundamental causes than a shift in trade.

By the end of the sixteenth century, fiscal strains had led the central government to seek extraordinary remedies. The *avarız*, an irregular tax previously used only for special cases of military emergency, became "an annual levy, made heavier from year to year" (Inalcik 1970b, 345). The capitation tax on Christians was raised sixfold during the period 1560–1590. To increase the revenues formerly collected by local *tımar* holders, the government pressured the tax farmers; but the abuses of the tax farmers then inflamed the provinces (McGowan 1981, 58; Itzkowitz 1972, 294).

Thus the failure of the Ottoman tax system laid the foundation for army revolts and popular uprisings. We see a strikingly similar pattern in the fiscal decay and government response that occurred in late Ming China.

MING CHINA

The ultimate failure of the Ming tax system was chiseled in stone in 1385, when the founding Hungwu emperor had the land tax quota carved in stone tablets. From that date, the land tax, which supplied roughly two-thirds of imperial revenues, remained unchanged "regardless of increases in population and land brought under cultivation" (R. Huang 1969, 86–87; 1974, 46–47). Local gentry concealed population increases from the central government simply by resubmitting past enumerations as current. The result, as Yim (1978, 15) notes in his careful study of official population data from sixteenth-century Henan Province, was "under-registration of the population on a gigantic scale" and a consequent fossilization of the official tax base.

In addition to land taxes, corvée labor and supplies of manufactures to the imperial court were organized by assigning these responsibilities to groups of approximately one hundred households, a system known as the *lijia* system. But "the *lijia* system was created for a static society. . . . The tax and corvée system of the early years of the dynasty was designed for a society with a stable population and very little circulation of reliable currency" (Littrup 1981, 60, 66). Population growth increased the administrative difficulties associated with this system, causing its effectiveness to decline. The most graphic example of this process was the decay of the army, which had similarly been designed to provide a fixed degree of manpower without large monetary outlays.

In the early Ming, the military was supposed to support itself by farming when not engaged in combat. But this self-sufficiency plan always fell short, and the army, consisting of men drawn from families proscribed for hereditary military service, subsisted on revenues drawn from its various locales of operation, supplemented by payments in paper money. As population growth cut into the ability of local prefectures to support local garrisons, and provisions were often in short supply, payments of rations and salaries were simply suspended. The result was mass desertion by soldiers. By the sixteenth century, the army units composed of military families—the *weiso* soldiery—had been reduced to little more than skeletons, with each force often only 10 percent of its prescribed strength (R. Huang 1974, 64–67; A. Chan 1982, 189–201).

As in the Ottoman Empire, locally supported military units were thus supplanted by a centrally paid mercenary force. Paying and supplying this army, which was concentrated on the northern frontier, became the crucial concern of the Ministry of Revenue. The required revenues were prodigious: the annual costs of the military force rose from less than five hundred thousand taels of silver (1 tael was roughly equivalent to 1.3 ounces) in the late fifteenth century to nearly four million taels in the early seventeenth century (A. Chan 1982, 127; R. Huang 1974, xiv, 285).

This revenue problem was met in part by commutation of taxes in kind to payment in silver. In the early Ming, taxes had been paid in goods, including grain, tea, charcoal, and silk cloth, and in services, including corvée labor in irrigation works, transport, postal service, and menial work in government offices. Cash played only a modest economic role, as paper and copper currency, easily counterfeited or inflated, were unreliable media of exchange. However, all these goods and services were assessed on the basis of fixed land tax quotas in each region; hence the assessments became increasingly obsolete as population grew and handicrafts, commerce, and highly intensive cultivation increased. In a series of reforms known as the "Single Whip," designed to give the government more control over its income, the complicated requisitions for materials, grain, and labor were gradually consolidated and commuted to payments in silver. But these reforms, carried out over a span of more than a century, were in many ways more of a burden than an aid to the Ming throne.

In 1436 seven southern districts, providing 15 percent of total land tax revenues, had their grain taxes commuted to silver, ostensibly to ease the burden of transporting their in-kind levies to Beijing. In fact, the commutation rate was set well below the market price of grain; the commutation thus resulted in a tax reduction for wealthy landowners in the region. A similarly inefficient commutation plagued the salt tax. The Ming government issued permits to merchants to sell salt, which was produced as a government monopoly by hereditary salt workers. In return, the merchants were to provide supplies to the military on the frontiers. A quota system, similar to the land tax quota, was established early in the dynasty to regulate salt production and sale. But as population grew, both the number of salt producers and the market demand increased. Instead of revising quotas, the Ming labeled the excess as "surplus" salt and sold it to merchants under a jury-rigged set of merchants' commissions and silver conversions. The salt monopoly thus became the basis for fabulous private fortunes earned by exploitation and corruption of the commission system for salt surpluses (R. Huang 1969, 95–97; Littrup 1981, 78).

Under the Wanli emperor, the grand secretary Zhang Juzheng (in office 1572–1582) attempted to restore the Ming treasury by further commutations. Taking advantage of a temporary peace with the Mongols on the northern frontier, Zhang reduced the army and prosecuted corruption and tax delinquency. More importantly, he ordered government use of corvée labor reduced by two-thirds, without reducing the corvée tax. Instead, the remainder was commuted to silver and hoarded in the imperial treasury (R. Huang 1974).

Thus, over the course of a century the tax system became gradually more monetized. Yet the reforms of the tax system failed to address the basic problem of Ming finance. Whether collected in kind or in cash, overall revenues were basically fixed, while expenses, particularly military expenses, continued to rise as steady inflation pushed costs upward: the basic pay of a soldier in the Ming armies rose from six taels of silver per year in the 1550s to eighteen taels by the early seventeenth century (R. Huang 1974, 285).

Moreover, the wealthiest areas, particularly the lower Yangzi delta, were precisely where the concentration of influential gentry made it difficult for the central government to enforce taxation (Fu 1981–1982, 75–76). False registration and collusion with local officials allowed wealthy landowners to evade taxes (F. Liang 1956; Tsurumi 1984; Marks 1984). Landlords sheltered their land from taxes by "giving" their land to officials and former officials, who were exempt from taxes. The latter would "manage" the estates in return for shares of the land. Landlords thus evaded taxes, while officials, whose salaries had never been adequate, accumulated lands through their "management" fees. This cooperation allowed landlords and gentry to protect themselves at the expense of the central government. The resources that could have averted disaster thus flowed out of the reach of government taxation. The tax burden then fell more heavily on the poorer regions of the northwest and on the poorer peasants of the south, while government revenues became ever more inadequate to meet current expenses (R. Huang 1969, 110).

A similar pattern of land concentration and landlord tax evasion occurred in the region around Beijing. There, "small holdings . . . which had been commonplace a century earlier, had virtually disappeared, transformed for the most part into Imperial demesnes, mortmains held by temples, and private estates"—all largely removed from imperial tax rolls. "As a result, revenues from the land tax continued to diminish throughout the sixteenth century" (Geiss 1979, 17–18).

From the 1590s, the government incurred annual deficits (Tong 1985). Through the end of the sixteenth century, the cash reserves accumulated under Zhang's administration staved off disaster, but these reserves were soon exhausted by renewed wars with Japan and the Manchus. In the seventeenth century, the government responded with a series of special tax "surcharges." Eunuchs were sent to the provinces to collect special revenues (Yang 1969, 13). By the 1640s, these surcharges amounted to a doubling or tripling of the local tax burdens (Hucker 1957, 135; Rossabi 1979, 187). But it is doubtful if these increases in the tax rate were ever realized. The provincial administration had been exhausted by poverty, as rising prices and fixed state revenues had led local administrators to rely on personal influence and corruption to salvage their own futures (J. Parsons 1970, xiii; Wakeman 1979, 43–44).

By the 1640s, several provinces had been lost to rebels, and the imperial treasury was empty. Unable to pay its own troops or to command the allegiance of local elites, the Ming dynasty succumbed, first to the internal revolt of deserting soldiers and rebellious peasants, and second to the desertion of Chinese officials. The latter's invitation to the Manchus revealed their preference for even a barbarian Confucian regime, if strong enough to restore order, over the corrupt and impotent Ming or the rule of popular rebels.

A FISCAL CRISIS, NOT A MONETARY CRISIS

It is sometimes suggested that in addition to internal factors, a collapse in China's trade with Europe contributed to the Ming decline (Atwell 1977). Europe sent American silver across the Atlantic and Indian oceans via Seville and Amsterdam, and across the Pacific via Manila, to China in exchange for silks, ceramics, and other luxuries. This trade faltered in the 1620s, recovered in the early 1630s, and then fell sharply in the late 1630s and early 1640s (Wakeman 1986, 4). Pierre Chaunu's famous comment on the Ming crisis expresses its purported connection to this decline in trade: "Unknown to itself, China was responding to the rhythms of Mexico and Peru" (cited in Adshead 1973, 276). But however tempting it may be to link China's fortunes to Europe's via the silver trade, attribution of Chinese economic difficulties to a fall in European bullion exports is quite hyperbolic, for it ignores the vast scale of the Chinese economy. Atwell (1977, 2) has estimated the volume of silver that reached China via European trade as generally 2–3 million ounces of silver per year in the early seventeenth century, with a peak year in 1597 of perhaps 13 million ounces. This figure needs to be set in the context of recent estimates of the national income of China in the mid-sixteenth century, which suggest a total volume of economic activity equivalent to roughly 825 million to 1.1 billion ounces of silver (Feuerwerker 1984, 300). Thus, the total volume of European trade was never more than just over 1 percent of China's economy, and it was on average only .2–.3 percent. The complete cessation of such trade would hardly have been noticeable in the overall economy.

Still, one might suggest that because the European trade was in silver bullion, it played a role far out of proportion to its scale in the economy, for it provided hard cash, the crucial lubricant of economic activity. But this assumption again bends under the vast weight of the Chinese economy. We have no idea of the total amount of silver circulating in late Ming China; thus, we have no precise measure of how much the fall in silver bullion imports from Europe actually affected China's money supply. However, we can compare the volume of silver imports with some specific figures from the Chinese economy. Needham and Huang (1974, 11) note that "before the end of the sixteenth century, the carrying of something like 30,000 ounces of silver by an individual on a business trip appears to have been quite common." Elvin (1972, 168) cites a seventeenth-century source who remarked that the "poorest" cloth merchants in Shanghai possessed a capital of ten thousand ounces of silver; the richest possessed several hundred thousand. For further comparison, R. Huang (1974, 81, 215) notes that a superintendent of the salt tax in the 1560s could make a personal income of nearly forty thousand ounces of silver a year, and that richer families in the Yangzi basin often kept hoards of several hundred thousand ounces of buried silver. Finally, Huang (1974, 275) estimates that the total tax revenue of the imperial government in the last quarter of the sixteenth century was forty-five million ounces of silver.

Noting that the volume of silver imports from Europe in the late sixteenth century was generally two to three million ounces per year, we now get a better sense of what this meant relative to China's monetary circulation. The total of a year's trade with European bullion ships would have provided enough silver either to (1) provide the capital for

100 substantial merchants or businessmen (in a population of 150 million persons!), *or* (2) finance the annual income of 25 superintendents of the salt tax or equivalent officials, *or* (3) provide the hoarded savings of 10 wealthy families in the Yangzi basin, *or* (4) finance 5 percent of the government's annual tax collection.

Moreover, China also exported silk and other products to Japan in return for silver, and imports of Japanese silver greatly exceeded those from European sources. Recent studies of Japanese and Chinese sources (Innes 1980; Yamamura and Kamiki 1983; Geiss 1979; Moloughney 1986; Moloughney and Xia 1989) have only begun to demonstrate the enormous volume of the indigenous Asian trading system. The silver trade with Japan grew steadily in the early decades of the seventeenth century, offsetting the European decline (Iwao 1976, 11). By the 1630s, Japanese silver exports to China reached 4 to 6 million ounces per year, several times the earlier flow of American bullion via Manila (Moloughney and Xia 1989, 63–65; Yamamura and Kamiki 1983, 353). Kobata (1965, 248), working from mine records, suggests that even this amount was less than the 7.4-million-ounces-per-year output of Japan's silver mines in the seventeenth century.

There was a slight fall in Japanese silver exports to China in the 1640s, on the order of 20 percent, before a recovery in the 1650s and 1660s to earlier highs, followed by a similar fall again in the 1670s and 1680s (Innes 1980, 379–380, 405, 410, 416); but at no time did silver imports to China cease to be higher after 1620 than before. However, by the 1640s decay of the imperial administration, provincial rebellions, and popular unrest had already disrupted Chinese economic activity, and it may well be that the decline in trade at this time merely reflects, rather than caused, China's internal disorders. There are two reasons to favor this explanation. First, the silver-copper and silver-gold exchange rates in China fell during these years: in 1630–1633 it took from 236 to 250 copper coins to purchase 16.875 grams (a standard unit) of silver, whereas in 1635–1639 it took only 188 copper coins (Atwell 1986); similarly, the value of silver to gold fell from a 1-to-4 ratio in 1580 to a 1-to-14 ratio in 1650. Rice prices in silver also peaked in the 1640s, at double the late-sixteenth-century level (Cartier 1969). All of these trends are hard to reconcile with a sharp fall in the supply of silver in circulation, which should have driven silver's value up; instead they suggest that the late 1640s saw a dishoarding of silver, along with shortages of rice, both signs of internal economic disruption. Second, after the

Manchus restored order, the silver trade with Japan quickly resumed: from 1648 to 1667 Japanese silver exports to China averaged almost two million ounces per year (Kobata 1981, 273). Although Japan put restrictions on European merchants in the late 1630s, which some scholars have interpreted as a contraction of trade, those restrictions are now understood as attempts to curtail Christian influence and to centralize trade, not to curtail it (Innes 1980, 3).

In short, the evidence suggests that internal disorders, not an external interruption of silver supplies, were at the root of the Ming crisis. Once Japan's silver trade is taken into account, it is evident that the contraction in imports followed, not preceded, the crisis. Europe's bullion trade with China was not large enough to be crucial to the workings of the Chinese economy, and any claim of a causal link between the decline in the European silver trade and the decline of the Ming dynasty must be viewed as an excess of Eurocentrism, rather than as a historical fact.

Indeed monetary factors in general had only a peripheral bearing on the Ming crisis. Silver imports to China grew steadily throughout the early seventeenth century, and though they peaked in the 1660s, they continued throughout the seventeenth century at a higher level than in the early 1600s. This monetary pattern does not fit the pattern of inflation, for prices rose most rapidly from the 1580s to the 1630s and 1640s and then steadily declined. Nor are the slight falls in the silver trade during the 1640s and 1670s correctly timed to account for the Ming decay; instead, these transitory trade fluctuations seem to have been caused by political difficulties—first the Ming collapse in the 1640s, then the War of the Three Feudatories (a resistance to Qing consolidation in South China) in the 1670s.

The critical fiscal problem in Ming China was that rising military costs collided with a decreasingly effective tax system. As Feuerwerker (1984, 306) remarks, "the Ming financial problem was less one of an unbearable tax burden than that the tax structure and administration could not raise enough revenue to meet critical expenses and collected what it did with a good deal of inefficiency and inequity."

In summary, the growing inadequacy of tax revenues in both China and the Ottoman Empire undermined these states' ability to support their armed forces. Moreover, efforts to close the gap between costs and revenues in the short term led to corruption and attempts to collect tax "surcharges" that antagonized all social groups. The outcome was a political crisis rooted in fiscal bankruptcy. This crisis was not due to overtaxation relative to the available resources of the society. In fact, the government's share of national wealth diminished. Rather, the crisis was due to an overall undertaxation as inflexible land-tax systems failed to capture growing output and tax evasion became increasingly common among influential elites.

Yet fiscal decay was not the sole source of political crisis; problems also arose from conflicts and disaffection among the elites.

ELITE COMPETITION AND CONFLICT

In both Ottoman Turkey and Ming China, the ecological shift created havoc in the traditional social order. Population growth and rising prices produced extraordinary social mobility, involving both "turnover"—the loss of influence and positions by traditional elites—and "displacement"—the exclusion of deserving aspirants from official positions. In both empires, while the central treasury and many traditional elite families were being squeezed by inflation, other families were acquiring wealth by exploiting rising prices and expanding markets. As a result, weakened central governments faced greatly increased demands for official favors and elite positions, as the newly wealthy sought recognition and official advancement, and impoverished families sought relief from misfortune. The strain of increased demands for limited positions produced a breakdown of normal channels of elite recruitment, with the impatient seeking to buy or force their way into higher positions, while those in office wallowed in corruption or sought to form defensive alliances to exclude newcomers. At the same time, the traditional educational systems for training the elites were overwhelmed by ever-increasing numbers of students, who faced diminishing opportunities for employment. In both cases, fierce competition, divisions, and disaffection among the elites dissipated state resources and threw the empires into turmoil.

THE OTTOMAN EMPIRE

Ottoman society was divided into two classes: the *askeri*, or ruling class, which included the entire military, administrative, and religious establishment; and the *reaya*, or producing class, which included the rest of the population, chiefly peasants, but also nomads, artisans, shopkeepers, and merchants. The *askeri*s were generally exempt from taxes, and were supported by the revenues drawn from the *reaya*s. The *askeri*s were uniformly Muslims; the *reaya*s included Muslims, Jews, and Christians, the latter comprising Greek Orthodox, Roman Catholics, and Coptic and Armenian Christians. In the ideals of Ottoman statecraft, the *reayas* produced the empire's wealth and paid the taxes that supported the *askeris*, while the *askeris* expanded and defended the empire, maintained order and enforced Islamic and imperial laws, and offered education and religious services, thus providing the conditions in which the *reayas* could be secure and prosper. Each group thus depended on the other, in what Ottoman statesmen called a "circle of equity."

In practice, of course, the *askeri* class was the chief beneficiary of the system. As Itzkowitz (1972, 40) observes, "The *askeris* zealously guarded their privileged position and looked to the sultan to maintain the dividing line between themselves and the rest of his subjects."

Initially, the *askeris* were drawn from the Turkish warriors who founded and expanded the empire. In the provinces, the Turkish warriors and their descendants continued to provide the *tımar*-holding cavalry. They were supplemented by absorption of local knights from conquered lands, especially in the Balkans, who generally converted to Islam after the Ottoman conquest and were assigned *tımars*. Although individual *tımars* themselves were not heritable, the son of a *tımar* holder could apply for assignment of a *tımar* and appointment to the army, and sons generally followed fathers into military careers in this fashion.

Recruitment and promotion to the highest ranks of the elite, however, were different and far more centralized processes. From the late fourteenth century, promising male youths from conquered, generally Christian, territories were selected to be slaves for the sultan. But these youths were not destined for menial slavery; they were converted to Islam and groomed for leading roles in the service of the state. The less promising were assigned to become soldiers in the elite imperial infantry—the janissaries. The more promising were trained in the sultan's palace schools, where they were taught Turkish, Arabic, Persian, and the skills of war and administration. The best obtained top posts in the army or civil administration, where they might become provincial governors or even grand viziers; others entered the imperial cavalry (*sipahi*) or became members of the palace staff (Itzkowitz 1972, 49–51).

These highest elites were totally dependent on, and hence completely loyal to, the sultan. They had no hereditary possessions, but relied on salaries paid by the sultan. Their children could be admitted to the palace schools only on the basis of merit. Alternatively, their offspring could enroll in the Muslim seminaries (*medreses*), which trained specialists in Islamic law, and possibly become judges (*kadıs*) in the Islamic courts.

Otherwise they could at best aspire to be *timariotes*, that is, holders of *timars*, and thus local administrators and cavalry in the Ottoman armies. This system of slave selection and training, the *devşirme* system, gave the state strict control over social mobility and the channels leading to elite positions. It produced a disciplined and highly skilled elite, united by their common training and dedicated to the Ottoman state. However, the system rested on the stability of the *timar* system. The *timars* provided the bulk of the armed forces and provincial local administration. This allowed the sultanate to keep the corps of imperial troops and Ottoman elites a small, cohesive group, concentrated in Istanbul where they could be closely supervised.

In the course of the sixteenth century, the decay of the *timar* system led to the stationing of janissaries in the provinces. There, the troops often intermarried with locally influential families, including *kadıs*, wealthy merchants, and tax farmers. Taking advantage of the state's need for cash, and using their influence with local judges and imperial troops, these families increased their control over government lands. Fewer and smaller *timars* were assigned to provincial cavalrymen, while more and larger *timars* came under the control of local elites and tax farmers (Cvetkova 1983a, 180–181). Tax farmers came to include large numbers of *reayas*, "enterprising individuals rising from every social stratum," ranging from wealthy merchants to former peasants and soldiers of fortune, "who achieved social preeminence by taking advantage of the opportunities in land administration and . . . tax collection" (Karpat 1974b, 91).

As tax farming spread, so did abuses. Using bribery and influence with central officials, tax farmers contrived to have their appointed domains classified as heritable leaseholds (*malikânes*), or even as outright private property (*mülk*). These holdings grew ever more valuable as grain prices rose, creating new wealth and new aspirations among the estate holders. Griswold (1985, 161) notes that in the late sixteenth century, the elite *reayas* "built lavish homes, invested in lands, but also put their wealth in . . . jewels, furs, and gold." Thus, alongside the old *timar* system there began to arise in the sixteenth and seventeenth centuries a class of landed local notables (*ayans*), which intermingled the *askeri* and *reaya* classes. Inalcik (1980a, 333) comments that "the farspread application of the *iltizam* [taxfarming] system in finance and administration, coupled with the rise of a new *multezim* class in the provinces [i.e., *ayans*], has to be considered one of the most important developments in Ottoman history after 1580."

The most successful of the *ayan*s created local dynasties, assembled their own armed supporters, and sought to influence the imperial government (Inalcik 1955, 224–225; 1972, 350–354; Itzkowitz 1972, 91; Karpat 1974b; Shaw 1976, 173–174). By the turn of the seventeenth century, this practice had caused "a drastic change in the criteria for the selection of elites; instead of an elite status decided by the ruling authority, there was a self-status-seeking effort by lower class people based on their economic power" (Karpat 1974b, 90). The result was a struggle over authority, status, and control of state lands between palace officials and provincial notables, with provincial governors and janissaries freely switching sides to promote their own interests.

Through coercion, bribery, or influence in the administration, both traditional *askeri*s and local notables sought to circumvent the traditional centralized training and promotion system and place their offspring and allies in key military and administrative posts. In the late sixteenth century, the British ambassador to Turkey noted that hardly a pasha or infidel in Istanbul failed to profit from the traffic in power and influence in high places (Griswold 1985, 160). As a result, the clear lines of authority and promotion that had once prevailed in the empire lapsed as newcomers infiltrated the palace and local administration: "The flexibility of the [Ottoman administrative] system in the mid-sixteenth century had turned into a non-system with no regular lines because almost anybody could move to almost any part of the [administrative] structure" (Kunt 1983, 67). Indeed, "the erosion of the system of military tenure at so many points led to ever growing confusion and litigation over rights to [estates], a process which sapped . . . military effectiveness (Cvetkova 1977, 167). Inalcik (1977, 39) notes that "in the seventeenth century, the rivalry between the *kapıkulları* [the sultan's official servants] and the so called 'upstarts' (*turedi*) emerged as one of the most important internal political issues." Increased social mobility was reflected in the number of "persons from new channels [who] kept flooding the system," which, combined with the diminished resources of the Ottoman state, created "a greater competition among an increasingly greater number of candidates for not many more, maybe even fewer, offices" (Kunt 1983, 76–77).

One of the most visible consequences of this increased mobility was the rapid turnover of officials, a problem that some contemporaries cited as a major factor in the Ottoman decline. In the early sixteenth century, district commanders stayed in office for several years at a time; as late as 1568–1574, 43 percent of them held the same post for three or more years. By 1632–1641, this figure had fallen to 11 percent, with 55 percent holding their post for one year or less. The frequent rotation also involved substantial periods out of office waiting for reassignment; these delays impoverished some officials and led others to attempt to increase their fortunes by unofficial means (Kunt 1983, 70–72). Bernard Lewis (1958, 113) remarks that by the early seventeenth century, "bureaucratic and religious institutions all over the Empire . . . suffered a catastrophic fall in efficiency and integrity . . . accentuated by the growing change in methods of recruitment, training, and promotion."

Such competition and intra-elite conflict often led to open revolts by provincial officials and magnates, and by janissary and *sipahi* groups. The most serious were the janissary revolts of 1622 and 1631–1632, which caused the sultan to flee Istanbul, and the Anatolian revolts of Abaza Mehemmed (1622–1628) and of Abaza Hasan Paşa (1657–1658). Under the strains of these uprisings, the Ottomans lost control of several eastern provinces—including Iraq, Syria, and the Crimea, as well as eastern Anatolia—for various periods (Griswold 1985; Shaw 1976, 190–196; V. Parry 1976, 142; Kurat 1976, 164–165). In addition to such open revolts, the central administration was plagued by factional divisions, which often resulted in the assassination of viziers and even of sultans (Shaw 1976, 170). The entire period 1617–1648 "can be described [as] a period of intrigue, of shifting alliances, and of spasmodic violence at the center of affairs" (Parry 1976, 135).

In sum, rising prices did more than merely undermine Ottoman central finances. By wreaking havoc with the *tımar* system and providing new wealth and opportunities to the provincial governors, military officers, and tax farmers who acquired control of government lands, the sustained price rise also created massive social mobility. As increasing numbers of aspirants to higher positions collided with each other and with the shortage of official positions, individuals pressed their claims for recognition and advancement by intrigue and corruption in the sultan's administration, and by open revolt in Istanbul and the provinces.

THE CHINESE GENTRY

Long-term ecological changes created similar strife among China's elite. In the sixteenth and early seventeenth centuries, increasing social mobility and competition produced factional divisions and intra-elite struggles that undermined Ming rule.

In imperial China, both local notables and state officials were traditionally drawn from the gentry—those families with scholars who had earned degrees in the imperial examination system. Most gentry families held land that they rented to peasants as a stable and secure source of income. However, land was generally divided among heirs, and over a few generations such division could easily diminish the landholdings of gentry families. At the same time, peasants, who could purchase clear and full title to their lands, might expand their holdings through good luck or hard work. Thus the difference between the gentry and the peasantry was not landholding per se, but rather the cultivation, prestige, and influence that came from success in the imperial exams. Scholars from poorer families often established ties to wealthy landowning families, with the latter hoping to benefit from the scholar's prestige, and perhaps from his influence if he obtained an official position. China also had vast numbers of merchants, particularly in the cities and along coastal and riverine trade routes. But in the early Ming, when taxes were collected largely in kind and the money economy was weak, most merchants had but modest fortunes. Merchant families could gain respect only by acquiring land, and could gain influence only by producing or allying with degree-holding scholars.

In theory, the system allowed a great deal of mobility, for any social class could produce scholars, who in turn could obtain degrees, prestige, and influence. In practice, however, the system was generally stable. Landed gentry families were better able to afford the lengthy training required to produce successful scholars, and successful scholars tended to protect and sustain the prosperity of their families. The gentry in turn depended on the efforts of a free and smallholding peasantry, who paid the taxes that supported the imperial system and local government, and paid the gentry directly for providing education, ceremonial services, and for some leasing of land and moneylending. The talented son of a peasant or merchant could be supported in his scholarly efforts and adopted by a gentry family, thus reinforcing the ideal of mobility while preserving the reality of gentry dominance. In a society with active but small-scale commerce and no great feudal-style landlords, the gentry readily dominated Chinese society.

These conditions of easy gentry dominance, based on a prosperous smallholding peasantry and small-scale commerce, were common in the early Ming dynasty. However, they gradually faded under the pressures of expanding population, market growth, and rising prices.

In the sixteenth century, inflation led more and more of the gentry to concern themselves with finance and profit-making activities in order to maintain their incomes (Brook, 1981, 198; W. Peterson 1979, 64–80). During the sixteenth and early seventeenth centuries, as the contemporary Guei Youguang (1506–1571) noted, "the status distinctions among scholars, peasants, and merchants became blurred" (deBary 1970, 173). Opportunities provided by greater commercialization of the economy and by rising prices allowed fortunate non-elite families to accumulate wealth, but posed problems for others. "The increase in trade, the use of silver . . . were resented and denounced by men whose interests rested on landholding and officeholding" (W. Peterson 1979, 70). An early-seventeenth-century gazeteer of Anhui Province wrote:

> Property and moral well being reached their peak in [1488–1505. By the mid-sixteenth century the situation differed]. As merchants and traders became more numerous, . . . property was exchanged. Prices fluctuated. Those who were able were successful. Those who were a bit slow were ruined. The family on the east might become rich while the family on the west was impoverished. The equilibrium between those of higher and lower status was lost. . . . By [the late sixteenth century] the situation differed even more. Instances of wealth from [commerce] were numerous. The rich became richer and the poor got poorer. Those who had risen were overbearing. Those who had fallen were skittish.
>
> (cited in W. Peterson 1979, 70–71)

Growing population meant land scarcity, smaller family holdings, and reduced surpluses for peasant farmers. In combination with rising taxation, these changes meant that peasants had great difficulty paying their taxes and rents. Wealthy merchants could then easily acquire their lands, for many peasants sought to escape taxation by offering themselves and their lands to wealthy patrons. The peasants thus gained security, but at the cost of becoming bonded laborers, often little better than serfs, on vast estates. The flow of land and labor to the newly wealthy in this fashion was so great, particularly in the highly commercialized economy of the Yangzi basin, that in some cases bondsmen were appointed as stewards and overseers for their masters and kept their own bonded laborers (McDermott 1981). Thus, the "rich became richer" and accumulated enormous landholdings, which, with the help from local gentry, were sheltered from imperial taxation.

By the sixteenth century, such commercial success could be translated directly into official status. Although the early Ming had strictly limited the number of lower-degree holders, the late Ming, in order to raise money, had taken to selling lower degrees and places in the Imperial Academy (Ho 1962, 175; A. Chan 1982, 290; Sakai 1970, 337). Money

invested in training, or occasionally in bribery, could bring higher degrees; Rawski (1972, 89) demonstrates that the commercial wealth of
Zhangzhou Prefecture in Fujian Province allowed it to go from producing 3 percent of the higher-degree holders in the province in 1513–1541
to producing 22 percent in 1544–1601. Dennerline (1981, 112–113),
in his study of elite families in Jiading Prefecture, a district transformed
by the rise of commercial cotton growing, notes that most of the elite
households in the seventeenth century were from lines that first began
holding office in the sixteenth century. Beattie (1979), in his study of
Anhui, similarly finds that most elite families of the late Ming and Qing
arose in the mid-to-late sixteenth century with the commercialization of
the local economy. In sum, "the sixteenth and early seventeenth centuries saw the apogee of upward mobility from the merchant families into
the bureaucracy" (deBary 1970, 172). The result was a vast swelling of
the lower levels of the official gentry; from 1400 to 1600, the number
of holders of the lowest (*shengyuan*) degree increased perhaps twenty-
fold (Atwell 1975).

As in Turkey, increased social mobility led to increased social competition and factionalism. "As the pool of literate men grew, a fierce
competition developed, as there was only a slow increase in the quotas
which had been imposed to keep the numbers who passed in the provincial and national examinations at levels commensurate with the bureaucracy's staffing requirements" (W. Peterson 1979, 54). Organized
factions, such as the Donglin party and the Restoration Society, sought
both to increase their representation among the officials and to build
local power bases among provincial gentry (Busch 1949–1955; Atwell
1975). They thus competed both with palace factions, which arose
around particular emperors, ministers, or imperial favorites, and with
local commercial interests. The struggle among local interests, state officials, reformist gentry and eunuch-led palace factions appears to have
become increasingly acute from the late sixteenth century. "Intense jock-
eying for power by rival factions and families in the late Ming countryside" grew with the "intense factionalism of court politics" (McDermott
1981, 700; Taniguchi 1980). Disgruntled gentry, rudely ousted in factional battles in the 1620s and 1630s, supported the northern and western revolts that toppled the dynasty in the 1640s, while factional
divisions led to the recall of able generals, the execution and assassination of able ministers, and the paralysis of the bureaucracy (Wakeman
1985, 1:229–237; Geiss 1979, 600).

As in Turkey, the turnover of key individuals caused "general bureaucratic chaos, with officials . . . being replaced with bewildering rapidity" (J. Parsons 1969, 225). Fifty grand secretaries (equivalent in rank to the grand vizier or prime minister) served the Ming from 1628 to 1644. The length of tenure for most officials decreased by two-thirds from the early to late Ming reigns, from an average of 10 years for county officials and 3.5–4.5 years for palace officials to an average of 3–3.5 years in the counties and .8–1.2 years at the top (Dennerline 1981, 25; J. Parsons 1969, 178).

What is most striking about the fall of the Ming, and the failure of restorationist attempts, is the inability of gentry, officials, and commercial interests to find common ground on which to mobilize for defense of the dynasty. Instead, support for the central government declined in favor of protecting local areas through private mobilization. By the mid-seventeenth century, the integration of local gentry and state officials was nonexistent (Dennerline 1981, 346; A. Chan 1982, 301; Struve 1984). Fiscal and military difficulties were thus fatally compounded by the lack of elite integration and the paralyzing factionalism that followed the sixteenth-century increases in social mobility.

EDUCATIONAL EXPANSION AND ELITE CONFLICT

Attention must also be directed to problems in the traditional channels of education and elite recruitment. The Ottomans had traditionally staffed their bureaucracy and military elite with slaves trained in the palace for state service. The palace schools trained both the janissary troops and the chief bureaucratic officials. The legal system and religious institutions were staffed by graduates of the Muslim seminaries. But by the late sixteenth century, both palace schools and seminaries were overburdened. The vast expansion of the janissaries and palace *sipahis* diluted the quality of the palace studentry; as janissaries moved to the provinces and allied with local magnates, wealth and family connections took precedence over education and merit in access to the palace schools and janissary ranks (Inalcik 1973a, 47; Itzkowitz 1972, 91–92). At the same time, as poor peasants flooded the Muslim seminaries, "a crisis of religious institutions [became] unavoidable, because the religious schools had overexpanded and enrolled far too many students for the number of jobs that were available" (Itzkowitz 1972, 96; Faroqhi 1973, 217). Unemployed students and seminarians demanded, and often seized, supplies from peasants in their respective locales. Many student groups became little better than bandits and joined in the revolts of the early seventeenth century (Cook 1972, 40; Barkan 1975, 28).

In China, population growth also led to a vast overexpansion of the student population relative to official jobs. There arose "a glut of candidates at higher level examinations . . . [that] engendered an increasing amount of social frustration," as well as a "deterioration of student quality" (Ho 1962, 179, 182). The problem was exacerbated by the sale of studentships in the Imperial Academy; one witness suggests that, by the early seventeenth century, two-thirds of the places in the Academy went to purchasers (A. Chan 1982, 291). Those who glutted the lower ranks of the educational system and "who failed to climb the upper rungs constituted a literate body whose capacity for discontent alarmed . . . imperial authorities toward the end of the Ming. Prominently involved in the urban demonstrations and 'party' movements of the late Ming, [students and lower-degree holders] were also frequently associated with peasant rebellions" (Wakeman 1975a, 3).

The problems posed by the overburdening and breakdown of the educational system in these states went far beyond the discontent among the ranks of students and underemployed degree holders. In the Chinese and Ottoman empires, the system of elite education and recruitment had served as the circulatory system through which the talented among local elites and central officials moved together, absorbed a common tradition, and channeled their aspirations. The breakdown of traditional systems of elite education and recruitment alienated local elites, turned talented men to the pursuit of private wealth rather than public honor, and destroyed the allegiance of existing elites, who saw responsible positions coming under the sway of purchasers and royal favorites. The overburdening of traditional elite education in the Ottoman state and in Ming China thus was a major factor in the disintegration of elite cohesion and of elite support for the state.

POPULAR UPRISINGS

The decay of central government finances and the disaffection of elites paved the way for the success of the popular uprisings that brought down the Ming Empire and wrested Asia Minor from the Ottomans in the mid-seventeenth century. In part, these revolts can be traced directly to the increase in landless and impoverished peasants that resulted from population growth, since this group served as the raw material for rebel

armies. But to characterize these disturbances as simple peasant uprisings or anti-tax revolts is an error that ignores their leadership and their
origins.

In Asia Minor the revolts in the countryside, known as the *celali*
revolts, found leaders among unemployed mercenary soldiers (*segbans*)
and even among provincial magnates who sought to increase their status.
Deserting soldiers and mercenaries formed bandit groups. In the absence
of strong government opposition, and with the cooperation of local magnates, religious students, and corrupt officials, these groups often grew
into semiautonomous regional power centers (Griswold 1985; Itzkowitz
1972, 92–93). Magnates or provincial officials could then lead their
forces against the central authorities, extorting titles, official positions,
or other rewards in "recognition" of their local authority. Increasing
numbers of landless peasants, pressured by population growth and the
rapacity of tax farmers, were also readily mobilized for uprisings against
the central government (Islâmoğlu 1987b, 117). The largest uprising was
that of Abaza Hasan Paşa in 1657–1658, which included a substantial
number of officials and founded a rebel government that posed a severe
threat to the Ottoman state (Kurat 1976, 165).

The effectiveness of the rural revolts was aided by urban revolts,
prompted by declining real wages in the face of inflation (Naff 1977,
14; Faroqhi 1984, 295–298; Murphey 1980, 167). Not only did the
janissaries of the capital frequently rise against the sultan, but urban
artisans staged protests as well, including a demonstration by 150,000
in Istanbul in 1651 against price manipulations (Inalcik 1973a, 161).

Similarly, in China it was unpaid mercenaries who, turning to banditry, initiated the rebel uprisings (Dardess 1972, 106). They were joined
by postal attendants whom the Ming had left unpaid and then fired as
an economy move; already mounted, these postal attendants became an
effective cavalry when they joined the rebel armies (Rossabi 1979). Peasants were often driven by hardship, particularly in the drought of 1628,
to cast their lot with the rebels, but it was the deserting soldiery of the
northern armies that formed the core of the rural revolts. These rural
rebellions were complemented by urban riots, involving artisans, laborers, students, and members of the gentry (Tanaka 1984; Yuan 1979,
283, 311–312), which recurred through the early seventeenth century.
Again, declining real wages lay behind the urban revolts, for as nominal
wages lagged far behind inflation, "the urban poor faced rising prices
and dwindling [real] incomes (Geiss 1979, 175). The Suzhou riot of
1626 was "an event of national significance; . . . it . . . drew the atten-

tion of the court and . . . gave a powerful display of gentry-commoner cooperation" (Yuan 1979, 292). As in Turkey, revolts that could be described as centered on cultivators, and hence truly "peasant revolts," were few, and limited largely to the uprisings of bonded laborers in the Yangzi region (Beattie 1979, 250–251; A. Chan 1982, 238; Adshead 1973, 274).

The uprisings of bonded laborers in the Yangzi basin deserve attention, however, for their distinctive social character. This was an area where extensive commercialization had been accompanied by the growth of popular literacy, and hence by the growth in circulation of popular encyclopedic and morality texts (Sakai 1970, 336–337; Handlin 1983). It was also an area influenced by the radical Taizhou school of Confucianism led by Wang Gen, who preached the equality of all men (deBary 1970, 168–173). The accounts of the uprisings of bonded laborers in this period thus have a strong social revolutionary flavor, reminiscent of Western accounts of revolution. A contemporary account of one uprising in Jiangxi relates that

> hundreds or thousands of them under rebel leaders . . . ripped up pairs of trousers to serve as flags. They sharpened their hoes into swords, and took to themselves the title of "Levelling Kings" declaring that they were levelling the distinction between masters and serfs, titled and mean, rich and poor. The tenants . . . broke into the homes of important families [and] would order the master to kneel. "We are all of us equally men. What right had you to call us serfs."
>
> (cited in Elvin 1973, 245–246)

Wiens adds that this revolutionary attitude was quite common among bondservants, and that rather than merely objecting to the level of taxation or rents, "the revolt of poor bondservants was in most cases aimed at overthrowing the existing order and abolishing the hereditary servility of bondservantry" (Wiens 1980, 27; 1979). However, it was not such bondservant revolts, concentrated in southern China, that brought down the Ming. That task was begun by the rebel armies of Li Zicheng, spearheaded by deserting soldiers and government employees, assisted by defections of the gentry elite, and completed by the Manchus. In both China and Turkey, it was thus chiefly the breakdown of the government mercenary forces and of the allegiance of provincial elites, not mere peasant suffering, that allowed popular uprisings to pose a fatal threat. Popular misery provided raw material, but it was unpaid soldiers and disaffected local officials who provided the leadership and were the most dangerous elements.

IDEOLOGICAL CHANGE: RELIGIOUS HETERODOXY
AND RADICALISM

The English Revolution has at times been so strongly associated with religious heterodoxy that some have labeled it a "Puritan revolution" (Gardiner 1970). Heterodox religious movements were not merely an English phenomenon, however; they were also a common element in Asia's seventeenth-century crises.

In the Ottoman Empire, the early seventeenth century witnessed the spread of Turkish popular literature, which implied the growth of a popular audience and the extension of literacy beyond the official class. Popular religion frequently took a heterodox turn, and struggles between orthodox and Sufi religious orders gained intensity and "rose to plague Ottoman society" (Shaw 1976, 206–207). As Woodhead (1987, 35) notes, in the early 1600s "Anatolian heterodox communities apparently caused as much unease to the sultans as did the Huguenots" to the kings of France. The mystic orders were successfully suppressed, although "their personal religion and extensive organization had provided a refuge for the mass of the people during periods of political anarchy." Moreover, the state's attack on religious heterodox groups proved a spur to rebellion, for "as the mystic *tekkes* were closed and their dervishes imprisoned, in desperation people accepted the leadership of the *celali* rebels" (Shaw 1976, 206–207). Thus, the period of social breakdown was accompanied by an increase in conflict between orthodox and heterodox strains of Islam, a conflict with links to political rebellion.

In China, the late Ming period was a time of extensive religious heterodoxies, reflecting both populist radical movements and elite movements associated with attempts at political reform through moral regeneration (deBary 1970, 1975). Sixteenth- and early-seventeenth-century China was marked by an expansion of elementary schooling and a rise in literacy, accompanied by a vast expansion of popular literature, from morality tales to novels (Ho 1962, 211–213; Atwell 1975; Sakai 1970, 336–337; A. Chan 1982, 101). As noted above, this period also saw the growth of the Taizhou school of Neo-Confucianism, "a kind of protest movement against the establishment, striking for its popular character and the revolutionary nature of its ideas" (deBary 1970, 168; Dennerline 1981, 155). The Taizhou school advocated the equality of all men, and "carried the intellectual torch to the masses. . . . In Kiangsu and Anhwei . . . we find agricultural tenants, firewood gatherers, potters, brick burners, stone masons, and men from other humble walks of life attending public lectures and chanting classics. Never before and never afterward, in traditional China, were so many people willing to accept their fellowmen for their intrinsic worth" (Atwell 1975, 336). DeBary (1970, 173) observes that "the growth of commerce and economic strength of the middle classes contributed to the self-confidence and optimism that is characteristic of Taizhou thought." The movement combined officials, merchants, and commoners in radical activism, whose most spectacular achievement was the Yangzi bondservant revolts discussed above.

More important for Ming politics, however, was the academy movement. Former officials and scholars, repelled by the corruption and failures of the state and the official educational system, set up academies for alternative training of Confucian scholars. Many drew their inspiration from the writings of the early-sixteenth-century heterodox scholar Wang Yangming, who advocated a moral purification of the individual based on self-examination. Far more than mere educational institutions, the academies became centers of political reform movements that sought to change the state through a return to "pure" Confucian practices.

The rate of founding of new academies accelerated sharply in the late Ming, rising from an average of 1.4 per year prior to the sixteenth century to 7.5 per year from 1506 to 1572 (Meskill 1982, 66). From the mid-sixteenth to the mid-seventeenth centuries, the academies were increasingly drawn into political conflicts as they sought to support reformist court factions, which resulted in repeated suppressions by the Ming state. Most famous was the Donglin Academy, whose members called for greater public morality in and out of government in an overt "moral crusade," drawing severe persecutions as a result (Busch 1949–1955; Hucker 1957). In 1625–1626 the Donglin Academy was brutally suppressed by the eunuch Wei Zhongxian, who dominated the emperor in those years and whom the Donglin had often attacked. Seven hundred Donglin sympathizers were purged from the government, the Donglin leaders were tortured and imprisoned, and the academy buildings were torn down. After Wei's removal by the new emperor in 1627, the Donglin was succeeded by the Fushe, a "study group" that resembled a formal political organization, with a published creed, membership list, national headquarters, and fund-raising and recruitment activities. Like the Donglin, the Fushe opposed corruption in government, supported reform-oriented officials, and even sought to aid its candidates in examinations and in obtaining official positions. In addition, the group "demonstrated its social commitment by championing education for the poor, . . . sponsoring public lectures, and accepting large numbers of members from humble backgrounds. The people responded by giving the group active support in several political battles" (Atwell 1975, 358). Although the group occasionally placed several members in high posts, the Ming government of the 1630s was too torn by factional divisions to mount a successful program of reform.

Parallels to the history of Puritanism are striking. Like the academy movement, Puritanism began as a movement for moral regeneration, the political aims of which were limited to purification of religious practice and of public and private morals. Moreover, the reasons for the appeal of Puritanism and the heterodox Confucian movements appear similar. Walzer (1974, 308–310) suggests that much of Puritanism's appeal to the gentry stemmed from the disorder of the social hierarchy caused by increased social mobility, Calvinism being "an appropriate option for anxiety-ridden individuals [seeking a sense of order]. Given the break-down of the old order, it is predictable that some Englishmen would make that choice." DeBary (1970, 173) similarly notes that the appeal of heterodox Confucian movements to Chinese gentry resulted from "the search for identity at a time when traditional roles have been ob-scured by rapid change and new energies can no longer be channeled along established lines." One can add that both movements were fed by the students from greatly expanded educational systems—the English universities and the Chinese academies and imperial schools—who had no other outlet. Lastly, the fate of both movements after the resolution of the political crises was similar. In Walzer's (1974, 302, 312, 320) words, "Puritan ideology was a response to real experience . . . a prac-tical effort to cope with personal and social problems. [But] the condi-tions of crisis and upheaval . . . did not endure, [leading to] the disappearance of the militant saints from English politics in the years after the Restoration. . . . After the Restoration, [Puritanism's] energy was drawn inward, its political aspirations forgotten; the saint gave way to the non-conformist." Similarly, after the Manchu Restoration, the academies, though continuing as centers of study, lost their political aspirations and reformist activism. Wakeman (1986, 16–17) notes that under the Manchus, "ethical philosophers became scholarly academi-cians and political leaders turned into bureaucratic administrators." By the late seventeenth century, the academies focused strictly on teaching the classics (Meskill 1982, 156–158). Though richly endowed, they be-came politically passive.

In sum, the contemporary and parallel careers of Puritanism and the academy movement, and to a lesser degree, Sufism, are highly sugges-tive. Especially in England and China, it appears that movements for moral regeneration were an attractive option in times of rapid social mobility and of state corruption and failure, and that the factional divisions among local and court interests made it likely that such moral reform efforts would become enmeshed in political struggles. Moreover, when the underlying social and political crises passed, the attractions of heterodoxy diminished, and its activist aspects waned.

The outcomes of these Asian crises were in many ways similar to the results of the European cases of state breakdown. In each case, the central administration was reorganized, and, even more striking, there were marked changes in rural class structure and local administration. I discuss these outcomes in more detail and compare them with the results of Western crises in the next chapter. But first, let us briefly move ahead in time. For in the East, as in the West, a second wave of state crises erupted from the late eighteenth to the mid-nineteenth centuries.

Two of these crises were quite "conventional" in terms of our model: the regional independence movements in the Ottoman Empire and the Taiping rebellion in China are almost textbook cases of how population growth undermined central authority. But the third crisis—the Meiji Restoration in Japan—occurred in a state whose population had been stable for over a century and a half. It thus poses a major challenge to our view of early modern state crises and deserves special attention.

C. COMPARISONS: THE NINETEENTH-CENTURY CRISES IN QING CHINA, THE OTTOMAN EMPIRE, AND TOKUGAWA JAPAN

THE ECOLOGICAL CYCLE AND SHORT-TERM RECOVERY

Both the Chinese and Ottoman empires reemerged as strong states in the late seventeenth and early eighteenth centuries, only to undergo once again administrative decay and provincial rebellions in the nineteenth century. Given the enormous, almost insurmountable, problems faced by these empires in the late sixteenth and early seventeenth centuries, it is worth inquiring how it was possible to restore imperial authority in the first place.

CHINESE REVIVAL AND PROSPERITY IN THE EARLY QING

From an early-seventeenth-century peak of perhaps 150 to 200 million inhabitants, China's population almost certainly declined in the course of the late Ming rebellions and the Manchu conquest. The northwest provinces of Shaanxi and Shanxi and the western province of Sichuan (which may have lost two-thirds of its population circa 1600) were devastated in the seventeenth-century revolts (Entenmann 1982, 59). The Manchu invasion wreaked further havoc, while adding the sparsely settled lands of Manchuria to the empire. Thus, after 1660 in "Szechuan, Yunnan, Kweichow, Shensi, and Kangsu, the phenomena of underpopulation and abundance of land were manifest" (Shang 1981–1982, 25). Indeed, the Shunzhi (1644–1661) and Kangxi (1661–1722) emperors introduced extensive land reclamation and resettlement programs (Guo 1982, 91).

With the return of ecological balance, social stability seems to have followed; at least, far less social mobility is evident in the later period. A study by Robert Marsh found that in the period 1685–1780 the percentage of officials from families with no prior officeholders was only half that in the period 1500–1684 (cited in Eberhard 1962, 29). Ho (1962, 114) similarly found reduced social mobility after 1673.

State finances improved as well, for prices declined in the late seventeenth century. The new tax levels that the Manchus established after their conquest therefore returned increasing levels of real income. Urban workers also benefited, as real wages moved to higher levels in the early Qing than they had been in the late Ming (Chao 1986, 218–219).

Although population likely recovered by the early eighteenth century and then began to expand, this expansion was at first accompanied by a vast increase in cultivated acreage. Under the peace imposed by the Manchus, Chinese territory was extended, and widespread migration to frontier and highland areas occurred. Even though by 1770 China's population was, at 270 million inhabitants, likely one-third larger than in 1600, cultivated area had probably risen by one-half (G. Wang 1984, 7). In addition, irrigation works were restored, and the best agricultural practices—including the use of improved strains of rice and the cultivation of sweet potatoes, peanuts, tomatoes, and other American crops—continued to spread, boosting output. Thus the early Qing was a time of increasing real incomes and vast commercial expansion. Contemporary gazetteers proclaimed an era of unprecedented prosperity.

OTTOMAN REVIVAL UNDER THE KÖPRÜLÜ

The Ottoman Empire had the advantage of controlling, in addition to overpopulated Turkey, the less burdened European territories of the Balkans and the Hungarian plain. Had the empire been confined to Asia

Minor, it most likely would have collapsed, as did the Ming in the seventeenth century. But the Ottomans, under the Köprülü dynasty of grand viziers, were able to raise armies from their Balkan territories to subdue Anatolia. These European territories, though also experiencing substantial population growth, evidently did not experience the same pressure of population outgrowing the supply of land. In the early seventeenth century, grain prices were lower in the Balkans than in Anatolia, there are fewer reports of landlessness and disorder, *çiftliks* (large de facto private estates) seem to have been less common than in Anatolia, tax receipts were higher, and some of the largest and richest *timars* were located in this region (McGowan 1981, 76, 113; Moutafchieva 1988, 32; Itzkowitz 1972, 44; Inalcik 1972, 353; 1978, 84). Thus the Köprülü had the resources needed to carry out an attack on corruption, discipline the janissaries, and restore order to the Ottoman territories.

The Köprülü were also aided by a return to ecological balance. Large areas of Anatolia had been depopulated by the *celali* uprisings (Inalcik 1978, 88); these were open for resettlement once order had been restored. In addition, the rapid population growth of the sixteenth century had ended. Issawi (1974, 107) estimates that the Ottoman population, which had risen from perhaps 12 million in 1520–1535 to 20 million by 1600, did not much exceed that level for another two centuries. Even in 1830, Istanbul's 600,000 inhabitants fell short of the previous peak in the seventeenth century (Issawi 1980, 17). There was an apparent decline in population after the early seventeenth century, perhaps in part owing to a return of the plague, followed by stagnation and revival only in the eighteenth century (Owen 1977, 146; McGowan 1981, 85, 113; Sugar 1977, 221–222). Not until the end of the eighteenth century, then, did population again attain the levels reached in 1600.

And with the cessation of rapid population growth, a measure of social stability seems to have returned as well. Zilfi (1983) notes that the religious hierarchy became far more stable, with fathers regularly followed by sons: a "new corporate stability" in the late seventeenth and eighteenth centuries thus replaced the "contest mobility" of the sixteenth century.

Under the Köprülü viziers from 1656 to 1700, and under the vigorous sultan Ahmet III (r. 1703–1730), social and fiscal order recovered (Shaw 1976, 202–211, 228–229). The power of the *ayans* (local notables) was curbed as villages were given communal responsibility for tax payments instead of being leased to tax farmers (Inalcik 1973a). Cooperation between local notables and the central authority replaced contention. A more stable elite, accompanied by and in part due to more stable prices, restored Ottoman military power to nearly the levels of the sixteenth century. In 1669, the Ottomans captured Crete. In 1683, the Turkish army was again besieging Vienna. Despite its setbacks in the Treaty of Karlowitz in 1699, "for almost fifty years in the eighteenth century the state enjoyed peace and prosperity and was able to regain some of the territories lost after the debacle of Vienna in 1683" (Karpat 1974b, 90). In 1711, the Turks administered a crushing defeat to Peter the Great on the river Pruth.

Although the years following the death of Suleyman the Magnificent (d. 1566) were ones of decay, and the early seventeenth century a period of great disorder, it would be a mistake to conclude that the entire span of over three-and-a-half centuries from the 1560s to the 1920s was a continuous slide into collapse. The Ottomans were indeed surpassed in economic and military might by the European states; but this was a *relative* rather than absolute decline, due more to the progress of northwest Europe than to continuous Ottoman dissolution. In the late seventeenth and early eighteenth centuries the Ottomans were once more a powerful foe of Europe, and they restored a measure of stability and prosperity at home.

We thus can speak of an "ecological cycle" underlying the instability, then recovery and return to greater stability, in both the Ottoman Empire and China from the sixteenth to the early eighteenth centuries. As we have seen, the seventeenth-century crises were a consequence of a growing imbalance between population and agricultural output. These ecological causes of the crises were largely self-correcting. The enormous destruction brought by the rebel armies—owing to epidemics and famine as much as to direct military action—depopulated entire regions, thus restoring the balance between population and land. And as in Europe, higher mortality in the late seventeenth and early eighteenth centuries meant that population growth remained slow. This slow growth gave these societies an opportunity to raise real incomes, and the states, reconstructed after the crisis, an opportunity to reassess taxation and improve relations with a now more stable elite.

From the mid-eighteenth century onward, however, the Ottoman and Chinese empires began to repeat the patterns of 1550–1660, resuming demographic growth, fiscal and economic decline, and social conflicts, all eventually leading again to civil wars.

RENEWED ECOLOGICAL PRESSURE AND REVOLTS

WHITE LOTUS AND TAIPING: REVOLTS IN QING CHINA

Nineteenth-century China presents the familiar pattern of demographic growth, inflation, elite competition, and popular uprisings conjoined to create a state crisis. Indeed, of all the cases of state breakdown in the early modern world, the crisis of the Qing regime in the late eighteenth to mid-nineteenth centuries is most often described by specialists as a case of state breakdown produced by population pressures on rigid institutions. For example, Susan Mann Jones and Philip Kuhn (1978, 110), in the *Cambridge History of China*, describe the fundamental causes of the late Qing rebellions as "an expanding population, without . . . the new kinds of economic and political growth whereby that population might be absorbed."

As already noted, the early Qing was a period of prosperity, in which demographic recovery was accompanied by increases in cultivated acreage and output. However, "diminishing returns were beginning to be felt by the end of the eighteenth century" (Jones and Kuhn 1978, 109). By 1850, China's population appears to have increased to nearly 400 million inhabitants, half again as many as in 1770 (Skinner 1987). But cultivated acreage had increased by only a quarter. Thus by 1850, the ratio of cultivated land to population, which had grown for over a century, had reversed trend and sunk even lower than it had been in the early seventeenth century (G. Wang 1984, 7; Perkins 1969, 16). In 1856 one Chinese observer, Wang Shiduo, was moved to make the observation cited at the head of this chapter: "The harm of overpopulation is that people are forced to plant cereals on mountain tops and to reclaim sandbanks and islets. . . . All the ancient forestry of Szechwan has been cut down and the virgin timber land of the aboriginal regions turned into farmland. Yet there is not enough for everybody. This proves that the resources of Heaven and Earth are exhausted" (cited in Overbeek 1974, 197).

It is no surprise that prices followed the same pattern as population movements. From the mid-seventeenth century to the early eighteenth century, rice prices first fell sharply and then slowly recovered. But the upward movement of prices accelerated dramatically after the mid-eighteenth century and rose sharply into the early nineteenth century. In the 1830s the price rise slowed as the purchase of opium apparently soaked up increasing amounts of Chinese spending. But for most of the century

after 1750, China experienced inflation unmatched since the early seventeenth century (Yeh-chien Wang 1973).

The combination of population expansion, commercial expansion,
and inflation affected the political and social structure much as it had
two centuries earlier. Strains on government finance mounted, the educational system became overburdened, elite competition increased, and
the populace struggled with land shortages.

The early Qing emperors, during the struggle with Ming loyalists,
overturned many of the tax privileges that officials and former officials
had used to shelter land. There was thus a vast expansion of the tax
rolls, and the government kept a far closer watch on remittances than
was possible under the decaying administration of the late Ming (Zelin
1984). As a result, the early eighteenth century was "a period of surplus
revenues for the Qing state, [of] bulging treasuries and a fat privy purse"
(Naquin and Rawski 1987, 218). The land taxes owed to the central
treasury were even fixed "in perpetuity" by the Kangxi emperor in
1713, a move that reflected the feelings of prosperity (Rowe 1985, 266).
Yet this move had two ill effects: first, taxes did not rise with the inflation
that set in later in the eighteenth century; second, taxes owed to the
central government did not rise with the increase in cultivated land and
population. Nor did the government turn to indirect taxes, despite the
vast expansion of commerce; in the 1750s, over 73 percent of tax revenues still came from land taxes, only 7 percent from customs duties, and
20 percent from the salt tax and miscellaneous revenues (Feuerwerker
1976, 91). As Naquin and Rawski (1987, 22) point out, "the state barely
began to tap the tax potential of the growing commerce, as it failed to
tax the expanding agricultural base." While the revenues owed to the
central government therefore lagged, local officials began to exact increasingly higher payments from local taxpayers to defray provincial and
district-level costs, including support for themselves and their retainers.
Some of this revenue enhancement was officially recognized and supported by the imperial government. But by the early nineteenth century,
there were "widespread shortages in official treasuries at all levels"
(Jones and Kuhn 1978, 128).

Lack of revenues brought declining efficiency in the administration
and the military. "The tasks of government began to outstrip the staff
and the budget, and, while officials turned to informal methods of obtaining funds, local elites took over more and more government functions" (Naquin and Rawski 1987, 11). Despite the doubling of popu-

lation, the number of official staff positions in the imperial bureaucracy remained the same. Thus by the later eighteenth century, "overworked officials [gave in.] Magistrates no longer oversaw local families
in managing irrigation, dispute mediation, philanthropy, tax collection, schools, granaries, and militias, as they had in the early Qing, but
yielded the initiative and responsibility to these elites. . . . This shift to
private management, already visible at the end of the eighteenth century,
gained rapid momentum in the nineteenth" (Naquin and Rawski 1987,
229).

   This less professional management was faced with an increasingly
difficult situation. As population grew and farming demands rose, irrigation systems were more beset, and silting and dike failure increased.
Demands for justice multiplied among peasants competing for land, and
between peasants and landlords as each group sought gains from rising
prices. Increasing numbers of elite aspirants fought for minor positions
in district offices and earned positions of influence and corruption as
mediators between overworked official appointees and local notables.
As P. Kuhn (1970, 51) remarks, the problem "was not simply that local
government was growing corrupt and decrepit. Rather, traditional
mechanisms of civil and military control were incapable of dealing with
a huge rural population in which traditional social relationships were
rent by an increasingly desperate economic competition."

   Military efficiency faltered as well, for the Manchu banner forces
had been settled on northern lands and guaranteed fixed incomes but
prohibited from pursuing other careers. Their fixed incomes were
sharply eroded by inflation. As a result, "the great majority became poor,
indebted, and unemployed; prices rose faster than stipends, and many
abandoned their land for the city" (Naquin and Rawski 1987, 141).
Imperial efforts to keep the bannermen ready were unavailing.

   Increased turnover and displacement among the recruits to the official bureaucracy exacerbated the administrative disarray. In the early
eighteenth century, as Ho (1962, 112–114) and Eberhard (1962, 29)
report, social mobility was apparently low, with very few obscure families receiving advanced degrees. But "because the eighteenth century
brought more opportunities to acquire wealth, the size of the elite,
broadly construed to include literati, merchants, and rich landlords, no
doubt grew in absolute terms and as a percentage of the total population." As a result, "the nouveaux riches and upwardly mobile . . . came
to dominate urban culture in the eighteenth century" (Naquin and
Rawski 1987, 124–125).

But this expanded pool of aspirants to elite positions could not be absorbed by the existing mechanisms of elite recruitment. Although official academies expanded to take more students, neither the examination system nor the formal bureaucracy grew apace. In the course of the eighteenth century, though the population roughly doubled, the number of final (*jinshi*) degrees awarded rose by only 33 percent, while the number of county-level posts increased only 13 percent. Thus, even though the number of degree holders shrank relative to the population, the number of offices available still did not keep pace with the number of qualified degree holders. Both the time and difficulty required to obtain a degree and, once obtained, to secure an official post increased (Naquin and Rawski 1987, 124). As a result, "political life in this era was characterized by fierce competition for advancement and security on all levels of public administration. That this competition should frequently take extra-legal form was probably ensured by the fact that formal mechanisms for mobility lagged behind the growth of population." The expansion of elite aspirants and of official schools meant "an overproduction of literate men in relation to the capacity of the economic and political systems to absorb and reward them" (Jones and Kuhn 1978, 110).

This familiar pattern resulted in downward mobility, displacement, and a drift toward radicalism among the elite. Naquin and Rawski (1987, 126, 155) rightly observe that "given the demographic reality . . . downward mobility was not only a fear but a patent social fact. . . . As competition for degrees and posts became increasingly fierce, dissidence and alienation from orthodox literati values came to be more and more frequently expressed by members of the scholar class. . . . Themes that had been sounded in the seventeenth century were revived." Nor was elite radicalism merely rhetorical. In the tax resistance movements of the 1840s and 1850s, prompted not by central government exactions but rather by the efforts of local magistrates and their assistants to extort additional funds from localities, "leadership often came from the lower elite—sheng-yuan and chien-sheng degree holders" (Jones and Kuhn 1978, 131). Hong Xiuquan, the leader of the Taiping rebellion, was a frustrated student who failed to pass the official exams.

Such dissident elites found ready followers. By the late eighteenth century, population growth in China's core regions was straining resources (Naquin and Rawski 1987, 106; Jones and Kuhn 1978, 109). In Hunan Province, as early as 1748 gazetteers complained of rising rents, land shortages, and "the growing pressure of population on a province that was exhausting the supply of readily cultivable land" (Perdue 1987, 88). Population growth led to the clearing and settlement of formerly wooded mountainsides; the resulting erosion increased the silting of irrigation works and produced disastrous flooding. In 1788, a turning point was reached in the ecology of the central Yangzi basin. Hampered by weak administration and heavy burdens of erosion, flood control simply failed to be maintained. Floods of the Yangzi and Han rivers punctuated the next century (Naquin and Rawski 1987, 167). As Jones and Kuhn (1978, 110) remark, "probably the most desperate crowding existed in the lower Yangtze provinces, soon to become the battleground" of the Taiping rebellion.

Misery in China's heartland led to massive migration to peripheral areas in the northwest, far west, and south. Such migration, however, did not provide an outlet that relieved social pressure; instead it added yet another set of tensions to China's already difficult situation. For the peripheral areas were of low fertility, and were already settled by various minority religious and ethnic groups. In the northwest, Rowe (1985, 252) notes that "tensions escalated as continued immigration and population growth strained the productivity of the land." In the west and the south, conflicts arose as ethnic Han Chinese competed for land with Muslims, Hakka Chinese, and other minorities. In all these peripheral areas, gentry settlement and control was relatively weak; thus, conflicts quickly produced increased banditry and violence. As a result, secret societies preaching various salvation religions and mobilizing their followers for mutual support drew increasing numbers of adherents. In the northwest highlands of Hubei, the White Lotus sect preached a variant of Buddhism; in the south, the Taiping movement, originated by Hakka Chinese, preached a variant of Christianity. Both movements became foci for rebellion.

In the late eighteenth and early nineteenth centuries, the Qing government moved to quell a number of revolts by ethnic minorities, and to put down the mounting power of heretical secret societies: there were actions against the Miao and Yao peoples in Hunan and Sichuan, against Muslims in southwest China and Turkestan, and against various secret societies in Guangdong, Hunan, Henan, Zhili, and Shandong. The largest of these was the White Lotus Rebellion, which lasted from 1796 to 1804 and included perhaps as many as three hundred thousand rebels (Feuerwerker 1975, 5–6).

These military actions exhausted the imperial treasury. It was not only that the revolts were extensive; enormous sums were also wasted because of corruption in the imperial administration. Although the rebels of the early nineteenth century were crushed, banditry and poverty continued to grow worse, while the central government continued to weaken owing to elite factional divisions and corruption. By the mid-nineteenth century, when the Qing moved to suppress the rapidly growing Taiping secret society, considerable numbers of peasants and elites were ready to abandon the weakening dynasty.

Victorious in their initial confrontation with imperial troops in 1850, the Taiping quickly gained adherents and spread throughout the Yangzi heartland. Gathering millions of peasants and thousands of elite supporters, the Taiping armies pushed the imperial forces back into northern China and established their own territory, centered on the old imperial capital of Nanjing. Had the Taiping merely attacked the "mandate of heaven" of the Qing and replaced the now weakened dynasty with a new one, it seems likely the Qing would have ended in the mid-nineteenth century (Michael and Chang 1966, 1:7).

What saved the dynasty was the eccentric leadership of the Taiping, for Hong had been heavily influenced by Christianity and had produced an anti-Confucian ideology that was also antilandlord. "In terms of its stated goals, the Taiping movement was indeed a profound social revolution" (P. Kuhn 1978, 279). This revolutionary program frightened off many potential gentry supporters. Hence, even though the official Qing forces were too weak to defend the dynasty, local notables organized regional militias to fight the Taiping. These orthodox, conservative militias spread throughout China, first nudging back the Taiping and then, finally, defeating it and the other early nineteenth-century rebellions. The dynasty thus was saved. But it had lost its initiative and remained dependent on local gentry militias. Since literally tens of millions perished in the Taiping wars, there was then a brief respite of recovery from the mid-nineteenth century population pressures. But when population and prices rocketed upward again toward the end of the century, thus increasing social conflicts throughout China, the stage was set for the collapse of the imperial government and the struggle among different warlord groups for control of China.

REVOLTS IN THE OTTOMAN EMPIRE

Kemal Karpat is preparing a definitive study of the revolts against Ottoman rule in the early nineteenth century, a work that emphasizes the key role of demographic change. In a preliminary outline of that work,

Karpat (1983, 386) notes that "the social, and to a considerable extent the political, history of the Ottoman state in the 19th century, including its disintegration and the accompanying rise of a series of autonomous or independent national states in the Balkans, was the consequence of population movements. One is struck . . . by the intimate relationship between the demographic factor and the socio-political changes in most of the Ottoman territories in the 19th century."

Without trying to anticipate the results of Karpat's forthcoming study, I wish to observe here that the Ottoman Empire also experienced the wave of state crises that swept the early modern world in the late eighteenth and early nineteenth centuries, just as it had experienced the prior wave two centuries before. The situation of the Ottoman Empire in the nineteenth century was similar to that of Hapsburg Spain in the seventeenth century: even though population in the core territory—in this case, Turkey—was moderate, rapid population growth in the periphery, in particular in the Balkans and the Arab territories, created imbalances in regional demands and state capacities, producing numerous regional revolts.

In the eighteenth and early nineteenth centuries, rapid population growth in the Balkans created new recruits for provincial rebellions and pushed prices upward, destabilizing both elite and imperial finances. The population of the province of Wallachia (in modern Romania), which had peaked at 300,000 inhabitants in 1560 before falling in the late sixteenth century, reached 700,000 by 1810, and 1 million by 1822 (Chirot 1976, 41, 83). The population of Greece more than doubled in the hundred years preceding 1821 (Spiridonakis 1977, 115–117). As a result, although prices had risen relatively slowly in much of the eighteenth century, they increased sharply from 1780 on. From 1800 to the 1840s, the price of wheat bread quadrupled, while that of rice tripled (Issawi 1980, 322–323, 337). This was true not only in Istanbul and the main Balkan capitals but also in Egypt. Egypt had experienced a "golden age" from 1740 to 1780, when food supplies were ample and society was at peace. This stability was largely due to a 25 percent population decline over the eighteenth century. But Egypt's population then grew from 3.9 million in 1800 to 5.5 million in 1860. The result was a "generalized economic crisis" marked by skyrocketing prices, administrative disarray, and famine (Raymond 1981, 697–699; Issawi 1982, 94). Only Anatolia itself grew more slowly, its population remaining virtually unchanged in the first third of the nineteenth century (Issawi 1982, 94).

By the last decade of the eighteenth century, inflation had set the local notables against the sultan's demands for more revenues. Thus, "the reign of Selim III (1789–1807) consisted of an incessant struggle against the *ayans* of Anatolia and the Balkans" (Karpat 1974b, 92). Selim's struggle helped to precipitate rebellion in Serbia (1803–1806) and resulted in his ouster by the janissaries (Karpat 1974b, 94). His successor, Mustafa IV, met the same fate the following year (Shaw 1976, 273–277).

Indeed, the entire early nineteenth century was a period of revolts and disorders, including those of Serbia, again, in 1815–1817, Romania and Greece in 1821, and Romania in 1848. In the 1830s the governor of Egypt, Muhammad Ali, revolted and seized control of Egypt and the near eastern territories as far north as Syria. Ali threatened to take his revolt to the sultanate itself, until, bowing to European pressure, he settled for virtually autonomous rule in Egypt under Ottoman suzerainty (Heyd 1970; Holt 1970).

The Ottomans were preserved in large measure through European diplomacy. Conceding Greek independence and Egyptian autonomy under informal European protectorates, the Ottomans in return received support for internal reforms. The leading *ayans* were destroyed in 1815, the janissaries abolished in 1826, the *vakıfs* (Islamic foundations) absorbed into the state structure, and the *tımar* system officially abolished in 1831. All of these reforms, and the development of a modern army and bureaucracy on European lines, helped to sustain Ottoman rule in Anatolia and the Balkans for another eight decades. But by the early nineteenth century, the Ottoman Empire had returned to the weakness of the early seventeenth century.

These very brief and schematic accounts of Ottoman and Chinese difficulties in the nineteenth century are only suggestive. They merely point out that a case can be, and often has been, made by scholars that the demographic/structural model provides a basis for understanding Asia's nineteenth-century state crises. As in Europe, therefore, the nineteenth-century crises appear to have roots similar to those of the seventeenth century.

But there is one case that is far more controversial, especially in terms of a demographic model of state crisis. The Meiji Restoration in 1868 in Japan has been the subject of vigorous debate. Was it a "revolution"? Did it have long-term causes? Was Japan becoming "better off" or "worse off" as the Tokugawa shogunate approached its end? In short, the same questions we have seen so often in regard to other state crises arise again in regard to Japan. But because of Japan's outstanding economic progress, scholars today are especially moved to ask how the Meiji Restoration differed from state crises in other Asian states where later economic and political development was much less rapid.

Our answers to these questions are straightforward. Though not quite a full social revolution, the Meiji Restoration was certainly a case of state breakdown. Like our other cases, Japan's Meiji Restoration did have long-term causes, which are explicable in terms of the demographic/ structural model, although with an interesting twist. Also like our other cases, asking whether "Japan" was becoming better or worse off is a poor approach; what mattered was that some elites were getting richer, while other elites, the central government, and many peasants and workers were becoming poorer. And the reason Japan after Meiji was able to accelerate its economic development has less to do with the *causes* of the Tokugawa crisis than with the manner in which the Meiji leaders responded to that crisis and interpreted Japan's future needs.

THE CAUSES OF STATE BREAKDOWN IN TOKUGAWA JAPAN

The Tokugawa regime arose in the early seventeenth century in the wake of a series of wars that united Japan under the warlord Tokugawa Ieyasu. In the preceding decades Japan had been ruled by a congeries of autonomous regional lords who nominally owed allegiance to the ancient imperial family in Kyoto. In fact, the emperor had only prestige, not power. He thus readily recognized the victorious Tokugawa as shogun, or lord general, of Japan. Tokugawa established his capital at Edo (modern Tokyo), from which he directly ruled the domains of his clan. These domains, which covered about one-quarter of Japan and included the richest agricultural lands, were administered by the shogun's own administration, the *bakufu*. The remainder of Japan was divided into semiautonomous regions, called *han*, which were ruled by other clans, some closely tied to the Tokugawa family, others more independent. Each *han* had its own administration, including taxation and commercial policy, run by the *han* lord, or daimyo. The daimyo were subject to varying degrees of control by the shogun. They could be disciplined by having the size of their *han* reduced, or by being deposed in favor of a successor. Daimyo were also required to make costly annual pilgrimages to Edo to attend the shogun's court and to leave family members as "hostages" in the capital. But they were permitted to run their domestic and *han* affairs as they saw fit, provided only that they maintained order and made contributions to the *bakufu* revenues when called upon.

The shogun and daimyo relied on a hereditary warrior elite—the samurai—to defend and administer their lands. Samurai were sharply distinguished from commoners. The latter had virtually no legal rights, were prohibited from carrying weapons, and—except for those peasants who acted as village headmen—were barred from any positions of authority. The vast majority of commoners were peasants who paid taxes in rice. These rice assessments were based on surveys taken at the beginning of the Tokugawa period, and were paid either to the daimyo who controlled the land or directly to the shogun. Samurai were then supported by rice stipends assigned to them by their masters.

The collapse of the Tokugawa shogunate in the 1860s in many ways paralleled the collapse of the English monarchy in the 1640s. The Tokugawa government, already in grave financial difficulties from the beginning of the nineteenth century, suffered virtual bankruptcy in the 1860s. The incursions of Western powers were merely occasions that revealed, not caused, the shogunate's weakness. In this sense, the Western incursions were much like the Scottish rebellion against England in 1638. And, as in England in the 1640s, many elite leaders responded to the government's weakness not by rallying to its support but rather by demanding change and by raising their own militias to oppose the central authority. In particular, the leaders of Satsuma and Choshu, two western *han*, developed modern armies that fought a brief and victorious civil war against the forces of the shogun. Although the Meiji Restoration is sometimes described as an elite movement or a "revolution from above" (Trimberger 1978), we should not misconstrue the scale of popular involvement. Tens of thousands of Japanese were enlisted in the armies of the shogun and of the rebel *han*, much as in the English civil wars. It is true that, as in England, the autonomous lower-class movements were not strong enough to force the rebel elite to adopt policies that favored workers or peasants. However, again as in England, cultivator and urban revolts were sufficient to alarm the elite, undermine confidence in the shogunate, and reinforce the belief that radical change was necessary to improve society.

After their victory, the leaders of the revolt dismantled the *bakufu* and *han* political structures, abolishing the shogunate and pensioning off the daimyo. The legal distinctions between samurai and commoners

were abolished. The new regime established a centralized Japanese government and strove to develop a modern industrialized economy. Yet
oddly, this institutional modernization was not justified in terms of the
triumph of modern constitutional and democratic ideas over traditional
rule. Instead, the leaders of the revolt affirmed their loyalty to the ancient authority of the imperial family, and justified their actions as having effected the "restoration" of the reigning Meiji emperor to power.
Indeed, the constitution finally adopted in 1889 "legalized [the em-
peror] as an absolute, sacred monarch, above the government and yet
the very embodiment of the state. The people of Japan were his subjects,
admonished to serve him loyally" (J. W. Hall 1970, 297). The destruction of the shogunate thus was undertaken in the name of a "return to
the past," under the sanction of an ancient, and supremely Japanese,
symbol (J. W. Hall 1970, 265). In practice, however, the emperor remained more a symbol than a ruler. The leaders of the revolt formed an
authoritarian oligarchy that, drawing on the sanctity of the emperor to
build strong nationalist support, ruled Japan and sponsored the development of a modern industrial and military complex. Success in wars
against China (1895) and Russia (1905) established post-Meiji Japan as
a Pacific power as it entered the twentieth century.

I shall return in chapter 5 to the paradoxical tension between the
dynamic institutional modernization brought by the Meiji Restoration,
on the one hand, and its conservative, traditional ideology, on the other.
At this point, however, let us concentrate on what caused the Tokugawa
state breakdown.

As in our previous cases, we can unravel this complex problem by
addressing three more basic questions: (1) What caused the Tokugawa's
financial failure? (2) What were the sources of elite discontent and rebellion? And (3) what created the potential for mass mobilization, both
as part of the rebel armies and as autonomous popular unrest? As before,
answers to these questions are best found by beginning with the demographic and economic trends of Tokugawa Japan.

THE EXCEPTION THAT PROVES THE RULE: DEMOGRAPHIC
STABILITY AND THE DEMOGRAPHIC/STRUCTURAL MODEL
OF STATE CRISIS

On first examination, the Meiji Restoration offers a clear refutation of
the demographic/structural model of state crisis. In Japan, population
was *stable* from 1721 to 1846 and increased only in the twenty years

preceding the Tokugawa crisis. Hanley and Yamamura (1977, 333) suggest that the net growth of Japan's population from 1721 to 1846 was no more than 3 percent, while the official shogunal figures show an increase of less than .5 percent (Hayami 1986a, 287). I have argued that in the seventeenth- and nineteenth-century crises in Europe, China, and the Ottoman Empire it took several generations of population growth, boosting population by 35 to 100 percent and producing pressure on food supplies and inflation, to undermine state finances and create elite dissension. How could these trends occur in a demographically *stable* setting?

In our other cases, we noted that governments had become largely dependent on fixed cash taxes on land. When prices rose, real tax revenues lagged. Similarly, many elites—such as European landlords who had let their land at fixed rents, Ottoman *timar* holders, and Chinese bannermen—depended on fixed cash revenues that also failed to respond to inflation, and hence suffered falling real incomes. The mechanism behind these trends was that as population growth ran ahead of economic output, particularly grain production, prices rose. Inflation then eroded the value of fixed cash incomes.

Tokugawa Japan had a rather different set of fiscal institutions. Taxes were collected primarily in grain, rather than in money. Taxes were set in terms of fixed volumes of rice (measured in *koku*) to be collected from each region, and the stipends of daimyo and samurai retainers were similarly set in fixed rice quantities. For example, a domain or *han* would be defined as a ten-thousand-*koku han* or a fifty-thousand-*koku han*, depending on its level of income. This fiscal system protected the elite and the *bakufu* from any increase in the relative price of rice. Indeed, elites could benefit if, as in our other cases, grain prices rose in relation to the prices of other goods and services.

But in Japan, the economic trends were also different than in our other cases. In Japan overall, population remained *stable* for more than a century after 1721, while grain production increased. As a result, the price of rice *fell* relative to the price of all other goods, and of labor. Since the *bakufu*, daimyo, and samurai all had to convert their rice stipends into clothing, construction, weapons, gifts, and other goods and services, and could only borrow money on the security of their rice stipends, they too faced *falling* real income and rising real interest rates. A reverse in *both* fiscal institutions *and* demographic and economic trends meant that the Japanese state and the elite found themselves in the same fix as their counterparts on the Eurasian mainland.

The combination of demographic trends and *political and economic structures* again provides the key to understanding the dynamics of state and elite conditions. Not population trends alone, but the manner in which demographic trends affected fiscal and social institutions, underlay social pressures. Thus Tokugawa Japan, with its opposite twists in both demography *and* structures, does not refute the model. Instead it is a demographic exception that reinforces the value of paying close attention to the *interaction* of demography and institutions.

We must also observe that the demographic exception is not as great as it first appears. Although Japan's total population growth was virtually nil from 1721 to 1846, this overall trend conceals considerable regional differences. The population of the shogun's own domains actually fell during this period, while the population of the *han* of Satsuma, Choshu, Tosa, and Hizen increased by 30 percent. Satsuma and Choshu grew the most rapidly, the former adding to its population by 62 percent (Hayami 1986a, 291; Hanley and Yamamura 1977, 333). These were precisely the *han* that led the successful rebellions against the Tokugawa; thus Japan does in some respects conform to the pattern we saw in seventeenth-century Spain and in the nineteenth-century Ottoman Empire, where rapidly growing peripheral territories rebelled against demographically and politically stable, but financially weakened, core regimes. Moreover, population did resume rapid growth from the 1830s. Thus the last decades of the Tokugawa were marked by rising prices and increasing pressure on land and wages.

Still, the fiscal problems of the Tokugawa state must be differently explained. In seventeenth-century Spain and the nineteenth-century Ottoman Empire, the central government had to hire and supply troops while prices were sharply rising. The Tokugawa *bakufu* suffered its fiscal crisis at the end of a century in which rice prices had generally fallen. Let us therefore look more closely at how demographic and economic trends undermined Tokugawa finances.

FINANCIAL DECAY IN THE BAKUFU

For the first hundred years following Tokugawa unification in 1600, peace and recovery from the civil wars resulted in considerable population growth, which put some pressure on rice production and prices. In this period, taxes in rice were fixed, and the shogun, daimyo, and their samurai retainers reaped the rewards of a growing economy in which they controlled the vital resource. Samurai, settled in the castle towns that served as the headquarters of the various *han*, became separated into a privileged caste distinct from commoners. The latter served as peasant cultivators or as merchants who supplied the castle towns and the major cities of Edo, Kyoto, and Osaka. Kept in a subservient position, merchants had the tasks of storing the rice, which was collected by the shogun and daimyo and paid to samurai retainers, and exchanging it for more varied foodstuffs and manufactured products. Silks and cottons, lacquerware and stoneware, processed foods and fine furnishings, as well as cash to pay the workers in the cities and rural castle towns all passed through the merchants' hands. Osaka, the merchants' city, became the central storehouse of the realm, while Edo became the political capital, and Kyoto, the cultural center. As urban merchant activity spread, Edo developed its own extensive merchant quarters and culture.

The first century of Tokugawa rule thus culminated in the prosperous Genroku period (1688–1704), in which shogunal dominance and samurai loyalty and efficiency were supported by a subservient but increasingly prosperous merchant class. But this political and social order did not survive the changing ecological conditions that followed.

Japan's population appears to have stabilized after 1720 as a result of later marriage and rising rates of nonmarriage among younger sons, abortion, and infanticide (Hanley and Yamamura 1977, 265–266; Skinner 1988; T. Smith 1977, 147). These were not acts of desperation, but simply means of increasing family fortunes. Thomas Smith (1977, 147) notes that for the village of Nakahara, as described in the Tokugawa registers, "both mortality and fertility . . . were low to moderate. What is surprising is that the practice [of infanticide] does not appear to have been primarily a response to poverty. . . . It gives the impression of a kind of family planning." Skinner's (1988) study of village populations in this period suggests that the rich practiced infanticide more often than the poor, having both a greater desire to regulate family fortunes and the resources to do without family labor.

The domestic peace brought by Tokugawa's unification increased the ease of commerce, despite the lack of innovations in transport technology (Sheldon 1958, 15). The spread of improved rice varieties, and later, the regional specialization of handicrafts, raised productivity considerably. Yasuba (1986, 218) reports that in the core regions of Japan rice output rose by 50 percent from 1727 to the early nineteenth century. And although productivity then leveled off after 1820, output in the peripheral areas continued to rise (Yasuba 1986, 218; L. Johnson 1983, 130–144). There were intermittent periods of harvest failure and famine in Tokugawa Japan, for the island nation was vulnerable to typhoons and earthquakes, and these created havoc in particular localities. But for the most part, stable population and rising rice output produced what was, by early modern standards, a prosperous nation (Hanley 1983; Yasuba 1986).

> This prosperity, however, did not flow to the shogun and samurai. So long as the urban population was increasing fairly rapidly, as had been the case during the seventeenth century, the rice price also tended to rise. But when the population boom ended early in the first quarter of the eighteenth century, a situation emerged wherein the rice price began a long, slow, descent while prices for all other commodities continued to rise. The daimyo and their retainer bands were thus caught in a vicious cycle. They strove to market more rice every year in Osaka and Edo—only to see its price fall, thereby driving them deeper into debt to merchants.
>
> (Bix 1986, 26–27)

Measured in silver, rice prices fell by over 25 percent merely from the last years of the seventeenth century to the early 1730s (Cartier 1981, 466). Thereafter, the shogun frequently recoined money, thus forcing merchants to pay more cash for rice; but the merchants simply passed the price rise through to their other products. Hence, although nominal prices rose almost tenfold over the course of the Tokugawa period, most of this increase was due to currency depreciation. The relative price of rice continued to fall (Sheldon 1958, 80; T. Smith 1973, 155; Takekoshi 1930, 2:297).

The early Tokugawa shoguns had enjoyed generous incomes. But as with the English gentry and Chinese officials, Japanese village headmen and daimyo conspired to freeze tax assessments so that the *bakufu*'s income remained roughly constant: the output and tax revenues from the shogun's domains were reported as the same in 1716–1725, 1776–1785, and 1841 and totaled about 1.4 million *koku* of rice (Takekoshi 1930, 2:306). Totman (1980, 352) argues that the wealth of Japan was sufficient to have allowed the shogun to meet military expenses in the 1860s, but the daimyo refused to cooperate with the shogun in his attempts to ascertain their incomes and levy taxes on their fiefs and stipends. Land that was reclaimed from waste, or farmed more intensively than before, or more productive—that is, by 1860, nearly all the land in Japan—was still taxed at the rates set in the seventeenth century. In addition, although agriculture had diversified to grow industrial crops such as plants for dyes and mulberry trees for silkworm production, these crops were rarely taxed at all (Vlastos 1986, 102). Again, inflexible taxation led to revenue shortfalls. By the late eighteenth century, virtually all of the daimyo, as well as the shogun, were heavily in debt to merchants, who had profited from the shift in relative prices favoring manufactures. From the 1780s, forced loans levied from merchants had become a key part of both *bakufu* and *han* finances (Sheldon 1958, 118–119; L. Johnson 1983, 110).

Through the eighteenth century, while shogunal finances were not as prosperous as in the seventeenth century when surpluses had been the rule, deficits were only intermittent, and income and expenses were roughly in balance. Loans from merchants and occasional recoinages solved short-term deficiencies. But by the nineteenth century the further decline in the value of rice revenues was causing annual shortfalls. Expenditures rose to several times the regular annual revenues (Honjo 1965, 270–275). More frequent and more massive recoinages became the key to the shogun's budget. But such massive currency depreciation provided no new real resources to meet the growing burdens of foreign defense.

The *bakufu* did attempt to rectify its finances by collecting more of its revenues in cash. But by the 1830s, the level of taxation had been so eroded by the past century of rice depreciation that changing a portion of rice levies to cash taxes at current prices did not solve the problem, for these measures did not make up for the past decline in the value of tax income. Worse yet, the commutations to cash occurred just as renewed population growth was beginning to raise prices and hence undermine cash taxation. Indeed, the tax commutations often were set by merchants at "past parity" rates that did not reflect current rising prices (Hanley and Yamamura 1977, 118–119). Thus fiscal stress grew, despite attempted reforms.

Takekoshi (1930, 2:349) remarks that "the Tokugawa shogunate lost its real strength in the eras of Bunkwa and Tempo [1804–1844], when it was in such financial distress." The attempted Bunkyu reforms, especially military reorganization, were crippled by "bakufu fiscal inadequacy" (Totman 1980, 30). Though unable to solve the financial problems, *bakufu* leaders did attempt to extort additional funds from daimyo; but they succeeded chiefly in turning many of the daimyo against the shogunate. Leaders of the western *han* of Choshu and Satsuma, in particular, turned to reforms to revive their own finances and weaponry, shifting the balance of power in Japan.

Takekoshi (1930, 2:349) comments that the shogunate "only nominally existed in 1868. Hence the battles of Fushimi and Toba might be said to have been the burial ceremony of the Shogunate corpse." Yet this nominal existence reflected not merely the shogun's hollow finances, but also the abandonment of the shogun by many of the elite, and the spread of disorders in the shogun's own domain.

ELITE MOBILITY AND DISSENSION

The samurai had begun as a military order akin to European knights, but they lost much of their essential purpose under the "pax Tokugawa." High-ranking samurai instead served the shogun and the daimyo as civil servants and administrators; low-ranking samurai served as teachers, priests, and household staff.

During the eighteenth century, the samurai, who were almost always paid by fixed rice stipends, saw the purchasing power of their incomes eroding. The merchants who profited from making loans and exchanging rice for manufactures soon dominated their nominal superiors in wealth. As Hayami (1986b, 10) notes, "no warrior in Tokugawa Japan acquired enormous wealth"—unless he gave up samurai status to become a merchant, a not infrequent practice. But those who remained samurai saw their positions steadily deteriorating. "Institutionally and individually the samurai class became the clients of commoners who, not infrequently, made humiliating demands before agreeing to refinance old loans" (Vlastos 1986, 166).

The financial distress of the samurai, and the rising fortune of the merchants, created a situation in which "during the first half of the nineteenth century the status system and status ideology slowly began to break down" (Bix 1986, xvii). Wealthy merchants acquired samurai status by purchase or by marriage into samurai families. Poor samurai took up trades and even manual arts. As early as 1780 a contemporary commentator on an uprising in Fukuyama *han*, where poor samurai had supported peasant demands to be allowed freely to pursue rural crafts, warned: "Only when civil and military arts are both maintained is the country secure and the government able to continue. Nowadays they are both abandoned and profits are pursued. Disasters follow one another and even good people are helpless to do anything about it" (cited in Bix 1986, 115). As Vlastos (1986, 166) comments, "it is difficult to explain the radicalism of the young samurai who seized power in 1868 . . . without taking into account the impoverishment of the samurai class."

The upward and downward mobility across the line separating samurai from commoners devalued the rank of samurai. As one samurai author noted in 1816, "nothing upset him more than the leveling out of class lines and distinctions" (cited in Jansen 1988a, 63). Yet, while a considerable amount of turnover marked the lower ranks of the samurai, the higher ranks hardened. This closing of opportunities for ascent within the samurai ranks created significant displacement among ambitious samurai who aspired to higher positions.

The last decades of the Tokugawa saw a vast expansion of elementary and higher academy schooling, partly because of population expansion after 1830, and partly because wealthy merchants sought to educate their families (Rubinger 1986, 196). But the graduates of the academies had little future beyond becoming schoolmasters or attendants to daimyo grandees. A severe stratification had set in within the samurai class by the nineteenth century (Jansen 1986, 74–75). While the higher ranks monopolized high *bakufu* and *han* offices and adopted distinctive dress and life-styles, the lower ranks, although educated and trained in the samurai code, were reduced to a marginal "service intelligentsia" (Huber 1981, 187–189, 227), with incomes that were often less than those of wealthy peasants.

It was precisely this service intelligentsia of younger, low-ranking samurai who formed the core of the Meiji leadership. Although the merchants of Tokugawa Japan had grown richer, it was not a "bourgeois" force that overthrew the shogunate. The merchants tended to be conservative, and they gained from loans to the *bakufu*. Even after the Meiji Restoration, the lead in rebuilding Japanese industry was not taken by former merchants but rather by samurai who took up careers in industry (G. Allen 1962). Thus, Huber (1981, 224) has noted that the rebel leaders in Japan chiefly resembled the Puritan radicals of England and the revolutionary journalists and minor civil servants of France in 1789, 1830, and 1848.

By the mid-nineteenth century, the shogunate faced difficulties on several fronts. Foreigners were seeking access to Japanese trade. Internally, finances were precarious, the traditional status system and gradations of wealth and power were in disarray, and popular uprisings were growing more frequent. This combination of ills led some *han* leaders to look to their own resources. In Choshu and Satsuma, younger, low-ranking samurai with radical ideas succeeded in gaining the patronage of the daimyo. As Totman (1980, 462–463) has pointed out, "feelings of status incongruence, han nationalism, and ethnic awareness became not semidiscordant matters but mutually reinforcing considerations. . . . By the 1860s a large number of men could reasonably believe that dramatic action leading to destruction of the bakufu would simultaneously bring recognition to themselves, glory to their families, triumph to their colleagues, honor to their lord, and salvation to emperor and nation."

Elite impatience for change was aided by popular disorders.

DIFFICULTIES IN THE TOWNS AND COUNTRYSIDE

As we have noted, the populace of Tokugawa Japan was prosperous by early modern standards. But there was considerable variation. The vagaries of family size and adaptation to commercial farming meant that some families prospered, while others did less well. Prosperous families succeeded in obtaining privileges as village headmen, by which they could further increase their landholdings and wealth. Although this disparity created recurrent local conflicts, it was not a serious problem in times of prosperity. But by the late Tokugawa, additional demands for taxes from hard-pressed *han* and *bakufu* leaders, together with renewed population growth and falling real wages after 1830, intensified conflicts. Indeed, Vlastos (1986, 159) states that "by the late Tokugawa period the intensity of conflict within villages and between the various strata of the peasant class superseded the conflict between ruler and ruled."

Moreover, in many parts of Japan peasants seeking higher incomes had turned to handicrafts, either by migrating to castle towns or taking up rural artisanship. In Choshu, half of peasant income was obtained from employment outside of agriculture (Hayami 1986a, 294). Yet those who depended on wages did poorly in the later decades of Tokugawa rule, since real wages, which had roughly doubled from 1730 to 1770, declined steadily from 1820 to 1868 (Hanley and Yamamura 1977, 111–13) as population began rapidly to increase.

Still, it was not the very poorest regions that had the worst conflicts. The pattern of popular protest in Japan is similar to that described earlier for England and France, where the truly destitute were not the main popular actors in early modern crises. In seventeenth-century England, the most vigorous supporters of Parliament were the "middling sort"— small husbandmen, artisans, and merchants, all dependent on the market—who felt their modest positions threatened by rising rents and food prices. In France, the peasants most active in the uprisings of 1789 were not those in the poorer areas of western and central France, but those in the more urban and prosperous northeast and Midi, where peasants supplemented their farm incomes with wage labor or produced wine for the market, and thus were most vulnerable to wage and price shifts. It is unsurprising, therefore, that J. White (1989) has found that late Tokugawa popular protests were most pronounced in precisely those counties that were most urban and in which smallholding peasants supplemented their incomes with artisanal labor; for in these areas peasants were most vulnerable to fluctuations in the market, especially to rising food prices.

There has long been controversy over the role of peasant revolts in the Tokugawa decline. Vlastos (1986, 20) noted that "the frequency and intensity of peasant protests peaked at the time of the Meiji Restoration," although he adds that "for the most part peasants were observers and not actors in the ensuing revolution." Borton (1968, iii) argued that popular protests played no direct role in the crisis, but were merely "disconnected incidents in which farmers demanded improvement in their economic status or elimination of unjust officials or feudal barons." Moreover, after 1837 conflicts between large and small peasants dominated; the revolts thus involved only limited portions of the village communities and were not direct anti-tax or anti-state revolts.

All of these claims about the peasantry may be true, but as we have seen in analyzing other state crises, it is not the direct actions of the poor per se that are important in the dynamics of state breakdown. Even disconnected rural uprisings can make the state appear incompetent or irresponsible; even sporadic food riots can alarm elites and lead to calls for change. Moreover, recruitment of popular groups by elites into rebel armies is facilitated by popular grievances against a regime. All of these factors played a role in the Tokugawa demise.

In 1866, high rice prices led to rural rebellions in the *bakufu* domains, and to urban food riots in Osaka, Kyoto, and Edo (Totman 1980, 221–222). Such riots distracted *bakufu* leaders and caused allies to waver in their support of a government that could not prevent such outbreaks (Harootunian 1988, 183). Moreover, Moulder (1977, 167) sharply observes that "during the Restoration, peasants played a part in national events for the first time during the Tokugawa period. During the 1850s and 1860s, several *han* had organized militias, enrolling men from the peasant and merchant classes as well as samurai. . . . It was armies of this sort, composed of peasants as well as samurai, that defeated the bakufu forces. For instance, a Tokugawa army was defeated in battle by 60,000 armed peasants" led by the Meiji rebels.

THE FALL OF THE TOKUGAWA BAKUFU: A DEMOGRAPHIC/ STRUCTURAL ACCOUNT

Of course, many of the most interesting and distinctive features of the Meiji Restoration—the unique blend of radical and traditional ideologies of the Restoration leaders and their success in transforming Japan into a modern industrial nation—cannot be brought within the simple demographic/structural framework. However, the model does help to account for several key features of the crisis. The financial difficulties of the *bakufu* stemmed from the falling value of its rice revenues. As is typical in the case of other early modern monarchies, the relatively fixed revenue system of the *bakufu* was undermined by changes in prices brought about by the marked change in the ecological balance between population and production. Similarly, the distress of the samurai elite was brought about by the collision of fixed stipends and a long-run change in prices. When one adds that popular mass mobilization potential was exacerbated by rising population and falling real wages after 1830, and that the *bakufu* faced foreign pressures that exposed its woeful finances, it is easy to understand that some sort of state crisis was likely.

What was unique and interesting about Japan is that the *long-run* decline in regime and elite finances was not due to population growth. Instead it was due to revenues *in kind* being undercut by rising production and *stable* population.

Japan had unique fiscal institutions, for it retained a dependency on in-kind tax collections long after most other states had adopted monetary taxation. But these institutions were just as rigid as other states' cash tax systems. Hence Japan's tax system was also vulnerable to changing ecological conditions; it merely acted in a different way. For states that depended on money taxes, population stability and declining grain prices were beneficial. But for the Tokugawa regime, with its rice-based taxes and elite stipends, population stability and declining grain prices were ruinous. In either case, we find the phenomenon of relatively inflexible social and political institutions being undermined by ecological shifts, which pave the way for state crises.

Japan therefore serves as an ideal example of how the demographic/ structural model differs from crude demographic schemes. The "rule" of my model is not that population growth per se is destabilizing, but that changing population/resource balances can wreak havoc with rigid fiscal and elite structures. Japan—where a century of population stability undermined fiscal institutions that were vulnerable to increases in grain output relative to population—is indeed the exception that proves the rule.

———————

In the preceding pages we have repeatedly restricted our vision to the *origins* of state breakdown, paying very little attention to the actual struggles for power and their outcomes. I have taken this approach because the origins of early modern state breakdown can be neatly grasped in terms of a single process, involving resource imbalances and inflexible institutions, that operated across a wide range of temporal and cultural contexts. In contrast, while struggles for power and outcomes also show consistent patterns, they cannot be readily explained in terms of resource shifts.

Resource imbalances can undermine existing states and social structures, but they do not dictate what will follow. The mobilization of supporters for change, and the reconstruction of the state and society, depend on how individuals diagnose the failings of the old regime and on their vision of how the future should unfold. Resource shifts may facilitate or hinder the reconstruction of states by certain actors, or along certain lines; but in setting the direction of change, ideology and culture play a unique and critical role. In particular, to understand why state breakdowns in the West often led to radical revolutions, while similarly caused state breakdowns in Asia more often led to conservative restorations, we need to examine these cultures' divergent views on the nature of change and of time itself.

FIVE

Ideology, Cultural Frameworks, Revolutionary Struggles, and State Reconstruction

Les origines de la Révolution sont une histoire; l'histoire de la Révolution en est une autre.

[The origins of the Revolution are one story; the story of the Revolution from that point onward is quite another.]

—D. Mornet

The study of culture has recently staged a resurgence in sociology and history. Structural studies of revolution, such as Skocpol's (1979), have been criticized for their neglect of ideological and cultural factors (Himmelstein and Kimmel 1981; Sewell 1985b; Arjomand 1986). To this point, I have placed a greater emphasis on structural factors in analyzing the episodes of state breakdown in early modern England, France, Turkey, and China and have given less attention to their ideological elements. The reason for this is straightforward: I have been concerned with elucidating the *origins* of state breakdown in each of these cases. And I have argued that ideological factors play mainly a supporting role in the breakdown of Old Regimes. It is chiefly *after* the initial breakdown of the state, during the ensuing power struggles and state reconstruction, that ideology and culture take leading roles.

I could therefore have ended this book here, commenting that revolutionary struggles and state reconstruction are major topics, each deserving of a book in its own right, in which ideology would be a key element. But to do so would leave the case studies offered here too much alike, and too materialistic. I thus cannot close without at least a brief look at the manner in which ideology and culture shaped the revolutionary struggles and state reconstruction that state breakdown initiated. This task is particularly important because the effects of culture and ideology created the key differences between the outcomes of Eastern and Western cases of state breakdown.

IDEOLOGY AND REVOLUTION: THEORIES AND PROBLEMS

Theorists of revolution have ascribed varied and often seemingly contradictory roles to ideology. Chalmers Johnson (1966) has argued that revolutionary ideology is radical and disruptive; in contrast, Calhoun (1982, 1983b) has argued that revolutionary ideology is often defensive and traditional. Rudé (1980) and Welch (1980) have made the point that popular groups usually have their own "folk" ideologies, which differ from those of elite revolutionary leaders. Yet Skocpol (1979) and Arjomand (1986) have argued that ideology serves to unify the opposition against the Old Regime.

Part of the problem in describing the role of ideology arises because ideology is highly fluid. Although one might hope that ideology would provide a clear guide to the intentions and actions of revolutionary leaders, in practice revolutionaries frequently shifted their policies in response to changing circumstances. And on many occasions, the twists and turns of the revolutionary struggle produced unforeseen results. English Puritans sought to create a community of saints, but England became a community dominated by soldiers when the civil wars ceased. Robespierre rose as a defender of the French Republic, but created a virtual dictatorship. It is hard to differ with Skocpol's (1979, 170) conclusion that "it cannot be argued that the cognitive content of . . . ideologies in any sense provides a predictive key to . . . the outcomes of revolutions."

Yet the inability to predict from prerevolutionary ideology to a precise postrevolutionary outcome hardly means that ideology is without effect. The major obstacle to understanding the role of ideology lies in the failure of most theorists of revolution to clearly distinguish the various *phases* through which a revolution unfolds. Not surprisingly, ideology evolves and plays different roles in the different phases of a revolution. Thus, one obtains contradictions if one tries to characterize the ideological thrust behind any state crisis—which generally comprises *many* ideologies, expressed by various groups at different stages of the crisis— as solely "radical" or "traditional," "unifying" or "divisive." And one generally fails in predicting from a prerevolutionary ideology to a postrevolutionary outcome if one proceeds as if a single "ideology" consistently lay behind the entire process.

We can analytically distinguish three phases in the process of revolution: prerevolution (the period leading up to state breakdown); revolutionary struggle and state reconstruction; and the stabilization of authority. Each phase involves conflict, but the contenders differ. In the first phase, the state is struggling to maintain control and keep the initiative in a situation of severe domestic and often international challenges; this phase is marked by increasing conflict over resources and growing opposition and discontent. In the second phase, the Old Regime state has lost the initiative and either collapses or struggles among the host of contenders who seek to establish a new monopoly of authority; this phase is marked by efforts to mobilize supporters, rapid-fire legislation and creation of economic and political structures, and often by civil war and a "reign of terror." In the third phase, one group has seized the initiative, gained the upper hand over its opponents, and moves to stabilize its authority; this phase is marked by state efforts to gain routine acceptance of the reconstructed political, religious, economic, and social institutions.

In reality, aspects of these phases may overlap and interpenetrate— for example, a guerrilla movement may enact legislation and build institutions in a "liberated" area before the central state falls. Yet if we focus on the fortunes of the central state, we may roughly note that in the first phase, the central state still wields (a diminishing) general authority; in the second phase, authority is unclear, and competing leaders control different areas or the allegiances of different groups and struggle to obtain generally recognized authority; and in the third phase, the central state (this time under new leadership and perhaps differently constructed) again wields general authority.

I have argued in the preceding chapters that the first phase is dominated by material and social forces: a combination of state fiscal crisis, elite disaffection due to turnover and displacement, and long-term changes in wages, landholding, urban concentration, and youthfulness of the population that increase the potential for mass mobilization. In this phase, ideological shifts occur that provide a focus for opposition to the Old Regime, but such shifts gain strength chiefly in response to material and social change.

Yet in the succeeding phases, when the institutional constraints of the Old Regime have collapsed, ideology and culture develop a momentum of their own. In fact, in the second and third phases, ideology and culture play the leading, rather than a following, role. Thus my view is similar to that of Arjomand (1986, 384), who argues that ideologies "cannot account for the collapse of the societal structure of domination to any significant degree. . . . On the other hand, [they] do shape the political order installed by the revolution to a significant extent."

Current debates leave us several problems regarding the role of ideology. (1) How does revolutionary ideology *develop*: Does the ideology within a particular revolution or rebellion tend to evolve and change? Do the conflicting ideologies of different groups—some radical, some traditional—tend to merge? If not, who carries the ideology or ideologies that have the critical impact? (2) How does ideology affect the *course* of revolution or rebellion: Does ideological development shift the nature and focus of revolutionary struggles? And (3), how does ideology affect the *outcome* of state breakdown: Why in some cases does state breakdown result in state reconstruction along lines designed to reinforce the old order, while in other cases state breakdown results in a radical remaking of beliefs and institutions?

The answers to these questions help to solve three historical puzzles: Why do revolutions characteristically show a "drift" from moderate to more extreme goals and actions? Why is *revolution*—in the sense of construction of a radically new political or social order on the ruins of its predecessor—a uniquely Western phenomenon in the early modern period? And why, given that diverse states experienced state breakdown, did Western states show more dynamic long-term development after such crises than did Eastern states?

As mentioned earlier, the role of ideology in revolutions and rebellions deserves a book in itself; this chapter is no more than a preliminary, suggestive, examination. Nonetheless, considerable gains in understanding can come from considering cases addressed in this book, and examining the role of ideology in the *distinct phases* of the revolutionary process: prerevolution, revolutionary struggle and state reconstruction, and stabilization of authority.

PREREVOLUTION: IDEOLOGY AS COMPLAINT AND MORAL CRITIQUE

The conditions that give rise to state breakdown—state fiscal distress, elite alienation and conflict, and unemployment, increased vagrancy, and associated riots and disorders among the populace—also give rise to a widespread perception that something has "gone wrong" in society. This perception may be expressed as complaints about specific conditions or state actions or, more broadly, as diagnoses and prescriptions for society's ills.

As Welch (1980) and Calhoun (1983b) have noted, popular reactions are often conservative in tone: complaints that traditional rights are being violated, or that landlords or employers are unfairly exploiting the people. These complaints often take the form of appeals to the ruler to reestablish "justice" and set things right. But this "conservative" diagnosis can easily prompt radical action, for peasants also have a communal and xenophobic ideology that pictures utopia as a village free from outside interference. Peasants may thus complain that, while they are loyal to the regime, they would like to see landlords, or at least their impositions, done away with. This is the ideology that lay behind much peasant activity once state breakdown allowed peasants to take matters into their own hands, as occurred in the English fens, the French northeast, and China's Yangzi basin.

Elites also voice their sense that society has gone astray by offering plans for renewal, and sometimes for transformation, of the Old Regime. Elite complaints may take the same tack as peasants', with criticism of "injustice" and demands that the ruler restore traditional balances among elites, the populace, and the state. We can call this form of complaint, following Welch, an ideology of "rectification." It has much in common with the popular grievances discussed above, although it generally deals with elite concerns (which may include putting the poor in their "proper" place). Yet elites are also capable of offering diagnoses that the Old Regime is not simply corrupt and in need of rectification; they may proclaim it fatally flawed and in need of replacement by a new order. Thus, for example, the Rump Parliament in England justified its formation of the Commonwealth by a declaration, claiming not only that Charles I was an evil monarch but also that "the monarchy had failed—not just in the recent crisis, but throughout its history—to provide England with political stability" (A Declaration of Parliament of England, 22 March 1648, cited in Pocock 1975, 377). We can call this form of complaint, again following Welch, an ideology of "transformation."

Prior to state breakdown, the weakness of the state invites diverse elements of society to press their own grievances. Thus various elites may press programs for rectification or transformation without consciously attempting to unite with other elite segments or popular groups. For example, English Puritans dreamed of the transformation of England into a more godly state, whereas conventional Anglicans sought mainly rectification of royal abuses of authority. French parlements sought rectification of royal tyranny, whereas leading professionals of the Third Estate hoped for a transformation of the social basis of elite politics. Chinese gentry of the Donglin and Fushe, and those who collaborated with the Manchus, sought in different ways a more effective central government. Anatolian *ayan*s sought more autonomy and rewards from the Ottoman sultanate, whereas the sultan's court sought to increase central control. At the same time, artisans may stage food riots, and peasants may stage land invasions, increase poaching, or withhold rents or tithes, without any thought other than to take advantage of propitious times to rectify personally felt injustices.

All of these actions, elite and popular, may precipitate further discussions of injustice and social ills. Elite groups are likely to form that identify themselves with the "true" order and moral reform. As Arjomand (1986, 402), following Walzer (1974), notes, "the fact that integrative social movements are reactions to social dislocation and normative disorder explains the salience of their search for cultural authenticity and their moral rigorism." English Puritans, French parlements, Chinese academy movements, and the authors of the Ottoman "retrenchment" literature exemplify the pretensions of higher cultural authenticity and moral rigor in times of disorder.

But once the state's fiscal and political woes reduce its authority to nil, the situation changes. Instead of merely pressing demands for change, or resisting state authority, elites (and sometimes the populace, where local control depends on the central state) find themselves with new opportunities and new rivals. The new opportunities appear in the state's loss of initiative and inability to enforce its views, allowing elites new scope for action. The new rivals appear in the form of competing elite segments and various regional and popular groups seeking to shape the social and political order and to replace the Old Regime.

Taking advantage of the new opportunities requires building coalitions and mobilizing support among the social and political fragments set free by the collapse of the Old Regime. It is thus at this point that revolutions characteristically see a flood of pamphlet literature and wildly shifting postures and alliances. Instead of particularistic complaints, sweeping social programs come to dominate discourse. New symbols are developed to represent the various viewpoints and factions that compete for allegiance. New enemies are defined, vilified, and condemned in order to sharpen differences and strengthen loyalties among competitors. In short, the revolutionary struggle has begun.

THE REVOLUTIONARY STRUGGLE AND STATE RECONSTRUCTION: IDEOLOGY AND ORGANIZATION

Old Regimes are typically a diverse lot of divided elements: religious, military, landlord, professional, and commercial elites; urban shopkeepers, artisans, and laborers; and rural peasants ranging from the well off to the destitute. Within each of these class designations, segments may be sharply divided by local origin, family background, relation to the Crown, degree of wealth or status, education, and religious beliefs. Thus in England differences between Arminian clergy and Puritan preachers, in France between liberal and conservative nobles, in China between court cliques and academic gentry, and in Turkey between provincial governors and palace elites were sharper and probably of greater political significance than the class divisions in these societies. What is important is that among this heterogeneity no group was liable to emerge as dominant on its own in the face of opposition by all groups; any contender seeking power needed to build what political scientists call a "dominant coalition," a group with sufficient solidarity and resources to defeat all possible combinations of opponents.

It should be clear that the formation of a dominant coalition is by no means a foregone conclusion. Where such a coalition does not form (prime examples are the French Fronde, the Sicilian and Neapolitan revolts against Hapsburg Spain, and the German Revolution of 1848) the Old Regime state can recover its authority by playing various social elements against one another.

In general, the first months following the fall of an Old Regime are a time of superficial unity, as all groups hope that their individual complaints will be rectified and their individual goals realized. This is the "honeymoon" period of exuberance that follows the realization that the Old Regime has lost its force.[1] But the honeymoon cannot last, for the problems that initiated state breakdown—fiscal crisis, elite competition, and popular deprivation—do not disappear and still require solutions. As popular groups almost invariably have only local concerns and goals, the task of building a dominant coalition to address these issues falls to members of the elite. Taking the various particular complaints and the various elite and folk ideologies, and forging from these elements an ideology with broad appeal, is critical to the construction of a dominant coalition.

Many different ideologies have played this leading role in revolutions—Puritanism, Jacobinism, Constitutionalism, Communism (Bolshevik, Maoist, Sandinist, and other national variants), and Islamic

---

1. In modern revolutions, this period of pervasive unity often begins before the collapse of the Old Regime; having learned the lesson of mobilization from past revolutions, regime opponents with diverse goals may nonetheless unite behind a broad "umbrella" organization, wherein the only clearly articulated goal is the end of the Old Regime. This kind of unity was evident in the last year of state breakdown in Nicaragua and also in Iran (Chavarría 1986; Green 1986).

fundamentalism. But behind this diversity, three broad themes can be discerned in the mobilization of revolutionary coalitions: rectification, redistribution, and nationalism. Revolutionary struggles are, for the most part, the story of how elite segments seek to appropriate and dominate one or more of these themes, while defeating similar attempts by their opponents.

Of course, such struggles are not waged merely in the abstract realm of ideas. It is not merely the content but also the particular organization that carries an ideology that is responsible for its success or failure. Thus, the role of revolutionary ideology is inseparable from the role of revolutionary organizations.

REVOLUTIONARY ORGANIZATION

To dominate a revolution, an ideology needs a well-organized carrier capable of interpreting that ideology for a mass audience. The ideologies of transformation that dominated Western revolutions—Puritanism, Jacobinism, and Bolshevism—and the ideologies of rectification that dominated some Western and most Eastern crises—those of the Counter-Reformation, the Chinese academy movement, and the Ottoman advice literature—were strongly held by only a small minority in each case. In England, "there was a revolutionary minority in Parliament, and an equally determined minority in the Army, in the towns, and in the countryside, which saw the crisis of 1640 as the dawn of a new day, the great climactic struggle for the New Jerusalem" (Underdown 1985, 3). In France, the Jacobins numbered a few hundred in each of the major cities and towns (M. Kennedy 1982). In China, the academy movement involved a few hundred elite scholars. In Counter-Reformation Europe, the ideology of resistance was articulated by a few hundred members of elite Church orders. How could these relatively few individuals play a dominant role in national crises? The key was their superior organization in comparison to their opponents and competitors.

In England, there existed in the early seventeenth century a close-knit network of gentry with Puritan sympathies. They knew each other, they socialized and intermarried, and they corresponded about the political and religious problems and opportunities of the day (W. Hunt 1983). When open conflict broke out in 1640–1642 and men sought to build new alliances amid the breakdown of the monarchy's traditional patronage network, the Puritan gentry were already equipped with a network for communication and action. Thus in Essex, for example, Puritan gentry were able to direct popular protests, which might have taken an antigentry turn, into anti-Catholic channels (W. Hunt 1983, 309). Throughout England, while most groups sought chiefly to defend their local interests, only the Puritans were able to offer a national program to oppose the king, a program based on defense of "authentic" English law and religion. It is thus not surprising that the Puritans utilized symbols of foreign threat: a need to throw off the "Norman yoke" of subjugation and a need to defend the "ancient constitution" and to fight off "papists." All of these steps are part of a typical ideological progression, in which elites seek to mobilize popular support by identifying themselves as custodians of a tradition more "authentic" and truly "national" than those of their opponents. Only then can "a movement originally concerned with issues of doctrine and ceremonial be broadened out to become a cultural orientation arousing the emotions of large numbers of people" (Fulbrook 1983, 10).

Similarly in the French Revolution, the Jacobins sought to identify themselves as the custodians of French "nationhood," as the true voice of the French "nation." They were able to do so, albeit briefly, in large measure because their national network of clubs in major towns allowed them to dominate the news from the capital and to offer a coherent program at a time of chaos. In contrast, the failure of the Fronde was in large measure due to the failure of any group to wrest the mantle of national symbol from the king (D. Parker 1983, 111), and thus to the inability of any elite group to integrate the opposition to the Crown. No one was able to unite the urban *officiers*, commercial and financial elites, and grand nobles, who exhausted each other and eventually turned to the monarchy to reestablish national order.

In China and Turkey, the seventeenth-century rectification movements remained elite movements. The provincial rebellions succeeded only in splitting the country, and although they temporarily damaged central authority, they offered no new symbols or organization to replace it. Indeed, rectification ideologies, in general, are incapable of mobilizing energies on a national scale, and hence incapable of successfully supplanting an Old Regime with a new order, *unless* they turn to redistributive or nationalist themes.

Why did Chinese and Turkish elites not turn to redistributive or nationalist themes? Part of the reason lies in the different elite structures of Eastern and Western states. We need to consider what kind of elites would adopt a redistributionist program or would seek to mobilize the populace around a national vision different from that which underpins the extant hierarchy. Skocpol (1979, 1986) has pointed out the key role of *marginal* elites in the French (1789), Russian (1917), and Chinese (1949) revolutions. Marginal elites are groups that have an upper-class education and access to national debates over political and social issues, yet at the same time are also restricted—by their personal circumstances or treatment by the Old Regime that is unrelated to their merit—from any prospect of active participation in the highest levels of government and society. Such marginal elites take the lead in articulating and seeking to implement alternative social orders; their presence or absence is thus a critical factor in the spread of "transformative" ideologies.

In the English Revolution, it was lay preachers—disdained by the king and the Arminian leaders of the Anglican Church, but believing themselves educationally equal and morally superior to the regular clergy—who articulated the vision of a Puritan commonwealth. In the French Revolution, as Darnton (1970) has shown, the fiercest attacks on the status of nobles came not from the leaders of the high Enlightenment (who were largely royalists) but rather from the lower ranks of journalists and provincial lawyers, men whose status as commoners and modest incomes limited them to secondary roles in the ancien régime. Seventeenth-century England and eighteenth-century France, as well as seventeenth-century Ottoman Turkey and late Ming China, had undergone expansions of education and literacy without commensurate expansion of elite positions, and thus they faced problems of blocked mobility and disaffection of elites. But in the former two cases, many of the aspirants to elite positions found their way blocked *on principle*, rather than merely by surplus of candidates or lack of merit. Thus under Charles I, Arminians (and sometimes Catholics) received preferment in Church and State; under Louis XV and Louis XVI, those of noble rank received privileged treatment. Of course, these barriers were not impenetrable; indeed, under James I in England and Louis XIV in France, positions were more numerous and aspirants fewer, so mobility was not so often blocked and principles were flexible enough to absorb outsiders. Still, by the 1630s in England, and the 1770s in France, displacement was sufficiently great, and the odious grounds of exclusion sufficiently in evidence, that many aspirants to elite positions perceived themselves to be marginalized by the principles espoused by the Old Regime. It was these elites who sought to implement a new vision of society, in which their place would not be limited by the principles of the traditional hierarchy.

In contrast, Ottoman Turkey and Ming China had no such principles excluding literati and provincial governors from higher status. Failure on examinations, corrupt preferment of favorites, and military and fiscal weaknesses that prevented the appointment of good men and limited the growth of elite positions were the only apparent reasons for failure of individuals to advance. Thus, in both these societies members of the elite fiercely criticized the leadership for corruption and incompetence, moral failure, and mismanagement. Favorites were excoriated (sometimes literally), and rectification movements developed a considerable elite following. But attacks on the principles of Ottoman and Confucian rule were limited to Sufis and eccentric scholars. There was no considerable body of marginal elites in Turkey or China who saw themselves as denied success by the very principles of the traditional order.

Thus, in Turkey and China the ideological appeals behind opposition to the state, and behind state reconstruction, rarely went beyond appeals for rectification of abuses. Elite and popular opposition to the Ming and Ottoman regimes were sufficient to destroy the authority of the state, but produced no clear alternative. In both cases, new dynasties of leaders—the Manchus who seized the throne in China, and the Köprülü viziers who ruled in the name of the Ottoman sultans—gained an opportunity to take power, but the coalitions of civil and military elites on which they based their rule were grounded in adherence to traditional ideals.

But in England and France, marginal elites sought to create popular support for a clear alternative to the Old Regime. Moderate reformers could initially wrest the initiative from the Old Regime state by promising to correct the worst flaws of Old Regime policies. Yet the degree of fiscal stress, elite demands, and popular grievances that had brought state breakdown were deeply rooted in long-term social changes; thus progress in satisfying demands for change were slow, and moderates were soon outflanked by marginal elites who articulated alternative principles calling for more extreme measures. Given a choice between moderates who sought merely to restore a more virtuous version of the Old Regime, and marginal elites who offered an alternative vision based on more popular principles, the populace generally could be mobilized against moderates and in favor of more extreme groups.

One popular principle was redistribution. Both marginal elites aggrieved at exclusion from official positions and popular groups aggrieved at falling living standards could find common cause in policies that redistributed the property of unpopular institutions or elites. Thus, overturning principles that restricted access to office, dispossessing holders of privileges, and disbursing either state or church wealth through land redistribution or expropriation of elites were policies that both responded to immediate pressures and built a coalition that gave radicals an edge in the competition for popular mobilization and pursuit of authority. Yet redistribution was inherently a short-lived basis for building a revolutionary coalition. Groups who received a boon often simply retired from further revolutionary activity. Moreover, an initial redistribution, once completed, had to be renewed to maintain fervor. But redistribution has its limits: the wealth of the privileged elite, when diluted and redistributed, is generally far from sufficient to relieve the wants of the general populace. Moreover, if the revolutionary leadership is to retain the support of skilled elites and middle groups, redistribution must stop far short of total equality. Thus, the redistributive basis for revolutionary mobilization, and groups that depend solely on it, become vulnerable, and a further alternative basis for popular mobilization is needed.

The ideal, and most common, alternative popular principle is nationalism.[2] By identifying the revolutionary leadership as the new carrier of authentic national aspirations and identity, revolutionaries can hope to maintain the loyalty of a broad, cross-class coalition. However, the creation of a new national identity is often ridden with conflict. Nationalism acquires its potency not simply from commonalities of ethnicity, or language, or territorial boundaries. Instead, the heart of nationalism is a principle of belonging *and exclusion* that distinguishes true members of the community from outsiders (J. Armstrong 1982, 5–6). Thus revolutionary nationalism seeks to identify supporters of the revolution as patriots, and opponents of the revolution—whether external or domestic—as enemies of the nation. Indeed, the identification and pursuit of enemies is often precisely what gives revolutionary nationalism its emotional appeal. Revolutionary ideology therefore often tends to an aggressive, intolerant nationalism. This characteristic helps to explain why the anxiety over counterrevolutionary "plots"—for example, purported papist plots in revolutionary England, and aristocratic plots in revolutionary France—played such a major role in revolutionary struggles. These plots formed a counterpoint to revolutionary nationalism, giving purpose and credibility to the revolutionary leadership and a sense of unity and virtue to their followers.

For this reason, the likelihood of war between a new revolutionary

---

2. By "nationalism" I mean allegiance to a community (possibly ethnic) that views itself as having a unique character, history, and destiny, in which "outsiders" cannot share, or only share to a secondary degree. This overlaps with, but differs from, mere "patriotism," which is more often associated with allegiance to a particular regime or territory.

state and its neighbors increases. Similarly, intolerant nationalism often leads to persecution of ethnic, religious, or regional minorities who find it difficult to be identified with the "nation" of the revolutionary leadership and its primary followers. This is a striking element of the evolution of revolutionary ideology. For in the prerevolutionary phase, when a diversity of complaints against the Old Regime are given voice, ethnic, religious, and regional minorities may assert their grievances and join in the broad chorus of opposition. Even in the initial honeymoon phase, moderates may offer such minority groups improvements in status as part of the rectification of Old Regime abuses. Yet if marginal elites succeed in pushing the revolution in alternative directions, and continuing struggles for power lead to nationalism as the leading principle for revolutionary mobilization, such minority groups may find themselves subject to persecutions even worse than were encountered under the Old Regime.

Ideology thus tends to develop in the course of a revolution. Initially, social and material change is likely to produce calls for rectification of Old Regime abuses. Such calls may be rooted in tradition and reflect a wide variety of elite and popular grievances. However, once the Old Regime loses the initiative, the struggle for power leads to heightened ideological as well as political conflict. Moderate reformers are likely first to win broad support for enactment of policies that rectify past abuses. But where marginal elites seek to articulate alternative principles for social and political rule, and particularly when such elites have access to organized networks for spreading their view, popular support for more extreme measures is likely to undermine moderates. More extreme leadership, turning first to redistributive measures and then to an aggressive, intolerant nationalism, is likely to result.

Let us look at the process of ideological evolution and its effects in more detail by examining the case of France in 1789–1800.

IDEOLOGY IN THE FRENCH REVOLUTION

Intense debate has raged on the role of ideology in the French Revolution, most recently in Furet's (1981) argument with Soboul (1975), and in the debate between Sewell (1985b) and Skocpol (1985). Where Soboul, following Marx, argued that the Enlightenment represented a unified, probourgeois program for reform, Furet claims this view is simply the outcome of taking literally the propaganda of the revolution's peak years of 1792–1794. For Furet, the verbiage of the revolution must be seen as a veil that shrouds the true motives of actors; indeed, "revolutionary times are precisely the most difficult to understand, since they are often periods when the veil of ideology hides most completely the real meaning of events" (1981, 159). Sewell (1985b, 66–67, 69) grants that Enlightenment ideology did not cause the breakdown of the Old Regime, but he nonetheless maintains that "once the crisis had begun, ideological contradictions contributed mightily to the deepening of the crisis into Revolution," and that certain actions, such as the abolition of feudal privileges on August 4, 1789, were moved forward by "an overwhelming urge for ideological consistency." Skocpol (1979, 1985), however, while conceding the importance of cultural idioms and ideologies in framing the symbolic accompaniments to actions, prefers to emphasize structural constraint over ideological autonomy, holding that political, economic, and social conditions limit which ideologies can succeed.

We can resolve many of these disputes by noting that as ideologies develop they can act as propaganda *and* as program, as impetus to action *and* as reaction to given conditions. But these twists and turns in the role of ideology are comprehensible only when we cease to consider revolutions as single events and recall that they are *processes* with multiple phases, in each of which ideology may play a different role. The guiding ideology of the French Revolution moved from an attack on privilege in general—led by representatives of all classes—to an attack on those individuals who claimed privilege—led by the representatives of the Third Estate—to an attack on anyone considered an "enemy of the nation"—led by the Jacobins—and finally, under Napoleon, to the pursuit of national glory.

Let us begin our examination of these changes by returning to the relation of ideology and organization, for there Furet (1981) makes a cogent contribution to an understanding of France's revolutionary struggle. Furet argues that the Enlightenment's influence on the revolution was at first not ideological, but organizational. The Enlightenment gave birth in France to a peculiar institution: the philosophical society. Born of the rise of literacy, of educated professionals with few official prospects seeking intellectual life, and of the desire of *anoblis* and *gentils-hommes* to compete in cosmopolitan sophistication, philosophical societies sprang up in all the major cities of eighteenth-century France.

The philosophical society was a new organizational form, where rank and birth were second to oratorical ability, and oratorical ability was employed for abstract argument. "It was a form of social life based on the principle that its members, in order to participate in it, must divest themselves of all concrete distinctions, and of their social existence"

(Furet 1981, 174). Moreover, it was a meeting place of the "dominant classes" that eschewed social divisions. "The highest social circles, the academies, the masonic lodges, the cafes and theatres, . . . gradually fused into an Enlightened society, very largely aristocratic yet also open to non-noble talent and money" (Furet 1981, 114). It was in this mixed company, not in the combat of classes, that the Old Regime notion of a society of corporate entities based on specific occupational and social interests melted away. "The philosophical society of the 'enlightened' type was the matrix of a new network of political relations that was to be the main characteristic and the outstanding innovation of the French Revolution" (Furet 1981, 175).

When the crisis that resulted in the calling of the Estates General arose, the philosophical society—which had been the mode in which all political problems and reforms had been discussed for the last decades— was the obvious model for the national debate. But the Estates General were essentially corporatist, their organization reflecting the traditional divisions of French society. What, then, could be more natural for the patriot party, led by a mix of nobility and non-noble talent that characterized the philosophical societies, than to ask that the Estates General be constituted along enlightened, rather than corporatist, lines? The request for voting by head and for double representation of the Third Estate therefore originated not in the demands of the hostile bourgeoisie against the nobility, but rather in the demands of the Enlightenment philosophical society against the old corporate organization. It was thus an organizational precedent, not merely a transformative vision, that, as Sewell (1985b, 65) notes, led "many of the Third Estate representatives . . . to see their estate as the germ of a National Assembly, rather than as a subordinate part of an ancient corporate body." In the pre-revolutionary phase of the French Revolution, therefore, enlightened nobles *and* non-nobles called for debates to be conducted with regard to merit, rather than social rank.

But the Crown's decision to call the Estates General in their traditional form, and the resulting electoral disputes, created a new situation. Struggles for power among factions of the elite crystallized along new organizational lines. As nobles and members of the Third Estate competed for control of the Estates General, language and myths were invented and employed to justify the various protagonists. As Furet (1981, 43) notes, "Revolutionary ideology [i.e., the attack on the nobility] was born . . . in the battles of the election itself. . . . Robespierre became Robespierre only when he had to win his seat as deputy for the Third

Estate from Arras. It was then that the young conformist invented the discourse of equality."

Conflicts over how the Estates General would be conducted arose from the different interests of various noble groups, bishops and clergy, members of the Third Estate, and the monarchy and its ministers. Forced on the defensive by the king, the Third Estate sought to recruit supporters by appealing to the general desire for change. But their ability to win supporters rested on their capacity, as in the case of the English Puritans, to present themselves as embodying the true interest of the nation as a whole. That presentation in turn came to rest, at first, on a limited platform of redistribution of tax burdens and seigneurial levies. But the National Assembly discovered, as revolutionary leaderships often do, that redistributive programs are inherently divisive, creating enemies as well as allies.

The events of 1789 had brought forth a complete anomaly in French history: a deliberative body, the National Assembly, empowered to debate and legislate fundamental laws. It was inevitable that such a body would need to adjudicate conflicts of interest and to reconcile opposing views. But no mechanisms for that process existed. Parties organized to forge legislative compromises and to orchestrate peaceful conflicts had yet to be developed. There was only one principle that all accepted for the resolution of conflicts, one principle that represented the legitimacy of the Assembly: the will of the people.

Thus the French Revolution sought to place the will of the people at the font of power. But because this was an administrative impossibility, the result was an ever-escalating struggle among the various nonrepresentative groups competing for "the exclusive right to embody the democratic principle" (Furet 1981, 77). The key struggle of the Jacobin period was precisely the struggle to gain the role of "voice of the people," a struggle carried out in large part by seeking to dominate the revolutionary dialogue. "Revolutionary activity par excellence was the production of maximalist language. . . . The constant raising of the ideological stakes was the rule of the game in the new system" (Furet 1981, 50, 55).

As the legitimating principle of the revolution was the will of the people, the enemy was embodied in its antiprinciple, the "aristocratic" or "counterrevolutionary" plot. "The 'aristocratic' plot thus became the lever of an egalitarian ideology that was both exclusionary and highly integrative" (Furet 1981, 55). It provided an enemy against which the masses could be mobilized to support whichever group was temporarily successful in seizing the role of representative of the popular will. The "plot" became ever-expanding as competing groups raised the volume and extremism of discourse (Higonnet 1981).

Furet perhaps exaggerates the degree to which the revolution created its own momentum, neglecting the importance of the international arena. The émigrés did have resources in the support of European monarchs, and the threat of counterrevolution (assisted by the king and queen themselves) was quite real. State breakdown provides opportunities for both revolution and counterrevolution, and conservatism and apathy are, initially, on the side of restoration of the traditional order. It is not simply, as Furet suggests, that the revolutionary rhetoric escalated the conflict. It is more accurate to say that every bout between revolutionaries and counterrevolutionaries (including the western rebels in the Vendée and the federalists in the center and south) led the revolutionaries to push the revolution further, to a point where there could be no turning back, and to purge more slackers from their midst. Coward's (1980, 161) remarks about the English Revolution seem to hold equally for the French Revolution: "The King's opponents were forced to become more radical because of the fear and distrust of counterrevolution, rather than by social, economic, or ideological forces." In short, the power struggle itself radicalized the revolution.

War was a natural outcome of this revolutionary struggle. At first, war was demanded as part of the crusade to renew French society and root out enemies. Thus in 1792 Vergniaud, the Assembly deputy from Bordeaux, declared: "We can see that the abrogation of this treaty [i.e., the peace treaty of 1763] is a revolution as necessary in foreign affairs, both for Europe and for France, as the destruction of the Bastille has been for our internal regeneration" (cited in Blanning 1986, 99). Later, war became essential for the revolution to continue. As Blanning (1986, 196) remarks, "in truth, war had become a way of life, even a matter of necessity for the Directory. Only war could keep ambitious generals and disruptive soldiers out of France, only war could keep the armies supplied and paid, only war could justify the repeated abuse of the constitution, only war could bring the regime some badly needed prestige."

The growing pursuit of internal and external enemies—the Reign of Terror and the war—were the natural outcome of the terms in which the revolutionary power struggles were framed. Thus, the Terror—both in the form of the guillotine and in the variety of repressive episodes raging over the civil war, sporadic assassinations, and spontaneous massacres perpetrated by revolutionary crowds—was neither merely a regrettable deviation brought into the revolution by the unfortunate pressures of a war launched by its enemies, nor a necessary step in the abolition of the feudal Old Regime. The war was itself a product of the revolution, because revolution could not be made without dealing with the threat of counterrevolution, which inevitably involved both conservative groups within France and their external allies. War was the preferred method of the revolutionary regime to harness patriotic support and to justify its extreme measures. And the feudal Old Regime was effectively a dead letter by 1790. But securing the leadership of the revolution, and winning popular support, depended on identifying and vanquishing "enemies of the nation." Terror arose because the power struggles of the revolution gave it life, because the way to rush to the head of "the people" was to serve them the heads of their enemies.

If the Reign of Terror was an inherent part of the process of revolution, so too military rule was its inevitable conclusion. For as Marx stated, "Napoleon was the last stand of revolutionary terror. . . . He carried the terror to its conclusion" (*The Holy Family*, cited in Furet 1981, 129). As purges and terror escalate, and as the radical party shrinks and turns to paranoid attacks on all outside the party's orthodox pale, the leaders of the people's attack on its enemies may become isolated and may be pushed aside by those desiring a surcease from terror. At this point, the terror may be repudiated. Yet the logic of the revolution has not then fully run its course. The terror derives from the struggle to embody the will of the people; its logical conclusion is the succeeding of the "leader of the people's attack on its enemies" by the "national hero," who in his or her own person represents the plebiscitary will of the nation. The democratic despot—despotic in authority, for both monarchical and republican rule have been discredited, but legitimized as representing the will of the people, the "nation": this is the principle of the revolution brought to its logical conclusion. Thus, Napoleon should not be regarded as the consolidator of a bourgeois revolution that brewed through the eighteenth century; Napoleon is the product of the new situation, the revolutionary situation, which was ushered in with the collapse of the Old Regime in 1789. The "type" of Napoleon—the democratically legitimized authoritarian ruler—was a product of the process of revolution.

Furet limits his discussion to the French Revolution. But the progress of rhetorical competition and the escalation leading to terror and democratic despotism that he describes are common to social revolutions: Napoleon succeeded Robespierre; Cromwell replaced Pym; Stalin succeeded Lenin; Chiang Kai-shek and, later, Mao Zedong replaced Sun Yat-sen.

IDEOLOGY AND THE COURSE OF REVOLUTION

Let us now recap. Historians have often puzzled over why revolutions characteristically show a progression to the "left," toward more extreme radicalism. The answer should now be clear. In the conditions of social dislocation that precede state breakdown, ideologies are a diverse mix: folk views of rectification, largely conservative but possibly with utopian elements; elite views of rectification, both conservative and transformative; and mostly, particularistic complaints of poor policies, injustice, corruption, bad ministers, and so forth. When the crisis reaches the point where the Old Regime is clearly breaking down and has lost the initiative, attempts are made to unite the opposition to the Old Regime by broad slogans that can bridge both the folk and the elite views of the problem and the various particularistic complaints. Examples include the call to defend the "rights of Englishmen and the true religion" in England in the 1640s; the call for the Estates General in France in 1787–1788; the slogan "Peace and Land" in Russia in 1916–1917; and the simple "Down with the Shah" and "Somoza Must Go" in contemporary Iran and Nicaragua. Such simple unifying slogans are not always present in revolutionary contexts. The Fronde in seventeenth-century France, for instance, was never able to unite its diverse elements. But such slogans, when they do occur, dominate the early stages of revolution, deferring conflicts and focusing enmity on the Old Regime.

The collapse of the Old Regime, however, creates a new situation, in the sense that competition is now open among formerly subordinate elite groups to dominate the polity and offer solutions to the problems that brought down the Old Regime. In this competition, groups that have prior national organization and programs are at an advantage. It is not necessarily their radical views that put them at the forefront; for example, the Puritan gentry in the 1630s and the Jacobin clubs in the 1780s were clearly moderate and reformist, not revolutionary (Cliffe 1984; M. Kennedy.1982). Rather, their organizational advantage allows them to take the lead in disseminating their viewpoint.

Nonetheless, their success in dominating the polity, given the lack of accepted institutions and of adequate military force, rests on their ability to win the allegiance of key groups. This means appealing to desires for rectification, redistribution, and national authenticity. Restriction of royal taxing authority and abolition of the prerogative courts in England, and reform of tax administration and abolition of feudal obligations in France, embodied rectification and redistributive ideologies. Yet rectification and redistribution are inherently limited tools for massive popular mobilization in a time of weak institutions. Rectification means different things to different groups, and one group's satisfaction is another's grievance. Higonnet's (1981, 245) description of the failure of republican ideology in France in the 1790s is apropos: "It did not seduce the poor, and it made the rich anxious." Similarly, redistribution is limited. Groups who receive a boon may then simply retire from revolutionary activity, as did France's peasants after 1789. A longer-lasting ideology is needed that welds disparate groups together in the revolutionary cause. For this purpose nationalism is ideal. Its fervor can be renewed by the search for "enemies" of the revolution, or more accurately, of the "people" or the "nation." Thus revolutions typically progress from initially moderate, to more radical redistributive, to more broadly nationalistic visions.[3]

This perspective makes it clear why revolutions are periods of heightened innovation and emphasis in relation to symbols and discourse; these latter are the means by which competing factions seek to stand out, claim popular attention, and establish identification with "authentic" national aspirations and character.

Moreover, it should also be evident why military dictatorship is often welcomed as an outcome of revolution. It is seen as plebiscitary leadership, and it appropriates the symbols that the revolution has developed to embody nationalist pride. It is thus generally not seen as a revival of the Old Regime; instead, it best embodies the fervent nationalism that is the common denominator to which most revolutions are eventually reduced.

Indeed, much the same struggle—to win allegiance and mobilize on the basis of loyalty to the "nation" rather than to the Old Regime—takes place in the armed forces of a nation during a revolution as takes place in the country at large. As Adelman (1985) has shown, recruitment to and promotion in revolutionary armies take on new principles, emphasizing talent, rectification of past abuses, redistribution of authority, and national service. The armies of the revolution thus embody its ideology; their eventual dominance is not merely a triumph of their own

---

3. Of course, nationalism can also be tapped by counterrevolution, and bloody reprisals against the people's "enemies" are also part of the successful suppression of rebellions, as, for example, in England following the failure of Monmouth's rising in 1685.

strength but also the final victory of the revolution, albeit in authoritarian form.

In short, many characteristics of ideology in revolutions depend not on the content of particular ideologies, but on the conditions of revolutionary struggle per se. We have seen that ideology can take on a *variety* of roles over the course of a revolution, and that if counterrevolutionary threats and factional struggles for power continue as a revolution unfolds, then the intensity of such power struggles will tend to produce more extremist revolutionary ideology and revolutionary action. For this reason the French Revolution of 1789, and the English Revolution of 1640, both developed in the direction of increasing radicalization; in contrast, the French Revolution of 1830—where counterrevolutionary threats were mild and revolutionary struggles quickly concluded—showed only a limited radical trend. More generally, the tendency of ideology to grow radical in response to revolutionary struggles explains why most revolutions often follow a similar course—moving from initially moderate to more extreme positions, and from rectification to redistribution to nationalism as their guiding principle—despite having ideologies of diverse content.

Yet "radical" need not mean "novel." "Radical" action and institutional change can take place under the banner of counterrevolutionary and conservative ideology, as well as under the banner of revolution. Of the four main cases of state breakdown described in this volume, only England in 1640 and France in 1789 produced avowedly revolutionary regimes, which aimed to abolish, rather than refurbish, the institutions of traditional rule. The other two instances of state breakdown, the Ming-Qing transition in China and the seventeenth-century Ottoman crisis, had outcomes of a different nature. To be sure, these cases too showed violent struggles for power, with radical phases of terror against regime opponents, and major changes in the rural social order and the institutions of government (which I describe in more detail below). But these cases, despite major institutional changes, did not show sharp *ideological* breaks with the past. Instead, the changes in institutions were framed and justified in terms of restoring the virtues of the past, rather than in terms of destroying the past to create a more virtuous future.

Thus, we need to ask why state breakdown resulted in revolutionary state reconstruction in some cases, but in conservative state reconstruction in others. This problem leads us to consider the role of broad cultural frameworks in the stabilization of authority under new, postbreakdown, regimes.

REVOLUTIONARY OUTCOMES: INSTITUTIONAL AND IDEOLOGICAL DIMENSIONS OF CHANGE

Any regime that comes to power following state breakdown is likely to be pressed by necessity to make a number of institutional changes. In regard to state fiscal and economic organization, the failure of the Old Regime makes it almost inevitable that fiscal institutions will be overhauled. In addition, as we observed earlier, if a revolution is dominated by a formerly marginal elite, that elite will likely overhaul the institutions of elite recruitment and access to power, changing the principles of the social order that they believe excluded them under the Old Regime and providing a justification for their newfound dominance. In addition, if changes in local landlord-cultivator relations have occurred, either as a result of the decay of old local practices or as a result of organized actions by cultivators, the new regime is likely to find it necessary to accept and institutionalize such new agrarian conditions.

In our four main cases of state breakdown—England, France, the Ottoman Empire, and China—such changes are widely evident. In each case, state finances were greatly strengthened by changes in the level and enforcement of taxation. Elite access to power was also changed, most radically in those countries where marginal elites played a key role. Thus in England, lay preachers succeeded, if only briefly, in abolishing the episcopacy; and in France, professionals succeeded in overturning the privileges of the nobility. In Qing China and the Ottoman Empire, significant, if less radical, changes in elite recruitment also took place. In China, a number of positions in the elite hierarchy were reserved for Manchu officials who rose by personal preferment rather than through the examination system. And in the Ottoman Empire, the recruitment of Christian youths for high office was largely replaced by recruitment of the offspring of the most loyal and distinguished of the sultan's officials. Finally, in every case except that of England, there were major changes in rural class structure, reflecting a combination of prior decay of older rural relations, direct action by cultivators, and state institutionalization of new rural economic and political structures.

Yet if institutional changes are often forced on a new regime, it seems that considerable latitude remains as to how such changes will be justified, and what will be the *ideological basis* for the restabilization of authority. In particular, the new regime would seem to be free to describe its actions as either a modification and correction of basically sound traditional institutions (conservative state reconstruction) or else as a totally new beginning, needed to replace obsolete traditional practices (revolutionary state reconstruction). Thus we need to explain why in some cases postbreakdown regimes justify their reconstruction by exalting, and in other cases by excoriating, tradition.

Let us briefly examine the outcomes of our four main cases of state breakdown. To enrich the comparison, let us also look at two cases of more modest state crisis and reconstruction, England in 1688–1689 and Japan during the Meiji Restoration. Once again, we will find the case of Japan to be a useful "exception" that clarifies more general relationships.

INSTITUTIONAL CHANGE

Perhaps the most striking finding from a comparison of the seventeenth-century crises in Turkey and China with the English and French revolutions is that one *cannot* maintain that the latter two experienced significant institutional changes whereas the former two experienced only a "crisis" or "breakdown" followed by a restoration of the institutions of the Old Regime. Instead, the degree of institutional change from the beginning to the end of the seventeenth century, particularly in the organization of rule in the countryside, was far greater in Turkey and China than in England, and comparable to that in eighteenth-century France.

In the English Revolution, although traditional Whig historiography has tended to see an emancipation of Parliament persisting after the Restoration, more recent and detailed investigations of Crown-Parliamentary relations after 1660 have questioned any change. Miller (1982, 23) asserts that members of Parliament were concerned to preserve the balanced constitution, not to change it or to seize executive initiative: "Far from pursuing a vision of parliamentary sovereignty, MP's struggled to make the old constitution work again." Institutional changes were relatively few. The royal prerogative courts were abolished, and the Crown budget was limited. However, "these restrictions on the monarchy . . . were perhaps less significant than the restrictions which were not imposed." Instead of seeking to reduce royal authority, after 1660 members of Parliament "seemed to go out of their way to build up the power of the Crown. . . . They abandoned Parliament's two main constitutional demands of 1641–48: a share in the King's choice of ministers and in control of the armed forces" (Miller 1979, 30). In short, in 1660 they went only back to the era of the Tudors, when the Crown lacked the independent resources for absolute rule and required the cooperation of Parliament to govern. There was *no* attempt to reach toward legislative supremacy. McInnes (1982, 379) concurs that "insofar as the Civil War had been fought to place further tangible limits on the Crown, it had proved a dismal failure." Even the institutional changes, such as abolition of the prerogative courts, achieved little, for the king still appointed royal judges who remained dismissible at will; and the king's control over the appointment of lord lieutenants, justices of the peace, and militia officers was restored, restoring much of his power over the counties. Real restrictions on royal power did not come until the Act for the Rights and Liberties of the Subject in 1701, while parliamentary prerogative did not emerge until the Hanoverian years (McInnes 1982, 383–389).

Continuity was even more emphatic at the level of country control. The administrative apparatus of justices of the peace, selected from local gentry, remained untouched by the revolution, while the prestige of the aristocracy underwent a sharp revival after midcentury (Hexter 1968, 72; Cannon 1984). The primacy of the Anglican Church was restored as well, and although Catholics and Nonconformists experienced some tolerance after 1660, it was not until after 1800 that they gained full political rights. In sum, at the local and national levels, an Englishman who fell asleep during Elizabeth I's reign in the 1570s and awoke in the reign of William III in the 1690s would have found little unfamiliar or shocking.

The same cannot be said regarding the French revolution. Although the great symbols of the revolution that had been used to establish its novelty—the new calendar, the disestablishment of the Catholic Church, and the repudiation of the aristocracy—had begun to lose their force under Napoleon and were ineffective by the 1820s, there were major administrative changes that lasted: the Napoleonic Code, the replacement of provinces as basic administrative units by *départements*, and new municipal governments. And there were lasting changes in rural administration: most notably, the local power of landlords to administer petty justice and exact seigneurial dues was swept away. More importantly, the Church ceased to be a major independent landlord and collector of tithes. But although there was much political change, there was no social revolution. No class was expropriated or lost its status. Under Napoleon, the richest landlords in France were still largely from the same noble families that had led France in wealth in the 1780s (Bergeron 1981, 125–129); and one has only to read Stendahl's great novel *Le rouge et le noir* to see the status retained by the aristocracy and the

Church in the early nineteenth century. Much of what we think of as "revolutionary" about both the English and the French revolutions has more to do with their language of mobilization and their temporary radical phases than with their permanent results.

How different were the Eastern cases? Interestingly, a Chinese or Ottoman Rip van Winkle who slept through the seventeenth century could not help but notice marked changes in his society's major administrative institutions.

The displacement of the Ming by the Qing brought immediate changes to the central administration; the presence of Manchu banner forces in the army and the joint authority of Manchu and Chinese officials in key roles were two striking innovations. Even more striking, however, were changes in local authority and class structure.

In 1661, the Qing achieved an administrative reform that changed the system of land registration and effectively abolished the ability of literati to shelter their lands, and those of allied landlord families, from taxation (Dennerline 1981, 323–325). This adjustment, crucial for the survival of the state, also greatly weakened the attraction of land as an investment. Thus the agricultural basin of the Yangzi shifted from large estates, usually held by wealthy landlords who were sheltered by degree holders and retired officials (the gentry proper) and worked by bonded laborers, to peasant smallholdings. As Marks (1984, 44–45) comments, "a new class structure ha[d] emerged, quite different from that of Ming times, that created new patterns of rural life." The power of the non-gentry landlord disappeared, and leverage over the peasant, other than that of the state, was obtained chiefly through moneylending and control of ceremonial and educational functions, all roles that attracted the gentry. Whereas prior to 1660 the Chinese countryside was dominated by a gentry-landlord alliance that owned vast estates, controlled bonded laborers, and brokered with state officials, after 1660 the gentry, with an economic role now almost wholly defined in terms of moneylending and administrative functions, stood alone between cultivators and the state bureaucracy. As Naquin and Rawski (1987, 120) firmly state, "the diminution of servile field labor and its replacement with contractual forms of tenancy ranks . . . as one of the major social and economic phenomena of the early Qing." Paradoxically, although the connection between gentry and landholding diminished, the power of the gentry increased with the virtual disappearance of a class that had loomed large in the sixteenth century: the landlords who held vast private estates (Wiens 1980, 4–5; Dennerline 1981, 3–4; Elvin 1973, 249). As Metzger

(1977, 9) remarks, "what can be called the 'privileged rural sector' of the Ming period largely died out," to be replaced by a more urban, more commercial, gentry elite.

In Ottoman Turkey, the Köprülü viziers who restored order in the late seventeenth century were able to restore many of the central administrative departments. Some permanent changes occurred: the *devşirme* system of official recruitment, whereby Christian youth were levied from the countryside and educated in palace schools, was abandoned in the early seventeenth century and did not return (Shaw 1976, 187). But as in China, the true structural transformation occurred at the local level.

In restoring state authority through repression of recalcitrant local officials, the Köprülü were not able to entirely restore the *tımar* system. Instead they found themselves forced to recognize and seek the aid of the local notables, the *ayan*s, who had arisen in the sixteenth and seventeenth centuries and whose numbers and significance greatly increased in the eighteenth. The rise of the *ayan*s "marked a structural change for the Ottoman feudal system [and] altered the relationship between the central authority and the provinces" (Naff 1977, 9). What differentiated the crisis of the seventeenth century in Ottoman Turkey from prior factional and dynastic civil wars in the fifteenth and sixteenth centuries was this transformation of local authority relations. An entire class—the *tımar*-holding cavalry, who held prebendal fiefs from the sultan in exchange for military service, sought success in war, and held political and military power in the countryside in the sixteenth century— was displaced by a new class, the *ayan*s. This new class held de facto private estates, either *çiftlik*s (big commercial farms) or trusteeship of *vakıf*s (religious foundations), gained wealth by tax farming and trade, and held political and military authority in the countryside in the eighteenth century (Inalcik 1977, 29–32; Cvetkova 1977, 167–169; Karpat 1974b).

In sum, in both Turkey and China the seventeenth century crises resulted in the disappearance of a class that had become a stumbling block to the state: large estate and bondservant-owning landlords in China, and prebendal military groups in Turkey. And in each case, the transformation entailed new rural class relationships: usurious and ceremonially dominant gentry exploiting small peasant proprietors in China, and locally rooted commercial landlords and tax farmers dominating villages in Turkey. Thus, the seventeenth-century crises in Asia resulted in changes, especially at the local level, far greater than were experienced in contemporary England, and comparable to those in eighteenth-century France.

It is also worthwhile to consider here the outcomes of the events of 1688–1689 in England and of 1868 in Japan. By our definition, the events of 1688–1689 in England, though constituting a political crisis, do not qualify as a case of state breakdown. Neither popular uprisings nor civil war took place, for thirty years of demographic stability and economic recovery had improved popular conditions and started to heal elite divisions. There was a crisis of authority, but it was caused by concern about the Crown's allegiance to the national religion, not by fiscal or military failure or by intra-elite struggles for social precedence. The authority of Parliament was reinforced and the terms of succession slightly changed, but there were no changes in elite status, in economic organization, or in the beliefs that justified the distribution of power and status. We can describe this event, in our earlier terminology of chapter 1, as (1,1,0,0,1,0,0,0). In the Meiji Restoration, there were clear intra-elite struggles between lower-class samurai intellectuals and officials, on the one hand, and more privileged upper-rank samurai, on the other, as these divisions had hardened into virtually hereditary strata (Huber 1981). There were also conflicts that did lead to civil war (although on a modest scale) between the shogunate and the leaders of the Choshu and Satsuma *han* in the southwest. The extent of popular uprisings in the years leading to the Restoration is much debated, but Bix (1986) argues persuasively that popular unrest in the 1860s was sufficiently widespread to reinforce elite doubts about the efficacy and virtue of the shogunate, and thus to contribute to its fall. I thus consider the Meiji Restoration a bona fide case of state breakdown. Given the vast changes in Japanese institutions that followed, we can describe the Meiji Restoration as (1,1,1,1,1,1,1,0). In sum, the Meiji Restoration had far more elements in common with the other cases of state breakdown than did the English Revolution of 1688.

What is remarkable about the Meiji Restoration is that, despite the large role played by marginal elites, namely the lower-ranking samurai, and despite the resulting dramatic changes in the principles of elite recruitment and in political and social institutions, the *ideology* of the restoration was explicitly conservative. No doubt the Meiji leaders developed an aggressively intolerant nationalism, as did the revolutionary leaders in England and France. But in the Western cases, such nationalism was a substitute for traditional royal authority, which, along with most traditional beliefs and institutions, was repudiated by the revolutionary extremists. In the Japanese case, nationalism was introduced as an *affirmation* of traditional political and religious symbols. Obedience to traditional authority (that of the emperor), rather than a challenge to traditional authority, was the leading principle of mobilization behind the Meiji leaders. Thus Japan demonstrates that the presence of marginal elites in the revolutionary leadership may be necessary, but is certainly not sufficient, to produce state reconstruction that embodies a revolutionary ideology.

For both the English Revolution of 1688 and the Meiji Restoration, the applicability of the label "revolution" has been hotly debated. Both events were proclaimed by their leaders as restorationist movements: the Declaration of Rights of 1689 was presented as merely listing "the knowne lawes and statutes and freedome of the Realme" (Schwoerer 1981, 296), while the Meiji leaders rested their legitimacy on the restoration of the authority of the emperor (A. Craig 1986; Jansen 1986; Totman 1980). Yet both have been cited as turning points in the histories of their nations: the English Revolution of 1688 is often held to have completed the task begun in 1640 and to have placed irrevocable limits on monarchical authority (Trevelyan 1953; Schwoerer 1981), while the Meiji oligarchs are hailed for having dismantled the strict status system and feudal partition of their country and having created a unified, modernizing government in Japan (Trimberger 1978; Huber 1981). Were these "revolutions," or not?

Posing the question in this manner manifests a common confusion, one stemming from the assumption that only events motivated by a revolutionary ideology can be significant turning points in history. In fact, the cases described in this chapter illustrate how the ideological and institutional components of state reconstruction can sharply *differ*. If we judge these cases by the ideological stance toward tradition shown in their most radical phase, then the Puritan and French revolutions stand alone in this group as revolutionary, while the Qing, the later Ottomans, and the English in 1688–1689 are avowedly nonrevolutionary. The Japanese, with their defense of the emperor but their condemnation of the shogunate and abolition of the special status of the samurai, stand somewhere in between. In contrast, if we judge these events by the degree of change that occurred in political institutions and agrarian class structure, viewed from the perspective of twenty to thirty years after the onset of state breakdown, then we have to label the Meiji Restoration as the "most" revolutionary, and the English Revolution of 1640 the least. The Ming, Ottoman, and French crises had perhaps equally "revolutionary" outcomes, and the English crisis of 1688–1689 somewhat less, all falling somewhere between the Japanese and English 1640 cases. Quite plainly, the usual assumption that revolutionary ideology and revolutionary results go together is mistaken.

In sum, state breakdown was generally followed by significant changes in political and agrarian institutions, whether in Europe or in Asia. Where marginal elites led state reconstruction, the principles of elite recruitment and social status differentiation were sharply altered. But only in the West was state breakdown followed by phases, however brief, of complete repudiation and abolition of traditional institutions. It is these phases, with their attempt to create a new society resting on new ideals, that strike many observers as constituting the essence of "revolution." Yet as we have seen, these phases cannot be traced to distinctive political or social causes for state breakdown itself, which were similar in both Eastern and Western cases. What, then, provided the outlook, and the language, that turned Western reactions to state breakdown in the direction of "revolution?"

IDEOLOGIES AND CULTURAL FRAMEWORKS:
ESCHATOLOGICAL OR CYCLICAL?

This know also, that in the last days perilous times shall come.

2 Tim. 3:1

What seems to differentiate the so-called great revolutions—for example, the Puritan Revolution, the French Revolution, the Russian Revolution, the Chinese Communist Revolution—from other similar instances of state breakdown and reconstruction is the profession of novelty during the phase of revolutionary struggle and state reconstruction. In this phase, traditional symbols, ceremonies, and marks of status are repudiated and replaced by new ones. This phase may fail to be institutionalized for any number of reasons: in England, there were the reluctance of Cromwell to treat the Protectorate of the Commonwealth as tantamount to a kingship and his failure to produce a worthy successor; in France, there were military exigencies that led to Napoleon's dominance and later defeat. Or this phase may be institutionalized through the success of revolutionary leaders in building an army and stable institutions, as in Russia and China. Some analysts of revolution have argued that events count as "great" revolutions only if they have this rejection of tradition and symbolic reconstruction (Eisenstadt 1978), and that other early modern crises involve merely rebellion and dynastic struggles, but no social change (Huntington 1968). As we have seen, these arguments underestimate the degree of institutional change that has occurred in other cases of state breakdown and reconstruction. However, whether or not it is fully institutionalized, an episode of sharp repudiation of tradition leaves a legacy of symbols and ideas that may have dynamic consequences in the future. Thus, the conditions governing the presence or absence of such an episode in the process of revolutionary struggle and state reconstruction deserve consideration.

All successors to fallen Old Regimes face similar problems and adopt broadly similar measures to deal with them: gaining support of key groups, rebuilding the army, increasing state centralization, reforming taxation, weakening the independence of elites, and reestablishing peasant proprietors to provide the basis needed for the revenue and manpower requirements of the state. But as we noted, revolutionary leaderships have some latitude about whether to present their solutions as modifications and corrections to a basically sound Old Regime, or as altogether new regimes that repudiate the old. Clearly, the choice depends to a large extent on how elites diagnose the failure of the Old Regime: Was it simply corrupt, mismanaged, and effete? Or was it a relic of past times, and thus no longer workable or legitimate in current circumstances?

To understand why elites may adopt one or the other stance, it is necessary to draw a distinction between "ideologies" and "cultural frameworks." This distinction has been developed by Swidler (1986) and Skocpol (1985). Both suggest that ideologies are values, meanings, and symbols that are self-consciously offered in contest with other sets of values, meanings, and symbols. Ideologies, then, are programmatic and belligerent. In contrast, there are "traditions" (Swidler) or "cultural idioms" (Skocpol). These are the taken-for-granted, background set of values, meanings, and symbols that are embodied in the dominant social, economic, religious, and political habits and institutions of a society. Except in times of social dislocation and conflict, they are not programmatic or belligerent; they are simply "there," part of every competent social actor's tool kit for social life. I prefer to use the term "cultural framework" for such background, taken-for-granted meanings and values so as to indicate the bounded and connected nature of a set of traditional symbols and beliefs.

Swidler (1986) has advanced our understanding of such cultural frameworks. She takes issue with Max Weber, who emphasized, most famously in *The Protestant Ethic*, the role of culture as a set of goals that guide individual behavior. Swidler has suggested that cultures provide not a coherent set of goals but rather a tool kit of meanings, values, and goals that individuals can use to construct life strategies. This notion of a tool kit helps make sense of the ideological struggles and manipulation that take place in revolutions. For example, seventeenth-century England had a variety of diverse traditions—Roman, Anglo-Saxon, Norman, constitutional, Catholic, Protestant, common law, and canon law—all kept alive in various village, county, court, and Church institutions and memories. Much of the ideological struggle in the English Revolution was over which of these elements would be selected and given emphasis. Charles I and Archbishop Laud were attempting, in the 1630s, to emphasize the hierarchical, Roman, and canon traditions for political and Church organization. The Long Parliament emphasized the constitutional, common law, and Protestant traditions. The more extreme revolutionaries sought to justify their case through references to "Anglo-Saxon freedoms" and communal traditions.

This multiplicity of symbols and traditions is a common aspect of major cultural frameworks. Eighteenth-century France had Roman, Frankish, Catholic, Protestant, and numerous regional traditions embodied in its legal, political, religious, social, and economic organizations. It was these traditions, melded into the Old Regime, that the ideology of the Enlightenment opposed. Ming China had Confucian, Buddhist, Taoist, and legalist traditions; Ottoman Turkey had a rich blend of Turkish, Arabic, Persian, Byzantine, and Egyptian elements. Japanese culture was more homogenous, but the Shinto religion had absorbed Buddhist elements, and by the eighteenth century the warrior ethic competed with an emerging urban commercial culture that had its own values.

One element in the cultural framework of the Western cases, however, was missing in the East. This was an eschatological view of history, rooted in the Judeo-Christian tradition. Where this tradition had penetrated, people were accustomed to thinking in apocalyptic terms, and to seeing history as secular rather than cyclic (Christiansen 1978). In eschatological thinking, history moves to a particular point in time, a time of judgment and destruction, from which a new, superior order will emerge (R. Bloch 1985, xi). Revolutionary leaders seeking freedom to maneuver, trying to bridge their plans to folk traditions, and casting about for legitimation of acts of violence against the old order turned to eschatological imagery, where it was available in the extant cultural framework, to describe the revolutionary struggle and the task of reconstruction.

For example, in Puritan England Sir Henry Vane wrote of the 1640s that "the time of the End, that is to say, the foretold-of day, in which Christ is to judge the World in Righteousness . . . is at the very doors." He was far from alone, as millenarian thinking was common among Puritan leaders, and Parliament ordered the translation and publication of millenarian texts (Cliffe 1984, 208; Underdown 1985, 259; Lamont 1969; R. Bloch 1985, 8). Capp (1972) found that 70 percent of the works in a sample drawn from the most prolific Presbyterian and Independent divines showed some millenarian content. In eighteenth-century France, millenarianism had become secularized, but the mode of thought was the same. Time would begin anew with the revolution, and man would be reborn—hence the new calendar, the new designation of "citizen," and the attempt by Robespierre to introduce new modes of public worship (Zerubavel 1981). Indeed, one of the curiosities of the French Revolution is that its secular millenarianism was not capable of drawing on ready-made symbols from the past, as Puritans drew on the Bible and constitutionalists drew on the mythic Saxon past and Magna Carta in England (although the French did draw on Roman republican traditions). Thus French revolutionary leaders strove mightily to create a new vocabulary of words, symbols, and ceremonies to distance their institutions from those of the Old Regime. Festivals were invented, clothing redesigned, and new credos and terms of address developed to demonstrate to all that they were living in a new age (Sewell 1985b). Of course, under cover of these revolutionary "incantations"—as L. Hunt (1984) labels them, *nation, patrie, vertu*—they were extending authority and centralizing the government. Nonetheless, it is these attempts to mark a symbolic caesura between the Old Regime and the era of the revolution that have stayed with us and have fixed in our minds the image of the French Revolution as a repudiation of the past.

Communist revolutions, though taking place throughout the world, have also employed Western eschatological imagery, albeit in the form given by Marx, with history progressing explicitly toward proletarian revolution. The Communist notion of linear and progressive history, with an accumulation of moral decay (the misery and alienation brought by the advance of capitalism) being purified by a transformative act of destruction, is, in broad outline, much the same as in earlier Western revolutions. Another parallel case, pointed out by Arjomand (1986), is the recent Iranian Revolution. Arjomand has shown that much of the radicalism of that event drew from the peculiar characteristics of Shi'ism, which is a uniquely eschatological strain of Islam. Arjomand (1986, 414) notes that "Shi'ite doctrine has an important millenarian tenet: the belief in the appearance of the Twelfth Imam as the Mahdi to redeem the world. . . . There can be no doubt that revolutionary political millenarianism played a crucial role in the motivation of the Iranian intelligentsia and other groups."

This eschatological element was an innovation of Judeo-Christian culture. As Eliade (1959, 104, 112) notes, Hebrew prophets were the first to articulate a "one-way" vision of time, and thus "succeeded in transcending the traditional vision of the cycle" that was found in Greek and Roman philosophy and throughout the Middle and Far East. The Hebrew vision was "taken up and amplified" by Christian belief. In Christianity, "periodic regeneration of the Creation is replaced by a single regeneration that will take place in an *in illo tempore* [a specific time in this world] to come."

In contrast, the cultural frameworks of Ming China, Ottoman Turkey (dominated by Sunni, not Shi'ite, Islamic doctrine), and Tokugawa Japan did not contain eschatological elements. "[Unlike] the Hebrew view of time as a linear passage from the creation to the end of the world," in Eastern cultures "significant events were thought of as occurring cyclically" (Gough 1968, 75). The cosmos itself was considered to be regulated by "cyclic cosmic time, with no beginning point" (Mote 1971, 20). The reigning view of history in all three cases—drawn in China from Neo-Confucian historical scholarship (which was borrowed by Japan) and the Buddhist doctrine of "return," and in the Ottoman state from the historical tradition of Ibn Khaldûn—was therefore cyclic. Chinese peasant revolts typically "looked back to a time of primitive justice" and idealized past dynasties (Chesneaux 1973, 15–16). Millenarian revolts in China, such as the White Lotus rebellion in the nineteenth century, adopted a Buddhist view of history as divided into great cycles (*kalpa*), at the end of which a holocaust would destroy the world and a new period would begin. But this view was not about progress, at least as the concept is understood in the West; it was instead about the destruction of evil and, it was hoped, the reconstruction of a primordial paradise (Naquin 1976, 10–11).

Chinese and Islamic elites also adopted a cyclic, though more empirical, view of history. They believed that dynasties rose and fell according to their greater or lesser fidelity to authentic Confucian or Islamic precepts of rule (Eisenstadt 1980a, 7; Itzkowitz 1972, 87–89). Thus, political crises in Chinese and Islamic empires were not diagnosed as final moments, calling for an "end" to the olden times; instead they were diagnosed as failures of virtue, calling for a more rigid adherence to traditional ideals. Institutions might be changed to achieve these goals, but the ideological "cover" was always a claim of greater authenticity and fidelity in regard to *traditional* symbols of authority. The same applies to Japan during the Meiji period.

Western analysts of revolution have shown a tendency to overemphasize the difference between Eastern and Western political crises by placing too great a stress on the presence or absence of one element—eschatological imagery—in the complex process of state breakdown, revolutionary struggle, and state reconstruction. Many elements of this process were common across all the cases we have studied here. And since considerable institutional change can take place under the "cover" of ideologically conservative state reconstruction, social scientists have often overlooked the extensive institutional change that occurred following Eastern political crises. However, the presence of eschatological elements in the cultural frameworks of seventeenth-century England and eighteenth-century France (as well as in the Marxist revolutions in twentieth-century Russia and China, and in the Shi'ite revolution in Iran) do give a unique aspect to these cases: an ideological episode that involves explicit repudiation of Old Regime symbols and institutions.

This repudiation of tradition is not solely a function of the cultural setting. In particular, the attempt to implant a "new" order depends on the conjunction of *two* characteristics, one structural and one ideological. First, there must be "marginal" elites who want not only to seize power but also to change the principles that they feel originally relegated them to marginal status. Second, there must be within the ideological framework of the society an eschatological element that can be utilized to cast the political struggle as a final end to the Old Regime, to be followed by the emergence of a new, more virtuous society.

History offers examples of millenarian populist movements that failed to draw the leadership of marginal elites from the national center—for example, the Islamic Mahdist and European medieval millenarian movements (N. Cohn 1970). Lacking elite leadership, these movements generally aimed simply at creating traditional anti-elite utopias or anarchism, rather than at remaking the state. There are also cases of marginal elites who took advantage of state breakdown to remake society, but outside of eschatological cultures, for example the Mamluk military leaders who took power in medieval Egypt, the lower-class samurai intellectuals who spearheaded the Meiji Restoration in Japan, and the Islamic nationalists who led the state transformation of Saudi Arabia in the early twentieth century. In all these cases, the reconstruction of society took place on the basis of appeals to ethnic nationalism and of reaffirmations of certain traditional elements that had been "corrupted" by the Old Regimes. One can also cite instances of state breakdown or political crisis where marginal elites were unable to wrest the mantle of "authentic" national leadership from the traditional regime, as in the Fronde and in Hapsburg Spain. In these cases as well, state reconstruction took place on the basis of conservative nationalism. Thus, it takes a combination of eschatological cultural elements and the leadership of marginal elites who are sufficiently well organized to gain some initial triumphs in the revolutionary struggles following state breakdown, to produce symbolic transformation and revolutionary political reconstruction. Without this combination, conservative state reconstruction is the likely outcome.

What bearing did this difference have on the respective histories of Eastern and Western nations? One clue to follow here is that the boundaries drawn between "East" and "West" are slightly misleading. England and France had dynamic futures after their revolutions, and China and Turkey entered long periods of stagnation. However, in the West, Spain too entered a period of relative stagnation after its seventeenth-century crisis, whereas in the East, Japan became dynamic after the Meiji Restoration. Thus, although state breakdown generally led to institutional change, not all change was equally fruitful. We therefore still need to ask what differentiated the long-term outcomes of the crises in England, France, and Japan, on the one hand, from those in China, the Ottoman Empire, and Spain, on the other.

CULTURAL CONFORMITY AND ITS CONSEQUENCES

Let us first consider the outcomes of the English and French revolutions. In each case, the monarchy was challenged, not merely in regard to its competence but also in regard to its right to exist. This challenge, although in both cases defeated, left a legacy of radical ideas that could be used to justify reforms and departures from tradition in the future. The English author James Harrington, in his celebrated *Oceana*, sought "to argue against any return to the traditional 'ancient' or 'balanced' constitution by showing that it had rested on foundations which had always been insecure and were now swept away" (Pocock 1975, 385).

Thomas Paine's arguments in *Rights of Man* reasserted the case that monarchy was a human institution, which was made during a particular historical period and could be unmade when circumstances warranted.

Since the monarchies were not permanently swept away by the revolutions, however, we may ask what such arguments accomplished. Their most valuable legacy was the hedge that they erected against absolute power. Western states could have succumbed to the elements of Imperial Rome in their heritage, still very much alive in the Catholic hierarchy and in the classical notions of Roman law, in which the ruler was granted absolute power for the sake of keeping order. But those revolutions in which political struggles involved the eschatological claims of marginal elites resulted in searches for alternative symbols and principles. These alternatives were built on the heritage of Roman republicanism, vague memories of Anglo-Saxon and Frankish communal freedoms, and, in place of Roman law, common law in England and Enlightenment constitutionalism on the Continent. These elements, once restored to the center of political discourse, did not disappear but instead remained as the basis of claims to what contemporaries called "liberty" (L. Stone 1980). The persistence of these claims continued to move English and French politics in the centuries following the revolutions and helped to secure continued openness and dynamism in their institutions. Claims to liberty also provided a shield behind which individuals could deploy their resources freely in new combinations and thus introduce innovations in the economy as well as in institutions (North 1981; J. A. Hall 1985; Goldstone 1987).

The importance of these ideological elements is evident when we turn to Spain, where the imperial and Church canon traditions were reasserted after the seventeenth-century crisis, and triumphed. Spain, after all, with its entrenched aristocracy and powerful Church, had no marginal elites able to supplant the traditional authorities. Nationalist claims motivated the Catalans, and tax demands motivated the Italian elite, to revolt. But in both countries traditional elites were frightened of the popular movements that threatened to emerge, and they turned back to royal authority (in Catalonia, first to the French Crown) for reinforcement of their positions (Elliott 1970). The stability of Castile, and the resubjugation of Catalonia and Italy, meant that the king retained the mantle of national authority, and no "eschatological" movement took root. Thus, the response to the crisis was a reassertion of traditional authority.

Kamen (1983, 251) notes that after the crisis, "the stimulation once provided by . . . humanism, Italian influences, [and] the American experience . . . faded and altered into a more subdued, occasionally aggressive, national chauvinism." Led by the Jesuits, the Counter-Reformation encouraged Catholic ideology and kept Enlightenment ideas at arm's length. Kamen (1980, 291, 313) thus points out that after 1650, "while other European universities in the late century were becoming more secularized, those of Spain were falling more under the influence of orders with a dogmatic interest in traditional Catholic philosophy. . . . The siege mentality which typified the 'closed society' of Hapsburg Spain induced the authorities to treat all non-Spanish influences as suspect." Institutional rigidity, dogmatic orthodoxy, and economic stagnation went together.

In China and the Ottoman Empire, as we have noted in discussing their cyclic view of history, the logical solution to the seventeenth-century crises was a reaffirmation of traditional orthodoxy. One does not find the notion that the state should be redesigned for new challenges; instead, all that was needed was a purging of corruption and a return to the institutions as they had operated at the height of each empire (Inalcik 1985, 95, 201; Wakeman 1985, 2:448–449). Thus, after 1650 the Ottoman and Chinese empires became more rigidly orthodox and conservative than they had been earlier; they eschewed novelties, while rewarding conformity to past habits (Plaks 1985, 551; Welch 1980, 92).

The early Ottomans had readily introduced innovations in their institutions and military technology. However, their tardy and ineffective following of European progress in military technology after 1650 stands "in marked contrast with the speed and inventiveness with which they accepted and adapted the European invention of artillery in the 15th century" (Lewis 1958, 116). Although the sultans continued to introduce some innovations in military techniques borrowed from the West, the Ottomans sought to keep their institutions pure; thus, "after a tolerant start . . . the Ottomans came positively to encourage obscurantist thought. This militated against the borrowing of western techniques and against native inventiveness" (E. Jones 1981b, 201). Sugar (1977, 251) adds that the "strict formalist orthodoxy of the Ottoman authorities . . . stifled intellectual activities." After the 1680s, the Ottoman religious authorities "especially maintained the superiority of . . . Islam, . . . heaping scorn upon the outside world. Innovation became a particular object of their wrath. . . . All eyes looked backwards" to the days of Ottoman greatness. The Ottomans believed they "had only to discover how things were done then and follow that example" (Itzkowitz 1972, 96–97, 107). Reformers focused on the traditional Islamic "circle of equity," a rigid prescription for the restoration of order. Reformers argued that "in Ottoman society everyone has his place [and] it was the sultan's function to keep everyone in his place" (Itzkowitz 1972, 79).

In China after 1650, "early Qing literati sought to reconstruct the ideal Confucian order . . . before it had been sullied with Buddhist and Taoist notions" (Naquin and Rawski 1987, 65). Many scholars therefore cooperated with the Qing as they sought to reinforce their rule through an increasingly authoritarian imposition of Confucian norms of conformity (Ho 1967; Kessler 1976). The Ming dynasty had at times tried to reinforce state control by stifling innovation and preserving traditional practices, most notably by failing to follow up the overseas voyages of the admiral Zheng He (A. Chan 1982, 387). But the Ming were not entirely successful in suppressing orthodoxy. For most of the Ming period, "official religion" was not merely Confucianism, but "a complex . . . and unstable collection of cults of various sorts: classical, pseudo-classical, popular, and Taoist" (R. Taylor 1990, 156). Ming Neo-Confucianism was rich in variations, and currents flowed out of state control, from the populist school of Taizhou to the puritan Donglin and Fushe (deBary 1970). But what the Ming attempted, the Qing accomplished. Late Ming syncretism was replaced by "a rather rigid Confucian intolerance of Buddhism and Taoism" (Ropp 1981, 47). For the Manchus,

the most effective long-range policy was to sponsor the very institutional and cultural system which . . . the leading social class of scholars and officials regarded as orthodox. [Hence] the ardent endorsement by the K'ang-hsi emperor and his successors of the conservative and passive aspects of social and political relationships in later Sung Neo-Confucianism as official orthodoxy. [By contrast,] in its formative stage the Sung Confucian state is known for its remarkable diversity of thought and policy and for its absence of officially endorsed orthodoxy. In spite of the Ming founder's choice of the Ch'eng-Chu school as orthodoxy, none of his successors showed any real concern for ideology. . . . It was under the alien Manchu rule that China became a strictly conformist "orthodox" state. [Indeed,] much of what we regard as the orthodox Confucian state and society is exemplified not by earlier Chinese dynasties, but by the Ch'ing period.

(Ho 1967, 192)

Confucian orthodoxy soon became smothering and intolerant. Enforced orthodoxy led to a passive conformity, and "invention was almost absent" (Elvin 1973, 193–194, 203). Traditional hierarchies were more rigidly defined. As G. Hamilton (1984, 415) comments, what increased in China after the Ming "was the codification of roles and role responsibilities." And as Ropp (1981, 47) observes, "whereas scholars in the seventeenth century were frequently aware of Western natural science . . . by the eighteenth century, Chinese scholarship was again isolated, self-contained, and introspective." Censorship, beginning in 1687 with book proscriptions, reached its height in 1774 with the literary inquisition, in which vast numbers of books were destroyed and their authors (and relatives) severely persecuted (Gernet 1982, 475).

In short, in the aftermath of the English and French revolutions, the legacy of the brief phases of repudiation of the past was to create symbols and ideologies that remained in contest with Old Regime authority, and that continued to make claims for institutional change and liberty. But in Spain, Ottoman Turkey, and China, the response to the seventeenth-century crises was to seek order by enforcing conformity to traditional norms, alternative claims being virtually absent. The latter nations became, to coin an awkward phrase, highly "role-prescriptive" societies, concerned with preserving themselves through ever-tighter prescriptions of role behavior and ever-tighter definitions of orthodoxy. State reconstruction and institutional reform on these terms successfully restored a measure of prosperity to each of these states, but they entered the late seventeenth and early eighteenth centuries without the dynamism of postrevolutionary England and France.

Thus we have a surprising result. It was not the degree of institutional change, but the ideological framework in which such change was embedded, that governed the dynamism of societies after state breakdown. Both Ottoman Turkey and Qing China showed considerable change, in both administrative institutions and agrarian class relations, in their postbreakdown state reconstruction. And in both cases, the result was a greatly strengthened state. But there was little further innovation, and their societies stagnated. Along with Counter-Reformation Spain, these societies were throttled by state-enforced *cultural conformity*, whereby states increased their domestic authority at the expense of future vitality. England experienced much less, and France only comparable, levels of institutional change after their state breakdowns. But they retained high levels of *ideological tension*. Thus, their postbreakdown states did not harden and stagnate, but instead showed a continuing dynamic evolution.

The case of Japan is more of a puzzle. Despite the absence of eschatological elements in the Meiji Restoration and the reconstruction and reform of the state under the aegis of a conservative ideology, Japan rapidly progressed to fight off the Western challenge and become an imperial power in its own right. But the apparent contradiction is easily resolved. Japan shows just the combination of an initial dramatic change in the principles and institutions of elite rule with a succeeding increase in conservatism and pressures for cultural conformity that one would expect in the case of state reconstruction by a marginal elite that lacked an eschatological ideology, and hence a source of ideological tension with traditional authority.

Thus, the Japanese case shows aspects of both revolutionary and conservative state reconstruction. First, despite the lack of novel ideology, the Meiji Restoration was led largely by a marginal elite—low-ranking samurai professionals—who sought to change the principles of Japanese social and political organization. In our other cases of conservative state reconstruction, marginal elites were absent. In Spain, Turkey, and China, though there were changes in class structure and political institutions, traditional elites continued to affirm the traditional status privileges and the superiority of the traditional empire; hence, foreign ideas and technology were rejected. But in Japan those elements of traditional Tokugawa rule that had fortified the high-ranking samurai—for example, the feudal organization and status hierarchy and the closure of Japan to outside influences—were done away with. Only those elements of tradition that did not threaten the new position of the formerly lower-class samurai—for example, emperor worship, ethnic nationalism, and strict deference and obedience to duly recognized authority—were retained and strengthened (Trimberger 1978).

Moreover, while discipline and the use of foreign technology, as well as the economic surpluses and entrepreneurial urban classes that had developed in the eighteenth and nineteenth centuries, allowed Japan to progress militarily, Japan became neither a state that favored liberty nor a center of economic innovation. It too became a nation that stressed recovery from crisis through greater conformity to traditional norms. As Pyle (1988, 674) points out, "the Meiji period bequeathed to modern Japan a powerful conservative tradition that dominated government and society." Barrington Moore (1966) has detailed how, despite success in maintaining independence against the West, Japan's failure to experience a marked break with its conformist, authoritarian traditions led to the triumph of fascist elements in the early twentieth century. It is well to remember that Japan's current constitution and liberties are to a significant degree attributable to the recovery from another case of state breakdown: following Japan's defeat in World War II, the United States imposed a new constitution embodying some very non-Japanese cultural elements.

Moore built his account of the development of modern states around the roles of agrarian change and revolution. The structural analysis in this book of the preconditions of state breakdown—which unites attention to long-term demographic trends, and their consequences for state finances and intra-elite competition, with consideration of mass mobilization potential—expands on Moore's study. But as this chapter demonstrates, we must also attend to the cultural frameworks and the triumphant ideologies that shape the outcomes of state breakdown and reconstruction. The ideologies that arise in revolutionary struggles, and their impact on state reconstruction, can influence the history of nations for centuries afterward.

CONCLUSIONS: THE VARYING ROLE OF CULTURE

The English and French revolutions were not the product of uniquely Western crises of capitalism or absolutism. They shared their basic causes with profoundly similar crises in the Eastern states of the Ottoman Empire and China. The divergence of Eastern and Western civilizations after the mid-seventeenth century thus cannot be simply attributed to a structural difference between Western "revolutions" and Eastern "peasant rebellions" or "dynastic crises." In terms of institutional changes, particularly changes in local class structure, more extensive changes followed the seventeenth-century crises in Ottoman Turkey and Ming China than followed the English Revolution. The entire question of the divergence of Eastern and Western economic and political development, of Western dynamism and Eastern stagnation in the early modern period, therefore needs reexamination. In particular, the manner in which Western Europe forged ahead of the advanced Eastern civilizations of Islam and China needs to be explained in a way that accommodates the similarities of the seventeenth-century crises in each.

Focusing on cultural frameworks and how they governed reactions to state crises and shaped state reconstruction provides an entry point for such an explanation. Different ideological legacies, embedded in state reconstruction after the seventeenth-century crises, profoundly influenced the later divergence of East and West.

I observed in chapter 1 that social theorists have tended to polarize debates about social change by arguing whether "material" or "cultural and ideological" factors are the primary agents of change. Clearly this false dilemma—asking whether history is governed by Marxist materialism or Hegelian idealism—fails to capture historical reality. A number of scholars have tried to overcome this dichotomy. Geertz (1973), N. Davis (1975), and Darnton (1984) have turned to deep analysis of texts or events, analysis designed to illustrate the creativity of individuals and groups in producing symbols and actions that both express and shape their material conditions. Other authors (Giddens 1982; Bourdieu 1984) have put forth general theories of culture that stress the ability of individuals to appropriate cultural elements and use them to reconstruct or reinforce material and institutional structures. All of these approaches attempt to free individuals from the determinism of materialist constraints, and also from the mechanical reproduction of a dominant culture. These approaches therefore have the virtue of avoiding either a simple socioeconomic or cultural determination of individual action. Yet they also are almost useless for long-term, causal historical explanation, for they tend to reduce to a halfway house between materialism and idealism, blandly asserting that, in general, individuals respond to both their material and their cultural environments with (more or less) creative responses that both reproduce and alter those environments.

But as we have just observed, the creative response to a changing environment is *not* constant. These theories of culture fail to appreciate temporal variation, that the role of culture may be quite different in particular concrete historical settings. At some times, as in politically stable periods, the level of cultural innovation may be low; at other times, as in prerevolutionary periods, ideological innovation may increase, but chiefly in response to material forces that create a social crisis. At still other times, as during state breakdown and the ensuing struggle for power, ideological creativity may rise to great heights and develop its own dynamics. And in the restabilization of authority after a breakdown, as the ideological creations of the power struggle become embedded in the postrevolutionary cultural framework, cultural patterns and ideologies may dominate the future possibilities for material as well as cultural change.

Interestingly, it was precisely those revolutions that failed to fully overcome traditional rule but did experience a phase of creative, tradition-repudiating ideology, namely England and France, that left a legacy of fruitful and dynamic tension in postbreakdown society. Although the Puritans and Jacobins faded after the revolutions, a part of their views remained in a rich stock of antitraditional symbols, institutions, and ideals. State reconstructions in those countries thus were continually challenged by claims to principles that hedged absolute authority. In contrast, the ideological response that occurred in tradition-reinforcing cases of state breakdown—as in the Ottoman Empire, China, and Hapsburg Spain—sought to purify and reaffirm traditional institutions. In these cases, the crisis was blamed on deviation from orthodoxy, and the new regimes sought to strip away variety in the extant cultural framework, purging elements perceived as heterodox. The reconstruction of state and social institutions allowed a recovery of traditional prosperity; but the impoverishing of the cultural framework of postbreakdown society reduced the basis for future dynamism and fundamental change. Meiji Japan was a hybrid case, as marginal elites did sweep away certain aspects of the traditional government and its status system, releasing resources for development and imperial expansion. But the Meiji Restoration still was framed in traditional and conservative ideology, which left a legacy of conservative and traditional emphases that continued to dominate much of political and social life.

In short, theories of culture that simply describe the interaction of individuals with cultural elements *in general* are gravely incomplete. Cultural frameworks act with particular power at the times when states are rebuilt or revised in times of state breakdown or crisis. A more complete theory of culture—as suggested by Wuthnow (1989) and Swidler (1986)—thus must recognize that cultural dynamics vary over time, becoming more fluid and more creative at some times, more rigid and more limiting at others.

These diverse outcomes suggest that macrosociology has unduly neglected the role of culture in shaping state structure and dynamics, particularly during periods of state crisis and reconstruction. Theories of social change must recognize that at some concrete historical junctures it is material forces, while at other such junctures it is *cultural* frameworks and ideologies, that play the dominant role in causing and directing change.

SIX

From Past to Present

> Our joint publications excited very little attention, and the only published notice of them which I can remember was by Professor Houghton of Dublin, whose verdict was that all that was new in them was false, and what was true was old.
>
> —*Charles Darwin (on the reception accorded his presentation, in collaboration with Alfred Wallace, of the theory of evolution by natural selection)*

This book has covered a wide range of subjects. Some of the conclusions I now draw follow directly from the findings presented. Others are more speculative, and more provocative. The former concern certain patterns in early modern history. The latter consider the future roles of population change, capitalism, and revolutions; the sources of the "Rise of the West"; and the much-debated current decline of the United States.

EARLY MODERN HISTORY: A WORLD HISTORY

My primary conclusion is quite beautiful in its parsimony. It is that *the periodic state breakdowns in Europe, China, and the Middle East from 1500 to 1850 were the result of a single basic process.* This process unfolded like a fugue, with a major trend giving birth to four related critical trends that combined for a tumultuous conclusion. The main trend was that population growth, in the context of relatively inflexible economic and social structures, led to changes in prices, shifts in resources, and increasing social demands with which agrarian-bureaucratic states could not successfully cope.

The four related critical trends were as follows: (1) Pressures increased on state finances as inflation eroded state income and population growth raised real expenses. States attempted to maintain themselves by raising revenues in a variety of ways, but such attempts alienated elites, peasants, and urban consumers, while failing to prevent increasing debt and eventual bankruptcy. (2) Intra-elite conflicts became more prevalent as larger families and inflation made it more difficult for some families to maintain their status, while expanding population and rising prices lifted other families, creating new aspirants to elite positions. With the state's fiscal weakness limiting its ability to provide for all who sought elite positions, considerable turnover and displacement occurred throughout the elite hierarchy, giving rise to factionalization as different elite groups sought to defend or improve their position. When central authority collapsed, most often as a result of bankruptcy, elite divisions came to the fore in struggles for power. (3) Popular unrest grew, as competition for land, urban migration, flooded labor markets, declining real wages, and increased youthfulness raised the mass mobilization potential of the populace. Unrest occurred in urban and rural areas and took the various forms of food riots, attacks on landlords and state agents, and land and grain seizures, depending on the autonomy of popular groups and the resources of elites. A heightened mobilization potential made it easy for contending elites to marshal popular action in their conflicts, although in many cases popular actions, having their own motivation and momentum, proved easier to encourage than to control. (4) The ideologies of rectification and transformation became increasingly salient. Spreading poverty and vagrancy, ever more severe and frequent harvest crises and food riots, and state ineffectiveness undermined the credibility of religious leaders associated with states and turned both elites and middling groups to heterodox religious movements in the search for reform, order, and discipline. The conjuncture of these four critical trends—state fiscal distress, intra-elite conflicts, heightened mass mobilization potential, and, deriving in part from the other three, increased salience of the folk and elite ideologies of rectification and transformation—combined to undermine stability on *multiple* levels of social organization.

This basic process was triggered all across Eurasia by the periods of sustained population increase that occurred in the sixteenth and early seventeenth centuries and again in the late eighteenth and early nineteenth centuries, thus producing worldwide waves of state breakdown. In contrast, in the late seventeenth and early eighteenth centuries populations did not grow, and the basic process and its four subthemes were absent. Political and social stability resulted. In the early nineteenth century, one should note, several European states had greatly increased their financial resources; thus, even though population growth initiated a similar pattern, the first critical trend was muted, and the ensuing state crises in 1830 and 1848 were less severe. But their kinship with the earlier wave of state crises, and with contemporary state crises in the Ottoman and Chinese empires, remains clear. After 1850, most western European states had increased the flexibility of their economies through industrialization, and of their administrative and social structures through political revolution or reform; thus, population growth lost its ability to trigger the processes that earlier had led to state breakdown. Russia, China, and the Ottoman Empire, however, with their still largely traditional economic, political, and social structures, remained vulnerable to population pressures, which continued through the nineteenth century and led to state breakdown in the early years of the twentieth.

The power of this argument lies not merely in its ability to explain the timing, and the widespread coincidence, of such crises. It lies especially in displaying the linkages—between population growth and price inflation, and between both these factors and state fiscal crisis, elite mobility and competition, and mass mobilization potential—that shaped the development and key features of these crises. Thus for example, the fact that the English and French revolutions were both preceded by periods of unusual social mobility and triggered by fiscal crises can be understood as similar responses to similar historical situations, rather than as mere coincidence or superficial analogy.

Indeed, it is fascinating to find so many trends that English, or French, or Chinese, or Ottoman specialists have claimed to be the product of unique conditions appearing again and again across time and space. Moreover, this consistency lays to rest many old shibboleths and tortured debates. Thus, we clearly and repeatedly find that revolution and rebellion were *not* due to excessively high taxation by rulers, or to a simple lack of social mobility, or chiefly to class conflict, or to general impoverishment of society as a whole. Instead we find consistently that fiscal crises were due to *undertaxation* as elites systematically evaded taxes, so that state revenues barely kept pace with inflation, and hence never kept pace with the increasing *real* wealth of their societies. We find everywhere that *high* social mobility—high rates of turnover and displacement—preceded crises, while *low* social mobility characterized times of stability. Rapid turnover among high officials, strains on elite education and recruitment, and conflicts over patronage are seen in all states and empires approaching crisis. *Factional conflict within the elites*, over access to office, patronage, and state policy, rather than conflict across classes, led to state paralysis and state breakdown. We also find consistently that elites succeeded in shifting the burden of taxation to the middling classes, and that the conditions of the working classes and peasants declined while elites and commercial classes grew richer. Thus, we consistently see a *polarization* of social wealth in the generations preceding crises. And the combination of declining state effectiveness, heightened conflicts over mobility, and increasing poverty at the bottom of the social scale raised the salience of reformist, disciplined, heterodox moral and philosophical schools, a salience that faded rapidly when these social trends ended. These trends are evident in the sixteenth and early seventeenth centuries, and in the eighteenth and early nineteenth centuries, across Eurasia. Certainly particular conditions in each society shaped the timing and magnitude of these trends. But in light of their near universal character, any claim that such trends were produced *solely* by unique local conditions is thoroughly undermined by the evidence.

Almost two decades ago, Lawrence Stone (1972, 26) wrote that "with both [the English and French] Revolutions, once historians have realized that their Marxist interpretation does not work very much better than the Whig, there has followed a period where there is nothing very secure to put in its place." I hope that the *demographic/structural* model can now take that place, as it explains the key features of both crises in better accord with the known facts than the Marxist or Whig views. It also deals far more effectively with the contemporary crises in China and the Middle East and avoids any of the objectionable teleology characteristic of other analyses.

There is no teleology because, although the basic processes and pressures that led to state breakdown occurred widely, the model allows that the precise responses to these pressures varied with the capacity of states to react, of elites to organize, and of popular groups to mobilize. Moreover, once state breakdown had begun, the struggle for power and the need for state reconstruction gave great scope to distinct ideologies, albeit constrained by existing cultural frameworks, to shape the future course of reaction or revolution. Thus, the same basic causal process gave rise to a range of outcomes, depending on the setting in which that process unfolded.

Historians have long debated whether the main causes of early modern revolutions and rebellions were social, economic, religious, or political cleavages. Such distinctions are illusory. Social and economic conflicts, religious heterodoxy, and political factionalization were not independent factors but related aspects of an underlying causal pattern. For a number of societies, this book demonstrates that the early modern crises were rooted in the simultaneous decline of traditional systems of taxation, elite training and recruitment, and popular living standards, and hence in the increased salience and appeal of heterodox ideologies, under the pressure of ecological change.

This model offers several advantages over the Marxist interpretation, its "revisionist" adversaries, and the more recent theories of revolution such as Skocpol's. First, the state appears as an autonomous actor in *three* respects: (1) as an economic actor whose strength is affected by trends in the economy such as inflation and by changing real costs of governance brought by population growth; (2) as a political actor whose strength is affected by the demands of international competition and the demands of domestic elite and popular groups; and (3) as a cultural actor whose strength (and pace of future development) is affected by the tensions—or lack thereof—between state-supported orthodoxy and alternative ideological claims. The Marxist interpretation tends to neglect the autonomy of political actions, the revisionists and Skocpol tend to neglect the impact of key shifts and cycles in economic history, and Skocpol and many Marxists tend to neglect the autonomy of cultural and ideological aspects of social change. The demographic/structural approach to state breakdown—combined with our analysis of the process of revolutionary struggles and their outcome—gives due attention to the economic, political, and cultural aspects of the state's relations with other states, elites, and popular groups.

Second, this analysis of elites identifies a variety of social conflicts, not just those between economically distinct classes. Instead, demographic and economic pressures are seen to create conflicts both *across* classes—between peasants and landlords and between urban artisans and urban oligarchies—and *within* classes—between factions of landed, merchant, professional, and religious groups. Recognition that social mobility can provide absorption or generate displacement and turnover, noting that the latter combination, in particular, generates intra-elite competition and conflict at a *multiplicity* of levels, allows a better understanding of the precise cleavages that broke across the Old Regimes when subjected to demographic pressure: reform versus conservative factions among ministerial, provincial, and town officials; bishops versus curés or preachers; international versus domestic merchants; older versus newer military officers; financiers versus professionals; and orthodox intellectuals versus heterodox reformers.

Understanding how demographic pressure gives rise to heightened elite competition also explains a particular, and heretofore puzzling, phenomenon: the simultaneous "boom" in university enrollments all across Europe and the overburdening of religious schools in the Ottoman Empire and of the imperial examination system in China in the late sixteenth and early seventeenth centuries, followed by the "bust" in those enrollments in Europe and an easing of educational strains in Asia in the late seventeenth and early eighteenth centuries. This sequence was followed by another "boom" in the late eighteenth and early nineteenth centuries. These booms and busts are too extreme to be explained by changes in population size per se. However, we need only recognize that the periods of growing population led to inflation, which created economic opportunities that, in turn, increased the number of people who considered themselves qualified to demand elite positions. At the same time, inflation and sharp resistance to increasing taxation limited each state's ability to increase the supply of elite positions. The result was heightened competition for such positions, which spurred a scramble for credentials. Conversely, periods of stable population gave rise to little social mobility, and stable family size allowed much of the demand for elite positions to be satisfied by simple inheritance or family succession. Thus, the demand for formal credentials went "bust." Whether examining education or broad-based elite conflicts, consideration of the *interaction* of demographic, economic, and political relationships is far more fruitful than asserting the centrality of purely class, or purely political, factors.

Third, the demographic/structural approach to popular uprisings allows considerable scope for attention to *regional* differences in conflicts that occur within a crisis. Thus, an awareness of how demographic pressures produce land shortages, rising rents, falling real wages, and a more youthful population helps to explain why banditry, urban riots, and rural rebellions would all become more likely following periods of sustained population increase in agrarian-bureaucratic states. However, the model dictates no particular form of popular unrest. Instead, the precise shape of popular action is determined by the way such pressures impinge on a particular region's distribution of resources and relationships between potential actors. Thus, one would expect different patterns of popular unrest in northern France, southwestern France, and rural England, for in each case the organization of peasants, and the resources of landlords, differed. Similarly, in China one would expect different patterns of popular unrest in the mountains of the west and in the waterways of the Yangzi delta. Regional differences, as well as international differences, are the logical outcome of a model in which similar *causal* forces, rooted in demographic change, act on a variety of *social structures* to produce various patterns of conflict.

Fourth, this analysis integrates material and cultural factors in a far richer way than do the Marxist or revisionist analyses, and in a way that rectifies Skocpol's underemphasis on ideologies. I argue that the material causes of state breakdown first give rise to evident decay in state effectiveness and increases in popular and elite discontent. This combination of decay and disaffection raises the salience of ideologies of rectification and transformation, which may be long-standing but dormant elements of the political culture. Clear shifts in discourse and the spread of heterodoxy thus precede state breakdown, though these derive primarily from the collision of economic, political, and social structures with demographic change. If state crisis leads to state breakdown, however, the struggle for power polarizes and radicalizes discourse, further shaping and giving vent to ideological conflicts. When a victor emerges and sets a course for state reconstruction, these ideologies have a powerful molding effect on the postrevolutionary state. Moreover, ideologies of state reconstruction reflect not only the struggle for power but also the broader cultural framework of the society at large.

Ideologies reflect the available elements for conceptualizing change. Thus, European societies (as well as non-European societies later affected by European ideas), because of their linear and eschatological notions of time, their stock of apocalyptic imagery, were likely to respond to state breakdown through innovation; whereas Asian societies, with their primarily cyclic notions of time, were likely to respond to state breakdown with conservative state reconstruction. In this argument, both material and ideal factors play a leading role, although they do so in different phases of the process of state breakdown and reconstruction. This model also has the advantage, in regard to the Marxist view of history, of *not* interpreting the relative stagnation of Asia after the seventeenth century as the "absence" of change relative to Europe; instead it is seen as the result of a different *direction* of change, because of its different response to a similar crisis. In this respect, the model suggests parallels between the responses to the seventeenth-century crises in Hapsburg Spain, the Ottoman Empire, and China that merit further study.

Fifth, the quantification of the conjunctural analysis in a simplified model (the *psi* model of instability) clearly demonstrated and accounted for the greater likelihood of state breakdown in particular decades. Indeed, as shown in figures 5, 8, and 12–14, the *psi* model explains the timing of the English Revolution, the French Revolution, and the nineteenth-century revolutions of France and Germany, while also accounting for the *absence* of state crises in England and France from 1660 to 1750, in early nineteenth-century Germany, and in mid-nineteenth century England. Many theories of revolution seek to explain crises, but they do not even try to explain stability. The model I have presented explains not only the crisis "peaks" but also the recession of political pressures and consequent stability when population growth ceased.

Finally, this model accomplishes its initial goal, which was to provide a causal explanation for a striking sequence of events that neither Marxists, nor revisionists, nor Skocpol even attempt to analyze, let alone explain: the periodic waves of state breakdown that rose and ebbed across all of temperate Eurasia from 1640 to 1850. The present model thereby restores a true sense of "world history" to the early modern era.

CAVEATS

In response one might well argue, in the critical spirit of Darwin's Professor Houghton, that this view contains little of value that is new. Historians of particular state crises, including L. Stone (1972), Wakeman (1975b), Langer (1969), and Hamerow (1958), have argued for decades that population growth was the key factor in their cases. And demographers, historians, social ecologists, and some political scientists (Keyfitz 1965; Hawley 1978; Moller 1964; Monter 1977; Matossian and Schaefer 1977; Herlihy 1980; G. Holmes 1986; Hirst 1986; Weiner 1971; North and Choucri 1975; Clinton 1973) have long sounded the clarion call for students of political conflict to pay more attention to demography. Of course, the point is at least as old as Plato, who suggested in *The Laws* (1952, 123) that birth control leads to more stable societies. Aristotle, in his treatise on politics (1967, 341–342), expressed it more succinctly: "If the number of children exceeds what the amount of property will support, [difficulties of inheritance] must necessarily follow. . . . It is a sorry thing that a large number of persons should be reduced from comfort to penury. It is difficult for men who have suffered that fate not to be revolutionaries."

But while many have pointed to the impact of demography, they have been extremely vague about precisely how it affects politics. Choucri (1974, 81) surveyed current research on political demography and complained that "propositions are generally put forth in discrete and disjointed fashion. Only occasionally is there an attempt to trace the reverberating effects of population throughout the system, to a culmination in violence [*sic*] behavior. . . . The major emphasis is placed upon population size, and only secondarily upon composition or distribution. . . . Combined or interactive effects . . . are almost never taken into account."

Among historians, while the French *Annales* school and its founder, Fernand Braudel, have vigorously brought the brute facts of demography into mainstream historical studies, C. Tilly (1984a, 72) still notes that "Braudel makes no significant effort either to analyze demographic dynamics or to incorporate them into his explanatory system." Indeed, although the *Annales* historians (particularly Le Roy Ladurie 1974a; Goubert 1960; and P. Bois 1960), as well as English and American historians associated with the journal *Past and Present* (e.g., Robert Brenner 1976, 1978), have delved deeply into how population change affects long-term social and economic change, virtually none has sought to link the demographic movements of the *longue durée* with great political events, such as the English and French revolutions. As Himmelfarb (1987), L. Stone (1984), and others have complained, specialists in the "new history" of population, urbanization, wage and price movements, social mobility, and the like often pay little attention to the "old history" of great political events.

In sum, the importance of demography in history is frequently voiced, but when we examine the work that has been done on state crises in early modern history we find, at best, vague pronouncements and, more commonly, outright denials of the key role of population change. All too often scholars look only at the overall growth of population as a measure of demographic effects. I have tried to make clear that indirect and marginal effects—price inflation, changes in landlessness and unemployment, urban migration, and survival of younger sons—generally have a magnitude many times greater than overall population growth. In addition, these indirect and marginal effects often interact, producing effects on state finances, social mobility, income distribution, and mass mobilization potential that cannot be appreciated or understood by examining overall population figures alone. I hope that an awareness of the long-term and, especially, the *interactive* consequences of population growth will henceforth play a greater role in the analysis of early modern history.

I do not wish to be too rigid or expansive in this claim. As J. R. T. Hughes (1968, 215) has stated, "Nothing, possibly, is more galling to the mature and careful historian than the appearance of a one-cause explanation of a long, complex, and tortuous sequence of historical events." No doubt the argument of this book will gall many. But I have tried to state, as clearly as possible, that this is not a one-cause model: population growth alone leads to no determinate end. It is the *interaction* of population growth with particular social, political, and economic institutions that produces crises. Where institutions are different, as the case of Tokugawa Japan clearly shows, population stability rather than growth can lead to crisis. Hence, as I have repeatedly stated, this book does not argue for a demographic model of state crises but rather for a *demographic/structural* model.

Nor does this model claim to explain all facets of revolutionary crises. It offers no more than an explanation of why *some kind of severe state crisis* was particularly likely in many states in the late sixteenth to midseventeenth centuries, and again in the late eighteenth to mid-nineteenth centuries, but not very likely during the century in between. To explain why particular individuals or groups took particular actions, one must refer to the contingent and particular details of each crisis. The greater the local detail of explanation required, the smaller the value of the present model and the greater the necessity of local and contingent explanation. The value of this model lies in the reverse direction: the broader the problem to be explained, the more valuable is the model. Thus, if one is seeking an explanation of why the English Revolution was coincident with the French Fronde and the fall of the Ming Dynasty; why the period of Louis XIV combined both heightened international military mayhem and domestic stability all across Europe; why, despite international peace, Europe, the Ottoman Empire, and China were all wracked by internal revolt in the nineteenth century, local and contingent details will get one only so far. If one asks why there were "Levellers" in the 1640s in *both* England and China; if one asks why fiscal crises and religious heterodoxy and the "discovery of poverty" and heightened social mobility show recurrent patterns across Eurasia, local explanations offer little. For these questions the demographic/structural model provides answers. In this respect, it assists us in comprehending the world history of the early modern era.

But history did not stop in 1850. Modern problems have historical roots, and insights gained from historical study can offer guidance for current dilemmas.

POPULATION GROWTH: A BLESSING OR A CURSE?

There is an old debate in demographic theory about whether there is an "ideal" level of population for a society, and whether increases in population are generally beneficial or detrimental to societal well-being. There have been famous pessimists, from Malthus to Keynes, and famous optimists, most recently Julian Simon and Ester Boserup, who have reiterated Dupréel's argument that "an increase in population is beneficial in itself, because it enhances competition and spurs individual initiative, and is thus a decisive factor in civilization and progress" (cited in Overbeek 1974, 118).

At first glance, the argument in this book appears pessimistic in tone, for population growth in early modern history was strongly associated with mass poverty, elite factionalism, and state crises. But this observation alone would be an excessively simple and misleading characterization of events. The actual matter of interest is not defined by movements of population alone, viewed as a single independent variable, but rather by a set of *balances*: between population and agrarian output, between elite recruitment and eligible aspirants, and between state tax revenues and state expenditures. It was not population growth per se but rather growth beyond the absorptive capacity of early modern economic, social, and political institutions that undid these delicate balances and ruptured the social order. The lesson of early modern history is not that population growth is bad but rather that inflexible social structures are bad, at least in the sense that they become highly unstable in the event of sustained demographic change.

What, then, are the policy implications to be drawn from this book with respect to the pressing issue of population growth in the developing world? Will population growth lead to continued political instability?

The answer is that population increases *probably will* lead to political crises, but they need not. The argument of this book can be neatly divided into two parts. First, there is a theory of the conditions that create a likelihood of state breakdown, drawing on a conjunctural model of crises. This theory asserts that massive state breakdown is likely to occur only when there are *simultaneously* high levels of distress and conflict at *several levels* of society—in the state, among elites, and in the populace. We examined this conjuncture empirically through the *psi* equation, which combined attention to trends in state fiscal distress, elite mobility and competition (including both turnover and displacement), and mass mobilization potential. A sustained rise in all three elements is associated with state breakdown; a rise in two of these elements can produce a state crisis leading to major reforms or modest state breakdown; a rise in any one alone is unlikely to end a regime. This theory can be simply summarized: high *psi* implies a high probability of state crisis. Second, there is a more historically delimited theory that seeks to explain *why psi* rose to high levels in most Eurasian states in the two periods 1550–1660 and 1770–1850, an explanation that rests on the interaction of demography and institutions.

Since the two parts are logically independent, we can approach the problems of contemporary population growth and instability through two questions: Is population growth likely to raise *psi* in today's world? And are there other forces that could raise *psi*, and hence other, more worrisome, sources of state breakdown?

In the early modern world, population growth was a threat to societies that were fundamentally agrarian. As Gellner (1983, 110) has pointed out, "agrarian society . . . unlike, it would seem, both its predecessor [hunter-gatherer society] and successor [industrial society] is Malthusian." Today, although many developing nations such as India, China, and most nations of Africa and northwest Latin America still have largely agrarian economies, they are no longer purely agrarian *societies*. That is to say, the wealth, political power, and military strength of each depend more on access to capital, technology, information, and often electoral support and foreign assistance than on mere ownership of acreage. Without access to foreign and urban markets, without capital for machinery, fertilizer, fuel, and transportation, large landholdings today are nearly worthless. Without access to national party organizations, large landowners can be, at best, local *caudillos* or bosses; small farmers and tenants can be, at best, restive local forces. Technological improvements that are available in agriculture, production, communication, and transportation dwarf anything that was available in the early modern world. Thus, population growth need not overwhelm modern societies, provided they can harness modern resources to absorb their population increases.

In these circumstances, the question of whether population growth will undo crucial balances that sustain social stability has more to do with government policy, capital availability, and local organization than with the simple arithmetic of bodies and land. Policies of cronyism and corruption that drain or unproductively concentrate capital, and policies of urban investment and price-skewing at the expense of rural infrastructure and economies, are likely to create the same conditions of high mass mobilization potential among impoverished cultivators that simple population growth produced in the seventeenth and nineteenth centuries. Conversely, policies that create a well-capitalized, productive, domestic agriculture, and that can supply employment to the rural sector and food and raw materials to world markets and the urban sector, can cope with quite rapid population growth. Japan under the Meiji oligarchs experienced rapid population increase, but state policies of the latter type served to maintain political stability (Nishikawa 1986, 426; Macpherson 1987).

Development policies often focus on raising GNP per capita. Clearly, this approach need not succeed in reducing *psi*, which is not a simple matter of total social wealth. We have seen that the nations and empires that encountered crisis suffered from *polarization* in their income distribution, from high social mobility that unsettled and divided elites, and from failure of the state to gain resources to cope with rising real expenses. Eighteenth-century France, for example, raised its GNP per capita. But a lagging agricultural sector, and problems in the distribution of income and taxation, still produced a crisis. Thus development policies, if they wish to help counter political instability as well as create growth, need to do more than just raise GNP. Measures such as land reform and support for small farmers, which reduce income polarization and urban migration, and foreign aid aimed at avoiding excessive government debt while providing government resources for housing, education, and other population-linked infrastructural expenses, are more politically stabilizing than investments in concentrated industries. One must also consider the ability of the state, church, business, and social institutions to employ ambitious elites at levels that correspond to their self-perceived qualifications. It is politically risky to create new, professional, educated elites without also creating ample political and economic opportunities for them. It is in these areas that demographic change poses problems to contemporary governments.

In fact, rapid population growth in many Third World countries has had two extremely important political effects: rapid urbanization and the growth of new professional and managerial elites. The extreme urbanization reflects a common economic bias, wherein development policies, pricing policies, and foreign investment increase economic opportunities in cities rather than in the countryside (Bates 1981; Kelley and Williamson 1984; Bradshaw 1985). Unfortunately, such rapid urbanization places enormous strains on the capacity of governments to provide services, political organization and control, and employment for urban residents. Under such conditions, dissident elites may find ready recruits to mobilize in anti-state movements. Tehran and Managua in 1979 thus had the same potential—in terms of mass mobilization in politically crucial sites—as Paris in 1789 or Vienna and Berlin in 1848.

Dissident elites may arise when expanding urban markets offer opportunities to entrepreneurs in manufacturing and services and an expanding educational system produces professional degree holders, while traditional military and landowning elites, or a particular ruler or clique, seeks to monopolize power. Stable balances within a landed oligarchy, or between elite segments under the orchestration of an authoritarian ruler, may be undone by a relatively sudden expansion of urban population and markets.

The demands of traditional elites to preserve their privileged position often clash with the demands of new elites and popular urban and rural groups for broad economic expansion. Development plans must then meet many agendas, from satisfying current and emerging elites to keeping pace with overall population growth. A combination of agrarian reform, guided productive investment, and compensation to traditional elites has sometimes successfully overcome this dilemma, as in Japan during the Meiji era.

However, states with less political clout and fewer resources often seek to defer difficult choices by borrowing. In early modern times, such a course might have led straightforwardly to a state fiscal crisis. But contemporary states have a greater ability to externalize deficits by inviting foreign investment, printing money, and manipulating exchange rates. Thus, in analyzing the "fiscal crisis" component of *psi* for modern states, we may see rising inflation, loss of control of the economy to foreign interests, or wild swings or divergences from parity in the local currency, instead of simple state financial difficulties. Nonetheless, all of these disrupt the flow of resources to states, or to elite and popular groups who look to the state for control of these matters. Thus broadly defined, fiscal or economic crises are a common outcome of states' attempts to utilize borrowing and currency controls to meet foreign competition and the demands of changing elites and growing populations.

Again, we come face to face with the problem of population change and its effects on political and economic *structures*. Early modern states failed to cope with population growth because their economic, fiscal, and social structures—rooted in simple agrarian techniques and in aristocratic status and political systems—lacked sufficient flexibility to deflect or absorb the conflicts produced by that growth. Contemporary states rarely face such simple economic and traditional status institutions, and their attendant constraints. Thus, they often *can* absorb population growth; the question is whether, at a given time, they adopt the policies that will actually allow them to do so (cf. Johnson and Lee 1987).

The tenets that favor stability are simple: do not adopt fiscal policies that rely on debts in excess of what the economy and tax system can reasonably be expected to sustain; do not adopt economic policies that encourage urban growth at a faster rate than housing, services, employment, and civic organization can develop; do not adopt educational policies that produce graduates in excess of the state's and the economy's ability to give them meaningful responsibilities; and do not adopt political policies that exclude from power newly rising groups that are growing in numbers and wealth. States often fail to follow these tenets because it is in the short-term interests of rulers or particular elites to acquire debts, to favor rapid urban expansion, to implement educational expansion, or to seek monopolization of power. The problem is that these short-term, and thus short-sighted, policies undermine political stability in the long run. How a current regime weighs the short-run versus the long-run consequences of its choices is often the key to whether its prospects for stability are brief or extend far into the future.

These tenets are *not* merely matters of economic expansion or development. One can have economically stagnant states that follow these tenets and yet remain politically stable economic backwaters—for example, North Korea. And one can have economically dynamic states that fail to follow these tenets for stability and hence encounter state crisis—for example, Iran.

From 1956 to 1976, the population of Iran increased from just over twenty million inhabitants to nearly thirty-five million, an increase of 75 percent in two decades (B. Clark 1972). During these decades, the Pahlavi regime adopted a rural land reform program that left three-fourths of rural families with inadequate land to support commercial farming, and it adopted pricing and credit policies that starved the rural sector while subsidizing urban populations. The cities were also the focus of development efforts financed by massive borrowing. The state thus drew population to the cities more rapidly than adequate services or regular employment could be supplied, developing a large population of aggrieved urban families who looked to the mosque and bazaar, rather than to the state and modern economic sector, for material benefits, moral authority, and community leadership. The number of university students increased tenfold, many of them educated overseas for lack of domestic facilities (Abrahamian 1980). Witnessing the moral dissolution and poverty in the urban slums, along with the concentration of wealth among the shah's family and associates, many elites and students became dismayed at the moral failures and corruption of the regime.

Counting on future oil wealth, the shah borrowed heavily, and sought to complement his development effort with a military buildup. These expenditures stretched both the state budget and the economy to the limit. The resulting inflation undermined middle- and working-class incomes. Finally, seeking to monopolize power, the shah excluded from politics the professional and managerial groups and civil servants on which his modernization efforts depended, and attacked the bazaar merchants and the traditional religious elite (Keddie 1981; Green 1986).

The result of these policies was mounting state debt, roaring inflation, and political exclusion that made enemies among the salaried middle class and the traditional religious leaders and bazaar merchants. When these elite groups allied and began to mobilize the urban masses against the shah's government, given the questionable ability of the army to act against a broad popular movement (as in France in 1830 and 1848), the breakdown of the shah's regime became imminent (Abrahamian 1980). The shah's fall was thus a product of misguided policies, not an inevitable outcome of rapid development or Islamic fundamentalism. However, once state breakdown had begun, there followed the familiar sequence: an initially moderate, widely supported movement for rectification, then struggles for popular mobilization and power, with victory attained by extremist leaders. These leaders were a formerly marginal elite—the fundamentalist wing of the Shi'ite clergy—who drew on an eschatological ideology. The revolutionary process culminated in an aggressive Iranian nationalism that produced persecution of minorities and other internal "enemies," as well as foreign war.

In sum, population growth does pose problems for modern states. But they are not insoluble problems, as many examples from the newly industrialized countries show. Whether or not population growth will lead to instability depends on the policies adopted by particular regimes. Poor policy choices can create exactly the "high *psi*" conditions—state fiscal crises, elite factionalization and alienation, and rising mass (particularly urban) mobilization potential—that make state crises likely. In contrast, careful policy choices can maintain "low *psi*" conditions, and hence political stability despite rapid economic growth.

Given the explosive population growth that has occurred in the Third World during the twentieth century, often without the benefit of rapid industrialization or flexible political institutions, it is not surprising that this is a "century of revolution" in Third World states. Although a decline in per capita wealth has occasionally been a problem, this has not been the primary factor in modern revolutions. Instead, problems of wealth distribution among the population, weak state finances, and competition among elites, exacerbated by explosive population increases and inappropriate policy responses, have undermined political stability. Wherever rulers or elites have been tempted to put their own short-term interests ahead of long-term political stability for their respective societies, the resulting policy choices have created, over a span of few decades, the ingredients for state crises.

We should thus not be surprised if population growth and state crises, though not inevitably linked, remain companion phenomena in the contemporary Third World.[1]

CAPITALISM: SAVIOR OR DESTROYER?

Just as there have been long-standing debates on whether or not population growth is desirable, there have been debates ever since Adam Smith's *Wealth of Nations* (1776) on whether or not capitalism—that is, economic organization through private ownership of capital and contracting of wage labor—is preferable to other economic systems. The two alternatives that are sometimes held as superior are the precapitalist freedoms of the independent peasant farmer or self-employed artisan and the postcapitalist communities of managed state socialism.

Academic social science has often been hostile to capitalism. It has been considered the destroyer of traditional values and of the incomes of farmers and workers, the cause of worsening inequality, and the key factor that undermined traditional states and led to revolutions. The breakdowns of the English state in 1640, the French state in 1789, and the Iranian state in 1979 have all been attributed to the excesses of capitalism.

But such arguments are belied by a wealth of evidence. We have shown in some detail why they are false for England and France and have just sketched why they are inadequate to account for the fall of the shah of Iran.

In fact, capitalism was the savior of the early modern economies from the pressures of population growth. It was precisely those states most affected by capitalism—England in the early nineteenth century, and

1. For a more detailed consideration of contemporary revolutions, see Goldstone, Gurr, and Moshiri (forthcoming).

France and Germany in the late nineteenth century—that first escaped the cycles of overpopulation and food riots and of land shortage and state breakdown that pervaded early modern history. Where capitalist development lagged and population bore down on the productive capacity of the land, as in Russia and China, vulnerability to revolutionary crises stretched into the late nineteenth and early twentieth centuries.

Regional and occupational analyses reveal the same patterns. Those workers most affected by capitalism—factory workers in northern England and northeastern France—were least involved in the revolutionary and reform crises of the nineteenth century, while those least affected by capitalist development—construction workers and furniture and cabinetmakers—manned the barricades. In the rural sector, the peasant farmer whose land became inadequate for his family over several generations of population growth gained no satisfaction or succor by being free of capitalism; whether in the seventeenth or the nineteenth century, rural unrest reflected the limitations of traditional agriculture in the face of demographic pressures. In contrast, access to fertilizers, railroads, and urban markets saved the commercial family farm for many generations, while urban factories produced the alternative jobs that relieved the plight of agrarian laborers in overcrowded countrysides.

In short, the advent of capitalism cannot be blamed for revolution, or even for poverty. Population growth in the context of inflexible economic and social institutions is fully capable on its own of producing income polarization, elite conflict, and state breakdown, as the cases of Ming China and Ottoman Turkey demonstrate. Indeed, capitalism can be a way out of the morass. Thus, to see capitalism as responsible for the evils of the early modern and modern eras, framed between a primitive workers' paradise in the past and a socialist workers' paradise in the future, is to engage in scapegoating sugarcoated with romanticism.

This is not to absolve capitalism from all sins. Private ownership of wealth can lead to stultifying monopolies of power and privilege. If capitalism is an engine of growth, it must nonetheless be oiled with basic freedoms and civil rights and fueled with opportunities allowing new individuals and ideas to rise. A terrible lesson of history is that without careful protection of freedom and opportunity, capitalism can readily produce fascism. Thus, one must also consider the roots of democracy. In this regard, the argument is often made that revolution, by breaking up concentrations of wealth and power, paves the way for democracy. But again, history tells a quite different story. Revolutions, in general, no more give rise to democracy than capitalism gives rise to revolutions.

REVOLUTIONS: THE DECLINE OF EMPIRES, NOT THE BIRTH OF DEMOCRACY

Eisenstadt (1978) has noted that the causes usually adduced to account for revolutions are quite similar to those used to explain the decline and fall of empires. We have seen in this book that there is good reason for this overlap: the factors behind the English and French revolutions were, in essence, the same factors behind the fall of the Ming Empire and the crises of the Ottoman Empire in the seventeenth and nineteenth centuries.

But this finding raises crucial questions, for revolution is generally thought to be the antithesis of imperial decline. Revolutions are new beginnings, whereas imperial declines are no more than losses of past glory. To say that the English and French revolutions resembled crises in Asian states thus forces us to ask whether the great revolutions of the West really were milestones in the "march of progress."

Here it is necessary to carefully separate cause and effect. In regard to the *causes* of revolutions, I heartily oppose the notion that revolutions were the necessary and desirable results of progressive forces confronting "blockages" to progress that must be overcome. Instead I have argued that state crises resulted from mismatches between the capacities of institutions and the demands made on them. In the great revolutions of the early modern era, such mismatches arose from cyclic ecological crises. In our day, revolutions and state crises stem primarily from policies that create such mismatches, though still, in part, from ecological pressures.

But once cases of state breakdown occurred, we can ask whether it was in any way helpful to economic and democratic development for existing authority structures to have been "shaken up." In other words, were the *effects* of state crises beneficial?

In regard to economic growth, the answer is generally negative in the short run, but indeterminate in the long run. In the short run, state breakdown produces enormously destructive struggles for power, which often lead to civil and international wars. The cost in human life alone is appalling: in the English civil wars, over 100,000 Englishmen out of a population of 5 million died, a ratio of roughly 1 in 50; in the French Revolution and Napoleonic Wars, 1.3 million died out of a population of 26 million, or 1 in 20; in the Mexican Revolution and civil wars of 1911–1920, over 2 million died out of a population of 17 million, or more than 1 in 10 (Goldstone 1986c, 207). The destruction of life and the economic disruption resulting from the more recent crises in Vietnam, Ethiopia, Afghanistan, Iran, and Central America are widely evident. What gains can be set against these enormous costs?

State crises and revolutions often led to the dispersion of assets that were highly concentrated in unproductive hands, especially those of the Church and conservative landlords. In addition, states were generally rebuilt with greater control over national resources. To the extent that postrevolutionary states were able to channel those resources into productive investments, postrevolutionary growth was quite rapid. Thus, Stalin's Russia and Mao's China did experience impressive, if direly painful to certain groups and individuals, levels of economic growth.

However, long-term growth depends not merely on the ability to produce wealth but also on the ability to develop *new ways* of producing wealth. A one-shot increase in productivity will increase production; but only *continuously* strong increases in productivity will sustain modern development. Where postrevolutionary states, moved by ongoing ideological tension over state authority, have developed institutions that protected individual liberty, and hence gave creative individuals leeway to innovate and experiment with new forms of business organization and new products, productivity growth was sustained. But where postrevolutionary states suppressed freedom, innovation was stifled, and economic growth slowed. We have noted that in this respect the state crises of northwestern Europe had different outcomes than the state crises of Asia and Spain. In all cases, states and economies revived after the crises, but in the latter cases the rate of further progress fell far short of that of the leading liberal states. Thus, whether or not economic growth in the *long* run benefits from state breakdown depends in large measure on whether state breakdown is followed by state reconstruction that protects or suppresses individual liberty.

I have noted that Western revolutions can be distinguished from Asian state breakdowns by the emergence of marginal elites who carried an eschatological ideology and who sought to make a new social order rather than merely fix the old one. The aspirations and ideals of these elites then formed a basis of future campaigns for liberalizing traditional societies. But these aspirations and ideals would not, in themselves, have been sufficient to raise democracy from the ruins of absolutist states. As we noted in the preceding chapter, the struggle for power that follows state breakdown tends to overwhelm moderate, and later, radical, efforts to rebuild the state. Instead, the common outcome of episodes of state breakdown is the thirst for order, and hence, within a decade or two, the rise of a nationalist populist dictatorship.

In England the state breakdown of 1640 was followed in the mid-1650s by military rule under Cromwell. Even after the Restoration of 1660, the result was a reactionary monarchy driven by a backlash against Puritan and parliamentary freedoms. In France, the state breakdown of 1789 was followed, a little over a decade later, by the Napoleonic Empire. And just two decades after the state breakdown of 1830, France was again ruled by an imperial despotism led by a Bonaparte. In Germany, the legacy of 1848 was the kaiser's bureaucratic and military empire. Even after the second German Revolution, in 1918, it took only a decade and a half for a nationalist dictatorship to emerge under Hitler. In Russia, socialist revolutionary fervor gave way to military nationalism under Stalin. And in Meiji Japan, although state breakdown had been only moderately severe, militarist nationalism supplanted the Meiji oligarchs by the early twentieth century.

In short, history shows an almost uniform tendency of episodes of state breakdown to culminate in populist, usually military, dictatorship. We have laid bare the reasons for this tendency in the preceding chapter: regardless of the aims or ideology of revolutionaries, the task of rebuilding state authority requires the broad-based mobilization of popular and elite groups to support a new regime, as well as the defeat of internal and often external opponents. The exigencies of this struggle generally lead to terror, disorder, and the growing dominance of military men. The rebuilt armies of the revolution embody its energy and ideals but have little patience with national democracy or individual freedom. The major difference between postrevolutionary populist despotisms has been whether they have sought to achieve their goals through protection and regulation of private property, which produces authoritarian and sometimes fascist regimes, or through ownership and control of public property, which produces communist regimes. In both kinds of events there may be spurts of economic growth. In both cases, too, the initial populist dictatorship tends to develop in the direction of despotism by a national party structure that transcends individual authoritarianism. In neither case is there established the individual liberty required to sustain innovation and development, nor the dispersal of political power required to sustain democracy (Diamond, Linz, and Lipset, 1988).

If revolutions and state crises have failed to bring about stable democratic liberal regimes, how have such regimes become established? The answer—another painful lesson of history, which I would rather not draw but cannot in good faith avoid—is that the crucial catalyst of democracy has most often been defeat in war. When absolutist regimes have been overthrown by revolutions, the tendency has been to substitute a new, more efficient, more populist despotism for the narrower, more traditional variety. But the discrediting of absolutist regimes by catastrophic military defeat has sometimes led elites and popular groups to withdraw their support from central authorities altogether and, where assisted by the occupying power, to rebuild regimes that place more emphasis on individual rights and republican institutions. Thus, it was not after 1640 that Parliament became secure—it was dismissed by Cromwell and again by Charles II. Rather, Parliament gained stability only after the successful invasion of England by William III in 1688. It was a compromise between the occupying power and the English elite, each of whom needed the other, that resulted in acts to secure triennial parliaments and in the Declaration of Rights. In France, it was not the revolutions of 1789, or 1830, or 1848 that secured stable democratic regimes. Napoleon III ruled the Third Empire for two decades; it was defeat by Prussia in 1870, and suppression of the Commune in 1871, that led to the relatively stable Third Republic. In Germany and Japan, it was defeat in World War II that secured stable democratic and liberal institutions. We have recently seen the same process take place in Argentina, where the discredit brought on a military regime by its defeat in the Falkland Islands created an opening for democratic politics to emerge.

In short, revolution is not part of the solution to authoritarianism and tyranny; instead it is part—indeed, a recurrent part—of the problem. To do away with tyranny, it is not enough for governments to weaken and be overthrown, for new tyrants generally take their places. Establishment of democracy requires a disenchantment with central authority in general, an army too weak or demoralized to impose its will on society, and a broad alliance between elites and popular groups in defense of individual freedoms. State breakdown, though it may begin with such conditions, quickly reverses them, producing a demand for a strong central authority to restore order, a renovated revolutionary army, and a sharp reaction by elites against populist claims for expanded shares of power and property. A decade or two after state breakdown, then, all the elements for a reemergent absolutism are in place. Defeat in war may produce the same effects, but it need not do so. If victorious opponents impose conditions that limit executive authority, reduce military strength and autonomy, and provide economic assistance that helps produce constructive alliances between economic elites and popular groups (omitting this last item was a signal failure of Allied treatment of Germany after World War I), then openings toward liberal democracy can be sustained. Both defeat in war and state breakdown offer opportunities to realize the goals of revolutionary marginal elites to build new societies. Ironically, where those goals include supplanting authoritarian regimes by liberal and democratic states, defeat in war rather than victory in revolution has been the most efficacious vehicle for achieving those aims.

It is therefore crucial for those who seek change to keep in mind that the political choices include a broader range than merely war, repression, or revolution. There have been cases in history where initial phases of dissent, demonstrations, and resistance to the state led not to revolution or repression but rather to successful reform. Where states were unusually bold, and capable of seeing the benefits to rulers as well as to the ruled in pursuing reforms, progress toward democracy has been made. Although such progress has sometimes seemed slow, it has cost far less in blood, and resulted in more durable and prosperous democratic regimes.

One case in point is the success of the English Reform Movement of 1828–1832, and succeeding Reform Bills, in enlarging democracy in response to a state crisis and averting state breakdown. The hallmark of the English Reform, however, is that it was not cosmetic reform— the concession of advisory status or the bestowal of economic palliatives to reformers. It was reform in a true spirit of compromise and sacrifice: the sharing of real power with new groups, in a way that diminished (although by no means curtailed) the power of the existing leadership. Because of the magnitude of that change, it was bitterly resisted. The House of Lords passed the Reform Bill only under threat of greater internal disorders, and with the suasion of the king. But it was also the magnitude of the parliamentary reform that defused immediate pressures for more violent change. Such compromise and sacrifice by political leadership is rare. A more recent case, also successful in avoiding state breakdown, is the settlement accepted by the white leaders of Southern Rhodesia (now Zimbabwe) under British pressure, which led to black rule (Scarritt forthcoming). In facing such volatile situations as today obtain in South Africa, China, and the Soviet Union, one hopes the lessons of history will be heeded. True power-sharing reforms can avert state breakdown and implant democracy. Cosmetic reforms cannot avert state breakdown; and state breakdown and revolution, although they may destroy the Old Regimes, are unlikely to mould a democratic pattern for the future.[2]

THE RISE OF THE WEST

Much of the world still seeks to emulate the economic success of the West. Much of the world also pays lip service to the ideals of individual liberty and democratic political institutions, although few nations have been able to achieve stable liberal democracies.

Why is the West different? The standard story of the "Rise of the West" relates that the West experienced true revolutions—in England and in France, in particular—that secured liberal democracy and overturned traditional obstacles to economic development. In addition, the

2. As this chapter is being written, the nations of Eastern Europe and the Soviet Union are experiencing a wave of political crises and transformations. All of these states experienced dramatic increases in the components of *psi* during the past two decades: state fiscal or economic distress; elite alienation and competition (between generally older, loyal, Communist party elites and generally younger, newly risen, reformist, technical, intellectual, and religious elites); and rising mass mobilization potential (increased urbanization, more youthful populations, and declining real incomes). In 1989, these underlying pressures for crisis burst forth, triggered by Soviet leader Mikhail Gorbachev's criticism and efforts at reform of the Soviet state. But it is far too early to know whether these transformations will be successful in creating stable democratic regimes.

At this time, only two conclusions seem merited. First, it is a mistake to seek a single historical analogue or precedent for all of the events of 1989. Certainly, the pressures for crisis, as suggested by rising *psi*, are evident throughout the communist world. Yet as I have stressed, the precise shape of any political crisis depends on how the different components of *psi* combine, *and* on how they interact with particular social and political structures. The events of 1989 range from moderate and swift transitions of power in Hungary and Czechoslovakia, resembling the French Revolution of 1830, to drawn-out power struggles with great potential for full-scale state breakdown in the Soviet Union. As the specific combination of pressures, and the particular social structures, in these nations are quite varied, we should expect considerable variation in the crises of 1989 and their outcomes. Second, although many fears have been voiced about the rise of nationalism, in a unified Germany or elsewhere in Eastern Europe, the preceding analysis suggests that aggressive nationalism is likely only as an outcome of extended power struggles. Thus this threat seems likely to arise only in Romania and in the Soviet Union. In Germany, the quick unification of East Germany under a stable, democratic, federal government should avert, rather than exacerbate, German nationalism.

In Communist China, an attempt at revolution led by intellectuals and workers in the capital city, but not generally supported in the countryside, was fiercely repressed by an army loyal to the state. The lack of severe fiscal stress on the Chinese government, and the failure of elite competition and alienation to reach a level at which the army leadership was aggrieved at the regime, led to the failure of the revolt. However, the pressures that underlay the crisis—growing economic difficulties, especially in the urban economy; alienation among elites, particularly intellectuals, students, and party officials; and an increasingly youthful, urban, and materially dissatisfied working class—continue, and it is likely that conflicts in China will reemerge. Should economic discontent spread to the countryside, or should the army leadership join other elites in opposing the Communist regime, the outcome could be quite different on the next occasion.

story goes on, the West was the first region of the world to develop industrial economies, and this accounted for its economic success; unfortunately, however, it did so through the vehicle of capitalist organization, which exacerbated social conflict and deprived and exploited the working class.

This story is false. As we have noted, revolutions tend to produce not democracy but authoritarianism. Democracy developed in the West through the combination of (1) visions of secular improvement and wider political participation articulated by marginal elites; (2) military defeats and occupations that discredited central authorities, forged broad elite coalitions in favor of republican institutions, and created opportunities for liberal ideas to bear fruit; and (3) reform legislation that expanded the franchise and guaranteed individual rights and liberties.[3] That we associate revolutions with democracy is an illusion that arose because revolutions offered marginal elites the greatest opportunities and incentives to invent and propagate democratic ideologies. We then ignore or treat as regrettable "deviations" the almost universal failure of revolutions to entertain such ideologies for more than a few years before succumbing to despotic rule.

Moreover, there is no evidence that the revolutions of 1640 in England and of 1789 in France were instrumental in removing blockages to economic development. The Revolution of 1640 did not change the social structure, property ownership, or legal basis for England's economic organization. The Revolution of 1789 unified administration and removed internal tariffs in France, but the fundamental blockages to French development were the climate, soil, and transportation constraints on French agriculture and the attachment of the labor force to the land. The latter factor was worsened by the revolution, and the former were unaffected. Prussia's reform movement of 1806–1812 and its institution of the Zollverein in 1834 were more effective promoters of economic development than any revolution in the West.

---

3. Although the American War of Independence is often cited as a revolution that established democracy, it was in fact merely a defense of existing democratic institutions against Britain's attempt to circumvent them to increase its revenues from the colonies. America's state and local democratic institutions, and those on a national level after 1776, were largely imported and modeled on those developed in Britain and securely established there only in 1689. Europe's other republics, such as Holland and Venice, were narrow aristocratic oligarchies that developed toward democracy only after Napoleonic occupation. The indigenous democracy of Switzerland developed as a result of local coalitions for military defense, stemming from the Everlasting League of cantons who defeated Leopold I of Hapsburg at Schwyz in 1315. For more detail on how "consensual elite settlements," which underpin democracy, arise, see Burton and Higley (1987b).

Furthermore, capitalism is not a regrettable and avoidable manner of achieving industrial progress but rather is essential for sustained economic growth. Wherever industrialism has been developed through state socialism rather than through capitalism or a mixed but predominantly capitalist economy, it has invariably failed to sustain independent growth at the pace of capitalist democracies. And as examples from the early modern era to modern day Kampuchea (Cambodia), Yugoslavia, and Ethiopia clearly show, eschewing capitalism is no guarantee of avoiding popular misery and social conflict. Nor, as Eastern Europe and China under Mao demonstrate, does eschewing capitalism end the deprivation and exploitation of industrial workers.

Finally, the standard story, focusing on the rise of strong nation-states, places too little emphasis on the rise of toleration and avoidance of rigid cultural conformity as factors in economic success. Not merely growth, but *innovation*, was crucial to the rise of the West. Such innovation flourished best where national cultures were leavened by toleration of individual liberty and free thinking about social and economic organization. Where states imposed a national orthodox culture and rejected toleration, innovation became relatively rare.

The standard story of the "Rise of the West" is false largely because it rests on a dire misunderstanding of early modern history, particularly of the causes of the major state crises. In presenting the great crises as triumphs of progress over institutional "blockages," rather than as cyclic crises that shook, but often failed to fundamentally change, rigid institutions and economies, the story has misread the nature of early modern revolutions and rebellions, substituting teleology and post hoc, ergo propter hoc, analysis for careful examination of the cyclic patterns of crises. Moreover, by overlooking the dynamics of revolutionary struggle that produce authoritarian outcomes, the story suggests that the act of revolution is sufficient to create democracy and economic progress. And by presenting the crises as produced by capitalism rather than by demographic/structural causes, capitalism has been vilified as a source of conflict to be avoided, instead of lauded as a means of overcoming the ecological imbalances responsible for most preindustrial crises and suffering.

The standard story is not only false; it is also tragic. For, taken as a guide, it has deluded literally billions of people. Throughout the twentieth century, people seeking to replace traditional authoritarian regimes with greater democracy have put their faith in revolution; nations seeking to achieve economic progress while avoiding social conflict have put their faith in state socialism and turned away from capitalism. Many societies thus have suffered the worst of both worlds, gaining for their vast efforts only authoritarian political regimes and stagnant economies. The success of the West lies in a combination of two factors, both of which emerged in complex and gradual fashion: personal freedom based on toleration, broad civic participation, and protection of individual rights; and capitalist economic organization. Without personal freedom and toleration providing scope for economic and social innovation, even private property-based economies—as in Qing China, the Ottoman Empire, and Bourbon Spain—remained rigid and stagnant rather than dynamic. Without capitalism, economic organization remains inefficient and unable to cope with changing demands. It is the *combination* of liberal freedoms and capitalism that is essential for success.

To trace the rise of freedom and capitalism is a task well beyond the scope of this book.[4] But even with the present focus on the narrower problem of the origins and dynamics of state crises, it should be clear from the analysis that state breakdown is not likely to produce freedom, and that seeking to implement state control of ideological orthodoxy rather than tolerance of individual conscience and freedom in the wake of a state crisis is liable to stifle, not accelerate, economic progress. The policies adopted by many nations that seek to emulate Western success—revolution followed by state control of culture and the economy—are thus dead wrong, and their failure is to be expected. Adoption of the opposite policies—political reform to broaden participation and secure individual rights, toleration of cultural pluralism, and a dominant economic role for capitalist organization—holds much greater promise.

THE DECLINE OF THE UNITED STATES

It is ironic that precisely when the above ideas are gaining wide acceptance, the leading exemplar of these ideas—the United States—is troubled by intimations of decline. Some symptoms are familiar from the

4. The history of freedom in the West awaits its definitive history, but an attempt is now underway under the editorship of J. H. Hexter and R. Davis. I point out the unique role played by cultural pluralism in the history of Western capitalism in Goldstone (1987). Most histories of industrial capitalism either are Marxist, and hence suffer from teleology and an overemphasis on class dynamics, or else are based on classical economics, and hence suffer from a neglect of culture and institutions. The efforts of North (1981) are a beginning, and the work of Collins (1986) makes considerable progress toward rectifying these difficulties. Nonetheless, a history of the development of Europe's industrial capitalism that avoids the Marxist and classical economic biases, and takes account of the exogenous cyclic processes of the early modern period, remains to be written.

preceding discussion of state crises—rising government debt and a polarization of incomes. Can the analysis in this volume shed any light on
these trends?

The United States' ills have sometimes been traced, using an oversim-
plified version of Paul Kennedy's (1987) model of state competition, to
excessive international military commitments, or "imperial overstretch." But this simple idea provides an incorrect diagnosis, even of
the past. The notion that imperial overstretch—a nation taking on commitments that exceeded its resources—was responsible for the decline
and fall of early modern states is profoundly mistaken. Overstretch may
apply to the campaigns of particular commanders, such as Napoleon's
Russian campaign, but it is not the reason for the crises that overturned
long-established early modern monarchies and imperial states. We have
noted that the English, Ottoman, and Ming Chinese states broke down
in the seventeenth century, and the French state in the late eighteenth
century, because of fiscal crises, elite factionalism, and rising mass mobilization potential. But in each case, within a few decades after the
crisis, these states enormously expanded their power and international
influence. Cromwell's navy wrested the seas from the Dutch, where the
early Stuarts had failed; the Ottomans again threatened Vienna in 1689
and soundly defeated Peter the Great in Russia in 1711; the Qing Empire
soon exceeded that of the Ming in territory and population; and Napoleon's empire far exceeded the Bourbons' wildest dreams. If the
Stuarts, Ottomans, Ming, and Bourbons had overstretched their nations'
capacities, how is it possible that their successors quickly reasserted or
even extended their international reach?

SELFISH ELITES AND NATIONAL DECAY

The answer is that these regimes fell because they had used their nation's
resources poorly. Inefficient tax systems failed to capture a growing
share of national wealth. We have noted that English gentry in the seventeenth century reduced their own assessments, privileged French nobility and bourgeois elites were exempt from the *taille*, Ottoman
magnates converted their lands to *vakıf*s or sought *malikâne*s, and
Chinese officials sheltered the land of dependents and associates. These
persistent efforts by elites to resist or evade taxation, despite being massively undertaxed, led to excessive state debts and reduced the state's
ability to respond to domestic demands and foreign threats. Straitened

state finances also restricted pay to officials, leading to corruption and rapid turnover in bureaucratic posts.

In short, a key difficulty faced by regimes in decline was *selfish elites*. Nations that were the richest countries in their day suffered fiscal crises because elites preferred to protect their private wealth, even at the expense of a deterioration of state finances, public services, and long-term international strength. By "selfish elites" I do not mean, of course, simply elites' aspirations to maintain disproportionate shares of wealth and power. That ambition is a universal constant. What I wish to emphasize is that in some eras in history, elites have identified their interests with the national state and the public weal, and they have been willing to tax themselves heavily to expand the influence and resources of their nation and its government. At other times, particularly times of elite insecurity owing to inflation and to rising social mobility and competition within their ranks, elites have turned into competing factions, driven by self-enrichment at the expense of their rivals and opponents, even when that meant starving the national state of resources needed for public improvements and international competitiveness.[5]

In addition, declining regimes were beset by factionalism within the elites that paralyzed decision making. Struggles for prestige and authority took precedence over a united approach to resolving fiscal and social problems. Among English gentry in Parliament, within the French Estates General and the National Assembly, among Ottoman officials, and within the ranks of Chinese scholars, partisanship prevailed over consensus—with disastrous results.

It is quite astonishing the degree to which the United States today is, in respect of its state finances and its elites' attitudes, following the path that led early modern states to crises. As in the past, inability to sustain international influence is merely symptomatic of deeper internal decay.

For example, lack of consensus among U.S. elites has virtually immobilized efforts to deal with a persistent federal budget deficit, and has hamstrung state action in many foreign policy theaters and in much domestic policy planning. The only consensus that has prevailed in the last decade is precisely that which history tells us is the most disastrous,

---

5. The fall of the Roman Empire in the West, while the empire continued to flourish for several more centuries in the East as the Byzantine Empire, may have been due to similar causes. Downey (1969, 81) observes that "the structure of the [Roman] government differed significantly in the East and West. In the West, the land-owning aristocrats . . . contribut[ed] much less than they should to the cost of the army and the government. The Eastern Empire, in contrast, . . . received in taxes a higher proportion of the national income than the Western government could enjoy."

namely, the consensus that private consumption should take precedence over all public expenses, and that raising taxes to realistic levels to meet state obligations should be fiercely resisted. Hence the U.S. government has been running a growing debt, sustained only by foreign borrowing.

The result has been just what the history of earlier states who have been denied adequate taxation and relied on debt would lead us to expect: private individuals among the elite have become enormously richer, while basic public services that support the economy as a whole—primary and secondary education, airports, trains, roads, and bridges—are neglected, overburdened, and deteriorating. Moreover, public officials have become ruinously underpaid compared to their counterparts in the private sector. The chief executive of a $3-billion-per-year automobile company may earn $20 million annually, whereas in public service, the secretary of defense, chief executive of a $300 billion per year operation, is paid less than $100,000 annually.[6] Lower-level public managers suffer in proportion. The 1984–1985 Commission on Executive, Legislative, and Judicial Salaries reported that from 1969 to 1985, while the real income of corporate executives rose 68 percent, the real income of top federal officials *declined* by 40 percent (Brauer 1988, 75). Thus, public officials have succumbed to subtle (and sometimes not-so-subtle) forms of corruption, using their government offices as launching pads to more lucrative private-sector jobs. One-third of recent presidential appointees to top government jobs have stayed for one and a half years or less; their *average* length of service is two years (Brauer 1988, 76). Professionalism, experience in office, and commitment to public service can not long survive such conditions.

It has become popular of late to lament the lack of ethics in public life. But how does one judge the ethics of a society that expects its public officials to pursue careers that pay only 5–10 percent of what their responsibilities and talents would merit elsewhere? I have seen modern Westerners chuckle at stories about the Chinese bureaucracy, which paid its officials ludicrously low official salaries, expecting them to make their living from private donations received in return for favorable use of their influence in office. But did the United States in the 1980s treat its top bureaucrats any differently?

The United States thus enters the 1990s with several evident problems: factional divisions among elites that undercut policy consensus, widespread resistance to realistic taxes, an overreliance on debt, and a

6. As of 1987, after a substantial raise in federal pay that took effect in January of that year, U.S. cabinet secretaries received an annual salary of $99,500 (Brauer 1988, 75).

polarization of private incomes while public services—and public servants—are grossly underfunded and losing their ability to support the
economy. The key element in this decay is not, as it is sometimes por-
trayed, a decay of American manufacturing ability or of American foreign power, or a threat of imminent economic catastrophe; instead it is
a steady erosion of public institutions and public services. This decay
threatens to undermine the social and infrastructural foundations that
supported American economic growth in the first three-quarters of this
century. If unchecked, it is certain that the long-term results, which are
now only slightly apparent but will accumulate rapidly in the coming
decades, will be a relative decline in the living standards, freedom of
decision, and international position of the United States as compared
with other industrialized nations. How did this impasse develop?

Part of the answer is again demographic: the impact of the U.S. "baby
boom." The cohort of individuals born from 1950 to the early 1960s
was exceptionally large. Economists have argued extensively over the
economic impact of this cohort (Easterlin 1980). However, two points
are sufficient to clarify recent developments. First, the growth in the
labor force halted the growth in real wages, making it sensible for corporations to substitute labor for capital, and thus to defer investment.
Second, the slow growth of investment, and hence of capital per worker,
has stalled productivity (Friedman 1988). This means, very simply, declining international competitiveness, and declining rates of per-capita
economic growth. At the same time, the overall expansion in the size of
the economy with the maturing of the baby boomers greatly increased
the economic opportunities for the few who did make it to the top. Thus
a successful minority shows remarkable incomes, while most baby
boomers find it difficult to match, much less surpass, the living standards of their parents. The economic "pinch" on the large baby-boom
cohort as it entered the marketplace and struggled for promotions has
led to greater competition within that cohort. Other things being equal,
therefore, it is understandable that members of this cohort devote more
attention to their own upward mobility as individuals and less to the
support of investments and taxation for public goods, such as education
and infrastructure, that will aid future generations but slightly reduce
their own immediate level of consumption. America in the wake of the
baby boom, therefore, has seen in milder form much the same syndrome
that was seen in early modern economies under pressures of rapid population growth: polarization of incomes, stagnant real wages, reluctance
to pay taxes, and greater struggles for personal advancement.

Since 1960 demands have grown for federal government action in a wide variety of fields—support of education, research, and medical care; protection of the environment; enforcement of safety in the workplace, in pharmaceuticals, in cosmetics and food additives, and in consumer goods; intervention against the distribution and use of narcotics; provision of a "safety net" for the poor; support for troubled family farmers; aid to state and local governments; provision and regulation of national transportation, including highway construction, airport management, and subsidies for rail and mass transit; provision of greatly expanded postal services; provision of national statistics, weather forecasting, library and information services; and provision of various guarantees and subsidies for private loans, pensions, mortgages, and savings institutions. All of these services, which are to provide for a population that has grown by 39 percent from 1960 to 1987, are *in addition* to the burdens of providing social security for a rapidly growing older population and providing national defense and foreign aid to protect and further the United States' international security in an increasingly complex world. In short, the *real* demands on the federal government have enormously increased. Yet the percentage of GNP collected by the federal government has *not* risen, but has *fallen* very slightly, from 1960 to 1987.[7] We thus find a familiar pattern—despite increasing demands on the state, taxation receives a declining share of national wealth. The result is the federal deficit and a public infrastructure increasingly unable to meet national needs.

Such trends and attitudes may be a short-term "blip" in American politics, with the post-baby-boom generation having different values. Unfortunately, to the extent that the current political majority—self-focused, and demanding state services but resisting taxation—supports state policies that accumulate an enormous debt burden, the next generation, regardless of its values, will face massive problems in reconciling state resources with state commitments. Aside from accumulated government debt, the neglect of problems in the water, fuel, and transportation infrastructure, in the accumulation of radioactive toxins from U.S. weapons programs, and in the U.S. banking system and other systems of state-guaranteed liability for private loans and pensions, has left a

7. The percent of GNP collected by the federal government has been remarkably constant, despite the increase in federal responsibilities. This percentage was 19.0 percent in 1960, 18.99 percent in 1970, 18.93 percent in 1980, and 18.87 percent in 1987. The data in this paragraph are from U.S. Bureau of the Census (1964, 1989a, 1989b).

legacy of currently unfunded government commitments running into the hundreds of billions of dollars.

Furthermore, once serious undertaxation and decay of public services and infrastructure has begun, a strong momentum sets in. As urban centers become unsafe, wealthier elites move to more isolated—even privately guarded—residential communities. As schools deteriorate, the middle and upper classes send their children to private schools. As public hospitals decay, the wealthier seek treatment from private faciliites. As roadways decline, there is talk of building private toll roads. All these trends—each entailing the substitution of private for formerly public services—create a situation in which those who are economically better off feel compelled to resist taxation, so that they can afford to live in more exclusive communities and send their children to private schools; moreover, they then become even more intolerant of taxes, since they no longer consume the public services that such taxation provides. Their heightened resistance to taxation then leads to further underfunding and deterioration of public services, which reinforce the trend of private substitution in an accelerating cycle. The long-term result is a loss of faith in the public sector, a greater polarization and fragmentation of society, and a loss of a sense of shared community. Once begun, a trend toward glorification of private consumption and denigration of the public sector thus gathers institutional momentum that can long outlast the value orientation that initiated the trend. For these reasons, the accumulation of government debt and the decay of public services is extremely difficult to reverse.

Early modern regimes, based on narrow imperial or monarchical authority, on traditional status systems with a limited ability to absorb new elites, and on a relatively inflexible agrarian economy, had only limited ability to cope with elite conflict and fiscal strains. Worse yet, early modern governments and their elites generally did not understand what was happening to their societies, and blamed each other for the ills brought by rising population and diminishing economic returns.

The United States has greater flexibility, and a greater number of options. Where in early modern states it took state breakdown and reconstruction to change traditional tax systems, to overhaul elite recruitment and status systems, and to restore the balance of population and productivity, the United States can accomplish such goals through elections, legislation, and innovation. Moreover, the problems of the United States are far milder. The United States is faced not with the threat of state breakdown but merely with the loss of relative international economic standing and political influence. Still, it must be noted that today's problems are not widely understood.

DEMOGRAPHIC OVERHANG AND THE COMING DECLINE

One clear sign of America's lack of understanding of the coming crisis is the nature of the debate over the federal deficit and budgeting for social security. The problem is often posed as an accounting issue—should the United States run a deficit? How many dollars, or bonds, does the U.S. need to save to ensure that social security claimants in the twenty-first century will receive their checks? Yet these questions overlook an obvious fact: the ability to pay off deficits and provide a secure retirement for the baby boomers depends primarily on future U.S. production. No matter how many dollars are "saved," *they will be useless to holders of government bonds or to those receiving social security checks unless the economy is producing enough goods and services for recipients to make desired purchases.*

If the funds placed in the hands of retirees are chasing too small a supply of goods and services, then social security disbursements will bring ruinous inflation rather than comfortable retirement. The deficit and social security questions are therefore not a matter of "saving," but one of *productivity*; a sound standard of living in the next century depends not on how many dollars will then be stashed in various accounts, but on how many goods and services the economy will then be *producing* for purchase.

We can examine more precisely America's needs in the way of productivity growth. In 1989, the U.S. labor force comprised 119 million individuals, who supported a retired population of 27.6 million. Thus the ratio of workers to retirees was 4.3:1. Thirty years from now, in 2020, when the baby-boom generation has retired, the ratio of workers to retirees is expected to be only 2.7:1. In order merely to maintain today's standard of living, then, each worker in 2020 will have to produce 59 percent *more* output to provide for both personal needs and those of the additional retirees. The change in the age structure thus creates a demographic overhang in the next thirty years, such that a 59 per cent increase in per capita productivity is required merely to stand still. This works out to a required annual increase in productivity of 1.6

percent. Any smaller increase will lead to an inevitable decline in living standards.[8]

From 1973 to 1988, U.S. productivity (real GNP per worker) rose by only 0.86 percent per year, or only *half* the rate needed to offset the demographic overhang.[9] Moreover, from 1990 to 2020 the United States will have greater burdens: payment of interest on the existing debt, rescue of the savings and loan industry, repair of current infrastructure, and cleanup of toxic wastes will entail spending hundreds of billions of dollars. Yet these expenditures will not raise productivity or living standards one iota—they are necessary simply to arrest drastic decline. To offset the demographic overhang, the United States will have to double the current rate of growth in productivity; that will require public investment to provide a skilled labor force and improved transportation, health care, and resource management. Improving productivity will also require massive private investment to equip the labor force with the latest capital and technology. The dilemma is therefore stark and simple: money must be found for government to make the expenditures needed to arrest drastic decline. Money must also be found for both the government and private industry to make productivity-raising investments.

At present, too few resources are going to such expenditures and investments; thus productivity growth is too small by half to offset the impact of the coming demographic overhang. American living standards are therefore set to decline over the next three decades.

Reversing this trend will require a very different set of commitments than those found among today's political elites.

WHAT THE U.S. REQUIRES: ENNOBLING LEADERSHIP

Why we have not already resolved these problems is simply understood: we have preferred the short-term benefits of policies that favor our consumption over the long-term policies that maintain a stable and developing economy over time. The history of societies that have followed

8. Data are from U.S. Department of Labor (1990), U.S. Department of Health and Human Services (1990), International Labor Office (1986), and U.S. Bureau of the Census (1989b). Retired population in 2020 is based on the projection of population aged sixty-five and over in U.S. Bureau of the Census (1989b).
9. Productivity gains have varied considerably in this period: .5 percent per annum from 1973 to 1979, then 1.1 percent to 1988. However, the latter period included rapid but short-lived gains during the initial recovery from the 1981–1982 recession. In 1987, productivity increase was .8 percent, about the average for the period since 1973 as a whole (Friedman 1988, 189, 206–207).

this course is plain to see—decay, decline, and internal turmoil or external defeat. The parallels between U.S. fiscal policy in the 1980s and French fiscal policy in the 1770s are startling. Both countries had economies easily strong enough to close their state budget deficits, with only slight increases in taxation. But both countries lacked the necessary political will to do so. Elites and popular groups, the former enjoying extraordinary riches owing to economic expansion that they considered their due, the latter under pressure owing to declining productivity, combined to resist further taxation. Each state resorted to borrowing, both international and domestic.

Forced to pay higher rates of interest than its neighbors, each state prided itself on the strength of its currency. At the same time, its higher interest rates discouraged productive investment and encouraged financial speculation. Faced with higher real interest rates, these countries invested less in new industrial capacity, and their productivity failed to keep pace with their competitors. Instead, investors turned to the high yields available on government bonds and more speculative investments. Financiers thus grew richer through lending to the state, while workers in traditional industries faced ever greater difficulties. In each case, the largest and wealthiest country in its area and era—France in eighteenth-century Europe, the United States in the twentieth-century world—lost ground to foreign economic competitors. France was shortly overtaken economically, despite its military strength, first by England and Belgium and later by Germany. The United States is now in danger of being overtaken economically by Japan and by the leading economies of Western Europe. In France by the 1780s, chronic borrowing reached a point at which the government was forced to borrow merely to pay the interest on its debt, a situation the United States will reach in the early 1990s given present trends. State fiscal weakness and income polarization led to elite factionalism and popular unrest in France; similar trends have led to elite factionalism in the United States, and may lead again to riots to complement the current gang warfare in U.S. inner cities.

To restore U.S. strength, a simple prescription is required: adequate taxation instead of debt to finance government, and improved funding of public services and officials; emphasis on investment and research to raise productivity over consumption; and consensus on domestic and foreign policy goals, so that sacrifices can be uniformly sought and efforts consistently directed. Unfortunately, that simple prescription is extremely difficult to fill. What is needed is leadership that is both effective *and* ennobling.

"Effective" leadership brings a variety of individuals and groups together to focus on a common cause. In this sense, Ronald Reagan was an extraordinarily effective leader. However, the causes that were the focus of his leadership in the period 1982–1988—achieving higher personal consumption and stronger national defense through replacement of taxation by state debt—did not require any sacrifice; instead they brought immediate satisfaction. The lowering of income taxes and the borrowing to increase spending on defense were policies aimed at emotional needs, namely, fears stemming from the inflation and the Iranian hostage crisis of 1978–1981. Reagan's policies were not aimed at the long-term needs of American society: increasing productivity and bringing personal, corporate, and government expenditures more in line with incomes, to allow a surplus for investment and future growth. Thus for example, borrowing money to pay defense engineers and military servicemen created jobs, including jobs for those restaurant, clerical, and other domestic service industries that served the communities with military facilities. But this job expansion did nothing to promote more efficient production of manufactures, services, or capital goods for the international marketplace.

"Ennobling" leadership brings a variety of individuals and groups together to focus on a common cause that does *not* immediately satisfy current desires. Instead, such leadership asks individuals and groups to make immediate sacrifices, and to tolerate immediate discomfort, by refocusing their interest on long-term gains. The policies needed to provide long-term gains for the U.S. economy, and long-term effectiveness of the United States in world leadership, are often pointed out. The United States must increase its investment and reduce its dependence on foreign borrowing. However, since investment equals total output plus borrowing minus consumption, simple arithmetic tells us we cannot get from here (low investment and high foreign borrowing) to there (high investment and low foreign borrowing) without *reducing* consumption, at least until our total output increases enough to reduce our borrowing requirement. The difficulty we have had in adopting such policies is not that the right measures are hard to find, but rather that the reduction in consumption cannot be implemented without effective and *ennobling* leadership to gain its acceptance. Unless the American public is convinced that some sacrifice of immediate consumption is necessary to prevent an inevitable economic and political decline of the nation, the necessary steps to restore U.S. strength cannot be taken.

To demand sacrifice is extremely difficult for any leader. It is ren-

dered easier by war or by depression. It is for this reason that great
leaders more easily emerge in such catastrophes—catastrophe predis-
poses people to be more open to ennobling leadership. The specter of
being left behind in international competition is rarely sufficient, for in
the short term this threat creates emotional needs that are satisfied by
aggressive trade policies and protectionism. This provides a path for
effective leadership that is not ennobling and does little for long-term
prosperity: restrictive trade policies that maintain a market for today's
products are of no use if tomorrow's economy does not produce goods
that are widely sought, such as video recorders or memory chips.

The prospects for the future economic and political standing of the
United States thus depend greatly on the emergence of leaders who can
truly lead, rather than merely satisfy, public opinion. Given the difficulties faced by the baby-boom generation, a reduction in consumption
will be difficult to achieve. The great challenge of American political
leadership in the 1990s is therefore to persuade Americans, whether or
not they experience a devastating recession, to make the sacrifices
needed to raise investment and the level of public goods.

The study of early modern history suggests that the current U.S.
course will lead to heightened factional conflict and economic weakness.
But it also suggests that such decline is not inevitable. Early modern
monarchies and empires declined because they lacked the flexibility to
respond to changing balances of population and resources. The United
States has the flexibility to respond; the question is whether it has the
will.

This book examines early modern history. But the processes that
shaped early modern history have not stopped; they have only grown
more complex by intertwining with new ones. We continue to build on
the legacies of the early modern period, and many people still seek to
mimic its successes and avoid its mistakes. But if I am correct, most social
theory has fundamentally misunderstood the dynamics of the early modern period. Not the growth of capitalism, but a periodic, cyclic imbalance between population growth and inflexible economic and political
systems, was responsible for the recurrent waves of state breakdown.
Not revolution, but the defeat of autocratic regimes in war or gradual
but meaningful reforms, provided the openings for stable democratic
politics. Given such misunderstandings, it is no surprise that the contemporary world is far from what we would like it to be.

We live in a world where capital and modern weaponry, political parties and information management, dominate. But achieving a balance between population and resources is still critical to improving the political stability and economic prospects of the world's nations. Our great advantage over our early modern predecessors is that modern technology has given us a greater range of choices, and modern political systems have given individuals greater opportunities to make their choices heard. Nonetheless, we have not been delivered from the responsibility of choice. Population growth in the face of limited resources can lead to selfishness and corruption, factionalism, income polarization, and fiscal decay. Or, the same conditions can be a spur to growth, *provided* that taxation is increased to keep pace with demands on government and prudent investments are made that raise productivity. For developing nations, emerging democracies, and industrialized nations—including the United States—the desirable, if difficult, choice should be clear.

In the past, rigid institutions and restricted political access, the favoring of private elite wealth through unrealistically low taxes and inadequate public investment, the stifling of individual freedom and economic initiative through state-imposed cultural conformity, and the failure to provide productive opportunities for the poor have produced growing inequity, elite factionalism, economic stagnation, and the decline and collapse of states and empires. In contrast, reforms made in the spirit of compromise and sacrifice, respect for individual liberty, democratic politics, and a capitalist economy—tempered with incentives for investment, taxation sufficient to provide for the public good, and assistance to the poor—have consistently marked the path to increasing material prosperity for diverse societies. Despite technological progress, similar policies will likely produce similar consequences in the future. We ignore the past at our peril.

Appendix

Compiling French and
English National Income and
Tax Tables (Tables 2 and 3)

French output is divided into agriculture, industry, and foreign trade. Marczewski (1965, 92) estimates total output in agriculture and industry in 1789 at 5.1 billion livres. Perroux's (1955, 61) estimate of shares in agriculture (73 percent of physical output) and industry (27 percent) for 1789 are then used to partition this total. This yields estimates of output in agriculture of 3.7 billion livres, and in industry of 1.4 billion livres. Riley (1986, 13) estimates that circa 1780 foreign trade contributed 6 percent to total output. If it contributed the same percentage in 1789, that would add .3 billion livres. Thus total physical output in 1789 is estimated at 5.4 billion livres. (This estimate, of course, excludes services.)

To obtain estimates of output in 1700, these figures were reduced by assuming total increases (in constant value) of 25 percent for agriculture and 80 percent for industry. The agriculture increase is based on tithe estimates of Le Roy Ladurie and Goy (1982, 175–176) as adjusted according to the discussion in the text. The increase in industry is based on Markovitch's (1976, 458–459) estimate of the increase in wool cloth production.

These constant value estimates were then further deflated to allow for inflation of 69 percent in agricultural prices and 47.2 percent in industrial prices. The agricultural price deflator is from a merging of Baulant's (1972) Paris wheat prices and Labrousse's (1970e, 9) national wheat prices. The series were merged by taking the average price for both series in the years 1730–1769 and then using the ratio to bring the Baulant series into terms comparable with the Labrousse index (the latter commences in 1726). The increase in average prices from the years 1700–1709 to 1780–1789 is then 69 percent. The industrial price deflator is taken from Markovitch's (1976, 459) data on the increase in finished wool cloth prices from 1716–1718 to 1785–1787, which was 47.2

percent. This figure does omit any possible changes in manufactured goods prices from 1700 to 1716–1718. However, since from 1730–1739 to 1780–1789 alone the price of wheat rose 67 percent, while that of linen cloth and wool cloth rose only 33 percent and 24 percent, respectively, it seems reasonable to assume that for the whole period 1700–1789 the rise in manufactures' prices was less than that of agricultural products. The change in the nominal value of trade was taken to be 400 percent from Crouzet's (1970, 261) estimate. With these adjustments, the value of output in 1700 (in 1700–1709 prices) is 1.8 billion livres in agriculture and .59 billion livres in trade and industry, for a total of 2.4 billion livres.

These figures were then converted to wheat equivalents using the Baulant/ Labrousse price series, at 9.04 livres/hectoliter in 1700–1709 and 15.28 livres/ hectoliter in 1780–1790 and then converted to bushels at 1 hl = 2.75 bu (Imp.).

Real output for both sectors for the years 1726, 1751, and 1775 was then interpolated, assuming linear real growth from 1700 to 1770 and no real growth thereafter. The assumption of no real growth after 1770 is suggested by Riley (1987, 237). It is consistent with the findings of Hufton (1974) and Labrousse (1958, 1984) that French agriculture was saturated after 1770, and that manufacturing entered a long period of recession. The real output figures were then converted to current prices using the Labrousse national wheat price averages for 1726–1729 for 1726, 1746–1755 for 1751, and 1770–1779 for 1775. (The abbreviated period for 1726 was chosen to stay within the period of stable currency.)

FRENCH TAXES

These figures are for ordinary revenues only and thus exclude revenues from borrowing, sale of offices, and special contributions. These figures also exclude sums collected from the population that did not reach the royal accounts, such as the profits of the tax farmers. However, they do include the entire sum levied for the direct taxes, before deductions for the costs of collection.

Figures for 1700 are from Forbonnais (1758, 4:167). Figures for other years are from Morineau (1980, 314). Morineau's last figures are for 1788, rather than 1789.

I have partitioned the total tax revenues into taxes on agriculture and taxes on industry and trade. I have construed as taxes on the land all direct taxes (taille, capitation, vingtièmes), the revenue from the royal domain, and the dons gratuits of the clergy and the pays d'état. I have construed as levies on industry and trade all taxes listed by Forbonnais as customs, excises, or "indirects," and all taxes listed by Morineau as "indirects" and "other." Since many of these taxes were paid by peasants, especially the salt taxes, this procedure overestimates the tax burden on industry and trade and underestimates that on agriculture. However, since the results still indicate an unfairly heavy burden on agriculture, these results can be viewed as conservative.

French population totals for 1700, 1775, and 1790 are from Dupâquier (1979, 34–37, 81). Population totals for 1726 and 1751 were interpolated from Dupâquier's estimates for 1720 and 1730, and 1750 and 1755, respectively.

ENGLISH OUTPUT AND TAXES

The data on English output in nominal terms, for 1700 and 1790, are from W. Cole (1981, 64). Cole divides output into agriculture, and trade and industry. Cole's nominal figures were converted to bushels of wheat equivalent using the index of wheat prices (average of Exeter, Winchester, and Eton) in B. Mitchell (1962, 486–487).

The data on English taxes in 1700 and 1790 are from B. Mitchell (1962, 386). I have construed as levies on agriculture the English land taxes, and as levies on trade and industry all other taxes (customs, excise, stamps, etc.). As with France, this procedure underestimates the burden on agriculture. However, since much less of the English consuming population was employed in agriculture, and most of the customs and excise taxes fell on manufactures rather than on staples (the salt tax, for example, was much smaller in England), the error is probably smaller than for France.

The data on English population in 1700 and 1790 are from Wrigley and Schofield (1981, 533–534).

Bibliography

Abbott, A. 1988. Transcending General Linear Reality. *Sociological Theory* 6:169–186.

Abel, W. 1973. *Crises agraires en Europe (XIIIe-XXe siécle)*. Rev. and enl. Translated from 2d German ed. Paris: Flammarion.

Abrahamian, E. 1980. Structural Causes of the Iranian Revolution. *MERIP Reports* 87:21–26.

———. 1982. *Iran: Between Two Revolutions*. Princeton, NJ: Princeton University Press.

Abrams, P. 1982. *Historical Sociology*. Shepton Mallet, Somerset: Open Books.

Abrams, P., and E. A. Wrigley, eds. 1978. *Towns in Societies: Essays in Economic History and Historical Sociology*. Cambridge: Cambridge University Press.

Abu-el-haj, R. A. 1987. Fitnah, Huruc Ala Al-Sultan, and Nasihat: Political Struggle and Social Conflict in Ottoman Society, 1560's–1700's. In *Comité international d'études pré-Ottomanes et Ottomanes VIe symposium*, edited by J.-L. Bacqué-Grammont and E. van Donzel, 186–191. Istanbul: Divit Press.

Abu-Lughod, J. 1989. *Before European Hegemony: The World-System, A.D. 1250–1350*. New York: Oxford University Press.

Adelman, J. R. 1985. *Revolution, Armies, and War: A Political History*. Boulder, CO: L. Rienner.

Adshead, S. A. M. 1973. The Seventeenth Century General Crisis in China. *Asian Profiles* 1:271–280.

———. 1974. An Energy Crisis in Early Modern China. *Ch'ing shih wen-t'i* 3(2):20–28.

Agulhon, M. 1976. La révolution et l'empire. In *Histoire de la France rurale*, edited by G. Duby and A. Wallon, 3:19–57. Paris: Editions du Seuil.

———. 1982. *The Republic in the Village: The People of the Var from the French*

Revolution to the Second Republic. Translated by J. Lloyd. Cambridge: Cambridge University Press.

————. 1983. *The Republican Experiment, 1848–1852*. Translated by J. Lloyd. Cambridge: Cambridge University Press.

Alexander, J. C., and B. Giesen. 1987. From Reduction to Linkage: The Long View of the Micro-Macro Link. In *The Micro-Macro Link*, edited by J. C. Alexander, B. Giesen, R. Münch, and N.J. Smelser, 1–42. Berkeley and Los Angeles: University of California Press.

Alldridge, N. 1986. The Population Profile of an Early Modern Town: Chester, 1547–1728. *Annales de Démographie Historique*, 115–131.

Allen, G. C. 1962. *A Short Economic History of Modern Japan, 1867–1837*. London: Allen and Unwin.

Allen, R. C. 1982. The Efficiency and Distributional Consequences of Eighteenth Century Enclosures. *Economic Journal* 92:937–953.

————. 1987a. *The "Capital Intensive Farmer" and the English Agricultural Revolution. A Reassessment*. Department of Economics, University of British Columbia, Vancouver, Discussion Paper no. 87–11.

————. 1987b. *Enclosure, Farming Methods, and Growth of Labor Productivity in the South Midlands*. Department of Economics, University of British Columbia, Vancouver, Discussion Paper no. 86–44.

————. 1988. The Price of Freehold Land and the Interest Rate in the Seventeenth and Eighteenth Centuries. *Economic History Review*, 2d ser., 41:33–50.

Allen, R. C., and C. O'Grada. 1988. On the Road Again with Arthur Young: English, Irish, and French Agriculture during the Industrial Revolution. *Journal of Economic History* 48:93–116.

Allison, K. J., M. W. Bereford, J. G. Hurst, et al. *Deserted Villages of Oxfordshire*. Leicester: Leicester University Press.

Alsop, J. D. 1982. The Theory and Practice of Tudor Taxation. *English Historical Review* 97:1–30.

Alter, G., and J. Riley. 1986. How to Bet on Lives: A Guide to Life Contingent Contracts in Early Modern Europe. *Research in Early Modern History* 10:1–53.

Amelang, J. S. 1982. The Purchase of Nobility in Castile, 1552–1700: A Comment. *Journal of European Economic History* 11:219–226.

Aminzade, R. 1981. *Class, Politics, and Early Industrial Capitalism*. Albany, NY: State University of New York Press.

Amman, P. 1975. *Revolution and Mass Democracy: The Paris Club Movement in 1848*. Princeton, NJ: Princeton University Press.

Anderson, P. 1974. *Lineages of the Absolutist State*. London: NLB.

Andrews, R. M. 1985. Social Structures, Political Elites, and Ideology in Revolutionary Paris, 1792–94: A Critical Evaluation of A. Soboul's *Les sansculottes parisiens en l'an II. Journal of Social History* 19:71–112.

Andriette, E. A. 1971. *Devon and Exeter in the Civil War*. Newton Abbot, Devon: David and Charles.

Antler, S.D. 1972. Quantitative Analysis of the Long Parliament. *Past and Present*, no. 56, 154–157.

Appleby, A. 1975a. Agrarian Capitalism or Seigneurial Reaction? The Northwest of England, 1500–1700. *American Historical Review* 80:574–594.
———. 1975b. Common Land and Peasant Unrest in Sixteenth Century England: A Comparative Note. *Peasant Studies* 4:20–23.
———. 1975c. Nutrition and Disease: The Case of London. *Journal of Interdisciplinary History* 6:1–22.
———. 1978. *Famine in Tudor and Stuart England.* Stanford: Stanford University Press.
———. 1979. Grain Prices and Subsistence Crises in England and France, 1590–1740. *Journal of Economic History* 43:865–888.
Ardant, G. 1965. *Théorie sociologique de l'impôt.* 2 vols. Paris: Imprimerie Nationale.
———. 1975. Financial Policy and Economic Infrastructure of Modern States and Nations. In *The Formation of National States in Western Europe,* edited by C. Tilly, 164–242. Princeton, NJ: Princeton University Press.
Aristotle. 1967. *The Politics of Aristotle.* Edited by E. Barker. Oxford: Oxford University Press.
Arjomand, S. A. 1985. Religion, Political Order, and Societal Change: With Special Reference to Shi'ite Islam. *Current Perspectives in Social Theory* 6:1–15.
———. 1986. Iran's Islamic Revolution in Comparative Perspective. *World Politics* 38:383–414.
Armengaud, A. 1976. Le rôle de la démographie. In *Histoire sociale et économique de la France,* edited by F. Braudel and E. Labrousse, 3:161–235. Paris: Presses Universitaires de France.
Armstrong, J. A. 1982. *Nations before Nationalism.* Chapel Hill, NC: University of North Carolina Press.
Armstrong, W. A. 1981a. The Influence of Demographic Factors on the Position of the Agricultural Laborer in England and Wales c. 1750–1914. *Agricultural History Review* 29: 71–82.
———. 1981b. The Trend of Mortality in Carlisle between the 1780s and the 1840s: A Demographic Contribution to the Standard of Living Debate. *Economic History Review,* 2d ser., 34:94–114.
Ashton, R. 1960. *The Crown and the Money Market, 1603–1640.* Oxford: Clarendon Press.
———. 1961. Charles I and the City. In *Essays in the Economic and Social History of Tudor and Stuart England,* edited by F. J. Fisher, 138–163. Cambridge: Cambridge University Press.
———. 1969. The Aristocracy in Transition. *Economic History Review,* 2d ser., 22:308–322.
———. 1978. *The English Civil War: Conservatism and Revolution, 1603–1649.* London: Weidenfeld and Nicolson.
———. 1979. *The City and the Court, 1603–1643.* Cambridge: Cambridge University Press.
———. 1984. *Reformation and Revolution, 1558–1660.* London: Granada.
Ashton, T. S. 1959. *An Economic History of England: The Eighteenth Century.* London: Methuen.

Ashton, T. S., and C. H. E. Philpin, eds. *The Brenner Debate: Agrarian Class Structure and Economic Development in Pre-industrial Europe.* Cambridge: Cambridge University Press.

Ashtor, E. 1981. Levantine Sugar Industry in the Later Middle Ages: A Case of Technological Decline. In *The Islamic Middle East, 700–1900*, edited by A. L. Udovitch, 91–132. Princeton, NJ: Darwin Press.

Aston, T., ed. 1967. *Crisis in Europe, 1560–1660.* New York: Doubleday.

Atkinson, R. F. 1978. *Knowledge and Explanation in History.* London: Macmillan.

Attman, A. 1981. *The Bullion Flow between Europe and the East, 1000–1750.* Translated by E. Green and A. Green. Göteberg: Kungl. Vetenskaps- och Vitterhetssamhället.

Atwell, W. S. 1975. From Education to Politics: The *Fu She.* In *The Unfolding of Neo-Confucianism*, edited by W. T. deBary, 333–368. New York: Columbia University Press.

———. 1977. Notes on Silver, Foreign Trade, and the Late Ming Economy. *Ch'ing shih wen-t'i* 3(8):1–33.

———. 1982. International Bullion Flows and the Chinese Economy circa 1530–1650. *Past and Present*, no. 95, 68–90.

———. 1986. Some Observations on the Seventeenth Century Crisis in China and Japan. *Journal of Asian Studies* 45:223–244.

Aubin, H., and W. Zorn. 1976. *Handbuch der deutschen Wirtschafts- und Sozialgeschichte.* 2 vols. Stuttgart: Klett-Cotta.

Aya, R. 1984. Popular Intervention in Revolutionary Situations. In *Statemaking and Social Movements: Essays in History and Theory*, edited by C. Bright and S. Harding, 318–343. Ann Arbor: University of Michigan Press.

Aylmer, G. E. 1961. *The King's Servants: The Civil Service of Charles I, 1625–1642.* London: Routledge and Kegan Paul.

———. 1965. *The Struggle for the Constitution, 1603–1689: England in the Seventeenth Century.* Rev. ed. London: Blandford Press.

———, ed. 1972. *The Interregnum: The Quest for Settlement, 1646–1660.* London: Macmillan.

———. 1975. *The Levellers in the English Revolution.* Ithaca, NY: Cornell University Press.

———. 1986. *Rebellion or Revolution? England, 1640–1660.* Oxford: Oxford University Press.

Aymard, M. 1982. From Feudalism to Capitalism in Italy: The Case That Doesn't Fit. *Review* 6:131–208.

Bacqué-Grammont, J.-L., and E. van Donzel, eds. 1987. *Comité international d'études pré-Ottomanes et Ottomanes VIe symposium.* Istanbul: Divit Press.

Baechler, J., J. A. Hall, and M. Mann, eds. 1988. *Europe and the Rise of Capitalism.* Oxford: Basil Blackwell.

Baehrel, R. 1961. *Une croissance: la Bas-Provence rurale (fin du XIVe siècle–1789). Essai d'économie historique statistique.* Paris: SEVPEN.

Bairoch, P. 1982. International Industrialization Levels from 1750 to 1980. *Journal of European Economic History* 11:269–334.

Baker, K. M. 1978. French Political Thought at the Accession of Louis XVI. *Journal of Modern History* 50:279–303.

———. 1987a. Politique et opinion publique sous l'ancien régime. *Annales, E.S.C.* 42:41–72.

———. 1987b. Introduction. In *The French Revolution and the Creation of Modern Political Culture*, edited by K. Baker, 1:xi–xxiv. Oxford: Pergamon Press.

———, ed. 1987c. *The French Revolution and the Creation of Modern Political Culture*. 2 vols. Oxford: Pergamon Press.

Banai, A., and Vryonis, S., eds. 1977. *Individualism and Conformity in Classical Islam*. Wiesbaden: Otto Harrassowitz.

Barber, E. G. 1955. *The Bourgeoisie in 18th Century France*. Princeton, NJ: Princeton University Press.

Barkan, Ö. L. 1957. Essai sur les données statistiques des registres de recensement dans l'empire Ottoman aux XVe et XVIe siècles. *Journal of the Economic and Social History of the Orient* 1:9–36.

———. 1963. The Social Consequences of Economic Crisis in Later Sixteenth Century Turkey. In *Social Aspects of Economic Development: International Conference on Social Aspects of Economic Development*, 17–36. Istanbul: Economic and Social Studies Conference Board.

———. 1970. Research on the Ottoman Fiscal Surveys. In *Studies in the Economic History of the Middle East*, edited by M. A. Cook, 163–171. London: Oxford University Press.

———. 1975. The Price Revolution of the Sixteenth Century: A Turning Point in the Economic History of the Near East. *International Journal of Middle East Studies* 6:3–28.

———, ed. 1983. *Contributions à l'histoire économique et sociale de l'empire Ottoman*. Louvain: Editions Peeters.

Barnes, T. 1961. *Somerset, 1625–1640*. Cambridge, MA: Harvard University Press.

Bates, R. 1981. *Markets and States in Tropical Africa*. Berkeley and Los Angeles: University of California Press.

Batho, G. 1967. Landlords in England: Noblemen, Gentlemen, Yeomen. In *The Agrarian History of England and Wales*, vol. 4. *1500–1640*, edited by J. Thirsk, 276–305. Cambridge: Cambridge University Press.

Baulant, M. 1972. Grain Prices in Paris, 1431–1788. In *Social Historians in Contemporary France: Essays from Annales*, edited by M. Ferro, 22–41. New York: Harper and Row.

Baumber, M. L. 1977. *A Pennine Community on the Eve of the Industrial Revolution: Keighly and Haworth between 1660 and 1740*. Keighly, Yorkshire: J. L. Crabtree.

Beasley, W. G. 1972. *The Meiji Restoration*. Stanford: Stanford University Press.

———. 1988. Meiji Political Institutions. In *The Cambridge History of Japan*, vol. 5: *The Nineteenth Century*, edited by M. B. Jansen, 618–673. Cambridge: Cambridge University Press.

Beattie, H. J. 1979. *Land and Lineage in China: A Study of T'ung-Ch'eng*

County Anhwei, in the Ming and Ch'ing Dynasties. Cambridge: Cambridge University Press.

Beck, T. 1981. The French Revolution and the Nobility: A Reconsideration. *Journal of Social History* 15:219–234.

———. 1983. Occupation, Taxes, and a Distinct Nobility under Louis Philippe. *European Studies Review* 13:403–422.

Beckett, J. V. 1977. English Landownership in the Later Seventeenth and Eighteenth Centuries: The Debate and The Problems. *Economic History Review*, 2d ser., 30:567–581.

———. 1982. The Decline of the Small Landowner in Eighteenth and Nineteenth Century England: Some Regional Considerations. *Agricultural History Review* 30:97–111.

———. 1983. The Debate over Farm Sizes in Eighteenth and Nineteenth Century England. *Agricultural History* 5:308–25.

———. 1986. *The Aristocracy in England, 1660–1914.* Oxford: Basil Blackwell.

Beer, B. L. 1982. *Rebellion and Riot: Popular Disorder in England during the Reign of Edward VI.* Kent, OH: Kent State University Press.

Behrens, C. B. 1962. Nobles, Privilege, and Taxes in France at the End of the Ancien Régime. *Economic History Review*, 2d ser., 15:451–475.

———. 1974. The Ancien Régime and the Revolution. *Historical Journal* 17:630–643.

———. 1985. *Society, Government, and the Enlightenment: The Experience of Eighteenth-Century France and Prussia.* New York: Icon Editions.

Beier, A. L. 1974. Vagrants and the Social Order in Elizabethan England. *Past and Present*, no. 64, 3–29.

———. 1983. *The Problem of the Poor in Tudor and Early Stuart England.* London: Methuen.

———. 1989. Poverty and Progress in Early Modern England. In *The First Modern Society,* edited by A. L. Beier, D. Cannadine, and J. M. Rosenheim, 201–239. Cambridge: Cambridge University Press.

Beier, A. L., and R. A. Finlay, eds. 1986. *London, 1500–1700: The Making of the Metropolis.* London: Longman.

Beier, A. L., D. Cannadine, and J. M. Rosenheim, eds. 1989. *The First Modern Society: Essays in English History in Honour of Lawrence Stone.* Cambridge: Cambridge University Press.

Beik, W. 1985. *Absolutism and Society in Seventeenth Century France.* Cambridge: Cambridge University Press.

———. 1987. Urban Factions and the Social Order during the Minority of Louis XIV. *French Historical Studies* 15:36–67.

Beldiceanu, N. 1980a. Le timar dans l'état Ottoman. In *Structures féodales et féodalisme dans l'occident méditerranéen, Xe au XIIIe siècle,* 743–753. Rome: Centre de la Recherche Scientifique et l'Ecole Française de Rome.

———.1980b. *Le timar dans l'état Ottoman, début XIVe-début XVIe siècle.* Wiesbaden: Otto Harrassowitz.

Beldiceanu-Steinherr, L., and J. L. Bacqué-Grammont. 1982. A propos de quelques causes de malaises sociaux en Anatoli centrale aux XVIe et XVIIe siècles. *Archivum Ottomanicum* 7:71–115.

Benecke, G. 1972. The Problem of Death and Destruction during the Thirty Years War: New Evidence from the Middle Western Front. *European Studies Review* 2:239–253.

Bengtsson, T., G. Fridlizius, and R. Ohlsson, eds. 1984. *Pre-industrial Population Change.* Stockholm: Almquist and Wiksell.

Bennett, M. K. 1968. British Wheat Yield per Acre for Seven Centuries. In *Essays in Agrarian History,* edited by W. Minchinton, 1:53–72. New York: Augustus M. Kelley.

Beresford, M. 1948. Glebe Terrers and Open-Field Leicestershire. *Transactions of the Leicester Archeological Society* 24:77–126.

———. 1954. *The Lost Villages of England.* London: Lutterworth.

———. 1961. Habitation vs. Improvement: The Debate on Enclosure by Agreement. In *Essays in the Economic and Social History of Tudor and Stuart England,* edited by F. J. Fisher, 15–39. Cambridge: Cambridge University Press.

Bergeron, L. 1981. *France Under Napoleon.* Translated by R. R. Palmer. Princeton, NJ: Princeton University Press.

Berkner, L. K., and F. F. Mendels. 1978. Inheritance Systems, Family Structures, and Demographic Patterns in Western Europe, 1700–1900. In *Historical Studies of Changing Fertility,* edited by C. Tilly, 209–223. Princeton, NJ: Princeton University Press.

Bernard, L. 1975. French Society and Popular Uprisings under Louis XIV. In *State and Society in Seventeenth Century France,* edited by R. F. Kierstead, 157–179. New York: New Viewpoints.

Berry, B. J. L., E. C. Conkling, and D. M. Ray. 1976. *Geography of Economic Systems.* Englewood Cliffs, N.J.: Prentice-Hall.

Best, G. 1982. *War and Society in Revolutionary Europe, 1770–1870.* Bungay, Suffolk: Fontana.

Bezucha, R. J. 1975. The Revolution of 1830 and the City of Lyons. In *1830 in France,* edited by J. M. Merriman, 119–138. New York: New Viewpoints.

———, ed. 1982. *Modern European Social History.* Lexington, MA: D.C. Heath.

———. 1983. The French Revolution of 1848 and the Social History of Work. *Theory and Society* 12:469–484.

Bien, D. 1974. La réaction aristocratique avant 1789: l'exemple de l'armée. *Annales, E.S.C.* 29:27–48, 29:505–534.

———. 1978. The Secretaires du Roi: Absolutism, Corps, and Privilege under the Ancien Régime. In *Vom Ancien Régime zur Französischen Revolution,* edited by E. Hinrichs, E. Schmitt, and R. Vierhaus, 153–168. Göttingen: Vandenhoeck and Rupert.

———. 1987. Office Corps and a System of State Credit: The Uses of Privilege under the Ancien Régime. In *The French Revolution and the Creation of Modern Political Culture,* edited by K. Baker, 1:89–113. Oxford: Pergamon Press.

510   Bibliography

Biraben, J.-N. 1985. Le point de l'enquete sur le mouvement de la population en France avant 1670. *Population* 40:47–70.

Biraben, J.-N., and D. Blanchet. 1982. Le mouvement naturel de la population en France avant 1670. Présentation d'une enquête par sondage. *Population* 37:1099–1132.

Biraben, J.-N., and N. Bonneuil. 1986. Population et économie en pays de Caux aux XVIe et XVIIe siècles. *Population* 41:937–960.

Bitton, D. 1969. *The French Nobility in Crisis, 1560–1640*. Stanford: Stanford University Press.

Bix, H. 1986. *Peasant Protest in Japan, 1590–1884*. New Haven: Yale University Press.

Blacker, J. C. 1957. Social Ambitions of the Bourgeoisie in Eighteenth Century France and Their Relation to Family Limitation. *Population Studies* 11:46–63.

Blackwood, B. G. 1978. *The Lancashire Gentry and the Great Rebellion, 1640–1660*. Manchester: Chatham Society.

Blanchard, I. 1986. The Continental European Cattle Trade, 1400–1600. *Economic History Review*, 2d ser., 29:427–460.

Blanning, T. C. W. 1986. *The Origins of the French Revolutionary Wars*. London: Longman.

———. 1987. *The French Revolution: Aristocrats versus Bourgeois?* Atlantic Highlands, NJ: Humanities Press.

Blaug, M. 1963. The Myth of the Old Poor Law and the Making of the New. *Journal of Economic History* 23:151–184.

Blayo, Y. 1975. Mouvement naturel de la population française de 1740 à 1829. *Population* (Numéro Special): 15–64.

Bloch, M. 1966. *French Rural History: An Essay on Its Basic Characteristics*. Translated by J. Sondheimer. Berkeley and Los Angeles: University of California Press.

Bloch, R. 1985. *Visionary Republic: Millennial Themes in American Thought, 1756–1800*. Cambridge: Cambridge University Press.

Bluche, R. 1976. The Social Origins of the Secretaries of State under Louis XIV, 1661–1715. In *Louis XIV and Absolutism*, edited by R. Hatton, 85–100. London: Macmillan.

Blum, C. 1986. *Rousseau and the Republic of Virtue: The Language of Politics in the French Revolution*. Ithaca, NY: Cornell University Press.

Bogucka, M. 1980. The Role of the Baltic Trade in European Development from the XVIth to the XVIIIth Centuries. *Journal of European Economic History* 9:27–35.

Bois, G. 1984. *The Crisis of Feudalism: Economy and Society in Eastern Normandy, c. 1300–1550*. Cambridge: Cambridge University Press.

Bois, J.-P. 1981. Les anciens soldats de 1715 à 1815. Problèmes et méthodes. *Revue Historique* 265:81–102.

Bois, P. 1960. *Paysans de l'ouest*. Le Mans: Maurice Vilaire.

Bonfield, L. 1981. Marriage Settlements 1660–1740: The Adoption of the Strict Settlement in Kent and Northamptonshire. In *Marriage and Society: Studies in the Social History of Marriage*, edited by R. B. Outhwaite, 101–116. London: European Publications.

———. 1986. Affective Families, Open Elites, and Family Settlement in Early Modern England. *Economic History Review*, 2d ser., 39:341–354.

Bonnell, V. 1983. *Roots of Rebellion*. Berkeley and Los Angeles: University of California Press.

Bonney, R. J. 1978a. *Political Change under Richelieu and Mazarin, 1624–1661*. Oxford: Oxford University Press.

———. 1978b. The French Civil War, 1649–53. *European Studies Review* 8:71–100.

———. 1979. The Failure of the French Revenue Farms, 1600–1660. *Economic History Review*, 2d ser., 32:11–32.

———. 1980a. Cardinal Mazarin and His Critics: The Remonstrances of 1652. *Journal of European Studies* 10:15–31.

———. 1980b. The English and French Civil Wars. *History* 65:365–382.

———. 1981. *The King's Debts: Finances and Politics in France, 1589–1661*. Oxford: Oxford University Press.

Borchardt, K. 1976. Wirtschaftliches, Wachstum, und Wechsellagen, 1800–1914. In *Handbuch der deutschen Wirtschafts- und Sozialgeschichte*, edited by H. Aubin and W. Zorn, 1:198–275. Stuttgart: Klett-Cotta.

Bordo, M. D., and L. Jonung. 1987. *The Long-Run Behavior of the Income Velocity of Money: The International Evidence*. Cambridge: Cambridge University Press.

Borton, H. 1968. *Peasant Uprisings: Japan of the Tokugawa Period*. 2d ed. New York: Paragon.

Boserup, E. 1981. *Population and Technological Change: A Study of Long-Term Trends*. Chicago: University of Chicago Press.

Bosher, J. F. 1970. *French Finances, 1770–1795: From Business to Bureaucracy*. Cambridge: Cambridge University Press.

———. 1972. The French Crisis of 1770. *History* 57:17–30.

———. 1973. "Chambres de justice" in the French Monarchy. In *French Government and Society: Essays in Memory of Alfred Cobban*, edited by J. F. Bosher, 19–40. London: Athlone Press.

Bossenga, G. 1986. From Corps to Citizenship: The *Bureaux des finances* before the French Revolution. *Journal of Modern History* 58:610–642.

———. 1987. City and State: An Urban Perspective on the Origins of the French Revolution. In *The French Revolution and the Creation of Modern Political Culture*, edited by K. Baker, 1:115–140. Oxford: Pergamon Press.

———. Forthcoming. The Politics of Privilege: Old Regime and Revolution in Lille. Cambridge: Cambridge University Press.

Botham, F. W., and E. H. Hunt. 1987. Wages in Britain during the Industrial Revolution. *Economic History Review*, 2d ser., 40:380–399.

Bourdieu, P. 1984. *Distinction: A Social Critique of the Judgement of Taste*. Translated by R. Nice. Cambridge, MA: Harvard University Press.

Bourgeois-Pichet, J. 1968. The General Development of the Population of France since the Eighteenth Century. In *Population and History*, edited by D. V. Glass and D. E. C. Eversley, 474–506. Chicago: Aldine.

Bowden, P. J. 1962. *The Wool Trade in Tudor and Stuart England*. London: Macmillan.

——. 1967a. Agricultural Prices, Farm Profits, and Rents. In *The Agrarian History of England and Wales*, vol. 4: *1500–1640*, edited by J. Thirsk, 593–695. Cambridge: Cambridge University Press.

——. 1967b. Statistical Appendix. In *The Agrarian History of England and Wales*, vol. 4: *1500–1640*, edited by J. Thirsk, 814–870. Cambridge: Cambridge University Press.

Boyer, G. K. 1986. The Old Poor Law and the Agricultural Labor Market in Southern England: An Empirical Analysis. *Journal of Economic History* 46:113–135.

Boyson, R. 1972. Industrialization and the Life of the Lancashire Factory Worker. In *The Long Debate on Poverty: Eight Essays on Industrialization and "the Condition of England,"* edited by R. M. Hartwell, 61–85. London: Institute of Economic Affairs.

Bradshaw, Y. 1985. Dependent Development in Black Africa: A Cross National Study. *American Sociological Review* 50:195–207.

Braude, B. 1979. International Competition and Domestic Cloth in the Ottoman Empire, 1500–1650: A Study in Underdevelopment. *Review* 2:437–454.

Braudel, F. 1966. *The Mediterranean and the Mediterranean World in the Age of Philip II*. Translated by S. Reynolds. 2 vols. New York: Harper and Row.

——. 1967. *Capitalism and Material Life, 1400–1800*. Translated by M. Kochan. New York: Harper and Row.

——. 1980. *On History*. Translated by S. Matthews. London: Weidenfeld and Nicolson.

Braudel, F., and E. Labrousse, eds. 1970–1980. *Histoire économique et sociale de la France*. 4 vols. Paris: Presses Universitaires de France.

Brauer, C. 1988. Lost in Transition. *Atlantic* 262:74–80.

Braun, R. 1975. Taxation, Sociopolitical Structure, and State-Building: Great Britain and Brandenburg-Prussia. In *The Formation of National States in Western Europe*, edited by C. Tilly, 243–327. Princeton, NJ: Princeton University Press.

Bray, F. 1986. *The Rice Economies: Technology and Development in Asian Societies*. Oxford: Basil Blackwell.

Brenner, Reuven. 1983. *History: The Human Gamble*. Chicago: University of Chicago Press.

Brenner, Robert. 1973. The Civil War Politics of London's Merchant Community. *Past and Present*, no. 58, 53–107.

——. 1976. Agrarian Class Structure and Economic Development in Preindustrial Europe. *Past and Present*, no. 70, 30–75.

——. 1978. The Agrarian Roots of European Capitalism. *Past and Present*, no. 97, 16–113.

Brenner, Y. S. 1961. The Inflation of Prices in Early Sixteenth Century England. *Economic History Review*, 2d ser., 14:225–239.

——. 1962. The Inflation of Prices in England, 1551–1650. *Economic History Review*, 2d ser., 15:266–284.

Brennig, J. J. 1983. Silver in Seventeenth Century Surat: Monetary Circulation and the Price Revolution in Mughal India. In *Precious Metals in the Late Medieval and Early Modern World*, edited by J. F. Richards, 477–496. Durham, NC: Carolina Academic Press.

Brewer, J., ed. 1980. *An Ungovernable People? The English and Their Law in the Seventeenth and Eighteenth Centuries.* New Brunswick, NJ: Rutgers University Press.

———. 1988. The English State and Fiscal Appropriation, 1688–1789. *Politics and Society* 16:335–386.

Bridbury, A. R. 1974. Sixteenth Century Farming. *Economic History Review*, 2d ser., 27:538–556.

Bridge, F. R., and R. Ballen. 1980. *The Great Powers and the European States System.* London: Longman.

Briggs, R. 1977. *Early Modern France, 1560–1715.* Oxford: Oxford University Press.

Brinton, C. 1965. *The Anatomy of Revolution.* Rev. ed. New York: Vintage Books.

Broad, J. 1979. Gentry Finances and the Civil War: The Case of the Buckinghamshire Verneys. *Economic History Review*, 2d ser., 32:183–200.

———. 1980. Alternate Husbandry and Permanent Pasture in the Midlands, 1650–1800. *Agricultural Review* 27:77–89.

Brook, T. 1981. The Merchant Network in Sixteenth Century China. *Journal of the Economic and Social History of the Orient* 24:165–214.

———. 1985. The Spacial Structure of Ming Local Administration. *Late Imperial China* 6:1–55.

Brooks, C. W. 1989. Interpersonal Conflict and Social Tensions: Civil Litigation in England, 1640–1830. In *The First Modern Society*, edited by A. L. Beier, D. Cannadine, and J. M. Rosenheim, 357–399. Cambridge: Cambridge University Press.

Bruhat, J. 1976. L'affirmation du monde du travail urbain. In *Histoire économique et sociale de la France*, edited by F. Braudel and E. Labrousse, 3:769–827. Paris: Presses Universitaires de France.

Bruijn, J. R., F. S. Gaashra, and I. Schöffler, eds. 1979. *Dutch-Asiatic Shipping in the 17th and 18th Centuries.* The Hague: Martinus Nijhoff.

Brustein, W. 1985. Class Conflict and Class Collaboration in Regional Rebellions, 1500–1700. *Theory and Society* 14:445–468.

———. 1986. Regional Social Orders in France and the French Revolution. *Comparative Social Research* 9:145–161.

Burke, P., and M. Kitch. 1976. Society and Social Groups in Sixteenth Century Europe. In *European History, 1500–1700.* London: Sussex Books.

Burton, M. G. 1984. Elites and Collective Protest. *Sociological Quarterly* 25:45–66.

Burton, M. G., and J. Higley. 1987a. Invitation to Elite Theory: The Basic Contentions Reconsidered. In *Power Elites and Organizations*, edited by G. W. Domhoff and T. R. Dye, 133–143. Beverly Hills, CA: Sage.

———. 1987b. Elite Settlements. *American Sociological Review* 52:295–307.

Busch, H. 1949–1955. The Tung-lin Academy and Its Political and Philosophical Significance. *Monumenta Serica* 14:1–163.

Butlin, R. A. 1979. The Enclosure of Open Fields and Extinction of Common Rights in England, circa 1600–1750. In *Change in the Countryside: Essays on Rural England, 1500–1900*, edited by H. S. A. Fox and R. A. Butlin, 65–82. London: Institute of British Geographers.

———. 1982. *The Transformation of Rural England, c. 1580–1800: A Study in Historical Geography.* Oxford: Oxford University Press.

Calhoun, C. J. 1982. *The Question of Class Struggle: Social Foundations of Popular Radicalism during the Industrial Revolution.* Chicago: University of Chicago Press.

———. 1983a. Industrialization and Social Radicalism. *Theory and Society* 12:485–504.

———. 1983b. The Radicalism of Tradition: Community Strength or Venerable Disguise and Borrowed Language? *American Journal of Sociology* 88:886–914.

———. 1989. Classical Social Theory and the French Revolution of 1848. *Sociological Theory* 7:210–225.

Cameron, I. A. 1977. The Police of Eighteenth Century France. *European Studies Review* 7:47–76.

Cameron, R., ed. 1970. *Essays in French Economic History.* Homewood, IL: Richard D. Irwin.

———. 1973. The Logistics of Economic Growth: A Note on Historical Periodization. *Journal of European Economic History* 2:145–148.

Campbell, B. M. S. 1981a. Commonfield Origins—The Regional Dimension. In *The Origins of Open Field Agriculture*, edited by T. Rowley, 112–129. London: Croom Helm.

———. 1981b. The Regional Uniqueness of English Field Systems: Some Evidence from Eastern Norfolk. *Agricultural Historical Review* 29:16–28.

———. 1983. Agricultural Progress in Medieval England: Some Evidence from Eastern Norfolk. *Economic History Review*, 2d ser., 36:26–46.

———. 1984. Inheritance and the Land Market in a Peasant Community. In *Land, Kinship, and Life-Cycle*, edited by R. M. Smith, 87–134. Cambridge: Cambridge University Press.

Campbell, M. 1942. *The English Yeoman under Elizabeth and the Early Stuarts.* New Haven: Yale University Press.

Canet, M. 1983. *Entre landes et bocage: Pleugueneuc et le pays Dolois au XVIIIème siècle.* Paris: ISI.

Cannadine, D. 1980. *Lords and Landlords: The Aristocracy and the Towns, 1774–1967.* Leicester: Leicester University Press.

Cannon, J. 1984. *Aristocratic Century: The Peerage of Eighteenth Century England.* Cambridge: Cambridge University Press.

Capp, B. S. 1972. *The Fifth Monarchy Men.* Totowa, NJ: Rowman and Littlefield.

Carlton, C. 1980. Three British Revolutions and the Personality of Kingship. In *Three British Revolutions: 1641, 1688, 1776*, edited by J. G. A. Pocock, 165–207. Princeton, NJ: Princeton University Press.

Caron, F. 1981. *Histoire économique de la France, XIXe-XXe siècles.* Paris: Armand Colin.

Carter, Jennifer. 1979. Law Courts and Constitution. In *The Restored Monarchy*, edited by J. R. Jones, 71–93. Totowa, NJ: Rowman and Littlefield.

Cartier, M. 1969. Notes sur l'histoire des prix en Chine du XIVe au XVIIe siècle. *Annales, E.S.C.* 24:876–879.

————. 1973. Nouvelles données sur la démographie chinoise a l'époque des Ming (1368–1644). *Annales, E.S.C.* 28:1341–1359.

————. 1979. La croissance démographique chinoise du XVIII siècle et l'enregistrement des Pao-Chia. *Annales de Démographie Historique*, 9–28.

————. 1981. Les importations de metaux monétaires en Chine: essai sur la conjoncture chinoise. *Annales, E.S.C.* 36:454–466.

Cavanaugh, G. J. 1974. Nobles, Privileges, and Taxes in France: A Revision Reviewed. *French Historical Studies* 8:681–692.

Chalkin, C. W., and M. A. Havinden, eds. 1974. *Rural Change and Urban Growth, 1500–1800: Essays in English Regional History in Honor of W. G. Hoskins*. London: Longman.

Challis, C. 1975. Spanish Bullion and Monetary Inflation in England in the Late Sixteenth Century. *Journal of European Economic History* 4:381–392.

————. 1978. *The Tudor Coinage*. Manchester: Manchester University Press.

Chambers, J. D. 1966. *Nottinghamshire in the Eighteenth Century: A Study of Life and Labour under the Squirearchy*. New York: Augustus M. Kelley.

————. 1967. Enclosure and Labour Supply in the Industrial Revolution. In *Agriculture and Economic Growth in England, 1650–1815*, edited by E. L. Jones, 94–127. London: Methuen.

————. 1972. *Population, Economy, and Society in Pre-industrial England*. London: Oxford University Press.

Chan, A. 1982. *The Glory and Fall of the Ming Dynasty*. Norman: Oklahoma University Press.

Chan, H. L. 1980. *Li Chih (1527–1602) in Contemporary Chinese Historiography: New Light on His Life and Works*. White Plains, NY: M. G. Sharpe.

Chan, W. T. 1967. Syntheses in Chinese Metaphysics. In *The Chinese Mind: Essentials of Chinese Philosophy and Culture*, edited by C. A. Moore, 132–147. Honolulu: East-West Center, University of Hawaii Press.

Chandaman, C. P. 1975. *The English Public Revenue, 1660–1688*. Oxford: Clarendon Press.

Chandler, T., and G. Fox. 1974. *3000 Years of Urban Growth*. New York: Academic Press.

Chang, C. L. 1962. *The Income of the Chinese Gentry*. Seattle: University of Washington Press.

Chao, K. 1977. *The Development of Cotton Textile Production in China*. Cambridge, MA: Harvard University Press.

————. 1981. New Data on Land Ownership Patterns in Ming-Ch'ing China— A Research Note. *Journal of Asian Studies* 40:719–734.

————. 1986. *Man and Land in the Chinese History: An Economic Analysis*. Stanford: Stanford University Press.

Charlesworth, A., ed. 1983. *An Atlas of Rural Protest in Britain, 1548–1900*. London: Croom Helm.

Chartier, R. 1982. Espace social et imaginaire social: les intellectuels frustrés au XVIIe siècle. *Annales, E.S.C.* 37:389–400.

Chartier, R., D. Julia, and M.-M. Compère. 1976. *L'éducation en France du XVIe au XVIIIe siècle.* Paris: Société d'Edition d'Enseignement Supérieur.

Chartres, J. A. 1977. *Internal Trade in England, 1500–1700.* London: Macmillan.

Chaudhuri, K. 1963. The East India Company and the Export of Treasure: The Early Seventeenth Century. *Economic History Review,* 2d ser., 16:23–38.

———. 1968. Treasure and Trade Balances: The East India Company's Export Trade, 1660–1720. *Economic History Review,* 2d ser., 21:480–502.

Chaunu, H., and P. Chaunu. 1953. Economie atlantique, économie-monde (1504–1650). *Cahiers d'histoire mondiale* 1:91–104.

———. 1974. The Atlantic Economy and the World Economy. In *Essays in European Economic History, 1500–1800,* edited by P. Earle, 113–126. Oxford: Clarendon Press.

Chaussinand-Nogaret, G. 1975. Aux origines de la révolution: noblesse et bourgeoisie. *Annales, E.S.C.* 30:265–278.

———. 1982. Un aspect de la pensée nobiliaire au XVIIIe siècle: <<l'antinobilism>>. *Revue D'histoire moderne et contemporaine* 29:442–452.

———. 1985. *The French Nobility in the Eighteenth Century: From Feudalism to Enlightenment.* Translated by W. Doyle. Cambridge: Cambridge University Press.

Chavarría, R. 1986. The Revolutionary Insurrection. In *Revolutions: Theoretical, Comparative, and Historical Studies,* edited by J. A. Goldstone, 152–158. San Diego: Harcourt Brace Jovanovich.

Chen, C. N. 1975. Flexible Bi-metallic Exchange Rates in China, 1650–1850. *Journal of Money, Credit, and Banking* 7:359–367.

Chesneaux, J. 1973. *Peasant Revolts in China.* Translated by C. A. Curwen. New York: Norton.

Chevalier, L. 1973. *Laboring Classes and Dangerous Classes.* Translated by F. Jellinek. Princeton, NJ: Princeton University Press.

Ch'ien, M. 1982. *Traditional Government in Imperial China: A Critical Analysis.* Translated by C. T. Hsueh and G. O. Totten. Hong Kong: Chinese University Press.

Chirot, D. 1976. *Social Change in a Peripheral Society: The Creation of a Balkan Society.* New York: Academic Press.

———. 1985. The Rise of the West. *American Sociological Review* 50:181–195.

Chorley, G. P. H. 1981. The Agricultural Revolution in Northern Europe, 1750–1880: Nitrogen, Legumes, and Crop Productivity. *Economic History Review,* 2d ser., 34:71–93.

Choucri, N. 1974. *Population Dynamics and International Violence: Propositions, Insights, and Evidence.* Lexington, MA: Lexington Books.

———, ed. 1984. *Multidisciplinary Perspectives on Population and Conflict.* Syracuse, NY: Syracuse University Press.

Choucri, N., and R. C. North. 1975. *Nations in Conflict: National Growth and International Violence.* San Francisco: W. H. Freeman.

Christiansen, P. 1976. The Causes of the English Civil War: A Reappraisal. *Journal of British Studies* 15:40–75.

———. 1978. *Reformers and Babylon: English Apocalyptic Visions from the Reformation to the Eve of the Civil War.* Toronto: University of Toronto Press.

Chuan, H. S. 1975. Tu Chien Silk Trade with Spanish America from the Late Ming to the Mid-Ch'ing Period. In *Studia Asiatica*, edited by L. G. Thompson, 99–117. San Francisco: Chinese Materials Center.

Church, C. 1977. Forgotten Revolutions. *European Studies Review* 7:95–106.

———. 1983. *Europe in 1830: Revolution and Political Change.* London: Allen and Unwin.

Cipolla, C. 1972. The So-called Price Revolution: Reflections on the Italian Situation. In *Economy and Society in Modern Europe: Essays from Annales*, edited by P. Burke, 43–46. New York: Harper and Row.

Cizakca, M. 1980. Price History and the Bursa Silk Industry: A Study of Ottoman Industrial Decline, 1550–1650. *Journal of Economic History* 40:533–550.

Clark, B. D. 1972. Iran: Changing Population Patterns. In *Populations of the Middle East and North Africa: A Geographical Approach*, edited by J. I. Clarke and W. B. Fisher, 68–96. London: University of London Press.

Clark, J. C. D. 1985. *English Society, 1688–1832: Ideology, Social Structure, and Political Practice during the Ancien Régime.* Cambridge: Cambridge University Press.

———. 1986. *Revolution and Rebellion: State and Society in England in the Seventeenth and Eighteenth Centuries.* Cambridge: Cambridge University Press.

Clark, P. 1976. Popular Protest and Disturbances in Kent, 1558–1640. *Economic History Review*, 2d ser., 29:365–382.

———. 1977. *English Provincial Society from the Reformation to the Revolution: Religion, Politics, and Society in Kent, 1500–1640.* Hassocks, Sussex: Harvester Press.

———. 1979a. Migration in England during the Late Seventeenth and Early Eighteenth Centuries. *Past and Present*, no. 83, 57–90.

———. 1979b. The "Ramoth-Gilead of the Good": Urban Change and Political Radicalism at Gloucester, 1540–1640. In *The English Commonwealth, 1547–1640: Essays in Politics and Society Presented to Joel Hurstfield*, edited by P. Clark, A. G. R. Smith, and N. Tyacke, 167–187. Leicester: Leicester University Press.

———. 1984. *Country Towns in Pre-industrial England.* New York: St. Martin's Press.

———, ed. 1985. *The European Crisis of the 1590s.* London: Allen and Unwin.

Clark, P., and P. Slack, eds. 1972. *Crisis and Order in English Towns, 1500–1700: Essays in Urban History.* London: Routledge and Kegan Paul.

———. 1976. *English Towns in Transition, 1500–1700.* London: Oxford University Press.

Clark, P., A. G. R. Smith, and N. Tyacke, eds. 1979. *The English Commonwealth, 1547–1640: Essays in Politics and Society Presented to Joel Hurstfield.* Leicester: Leicester University Press.

Clarkson, L. A. 1972. *The Pre-industrial Economy in England, 1500–1700.*
New York: Schocken Books.

Clay, C. 1981a. Property Settlements, Financial Provision for the Family, and
Sale of Land by the Greater Landowners. *Journal of British Studies* 21:18–
38.

———. 1981b. Lifeleasehold in the Western Counties of England, 1650–1750.
Agricultural History Review 29:83–96.

———. 1984. *Economic Expansion and Social Change: England, 1500–1700.*
2 vols. Cambridge: Cambridge University Press.

Cliffe, J. T. 1984. *The Puritan Gentry.* London: Routledge and Kegan Paul.

Clifton, R. 1973. Fear of Popery. In *The Origins of the English Civil War*, edited
by C. Russell, 144–167. New York: Barnes and Noble.

Clinton, R. L., ed. 1973. *Population and Politics.* Lexington, MA: D.C. Heath.

Clinton, R. L., W. S. Flash, and R. K. Godwin, eds. 1972. *Political Science in
Population Studies.* Lexington, MA: D.C. Heath.

Clout, H., ed. 1977. *Themes in the Historical Geography of France.* New York:
Academic Press.

———. 1980. *Agriculture in France on the Eve of the Railway Age.* London:
Croom Helm.

———. 1983. *The Land of France, 1815–1914.* London: Allen and Unwin.

Coale, A. J. 1956. The Effects of Changes in Mortality and Fertility on Age
Composition. *Milbank Memorial Fund Quarterly* 34:79–114.

Cobb, R. C. 1967. The Police, the Repressive Authorities, and the Beginning of
the Revolutionary Crisis in Paris. *Welsh History Review* 3:427–440.

Cobb, R., and G. Rudé. 1965. The Last Popular Movement of the Revolution
in Paris: The "Journées" of Germinal and of Prairial of Year III. In *New
Perspectives on the French Revolution*, edited by J. Kaplow, 254–276. New
York: John Wiley.

Cobban, A. 1957. *History of Modern France.* 3 vols. Baltimore, MD: Penguin.

———. 1964. *The Social Interpretation of the French Revolution.* Cambridge:
Cambridge University Press.

———. 1967. The "Middle Class" in France, 1816–1848. *French Historical
Studies* 5:41–52.

Cohen, I. B. 1984. *Revolution in Science.* Cambridge, MA: Belknap Press.

Cohen, J. S., and M. L. Weitzman. 1975. Enclosures and Depopulation: A Marx-
ian Analysis. In *European Peasants and Their Markets*, edited by W. N. Parker
and E. L. Jones, 161–178. Princeton, NJ: Princeton University Press.

Cohn, N. 1970. *The Pursuit of the Millennium: Revolutionary Millenarians and
Mystical Anarchists of the Middle Ages.* New York: Oxford University Press.

Cohn, S., and K. Markides. 1977. The Location of Ideological Socialization and
Age-based Recruitment into Revolutionary Movements. *Social Science
Quarterly* 58:462–471.

Cole, James H. 1986. *Shaoshing: Competition and Cooperation in Nineteenth
Century China.* Tucson: University of Arizona Press.

Cole, W. A. 1981. Factors in Demand, 1700–80. In *The Economic History of
Britain since 1700*, edited by R. Floud and D. McCloskey, 36–65. Cambridge: Cambridge University Press.

Coleman, D.C. 1960. *The Domestic System in Industry*. London: Routledge and Kegan Paul.

——. 1976. Labour in the English Economy of the Seventeenth Century. In *Seventeenth Century England: Society in an Age of Revolution*, edited by P. A. Seaver, 111–138. New York: New Viewpoints.

——. 1977. *The Economy of England, 1450–1750*. Oxford: Oxford University Press.

Coleman, D. C., and A. H. John, eds. 1976. *Trade, Government, and Economy in Pre-industrial England*. London: Weidenfeld and Nicolson.

Coles, P. 1968. *The Ottoman Impact on Europe*. London: Thames and Hudson.

Colley, Linda. 1982. *In Defense of Oligarchy: The Tory Party, 1714–60*. Cambridge: Cambridge University Press.

Collins, R. 1980. Weber's Last Theory of Capitalism: A Systematization. *American Sociological Review* 45:925–942.

——. 1981. *Sociology since Midcentury: Essays in Theory Cumulation*. New York: Academic Press.

——. 1986. *Weberian Sociological Theory*. Cambridge: Cambridge University Press. Collinson, Patrick. 1982. *The Religion of Protestants: The Church in English Society*. New York: Oxford University Press.

Compère, M.-M., and D. Julia. 1984. *Les collèges françaises, 16e–18e siècles*. Paris: INRP and CNRS.

Cook, M. A. 1972. *Population Pressure in Rural Anatolia, 1450–1600*. New York: Oxford University Press.

——, ed. 1976. *A History of the Ottoman Empire to 1730*. Cambridge: Cambridge University Press.

Cooper, J. P. 1967. The Social Distribution of Land and Men in England, 1436–1700. *Economic History Review*, 2d ser., 20:419–440.

——. 1978. In Search of Agrarian Capitalism. *Past and Present*, no. 80, 20–65.

Cooper, R. 1982. William Pitt, Taxation, and the Needs of War. *Journal of British Studies* 22:94–103.

Corcia, J. di. 1978. Bourg, Bourgeois, Bourgeois de Paris from the Eleventh to the Eighteenth Century. *Journal of Modern History* 50:207–233.

Corfield, P. 1982. *The Impact of English Towns, 1700–1800*. Oxford: Oxford University Press.

Cornwall, J. 1962. English Country Towns in the Fifteen-Twenties. *Economic History Review*, 2d ser., 15:54–69.

——. 1970. English Population in the Early Sixteenth Century. *Economic History Review*, 2d ser., 22:32–44.

——. 1977. *Revolt of the Peasantry, 1549*. London: Routledge and Kegan Paul.

——. 1988. *Wealth and Society in Early Sixteenth Century England*. London: Routledge and Kegan Paul.

Corrigan, P., and D. Sayer. 1985. *The Great Arch: English State Formation as Cultural Revolution*. Oxford: Basil Blackwell.

Corvisier, A. 1979. *Armies and Societies in Europe, 1494–1789*. Translated by A. Sidall. Bloomington: Indiana University Press.

Coveney, P. J., ed. 1977. *France in Crisis, 1620–1675*. Totowa, NJ: Rowman and Littlefield.

Coward, B. 1980. *The Stuart Age*. London: Longman.

———. 1986. Was There an English Revolution in the Middle of the Seventeenth Century? In *Politics and People in Revolutionary England*, edited by C. Jones, M. Newitt, and S. Roberts, 9–39. Oxford: Basil Blackwell.

Cowie, L. 1977. *Sixteenth Century Europe*. Edinburgh: Oliver and Boyd.

Crafts, N. F. R. 1977. Determinants of the Rate of Parliamentary Enclosure. *Explorations in Economic History* 14:227–249.

———. 1978. Enclosure and Labor Supply Revisited. *Explorations in Economic History* 15:172–183.

———. 1980. Income Elasticities of Demand and the Release of Labour by Agriculture during the British Industrial Revolution. *Journal of European Economic History* 9:153–168.

———. 1983. British Economic Growth, 1700–1831: A Review of the Evidence. *Economic History Review*, 2d ser., 36:177–199.

———. 1984. Economic Growth in France and Britain, 1830–1910: A Review of the Evidence. *Journal of Economic History* 44:49–67.

———. 1985. English Workers' Real Wages during the Industrial Revolution: Some Remaining Problems. *Journal of Economic History* 45:139–144.

Crafts, N. F. R., and N. J. Ireland. 1976. A Simulation of the Impact of Changes in Age at Marriage before and during the Advent of Industrialization in England. *Population Studies* 30:495–510.

Craig, A. M. 1961. *Choshu in the Meiji Restoration*. Cambridge, MA: Harvard University Press.

———. 1986. The Central Government. In *Japan in Transition: From Tokugawa to Meiji*, edited by M. B. Jansen and G. Rozman, 36–37. Princeton, NJ: Princeton University Press.

Craig, G. A. 1966. *Europe since 1815*. New York: Holt, Rinehart and Winston.

Crawcour, E. S. 1988. Economic Change in Nineteenth Century Japan. In *The Cambridge History of Japan*, vol. 5: *The Nineteenth Century*, edited by M. B. Jansen, 569–617. Cambridge: Cambridge University Press.

Crawford, R. B. 1961–1962. Eunuch Power in the Ming Dynasty. *T'oung Pao* 49:115–148.

Croot, P., and D. Parker. 1978. Agrarian Class Structure and Economic Development. *Past and Present*, no. 78, 37–47.

Cross, H. E. 1983. South American Bullion Production and Export, 1550–1750. In *Precious Metals in the Later Medieval and Early Modern World*, edited by J. F. Richards, 397–423. Durham, NC: Carolina Academic Press.

Crouzet, F. 1970. An Annual Index of French Industrial Production in the Nineteenth Century. In *Essays in French Economic History*, edited by R. Cameron, 245–278. Homewood, IL: Richard D. Irwin.

———. 1980. Economic Growth in Britain and France. In *Britain and France: Ten Centuries*, edited by D. Johnson, F. Crouzet, and F. Bedarida, 187–195. Folkestone, Kent: William Dawson.

Cubells, M. 1982. La politique d'anoblissement de la monarchie en Provence de 1715 à 1789. *Annales du Midi* 94:173–196.

Curtis, M. 1959. *Oxford and Cambridge in Transition, 1558–1642.* Oxford: Oxford University Press.

————. 1962. The Alienated Intellectuals of Early Stuart England. *Past and Present,* no. 23, 25–43.

Cvetkova, B. 1977. Problems of the Ottoman Empire in the Balkans from the Sixteenth to the Eighteenth Century. In *Studies in Eighteenth Century Islamic History,* edited by T. Naff and R. Owen, 165–169. Carbondale: Southern Illinois University Press.

————. 1983a. Early Ottoman *Tahrir Defters* as a Source for Studies on the History of Bulgaria and the Balkans. *Ottoman Archivum* 8:133–213.

————. 1983b. Le crédjt dans les Balkans, XVIe–XVIIe siècles. In *Contributions à l'histoire économique et sociale de l'empire Ottoman,* edited by Ö. L. Barkan, 299–308. Louvain: Editions Peeters.

Dallas, G. 1982. *The Imperfect Peasant Economy: The Loire Country, 1800–1914.* Cambridge: Cambridge University Press.

Daly, J. 1984. The Implications of Royalist Politics, 1642–46. *Historical Journal* 27:745–755.

Darby, H. C., ed. 1973a. *A New Historical Geography of England.* Cambridge: Cambridge University Press.

————. 1973b. Age of the Improver, 1600–1800. In *A New Historical Geography of England,* edited by H. C. Darby, 302–388. Cambridge: Cambridge University Press.

Dardess, J. W. 1972. The Late Ming Rebellions: Peasants and Problems of Interpretation. *Journal of Interdisciplinary History* 3:103–117.

Darnton, R. 1970. The High Enlightenment and the Low Life of Literature in Pre-revolutionary France. *Past and Present,* no. 51, 81–115.

————. 1984. *The Great Cat Massacre and Other Episodes in French Cultural History.* New York: Basic Books.

Daumard, A. 1963. *La bourgeoisie parisienne de 1815 à 1848.* Paris: SEVPEN.

Daumard, A., F. Locaccioni, G. Dupeaux, J. Herpin, J. Godechot, and J. Sentou. 1973. *Les fortunes françaises au XIXe siècle.* Paris: Mouton.

David, P. 1975. *Technical Choice, Innovation, and Economic Growth.* Cambridge: Cambridge University Press.

Davies, A. 1964. The Origins of the French Peasant Revolution of 1789. *History* 49:24–41.

Davies, C. S. L. 1964. Provisions for Armies, 1509–1550: A Study in the Effectiveness of Early Tudor Government. *Economic History Review,* 2d ser., 17:234–248.

————. 1969. Révoltes populaires en Angleterre (1500–1700). *Annales, E.S.C.* 24:24–60.

————. 1973. Peasant Revolt in France and England: A Comparison. *Agricultural History Review* 21:122–134.

Davies, J. C. 1962. Toward a Theory of Revolution. *American Sociological Review* 27:5–19.

Davies, M. G. 1977. Country Gentry and Falling Rents in the 1660s and 1670s. *Midland History* 4:86–96.

Davis, K. 1971. The World's Population Crisis. In *Contemporary Social Prob-*

lems, edited by R. K. Merton and R. Nisbet, 363–406. New York: Harcourt Brace Jovanovich.

Davis, N. Z. 1975. *Society and Culture in Early Modern France*. Stanford: Stanford University Press.

Davis, R. 1966. The Rise of Protection in England, 1689–1786. *Economic History Review*, 2d ser., 19:306–317.

————. 1967. *A Commercial Revolution: English Overseas Trade in the Seventeenth and Eighteenth Centuries*. London: The Historical Association.

————. 1970. English Imports from the Middle East. In *Studies in the Economic History of the Middle East*, edited by M. A. Cook, 193–206. London: Oxford University Press.

————. 1973. *English Overseas Trade, 1500–1700*. London: Macmillan.

————. 1979. *The Industrial Revolution and Britain's Overseas Trade*. Leicester: University of Leicester Press.

Deane, P., and W. A. Cole. 1969. *British Economic Growth, 1688–1959*. 2d ed. Cambridge: Cambridge University Press.

deBary, W. T. 1957. Chinese Despotism and the Confucian Ideal: A Seventeenth Century View. In *Chinese Thought and Institutions*, edited by J. K. Fairbank, 163–203. Chicago: University of Chicago Press.

————. 1970. Individualism and Humanitarianism in Late Ming Thought. In *Self and Society in Ming Thought*, edited by W. T. deBary, 145–247. New York: Columbia University Press.

deBary, W. T. et al. 1975. *The Unfolding of Neo-Confucianism*. New York: Columbia University Press.

Defourneaux, M. 1970. *Daily Life in Spain in the Golden Age*. Translated by N. Branch. Stanford: Stanford University Press.

DeGroot, A. H. 1978. *The Ottoman Empire and the Dutch Republic*. Leiden: Nederlands Historisch-Archeologisch Instituut.

Dennerline, J. 1981. *The Chia-ting Loyalists: Confucian Leadership and Social Change in Seventeenth Century China*. New Haven: Yale University Press.

Derouet, B. 1980. Une démographie differentielle: clés pour un système autorégulateur des populations rurales d'ancien régime. *Annales, E.S.C.* 35:3–41.

Desan, S. 1988. Redefining Revolutionary Liberty: The Rhetoric of Religious Revival during the French Revolution. *Journal of Modern History* 60:1–27.

de Vries, J. 1976. *Europe in an Age of Crisis, 1650–1750*. Cambridge: Cambridge University Press.

————. 1984. *European Urbanization, 1500–1800*. Cambridge, MA: Harvard University Press.

Dewald, J. 1987. *Pont-St-Pierre, 1398–1789: Lordship, Community, and Capitalism in Early Modern France*. Berkeley and Los Angeles: University of California Press.

Deyon, P. 1975. Relations between the French Nobility and the Absolute Monarchy during the First Half of the Seventeenth Century. In *State and Society in Seventeenth Century France*, edited by R. F. Kierstead, 25–43. New York: New Viewpoints.

————. 1976. Manufacturing Industries in Seventeenth Century France. In

Louis XIV and Absolutism, edited by R. Hatton, 226–242. London: Macmillan.

Diamond, L., J. J. Linz, and S. M. Lipset. 1988. Democracy in Developing Countries: Facilitating and Obstructing Factors. In *Freedom in the World: Political Rights and Civil Liberties, 1987–88*, edited by R. D. Gastil, 229–258. New York: Freedom House.

Dickson, P. G. M. 1967. *The Financial Revolution in England: A Study in the Development of Public Credit, 1688–1756*. New York: St. Martin's Press.

Dietrich, C. 1972. Cotton Culture and Manufacture in Early Ch'ing China. In *Economic Organization in Chinese Society*, edited by W. E. Willmott, 105–136. Stanford: Stanford University Press.

Dietz, B. 1986. Overseas Trade and Metropolitan Growth. In *London, 1500–1700: The Making of the Metropolis*, edited by A. L. Beier and R. A. Finlay, 115–140. London: Longman.

Dietz, F. 1964. *English Public Finance, 1485–1641*. 2d ed. 2 vols. New York: Barnes and Noble.

Dillon, M. 1978. Jingdezhen as a Ming Industrial Center. *Ming Studies* 6:37–44.

Dimberg, R. 1974. *The Sage and Society: The Life and Thought of Ho Hsin-Yin*. Honolulu: University of Hawaii Press.

Dix, R. 1983. The Varieties of Revolution. *Comparative Politics* 15:281–293.

Dobb, M. 1946. *Studies in the Development of Capitalism*. London: Routledge and Kegan Paul.

Dobson, R. B. 1977. Population Decline in Late Medieval England. *Transactions of the Royal Historical Society*, 5th ser., 27:1–22.

Dodgshon, R. A., and R. A. Butlin, eds. 1978. *An Historical Geography of England and Wales*. New York: Academic Press.

Dols, M. W. 1977. *The Black Death in the Middle East*. Princeton, NJ: Princeton University Press.

———. 1979. The Second Plague Pandemic and Its Recurrences in the Middle East, 1347–1894. *Journal of the Economic and Social History of the Orient* 22:162–189.

Dominguez Ortiz, A. 1971. *The Golden Age of Spain, 1516–1659*. New York: Basic Books.

Dovring, F. 1965. The Transformation of European Agriculture. In *The Cambridge Economic History of Europe*, edited by H. J. Habakkuk and M. Postan, 6:604–672. Cambridge: Cambridge University Press.

Dow, F. D. 1985. *Radicalism in the English Revolution, 1640–1660*. Oxford: Basil Blackwell.

Dowell, S. 1884. *A History of Taxation and Taxes in England from the Earliest Times to the Present Day*. 2 vols. London: Longman, Green.

Downey, G. 1969. *The Late Roman Empire*. New York: Holt, Rinehart and Winston.

Doyle, W. 1970. The Parlements of France and the Breakdown of the Old Regime, 1771–1788. *French Historical Studies* 6:415–458.

———. 1972. Was There an Aristocratic Reaction in Pre-revolutionary France? *Past and Present*, no. 57, 97–122.

———. 1974. *The Parlement of Bordeaux and the End of the Old Regime, 1771–1790.* London: Ernest Benn.

———. 1978. *The Old European Order, 1660–1800.* Oxford: Oxford University Press.

———. 1980. *Origins of the French Revolution.* Oxford: Oxford University Press.

———. 1984. The Price of Offices in Pre-revolutionary France. *Historical Journal* 27:831–860.

———. 1986. *The Ancien Régime.* Atlantic Highlands, NJ: Humanities Press.

———. 1989. *The Oxford History of the French Revolution.* Oxford: Clarendon Press.

Dray, W. H. 1964. *Philosophy of History.* Englewood Cliffs, NJ: Prentice-Hall.

Droz, J. 1967. *Europe between Revolutions, 1815–1848.* Translated by R. Baldick. New York: Harper and Row.

Duby, G., and A. Wallon, eds. 1975–1976. *Histoire de la France rurale.* 4 vols. Paris: Editions du Seuil.

DuFraisse, R. 1982. Elites anciennes et élites nouvelles dans les pays de la rive gauche du Rhin à l'époque napoléonienne. *Annales Historique de la Révolution Française* 248:244–283.

Dunstan, H. 1975. The Late Ming Epidemics: A Preliminary Survey. *Ch'ing shih wen-t'i* 3(3):1–59.

Dupâquier, J. 1970. French Population in the 17th and 18th Centuries. In *Essays in French Economic History*, edited by R. Cameron, 150–169. Homewood, IL: Richard D. Irwin.

———. 1978. Révolution française et révolution demographique. In *Vom Ancien Régime zur Französischen Revolution*, edited by E. Hinrichs, E. Schmitt, and R. Vierhaus, 233–260. Göttingen: Vandenhoeck and Rupert.

———. 1979. *La population française aux XVIIe et XVIIIe siècles.* Paris: Presses Universitaires de France.

———. 1989. Demographic Crises and Subsistence Crises in France, 1650–1725. In *Famine, Disease and the Social Order in Early Modern Society*, edited by J. Walter and R. Schofield, 189–199. Cambridge: Cambridge University Press.

Dupâquier, J., et al. 1988. *Histoire de la population française.* 4 vols. Paris: Presses universitaires de France.

Dupeaux, G. 1976. *French Society, 1789–1970.* London: Methuen.

Durand, Y. 1966. Recherches sur les salaires des maçons à Paris au XVIIIe siècle. *Revue d'Histoire Economique et Sociale* 44:468–480.

Dyer, A. D. 1973. *The City of Worcester in the Sixteenth Century.* Leicester: Leicester University Press.

———. 1979. Growth and Decay in English Towns, 1500–1700. *Urban History Yearbook*, 60–72.

———. 1981. Seasonality of Baptisms: An Urban Approach. *Local Population Studies*, no. 27, 26–34.

Dyer, C. 1982. Deserted Medieval Villages in the West Midlands. *Economic History Review*, 2d ser., 35:19–34.

Earle, P., ed. 1974. *Essays in European Economic History, 1500–1800.* Oxford: Clarendon Press.

Easterlin, R. 1980. *Birth and Fortune*. Chicago: University of Chicago Press.

Eberhard, W. 1962. *Social Mobility in Traditional China*. Leiden: E. J. Brill.

Ebrey, P. 1983. Types of Lineage in Ch'ing China: A Re-Examination of the Chang Lineage of T'ung-ch'eng. *Ch'ing shih wen-t'i* 4(9):1–20.

Echeverria, D. 1972. The Pre-revolutionary Influence of Rousseau's *Contrat Social*. *Journal of the History of Ideas* 33:543–560.

———. 1985. *The Maupeou Revolution*. Baton Rouge: Louisiana State University Press.

Eckstein, S. 1982. The Impact of Revolution on Social Welfare in Latin America. *Theory and Society* 11:43–94.

Edeen, A. 1986. The Soviet Civil Service: Its Composition and Its Status. In *Revolutions: Theoretical, Comparative, and Historical Studies*, edited by J. A. Goldstone, 238–247. San Diego: Harcourt Brace Jovanovich.

Edmonds, B. 1983. Federalism and Urban Revolt in France in 1793. *Journal of Modern History* 55:22–53.

Egret, J. 1965a. The Origins of the Revolution in Brittany (1788–1789). In *New Perspectives on the French Revolution*, edited by J. Kaplow, 136–152. New York: John Wiley.

———. 1965b. The Pre-Revolution in Provence. In *New Perspectives on the French Revolution*, edited by J. Kaplow, 153–169. New York: John Wiley.

———. 1968. Was the Aristocratic Revolt Aristocratic? In *The French Revolution: Conflicting Interpretations*, edited by F. A. Kafker and J. M. Laux, 37–49. New York: Random House.

———. 1977. *The French Pre-Revolution, 1787–88*. Translated by W. D. Camp. Chicago: University of Chicago Press.

Eisenstadt, S. N. 1963. *The Political Systems of Empires*. London: Macmillan.

———. 1978. *Revolutions and the Transformation of Societies: A Comparative Study of Civilizations*. New York: Free Press.

———. 1980a. *This Worldly Transcendentalism and the Structuring of the World: Weber's "Religion of China" and the Format of Chinese History and Civilization*. Jerusalem: Eliezer Kaplan School of Economics and Social Sciences of the Hebrew University.

———. 1980b. Comparative Analysis of State Formation in Historical Contexts. *International Social Science Journal* 32:624–654.

———. Forthcoming. Patterns of Conflict and Conflict Resolution in Japan: Some Comparative Indications. In *Japanese Models of Conflict Resolution*, edited by S. N. Eisenstadt and E. Ben Ari. London: Routledge and Kegan Paul.

Eisenstein, E. 1968. Was the Bourgeois Revolt Bourgeois? in *The French Revolution: Conflicting Interpretations*, edited by F. A. Kafker and J. M. Laux, 50–69. New York: Random House.

Eisner, R. 1986. *How Real is the Federal Deficit?* New York: Free Press.

Eliade, M. 1959. *Cosmos and History: The Myth of the Eternal Return*. New York: Harper and Brothers.

Elliott, J. H. 1963a. *Imperial Spain, 1469–1716*. New York: New American Library.

———. 1963b. *The Revolt of the Catalans*. Cambridge: Cambridge University Press.

————. 1970. Revolts in the Spanish Monarchy. In *Preconditions of Revolution in Early Modern Europe*, edited by R. Forster and J. P. Greene, 109–130. Baltimore, MD: Johns Hopkins University Press.

————. 1977. Self-Perception and Decline in Early Seventeenth Century Spain. *Past and Present*, no. 74, 48–61.

————. 1984. *Richelieu and Olivares*. Cambridge: Cambridge University Press.

Ellis, G. 1978. The Marxist Interpretation of the French Revolution. *English Historical Review* 93:353–376.

Ellis, J. 1974. *Armies in Revolution*. New York: Oxford.

Elman, B. A. 1984. *From Philosophy to Philology: Intellectual and Social Aspects of Change in Late Imperial China*. Cambridge, MA: Council on East Asian Studies.

Elster, J. 1983. *Explaining Technical Change: A Case Study in the Philosophy of Science*. Cambridge: Cambridge University Press.

Elton, G. R. 1974a. *England under the Tudors*. London: Methuen.

————. 1974b. *Studies in Tudor and Stuart Politics and Government: Papers and Reviews, 1946–1972*. 2 vols. Cambridge: Cambridge University Press.

————. 1977. *Reform and Reformation: England, 1509–1558*. Cambridge, MA: Harvard University Press.

Elvin, M. 1972. The High-Level Equilibrium Trap: The Causes of the Decline of Invention in the Traditional Chinese Textile Industries. In *Economic Organization in Chinese Society*, edited by W. E. Willmott, 137–172. Stanford: Stanford University Press.

————. 1973. *The Pattern of the Chinese Past*. Stanford: Stanford University Press.

————. 1977. Marketing Towns and Waterways: The County of Shanghai from 1480 to 1910. In *The City in Late Imperial China*, edited by G. W. Skinner, 441–473. Stanford: Stanford University Press.

————. 1984. Why China Failed to Create an Endogenous Industrial Capitalism: A Critique of Max Weber's Explanation. *Theory and Society* 13:379–391.

————. 1988. China as a Counterfactual. In *Europe and the Rise of Capitalism* edited by J. Baechler, J. Hall, and M. Mann, 101–112. Oxford: Basil Blackwell.

Emery, F. V. 1973. England circa 1600. In *A New Historical Geography of England*, edited by H. C. Darby, 248–301. Cambridge: Cambridge University Press.

Engrand, C. 1982. Paupérisme et condition ouvrière dans la seconde moitié du XVIIIe siècle: l'exemple amienois. *Revue d'histoire moderne et contemporaine* 29:376–410.

Entenmann, R. E. 1982. Migration and Settlement in Sichuan, 1644–1796. Ph.D. diss., Harvard University.

Epstein, J., and D. Thompson, eds. 1982. *The Chartist Experience: Studies in Working Class Radicalism and Culture, 1830–1860*. London: Macmillan.

Erder, L. 1975. The Measurement of Preindustrial Population Changes: The Ottoman Empire from the 15th to the 17th Century. *Middle Eastern Studies* 11:284–301.

Erder, L., and S. Faroqhi. 1979. Population Rise and Fall in Anatolia, 1550–1620. *Middle Eastern Studies* 15:322–345.

———. 1980. The Development of the Anatolian Urban Network during the Sixteenth Century. *Journal of the Economic and Social History of the Orient* 23:265–303.

Esler, A. 1972. Youth in Revolt: The French Generation of 1830. In *Modern European Social History*, edited by R. J. Bezucha. Lexington, MA: D.C. Heath.

Evans, E. 1983. *The Forging of the Modern State: Early Industrial Britain, 1783–1870.* London: Longman.

Evans, J. T. 1979. *Seventeenth Century Norwich: Politics, Religion, and Government, 1620–1690.* Oxford: Clarendon Press.

Everitt, A. 1967a. The Marketing of Agricultural Produce. In *The Agrarian History of England and Wales*, vol. 4: *1500–1640*, edited by J. Thirsk, 466–592. Cambridge: Cambridge University Press.

———. 1967b. Farm Laborers. In *The Agrarian History of England and Wales*, vol. 4: *1500–1640*, edited by J. Thirsk, 396–465. Cambridge: Cambridge University Press.

———. 1968. The County Community. In *The English Revolution, 1600–1660*, edited by E. W. Ives, 48–63. New York: Harper and Row.

———. 1969. *Change in the Provinces: The Seventeenth Century.* Leicester: Leicester University Press.

———. 1973. The Local Community and the Great Rebellion. In *The Historical Association Book of the Stuarts*, edited by K. H. D. Haley, 74–101. New York: St. Martin's Press.

Faber, J. A., H. K. Roessingh, B. H. Slicher van Bath, A. N. van de Woude, and R. J. van Xanten. 1965. Economic Developments and Population Changes in the Netherlands up to 1800. In *Third International Conference of Economic History*, edited by D. E. C. Eversley, 67–78. Paris: Mouton.

Fairbank, J. K., E. O. Reischauer, and A. M. Craig. 1965. *A History of East Asia Civilization.* 2 vols. Boston: Houghton Mifflin.

Fairchilds, C. 1976. *Poverty and Charity in Aix-en-Provence, 1640–1789.* Baltimore, MD: Johns Hopkins University Press.

Farmer, E. L. 1990. Social Regulations of the First Ming Emperor: Orthodoxy as a Function of Authority. In *Orthodoxy in Late Imperial China*, edited by K. C. Liu, 103–125. Berkeley and Los Angeles: University of California Press.

Farnell, J. E. 1977. The Social and Intellectual Basis of London's Role in the English Civil Wars. *Journal of Modern History* 49:641–660.

Faroqhi, S. 1973. Social Mobility and the Ottoman 'Ulema in the Late Sixteenth Century. *International Journal of Middle East Studies* 4(2):204–218.

———. 1977. Rural Society in Anatolia and the Balkans during the Sixteenth Century, parts 1 and 2. *Turcica* 9:161–196, 11:103–153.

———. 1979a. Notes on the Introduction of Cotton and Cotton Cloth in Sixteenth and Seventeenth Century Anatolia. *Journal European Economic History* 8:405–417.

———. 1979b. Sixteenth Century Periodic Markets in Various Anatolian Sancaks. *Journal of the Economic and Social History of the Orient* 22:32–80.

———. 1979–1980. Taxation and Urban Activities in Sixteenth Century Anatolia. *International Journal of Turkish Studies* 1:19–53.

———. 1980. Land Transfer, Land Dispute, and Askeri Holdings in Ankara (1592–1600). In *Memorial Ömer Lüfti Barkan*, edited by H. Inalcik, 87–99. Paris: Librarie d'Amérique et d'Orient Adrien Maisonneuve.

———. 1984. *Towns and Townsmen in Ottoman Anatolia*. New York: Cambridge University Press.

———. 1986a. *Peasants, Dervishes, and Traders in the Ottoman Empire*. London: Variorum.

———. 1986b. The Venetian Presence in the Ottoman Empire (1600–1630). *Journal of European Economic History* 15:345–384.

Farris, N.M. 1987. Remembering the Future, Anticipating the Past: History, Time, and Cosmology among the Maya of Yucatan. *Comparative Studies in Society and History* 29:566–593.

Fay, C. R. 1932. *The Corn Laws and Social England*. Cambridge: Cambridge University Press.

Feher, F. 1985. The French Revolution: Between Class Identity and Universalist Illusions. *Review* 8:335–351.

Fei, H. T. 1946. Peasantry and Gentry: An Interpretation of Chinese Social Structure and Its Changes. *American Journal of Sociology* 52:1–17.

Felloni, G. 1977. Italy. In *An Introduction to the Sources of European Economic History, 1500–1800*, edited by C. Wilson and G. Parker, 1–36. Ithaca, NY: Cornell University Press.

Feuerwerker, A. 1975. *Rebellion in Nineteenth Century China*. Ann Arbor: Center for Chinese Studies, University of Michigan.

———. 1976. *State and Society in Eighteenth Century China: The Ch'ing Empire in Its Glory*. Ann Arbor: Center for Chinese Studies, University of Michigan.

———, ed. 1982. *Chinese Social and Economic History from the Song to 1900*. Ann Arbor: Center for Chinese Studies, University of Michigan.

———. 1984. State and Economy in Late Imperial China. *Theory and Society* 13:297–326.

Fiette, S. 1982. Propriétaire et exploitants dans un grand domaine du Lauragais à la fin de l'ancien régime et au dèbut de la révolution. *Revue d'histoire moderne et contemporaine* 29:177–213.

Fincham, K. 1984. The Judge's Decision on Ship Money in February 1637: The Reaction of Kent. *Historical Journal* 57:230–236.

Fincham, K., and P. Lake. 1985. The Ecclesiastical Policy of King James I. *Journal of British Studies* 24:169–207.

Finlay, R. 1981a. *Population and Metropolis: The Demography of London, 1580–1650*. Cambridge: Cambridge University Press.

———. 1981b. Differential Child Mortality in Pre-industrial England: The Example of Cartmel, Cumbria, 1600–1750. *Annales de Démographie Historique*, 67–79.

Finlay, R., and B. Shearer. 1986. Population Growth and Suburban Expansion. In *London, 1500–1700: The Making of the Metropolis*, edited by A. L. Beier and R. A. Finlay, 37–59. London: Longman.

Finlayson, M. G. 1983. *Historians, Puritanism, and the English Revolution.* Toronto: University of Toronto Press.

Fisher, F. J. 1935. The Development of the London Food Market, 1540–1640. *Economic History Review,* 2d ser., 5:46–64.

———, ed. 1961. *Essays in the Economic and Social History of Tudor and Stuart England.* Cambridge: Cambridge University Press.

———. 1965. Influenza and Inflation in Tudor England. *Economic History Review,* 2d ser., 18:120–129.

———. 1968. The Growth of London. In *The English Revolution, 1600–1660,* edited by E. W. Ives, 76–86. New York: Harper and Row.

———. 1971. London as an Engine of Economic Growth. In *Britain and the Netherlands,* vol. 4: *Metropolis, Dominion and Province,* edited by J. S. Bromley and E. H. Kossman, 3–16. The Hague: Martinus Nijhoff.

Fisher, I. 1911. *The Purchasing Power of Money.* London: Macmillan.

Fletcher, A. 1973. *Tudor Rebellions.* Harlow, Essex: Longman.

———. 1975. *A County Community in Peace and War: Sussex, 1600–1660.* London: Longman.

———. 1981. *The Outbreak of the English Civil War.* London: Edward Arnold.

———. 1983. Parliament and People in Seventeenth Century England. *Past and Present,* no. 98, 151–155.

———. 1986. *Reform in the Provinces: The Government of Stuart England.* New Haven: Yale University Press.

Fletcher, A., and J. Stevenson, eds. 1985. *Order and Disorder in Early Modern England.* Cambridge: Cambridge University Press.

Fletcher, J. F., Jr. 1985. Integrative History: Parallels and Interconnections in the Early Modern Period, 1500–1800. *Journal of Turkish Studies* 9:37–58.

Flinn, M. 1981. *The European Demographic System, 1500–1820.* Baltimore, MD: Johns Hopkins University Press.

Floud, R., and D. McCloskey, eds. 1981. *The Economic History of Britain since 1700.* 2 vols. Cambridge: Cambridge University Press.

Flynn, D. 1978. A New Perspective on the Spanish Price Revolution: The Monetary Approach to the Balance of Payments. *Explorations in Economic History* 15:388–406.

Fogel, R. W., and G. R. Elton. 1983. *Which Road to the Past: Two Views of History.* New Haven: Yale University Press.

Forbonnais, F. V. D. de. 1758. *Recherches et considérations sur les finances de France depuis 1596 jusqu'en 1721.* 4 vols. Liège.

Forrest, A. 1981. *The French Revolution and the Poor.* Oxford: Basil Blackwell.

Forstenzer, T. R. 1981. *French Provincial Police and the Fall of the Second Republic.* Princeton, NJ: Princeton University Press.

Forster, R. 1963. The Provincial Noble: A Reappraisal. *American Historical Review* 68:681–691.

———. 1970. Obstacles to Agricultural Growth in Eighteenth Century France. *American Historical Review* 75:1600–1615.

———. 1971. *The Nobility of Toulouse in the Eighteenth Century.* New York: Octagon Books.

———. 1976. The Survival of the Nobility during the French Revolution. In

French Society and the Revolution, edited by D. Johnson, 132–147. New York: Cambridge University Press.

———. 1980. The French Revolution and the New Elite, 1800–1850. In *The American and European Revolutions, 1776–1848*, edited by J. Pelenski, 182–207. Iowa City: University of Iowa Press.

———. 1981. *Merchants, Landlords, Magistrates: The Depont Family in Eighteenth Century France*. Baltimore, MD: Johns Hopkins University Press.

Forster, R., and J. Greene, eds. 1970. *Preconditions of Revolution in Early Modern Europe*. Baltimore, MD: Johns Hopkins University Press.

Forster, R., and O. Ranum, eds. 1977. *Rural Society in France: Selections from the Annales*. Translated by E. Forster and P. M. Ranum. Baltimore, MD: Johns Hopkins University Press.

Foster, J. 1974. *Class Struggle and the Industrial Revolution*. London: Weidenfeld and Nicolson.

Fox, E. 1971. *History in Geographic Perspective: The Other France*. New York: Norton.

Fox, H. S. A. 1981. Approaches to the Adoption of the Midland System. In *The Origins of Open Field Agriculture*, edited by T. Rowley, 64–111. London: Croom Helm.

———. 1975. The Chronology of Enclosure and Economic Development in Medieval Devon. *Economic History Review*, 2d ser., 28:181–202.

Fox, H. S. A., and R. A. Butlin, eds. 1979. *Change in the Countryside: Essays on Rural England, 1500–1900*. London: Institute of British Geographers.

Fox-Genovese, E. 1976. *The Origins of Physiocracy: Economic Revolution and Social Order in Eighteenth Century France*. Ithaca, NY: Cornell University Press.

Franz, G. 1976. Landwirtschaft, 1800–1850. In *Handbuch der deutschen Wirtschafts- und Sozialgeschichte*, edited by H. Aubin and W. Zorn, 1:276–320. Stuttgart: Klett-Cotta.

Frêche, G. 1973. La population de la région Toulousaire sous l'ancien régime. In *Sur la population française au XVIIIe et au XIXe siècles*, 251–269. Paris: Société de Démographie Historique.

———. 1974. *Toulouse et la région Midi-Pyrénées au siècle de Lumières (vers 1670–1789)*. Paris: Cujas.

Fridlizius, G. 1979. Population, Enclosure, and Property Rights. *Economy and History* 22:3–37.

Friedman, B. M. 1988. *Day of Reckoning: The Consequences of American Economic Policy under Reagan and After*. New York: Random House.

Frost, P. 1981. Yeomen and Metalsmiths: Livestock in the Dual Economy in South Staffordshire, 1560–1720. *Agricultural History Review* 29:29–41.

Fu I. L. 1981–1982. A New Assessment of the Rural Social Relationship in Late Ming and Early Ch'ing China. *Chinese Studies in History* 15:62–92.

Fulbrook, M. 1982. The English Revolution and the Revisionist Revolt. *Social History* 7:249–264.

———. 1983. *Piety and Politics*. Cambridge: Cambridge University Press.

———. 1984. Legitimation Crisis and the Early Modern State: The Politics of Religious Toleration. In *Religion and Society in Early Modern Europe, 1500-1800*, edited by K. von Greyerz, 146–156. Boston: Allen and Unwin.

Furet, F. 1971. Le catéchisme révolutionnaire. *Annales, E.S.C.* 26:255–189.

———. 1978. Les élections de 1789 à Paris: le tiers état et la naissance d'une classe dirigeante. In *Vom Ancien Régime zur Französischen Revolution*, edited by E. Hinrichs, E. Schmitt, and R. Vierhaus, 188–206. Göttingen: Vandenhoeck and Rupert.

———. 1981. *Interpreting the French Revolution*. Translated by E. Forster. Cambridge: Cambridge University Press.

Furet, F., and D. Richet. 1970. *The French Revolution*. Translated by S. Hardman. New York: Macmillan.

Gagnol, P. 1974 [1911]. *Ladîme ecclesiastique en France au XVIIIe siècle*. Geneva: Slatkine-Megariotis Reprints.

Galassi, F. L. 1986. Reassessing Mediterranean Agriculture: Retardation and Growth in Tuscany, 1870–1914. *Rivista de Storia Economica*, 2d ser., 3:90–121.

Galloway, P. 1986. Long Term Fluctuations in Climate and Population. *Population and Development Review* 12:1–24.

Gardiner, P., ed. 1974. *The Philosophy of History*. Oxford: Oxford University Press.

Gardiner, S. R. 1970. *The First Two Stuarts and the Puritan Revolution*. New York: Thomas Y. Cromwell, Apollo Editions.

Garnot, B. 1983. *Vivre et mourir dans une ville d'Eure-et-Loir au XVIIIème siècle: l'exemple de Chartres*. Chartres: Centre National de Documentation Pédagogique.

Garrier, G. 1973. *Paysans du Beaujolais et du Lyonnais, 1800–1970*. Grenoble: Presses Universitaires de Grenoble.

Gash, N. 1979. *Aristocracy and People: Britain, 1815–1865*. London: Edward Arnold.

Gates, J. M. 1986. Toward a History of Revolution. *Comparative Studies in Society and History* 28:535–544.

Gath, D. J., and J. W. McKenna, eds. 1977. *Tudor Rule and Revolution: Essays for G. R. Elton from His American Friends*. Cambridge: Cambridge University Press.

Gauthier, F. 1977. *La voie paysanne dans la révolution française*. Paris: F. Maspero.

Geertz, C. 1973. *The Interpretation of Culture*. New York: Basic Books.

Geiss, J. P. 1979. Peking under the Ming, 1368–1644. Ph.D. diss., Princeton University.

———. 1988. The T'ai-ch'ang, T'ien-ch'i, and Ch'ung-chen Reigns, 1620–1644. In *The Cambridge History of China*, edited by F. W. Mote and D. Twitchett, 4:586–640. Cambridge: Cambridge University Press.

Gellner, E. 1983. *Nations and Nationalism*. Oxford: Basil Blackwell.

George, A. L. 1979. The Causal Nexus between Cognitive Beliefs and Decision-making Behavior: The Operational Code Belief System. In *Psychological*

Models in International Politics, edited by L. S. Flakowski, 95–124. Boulder, CO: Westview Press.

Gernet, J. 1982. *A History of Chinese Civilization*. Cambridge: Cambridge University Press.

Gibb, H., and H. Bowen. 1950. *Islamic Society and the West*. 2 vols. London: Oxford University Press.

Giddens, A. 1976. *New Rules of Sociological Method*. London: Hutchinson.

———. 1979. *Central Problems in Social Theory*. London: Macmillan.

———. 1982. *Profiles and Critique in Social Theory*. Berkeley and Los Angeles: University of California Press.

Giesey, R. E. 1977. Rules of Inheritance and Strategies of Mobility in Prerevolutionary France. *American Historical Review* 82:271–289.

———. 1983. State-Building in Early Modern France: The Role of Royal Officialdom. *Journal of Modern History* 55:191–207.

Gillis, J. R. 1971. *The Prussian Bureaucracy in Crisis, 1840–1860*. Stanford: Stanford University Press.

———. 1974. *Youth and History*. New York: Academic Press.

———. 1977. *The Development of European Society, 1770–1870*. Boston: Houghton Mifflin.

Glass, D. V., and R. Revelle, eds. 1972. *Population and Social Change*. London: Edward Arnold.

Glassman, D., and A. Redish. 1985. New Estimates of the Money Stock in France, 1493–1680. *Journal of Economic History* 40:31–46.

Gleason, J. H. 1969. *The Justices of the Peace in England, 1558–1640*. Oxford: Oxford University Press.

Glenn, N. 1976. Cohort Analysts' Futile Quest: Statistical Attempts to Separate Age, Period, and Cohort Effects. *American Sociological Review* 41:900–904.

Godechot, J. 1970. *Les révolutions, 1770–1799*. Paris: Presses Universitaires de France.

———. 1971. *The Counter-Revolution: Doctrine and Action, 1789–1804*. Translated by S. Attanasio. Princeton, NJ: Princeton University Press.

Goitein, S.D. 1977. Individualism and Conformity in Classical Islam. In *Individualism and Conformity in Classical Islam*, edited by A. Banani and S. Vryonis, 3–18. Wiesbaden: Otto Harrassowitz.

Goldfrank, W. L. 1979. Theories of Revolution and Revolution without Theory: The Case of Mexico. *Theory and Society* 7:135–165.

Goldstone, J. A. 1980. Theories of Revolution: The Third Generation. *World Politics* 32:425–453.

———. 1982. The Comparative and Historical Study of Revolutions. *Annual Review of Sociology* 8:187–207.

———. 1983. Capitalist Origins of the English Revolution: Chasing a Chimera. *Theory and Society* 12:143–180.

———. 1984. Urbanization and Inflation: Lessons from the English Price Revolution of the Sixteenth and Seventeenth Centuries. *American Journal of Sociology* 89:1122–1160.

———. 1985. Revolutions. In *The International Social Science Encyclopedia*,

edited by A. Kuper and J. Kuper, 705–707. London: Routledge and Kegan Paul.
————. 1986a. The Demographic Revolution in England: A Reexamination. *Population Studies* 49:5–33.
————, ed. 1986b. *Revolutions: Theoretical, Comparative, and Historical Studies*. San Diego: Harcourt Brace Jovanovich.
————. 1986c. The Outcomes of Revolutions. In *Revolutions: Theoretical, Comparative, and Historical Studies*, edited by J. A. Goldstone, 207–208. San Diego: Harcourt Brace Jovanovich.
————. 1987. Cultural Orthodoxy, Risk, and Innovation: The Divergence of East and West in the Early Modern World. *Sociological Theory* 5:119–135.
————. 1988. Regional Ecology and Agrarian Development in England and France. *Politics and Society* 16:287–334.
————. Forthcoming. The Causes of Long Waves in Early Modern Economic History. In *The Vital One: Essays in Honor of Jonathan R. T. Hughes*, edited by J. Mokyr. Greenwich, CT: JAI Press.
Goldstone, J. A., T. R. Gurr, and F. Moshiri, eds. Forthcoming. *Revolutions of the Late 20th Century*. Boulder, CO: Westview Press.
Goodman, D., and M. Redclift. 1982. *From Peasant to Proletarian: Capitalist Development and Agrarian Transition*. Oxford: Basil Blackwell.
Goody, J., J. Thirsk, and E. P. Thompson, eds. 1976. *Family and Inheritance: Rural Society in Western Europe, 1200–1800*. Cambridge: Cambridge University Press.
Gordus, A., and J. P. Gordus. 1981. Potosi Silver and Coinage in Early Modern Europe. In *Precious Metals in the Age of Expansion: Papers of the XIVth International Congress of the Historical Sciences*, edited by H. Kellenbenz, 225–241. Stuttgart: Klett-Cotta.
Gottfried, R. S. 1978. *Epidemic Disease in Fifteenth Century England: The Medical Response and the Demographic Consequences*. New Brunswick, NJ: Rutgers University Press.
————. 1982. *Bury St. Edmunds and the Urban Crisis, 1290–1539*. Princeton, NJ: Princeton University Press.
Goubert, P. 1960. *Beauvais et le Beauvaisis de 1600 à 1730*. Paris: SEVPEN.
————. 1965. Recent Theories and Research in French Population between 1500 and 1700. Translated by M. Hilton. In *Population in History: Essays in Historical Demography*, edited by D. Glass and D. E. C. Eversley, 457–473. Chicago: Aldine.
————. 1967. The French Peasantry of the Seventeenth Century: A Regional Example. In *Crisis in Europe, 1560–1660*, edited by T. Aston, 150–176. Garden City, NY: Doubleday/Anchor Books.
————. 1970a. Historical Demography and the Reinterpretation of Early Modern French History. *Journal of Interdisciplinary History* 1:37–48.
————. 1970b. Les fondements demographiques; les campagnes françaises. In *Histoire économique et sociale de la France*, edited by F. Braudel and E. Labrousse, 2:9–160. Paris: Presses Universitaires de France.
————. 1970c. Le ≪tragique≫ XVIIe siècle. In *Histoire économique et sociale*

de la France, edited by F. Braudel and E. Labrousse, 2:330–366. Paris: Presses Universitaires de France.

———. 1973a. *The Ancien Regime: French Society, 1600–1750.* Translated by S. Cox. New York: Harper and Row.

———. 1973b. *L'ancien régime: les pouvoirs.* Paris: Armand Colin.

———. 1977a. Life and Death in a Peasant Village. In *The Peasantry in the Old Regime: Conditions and Protests*, edited by I. Woloch, 9–12. Huntington, NY: Robert E. Krieger.

———. 1977b. Family and Province: A Contribution to the Knowledge of Family Structure in Modern France. *Journal of Family History* 2:179–195.

———. 1986. *The French Peasantry in the Seventeenth Century.* Translated by I. Patterson. Cambridge: Cambridge University Press.

Gough, K. 1968. The Implications of Literacy in Traditional China and India. In *Literacy in Traditional Societies*, edited by J. Goody, 69–84. Cambridge: Cambridge University Press, 1968.

Gould, J. P. 1962. Agricultural Fluctuations and the English Economy in the Eighteenth Century. *Journal of Economic History* 22:313–333.

Gould, S. J. 1986. Cardboard Darwinism. *New York Review of Books* 33:47–54.

———. 1988. Mighty Manchester. *New York Review of Books* 35:32–35.

Gouldner, A. W. 1983. Artisans and Intellectuals in the German Revolution of 1848. *Theory and Society* 12:521–532.

Graham, G. 1983. *Historical Explanation Reconsidered.* Aberdeen: Aberdeen University Press.

Granovetter, M. 1978. Threshold Models of Collective Behavior. *American Journal of Sociology* 83:1420–1443.

Grantham, G. 1978. The Diffusion of the New Husbandry in France, 1815–1840. *Journal of Economic History* 38:311–337.

Green, J. D. 1986. Countermobilization in the Iranian Revolution. In *Revolutions: Theoretical, Comparative, and Historical Studies*, edited by J. A. Goldstone, 127–138. San Diego: Harcourt Brace Jovanovich.

Greenlaw, R. W., ed. 1958. *The Economic Origins of the French Revolution.* Boston, MA: D.C. Heath.

———, ed. 1975. *The Social Origins of the French Revolution.* Lexington, MA: D.C. Heath.

Grenier, J-Y. 1984. Quelques éléments pour une étude des liens entre conjoncture économique et conjoncture démographique aux XVIIe et XVIIIe siècles. *Annales de Démographie Historique*, 175–199.

Grenville, J. A. S. 1976. *Europe Reshaped, 1848–1878.* Hassocks, UK: Harvester Press.

Grigg, D. B. 1963. Small and Large Farms in England and Wales: Their Size and Distribution. *Geography* 48:268–279.

———. 1966. *The Agricultural Revolution in South Lincolnshire.* Cambridge: Cambridge University Press.

———. 1980. *Population Growth and Agrarian Change.* Cambridge: Cambridge University Press.

Grim, T. 1969. Ming Educational Intendants. In *Chinese Government in Ming*

Times: Seven Studies, edited by C. Hucker, 129–148. New York: Columbia University Press.

Griswold, W. J. 1985. *The Great Anatolian Rebellion, 1591–1611*. Berlin: Klaus Schwarz.

Grove, L., and C. Daniels, eds. 1984. *State and Society in China: Japanese Perspectives on Ming-Qing Social and Economic History*. Tokyo: University of Tokyo Press.

Grove, L., and J. W. Esherick. 1980. From Feudalism to Capitalism: Japanese Scholarship on the Transformation of Chinese Rural Society. *Modern China* 6:397–438.

Gruder, V. R. 1968. *The Royal Provincial Intendants: A Governing Elite in Eighteenth Century France*. Ithaca, NY: Cornell University Press.

———. 1984a. Paths to Political Consciousness: The Assembly of Notables and the Pre-Revolution in France. *French Historical Studies* 13:323–355.

———. 1984b. A Mutation in Elite Political Culture: The French Notables and the Defense of Property and Participation, 1787. *Journal of Modern History* 56:598–634.

Guéry, A. 1978. Les finances de la monarchie française sous l'ancien régime. *Annales, E.S.C.* 33:216–239.

Gugler, J. 1982. The Urban Character of Contemporary Revolutions. *Studies in Comparative International Development* 17:60–73.

Guo, S. 1982. Wasteland Reclamation Policies and Achievements during the Reigns of Shunzhi (1644–1661) and Kangxi (1662–1722). In *Chinese Social and Economic History from the Song to 1900*, edited by A. Feuerwerker, 91–92. Ann Arbor: Center for Chinese Studies, University of Michigan.

Gurr, T. R. 1970. *Why Men Rebel*. Princeton, NJ: Princeton University Press.

———. 1986. The Political Origins of State Violence and Terror: A Theoretical Analysis. In *Government Violence and Repression: An Agenda for Research*, edited by M. Stohl and G. A. Lopez, 45–71. New York: Greenwood Press.

Gutman, M. P. 1977. Putting Crises in Perspective: The Impact of War on Civilian Populations in the Seventeenth Century. *Annales de Démographie Historique*, 101–127.

Habakkuk, J. H. 1960. The English Land Market in the Eighteenth Century. In *Britain and the Netherlands*, edited by J. S. Bromley and E. H. Kossman, 154–173. London: Chatto and Windus.

———. 1979. The Rise and Fall of English Landed Families, 1600–1800. *Transactions of the Royal Historical Society*, 5th ser., 29:187–207.

Haberman, M. 1986. Invisible Handshakes in Lancashire: Cotton Spinning in the First Half of the Nineteenth Century. *Journal of Economic History* 46:987–1009.

Hagen, W. W. 1986. Working for the Junker: The Standard of Living of Manorial Laborers in Brandenburg, 1584–1810. *Journal of Modern History* 58:1443–1458.

———. 1989. Seventeenth-Century Crisis in Brandenburg: The Thirty Years' War, the Destabilization of Serfdom, and the Rise of Absolutism. *American Historical Review* 94:302–335.

Hajnal, J. 1965. European Marriage Patterns in Perspective. In *Population in*

History, edited by D. V. Glass and D. E. C. Eversley, 101–143. Chicago: Aldine.

———. 1982. Two Kinds of Pre-industrial Household Formation Systems. *Population and Development Review* 8:449–494.

Halèvi, R. 1984. Les représentations de la démocratie maçonnique au XVIIIe siècle. *Revue d'Histoire Moderne et Contemporaine* 31:571–596.

Hall, A. R. 1983. *The Revolution in Science, 1500–1750*. London: Longman.

Hall, J. A. 1985. *Powers and Liberties: The Causes and Consequences of the Rise of the West*. Berkeley and Los Angeles: University of California Press.

Hall, J. W. 1970. *Japan: From Prehistory to Modern Times*. New York: Dell.

Hamashima, A. 1980. The Organization of Water Control in the Kiangnan Delta in the Ming Period. *Acta Asiatica* 38:69–92.

Hamerow, T. S. 1958. *Restoration, Revolution, Reaction: Economics and Politics in Germany, 1815–1871*. Princeton, NJ: Princeton University Press.

———. 1983. *The Birth of a New Europe: State and Society in the Nineteenth Century*. Chapel Hill: University of North Carolina Press.

Hamilton, E. 1934. *American Treasure and the Price Revolution in Spain*. Cambridge, MA: Harvard University Press.

Hamilton, G. 1984. Patriarchalism in Imperial China and Western Europe: A Revision of Weber's Sociology of Domination. *Theory and Society* 13:393–426.

———. 1985. Why No Capitalism in China: Negative Questions in Comparative Historical Sociology. In *Max Weber in Asian Studies*, edited by A. Buss, 65–89. Leiden: E. J. Brill.

Hamilton, G., and J. Walton. 1988. History in Sociology. In *The Future of Sociology*, edited by E. F. Borgatta and K. S. Cook, 181–199. Newbury Park, CA: Sage.

Hammarström, I. 1957. The Price Revolution of the Sixteenth Century: Some Swedish Evidence. *Scandinavian Economic History Review* 5:118–154.

Hampson, N. 1963. *A Social History of the French Revolution*. Toronto: University of Toronto Press.

———. 1978. The Enlightenment and the Language of the French Nobility in 1789: The Case of Arras. In *Studies in the French Eighteenth Century*, edited by D. J. Messop, G. E. Rodmill, and D. B. Wilson, 81–91. Durham: University of Durham Press.

———. 1983. *Will and Circumstance: Montesquieu, Rousseau, and the French Revolution*. London: Duckworth.

Handlin, J. F. 1983. *Action in Late Ming Thought: The Reorientation of Lu K'un and Other Scholar-Officials*. Berkeley and Los Angeles: University of California Press.

Hanley, S. B. 1983. A High Standard of Living in 19th Century Japan: Fact or Fantasy? *Journal of Economic History* 43:183–192.

Hanley, S. B., and K. Yamamura. 1977. *Economic and Demographic Change in Preindustrial Japan, 1600–1868*. Princeton, NJ: Princeton University Press.

Harootunian, H. D. 1988. Late Tokugawa Culture and Thought. In *The Cambridge History of Japan*, vol. 5: *The Nineteenth Century*, edited by M. B. Jansen, 168–258. Cambridge: Cambridge University Press.

Harris, J. R., and V. Samaraweera. 1984. Economic Dimensions of Conflict. In *Multidisciplinary Perspectives on Population and Conflict*, edited by N. Choucri, 123–156. Syracuse, NY: Syracuse University Press.

Harris, R. 1970. Necker's *Compte rendu* of 1781: A Reconsideration. *Journal of Modern History* 42:161–183.

———. 1976. French Finances and the American War, 1777–83. *Journal of Modern History* 58:233–258.

———. 1979. *Necker, Reform Statesman of the Ancien Régime*. Berkeley and Los Angeles: University of California Press.

———. 1986. *Necker and the Revolution of 1789*. Lanham, MD: University Press of America.

Hartwell, R. M. 1966. Markets, Technology, and the Structure of Enterprise in the Development of the Eleventh Century Chinese Iron and Steel Industry. *Journal of Economic History*. 26:29–58.

———, ed. 1972. *The Long Debate on Poverty: Eight Essays on Industrialization and "The Condition of England."* London: Institute of Economic Affairs.

———. 1982. Demographic, Political, and Social Transformations of China, 750–1550. *Harvard Journal of Asiatic Studies* 42:365–442.

Hatcher, J. 1977. *Plague, Population, and the English Economy, 1348–1530*. London: Macmillan.

———. 1986. Mortality in the Fifteenth Century: Some New Evidence. *Economic History Review*, 2d ser., 39:19–38.

Hauser, P. M., ed. 1979. *World Population and Development: Challenges and Prospects*. Syracuse, NY: Syracuse University Press.

Havinden, M. A. 1967. Agricultural Progress in Open-Field Oxfordshire. In *Agriculture and Economic Growth in England, 1650–1815*, edited by E. L. Jones, 66–79. London: Methuen.

Hawley, A. 1978. Presidential Address—Cumulative Change in Theory and in History. *American Sociological Review* 43:787–796.

Hayami, A. 1986a. Population Changes. In *Japan in Transition: From Tokugawa to Meiji*, edited by M. B. Jansen and G. Rozman, 280–317. Princeton, NJ: Princeton University Press.

———. 1986b. A Great Transformation: Social and Economic Change in Sixteenth and Seventeenth Century Japan. *Bonner Zeitschrift für Japanologie* 8:3–13.

Hazard, P. 1963. *The European Mind (1680–1715)*. Translated by J. L. May. London: Hollis and Carter.

Heffer, J., J. Mairesse, and J.-M. Chanut. 1986. La culture du blé au milieu du XIXe siècle: rendement, prix, salaires, et autre coûts. *Annales, E.S.C.* 41:1273–1302.

Hellmont, W. 1970–1971. On Ming Orthodoxy. *Monumenta Serica* 29:1–26.

Hempel, C. G. 1942. The Function of General Laws in History. *Journal of Philosophy* 39:35–48.

Henry, L., and Y. Blayo. 1975. La population de la France de 1740 à 1860. *Population* (Numéro Special): 71–92.

Herlihy, D. 1980. *Cities and Society in Medieval Italy*. London: Variorum Reprints.

Hershlag, Z. Y. 1980. *Introduction to the Modern Economic History of the Middle East*. Leiden: E. J. Brill.

Hess, A. C. 1974. Comment on McNeill. In *The Ottoman State and Its Place in World History*, edited by K. Karpat, 47–50. Leiden: E. J. Brill.

Hexter, J. H. 1961. *Reappraisals in History*. Evanston, IL: Northwestern University Press.

———. 1968. The English Aristocracy, Its Crisis, and the English Revolution, 1558–1660. *Journal of British Studies* 8:22–78.

———. 1978. Power Struggles, Parliaments, and Liberty in Early Stuart England. *Journal of Modern History* 50:1–50.

Hey, D. 1974. *An English Rural Community: Myddle under the Tudors and Stuarts*. Leicester: Leicester University Press.

Heyd, U. 1970. The Later Ottoman Empire in Rumelia and Anatolia. In *The Cambridge History of Islam*, edited by P. M. Holt, A. K. S. Lambton, and B. Lewis, 1:354–373. Cambridge: Cambridge University Press.

Heywood, C. 1981. The Role of the Peasantry in French Industrialization. *Economic History Review*, 2d ser., 34:359–376.

Hibbard, C. 1983. *Charles I and the Popish Plot*. Chapel Hill: University of North Carolina Press.

Higgs, D. 1981. Social Mobility and Hereditary Titles in France, 1814–1830: The *Majorats-sur-demande*. *Histoire Sociale* 14:29–48.

Higonnet, P. 1981. *Class, Ideology, and the Rights of Nobles during the French Revolution*. Oxford: Oxford University Press.

Hill, C. 1940. *The English Revolution, 1640*. London: Lawrence and Wishart.

———. 1961. *The Century of Revolution, 1603–1714*. New York: Norton.

———. 1972. *The World Turned Upside Down: Radical Ideas during the English Revolution*. New York: Viking.

———. 1975. *Change and Continuity in Seventeenth Century England*. Cambridge, MA: Harvard University Press.

———. 1980. A Bourgeois Revolution? In *Three British Revolutions: 1641, 1688, 1776* edited by J. G. A. Pocock, 109–139. Princeton, NJ: Princeton University Press.

Hilton, R. 1982. Towns in Societies. *Urban History Yearbook*, 7–13.

Himmelfarb, G. 1987. *The New History and the Old*. Cambridge, MA: Harvard University Press, Belknap Press.

Himmelstein, J., and M. S. Kimmel. 1981. States and Revolutions: The Implications and Limits of Skocpol's Structural Model. *American Journal of Sociology* 86:1145–1154.

Hinrichs, E., E. Schmitt, and R. Vierhaus, eds. 1978. *Vom Ancien Régime zur Französischen Revolution*. Göttingen: Vandenhoeck and Rupert.

Hirst, D. 1975. *The Representative of the People?* Cambridge: Cambridge University Press.

———. 1978. Unanimity in the Commons, Aristocratic Intrigues, and the Origins of the English Civil War. *Journal of Modern History* 50:51–71.

————. 1986. *Authority and Conflict: England, 1603–1658.* Cambridge, MA: Harvard University Press.

Ho, P. T. 1954. The Salt Merchants of Yang-chou: A Study of Commercial Capitalism in Eighteenth Century China. *Harvard Journal of Asiatic Studies* 17:130–168.

————. 1959. *Studies on the Population of China.* Cambridge, MA: Harvard University Press.

————. 1962. *The Ladder of Success in Imperial China.* New York: Columbia University Press.

————. 1967. The Significance of the Ch'ing Period in Chinese History. *Journal of Asian Studies* 26:189–196.

Hobsbawm, E. J., 1962. *The Age of Revolution, 1789–1848.* New York: Mentor.

————. 1965. The Crisis of the Seventeenth Century. In *Crisis in Europe, 1560–1660,* edited by T. Aston, 5–58. New York: Basic Books.

Hobsbawm, E. J., and G. Rudé. 1969. *Captain Swing.* London: Lawrence and Wishart.

Hochberg, L. 1984. The English Civil War in Geographical Perspective. *Journal of Interdisciplinary History* 14:729–750.

Hodges, R., and D. Whitehouse. 1983. *Mohammed, Charlemagne, and the Origins of Europe.* Ithaca, NY: Cornell University Press.

Hoffman, J., ed. 1839. *Die Bevölkerung des Preussischen Staats.* Berlin.

Hoffman, P. T. 1986. Taxes and Agrarian Life in Early Modern France: Land Sales, 1550–1730. *Journal of Economic History* 46:37–55.

————. 1988. Institutions and Agriculture in Old Regime France. *Politics and Society* 16:241–264.

Hohenberg, P. 1972. Change in Rural France in the Period of Industrialization, 1830–1914. *Journal of Economic History* 32:219–240.

Holderness, B. A. 1974. The English Land Market in the 18th Century: The Case of Lincolnshire. *Economic History Review,* 2d ser., 27:557–576.

Hollingsworth, T. H. 1965. *The Demography of the English Peerage.* London: London School of Economics.

————. 1977. Mortality in the British Peerage Families since 1600. *Population* (Numéro Spécial): 323–352.

Holmes, C. 1974. *The Eastern Association in the English Civil War.* Cambridge: Cambridge University Press.

————. 1980. *Seventeenth Century Lincolnshire.* Lincoln: Society for Lincolnshire History and Archeology.

Holmes, G. 1969. *Britain after the Glorious Revolution, 1689–1714.* London: Macmillan.

————. 1986. *Politics, Religion, and Society in England, 1679–1742.* London: Hambleton Press.

Holt, P. M. 1970. The Later Ottoman Empire in Egypt and the Fertile Crescent. In *The Cambridge History of Islam,* edited by P. M. Holt, A. K. S. Lambton, and B. Lewis, 1:374–393. Cambridge: Cambridge University Press.

Holton, R. J. 1978. The Crowd in History: Some Problems of Theory and Method. *Social History* 3:219–233.

Homans, G. C. 1961. *Social Behavior: Its Elementary Forms*. New York: Harcourt, Brace and World.

Homer, S. 1963. *A History of Interest Rates*. New Brunswick, NJ: Rutgers University Press.

Honjo, E. 1965. *The Social and Economic History of Japan*. New York: Russell and Russell.

Hood, J. N. 1979. Revival and Mutation of Old Rivalries in Revolutionary France. *Past and Present*, no. 82, 82–115.

Horn, P. 1980. *The Rural World, 1780–1850*. London: Hutchinson.

Horwitz, H. 1977. *Parliament, Policy, and Politics in the Reign of William III*. Manchester: Manchester University Press.

Hoshi, A. 1980. Transportation in the Ming Period. *Acta Asiatica* 38:1–30.

Hoskins, W. H. 1953. The Rebuilding of Rural England, 1570–1640. *Past and Present*, no. 4, 44–58.

———. 1963. *Provincial England: Essays in Social and Economic History*. London: Macmillan.

———. 1964. Harvest Fluctuations and English Economic History, 1480–1619. *Agricultural History Review* 12:28–46.

———. 1968. Harvest Fluctuations and English Economic History, 1620–1759. *Agricultural History Review* 16:15–31.

Hoszowski, S. 1972. Central Europe and the Sixteenth and Seventeenth Century Price Revolution. In *Economy and Society in Modern Europe: Essays from Annales*, edited by P. Burke, 85–103. New York: Harper and Row.

Hou, C. M., and T. S. Yu, eds. 1979. *Modern Chinese Economic History: Proceedings of the Conference on Modern Chinese Economic History, Academia Sinica, Taipei, Taiwan, Republic of China, Aug. 26–29*. Taipei: Institute of Economics, Academia Sinica.

Houdaille, J. 1982. Reconstitution des familles de Rosny-sou-Bois de 1620 à 1669. *Population* 37:412–418.

Hourani, A. 1974. The Ottoman Background of the Modern Middle East. In *The Ottoman State and Its Place in World History*, edited by K. Karpat, 61–78. Leiden: E. J. Brill.

Howard, M. 1976. *War in History*. Oxford: Oxford University Press.

Howell, R. 1979. The Structure of Urban Politics in the English Civil War. *Albion* 11:111–127.

———. 1982. Neutralism, Conservatism, and Political Alignment in the English Revolution: The Case of the Towns, 1642–9. In *Reactions to the English Civil War, 1642–1649*, edited by J. Morill, 67–87. London: Macmillan.

Hsiao, K. C. 1960. *Rural China: Imperial Control in the Nineteenth Century*. Seattle: University of Washington Press.

Hsieh, Y. W. 1967. Filial Piety and Chinese Society. In *The Chinese Mind*, edited by C. A. Moore, 167–187. Honolulu: East-West Center, University of Hawaii Press.

Hu, S. 1967. The Scientific Spirit and Method in Chinese Philosophy. In *The Chinese Mind*, edited by C. A. Moore, 104–131. Honolulu: East-West Center, University of Hawaii Press.

Huang, P. 1985. *The Peasant Economy and Social Change in North China.* Stanford: Stanford University Press.

Huang, R. 1969. Fiscal Administration during the Ming Dynasty. In *Chinese Government in Ming Times: Seven Studies*, edited by C. O. Hucker, 73–128. New York: Columbia University Press.

————. 1974. *Taxation and Governmental Finance in Sixteenth Century Ming China.* Cambridge: Cambridge University Press.

————. 1986. The History of the Ming Dynasty and Today's World. *Chinese Studies in History* 19:3–36.

Huber, T. M. 1981. *The Revolutionary Origins of Modern Japan.* Stanford: Stanford University Press.

Hucker, C. O. 1957. The Tung-lin Movement of the Late Ming Period. In *Chinese Thought and Institutions*, edited by J. K. Fairbank, 132–162. Chicago: University of Chicago Press.

————, ed. 1969. *Chinese Government in Ming Times: Seven Studies.* New York: Columbia University Press.

Hufton, O. H. 1967. *Bayeux in the Late Eighteenth Century: A Social Study.* Oxford: Clarendon Press.

————. 1974. *The Poor of Eighteenth Century France.* Oxford: Oxford University Press.

————. 1979. The Seigneur and the Rural Community in Eighteenth Century France: The "Seigneurial Reaction," a Reappraisal. *Transactions of the Royal Historical Society*, 5th ser., 29:21–40.

————. 1980. *Europe: Privilege and Protest, 1730–1789.* Ithaca, NY: Cornell University Press.

————. 1981. Women, Work, and Marriage in Eighteenth Century France. In *Marriage and Society: Studies in the Social History of Marriage*, edited by R. B. Outhwaite, 186–203. London: European Publications.

Hughes, A. 1987. *Politics, Society, and Civil War in Warwickshire, 1620–1660.* Cambridge: Cambridge University Press.

Hughes, J. R. T. 1968. Wicksell on the Facts: Prices and Interest Rates, 1844 to 1914. In *Value, Capital, and Growth: Papers in Honour of Sir John Hicks*, edited by J. N. Wolfe, 215–256. Edinburgh: University of Edinburgh Press.

Hunt, D. 1983. Theda Skocpol and the Peasant Route. *Socialist Review* 70:121–144.

————. 1984. Peasant Politics in the French Revolution. *Social History* 9:277–299.

————. 1988. Peasant Movements and Communal Property during the French Revolution. *Theory and Society* 17:179–210.

Hunt, E. H. 1986. Industrialization and Regional Inequality: Wages in Britain, 1760–1914. *Journal of Economic History* 4:935–966.

Hunt, L. 1978. *Revolution and Urban Politics in Provincial France.* Stanford: Stanford University Press.

————. 1984. *Politics, Culture, and Class in the French Revolution.* Berkeley and Los Angeles: University of California Press.

————, ed. 1989. *The New Cultural History.* Berkeley and Los Angeles: University of California Press.

Hunt, W. 1983. *The Puritan Moment: The Coming of Revolution in an English County.* Cambridge, MA: Harvard University Press.

Huntington, S. P. 1968. *Political Order in Changing Societies.* New Haven: Yale University Press.

Huppert, G. 1977. *Les Bourgeois Gentilshommes: An Essay on the Definition of Elites in Renaissance France.* Chicago: University of Chicago Press.

Hurstfield, J. 1979. *The Illusion of Power in Tudor Politics.* London: Athlone Press.

Hutteroth, W. 1980. The Demographic and Economic Organization of the Southern Syrian Sançaks in the Late Sixteenth Century. In *Social and Economic History of Turkey, 1071–1920,* edited by O. Okyar and H. Inalcik, 35–47. Ankara: Hacettepe University Press.

Hutton, R. 1985. *The Restoration: A Political and Religious History of England and Wales, 1658–1667.* Oxford: Clarendon Press.

Inalcik, H. 1955. Land Problems in Turkish History. *Muslim World* 45:221–228.

———. 1969a. Capital Formation in the Ottoman Empire. *Journal of Economic History* 29:97–140.

———. 1969b. L'empire Ottoman. *Actes du Ier congrès international des études balkaniques et sud-est européennes* 3:75–103.

———. 1970a. The Ottoman Economic Mind and Aspects of the Ottoman Economy. In *Studies in the Economic History of the Middle East,* edited by M. A. Cook, 207–218. London: Oxford University Press.

———. 1970b. The Heyday and Decline of the Ottoman Empire. In *The Cambridge History of Islam,* edited by P. M. Holt, A. K. S. Lambton, and B. Lewis, 1:324–353. Cambridge: Cambridge University Press.

———. 1972. The Ottoman Decline and Its Effects upon the *Reaya.* In *Aspects of the Balkans: Continuity and Change,* edited by H. Birnbaum and S. Vryonis, Jr., 338–354. The Hague: Mouton.

———. 1973a. *The Ottoman Empire: The Classical Age, 1300–1600.* Translated by N. Itzkowitz and C. Imber. New York: Praeger.

———. 1973b. Istanbul. In *Encyclopaedia of Islam,* edited by E. van Donzel, B. Lewis, and C. Pellat, 4:224–248. Leiden, E. J. Brill.

———. 1974. The Turkish Impact on the Development of Modern Europe. In *The Ottoman State and Its Place in World History,* edited by K. Karpat, 51–57. Leiden: E. J. Brill.

———. 1976. The Rise of the Ottoman Empire. In *A History of the Ottoman Empire to 1730,* edited by M. A. Cook, 10–53. Cambridge: Cambridge University Press.

———. 1977. Centralization and Decentralization in Ottoman Administration. In *Studies in Eighteenth Century Islamic History,* edited by T. Naff and R. Owen, 27–52. Carbondale: Southern Illinois University Press.

———. 1978. Impact of the *Annales* School on Ottoman Studies and New Findings. *Review* 1:69–96.

———. 1980a. Military and Fiscal Transformation in the Ottoman Empire, 1600–1700. *Archivum Ottomanicum* 6:283–338.

———. 1980b. Ottoman Social and Economic History: A Review. In *Social and*

Economic History of Turkey, 1071–1920, edited by O. Okyar and H. Inalcik, 1–8. Ankara: Hacettepe University Press.

———, ed. 1980c. *Memorial Ömer Lütfi Barkan*. Paris: Librairie d'Amérique et d'Orient Adrien Maisonneuve.

———. 1985. *Studies in Ottoman Social and Economic History*. London: Variorum Reprints.

Ingram, M. 1984. Religion, Communities, and Moral Discipline in Late Sixteenth Century England: Case Studies. In *Religion and Society in Early Modern Europe, 1500–1800*, edited by K. von Greyerz, 177–193. Boston: Allen and Unwin.

Inkster, I. 1983. Technology as the Cause of the Industrial Revolution: Some Comments. *Journal of European Economic History* 12:651–657.

Innes, R. L. 1980. The Door Ajar: Japan's Foreign Trade in the Seventeenth Century. Ph.D. diss., University of Michigan.

International Labor Office. 1986. *Economically Active Population: Estimates and Projections, 1950–2025*. Geneva: ILO.

Islâmoğlu, H. 1979. Population Pressure in Rural Anatolia, 1450–1600: A Critique of the Present Paradigm in Ottoman History. *Review of Middle East Studies* 3:120–135.

———. 1987a. 'Oriental Despotism' in World-System Perspective. In *The Ottoman Empire and the World-Economy*, edited by H. Islâmoğlu, 1–24. Cambridge: Cambridge University Press.

———. 1987b. State and Peasants in the Ottoman Empire: A Study of Peasant Economy in North-central Anatolia during the Sixteenth Century. In *The Ottoman Empire and the World-Economy*, edited by H. Islâmoğlu, 101–159. Cambridge: Cambridge University Press.

Islâmoğlu, H., and S. Faroqhi. 1979. Crop Patterns and Agricultural Production Trends in Sixteenth Century Anatolia. *Review* 2:401–436.

Islâmoğlu, H., and Ç. Keyder. 1977. Agenda for Ottoman History. *Review* 1:31–56.

Issawi, C. 1974. The Ottoman Empire in the European Economy, 1600–1914: Some Observations and Many Questions. In *The Ottoman State and Its Place in World History*, edited by K. Karpat, 107–117. Leiden: E. J. Brill.

———. 1980. *The Economic History of Turkey, 1800–1914*. Chicago: University of Chicago Press.

———. 1982. *An Economic History of the Middle East and North Africa*. New York: Columbia University Press.

Itzkowitz, N. 1972. *Ottoman Empire and Islamic Tradition*. New York: Knopf.

———. 1977. Men and Ideas in the Eighteenth Century Ottoman Empire. In *Studies in Eighteenth Century Islamic History*, edited by T. Naff and R. Owen, 15–26. Carbondale: Southern Illinois University Press.

Iwao, S. 1976. Japanese Foreign Trade in the 16th and 17th Centuries. *Acta Asiatica* 30:1–18.

Jackson, R. V. 1985. Growth and Deceleration in English Agriculture, 1660–1790. *Economic History Review*, 2d. ser., 38:333–351.

———. 1987. The Structure of Pay in 19th Century Britain. *Economic History Review*, 2d ser., 40:561–570.

Jacquart, J. 1974a. *La crise rurale en Ile-de-France, 1550–1670.* Paris: Armand Colin.

———. 1974b. French Agriculture in the Seventeenth Century. In *Essays in European Economic History, 1500–1800,* edited by P. Earle, 165–184. Oxford: Clarendon Press.

———. 1975. La rente foncière: indice conjoncturel? *Revue Historique,* no. 504, 355–76.

Jago, C. 1979. The Crisis of the Aristocracy in Seventeenth Century Castile. *Past and Present,* no. 84, 60–90.

James, M. 1974. *Family, Lineage, and Civil Society: A Study of Society, Politics, and Mentality in the Durham Region, 1500–1640.* Oxford: Clarendon Press.

Jansen, M. B. 1986. The Ruling Class. In *Japan in Transition: From Tokugawa to Meiji,* edited by M. B. Jansen and G. Rozman, 68–90. Princeton, NJ: Princeton University Press.

———. 1988a. Japan in the Early Nineteenth Century. In *The Cambridge History of Japan,* vol. 5: *The Nineteenth Century,* edited by M. B. Jansen, 50–115. Cambridge: Cambridge University Press.

———. 1988b. The Meiji Restoration. In *The Cambridge History of Japan,* vol. 5: *The Nineteenth Century,* edited by M. B. Jansen, 308–366. Cambridge: Cambridge University Press.

Jansen, M. B., and G. Rozman, eds. 1986. *Japan in Transition: From Tokugawa to Meiji.* Princeton, NJ: Princeton University Press.

Jarausch, K. J. 1974. The Sources of German Student Unrest. In *The University in Society,* vol. 2: *Europe, Scotland, and the United States from the Sixteenth to the Twentieth Century,* edited by L. Stone, 533–570. Princeton, NJ: Princeton University Press.

———. 1982. *Students, Society, and Politics in Imperial Germany: The Rise of Academic Illiberalism.* Princeton, NJ: Princeton University Press.

Jardin, A., and A.-J. Tudesq. 1983. *Restoration and Reaction, 1815–1848.* Translated by E. Forster. Cambridge: Cambridge University Press.

Jasso, G. 1988. Principles of Theoretical Analysis. *Sociological Theory* 6:1–20.

Jeanin, P. 1982. The Seaborne and Overland Trade Routes of Northern Europe in the XVIth and XVIIth Centuries. *Journal of European Economic History* 11:5–60.

Jenkins, P. 1983. *The Making of a Ruling Class: The Glamorgan Gentry, 1640–1790.* New York: Cambridge University Press.

Jennings, R. C. 1973. Loan and Credit in Early 17th Century Judicial Records: The Sharia Court of Anatolian Kayseri. *Journal of the Economic and Social History of the Orient* 16:168–216.

———. 1976. Urban Population in Anatolia in the Sixteenth Century. *International Journal of Middle East Studies* 7:21–57.

———. 1980. Firearms, Bandits, and Gun Control. *Archivum Ottomanicum* 6:339–358.

———. 1983. The Population, Society, and Economy of the Region of *Erciyeş dağı* in the 16th Century. In *Contributions à l'histoire économique et sociale de l'empire Ottoman,* edited by Ö. L. Barkan, 149–250. Louvain: Editions Peeters.

Jervis, R., N. Lebow, and J. G. Stein, eds. 1985. *Psychology and Deterrence.* Baltimore, MD: Johns Hopkins University Press.

John, A. H. 1978. The Course of Agricultural Change, 1660–1760. In *Essays in Agrarian History*, edited by W. E. Minchinton, 1:221–253. New York: Augustus M. Kelley.

Johnson, C. 1966. *Revolutionary Change.* Boston: Little, Brown.

Johnson, C. H. 1975a. Economic Change and Artisan Discontent: The Tailors' History, 1800–48. In *Revolution and Reaction: 1848 and the Second French Republic*, edited by R. Price, 87–114. London: Croom Helm.

———. 1975b. The Revolution of 1830 in French Economic History. In *1830 in France*, edited by J. Merriman, 139–189. New York: New Viewpoints.

Johnson, D., ed. 1976. *French Society and the Revolution.* New York: Cambridge University Press.

Johnson, D., F. Crouzet, and F. Bedarida, eds. 1980. *Britain and France: Ten Centuries.* Folkestone, Kent: William Dawson.

Johnson, D., A. J. Nathan, and E. S. Rawski. 1985. *Popular Culture in Later Imperial China.* Berkeley and Los Angeles: University of California Press.

Johnson, D. G., and R. D. Lee, eds. 1987. *Population Growth and Economic Development: Issues and Evidence.* Madison: University of Wisconsin Press.

Johnson, H. C. 1986. *The Midi in Revolution: A Study of Regional Political Diversity, 1789–1793.* Princeton, NJ: Princeton University Press.

Johnson, L. L. 1983. Patronage and Privilege: The Politics of Provincial Capitalism in Tokugawa Japan. Ph.D. diss., Stanford University.

Jones, C. 1982. *Charity and "Bienfaisance": The Treatment of the Poor in the Montpellier Region, 1740–1815.* Cambridge: Cambridge University Press.

Jones, E. L. 1974. *Agriculture and the Industrial Revolution.* Oxford: Basil Blackwell.

———. 1968. Agriculture and Economic Growth in England, 1660–1750: Agricultural Change. In *Essays in Agrarian History*, edited by W. E. Minchinton, 1:203–220. New York: Augustus M. Kelley.

———. 1970. English and European Agricultural Development, 1650–1750. In *The Industrial Revolution*, edited by R. M. Hartwell, 42–76. Oxford: Basil Blackwell.

———. 1981a. Agriculture, 1700–1800. In *The Economic History of Britain since 1700*, edited by R. Floud and D. McCloskey, 1:66–86. Cambridge: Cambridge University Press.

———. 1981b. *The European Miracle.* Cambridge: Cambridge University Press.

Jones, E. L., and M. J. R. Healey. 1974. Wheat Yields in England, 1815–1859. In *Agriculture and the Industrial Revolution.* Cambridge: Cambridge University Press.

Jones, G. S. 1983a. *Languages of Class: Studies in English Working Class History, 1832–1882.* Cambridge: Cambridge University Press.

———. 1983b. The Midcentury Crisis and the 1848 Revolutions. *Theory and Society* 12:505–520.

Jones, J. R. 1972. *The Revolution of 1688 in England.* London: Weidenfeld and Nicolson.

———. 1978. *Court and Country: England, 1658–1714.* Cambridge, MA: Harvard University Press.

Jones, P. 1981. *The 1848 Revolutions.* London: Longman.

Jones, S. M., and P. A. Kuhn. 1978. Dynastic Decline and the Roots of Rebellion. In *The Cambridge History of China,* vol. 10: *Late Ch'ing, 1800–1911, Part 1,* edited by D. Twitchett and J. K. Fairbank, 107–162. Cambridge: Cambridge University Press.

Jorberg, L. 1972. *A History of Prices in Sweden, 1732–1914.* Lund: CWK Gleerup.

Jorgenson, J. 1963. Denmark's Relations with Lübeck and Hamburg in the Seventeenth Century. *Scandinavian Economics History Review* 9:73–116.

Kafker, F. A., and J. M. Laux, eds. 1968. *The French Revolution: Conflicting Interpretations.* New York: Random House.

Kagan, R. L. 1974. *Students and Society in Early Modern Spain.* Baltimore, MD: Johns Hopkins University Press.

———. 1975. Law Students and Legal Careers in Eighteenth Century France. *Past and Present,* no. 68, 38–72.

Kamen, H. 1971. *The Iron Century: Social Change in Europe, 1550–1660.* New York: Praeger.

———. 1980. *Spain in the Later Seventeenth Century, 1665–1700.* London: Longman.

———. 1983. *Spain, 1469–1714: A Society of Conflict.* London: Longman.

Kamien, M., and N. Schwartz. 1975. Market Structure and Innovation: A Survey. *Journal of Economic Literature* 13:1–37.

Kaplan, S. L. 1976. *Bread, Politics, and Political Economy in the Reign of Louis XV.* 2 vols. The Hague: Mouton.

———. 1985. The Paris Bread Riot of 1725. *French Historical Studies* 14:23–56.

Kaplow, J., ed. 1965. *New Perspectives on the French Revolution: Readings in Historical Sociology.* New York: John Wiley and Sons.

———, ed. 1971. *France on the Eve of Revolution: A Book of Readings.* New York: John Wiley.

———. 1972. *The Names of Kings: The Parisian Laboring Poor in the Eighteenth Century.* New York: Basic Books.

Karpat, K. H. 1968. The Land Regime, Social Structure, and Modernization in the Ottoman Empire. In *The Beginnings of Modernization in the Middle East: The Nineteenth Century,* edited by W. R. Polk and R. L. Chambers, 69–90. Chicago: University of Chicago Press.

———. 1972. The Transformation of the Ottoman State, 1789–1908. *International Journal of Middle East Studies* 3:243–281.

———. 1973a. *Social Change and Politics in Turkey.* Leiden: E. J. Brill.

———. 1973b. *An Inquiry into the Social Foundations of Nationalism in the Ottoman State.* Princeton, NJ: Center of International Studies.

———. 1974a. Introduction. In *The Ottoman State and Its Place in World History,* edited by K. Karpat, 1–14. Leiden: E. J. Brill.

———. 1974b. The Stages of Ottoman History: A Structural Comparative Approach. In *The Ottoman State and Its Place in World History*, edited by K. Karpat, 79–98. Leiden: E. J. Brill.

———, ed. 1974c. *The Ottoman State and Its Place in World History*. Leiden: E. J. Brill.

———. 1983. Population Movements in the Ottoman State in the Nineteenth Century: An Outline. In *Contributions a l'histoire économique et sociale de l'empire Ottoman*, edited by Ö. L. Barkan, 386–428. Louvain: Editions Peeters.

———. 1985. *Ottoman Population, 1830–1914: Demographic and Social Characteristics*. Madison: University of Wisconsin Press.

Kaufhold, K. H. 1976. Handwerk und Industrie, 1800–1850. In *Handbuch der deutschen Wirtschafts- und Sozialgeschichte*, edited by H. Aubin and W. Zorn, 1:321–368. Stuttgart: Klett-Cotta.

Kearney, H. 1970. *Scholars and Gentlemen: Universities and Society in Preindustrial Britain*. London: Faber.

Keddie, N. 1981. *Roots of Revolution: An Interpretive History of Modern Iran*. New Haven: Yale University Press.

Kellenbenz, H., ed. 1981. *Precious Metals in the Age of Expansion: Papers of the XIVth International Congress of the Historical Sciences.* Stuttgart: Klett-Cotta.

Kelley, A. C., and J. G. Williamson. 1984. *What Drives Third World City Growth? A Dynamic General Equilibrium Approach*. Princeton, NJ: Princeton University Press.

Kelley, W. R., and O. R. Galle. 1984. Social Perspectives and Evidence on the Links between Population and Conflict. In *Multidisciplinary Perspectives on Population and Conflict*, edited by N. Choucri, 9–22. Syracuse, NY: Syracuse University Press.

Kemp, T. 1971. *Economic Forces in French History*. London: Dennis Dobson.

———. 1985a. Some Recent Contributions to European Economic History. *European History Quarterly* 15:237–248.

———. 1985b. French Economic Performance: Some New Views Critically Examined. *European History Quarterly* 15:473–88.

Kennedy, M. L. 1982. *The Jacobin Clubs in the French Revolution: The First Years*. Princeton, NJ: Princeton University Press.

———. 1984. The Best and Worst of Times: The Jacobin Club Network from October 1791 to June 2, 1793. *Journal of Modern History* 56:635–666.

Kennedy, P. M. 1987. *The Rise and Fall of the Great Powers: Economic Change and Military Conflict from 1500 to 2000*. New York: Random House.

Kennedy, W. 1913. *English Taxation, 1640–1799: An Essay on Policy and Opinion*. London: G. Bell.

Kent, J. R. 1981. Population Mobility and Alms: Poor Migrants in the Midlands during the Early Seventeenth Century. *Local Population Studies*, no. 27, 35–51.

Kenyon, J. P. 1978. *Stuart England*. Harmondsworth, Middlesex: Pelican.

Kerridge, E. 1962. The Movement of Rent, 1540–1640. In *Essays in Economic History*, edited by E. M. Carus-Wilson, 2:208–226. London: Edward Arnold.

————. 1967. *The Agricultural Revolution*. London: Allen and Unwin.

————. 1968. Turnip Husbandry in High Suffolk. In *Essays in Agrarian History*, edited by W. E. Minchinton, 1:143–146. New York: Augustus M. Kelley.

————. 1973. *The Farmers of Old England*. London: Allen and Unwin.

Kessler, L. 1976. *K'ang-Hsi and the Consolidation of Ch'ing Rule, 1661–1684*. Chicago: University of Chicago Press.

Kettering, S. 1986. *Patrons, Brokers, and Clients in Seventeenth Century France*. New York: Oxford University Press.

Keyfitz, N. 1965. Political-economic Aspects of Urbanization in Southeast Asia. In *The Study of Urbanization*, edited by P. Hauser and L. F. Schnore, 265–310. New York: John Wiley.

Khaldûn, I. 1967. *The Muqaddimah*. Translated by F. Rosenthal, edited by N.J. Dawood. Princeton, NJ: Princeton University Press.

Kiel, M. 1987. Population Growth and Road Production in Sixteenth Century Athens and Attica according to the Ottoman *Tahrir Defters*. In *Comité international d'études pré-Ottomanes et Ottomanes VIe symposium*, edited by J.-L. Bacqué-Grammont and E. van Donzel, 115–133. Istanbul: Divit Press.

Kiernan, V. 1980. *State and Society in Europe, 1550–1650*. Oxford: Basil Blackwell.

Kierstead, R. F., ed. 1975. *State and Society in Seventeenth Century France*. New York: New Viewpoints.

Kimmel, M. S. 1988. *Absolutism and Its Discontents*. New Brunswick, NJ: Transaction Books.

Kishimoto-Nakayama, M. 1984. The Kangxi Depression and Early Qing Local Markets. *Modern China* 10:227–256.

Kishlansky, M. 1977. The Emergence of Adversary Politics. *Journal of Modern History* 49:617–640.

————. 1979. *The New Model Army*. Cambridge: Cambridge Unviversity Press.

————. 1986. *Parliamentary Selection*. Cambridge: Cambridge University Press.

Kiss, I. 1980. Money, Prices, Values, and Purchasing Power from the XVIth to the XVIIIth Century. *Journal of European Economic History* 9: 459–490.

Kitchen, M. 1978. *The Political Economy of Germany, 1815–1914*. Montreal: McGill-Queens University Press.

Klein, D. M. 1987. Causation in Sociology Today: A Revised View. *Sociological Theory* 5:19–26.

Knafla, L. A. 1972. The Matriculation Revolution and Education at the Inns of Court in Renaissance England. In *Tudor Man and Institutions*, edited by A. J. Slavin, 232–264. Baton Rouge: Louisiana State University Press.

Kobata, A. 1965. The Production and Uses of Gold and Silver in Sixteenth and Seventeenth Century Japan. *Economic History Review*, 2d ser., 18:245–266.

————. 1981. Production and Trade in Gold, Silver, and Copper in Japan, 1450–1750. In *Precious Metals in the Age of Expansion: Papers of the XIVth International Congress of the Historical Sciences*, edited by H. Kellenbenz, 273–276. Stuttgart: Klett-Cotta.

Koch, H. W. 1978. *A History of Prussia*. London: Longman.

Köllmann, W. 1976a. The Population of Germany in the Age of Industrialism.

In *Population Movements in Modern European History*, edited by H. Moller, 100–108. New York: Macmillan.

———. 1976b. Bevölkerungsgeschichte, 1800–1970. In *Handbuch der deutschen Wirtschafts- und Sozialgeschichte*, edited by H. Aubin and W. Zorn, 1:9–50. Stuttgart: Klett-Cotta.

Kondratieff, N.C. 1950. The Long Waves in Economic Life. In *Readings in Business Cycle Theory*, selected by a Committee of the American Economic Assocation, 20–42. London: Allen and Unwin.

Kovacsics, J. The Population of Hungary in the Eighteenth Century (1720–1876). *Third International Conference of Economic History*, edited by D. E. C. Eversley, 136–145. Paris: Mouton.

Kranzberg, M., ed. 1959. *1848: A Turning Point?* Boston: D.C. Heath.

Krause, J. T. 1959. Some Implications of Recent Work in Historical Demography. *Comparative Studies in Society and History* 1:164–188.

Kuczynski, J. 1947. *Die Geschichte der Lage der Arbeiter in Deutschland von 1800 bis in die Gegenwart*. Berlin: Freie Gewerkschaft.

Kuhn, D. 1981. Silk Technology in the Sung Period (960–1278 A.D.). *T'oung Pao* 47:48–90.

Kuhn, P. 1970. *Rebellion and Its Enemies in Late Imperial China*. Cambridge, MA: Harvard University Press.

———. 1977. Origins of the Taiping Vision of a Chinese Rebellion. *Comparative Studies in Society and History* 19:350–366.

———. 1978. The Taiping Rebellion. In *The Cambridge History of China*, vol. 10: *Late Ch'ing, 1800–1911, Part 1*, edited by D. Twitchett and J. K. Fairbank, 264–317. Cambridge: Cambridge University Press.

Kunt, I. M. 1974. Ethnic-regional (*Cins*) Solidarity in the Seventeenth Century Ottoman Establishment. *International Journal of Middle East Studies* 5:233–239.

———. 1983. *The Sultan's Servants: The Transformation of Ottoman Provincial Government, 1550–1650*. New York: Columbia University Press.

Kurat, A. N. 1976. The Reign of Mehmed IV, 1648–87. In *A History of the Ottoman Empire to 1730*, edited by M. A. Cook, 157–177. Cambridge: Cambridge University Press.

Kussmaul, A. 1981. *Servants in Husbandry in Early Modern England*. Cambridge: Cambridge University Press.

———. 1985a. Agrarian Change in Seventeenth Century England: The Economic Historian as Paleontologist. *Journal of Economic History* 45:1–30.

———. 1985b. Time and Space, Hoofs and Grain: The Seasonality of Marriage in England. *Journal of Interdisciplinary History* 15:755–779.

Kuznets, S. 1966. *Modern Economic Growth*. New Haven: Yale University Press.

Labrousse, E. 1958. The Crisis in the French Economy at the End of the Old Regime. In *The Economic Origins of the French Revolution*, edited by R. Greenlaw, 59–92. Boston: D.C. Heath.

———. 1964. *Le mouvement ouvrier et les idées sociales en France de 1815 à la fin du XIXe siècle*. Paris: Centre de Documentation Universitaire.

———. 1970a. Les bons prix agricoles du XVIIIe siècle. In *Histoire économique et sociale de la France*, edited by F. Braudel and E. Labrousse, 2:367–416. Paris: Presses Universitaires de France.

———. 1970b. L'expansion agricole: la monté de la production. In *Histoire économique et sociale de la France*, edited by F. Braudel and E. Labrousse, 2:417–472. Paris: Presses Universitaires de France.

———. 1970c. Aperçu de la répartition sociale de l'expansion agricole. In *Histoire économique et sociale de la France*, edited by F. Braudel and E. Labrousse, 2:473–498. Paris: Presses Universitaires de France.

———. 1970d. Les ruptures periodiques de la prosperité: Crise économique du XVIIIe siècle. In *Histoire économique et sociale de la France*, edited by F. Braudel and E. Labrousse, 2:529–563. Paris: Presses Universitaires de France.

———. 1970e. *Le prix du froment en France au temps de la monnaie stable (1726–1913)*. Paris: SEVPEN.

———. 1978. A Review of the Allocation of Industrial Expansion among Social Classes. *Review* 2:149–178.

———. 1984 [1933]. *Equisse du mouvement des prix et des revenus en France au XVIIIe siècle*. 2 vols. Paris: Editions des Archives Contemporaines.

Lachman, R. 1987. *From Manor to Market: Structural Change in England, 1536–1640*. Madison: University of Wisconsin Press.

Lamont, W. 1969. *Godly Rule*. London: Macmillan.

Lamont, W., and S. Oldfield. 1975. *Politics, Religion, and Literature in the Seventeenth Century*. London: J. M. Dent.

Lampe, J. R., and M. R. Jackson. 1982. *Balkan Economic History, 1550–1950*. Bloomington: Indiana University Press.

Landau, N. 1984. *The Justices of the Peace, 1679–1760*. Berkeley and Los Angeles: University of California Press.

Landers, J. 1987. Mortality and Metropolis: The Case of London, 1670–1830. *Population Studies* 41:59–76.

Landers, J., and A. Monzos. 1988. Burial Seasonality and Causes of Death in London, 1670–1819. *Population Studies* 42:59–84.

Landes, D. S. 1950. The Statistical Study of French Crises. *Journal of Economic History* 10:195–211.

———. 1969. *The Unbound Prometheus: Technological Change and Industrial Development in Western Europe from 1750 to the Present*. Cambridge: Cambridge University Press.

Lane, F. C. 1966. *Venice and Its History*. Baltimore, MD: Johns Hopkins University Press.

Lang, R. G. 1974. Social Origins and Social Aspirations of Jacobean London Merchants. *Economic History Review*, 2d ser., 27:28–47.

Langer, W. 1966. The Pattern of Urban Revolution in 1848. In *French Society and Culture since the Old Regime*, edited by E. Accomb and M. Brown, 89–118. New York: Holt, Rinehart and Winston.

———. 1969. *Political and Social Upheaval, 1832–1852*. New York: Harper and Row.

Langford, P. 1988. Property and Virtual Representation in Eighteenth Century England. *Historical Journal* 31:83–115.

Lapidus, I. M. 1975. Hierarchies and Networks: A Comparison of Chinese and Islamic Societies. In *Conflict and Control in Late Imperial China*, edited by F. Wakeman and C. Grant, 26–42. Berkeley and Los Angeles: University of California Press.

Large, P. 1984. Urban Growth and Agricultural Change in the West Midlands during the Seventeenth and Eighteenth Centuries. In *Country Towns in Pre-industrial England*, edited by P. Clark, 169–189. New York: St. Martin's Press.

Lash, S., and S. Whimster. 1987. *Max Weber, Rationality, and Modernity*. London: Allen and Unwin.

Laslett, P. 1971. *The World We Have Lost*. New York: Charles Scribner.

Lattimore, O. 1951. *Inner Asian Frontiers of China*. Boston: Beacon Press.

Laurent, R. 1970. *Octroi* Archives as Sources of Urban Social and Economic History. In *Essays in French Economic History*, edited by R. Cameron, 279–285. Homewood, IL: Dorsey.

————. 1976. Tradition et progrés: le secteur agricole. In *Histoire économique et sociale de la France*, edited by F. Braudel and E. Labrousse, 3:619–738. Paris: Presses Universitaires de France.

Lázaro Ruíz, M., P. A. Gurria García, and F. Brumont. 1988. La population de La Riója. *Annales de Démographie Historique*, 221–241.

Le Bas, C. 1984. *Histoire sociale des faits économiques: la France au XIXe siècle*. Lyon: Presses Universitaires de Lyon.

Lebow, R. N. 1981. *Between Peace and War: The Nature of International Crises*. Baltimore, MD: Johns Hopkins University Press.

Lebrun, F. 1980. Les crises démographiques en France aux XVIIe et XVIIIe siècles. *Annales, E.S.C.* 35:205–234.

Lee, J. 1982. Food Supply and Population Growth in Southwest China, 1250–1600. *Journal of Asian Studies* 41:711–746.

Lee, R. D. 1974. Estimating Series of Vital Rates and Age Structure from Baptisms and Burials: A New Technique, with Applications to Pre-industrial England. *Population Studies* 28:495–512.

————. 1978. Models of Pre-industrial Dynamics with Applications to England. In *Historical Studies of Changing Fertility*, edited by C. Tilly, 155–208. Princeton, NJ: Princeton University Press.

————. 1980. A Historical Perspective on Economic Aspects of the Population Explosion: The Case of Pre-industrial England. In *Population and Economic Change in Developing Countries*, edited by R. A. Easterlin, 517–557. Chicago: University of Chicago Press.

————. 1985. Population Homeostasis and English Demographic History. *Journal of Interdisciplinary History* 15:635–660.

Lee, W. R. 1977. *Population Growth, Economic Development, and Social Change in Bavaria, 1750–1850*. New York: Arno Press.

————. 1979. Germany. In *European Demography and Economic Growth*, edited by W. R. Lee, 144–195. New York: St. Martin's Press.

————. 1984. Mortality Levels and Agrarian Reform in Early Nineteenth Century Prussia: Some Regional Evidence. In *Pre-industrial Population Change*, edited by T. Bengtsson, G. Fridlizius, and R. Ohlsson, 161–190. Stockholm: Almquist and Wiksell.

Lefebvre, G. 1947. *The Coming of the French Revolution*. Translated by R. R. Palmer. Princeton, NJ: Princeton University Press.

———. 1965a. The Movement of Prices and the Origins of the French Revolution. In *New Perspectives on the French Revolution: Readings in Historical Sociology*, edited by J. Kaplow, 103–135. New York: John Wiley.

———. 1965b. Revolutionary Crowds. In *New Perspectives on the French Revolution: Readings in Historical Sociology*, edited by J. Kaplow, 173–190. New York: John Wiley.

———. 1972 [1924]. *Les paysans du nord pendant la révolution française*. Paris: Armand Colin.

———. 1973. *The Great Fear of 1789: Rural Panic in Revolutionary France*. Translated by J. White. Princeton, NJ: Princeton University Press.

———. 1977. The Place of the Revolution in the Agrarian History of France. In *Rural Society in France: Selections from the Annales*, edited by R. Forster and O. Ranum, translated by E. Forster and P. M. Ranum, 31–49. Baltimore, MD: Johns Hopkins University Press.

Leffler, P. K. 1985. French Historians and the Challenge to Louis XIV's Absolutism. *French Historical Studies* 14:1–22.

Le Goff, T. J. A. 1981. *Vannes and Its Region: A Study of Town and Country in Eighteenth Century France*. Oxford: Clarendon Press.

Lemaître, N. 1978. *Un horizon bloqué: Ussel et la montagne Limousine aux XVIIe et XVIIIe siècles*. Ussel: Musée du Pays d'Ussel.

Lemmings, D. 1985. The Student Body of the Inns of Court under the Later Stuarts. *Bulletin of the Institute of Historical Research* 58:149–66.

Lemoigne, Y. 1965. Population and Provisions in Strasbourg in the Eighteenth Century. In *New Perspectives on the French Revolution: Readings in Historical Sociology*, edited by J. Kaplow, 47–67. New York: John Wiley.

Léon, P. 1970. L'élan industriel et commercial. In *Histoire économique et sociale de la France*, edited by F. Braudel and E. Labrousse, 2:499–528. Paris: Presses Universitaires de France.

Leonard, E. M. 1962. The Enclosure of Common Fields in the Seventeenth Century. In *Essays in Economic History*, edited by E. M. Carus-Wilson, 2:227–256. London: Edward Arnold.

Lequin, Y., ed. 1984. *Histoire de français XIXe-XXe siècles*. Paris: Armand Colin.

Le Roy Ladurie, E. 1974a. *The Peasants of Languedoc*. Translated by J. Day. Urbana: University of Illinois Press.

———. 1974b. Révoltes et contestations rurales en France de 1675 à 1788. *Annales, E.S.C.* 29:6–22.

———. 1975. De la crise ultime à la vraie croissance. In *Histoire rurale de la France*, edited by G. Duby and A. Wallon, 2:359–441. Paris: Editions du Seuil.

———. 1976. A System of Customary Law: Family Structures and Inheritance Customs in Sixteenth Century France. In *Family and Society: Selections from the Annales*, edited by R. Forster and O. Ranum, translated by E. Forster and P. M. Ranum, 75–103. Baltimore, MD: Johns Hopkins University Press.

———. 1977. Les masses profondes: la paysannerie. In *Histoire économique et sociale de la France*, edited by F. Braudel and E. Labrousse, 1:483–872. Paris: Presses Universitaires de France.

———. 1978. Les paysans français au XVIIIe siècle, dans la perspective de la revolution française. In *Vom Ancien Régime zur Französischen Revolution*, edited by E. Hinrichs, E. Schmitt, and R. Vierhaus, 261–278. Göttingen: Vandenhoeck and Rupert.

———. 1979. *The Territory of the Historian*. Translated by B. Reynolds and S. Reynolds. Hassocks, Sussex: Harvester Press.

———. 1981. *The Mind and Method of the Historian*. Translated by B. Reynolds and S. Reynolds. Hassocks, Sussex: Harvester Press.

———. 1987. *The French Peasantry, 1450–1660*. Translated by A. Sheridan. Berkeley and Los Angeles: University of California Press.

Le Roy Ladurie, E., and J. Goy. 1982. *Tithe and Agrarian History from the Fourteenth to the Nineteenth Centuries: An Essay in Comparative History*. Cambridge: Cambridge University Press.

Levi, M. 1988. *Of Rule and Revenue*. Berkeley and Los Angeles: University of California Press.

Levine, D. 1984. Production, Reproduction, and the Proletarian Family in England, 1500–1851. In *Proletarianization and Family History*, edited by D. Levine, 87–127. New York: Academic Press.

Lévy, C., and L. Henry. 1960. Ducs et pairs sous l'ancien régime. *Population* 15:807–830.

Levy, F. J. 1982. How Information Spread among the Gentry, 1550–1640. *Journal of British Studies* 21:2–25.

Lévy-Leboyer, M. 1968. La croissance économique en France au XIXe siècle. *Annales, E.S.C.* 23:788–807.

———. 1970. L'héritage de Simiand: prix, profit, et termes d'échange au XIXe siècle. *Revue Historique* 94:77–120.

Lévy-Leboyer, M., and F. Bourguignon. 1985. *L'économie française au XIX siècle*. Paris: Economica.

Lewis, B. 1958. Some Reflections on the Decline of the Ottoman Empire. *Studia Islamica* 9:111–127.

———. 1962. Ottoman Observers of Ottoman Decline. *Islamic Studies* 1:71–87.

Lewis, G., and C. Lucas, eds. 1983. *Beyond the Terror*. Cambridge: Cambridge University Press.

Liang, C. C. 1959. *Intellectual Trends in the Ch'ing Period*. Translated by I. C. Y. Hsu. Cambridge, MA: Harvard University Press.

Liang, F. 1956. The Ten-Part Tax System of the Ming. In *Chinese Social History*, edited by E. Sun and J. de Francis, 271–280. Washington, DC: American Council of Learned Societies.

Lincoln, B., ed. 1985. *Religion, Rebellion, Revolution: An Interdisciplinary and Cross-cultural Collection of Essays*. New York: St. Martin's Press.

Lindert, P. 1985. English Population, Wages, and Prices, 1541–1913. *Journal of Interdisciplinary History* 15:609–634.

Lindert, P., and J. Williamson. 1983. English Living Standards during the Industrial Revolution: A New Look. *Economic History Review*, 2d ser., 36:1–25.

———. 1985. English Workers' Real Wages: A Reply to Crafts. *Journal of Economic History* 45:145–158.

Lindley, K. 1982. *Fenland Riots and the English Revolution*. London: Heinemann.

———. 1986. London and Popular Freedom in the 1640s. In *Freedom and the English Revolution*, edited by R. C. Richardson and G. M. Ridden, 111–150. Manchester: Manchester University Press.

Lis, C., and H. Soly. 1977. *Poverty and Capitalism in Pre-industrial Europe*. Translated by J. Coonan. Atlantic Highlands, NJ.: Humanities Press.

Littrup, L. 1981. *Sub-bureaucratic Government in China in Ming Times: A Study of Shandong Province in the Sixteenth Century*. Oslo: Universitetsforlaget, Institute for Comparative Research in Human Culture.

Liu, K. C., ed. 1990. *Orthodoxy in Late Imperial China*. Berkeley and Los Angeles: University of California Press.

Liu, P., and K. Hwang. 1977. Population Change and Economic Development in Mainland China since 1400. In *Modern Chinese Economic History*, edited by C. Hou and T. Yu, 61–81. Taipei: Institute of Economics, Academia Sinica.

Livi-Bacci, M. 1989. *Population and Nutrition: Antagonism and Adaptation*. Cambridge: Cambridge University Press.

Lloyd, C. 1986. *Explanation in Social History*. Oxford: Basil Blackwell.

Lloyd, H. A. 1968. *The Gentry of South-west Wales, 1540–1640*. Cardiff: University of Wales Press.

Lodhi, A. Q., and C. Tilly. 1973. Urbanization, Crime, and Collective Violence in 19th Century France. *American Journal of Sociology* 79:296–318.

Lublinskaya, A. D. 1968. *French Absolutism: The Crucial Phase, 1620–29*. Translated by B. Pearce. Cambridge: Cambridge Unversity Press.

Lucas, C. 1973. Nobles, Bourgeois, and the Origins of the French Revolution. *Past and Present*, no. 60, 84–126.

———. 1978. The Problem of the Midi in the French Revolution. *Transactions of the Royal Historical Society*, 5th ser., 28, 1–26.

Lucas, P. 1962. Blackstone and the Reform of the Legal Profession. *Economic History Review*, 2d ser., 77:456–496.

Lynch, J. 1981. *Spain under the Habsburgs*. 2d ed. 2 vols. New York: New York University Press.

Lyons, M. 1975. The 9 Thermidor: Motives and Effects. *European Studies Review* 5:123–146.

———. 1978. *Revolution in Toulouse*. Bern: Peter Lang.

Macaulay, T. B. 1913–1915. *History of England from the Accession of James II*. London: Macmillan.

MacCaffery, W. 1958. *Exeter, 1540–1640*. Cambridge, MA: Harvard University Press.

McCahill, M. W. 1981. Peerage Creations and the Changing Character of the British Nobility, 1750–1850. *Economic History Review* 96:259–284.

McCarthy, J. 1976. Nineteenth Century Egyptian Population. *Middle Eastern Studies* 12(3):1–40.

———. 1983. *Muslims and Minorities: The Population of Ottoman Anatolia and the End of the Empire.* New York: New York University Press.

McCloskey, D. 1975. The Economics of Enclosure: A Market Analysis. In *European Peasants and Their Markets*, edited by W. Parker and E. Jones, 123–160. Princeton: Princeton University Press.

———. 1985. The Industrial Revolution, 1780–1860: A Survey. In *The Economics of the Industrial Revolution*, edited by J. Mokyr, 53–74. Totowa, NJ: Rowman and Allanheld.

McDermott, J. P. 1981. Bondservants during the Late Ming. *Journal of Asian Studies* 40:675–702.

McDougall, W. A. 1986. "Mais ce n'est pas l'histoire." Some Thoughts on Toynbee, McNeill, and the Rest of Us. *Journal of Modern History* 58:19–42.

McEvedy, C., and R. Jones. 1978. *Atlas of World Population History.* Harmondsworth, Middlesex: Penguin.

McGiffert, M. 1980. Covenant, Crown, and Commons in Elizabethan Puritanism. *Journal of British Studies* 20:32–52.

McGowan, B. 1981. *Economic Life in Ottoman Europe.* Cambridge: Cambridge University Press.

Machiavelli, N. 1952. *The Prince.* Translated by W. K. Marriott. Chicago: Encyclopaedia Britannica Books.

McInnes, A. 1982. When Was the English Revolution? *History* 67:377–392.

McKendrick, N., J. Brewer, and J. H. Plumb. *The Birth of a Consumer Society: The Commercialization of Eighteenth Century England.* Bloomington: Indiana University Press.

McManners, J. 1960. *French Ecclesiastical Society under the Old Regime: A Study of Angers in the Eighteenth Century.* Manchester: Manchester University Press.

McNeill, W. 1977. *Plagues and Peoples.* New York: Doubleday.

———. 1982. *The Pursuit of Power.* Chicago: University of Chicago Press.

Macpherson, W. J. 1987. *The Economic Development of Japan, c. 1868–1914.* New York: Macmillan.

Maczaky, A. 1976. Money and Society in Poland and Lithuania in the Sixteenth and Seventeenth Centuries. *Journal of European Economic History* 1:69–104.

Maddalena, A. de. 1974. Rural Europe, 1500–1750. In *Fontana Economic History of Europe*, vol. 2: *The Sixteenth and Seventeenth Centuries*, edited by C. Cipolla, 273–353. Glasgow: Fontana/Collins.

Major, J. R. 1975. Henry IV and Guyenne: A Study Concerning Origins of Royal Absolutism. In *State and Society in Seventeenth Century France*, edited by R. Kierstead, 2–24. New York: New Viewpoints.

———. 1980. *Representative Government in Early Modern France.* New Haven: Yale University Press.

————. 1981. Noble Income, Inflation, and the Wars of Religion in France. *American Historical Review* 86:21–48.

Malowist, M. 1972. Movements of Expansion in Europe in the Sixteenth and Seventeenth Centuries. In *Economy and Society in Early Modern Europe: Essays from Annales*, edited by P. Burke, 104–112. London: Routledge and Kegan Paul.

Mandel, E. 1980. *Long Waves of Capitalist Development: The Marxist Interpretation*. Cambridge: Cambridge University Press.

Mandrou, R. 1978. *Louis XIV et son temps: 1661–1715*. 2d ed. Paris: Presses Universitaires de France.

Mann, M. 1986. *The Sources of Social Power*, vol. 1: *A History of Power from the Beginning to A. D. 1760*. Cambridge: Cambridge University Press.

————. 1988. *State, War and Capitalism*. Oxford: Basil Blackwell.

Manning, B. 1976. *The English People and the English Revolution, 1640–49*. London: Heinemann.

Mantelli, R. 1984. The Sale of Crown Lands in Spain in the Early Modern Era. *Journal of European Economic History* 13:201–205.

Mantoux, Paul. 1903. Histoire et sociologie. *Revue de Synthèse Historique* 1:121–140.

Mantran, R. 1962. *Istanbul dans la seconde moitié du XVIIe siècle*. Paris: Adrien Maisonneuve.

————. 1977. The Transformation of Trade in the Ottoman Empire in the Eighteenth Century. In *Studies in Eighteenth Century Islamic History*, edited by T. Naff and R. Owen, 217–220. Carbondale: Southern Illinois University Press.

————. 1980. Politique, économie et monnaie dans l'empire Ottoman au XVIIème siècle. In *Social and Economic History of Turkey, 1071–1920*, edited by O. Okyar and H. Inalcik, 123–125. Ankara: Hacettepe University Press.

————. 1984. *L'empire Ottoman du XVI au XVIII siècle: Administration, économie, société*. London: Variorum.

Marczewski, J. 1961. Some Aspects of the Economic Growth of France, 1660–1958. *Economic Development and Cultural Change* 9:369–387.

————. 1965. *Introduction à l'histoire quantitative*. Geneva: Droz.

Mardin, Şerif. 1969. Power, Civil Society, and Culture in the Ottoman Empire. *Comparative Studies in Society and History* 11:258–281.

Margadant, T. 1975. Modernisation and Insurgency in December 1951: A Case Study of the Drôme. In *Revolution and Reaction: 1848 and the Second French Republic*, edited by R. Price, 254–279. London: Croom Helm.

————. 1979. *French Peasants in Revolt: The Insurrection of 1851*. Princeton, NJ: Princeton University Press.

————. 1984. Tradition and Modernity in Rural France during the Nineteenth Century. *Journal of Modern History* 56:667–697.

Margerison, K. 1987. History, Representative Institutions, and Political Rights in the French Pre-Revolution (1787–89). *French Historical Studies* 15:68–98.

Marion, M. 1914. *Histoire financière de la France depuis 1715*. Paris: A. Rousseau.

Markoff, J. 1985. Rural Revolt and the French Revolution. *American Sociological Review* 50:761–782.

———. 1988. Peasant Grievances and Peasant Insurrection: France in 1789. Paper presented at the annual meeting of the American Sociological Association, Atlanta, GA.

Markoff, J., and G. Shapiro. 1985. Consensus and Conflict at the Onset of Revolution: A Quantitative Study of France in 1789. *American Journal of Sociology* 91:28–53.

Markovitch, T. 1970. The Dominant Sectors of French Industry. In *Essays in French Economic History*, edited by R. Cameron, 226–244. Homewood, IL: Richard D. Irwin.

———. 1976. *Histoire des industries françaises: les industries lainières de Colbert à la révolution*. Geneva: Droz.

Marks, R. 1984. *Rural Revolution in South China*. Madison: University of Wisconsin Press.

Marmé, M. 1981. Population and Possibility in Ming (1368–1644) Suzhou: A Quantified Model. *Ming Studies* 12:29–64.

Marx, K. 1935. *The Eighteenth Brumaire of Louis Napoleon*. New York: International Publishers.

———. 1964. *The Class Struggles in France, 1848–50*. New York: International Publishers.

Mathiez, A. 1928. *The French Revolution*. Translated by C. Phillips. New York: Knopf.

Matossian, M., and W. Schaefer. 1977. Family, Fertility, and Political Violence, 1700–1900. *Journal of Social History* 11:137–178.

Matthias, P., ed. 1972a. *Science and Society, 1600–1900*. Cambridge: Cambridge University Press.

———. 1972b. Who Unbound Prometheus? Science and Technical Change, 1600–1800. In *Science and Society, 1600–1900*, edited by P. Matthias, 54–80. Cambridge: Cambridge University Press.

———. 1979. The People's Money in the Eighteenth Century: The Royal Mint, Trade Tokens, and the Economy. In *The Transformation of England: Essays in the Economic and Social History of England in the Eighteenth Century*, edited by P. Matthias, 190–208. New York: Columbia University Press.

Matthias, P., and P. O'Brien. 1976. Taxation in Britain and France, 1715–1810: A Comparison of the Social and Economic Incidence of Taxes Collected for the Central Government. *Journal of European Economic History* 5:601–650.

Mauro, F., and G. Parker. 1977. Spain. In *An Introduction to the Sources of European Economic History, 1500–1800*, edited by C. Wilson and G. Parker, 37–62. Ithaca, NY: Cornell University Press.

Mayer, J. 1953. La croissance économique française: la structure de l'économie française à trois époques éloignées: 1788, 1845, 1885. In *Income and Wealth*, edited by M. Gilbert, 3d. ser., 67–100. Cambridge: Cambridge University Press.

Maza, S.C. 1983. *Servants and Masters in Eighteenth Century France: The Uses of Loyalty.* Princeton, NJ: Princeton University Press.

———. 1987. Le tribunal de la nation: les mémoires judiciaires et l'opinion publique à la fin de l'ancien régime. *Annales, E.S.C.* 42:73–90.

Mazauric, C. 1970. *Sur la révolution française: contributions à l'histoire de la révolution bourgeoise.* Paris: Editions Sociales.

Merriman, J. M. 1963. *Six Contemporaneous Revolutions.* Hamden, CT: Archon Books.

———. 1975a. The *Demoiselles* of the Ariège, 1829–31. In *1830 in France,* edited by J. Merriman, 87–118. New York: New Viewpoints.

———, ed. 1975b. *1830 in France.* New York: New Viewpoints.

———. 1978. *The Agony of the Republic: The Repression of the Left in Revolutionary France, 1848–51.* New Haven: Yale University Press.

Meskill, J., ed. 1965. *The Pattern of Chinese History: Cycle, Development, or Stagnation?* Boston: D.C. Heath.

———. 1982. *Academies in Ming China: An Historical Essay.* Tucson: University of Arizona Press.

Metzger, T. 1977. On the Historical Roots of Economic Modernization in China: The Increasing Differentiation of the Economy from the Polity during Late Ming and Early Ch'ing Times. In *Modern Chinese Economic History,* edited by C. Hou and T. Yu, 3–14. Taipei: Institute of Economics, Academia Sinica.

Meuvret, J. 1971. *Etudes d'histoire économique.* Paris: Armand Colin.

———. 1974. Monetary Circulation and the Use of Coinage in Sixteenth and Seventeenth Century France. In *Essays in European Economic History, 1500–1800,* edited by P. Earle, 89–99. Oxford: Clarendon Press.

———. 1976. Fiscalism and Public Order under Louis XIV. In *Louis XIV and Absolutism,* edited by R. Hatton, 199–225. London: Macmillan.

Meyer, J. 1977. La noblesse française au XVIIIe siècle: aperçu des problèmes. *Acta Poloniae Historica* 36:7–45.

———. 1978. La noblesse parlementaire bretonne face à la pré-révolution et aux débuts de la révolution: du témoignage à la statistique. In *Vom Ancien Régime zur Französischen Revolution,* edited by E. Hinrichs, E. Schmitt, and R. Vierhaus, 279–317. Göttingen: Vandenhoeck and Rupert.

———. 1984. Un destin de grand négociant: Descazaux du Halley. In *La France d'ancien régime: études réunies en l'honneur de Pierre Goubert,* edited by the Société de Démographie Historique, 2:463–470. Paris: Editions Privat.

Michael, F., and C. L. Chang. 1966. *The Taiping Rebellion: History and Documents.* 3 vols. Seattle: University of Washington Press.

Michelet, J. 1967. *History of the French Revolution.* Edited by G. Wright. Chicago: University of Chicago Press.

Migdal, J. S. 1974. *Peasants, Politics, and Revolution: Pressures toward Political and Social Change in the Third World.* Princeton, NJ: Princeton University Press.

Miller, J. 1979. The Later Stuart Monarchy. In *The Restored Monarchy, 1660–1688*, edited by J. R. Jones, 30–47. Totowa, NJ: Rowman and Littlefield.

———. 1982. Charles II and His Parliaments. *Transactions of the Royal Historical Society*, 5th ser., 32:1–23.

———. 1983. *The Glorious Revolution*. London: Longman.

———. 1984. The Potential for Absolutism in Late Stuart England. *History* 69:187–204.

———. 1987. *Bourbon and Stuart: Kings and Kingship in France and England in the Seventeenth Century*. New York: F. Watts.

Milward, A., and S. B. Saul. 1973. *The Economic Development of Continental Europe, 1780–1870*. London: Allen and Unwin.

Minchinton, W. E., ed. 1968. *Essays in Agrarian History*. 2 vols. New York: Augustus M. Kelley.

———, ed. 1969. *The Growth of English Overseas Trade: The Seventeenth and Eighteenth Centuries*. London: Methuen.

Mingay, G. E. 1961–1962. The Size of Farms in the 18th Century. *Economic History Review*, 2d ser., 14:469–488

———. 1972. The Transformation of Agriculture. In *The Long Debate on Poverty: Eight Essays on Industrialisation and the "Condition of England,"* edited by R. M. Hartwell, 23–57. London: Institute of Economic Affairs.

———. 1976. *The Gentry: The Rise and Fall of a Ruling Class*. London: Longman.

Miskimin, H. A. 1975. Population Growth and the Price Revolution in England. *Journal of European Economic History* 4:179–186.

———. 1977. *The Economy of Later Renaissance Europe, 1460–1600*. Cambridge: Cambridge University Press.

———. 1979. The Impact of Credit on Sixteenth Century English Industry. In *The Dawn of Modern Banking*, edited by the Center for Medieval and Renaissance Studies, UCLA, 275–289. New Haven: Yale University Press.

Mitchell, B. 1962. *English Historical Statistics*. Cambridge: Cambridge University Press.

———. 1975. *European Historical Statistics, 1750–1970*. London: Macmillan.

Mitchell, H. 1973. Counterrevolutionary Mentality and Popular Revolution: Two Case Studies. In *French Government and Society: Essays in Memory of Alfred Cobban*, edited by J. F. Bosher, 231–260. London: Athlone Press.

Mitchison, R. 1965. The Movement of Scottish Corn Prices in the Seventeenth and Eighteenth Centuries. *Economic History Review* 2d ser., 18:278–291.

Mokyr, J. 1985a. Demand versus Supply in the Industrial Revolution. In *The Economics of the Industrial Revolution*, edited by J. Mokyr, 97–118. Totowa, NJ: Rowman and Allenheld.

———, ed. 1985b. *The Economics of the Industrial Revolution*. Totowa, NJ: Rowman and Allanheld.

———. 1988. Is There Still Life in the Pessimist Case? Consumption during the Industrial Revolution, 1790–1850. *Journal of Economic History* 48:69–92.

Molinier, A. 1985. *Stagnations et croissance: le vivarais aux XVIIe-XVIIIe siècles*. Paris: Ecole des Hautes Etudes en Sciences Sociales.

Moller, H. 1964. Population and Society during the Old Regime, c. 1640–1770. In *Population Movements in Modern European History*, edited by H. Moller, 19–41. New York: Macmillan.

———. 1968. Youth as a Force in the Modern World. *Comparative Studies in Society and History* 10:238–260.

Moloughney, B. 1986. Silver, State, and Society: A Monetary Perspective in China's Seventeenth Century Crisis. M. A. thesis, University of Canterbury.

Moloughney, B., and W. Xia. 1989. Silver and the Fall of the Ming: A Reassessment. *Papers on Far Eastern History* (Australian National University) 40:51–78.

Mols, R. S. J. 1958. *Introduction à la demographie historique des villes d'Europe du XIV au XVIII siecle*. 3 vols. Louvain: Publications Universitaires de Louvain.

Mommsen, W. 1987. Personal Conduct and Societal Change: Toward a Reconstruction of Max Weber's Concept of History. In *Max Weber, Rationality, and Modernity*, edited by S. Lash and S. Whimster, 35–51. London: Allen and Unwin.

Monter, E. W. 1977. Historical Demography and Religious History in Sixteenth Century Geneva. *Journal of Interdisciplinary History* 9:399–927.

Moore, B., Jr. 1966. *Social Origins of Dictatorship and Democracy*. Boston: Beacon Press.

Moore, C. A., ed. 1967. *The Chinese Mind: Essentials of Chinese Philosophy and Culture*. Honolulu: East-West Center, University of Hawaii Press.

Moreau, J.-P. 1958. *La vie rurale dans le sud-est du bassin parisien*. Paris: Société des Belles Lettres.

Mori, M. 1980. The Gentry in the Ming Period: An Outline of the Relations between the *Shih-ta-fu* and Local Society. *Acta Asiatica* 38:31–53.

Morineau, M. 1968. D'Amsterdam à Seville: de quel réalité l'histoire de prix est-elle le miroir? *Annales, E.S.C.* 23:178–205.

———. 1970a. *Les faux-semblants d'un démarrage économique: agriculture et démographie en France au XVIII siècle*. Paris: Armand Colin.

———. 1970b. Was There an Agricultural Revolution in 18th Century France? In *Essays in French Economic History*, edited by R. Cameron, 170–182. Homewood, IL: Richard D. Irwin.

———. 1976. The Agricultural Revolution in Nineteenth Century France: A Comment. *Journal of Economic History* 36:436–437.

———. 1977. France. In *An Introduction to the Sources of European Economic History*, edited by C. Wilson and G. Parker, 155–189. Ithaca, NY: Cornell University Press.

———. 1978. Trois contributions au colloque de Göttingen. In *Vom Ancien Régime zur Französischen Revolution*, edited by E. Hinrichs, E. Schmitt, and R. Vierhaus, 374–419. Göttingen: Vandenhoeck and Rupert.

———. 1980. Budgets de l'état et gestation des finances royales en France au dix-huitième siècle. *Revue Historique* 264:289–336.

———. 1981. History and Tithes. *Journal of European Economic History* 10:437–480.

———. 1985. *Incroyables gazettes et fabuleaux métaux.* Cambridge: Cambridge University Press.

Mornet, D. 1933. *Les origines intellectuelles de la révolution française 1715-1787.* Paris: Armand Colin.

Morrill, J. S. 1974. *Cheshire, 1630–1660: County Government and Society during the English Revolution.* Oxford: Oxford University Press.

———. 1976. *The Revolt of the Provinces: Conservatives and Radicals in the English Civil War, 1630–1650.* London: Allen and Unwin.

Mote, F. W. 1961. The Growth of Chinese Despotism: A Critique of Wittfogel's Theory of Oriental Despotism as Applied to China. *Oriens Extremus* 8:1–41.

———. 1971. *Intellectual Foundations of China.* New York: Knopf.

Mote, F. W., and D. Twitchett, eds. 1988. *The Cambridge History of China,* vol. 7: *The Ming Dynasty, 1368–1644.* Cambridge: Cambridge University Press.

Moulder, F. V. 1977. *Japan, China, and the Modern World Economy: Toward a Reinterpretation of East Asian Development, ca. 1600 to ca. 1918.* Cambridge: Cambridge University Press.

Mousnier, R. 1951. L'évolution des finances publiques en France et en Angleterre pendent les guerres de la Ligue d'Augsbourg et de la succession d'Espagne. *Revue Historique* 205:1–23.

———. 1970a. The Fronde. In *The Preconditions of Revolution in Early Modern Europe,* edited by J. Greene and R. Forster, 131–159. Baltimore, MD: Johns Hopkins University Press.

———. 1970b. *Peasant Uprisings in Seventeenth Century France, Russia, and China.* Translated by B. Pearce. New York: Harper and Row.

———. 1973. *Social Hierarchies, 1450 to the Present,* edited by M. Clarke. Translated by P. Evans. London: Croom Helm.

———. 1977. *Conjoncture* and Circumstance in Popular Uprisings. In *The Peasantry in the Old Regime,* edited by I. Woloch, 52–58. Huntington, NY: Robert E. Krieger.

———. 1979. *The Institutions of France under the Absolute Monarchy, 1598–1789.* Translated by B. Pearce. 2 vols. Chicago: University of Chicago Press.

———. 1982. Les fidelités et les clientèles en France aux XVIe, XVIIe, et XVIIIe siècles. *Histoire Sociale* 15:35–46.

———. 1984. Quelques remarques pour une comparaison des monarchies absolues en Europe et en Asie. *Revue Historique* 551:29–44.

Moutafchieva, V. P. 1988. *Agrarian Relations in the Ottoman Empire in the 15th and 16th Centuries.* New York: Columbia University Press.

Murphey, R. 1980. The Construction of a Fortress at Mosul in 1631. In *Social and Economic History of Turkey, 1071–1920,* edited by O. Okyar and H. Inalcik, 163–172. Ankara: Hacettepe University Press.

———. 1983. The Ottoman Attitude toward the Adoption of Western Technology: The Role of the *Efrence* Technicians in Civil and Military Applications. In *Contributions à l'histoire économique et sociale de l'empire Ottoman,* edited by Ö. L. Barkan, 287–298. Louvain: Editions Peeters.

Myers, R. 1974. Some Issues on Economic Organization during the Ming and Ch'ing Periods: A Review Article. *Ch'ing shih wen-t'i* 3(2):77–93.

———. 1982. Customary Law, Markets, and Resource Transactions in Late Imperial China. In *Explorations in the New Economic History*, edited by R. L. Ransom, R. Sutch, and G. M. Walton, 273–298. New York: Academic Press.

———. 1980. *The Chinese Economy, Past and Present.* Belmont, CA: Wadsworth.

Nadal, J. 1984. *La población española (siglos XVI a XX).* Edición corregida y aumentada. Barcelona: Editorial Ariel.

Nader, H. 1977. Noble Income in Sixteenth Century Castile: The Case of the Marquises of Mondéjar, 1480–1580. *Economic History Review*, 2d ser., 30:411–428.

Naff, T. 1977. The Central Administration, the Provinces, and External Relations: Introduction. In *Studies in Eighteenth Century Islamic History*, edited by T. Naff and R. Owen, 3–14. Carbondale: Southern Illinois University Press.

Nagata, Y. 1976. *Some Documents on the Big Farms of the Notables in Western Anatolia.* Tokyo: Institute for the Study of Languages and Culture of Asia and Africa.

Namboodiri, Krishnan. 1988. Ecological Demography: Its Place in Sociology. *American Sociological Review* 53:619–633.

Namier, L. B. 1959. 1848: Seed Plot of History. In *1848: A Turning Point?* edited by M. Kranzberg, 64–70. Boston: D.C. Heath.

———. 1964. *The Revolution of the Intellectuals.* Garden City, NY: Anchor Books.

Naquin, S. 1976. *Millenarian Rebellion in China: The Eight Trigrams Uprising of 1813.* New Haven: Yale University Press.

Naquin, S., and E. S. Rawski. 1987. *Chinese Society in the Eighteenth Century.* New Haven: Yale University Press.

Needham, J., and R. Huang. 1974. The Nature of Chinese Society: A Technical Interpretation. *Journal of Oriental Studies* 12:1–16.

Neveux, H. 1980. *Vie et déclin d'une structure économique: les grains du Cambrésis, fin du XIVe-debut du XVIIe siècle.* Paris: Ecole des Hautes Etudes en Sciences Sociales.

———. 1984. La gestion des grandes fermes du bassin parisien, XIVe-XVIe siècles: problèmes d'une difficile synthèse. In *La France d'ancien régime: études réunies en l'honneur de Pierre Goubert*, edited by the Société de Démographie Historique, 2:491–496. Paris: Editions Privat.

Newell, W. H. 1973. The Agricultural Revolution in Nineteenth Century France. *Journal of Economic History* 33:697–731.

———. 1977. *Population Change and Agricultural Development in Nineteenth Century France.* New York: Arrow Press.

Newman, E. L. 1975. What the Crowd Wanted in the French Revolution of 1830. In *1830 in France*, edited by J. Merriman, 17–40. New York: New Viewpoints.

Nichols, E. 1986. Skocpol on Revolution: Comparative Analysis vs. Historical Conjuncture. *Comparative Social Research* 9:163–186.

Nières, C. 1984. Une province et ses villes: la Bretagne au XVIIIe siècle. In *La France d'ancien régime: études réunies en l'honneur de Pierre Goubert*, edited by the Société de Démographie Historique, 2:509–517. Paris: Editions Privat.

Nishijima, S. 1984. The Formation of the Early Chinese Cotton Industry. In *State and Society in China: Japanese Perspectives on Ming-Qing Social and Economic History*, edited by L. Grove and C. Daniels, 17–77. Tokyo: University of Tokyo Press.

Nishikawa, S. 1986. Grain Consumption: The Case of Choshu. In *Japan in Transition: From Tokugawa to Meiji*, edited by M. B. Jansen and G. Rozman, 421–466. Princeton, NJ: Princeton University Press.

Norden, J. 1607. *The Surveyor's Dialogue*. London: H. Astley.

North, D. 1981. *Structure and Change in Economic History*. New York: Norton.

North, R. C., and N. Choucri. 1975. *Nations in Conflict: National Growth and International Violence*. San Francisco: W. H. Freeman.

Oberschall, A. 1973. *Social Conflict and Social Movements*. Englewood Cliffs, NJ: Prentice-Hall.

O'Boyle, L. 1966. The Middle Class in Western Europe. *American Historical Review* 71:826–845.

———. 1970. The Problem of an Excess of Educated Men in Western Europe, 1800–1850. *Journal of Modern History* 42:471–495.

O'Brien, P. 1977. Agriculture and the Industrial Revolution. *Economic History Review*, 2d ser., 30:166–181.

———. 1988. The Political Economy of British Taxation, 1660–1818. *Economic History Review*, 2d ser., 41:411–432.

O'Brien, P., and Ç. Keyder. 1978. *Economic Growth in Britain and France: Two Paths to the Twentieth Century*. London: Allen and Unwin.

Okyar, O. 1980. Ottoman Economic Growth during the Sixteenth Century. In *Social and Economic History of Turkey, 1071–1920*, edited by O. Okyar and H. Inalcik, 111–116. Ankara: Hacettepe University Press.

Olson, M. 1965. *The Logic of Collective Action*. Cambridge, MA: Harvard University Press.

———. 1982. *The Rise and Decline of Nations*. New Haven: Yale University Press.

Ooms, H. 1985. *Tokugawa Ideology*. Princeton, NJ: Princeton University Press.

Outhwaite, R. B. 1969. *Inflation in Tudor and Early Stuart England*. London: Macmillan.

Overbeek, J. 1974. *History of Population Theories*. Rotterdam: Rotterdam University Press.

Overmyer, Daniel L. 1984. Attitudes toward the Ruler and State in Chinese Popular Religion Literature: Sixteenth and Seventeenth Century *Pao-Chüan*, *Harvard Journal of Asiatic Studies* 44:347–379.

Overton, M. 1979. Estimating Crop Yields from Probate Inventories: An Example from East Anglia, 1585–1735. *Journal of Economic History* 39:363–378.

———. 1983. An Agricultural Revolution, 1650–1750. Paper presented at the Economic History Society Conference, Canterbury, U.K.

Owen, R. 1975. The Middle East in the Eighteenth Century. *Review of Middle East Studies* 1:101–112.

———. 1977. Resources, Population, and Wealth: Introduction. In *Studies in Eighteenth Century Islamic History*, edited by T. Naff and R. Owen, 133–151. Carbondale: Southern Illinois University Press.

———. 1981. *The Middle East in the World Economy, 1800–1914*. London: Methuen.

Ozouf, M. 1984. War and Terror in French Revolutionary Discourse. *Journal of Modern History* 56:579–597.

Paas, M. W. 1981. *Population Change, Labor Supply, and Agriculture in Augsberg 1480–1618*. New York: Arno Press.

Pach, Z. P. 1972. Sixteenth Century Hungary: Commercial Activity and Market Production by the Nobles. In *Economy and Society in Early Modern Europe: Essays from Annales*, edited by P. Burke, 113–133. London: Routledge and Kegan Paul.

Paige, J. M. 1975. *Agrarian Revolution: Social Movements and Export Agriculture in the Underdeveloped World*. New York: Free Press.

Palliser, D. M. 1983. *The Age of Elizabeth: England under the Later Tudors, 1547–1603*. London: Longman.

Palmer, R. R. 1959–1964. *The Age of the Democratic Revolution*. 2 vols. Princeton, NJ: Princeton University Press.

———. 1977. Lefebvre's Interpretation of the Peasant Revolution. In *The Peasantry in the Old Regime: Conditions and Protests*, edited by I. Woloch, 98–103. Huntington, NY: Robert E. Krieger.

———. 1985. *The Improvement of Humanity: Education and the French Revolution*. Princeton, NJ: Princeton University Press.

Parker, D. 1983. *The Making of French Absolutism*. New York: St. Martin's Press.

Parker, G. 1974. The Emergence of Modern Finance in Europe, 1500–1730. In *The Fontana Economic History of Europe*, vol. 2: *The Sixteenth and Seventeenth Centuries*, edited by C. Cipolla, 527–594. Glasgow: Collins/Fontana.

———. 1976. The Military Revolution, 1560–1660: A Myth? *Journal of Modern History* 48:195–214.

———. 1979. *Europe in Crisis, 1598–1648*. Ithaca, NY: Cornell University Press.

Parker, G., and L. Smith, eds. 1978. *The General Crisis of the Seventeenth Century*. London: Routledge and Kegan Paul.

Parker, W. L. 1984. *Europe, America, and the Wider World: Essays on the Economic History of Western Capitalism*, vol. 1: *Europe and the World Economy*. Cambridge: Cambridge University Press.

Parry, J. H. 1963. *The Age of Reconnaissance*. London: Weidenfeld and Nicolson.

Parry, V. 1976. The Period of Murad IV, 1617–1648. In *A History of the Ot-*

toman Empire to 1730, edited by M. A. Cook, 133–156. Cambridge: Cambridge University Press.

Parry, V., and M. E. Yapp, eds., 1975. *War, Technology, and Society in the Middle East*. London: Oxford University Press.

Parsons, J. B. 1963. The Ming Dynasty Bureaucracy: Aspects of Background Forces. *Monumenta Serica* 22:343–406.

———. 1969. The Ming Dynasty Bureaucracy: Aspects of Background Forces. In *Chinese Government in Ming Times: Seven Studies*, edited by C. O. Hucker, 175–231. New York: Columbia University Press.

———. 1970. *Peasant Rebellions of the Late Ming Dynasty*. Tucson: University of Arizona Press.

Parsons, T. 1937. *The Structure of Social Action*. New York: Free Press.

Patten, J. 1978. *English Towns, 1500–1700*. Hamden, CT: Archon Books.

Pearce, B. 1942. Elizabethan Food Policy and the Armed Forces. *Economic History Review*, 2d ser., 12:39–46.

Pearl, V. 1961. *London and the Outbreak of the Puritan Revolution*. Oxford: Oxford University Press.

Pennington, D. H. 1970. *Seventeenth Century Europe*. London: Longman.

Perdue, P. C. 1982. Water Control in the Dongting Lake Region during the Ming and Qing Periods. *Journal of Asian Studies* 41:747–765.

———. 1987. *Exhausting the Earth: State and Peasant in Hunan, 1500–1850*. Cambridge, MA: Council on East Asian Studies.

Perkin, H. 1969. *The Origins of Modern English Society, 1780–1880*. London: Routledge and Kegan Paul.

Perkins, D. D. 1967. Government as an Obstacle to Industrialization: The Case of Nineteenth Century China. *Journal of Economic History* 27:478–492.

———. 1969. *Agricultural Development in China, 1368–1968*. Chicago: Aldine.

———, ed. 1975. *China's Modern Economy in Historical Perspective*. Stanford: Stanford University Press.

Perrenoud, A. 1985. Le biologique et l'humain dans le déclin séculaire de la mortalité. *Annales, E.S.C.* 40:113–135.

Perrot, J.-C., and S. J. Woolf. 1984. *State and Statistics in France, 1789–1815*. New York: Harwood Academic Publishers.

Perroux, F. 1955. Prise de vue sur la croissance de l'économie française, 1780–1950. *Income and Wealth* 5:41–78.

Petersen, E. L. 1967. *The Crisis of the Danish Nobility, 1580–1660*. Odense, Denmark: Odense University Press.

Peterson, W. P. 1975. Fang I-chih: Western Learning and the Investigation of Things. In *The Unfolding of Neoconfucianism*, edited by W. T. deBary, 369–411. New York: Columbia University Press.

———. 1976. From Interest to Indifference: Fang I-chih and Western Learning. *Ching shih wen-t'i* 3(5):72–85.

———. 1979. *Bitter Gourd: Fang I-chih and the Impetus for Intellectual Change*. New Haven: Yale University Press.

———. 1980. Chinese Scientific Philosophy and Some Attitudes Toward

Knowledge about the Realm of Heaven and Earth. *Past and Present*, no. 87, 20–30.

Phelps Brown, E. H., and S. Hopkins. 1957. Wage Rates and Prices: Evidence for Population Pressure in the Sixteenth Century. *Economica*, n.s., 24: 289–306.

———. 1962a. Seven Centuries of Building Wages. In *Essays in Economic History*, edited by E. Carus-Wilson, 2:168–178. London: Edward Arnold.

———. 1962b. Seven Centuries of the Prices of Consumables, Compared with Builders' Wage-Rates. In *Essays in Economic History*, edited by E. Carus-Wilson, 2:179–196. London: Edward Arnold.

Phillips, W. D. 1978. State Service in Fifteenth Century Castile: A Statistical Study of Royal Appointees. *Societas* 8:115–136.

Pike, R. 1972. *Aristocrats and Traders: Sevillian Society in the Sixteenth Century*. Ithaca, NY: Cornell University Press.

Pinand, P.-F. 1982. La recette des finances, 1789–1865: essai d'histoire administrative. *Revue d'Histoire Moderne et Contemporaine* 29:584–598.

Pinkney, D. H. 1964. The Crowd in the French Revolution of 1830. *American Historical Review* 70:1–17.

———. 1972. *The French Revolution of 1830*. Princeton, NJ: Princeton University Press.

———. 1986. *Decisive Years in France: 1840–1847*. Princeton, NJ: Princeton University Press.

Plaks, A. 1985. After the Fall: Hsing-shih Yin-yuan Chuan and the Seventeenth Century Chinese Novel. *Harvard Journal of Asiatic Studies* 45:543–580.

Plato. 1952. *The Laws*. Translated by B. Jowett. Chicago: Britannica Great Books.

Plumb, J. H. 1967. *The Growth of Stability in England, 1675–1725*. London: Macmillan.

Pocock, J. G. A. 1975. *The Machiavellian Moment: Florentine Political Thought and the Atlantic Republican Tradition*. Princeton, NJ: Princeton University Press.

Polk, W. R., and R. L. Chambers. 1968. *The Beginnings of Modernization in the Middle East: The Nineteenth Century*. Chicago: University of Chicago Press.

Poos, L. R. 1985. The Rural Population of Essex in the Later Middle Ages. *Economic History Review*, 2d ser., 38:515–530.

Popkin, S. 1979. *The Rational Peasant: The Political Economy of Rural Society in Vietnam*. Berkeley and Los Angeles: University of California Press.

Porch, D. 1974. *Army and Revolution: France, 1815–1848*. London: Routledge and Kegan Paul.

Porchnev, B. 1963. *Les soulèvements populaires en France de 1623 à 1648*. Paris: SEVPEN.

Post, J. D. 1977. *The Last Great Subsistence Crisis in the Western World*. Baltimore: Johns Hopkins University Press.

———. 1985. *Food Shortage, Climatic Variability, and Epidemic Disease in Preindustrial Europe: The Mortality Peak in the Early 1740's*. Ithaca, NY: Cornell University Press.

Postan, M. M. 1972. *The Medieval Economy and Society*. Harmondsworth, Middlesex: Penguin.

Postan, M. M., and J. Hatcher. 1978. Population and Class Relations in Feudal Society. *Past and Present*, no. 78, 24–37.

Pound, J. 1971. *Poverty and Vagrancy in Tudor England*. Essex: Longman.

Pounds, N.J. 1979. *An Historical Geography of Europe, 1500–1840*. Cambridge: Cambridge University Press.

Poussou, J.-P. 1980. Les crises démographiques en milieu urbain: l'exemple de Bordeaux (fin XVIIe-fin XVIIIe siècle). *Annales, E.S.C.* 35:235–252.

Prall, S. E. 1972. *The Bloodless Revolution: England, 1688*. New York: Anchor Books.

Prest, W. 1972. *The Inns of Court under Elizabeth I and the Early Stuarts, 1590–1640*. London: Longman.

———. 1986. *The Rise of the Barristers: A Social History of the English Bar*. Oxford: Clarendon Press.

Price, R. 1972. *The French Second Republic: A Social History*. Ithaca, NY: Cornell University Press.

———. 1975a. Introduction. In *1848 in France*, edited by R. Price, 11–51. Ithaca, NY: Cornell University Press.

———, ed. 1975b. *Revolution and Reaction: 1848 and the Second French Republic*. London: Croom Helm.

———. 1981. *An Economic History of Modern France, 1730–1914*. London: Macmillan.

———. 1983a. *The Modernization of Rural France*. New York: St. Martin's Press.

———. 1983b. Poor Relief and Social Crisis in Mid-Nineteenth Century France. *European Studies Review* 13:423–454.

Prost, A. 1968. *Histoire de l'enseignement en France, 1800–1967*. Paris: Armand Colin.

Protho, I. 1979. *Artisans and Politics in Early Nineteenth Century London*. Folkestone, Kent: Harvester Press.

Prussia. Statistisches Bureau zu Berlin. 1849. *Tabellen und amtliche Nachrichten über den Preussischen Staat für das Jahr 1849*. Berlin: Druck und Verlag.

Pyle, K. B. 1988. Meiji Conservatism. In *The Cambridge History of Japan*, vol. 5: *The Nineteenth Century*, edited by M. B. Jansen, 674–720. Cambridge: Cambridge University Press.

Pythian-Adams, C. 1978. Urban Decay in Late Medieval England. In *Towns in Societies: Essays in Economic History and Historical Sociology*, edited by P. Abrams and E. A. Wrigley, 159–186. Cambridge: Cambridge University Press.

———. 1979. *Desolation of a City: Coventry and the Urban Crisis of the Late Middle Ages*. Cambridge: Cambridge University Press.

Qian, W-Y. 1985. *The Great Inertia: Scientific Stagnation in Traditional China*. London: Croom Helm.

Rabb, T. K. 1962. The Effect of the Thirty Years War on the German Economy. *Journal of Modern History* 34:40–51.

————. 1975. *The Struggle for Stability in Early Modern Europe*. New York: Oxford University Press.

————. 1981. Revisionism Revised: The Role of the Commons. *Past and Present*, no. 92, 55–78.

Ragin, C. C. 1987. *The Comparative Method: Moving beyond Qualitative and Quantitative Strategies*. Berkeley and Los Angeles: University of California Press.

Ramsey, P., ed. 1971. *The Price Revolution in Sixteenth Century England*. London: Methuen.

Rawski, E. S. 1972. *Agricultural Change and the Peasant Economy of South China*. Cambridge, MA: Harvard University Press.

Raymond, A. 1972. Les grandes épidémies de peste au Caïre aux XVIIe et XVIIIe siècles. *Bulletin d'Etudes Orientales* 25:203–210.

————. 1981. The Economic Crisis of Egypt in the Eighteenth Century. In *The Islamic Middle East, 700–1900: Studies in Economic and Social History*, edited by A. L. Udovitch, 687–707. Princeton, NJ: Darwin Press.

Rebaudo, D. 1979. Le mouvement annuel de la population française rurale de 1670 à 1740. *Population* 34:589–606.

Reinhard, M., A. Armengaud, and J. Dupâquier. 1968. *Histoire générale de la population mondiale*. Paris: Editions Montchrestien.

Reischauer, E. O., and J. K. Fairbank. 1960. *East Asia: The Great Tradition*. Boston: Houghton Mifflin.

Rejai, M., and K. Phillips. 1979. *Leaders of Revolution*. Beverly Hills, CA: Sage.

————. 1983. *World Revolutionary Leaders*. New Brunswick, NJ: Rutgers University Press.

Richards, J. F., ed. 1983. *Precious Metals in the Late Medieval and Early Modern World*. Durham, NC: Carolina Academic Press.

Richardson, R. C. 1973. Puritanism and the Ecclesiastical Authorities in the Case of the Diocese of Chester. In *Politics, Religion, and the English Civil War*, edited by B. Manning, 3–36. New York: St. Martin's Press.

————. 1977 *The Debate on the English Revolution*. London: Methuen.

Richet, D. 1970. Economic Growth and Its Setbacks in France from the Fifteenth to the Eighteenth Centuries. In *Essays in French Economic History*, edited by R. Cameron, 180–211. Homewood, IL: Richard D. Irwin.

Riley, J. 1984. Monetary Growth and Price Stability: France, 1650–1700. *Journal of Interdisciplinary History* 15:235–254.

————. 1986. *The Seven Years' War and the Old Regime in France: The Economic and Financial Toll*. Princeton, NJ: Princeton University Press.

————. 1987. French Finances, 1727–68. *Journal of Modern History* 59:209–243.

Riley, J., and J. McCusker. 1983. Money Supply, Economic Growth, and the Quantity Theory of Money: France, 1650–1788. *Explorations in Economic History* 20:274–293.

Ringrose, D. R. 1983. *Madrid and the Spanish Economy, 1560–1850*. Berkeley and Los Angeles: University of California Press.

Roberts, B. K. 1973. Field Systems of the West Midlands. In *Studies of Field*

Systems in the British Isles, edited by A. Baker and R. Butlin, 188–231. Cambridge: Cambridge University Press.

Roberts, C. 1977a. The Earl of Bedford and the Coming of the English Revolution. *Journal of Modern History* 49:600–616.

———. 1977b. The Constitutional Significance of the Financial Settlement of 1690. *Historical Journal* 20:59–76.

Roberts, J. M. 1978. *The French Revolution.* Oxford: Oxford University Press.

Roberts, M. 1973. *Sweden's Age of Greatness, 1632–1718.* New York: St. Martin's Press.

Robin, R. 1970. *La société française en 1789: Semur-en-Auxois.* Paris: Plon.

Roche, Daniel. 1979. Nouveaux Parisiens au XVIIIe siècle. *Cahiers d'Histoire* 24:3–20.

———. 1987. Académie et politique au siècle des lumières: les enjeux practiques de l'immortalité. In *The French Revolution and the Creation of Modern Political Culture,* edited by K. M. Baker, 1:331–343. Oxford: Pergamon Press.

Roden, D. 1973. Field Systems of the Chiltern Hills and Their Environs. In *Studies of Field Systems in the British Isles,* edited by A. Baker and R. Butlin, 325–376. Cambridge: Cambridge University Press.

Roebuck, P. 1980. *Yorkshire Baronets, 1640–1760: Families, Estates, and Fortunes.* Oxford: Oxford University Press.

Roehl, R. 1976. French Industrialization: A Reconsideration. *Explorations in Economic History* 13:233–281.

Romano, R. 1978. Between the Sixteenth and Seventeenth Centuries. In *The General Crisis of the Seventeenth Century,* edited by G. Parker and L. Smith, 165–225. London: Routledge and Kegan Paul.

Ronan, C. A. and J. Needham. 1981. *The Shorter Science and Civilization in China.* 2 vols. Cambridge: Cambridge University Press.

Root, H. 1982. En Bourgogne: l'état et la communauté rurale, 1661–1789. *Annales, E.S.C.* 37:288–302.

———. 1985. Challenging the Seigneurie: Community and Contention on the Eve of the French Revolution. *Journal of Modern History* 57:652–681.

———. 1987. *Peasants and King in Burgundy: Agrarian Foundations of French Absolutism.* Berkeley and Los Angeles: University of California Press.

Ropp, P. S. 1981. *Dissent in Early Modern China and Ch'ing Social Criticism.* Ann Arbor: University of Michigan Press.

Rosenbaud, L. N. 1985. Productivity and Labor Discipline in the Montgolfier Paper Mill, 1780–1805. *Journal of Economic History* 45:435–443.

Rosenberg, H. 1958. *Bureaucracy, Aristocracy, and Autocracy: The Prussian Experience, 1660–1815.* Boston: Beacon Press.

Rosenberg, N. 1969. The Direction of Technological Change. *Economic Development and Cultural Change* 17:1–24.

———. 1971. *The Economics of Technological Change.* Harmondsworth, Middlesex: Penguin.

———. 1982. *Inside the Black Box: Technology and Economics.* Cambridge: Cambridge University Press.

Rosenheim, J. M. 1989. County Governance and Elite Withdrawal in Norfolk,

1660- 1720. In *The First Modern Society: Essays in English History in Honour of Lawrence Stone*, edited by A. L. Beier, D. Cannadine, and J. M. Rosenheim, 95–125. Cambridge: Cambridge University Press.

Rossabi, M. 1979. Muslim and Central Asian Revolts. In *From Ming to Ch'ing: Conquest, Region, and Continuity in Seventeenth Century China*, edited by J. D. Spence and J. E. Wills, Jr., 167–200. New Haven: Yale University Press.

Rowe, W. T. 1985. Approaches to Modern Chinese Social History. In *Reliving the Past: The Worlds of Social History*, edited by O. Zunz, 236–296. Chapel Hill: University of North Carolina Press.

Rowley, T., ed. 1981. *The Origins of Open Field Agriculture*. London: Croom Helm.

Rowney, D. K. 1982. Structure, Class, and Career: The Problem of Bureaucracy and Society in Russia, 1801–1917. *Social Science History* 6:87–110.

Rozman, G., ed. 1981. *Modernization of China*. New York: Free Press.

———. 1982. *Population and Marketing Settlements in Ch'ing China*. New York: Cambridge University Press.

———. 1988. Social Change. In *The Cambridge History of Japan*, vol. 5: *The Nineteenth Century*, edited by M. B. Jansen, 499–568. Cambridge: Cambridge University Press.

Rubinger, R. 1986. Education: From One Room to One System. In *Japan in Transition: From Tokugawa to Meiji*, edited by M. B. Jansen and G. Rozman, 195–230. Princeton, NJ: Princeton University Press.

Rubinstein, W. D. 1983. The End of "Old Corruption," 1780–1860. *Past and Present*, no. 101, 55–86.

Rudé, G. 1964. *The Crowd in History: A Study of Popular Disturbances in France and England 1730–1848*. New York: Riley.

———. 1971. The Preindustrial Crowd. In *Paris and London in the Eighteenth Century*, edited by G. Rudé, 17–34. New York: Viking Press.

———. 1972. *Debate on Europe, 1815–1850*. New York: Harper and Row.

———. 1973. The Growth of Cities and Popular Revolt, 1750–1850, with Particular Reference to Paris. In *French Government and Society: Essays in Memory of Alfred Cobban*, edited by J. F. Bosher, 166–190. London: Athlone Press.

———. 1975. The Outbreak of the French Revolution. In *The Social Origins of the French Revolution*, edited by R. Greenlaw, 3–16. Lexington, MA: D.C. Heath.

———. 1980. *Ideology and Popular Protest*. New York: Pantheon Books.

Rule, J., and C. Tilly. 1972. 1830 and the Unnatural History of Revolution. *Journal of Social Issues* 28:49–76.

———. 1975. Political Process in Revolutionary France, 1830–32. In *1830 in France*, edited by J. Merriman, 41–85. New York: New Viewpoints.

Russell, C., ed. 1973. *The Origins of the English Civil War*. London: Macmillan.

———. 1979. *Parliaments and English Politics*. Oxford: Clarendon Press.

———. 1982. Monarchies, Wars, and Estates in England, France, and Spain, c. 1580–c. 1640. *Legislative Studies Quarterly* 7:205–220.

———. 1987. The British Problem and the English Civil War. *History* 72:395–415.

————. 1988. The British Background to the Irish Rebellion of 1641. *Historical Research* 61:166–182.

Ruttan, V. 1978. Structural Retardation and the Modernization of French Agriculture: A Skeptical View. *Journal of Economic History* 38:714–728.

Sagarra, E. 1980. *An Introduction to Nineteenth Century Germany*. London: Longman.

Sahillioğlu, H. 1983. The Role of International Monetary and Metal Movements in Ottoman Monetary History, 1300–1750. In *Precious Metals in the Later Medieval and Early Modern World*, edited by J. F. Richards, 269–304. Durham, NC: Carolina Academic Press.

Saint-Jacob, P. 1960. *Les paysans de la Bourgogne du nord au dernier siècle de l'ancien régime*. Paris: Société des Belles Lettres.

Saito, O. 1986. The Rural Economy: Commercial Agriculture, By-Employment, and Wage-Work. In *Japan in Transition: From Tokugawa to Meiji*, edited by M. B. Jansen and G. Rozman, 400–420. Princeton, NJ: Princeton University Press.

Sakai, T. 1970. Confucianism and Popular Educational Works. In *Self and Society in Ming Thought*, edited by W. T. deBary, 331–366. New York: Columbia University Press.

Salmon, J. H. M. 1981. Storm over the Noblesse. *Journal of Modern History* 53:242–255.

Sayer, D. 1985. This Scepter'd Isle: State Formation and the Making of the English Ruling Class: An Argument. Glasgow University. Typescript.

Scarritt, J. Forthcoming. Zimbabwe: Revolutionary Violence Resulting in Reform. In *Revolutions of the Late 20th Century*, edited by J. A. Goldstone, T. R. Gurr, and F. Moshiri. Boulder, CO: Westview Press.

Schalk, E. 1976. The Appearance and Reality of Nobility in France during the Wars of Religion: An Example of How Collective Attitudes Can Change. *Journal of Modern History* 48:19–31.

————. 1982. Ennoblement in France from 1350 to 1660. *Journal of Social History* 16:101–110.

Schama, S. 1989. *Citizens: A Chronicle of the French Revolution*. New York: Knopf.

Scheaper, T. 1980. *The Economy of France in the Second Half of the Reign of Louis XIV*. Montreal: Interuniversity Center for European Studies.

Schelling, T. C. 1960. *The Strategy of Conflict*. London: Oxford University Press.

Schmookler, J. 1971. Economic Sources of Inventive Activity. In *The Economics of Technological Change*, edited by N. Rosenberg, 117–136. Harmondsworth, Middlesex: Penguin.

Schofield, R. S. 1964. King, Parliament, and Society under the Tudors: The Question of Taxation. Cambridge University. Typescript.

————. 1976. The Relationship between Demographic Structure and Environment in Pre-industrial Western Europe. In *Sozialgeschichte der Familie in der Neuzeit Europas*, edited by W. Conze, 147–160. Stuttgart: Ernst Klett.

————. 1988. Taxation and the Political Limits of the Tudor State. In *Law and Government under the Stuarts*, edited by C. Cross, D. Loads, and J. J. Scarisbrick, 227–256. Cambridge: Cambridge University Press.

Schumpeter, J. A. 1934. *The Theory of Economic Development*. Oxford: Oxford University Press.

——. 1939. *Business Cycles*. 2 vols. New York: McGraw-Hill.

Schwartz, B. 1959. Foreword. In C. C. Liang, *Intellectual Trends in the Ch'ing Period*, translated by I. C. Y. Hsu. Cambridge, MA: Harvard University Press.

Schwartz, L. D. 1985. The Standard of Living in the Long Run: London, 1700–1860. *Economic History Review*, 2d ser., 38:24–41.

Schwartz, R. M. 1988. *Policing the Poor in Eighteenth Century France*. Chapel Hill: University of North Carolina Press.

Schwarz, M. L. 1982. Lay Anglicanism and the Crisis of the English Church in the Early Seventeenth Century. *Albion* 14:1–19.

Schwoerer, L. G. 1981. *The Declaration of Rights, 1689*. Baltimore, MD: Johns Hopkins University Press.

Scott, J. C. 1976. *The Moral Economy of the Peasant*. New Haven: Yale University Press.

——. 1985. *Weapons of the Weak*. New Haven: Yale University Press.

Scott, S. 1978. *The Response of the Royal Army to the French Revolution: The Role and Development of the Line Army, 1787–1793*. Oxford: Oxford University Press.

Sée, H. 1958. The Peasants and Agriculture. In *The Economic Origins of the French Revolution*, edited by R. W. Greenlaw, 49–58. Boston: D.C. Heath.

Sen, A. K. 1981 *Poverty and Famines: An Essay on Entitlement and Deprivation*. Oxford: Oxford University Press.

Sewell, W., Jr. 1980. *Work and Revolution in France: The Language of Labor from the Old Regime to 1848*. Cambridge: Cambridge University Press.

——. 1985a. *Structure and Mobility: The Men and Women of Marseilles, 1820–1870*. Cambridge: Cambridge University Press.

——.1985b. Ideologies and Social Revolutions: Reflections on the French Case. *Journal of Modern History* 57:57–85.

Shaffer, J. W. 1982. *Family and Farm: Agrarian Change and Household Organization in the Loire Valley, 1500–1900*. Albany: SUNY Press.

Shang, J. 1981–1982. The Process of Economic Recovery, Stabilization, and Its Accomplishments in the Early Ch'ing. *Chinese Studies in History* 15:19–62.

Shapiro, G., and P. Dawson. 1972. Social Mobility and Political Radicalism: The Case of the French Revolution of 1789. In *The Dimensions of Quantitative Research in History*, edited by W. O. Aydelotte, A. G. Bogue, and R. W. Fogel, 159–191. Princeton, NJ: Princeton University Press.

Sharp, B. 1980. *In Contempt of All Authority: Rural Artisans and Riot in the West of England, 1586–1660*. Berkeley and Los Angeles: University of California Press.

Sharpe, J. A. 1982. *Crime in Seventeenth Century England: A County Study*. New York: Cambridge University Press.

Sharpe, K. 1978a. Parliamentary History, 1603–1629: In or Out of Perspective? In *Faction and Parliament: Essays on Early Stuart History*, edited by K. Sharpe, 1–42. Oxford: Clarendon Press.

——, ed. 1978b. *Faction and Parliament: Essays on Early Stuart History*. Oxford: Clarendon Press.

Shaw, S. J. 1975. The Nineteenth Century Ottoman Tax Reforms and Revenue System. *International Journal of Middle East Studies* 6:421–459.

———. 1976. *History of the Ottoman Empire and Modern Turkey*, vol. 1: Empire of the Gazis: The Rise and Decline of the Ottoman Empire 1280–1808. Cambridge: Cambridge University Press.

Sheldon, C. D. 1958. *The Rise of the Merchant Class in Tokugawa Japan, 1600-1868*. Locust Valley, NY: J. J. Augustin.

Shiba, Y. 1977. Ningpo and Its Hinterland. In *The City in Late Imperial China*, edited by G. W. Skinner, 391–439. Stanford: Stanford University Press.

Shulim, J. 1981. The Continuing Controversy over the Etiology and Nature of the French Revolution. *Canadian Journal of History* 16:357–378.

Sigmann, J. 1973. *Eighteen Forty Eight: The Romantic and Democratic Revolution in Europe*. Translated by L. F. Edwards. London: Allen and Unwin.

Simiand, F. 1932. *Les fluctuations économiques à longue période et la crise mondiale*. Paris: Félix Alcan.

Simon, J. 1986. *Theory of Population and Economic Growth*. Oxford: Basil Blackwell.

Siraut, M. 1981. Physical Mobility in Elizabethan Cambridge. *Local Population Studies*, no. 27, 65–70.

Skinner, G. W. 1985. The Structure of Chinese History. *Journal of Asian Studies* 44:271–292.

———. 1987. Sichuan's Population in the Nineteenth Century: Lessons from Disaggregated Data. *Late Imperial China* 8:1–79.

———. 1988. Reproductive Strategies, the Domestic Cycle, and Fertility among Japanese Villagers, 1717–1869. Paper presented at the Rockefeller Foundation Workshop on Women's Status in Relation to Fertility and Mortality, Bellagio, Italy.

Skipp, V. 1978. *Crisis and Development: An Ecological Case Study of the Forest of Arden, 1570–1674* Cambridge: Cambridge University Press.

———. 1981. The Evolution of Settlement and Open Field Topography in North Arden down to 1300. In *The Origins of Open Field Agriculture*, edited by T. Rowley, 163–183. London: Croom Helm.

Skocpol, T. 1979. *States and Social Revolutions*. Cambridge: Cambridge University Press.

———, ed. 1984. *Vision and Method in Historical Sociology*. Cambridge: Cambridge University Press.

———. 1985. Cultural Idioms and Political Ideologies in the Revolutionary Reconstruction of State Power: A Rejoinder to Sewell. *Journal of Modern History* 57:86–96.

———. 1986. Comments on Culture and Ideology in Revolutions. Lecture at Emory University, Atlanta, GA.

Slack, P. A. 1974. Vagrants and Vagrancy in England, 1598–1664. *Economic History Review*, 2d ser., 27:360–379.

Slicher van Bath, B. H. 1960. The Rise of Intensive Husbandry in the Low Countries. In *Britain and the Netherlands*, edited by J. S. Bromley and E. H. Kossman, 130–153. London: Chatto and Windus.

———. 1963. *The Agrarian History of Western Europe, 500–1850*. New York: St. Martin's Press.

Smelser, N.J. 1963. *Theory of Collective Behavior.* New York: Free Press.

Smith, A. 1937 [1776]. *An Inquiry into the Nature and Causes of the Wealth of Nations.* Edited by E. Cannan. New York: Modern Library.

Smith, A. G. R. 1984. *The Emergence of a Nation-State: The Commonwealth of England, 1529–1660.* London: Longman.

Smith, A. H. 1974. *County and Court: Government and Politics in Norfolk, 1558–1603.* Oxford: Clarendon Press.

Smith, R. J. 1990. Ritual in Ch'ing China. In *Orthodoxy in Late Imperial China,* edited by K. C. Liu, 281–310. Berkeley and Los Angeles: University of California Press.

Smith, R. M., ed. 1984a. *Land, Kinship, and the Life-cycle.* Cambridge: Cambridge University Press.

———. 1984b. Families and Their Property in Rural England, 1250–1800. In *Land, Kinship, and the Life-Cycle,* edited by R. M. Smith, 1–87. Cambridge: Cambridge University Press.

Smith, S. 1973. The London Apprentices as Seventeenth Century Adolescents. *Past and Present,* no. 61, 149–161.

———. 1979. Almost Revolutionaries: The London Apprentices during the Civil Wars. *Huntington Library Quarterly* 42:313–328.

Smith, T. C. 1973. Pre-modern Economic Growth: Japan and the West. *Past and Present,* no. 60, 127–160.

———. 1977. *Nakahara: Family, Farming, and Population in a Japanese Village, 1717–1830.* Stanford: Stanford University Press.

Smuts, R. M. 1989. Public Ceremony and Royal Charisma: the English Royal Entry in London, 1485–1642. In *The First Modern Society: Essays in English History in Honour of Lawrence Stone,* edited by A. L. Beier, D. Cannadine, and J. M. Rosenheim, 64–97. Cambridge: Cambridge University Press.

Snell, K. 1985. *Annals of the Laboring Poor: Social Change and Agrarian England, 1660–1900.* Cambridge: Cambridge University Press.

Soboul, A. 1975. *The French Revolution, 1789–1799: From the Storming of the Bastille to Napoleon.* Translated by A. Forrest and C. Jones. New York: Vintage Books.

———. 1976. Georges Lefebvre et l'histoire agraire de la révolution. In *Problèmes paysans de la révolution (1789–1848),* edited by A. Soboul, 431–440. Paris: F. Maspero.

———. 1977a. *A Short History of the French Revolution, 1789–1799.* Translated by G. Symcox. Berkeley and Los Angeles: University of California Press.

———. 1977b. Persistence of "Feudalism" in the Rural Society of Nineteenth Century France. In *Rural Society in France: Selections from the Annales,* edited by R. Forster and O. Ranum, translated by E. Forster and P. M. Ranum, 50–71. Baltimore, MD: Johns Hopkins University Press.

———. 1982. Les philosophes, l'ancien régime, et la révolution. *Canadian Journal of History* 17:409–424.

Société de Démographie Historique. 1984. *La France d'ancien régime: études réunies en l'honneur de Pierre Goubert.* 2 vols. Paris: Editions Privat.

Solow, R. 1971. Technical Change and the Aggregate Production Function. In

The Economics of Technological Change, edited by N. Rosenberg, 117–136. Harmondsworth, Middlesex: Penguin.

Soltow, L. 1981. The Distribution of Property Values in England and Wales in 1798. *Economic History Review*, 2d ser., 34:60–70.

Somerville, J. P. 1986. *Politics and Ideology in England, 1603–1640.* London: Longman.

Sonenscher, M. 1985. Les sans-culottes de l'an 2: repenser le langage du travail dans la France révolutionnaire. *Annales, E.S.C.* 40:1087–1108.

Speck, W. A. 1977. *Stability and Strife: England, 1714–1760.* Cambridge, MA: Harvard University Press.

Spence, J. D. 1966. *Ts'ao Yin and the K'ang-hsi Emperor: Bondservant and Master.* New Haven: Yale University Press.

Spence, J. D., and J. E. Wills, Jr. 1979. *From Ming to Ch'ing: Conquest, Region, and Continuity in Seventeenth Century China.* New Haven: Yale University Press.

Spiridonakis, B. G. 1977. *Essays on the Historical Geography of the Greek World in the Balkans during the Turkokratia.* Thessaloniki, Greece: Institute for Balkan Studies.

Spitzer, A. B. 1987. *The French Generation of 1820.* Princeton, NJ: Princeton University Press.

Spufford, M. 1974. *Contrasting Communities: English Villagers in the Sixteenth and Seventeenth Centuries.* Cambridge: Cambridge University Press.

———. 1976. Peasant Inheritance Customs and Land Distribution in Cambridgeshire from the Sixteenth to the Eighteenth Centuries. In *Family and Inheritance*, edited by J. Goody, J. Thirsk, and E. P. Thompson, 156–176. Cambridge: Cambridge University Press.

Stadelmann, R. 1975. *Social and Political History of the German 1848 Revolution.* Translated by J. G. Chastain. Athens: Ohio State University Press.

Starr, P. 1982. *The Social Transformation of American Medicine.* New York: Basic Books.

Stearns, P. 1974. *1848: The Revolutionary Tide in Europe.* New York: Norton.

Steensgaard, N. 1973. *The Asian Trade Revolution of the Seventeenth Century.* Chicago: University of Chicago Press.

Stevenson, D. 1973. *The Scottish Revolution, 1637–1644.* Newton Abbot, Devon: David and Charles.

Stewart-McDougall, M. L. 1984. *The Artisan Republic: Revolution, Reaction, and Resistance in Lyon, 1848–51.* Montreal: McGill-Queen's University Press.

Stinchcombe, A. 1978. *Theoretical Methods in Social History.* New York: Academic Press.

Stoianovich, T. 1953. Land Tenure and Related Sections of the Balkan Economy, 1600–1800. *Journal of Economic History* 13:398–411.

Stone, B. 1981. *The Parlement of Paris, 1774–1789.* Chapel Hill: University of North Carolina Press.

———. 1986. *The French Parlements and the Crisis of the Old Regime.* Chapel Hill: University of North Carolina Press.

Stone, L. 1965. *The Crisis of the Aristocracy, 1558–1641.* Oxford: Oxford University Press.

———. 1972. *The Causes of the English Revolution, 1529–1642.* New York: Harper and Row.

———. 1974. The Size and Composition of the Oxford Student Body, 1580–1909. In *The University in Society,* vol. 1: *Oxford and Cambridge from the Fourteenth to the Early Eighteenth Centuries,* edited by L. Stone, 3–110. Princeton, NJ: Princeton University Press.

———. 1976. Social Mobility in England, 1500–1700. In *Seventeenth Century England,* edited by P. Seaver, 25–70. New York: New Viewpoints.

———. 1980. The Results of the English Revolutions of the Seventeenth Century. In *Three British Revolutions: 1641, 1688, 1776,* edited by J. G. A. Pocock, 23–108. Princeton, NJ: Princeton University Press.

———. 1984. The New Eighteenth Century. *New York Review of Books* 31:42–48.

Stone, L., and J. C. F. Stone. 1984. *An Open Elite? England, 1540–1880.* Oxford: Clarendon Press.

Stone, R. 1987. *Some Seventeenth Century Econometrics: Consumers' Behaviour.* Cahiers du Département d'Econométrie, no. 87.08. University of Geneva.

Stradling, R. A. 1981. *Europe and the Decline of Spain.* London: Allen and Unwin.

Straka, G. M., ed. 1973. *The Revolution of 1688 and the Birth of the English Political Nation.* 2d ed. Lexington, MA: D.C. Heath.

Struve, L. 1982. The Hsu Brothers and Semi-official Patronage of Scholars in the K'ang-hsi Period. *Harvard Journal of Asiatic Studies* 42:231–266.

———. 1984. *The Southern Ming, 1644–1662.* New Haven: Yale University Press.

Styles, P. 1978. *Studies in Seventeenth Century West Midlands History.* Kineton, Warwickshire: Roundwood Press.

Sugar, P. F. 1977. *Southeastern Europe under Ottoman Rule, 1354–1804.* Seattle: University of Washington Press.

Sullivan, R. J. 1984. Measurement of English Farming Technological Change, 1523–1900. *Explorations in Economic History* 21:270–289.

Sun, E-T. Z. 1972. Sericulture and Silk Textile Production in Ch'ing China. In *Economic Organization in Chinese Society,* edited by W. E. Willmott, 79–108. Stanford: Stanford University Press.

Supple, B. 1959. *Commercial Crisis and Change in England, 1600–1642.* Cambridge: Cambridge University Press.

Sussman, G. D. 1977. The Glut of Doctors in Mid-Nineteenth Century France. *Comparative Studies in Society and History* 19:287–304.

Sutherland, D. 1982. *The Chouans: The Social Origins of Popular Counter-revolution in Upper Brittany, 1770–1796.* Oxford: Clarendon Press.

———. 1986. *France, 1789–1815: Revolution and Counter-revolution.* New York: Oxford University Press.

Swidler, A. 1986. Culture in Action: Symbols and Strategies. *American Sociological Review* 51:273–286.

Százdi, A. 1981. Preliminary Estimates of Gold and Silver Production in America, 1501–1610. In *Precious Metals in the Age of Expansion: Papers of the XIVth International Congress of the Historical Sciences*, edited by H. Kellenbenz, 151–223. Stuttgart: Klett-Cotta.

Tackett, T. 1977. *Priest and Parish in Eighteenth Century France: A Social and Political Study of the Curés in a Diocese of Dauphine, 1750–1791*. Princeton, NJ: Princeton University Press.

———. 1982. The West in France in 1789: The Religious Factor in the Origins of the Counter-revolution. *Journal of Modern History* 54:715–745.

———. 1984. Les revenues des curés à la fin de l'ancien régime: équisse d'une géographie. In *La France d'ancien régime: études réunies en l'honneur de Pierre Goubert*, edited by the Société de Démographie Historique, 2:665–671. Paris: Editions Privat.

———. 1989. Nobles and Third Estate in the Revolutionary Dynamic of the National Assembly, 1789–1790. *American Historical Review* 94:271–301.

Taeuber, I. B. 1948. Population and Political Instabilities in Underdeveloped Areas. In *Population and World Politics*, edited by P. Hauser, 237–259. Glencoe, IL: Free Press.

———. 1958. *The Population of Japan*. Princeton, NJ: Princeton University Press.

Takekoshi, Y. 1930. *The Economic Aspects of the History of the Civilization of Japan*. 3 vols. London: Allen and Unwin.

Tanaka, M. 1984. Popular Uprisings, Rent Resistance, and Bondservant Rebellions in the Late Ming. In *State and Society in China: Japanese Perspectives on Ming-Qing Social and Economic History*, edited by L. Grove and C. Daniels, 165–214. Tokyo: University of Tokyo Press.

Tang, A. M. 1979. China's Agricultural Legacy. *Economic Development and Cultural Change* 28:1–22.

Taniguchi, K. 1980. Peasant Rebellions in the Late Ming. *Acta Asiatica* 38:54–68.

Tardanico, R. 1985. State Dependency and Nationalism: Revolutionary Mexico, 1924–28. *Comparative Studies in Society and History* 24:400–423.

Tawney, R. H. 1941. The Rise of the Gentry, 1558–1640. *Economic History Review* 11:1–38.

Taylor, A. J. P. 1959. 1848: The Year of German Liberalism. In *1848: A Turning Point?* edited by M. Kranzberg, 24–39. Boston: D.C. Heath.

———. 1980. *Revolutions and Revolutionaries*. London: Hamish Hamilton.

Taylor, G. V. 1962. The Paris Bourse on the Eve of the Revolution, 1781–89. *American Historical Review* 67:956–977.

———. 1964. Types of Capitalism in Eighteenth Century France. *English Historical Review* 79:478–497.

———. 1972a. Revolutionary and Nonrevolutionary Content in the *Cahiers* of 1789: An Interim Report. *French Historical Studies* 7:479–502.

———. 1972b. Noncapitalist Wealth and the Origins of the French Revolution. *American Historical Review* 72:469–496.

Taylor, M., ed. 1988. *Rationality and Revolution*. Cambridge: Cambridge University Press.

Taylor, R. 1990. Official and Popular Religion and the Political Organization of Chinese Society in the Ming. In *Orthodoxy in Late Imperial China*, edited by K. C. Liu, 126–157. Berkeley and Los Angeles: University of California Press.

Telford, T. A. N.d.a. Marital Fertility in the Ming-Qing Transition: Tongcheng County, 1520–1661. California Institute of Technology. Typescript.

———. N.d.b. Fertility and Population Growth in the Lineages of Tongcheng County, 1520–1661. California Institute of Technology. Typescript.

Temple, N. 1975. The Control and Exploitation of French Towns du. ng the Ancien Régime. In *State and Society in Seventeenth Century France*, edited by R. F. Kierstead, 67–93. New York: New Viewpoints.

Tepaske, J. J. 1983. New World Silver, Castile, and the Philippines, 1590–1800. In *Precious Metals in the Later Medieval and Early Modern World*, edited by J. F. Richards, 425–445. Durham, NC: Carolina Academic Press.

Thirsk, J. 1961. Industries in the Countryside. In *Essays in the Economic and Social History of Tudor and Stuart England*, edited by F. J. Fisher, 70–88. Cambridge: Cambridge University Press.

———. 1967a. Enclosing and Engrossing. In *The Agrarian History of England and Wales*, vol. 4: *1500–1640*, edited by J. Thirsk, 205–255. Cambridge: Cambridge University Press.

———, ed. 1967b. *The Agrarian History of England and Wales*, vol. 4: *1500–1640*. Cambridge: Cambridge University Press.

———. 1976. Seventeenth Century Agricultural Change. In *Seventeenth Century England: Society in an Age of Revolution*, edited by P. Seaver, 71–110. New York: New Viewpoints.

———, ed. 1984. *The Agrarian History of England and Wales*, vol. 5, pt. 1: *1640–1750—Regional Farming Systems*. Cambridge: Cambridge University Press.

———, ed. 1985. *The Agrarian History of England and Wales*, vol. 5, pt. 2: *1640–1750—Agrarian Change*. Cambridge: Cambridge University Press.

Thirsk, J., and J. P. Cooper, eds. 1972. *Seventeenth Century Economic Documents*. Oxford: Clarendon Press.

Tholfson, T. R. 1984. *Ideology and Revolution in Modern Europe: An Essay on the Role of Ideas in History*. New York: Columbia University Press.

Thomas, B. 1985a. Escaping from Constraints: The Industrial Revolution in a Malthusian Context. *Journal of Interdisciplinary History* 15:729–753.

———. 1985b. Food Supply in the United Kingdom during the Industrial Revolution. In *The Economics of the Industrial Revolution*, edited by J. Mokyr, 137–150. Totowa, NJ: Rowman and Allanheld.

Thomas, D. 1983. Financial and Administrative Developments. In *Before the English Civil War: Essays on Early Stuart Politics*, edited by H. Tomlinson, 103–122. New York: St. Martin's Press.

Thompson, E. P. 1963. *The Making of the English Working Class*. New York: Pantheon Books.

Thompson, I. A. A. 1979. The Purchase of Nobility in Castile. *Journal of European Economic History* 8:313–360.

Tilly, C. 1967. *The Vendée*. New York: John Wiley.

————. 1972. How Protest Modernized in France. In *The Dimensions of Quantitative Research in History*, edited by W. Aydelotte, A. Bogue, and R. Fogel, 192–253. Princeton, NJ: Princeton University Press.

————, ed. 1975. *The Formation of National States in Western Europe*. Princeton, NJ: Princeton University Press.

————. 1976. Does Modernization Breed Revolution? *Comparative Politics* 5:425–447.

————. 1978. *From Mobilization to Revolution*. Reading, MA: Addison-Wesley.

————. 1981. *As Sociology Meets History*. New York: Academic Press.

————. 1984a. *Big Structures, Large Processes, and Huge Comparisons*. New York: Russell Sage.

————. 1984b. Democratic Origins of the European Proletariat. In *Proletarianization and Family History*, edited by D. Levine. 1–85. New York: Academic Press.

————. 1985. Retrieving European Lives. In *Reliving the Past: The Worlds of Social History*, edited by O. Zunz, 11–52. Chapel Hill: University of North Carolina Press.

————. 1986. *The Contentious French*. Cambridge, MA: Harvard University Press, Belknap Press.

Tilly, C., and L. H. Lees. 1975. The People of June 1848. In *Revolution and Reaction: 1848 and the Second French Republic*, edited by R. Price, 170–207. London: Croom Helm.

Tilly, C., L. Tilly, and R. Tilly. 1975. *The Rebellious Century, 1830–1930*. Cambridge, MA: Harvard University Press.

Tilly, L. 1971. The Food Riot as a Form of Political Conflict in France. *Journal of Interdisciplinary History* 2:23–57.

Tocqueville, A. de. 1955 [1856]. *The Old Regime and the French Revolution*. Translated by S. Gilbert. New York: Doubleday.

————. 1970 [1893]. *Recollections*. Translated by G. Lawrence. London: MacDonald.

Tomlinson, H., ed. 1983. *Before the English Civil War: Essays on Early Stuart Politics and Government*. New York: St. Martin's Press.

Tong, J. W. 1985. Collective Violence in a Pre-modern Society: Rebellion and Banditry in the Ming Dynasty (1368–1644). Ph.D. diss., University of Michigan.

Totman, C. 1980. *The Collapse of the Tokugawa Bakufu, 1862–1868*. Honolulu: University of Hawaii Press.

————. 1985. *The Origins of Japan's Modern Forests: The Case of Akita*. Honolulu: University of Hawaii Press.

Toutain, J. C. 1961. *La produit de l'agriculture française de 1700 à 1958*. Paris.

————. 1963. *La population de la France de 1700 à 1959*. Paris: ISEA.

Traugott, M. 1983. The Mid-Nineteenth Century Crisis in France and England. *Theory and Society* 12:455–468.

————. 1985. *Armies of the Poor: Determinants of Working Class Participation in the Parisian Insurrection of 1848*. Princeton, NJ: Princeton University Press.

Trevelyan, G. M. 1953. *History of England*. Garden City, NY: Doubleday/Anchor.

Trevor-Roper, H. R. 1953. *The Gentry, 1540–1640*. Cambridge: Cambridge University Press.

———. 1965. The General Crisis of the Seventeenth Century. In *Crisis in Europe, 1560–1660*, edited by T. Aston, 57–96. New York: Basic Books.

Trimberger, E. K. 1978. *Revolution from Above*. New Brunswick, NJ: Transaction Books.

Trotsky, L. 1932. *History of the Russian Revolution*. Translated by M. Eastman. New York: Simon and Schuster.

Tsurumi, N. 1984. Rural Control in the Ming Dynasty. In *State and Society in China: Japanese Perspectives on Ming-Qing Social and Economic History*, edited by L. Grove and C. Daniels, 245–277. Tokyo: University of Tokyo Press.

Tunzelman, G. N. von. 1985. The Standard of Living Debate and Optimal Economic Growth. In *The Economics of the Industrial Revolution*, edited by J. Mokyr, 207–226. Totowa, NJ: Rowman and Allanheld.

Turner, D. 1978. A Lost Seventeenth Century Demographic Crisis? The Evidence of Two Contexts. *Local Population Studies* 21:11–18.

Turner, M. 1976. Parliamentary Enclosure and Population Change in England, 1750–1830. *Explorations in Economic History* 13:463–468.

———. 1980. *English Parliamentary Enclosure: Its Historical Geography and Economic History*. Folkestone, Kent: William Dawson.

———. 1982. Agricultural Productivity in England in the Eighteenth Century: Evidence from Crop Yields. *Economic History Review*, 2d ser., 35:489–510.

———. 1983. Sitting on the Fence of Parliamentary Enclosure: A Regressive Social Tax with Problematic Efficiency Gains. Paper presented at the Economic History Society Conference, Canterbury, United Kingdom.

———. 1984. *Enclosure in Britain, 1750–1830*. London: Macmillan.

Turner, R. S. 1980. The *Bildungsbürgertum* and the Learned Professions in Prussia, 1770–1830: The Origins of a Class. *Histoire Sociale* 13:105–136.

Tusser, T. 1573. *Five Hundred Pointes of Good Husbandrie*. London: Company of Stationers.

Twitchett, D., and J. K. Fairbank. 1978- . *The Cambridge History of China*. 14 vols. Cambridge: Cambridge University Press.

Udovitch, A. L., ed. 1981. *The Islamic Middle East, 700–1900: Studies in Economic and Social History*. Princeton, NJ: Darwin Press.

Underdown, D. 1973. *Somerset in the Civil War and Interregnum*. Newton Abbot, Devon: David and Charles.

———. 1981. The Problem of Popular Allegiance in the English Civil War. *Transactions of the Royal Historical Society*, 5th ser., 31:69–94.

———. 1985. *Pride's Purge: Politics in the Puritan Revolution*. London: Allen and Unwin.

———. 1987. *Revel, Riot, and Rebellion*. Oxford: Oxford University Press.

U.S. Bureau of the Census. 1964. *Statistical Abstract of the United States*. 84th ed. Washington, DC: U.S. Government Printing Office.

————. 1989a. *Statistical Abstract of the United States.* 109th ed. Washington, DC: U.S. Government Printing Office.

————. 1989b. *Projections of the Population of the United States by Age, Sex, and Race: 1988 to 2080.* By G. Spencer. Current Population Reports, Population Estimates, and Projections, Series P-25, no. 1018. Washington, DC: U.S. Government Printing Office.

U.S. Department of Health and Human Services. Social Security Administration. 1990. *Social Security Bulletin 53*, no 1. Washington DC: U.S. Government Printing Office.

U.S. Department of Labor. Bureau of Labor Statistics. 1990. *Employment and Earnings, February 1990.* Washington, DC: U.S. Government Printing Office.

van Creveld, M. 1989. *Technology and War: From 2000 B.C. to the Present.* New York: Free Press.

van der Sprenkel, O. B. The Geographical Background of the Ming Civil Service. *Journal of the Economic and Social History of the Orient* 55:302–336.

van der Wee, H. 1977. Monetary, Credit and Banking Systems. In *The Cambridge Economic History of Europe*, vol. 5: The Economic Organization of Modern Europe, *edited by E. Rich and C. Wilson*, 290–393. Cambridge: Cambridge University Press.

van Dillen, J. G. 1974. Economic Fluctuations and Trade in the Netherlands, 1650–1750. In *Essays in European Economic History, 1500–1800*, edited by P. Earle, 199–212. Oxford: Clarendon Press.

van Donzel, E., B. Lewis, and C. Pellat, eds. 1973. *The Encyclopaedia of Islam.* Leiden: E. J. Brill.

van Houtte, J., and L. van Buyten. 1977. The Low Countries. In *An Introduction to the Sources of European Economic History*, edited by C. Wilson and G. Parker, 81–114. Ithaca, NY: Cornell University Press.

van Kley, D. 1975. *The Jansenists and the Expulsion of the Jesuits from France, 1757–65.* New Haven: Yale University Press.

————. 1984a. Christianity, Christian Interpretation, and the Origins of the French Revolution. In *History and Historical Understanding*, edited by C. T. McIntire and R. A. Wells, 103–123. Grand Rapids, MI: William Eerdmans.

————. 1984b. *The Damien's Affair and the Unraveling of the Ancient Regime, 1750–1770.* Princeton, NJ: Princeton University Press.

Verlinden, C., J. Craegbeckx, and E. Scholliers. 1972. Price and Wage Movements in Belgium in the Sixteenth Century. In *Economy and Society in Early Modern Europe: Essays from Annales*, edited by P. Burke, 55–84. London: Routledge and Kegan Paul.

Vicens Vives, J. 1969. *An Economic History of Spain.* Translated by F. M. López-Morilla. Princeton, NJ: Princeton University Press.

Vidalenc, J. 1970. *La société française de 1815 à 1848.* Paris: Rivière.

Vilar, P. 1976. *A History of Gold and Money, 1450–1920.* Translated by J. White. London: NLB.

Vlastos, S. 1986. *Peasant Protests and Uprisings in Tokugawa Japan.* Berkeley and Los Angeles: University of California Press.

Vogel, H. U. 1987. Chinese Central Monetary Policy, 1644–1800. *Late Imperial China* 8:1–52.

von Greyerz, K., ed. 1984. *Religion and Society in Early Modern Europe, 1500– 1800.* Boston: Allen and Unwin.

Vovelle, M. 1977. Le tournant des mentalités en France, 1750–1789. *Social History* 5:605–629.

———. 1978. La sensibilité pré-révolutionnaire. In *Vom Ancien Régime zur Französischen Revolution*, edited by E. Hinrichs, E. Schmitt, and R. Vierhaus, 516–538. Göttingen: Vandenhoeck and Rupert.

———. 1980. *Ville et campagne au 18e siècle.* Paris: Editions Sociales.

———. 1984. *The Fall of the French Monarchy, 1787–1792.* Translated by S. Burke. Cambridge: Cambridge University Press.

Vryonis, S. 1977. Cultural Conformity in Byzantine Society. In *Individualism and Conformity in Classical Islam*, edited by A. Banai and S. Vryonis, 115– 144. Wiesbaden: Otto Harrassowitz.

Wake, C. H. H. 1979. The Changing Pattern of Europe's Pepper and Spice Imports, 1400–1700. *Journal of European Economic History* 8:360–404.

Wakeman, F., Jr. 1972. The Price of Autonomy: Intellectuals in Ming and Ch'ing Politics. *Daedalus* 101:35–70.

———. 1975a. The Evolution of Local Control in Late Imperial China. In *Conflict and Control in Late Imperial China*, edited by F. Wakeman and C. Grant, 1–25. Berkeley and Los Angeles: University of California Press.

———. 1975b. *The Fall of Imperial China.* New York: Free Press.

———. 1977. Rebellion and Revolution: The Study of Popular Movements in Chinese History. *Journal of Asian Studies* 36:201–238.

———. 1979. The Shun Interregnum of 1644. In *From Ming to Ch'ing: Conquest, Region, and Continuity in Seventeenth Century China*, edited by J. D. Spence and J. E. Wills, Jr., 39–88. New Haven: Yale University Press.

———. 1985. *The Great Enterprise: The Manchu Reconstruction of Imperial Order in Seventeenth Century China.* 2 vols. Berkeley and Los Angeles: University of California Press.

———. 1986. China and the Seventeenth Century Crisis. *Late Imperial China* 7:1–26.

Walker, H. A. 1987. Spinning Gold from Straw: On Cause, Law, and Probability. *Sociological Theory* 5:28–33.

Wallerstein, I. 1974. *The Modern World System*, vol. 1: *Capitalist Agriculture and the Origins of the European World Economy in the Sixteenth Century.* New York: Academic Press.

———. 1980. *The Modern World System*, vol. 2: *Mercantilism and the Consolidation of the European World Economy, 1600–1750.* New York: Academic Press.

———. 1984. Long Waves as Capitalist Process. *Review* 7:559–575.

———. 1989. *The Modern World System*, vol. 3: *The Second Era of Great Expansion of the Capitalist World Economy, 1730s–1840s.* San Diego: Academic Press.

Walter, J. 1980. Grain Riots and Popular Attitudes toward the Law: Maldon and the Crisis of 1629. In *An Ungovernable People?* edited by J. Brewer, 47– 84. New Brunswick, NJ: Rutgers University Press.

Walter, J., and K. Wrightson. 1976. Dearth and the Social Order in Early Modern England. *Past and Present*, no. 71, 22–42.

Walter, J., and R. Schofield, eds. 1989. *Famine, Disease, and the Social Order in Early Modern Society*. Cambridge: Cambridge University Press.

Walton, J. 1984. *Reluctant Rebels*. New York: Columbia University Press.

Walzer, M. 1974. *The Revolution of the Saints*. New York: Atheneum.

Wang, G. 1984. The Chinese Urge to Civilize: Reflections on Change. *Journal of Asian History* 18:1–34.

Wang, Yeh-chien. 1973. *Land Taxation in Imperial China, 1750–1911*. Cambridge, MA: Harvard University Press.

Wang, Yü-ch'üan. 1936. The Rise of Land Tax and the Fall of Dynasties in Chinese History. *Pacific Affairs* 9:201–220.

Waquet, J.-C. 1982. Who Profited from the Alienation of Public Revenues in the Ancien Régime? Some Reflections on the Examples of France, Piedmont, and Naples in the XVIIth and XVIIIth centuries. *Journal of European Economic History* 11:665–673.

Watkins, S. C., and J. Mencken. 1985. Famines in Historical Perspective. *Population and Development Review* 11:647–675.

Watson, A. M. 1981. A Medieval Green Revolution: New Crops and Farming Techniques in the Early Islamic World. In *The Islamic Middle East, 700–1900: Studies in Economic and Social History*, edited by A. L. Udovitch, 29–58. Princeton, NJ: Darwin Press.

Watson, I. 1983. *Agricultural Innovation in the Early Islamic World*. Cambridge: Cambridge University Press.

Weary, W. 1977. The House of La Tremoille, Fifteenth through Eighteenth Centuries: Change and Adaptation in a French Noble Family. *Journal of Modern History* 49 (suppl.): 1001–1038.

Weber, A. F. 1963. *The Growth of Cities in the 19th Century*. New York: Macmillan.

Weber, M. 1951. *The Religion of China*. Translated by H. Gerth. New York: Free Press.

———. 1958. *The Protestant Ethic and the Spirit of Capitalism*. Translated by T. Parsons. New York: Scribner.

———. 1961. *General Economic History*. Translated by F. Knight. New York: Collier-Macmillan.

———. 1978. *Economy and Society*. Edited by G. Roth and C. Wittich. Berkeley and Los Angeles: University of California Press.

Weiner, M. 1971. Political Demography: An Inquiry into the Political Consequences of Population Change. In *Rapid Population Growth: Consequences and Policy Implications*, compiled by the National Academy of Sciences, 567–617. Baltimore, MD: Johns Hopkins University Press.

Weir, D. R. 1982. Fertility Transition in Rural France 1740–1829. Ph.D. diss., Stanford University.

———. 1989a. Tontines, Public Finance, and Revolution in France and England, 1688–1789. *Journal of Economic History* 49:95–124.

———. 1989b. Markets and Mortality in France, 1600–1789. In *Famine, Disease, and the Social Order in Early Modern Society*, edited by J. Walter and R. Schofield, 201–234. Cambridge: Cambridge University Press.

Welch, C. 1980. *Anatomy of Rebellion*. Albany, NY: SUNY Press.

Wesson, R. 1978. *State Systems: International Pluralism, Politics, and Culture*. New York: Free Press.

White, E. N. 1989. Was There a Solution to the *Ancien Régime*'s Financial Dilemma? *Journal of Economic History* 49:545–568.

White, J. W. 1988a. Rational Rioters: Leaders, Followers, and Popular Protest in Early Modern Japan. *Politics and Society* 16:35–69.

———. 1988b. State Growth and Popular Protest in Tokugawa Japan. *Journal of Japanese Studies* 14:1–26.

———. 1989. Economic Development and Sociopolitical Unrest in Nineteenth Century Japan. *Economic Development and Cultural Change* 37:231–260.

White, L. 1962. *Medieval Technology and Social Change*. Oxford: Clarendon Press.

Wick, D. L. 1987. *A Conspiracy of Well-intentioned Men: The Society of Thirty and the French Revolution*. New York: Garland.

Wiens, M. 1979. Masters and Bondservants: Peasant Rage in the Seventeenth Century. *Ming Studies* 8:57–64.

———. 1980. Lord and Peasant: The Sixteenth to the Eighteenth Centuries. *Modern China* 6:3–39.

Wilkinson, E. P. 1980. *Studies in Chinese Price History*. New York: Garland.

Williams, A. 1979. *The Police of Paris, 1718–1789*. Baton Rouge: Louisiana State University Press.

Williams, P. 1979. *The Tudor Regime*. Oxford: Clarendon Press.

Williamson, J. 1984. Why Was British Growth So Slow during the Industrial Revolution? *Journal of Economic History* 44:687–712.

Wilson, C., and G. Parker, eds. 1977. *An Introduction to the Sources of European Economic History, 1500–1800*. Ithaca, NY: Cornell University Press.

Wittfogel, K. A. 1957. *Oriental Despotism: A Comparative Study of Total Power*. New Haven: Yale University Press.

Wolf, E. 1969. *Peasant Wars of the Twentieth Century*. New York: Harper and Row.

Woloch, I., ed. 1977. *The Peasantry in the Old Regime: Conditions and Protests*. Huntington, NY: Robert E. Krieger.

Wong, R. B. 1982. Food Riots in the Qing Dynasty. *Journal of Asian Studies* 41:767–788.

———. 1983. Les émeutes de subsistance en Chine et en Europe occidentale. *Annales, E.S.C.* 38:234–258.

Wonnacott, R. J., and T. H. Wonnacott. 1979. *Econometrics*. New York: John Wiley.

Wood, J. 1976. The Decline of the Nobility in Sixteenth and Early Seventeenth Century France: Myth or Reality. *Journal of Modern History* 48 (suppl.): 1–30.

———. 1977. Demographic Pressure and Social Mobility among the Nobility of Early Modern France. *Sixteenth Century Journal* 8:3–16.

Woodhead, C. 1987. "The Present Terror of the World?" Contemporary Views of the Ottoman Empire, c. 1600. *History* 72:20–37.

Woodward, D. 1981. Wage Rates and Living Standards in Pre-industrial England. *Past and Present*, no. 91, 28–46.

Woolrych, A. 1968. Puritanism, Politics, and Society. In *The English Revolution, 1600–1660*, edited by E. W. Ives, 87–100. New York: Harper and Row.

———. 1980. Court, Country, and City Revisited. *History* 65:236–245.

———. 1983. *England without a King, 1649–1660*. London: Methuen.

Wordie, J. R. 1983. The Chronology of English Enclosure. *Economic History Review*, 2d ser., 36:483–505.

Wright, G., and G. Saxonhouse, eds. 1984. *Technique, Spirit, and Form in the Making of Modern Economics: Essays in Honor of William N. Parker.* Greenwich, CT: JAI Press.

Wrightson, K., and D. Levine. 1979. *Poverty and Piety in an English Village: Terling, 1525–1700.* New York: Academic Press.

Wrigley, E. A. 1969. *Population and History.* New York: McGraw-Hill.

———. 1972. The Process of Modernization and the Industrial Revolution in England. *Journal of Interdisciplinary History* 3:225–259.

———. 1978. A Simple Model of London's Importance in Changing English Society and Economy, 1650–1750. In *Towns in Societies*, edited by P. Abrams and E. A. Wrigley, 215–244. Cambridge: Cambridge University Press.

———. 1983. The Growth of Population in Eighteenth Century England: A Conundrum Resolved. *Past and Present*, no. 98, 121–150.

———. 1985. The Fall of Marital Fertility in Nineteenth Century France: Example or Exception? *European Journal of Population* 1:31–60.

Wrigley, E. A., and R. Schofield. 1981. *The Population History of England, 1541–1871.* Cambridge, MA: Harvard University Press.

Wu, J. C. H. 1967. Chinese Legal and Political Philosophy. In *The Chinese Mind: Essentials of Chinese Philosophy and Culture*, edited by C. A. Moore, 213–237. Honolulu: East-West Center, University of Hawaii Press.

Wu, S. 1970. *Communication and Imperial Control in China.* Cambridge, MA: Harvard University Press.

———. 1979. *Passage to Power: K'ang-hsi and His Heir-Apparent, 1661–1722.* Cambridge, MA: Harvard University Press.

Wuthnow, R. 1985. State Structure and Ideology. *American Sociological Review* 50:799–821.

———. 1987. *Meaning and Moral Order: Explorations in Cultural Analysis.* Berkeley and Los Angeles: University of California Press.

———. 1989. *Communities of Discourse: Ideology and Social Structure in the Reformation, the Enlightenment, and European Socialism.* Cambridge, MA: Harvard University Press.

Wyczanski, A. 1960. Le niveau de la récolte des céréales en Pologne du XVI au XVIII siècle. In *First International Conference on Economic History*, 585–590. Paris: Mouton.

Wyndham, K. 1979. Crown Land and Royal Patronage in Mid-Sixteenth Century England. *Journal of British Studies* 19:18–34.

Yamamura, K. 1967. The Role of the Samurai in the Development of Modern Banking in Japan. *Journal of Economic History* 27:198–220.

Yamamura, K., and T. Kamiki. 1983. Silver Mines and Sung Coins: A Monetary History of Medieval and Modern Japan in International Perspective. In *Precious Metals in the Later Medieval and Early Modern World*, edited by J. F. Richards, 329–362. Durham, NC: Carolina Academic Press.

Yang, L. 1969. Ming Local Administration. In *Chinese Government in Ming Times: Seven Studies*, edited by C. O. Hucker, 1–22. New York: Columbia University Press.

Yasuba, Y. 1986. Standard of Living in Japan before Industrialization: From What Level Did Japan Begin? A Comment. *Journal of Economic History* 46:217–224.

Yelling, J. A. 1973. Change in Crop Production in East Worcestershire, 1540–1867. *Agriculture Historical Review* 2:24–26.

———. 1977. *Common Field and Enclosure in England, 1450–1800.* London: Macmillan.

———. 1982. Rationality in Common Fields. *Economic History Review*, 2d ser., 35:409–415.

Yim, S. 1978. Famine Relief Statistics as a Guide to the Population of Sixteenth Century China: A Case Study of Honan Province. *Ch'ing shih wen-t'i* 3(9):1–30.

Young, A. 1971 [1792]. Travels during the Years 1787, 1788, and 1789. In *France on the Eve of Revolution: A Book of Readings*, edited by J. Kaplow, 121–136. New York: John Wiley.

Yuan, T. 1978a. The Porcelain Industry at Ching-te-chen, 1550–1700. *Ming Studies Newsletter*, no. 6, 45–53.

———. 1978b. Continuities and Discontinuities in Chinese Agriculture, 1550–1700. *Ming Studies Newsletter*, no. 7, 35–51.

———. 1979. Urban Riots and Disturbances. In *From Ming to Ch'ing: Conquest, Region, and Continuity in Seventeenth Century China*, edited by J. D. Spence and J. E. Wills, Jr., 277–320. New Haven: Yale University Press.

———. 1981. The Silver Trade between America and China, 1550–1700. In *Precious Metals in the Age of Expansion: Papers of the XIVth International Congress of the Historical Sciences*, edited by H. Kellenbenz, 268–272. Stuttgart: Klett-Cotta.

Zagorin, P. 1969. *The Court and the Country.* Cambridge: Cambridge University Press.

———. 1982. *Rebels and Rulers.* 2 vols. Cambridge: Cambridge University Press.

Zakythinos, D. A. 1976. *The Making of Modern Greece.* Translated by J. Stone. Totowa, NJ: Rowman and Littlefield.

Zaret, D. 1985. *The Heavenly Contract: Ideology and Organization in Prerevolutionary Puritanism.* Chicago: University of Chicago Press.

Zelin, M. 1984. *The Magistrate's Tael: Rationalizing Fiscal Reform in Eighteenth Century Ch'ing China.* Berkeley and Los Angeles: University of California Press.

Zeller, O. 1983. *Les recensements lyonnais de 1597 et 1636.* Lyon: Presses Universitaires de Lyon.

Zen Sun, E. T., and J. de Francis, eds. 1956. *Chinese Social History: Translations of Selected Studies*. Washington, DC: Octagon Books.

Zerubavel, E. 1981. *Hidden Rhythms: Schedule and Calendars in Social Life*. Chicago: University of Chicago Press.

Zilfi, M. C. 1983. Elite Circulation in the Ottoman Empire: Great Mollas of the Eighteenth Century. *Journal of the Economic and Social History of the Orient* 26:318–364.

Zimmerman, E. 1979. Crises and Crisis Outcomes: Towards a New Synthetic Approach. *European Journal of Political Research* 7:67–115.

———. 1983. *Political Violence, Crises, and Revolutions: Theories and Research*. Boston: G. K. Hall.

Zolberg, A. R. 1980. Strategic Interactions and the Formation of Modern States: France and England. *International Social Science Journal* 32:687–716.

Zunz, O., ed. 1985. *Reliving the Past: The Worlds of Social History*. Chapel Hill: University of North Carolina Press.

Zurndorfer, H. T. 1981. The Hsin-an Ta-tsu Chih and the Development of Chinese Gentry Society, 800–1600. *T'oung Pao* 67:154–215.

———. 1983. Violence and Political Protest in Ming and Qing China. *International Review of Social History* 28:304–319.

———. 1984. Local Lineages and Local Development: A Case Study of the Fan Lineage, Hsui-ming hsien, Hui-chou (800–1500). *T'oung Pao* 70:18–59.

Index

The following abbreviations are used in the index subheadings:

c.	century
Ch.	China, Chinese
e.m.e.	early modern era
Eng.	England, English
Fr.	France, French
O.E.	Ottoman Empire
Rev., rev.	Revolution/s

Centuries are represented by numbers, e.g., "17th c." for seventeenth century. References to figures and maps are printed in italic type; references to tables are printed in boldface type.